Better Homes and Gardens®

new baking book

Better Homes and Gardens® Books
Des Moines, Iowa

Better Homes and Gardens® Books
An imprint of Meredith® Books

New Baking Book
Editors: Jennifer Dorland Darling, Lisa Holderness
Contributing Editors: Linda J. Henry, Shelli McConnell, Winifred Moranville, Paul E. Piccuito,
    Sarah Reynolds, Spectrum Communication Services, Inc., Joyce Trollope, Mary Major Williams
Contributing Writer: Lisa Kingsley
Associate Art Director: Lynda Haupert
Contributing Graphic Designer: Angie Hoogensen
Copy Chief: Catherine Hamrick
Copy and Production Editor: Terri Fredrickson
Contributing Copy Editors: Sheila Mauck, Angela K. Renkoski
Contributing Proofreaders: Kathy Roth Eastman, Gretchen Kauffman, Susie Kling, Mary Pas
Electronic Production Coodinator: Paula Forest
Editorial and Design Assistants: Judy Bailey, Treesa Landry, Karen Schirm
Test Kitchen Director: Sharon Stilwell
Test Kitchen Home Economists: Marilyn Cornelius, Product Supervisor; Patricia Beebout; Judy Comstock;
    Jill Hoefler; Maryellyn Krantz; Jan Miller; Deb Parenza; Kay Springer; Colleen Weeden; Lori Wilson
Contributing Food Stylists: Lynn Blanchard, Diana Nolin, Jennifer Peterson
Contributing Photographers: Peter Krumhardt, Scott Little, Andy Lyons (including cover), Greg Strelecki
Contributing Prop Stylist: Dana Etzel
Production Director: Douglas M. Johnston
Production Manager: Pam Kvitne
Assistant Prepress Manager: Marjorie J. Schenkelberg

Meredith® Books
Editor in Chief: James D. Blume
Design Director: Matt Strelecki
Managing Editor: Gregory H. Kayko
Executive Food Editor: Lisa Holderness

Director, Sales & Marketing, Retail: Michael A. Peterson
Director, Sales & Marketing, Special Markets: Rita McMullen
Director, Sales & Marketing, Home & Garden Center Channel: Ray Wolf
Director, Operations: George A. Susral

Vice President, General Manager: Jamie L. Martin

Better Homes and Gardens® Magazine
Editor in Chief: Jean LemMon
Executive Food Editor: Nancy Byal

Meredith Publishing Group
President, Publishing Group: Christopher M. Little
Vice President, Consumer Marketing and Development: Hal Oringer

Meredith Corporation
Chairman and Chief Executive Officer: William T. Kerr

Chairman of the Executive Committee: E.T. Meredith III

Our seal assures you that every recipe in the
New Baking Book has been tested in the
Better Homes and Gardens® Test Kitchen.
This means that each recipe is practical and
reliable, and meets our high standards of
taste appeal. We guarantee your satisfaction
with this book for as long as you own it.

All of us at Better Homes and
Gardens® Books are dedicated to
providing you with the information
and ideas you need to create delicious
foods. We welcome your comments
and suggestions. Write to us at:
Better Homes and Gardens® Books,
Cookbook Editorial Department,
1716 Locust St., Des Moines, IA
50309-3023.

If you would like to order additional
copies of any of our books, check
wherever books are sold.

CONTENTS

Pictured on the front cover: Cinnamon Rolls (page 378)
Pictured on page 1: *left,* Pecan Drops (page 189) and Browned Butter Cookies (page 188)
   center, Raspberry-Lemon Tartlets (page 86)
   right, Classic Ricotta Cheesecake (page 166)
Pictured on page 4: *top left,* Sour Cream, Raisin, and Pear Pie (page 74)
   lower left, Pumpkin-Praline Muffins (page 326) and Peach-Brown Sugar Muffins (page 327)
   right, Double-Swirl Apple Bread (page 358)

INTRODUCTION

Sure, it's easier to buy bread, cakes, cookies, and other baked goods from the baker or the grocery store. But home baking comes from the heart. It connects you with family and friends as well as traditions—handed down, learned, or new. In creating this book, we wanted to capture the rich, emotional experience of baking while presenting our largest, most comprehensive collection of baking recipes and information.

So, we asked people nationwide why they still choose to pull out a rolling pin and heat up the oven. "Baking is fun, cooking is everyday," said one individual. Another baker added, "It's rewarding when your kids get excited and say your cookies are the best, even if you burn a batch."

Now, *Better Homes and Gardens® New Baking Book* puts all the pleasures of baking between two covers. More than 600 recipes,

including must-have basics and hundreds of new ideas, will challenge seasoned cooks while inspiring novices. Count on instructional photos and tips throughout, too. Whatever your specialty, you will find it here: from cobblers and crisps to pies and pastries, from cakes and cookies to showy desserts, from holiday classics to breads for every occasion—including breakfast, dinner, snack time, high tea, and parties. Even the young aspiring baker can grab a stool and perch next to mom while poring over the "Baking with Kids" chapter.

Better Homes and Gardens® New Baking Book truly becomes yours once you have pressed your fingertips into dough and caught aromas wafting from the kitchen and throughout the house. After all, these recipes—with their marvelous flavors and textures—are personal gifts to lovingly shape and bestow.

baking basics

BAKING BASICS

You wouldn't build a house without a good set of plans, an understanding of the materials and techniques, and the right tools. Mastering the art of baking is no different. Whether you're making your first cake or your hundredth loaf of bread, there's no substitute for a trusted recipe and a good resource tool to rely on when you have questions. This chapter is full of information about common ingredients, measuring methods, mixing techniques, equipment, and bakeware that can help make your baking successful the first time—and every time.

Many of the recipes in this book are marked with one of the following symbols. These symbols designate recipes that are Best-Loved favorites, Low-Fat, and Easy to prepare, helping you choose recipes that fit your preferences, time limits, and dietary needs.

BEST-LOVED A Best-Loved recipe is one that is either so outstanding it gained instant favor among our food editors and Test Kitchen home economists or has been in the *Better Homes and Gardens* archives for many years and is a classic.

LOW-FAT A Low-Fat recipe is just that: low in fat, which by our definition, means it contains 3 to 5 grams of fat per serving.

EASY An Easy recipe is a comparatively simple one when you consider the entire collection of recipes in the chapter. It might have relatively few ingredients or might require only one bowl to prepare, for instance.

NUTRITION FACTS

With each recipe, we give important nutrition information. The calorie count of each serving and the amount, in grams, of fat, saturated fat, cholesterol, sodium, carbohydrates, fiber, and protein will help you keep tabs on what you eat. You can check the levels of each recipe serving for vitamin A, vitamin C, calcium, and iron. These are noted in percentages of the Daily Values. The Daily Values are dietary standards determined by the Food and Drug Administration (FDA).

HOW WE ANALYZE

Our Test Kitchen uses a computer analysis of each recipe to determine the nutritional value of a single serving. Here's how:
■ When ingredient options appear in a recipe (such as milk or half-and-half), we use the first one mentioned for analysis. The ingredient order does not mean we prefer one ingredient.
■ When milk is an ingredient in a recipe, the analysis is calculated using 2-percent milk.
■ The analysis does not include optional ingredients.
■ We use the first serving size listed when a range is given (such as "Makes 4 to 6 servings.")

RECIPE TIME ESTIMATES

The timings listed with each recipe should be used as general guidelines. Consider the following points as well.
■ Preparation (Prep) times with recipes are rounded to the nearest 5-minute increment.
■ Listings include the time to chop, slice, or otherwise prepare ingredients.
■ When a recipe gives an ingredient option, the calculations use the first ingredient.
■ Timings assume some steps are performed simultaneously.
■ The preparation of optional ingredients is not included.

EQUIPMENT

Using the right equipment is one way to guarantee a successful and enjoyable baking experience.

■ **Electric mixers.** These machines make life in the kitchen a whole lot easier. Portable (handheld) electric mixers are perfect for light jobs and short mixing periods, like whipping cream. For heavy-duty jobs and long mixing periods, a freestanding electric mixer works best, and it leaves you free to proceed with another part of the recipe. Some heavy-duty brands with dough hooks even take the effort out of kneading bread.

■ **Food processors.** Food processors can blend, chop, and puree as does a blender, but they also slice and shred. Some brands can even mix batters and knead bread and blend pastry (check your owner's manual to see what your model can do).

■ **Bakeware.** Bakeware is made in a range of materials: aluminum, tin, stainless steel, black steel, glass, and pottery. Both the material and the finish affect the final product. Shiny bakeware reflects heat, slowing the browning process. On the other hand, dark and dull-finish bakeware absorbs more heat, increasing the amount of browning. Here are some rules of thumb: Shiny bakeware, including aluminum, tin, and stainless steel, will result in thinner cake crusts and softer-set cookies that spread more. Dark or dull-finish bakeware, including dull aluminum or tin and glass, will give you heavier cake crusts, piecrusts that are evenly browned underneath as well as on top, crisp and nicely browned bread crusts, and crisper cookies. Black steel pans give breads a crisp dark crust and often are used for French bread sticks to give them their distinctive crunch. Essential bakeware includes:

Baking pans: 9×9×2-inch, 11×7×1½-inch, 13×9×2-inch

Baking sheets: 15×12-inch

Cake pans (round): 8×1½-inch, 9×1½-inch

Casserole dishes: in various sizes

Custard cups: 6 ounces each

Glass baking dishes: 1½-quart, 2-quart, 3-quart

Jelly-roll pan: 15×10×1-inch

Loaf pans: 8×4×2-inch, 9×5×3-inch

Muffin pan

Pie plate: 9-inch

Pizza pan or stone

Rectangular pans: 12×7×1½-inch, 13×9×2½-inch

Springform pan: 8- or 9-inch

Square pan: 8×8×2-inch or 9×9×2-inch

Tube pan: 10-inch (plain and fluted)

MEASURING

Baking is both an art and a science. To satisfy the scientific part, you must be correct and consistent when measuring ingredients. Not all ingredients are measured the same way.

■ **Liquids.** Use a glass or clear plastic liquid measuring cup on a

level surface. Bend down so your eye is level with the marking on the cup (see photo, lower left). When a liquid is measured in a measuring spoon, fill the spoon to the top, but don't let it spill over. Don't pour liquid ingredients over the other ingredients, in case you spill.

■ **Sugar.** Granulated or powdered sugar should be

spooned into a dry measuring cup and leveled off. Brown sugar, on the other hand, is pressed firmly into a dry measure so it holds the shape of the cup when it is turned out (see photo, above).

■ **Flour.** Proper measuring of flour is critical. Too much flour can

cause baked goods to turn out dry or sauces to become too thick. To measure flour, stir it in the bag or canister to lighten it. Except for cake flour, sifting is not necessary. Gently spoon flour into a dry measuring cup or a measuring spoon. Level it off the top with the straight side of a knife (see photo, above).

■ **Shortening.** Solid shortening is measured by pressing it firmly into a dry measuring cup or spoon with a rubber scraper (see photo, below), then leveling the excess off with a straight edge.

■ **Butter.** Butter is often packaged in stick form, with markings on the paper or foil wrapper indicating tablespoon and cup measures. Use a sharp

knife to cut off the amount needed (see photo, below). If the wrapper isn't marked, measure it as you would shortening.

■ **Spices.** Lightly fill the correct spoon just to the top with spice. A dash is less than ⅛ teaspoon, which is the smallest amount

you can measure accurately using a standard measuring spoon. A dash often is used when calling for dry seasonings or salt. Shake or sprinkle the ingredient into the palm of your hand so you can see how much you've got; add it to suit your taste.

HIGH-ALTITUDE ADJUSTMENTS

Ingredient	3,000 feet	5,000 feet	7,000 feet
Liquid: add for each cup	1 to 2 tablespoons	2 to 4 tablespoons	3 to 4 tablespoons
Baking powder: decrease for each teaspoon	⅛ teaspoon	⅛ to ¼ teaspoon	¼ teaspoon
Sugar: decrease for each cup	0 to 1 tablespoon	0 to 2 tablespoons	1 to 3 tablespoons

BAKING AT HIGH ALTITUDES

Baking at high altitudes requires some adjustments to standard recipes.

■ **Cakes.** If you live at or more than 3,000 feet above sea level, use the chart above to adjust the cake ingredients listed. Try the smaller amounts first; make any necessary adjustments next time around. When baking a cake, increase the oven temperature about 20 degrees and decrease the baking time slightly to keep it from expanding too much. For cakes leavened by air, such as angel food, beat the egg whites only to soft peaks. Otherwise, your cakes may expand too much (because the air pressure is less). If you're making a cake that contains a large amount of fat or chocolate—a cup or more—you may need to reduce the shortening by 1 to 2 tablespoons and add an egg to prevent the cake from falling. The leavening, sugar, and liquid in cakes leavened with baking powder or baking soda may need adjustment, too (see chart, above).

■ **Cookies, biscuits, and muffins.** Cookies, biscuits, and muffins are more stable than cakes and need little adjustment at high altitudes. If you feel it is necessary, experiment by slightly reducing the sugar and baking powder and increasing the liquid. For cookies, increase the oven temperature about 20 degrees and slightly decrease the baking time. This will keep your cookies from drying out.

■ **Yeast doughs.** If you're working with a yeast dough, allow unshaped dough to rise according to recipe directions; punch dough down. Repeat rising step once more before shaping dough. If dough seems dry, add more liquid and reduce the amount of flour the next time you make the recipe. Because flours tend to be drier at high altitudes, sometimes they absorb more liquid.

■ **Further information.** For more information on cooking at high altitudes, contact your county extension agent or write: Colorado State University Food Science Extension Office Fort Collins, CO 80523–1571. (Please use this address only for questions related to high-altitude cooking.)

EGGS

■ **Separating eggs.** To separate a yolk from the white, use an egg separator (see photo, below). Separating the egg yolk from the egg white by passing the yolk from shell to shell is not considered safe.

■ **Egg safety.** Eating uncooked or slightly cooked eggs can be hazardous, especially to people vulnerable to salmonella such as the elderly, infants, children, pregnant women, and the seriously ill. Commercial forms of egg products are safe because they are pasteurized, which destroys salmonella bacteria.

■ **Using egg substitutes.** Refrigerated or frozen egg substitutes are easy to use, readily available, and enable anyone on a cholesterol-restricted diet to enjoy great baked goods that contain eggs. These products are based on egg whites and contain no fat or cholesterol. When baking with an egg substitute, use ¼ cup of either refrigerated or frozen egg product for each whole egg called for in the recipe for most cookies, cakes, and muffins. Do not, however, use an egg substitute when the recipe you are making relies on air being whipped into eggs to leaven it, such as a sponge cake.

EGG EQUIVALENCE CHART

If you use an egg size other than large, you may need to increase or decrease the number of eggs you use in our recipes. Use these suggested alternatives:

1 large egg	=	1 jumbo, extra-large, medium, or small egg
2 large eggs	=	2 jumbo, 2 extra-large, 2 medium, or 3 small eggs
3 large eggs	=	2 jumbo, 3 extra-large, 3 medium, or 4 small eggs
4 large eggs	=	3 jumbo, 4 extra-large, 5 medium, or 5 small eggs
5 large eggs	=	4 jumbo, 4 extra-large, 6 medium, or 7 small eggs

■ **Beating eggs.** Beating eggs to the just-right stage is critical for many recipes.

Slightly beaten eggs: Use a fork to beat the whole egg until the yolk and white are combined and no streaks remain (a).

Soft peaks: Place the egg whites in a clean glass or metal bowl (do not use plastic). Beat with an electric mixer on medium speed or with a rotary beater until they form peaks with tips that curl over when the beaters are lifted (b). Be careful as you separate your eggs—even just a tiny speck of fat, oil, or yolk in the bowl will prevent the whites from whipping. For the best results, separate your eggs and let the whites sit at room temperature for 30 minutes first.

Stiff peaks: Continue beating egg whites on high speed until they form peaks with tips that stand straight when the beaters are lifted (c).

Beating egg yolks: Beat the egg yolks with an electric mixer on high speed for about 5 minutes or until they are thick and lemon-colored (d).

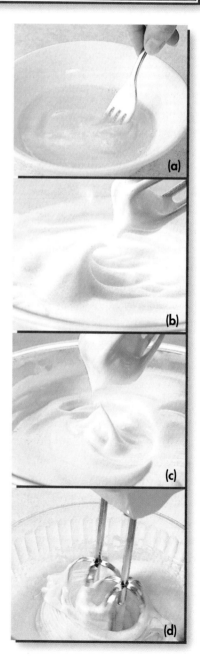

(a)

(b)

(c)

(d)

FATS AND OILS

Baked products such as cakes and cookies rely on fats for flavor and tenderness.

■ **Butter.** Nothing beats the flavor and richness that butter adds to baked goods. For all of the recipes in this book, we recommend using butter rather than margarine (see tip, right). What doesn't make a difference is whether you use salted or unsalted butter (although if you use unsalted butter, you may want to increase the amount of salt in the recipe).

■ **Margarine.** Margarine, made from vegetable oil or animal fat, was developed in the late 1800s as a substitute for butter. For all of the recipes in this book, we recommend using butter.

■ **Shortening.** Shortening is a solid fat that has been made from vegetable oils. It's often used for tender, flaky piecrusts and biscuits. It now comes packaged in sticks marked conveniently with tablespoon and cup measurements. Shortening can be stored at room temperature for up to a year. Plain and butter-flavored types are available; use whichever you prefer.

■ **Cooking oils, flavored oils.** For baking, these cannot be used interchangeably with solid fats because they are unable to hold air when beaten. Mildly flavored vegetable oils generally are made from corn, soybeans, sunflower seeds, or peanuts and have a pale color. Nut oils, such as walnut oil, have a pronounced nutty flavor and can be darker in color. Olive oil is used primarily in baking recipes for focaccia, pizza doughs, breads, and the occasional cake.

WHY NOT MARGARINE?

Technically, anything on your supermarket shelf labeled "margarine" must be at least 80 percent vegetable oil or fat, which—if used in baking in place of butter—will provide satisfactory results. However, there are so many margarine look-alikes on the market—and their labeling can be so tricky—it can be confusing as to which is a true margarine. Any margarinelike product that has less than 80 percent vegetable oil or fat contains additional water and milk solids and can make your baked goods soggy or rock-hard. If you do elect to use a true margarine, your rolled cookie dough, for instance, will be softer than if you use butter. You may need to chill it in the freezer to make it workable. Also, it's critical to use butter in baked goods that rely strictly on butter for flavor, such as genoise and pound cake. Shortbread should only be made with butter to retain its characteristic butter flavor, richness, and dense crumb. Streusel toppings, too, shouldn't be made with margarine because they don't crisp up as they do when they're made with butter.

FLOURS AND GRAINS

Flours are essential to many baked products. Many cereals, roots, and seeds are milled to make flour, although wheat is the most popular and contains the gluten necessary to give baked goods their structure. Some flours are made from soft wheats, some from hard wheats, and others are a combination of the two. Each type of flour affects the crumb texture of baked products differently.

■ **All-purpose flour.** This flour is made from a blend of soft and hard wheat flours and, as its name implies, is used as a multipurpose flour in a range of baked goods. However, different manufacturers use varying proportions of hard and soft wheats, so the protein level in all-purpose flours ranges from 9 to 15 grams per cup.

When baking yeast breads, use an all-purpose flour or a bread flour with at least 2¾ grams of protein per ¼ cup because high-protein flours tend to produce finer textured, higher volume yeast breads. To find out how much protein an all-purpose flour contains, check the amount of protein in grams per cup on the flour bag's nutrition label.

For information on bleached versus unbleached flour, see the tip on page 12.

■ **Cake flour.** Cake flour is made from soft wheat and produces a tender, delicate crumb because the gluten is less elastic. Many bakers use it for angel food and chiffon cakes. All the recipes in this cookbook were perfected using all-purpose flour. If you would like to use cake flour instead, sift it before measuring. Use 1 cup plus 2 tablespoons of cake flour for every 1 cup of all-purpose flour.

■ **Self-rising flour.** Self-rising flour is an all-purpose flour that contains baking powder, baking soda, and salt. You can use it as a substitute for all-purpose flour in quick bread recipes, but omit the salt, baking powder, and baking soda from the recipe.

■ **Bread flour.** Bread flour contains more gluten and protein than all-purpose flour, making it ideal for baking breads. When rubbed between your fingers, it feels a bit more granular than all-purpose flour. When used instead of all-purpose flour, you usually need less. If you use a bread machine, use bread flour instead of all-purpose flour for the best results. Or, use all-purpose flour and add 1 or 2 tablespoons of gluten flour (available at grocery or natural food stores).

■ **Specialty flours.** Specialty flours, such as whole wheat or graham, rye, oat, buckwheat, and soy, generally are combined with all-purpose flour in baked products because none has sufficient gluten to provide the right amount of elasticity on its own.

■ **Whole wheat.** Whole wheat or graham flours are processed less than plain flour and, therefore, retain more of their nutrients and fiber.

■ **Rye flour.** Rye flour is a traditional ingredient in many breads, cakes, and pastries of Northern and Eastern Europe. The gluten in rye flour adds stickiness to the dough but lacks

---

BLEACHED VS. UNBLEACHED

What's the difference between bleached and unbleached flour? They're both all-purpose, which means they're equally good for making most baked goods. The difference is that bleached flour has been made chemically whiter in appearance than unbleached flour. The bleaching process does compromise some of the flour's nutrients, but they are often added back to the flour. Which flour you choose is a personal preference. Some bakers like their white cake and bread as white as they can be; others prefer their flour to be processed as little as possible.

---

the elasticity of wheat flour gluten. Using a large proportion of rye flour to wheat flour results in a more compact product.

■ **Oat flour.** Oat flour can be purchased or made by grinding rolled oats to a fine powder in a food processor, ½ cup at a time.

■ **Soy flour.** Soy flour is a cream colored, strong flavored flour that is a rich source of protein and iron and contains no gluten. Baked products made with soy flour brown more quickly, so you may have to reduce the baking temperature depending on the amount used.

■ **Storing flour.** All-purpose flour should be stored in an airtight container in a cool, dry place for up to 10 to 15 months. Whole wheat and other whole grain flours may be stored for up to 5 months. For longer storage, refrigerate or freeze the flour in a moisture- and vaporproof container. Be sure to warm chilled flour to room temperature before using in yeast breads so it does not slow down the rising of the bread.

LEAVENINGS

Leavening agents add lightness to baked goods by "raising" them. Common leavens include yeast, baking powder, and baking soda. Steam, which forms when the liquid in the batter or dough heats up, also can cause a product to expand.

■ **Yeast.** Yeast is a one-celled organism that wakes up and goes into action when it's combined with a warm liquid and sugar or starch. It produces little bubbles of carbon dioxide gas that get trapped in your dough and make it rise. There are three forms of yeast available: active dry, quick-rising, and compressed. Active dry yeast is the most popular form. These tiny, dehydrated granules are mixed with flour or dissolved in warm water before they're used. Quick-rising yeast (sometimes called fast-rising or instant yeast) is a more active strain of yeast. It's usually mixed with the dry ingredients before the warm liquids are added. Quick-rising yeast cuts rising time by about one-third. The first rising will take about 10 to 15 minutes less; the second rising will be shortened, too. Quick-rising yeast can be substituted for active dry yeast, except in recipes requiring the dough to rise in the refrigerator and in doughs using sourdough starter. Compressed yeast, also called fresh yeast, comes in small, foil-wrapped square cakes. Soften it in warm water according to the package directions.

■ **Baking powder and soda.** Baking powder and baking soda are chemical leavening agents that produce carbon dioxide just as yeast does. Double-acting baking powder produces gases in two stages: first, when liquids are added and, second, during baking. Baking soda creates carbon dioxide bubbles instantly when it's mixed with acidic ingredients such as buttermilk, sour cream, or fruit juices. Any recipe that uses only baking soda as leaven should be baked immediately, before all those bubbles deflate.

DAIRY PRODUCTS

Milk and milk products are used in baking to provide moisture, flavor, and color and to activate the leavening agents. Because whole, low-fat, and skim milk vary only in fat content, you can use them interchangeably in baking. Whole milk may, however, result in a richer flavor than skim milk.

■ **Buttermilk.** Buttermilk is low-fat or skim milk to which a bacterial culture has been added. It is low in fat, thick, and creamy, with a mildly acidic taste. Sour milk, made from milk and lemon juice or vinegar, can be substituted for buttermilk (see tip, page 329).

WHIPPED CREAM FROSTING

Sweetened whipped cream makes a wonderful frosting on a cake, but unless it's stabilized, it doesn't hold its shape for long once it's piped through a pastry bag. Here's how to make it retain its shape for up to 2 days: In a glass measuring cup stir together 1 tablespoon cold water and ½ teaspoon unflavored gelatin. Let stand for 2 minutes. Place the measuring cup in a saucepan of boiling water. Cook and stir about 1 minute or until the gelatin is completely dissolved. In a bowl beat 1 cup whipping cream and 2 tablespoons sugar with an electric mixer on medium speed while gradually drizzling the gelatin over the cream mixture. Continue beating the cream mixture until stiff peaks form. Makes 2 cups (can be doubled).

■ **Whipping cream.** Whipping cream contains between 30 and 49 percent fat and can be beaten to form peaks that retain their shape. To speed up whipping, chill the bowl and beaters first.

■ **Light cream.** Light cream or table cream contains 10 to 30 percent fat, which is not sufficient for whipping.

■ **Half-and-half.** A mixture of milk and cream, half-and-half can be used instead of light cream in most recipes.

■ **Evaporated milk.** Evaporated milk is milk that has had 60 percent of its water removed. It is sold in cans and can be stored at room temperature until opened. Do not use evaporated milk as a substitute for sweetened condensed milk. It may be substituted for other milk products if you reconstitute it using 2 parts evaporated milk to 3 parts water (for example, ½ cup evaporated milk to ¾ cup water).

■ **Sweetened condensed milk.** Sweetened condensed milk is milk that has had about 50 percent of its water removed and, like evaporated milk, is sold in cans and can be stored at room temperature until opened. Because sweetened condensed milk also has about 40 percent added sugar, it is not a suitable substitute for other milks.

■ **Nonfat dry milk.** Nonfat dry milk has both the fat and water removed. Mix nonfat milk powder with water according to package directions to form milk. Some of the recipes in this cookbook call for it as a dry ingredient to add richness to baked products.

SWEETENERS

Sweeteners are essential for adding flavor, tenderness, and a bit of browning to baked goods. They may be either granular, as in granulated white and brown sugar, or liquid, as in honey, corn syrup, and molasses.

■ **Granulated, or white, sugar.** Granulated, or white, sugar is the most common sweetener used in baking. It is made from sugarcane or sugar beets. White sugar is most commonly available in what is called fine granulation, but it also comes in superfine (also called ultrafine or caster sugar), a finer grind of sugar that dissolves readily, making it ideal for frosting, meringues, and drinks. Pearl or coarse sugar is just that—a coarser granulation best used for decorating cookies and other baked goods.

■ **Brown sugar.** Brown sugar is a processed mixture of granulated sugar and molasses which gives it its distinctive flavor and color. Brown sugar is available in both light and dark varieties; dark brown sugar has the stronger flavor. Recipes in this cookbook were tested using light brown sugar, unless specified otherwise. You can substitute granulated sugar measure for measure for brown sugar, except in products where color and flavor might be important, such as a caramel sauce. In baked products that use baking powder or baking soda, add ¼ teaspoon more baking soda for each cup of brown sugar used in place of granulated sugar.

■ **Powdered sugar.** Powdered sugar, also known as confectioner's sugar, is granulated sugar that has been milled to a fine powder then mixed with cornstarch to prevent lumping. Sift powdered sugar before using and do not substitute it for granulated sugar.

■ **Honey.** Honey is made by bees from all sorts of flower nectars.

HOW TO SKIN A HAZELNUT

Hazelnuts—long popular in Europe (especially in combination with chocolate)—have been gaining many fans in North America in the last few years with their rich, sweet taste. For most uses, hazelnuts need to have their bitter brown cloak of skin removed before they're stirred into a cake batter or sprinkled over a tart. Here's how: Spread shelled hazelnuts on an ungreased cookie sheet and toast in a 350° oven for 10 to 15 minutes, stirring occasionally, until the skins begin to flake. Remove from the oven and place a handful of nuts at a time in a clean, dry cotton kitchen towel and rub vigorously until the skins come off.

It adds moisture, sweetness, and a characteristic flavor to baked goods. Because it caramelizes more quickly and at lower temperatures than sugar, honey causes baked goods to brown more quickly. Although it is available in whipped forms, the recipes in this cookbook refer to pure, unwhipped honey.

■ **Corn syrup.** Corn syrup is a heavy syrup that has half the sweetness of sugar. It is available in light and dark varieties. Like dark brown sugar, dark corn syrup has the stronger flavor.

■ **Molasses.** Although it is primarily used for flavoring gingersnaps and gingerbread, molasses—a thick, dark brown syrup generally made from the juice pressed from sugarcane during refining—adds sweetness to baked goods, too. Molasses comes in light and dark varieties. The two forms are interchangeable, so choose one depending on how much molasses flavor you like.

NUTS

Whole or chopped, plain or salted, nuts add an appealing crunch and rich flavor to any baked product.

■ **Almonds.** Almonds are a flat, oval-shaped nut with a reddish brown skin that can be removed by blanching. The smooth, light-colored meat has a mild, yet rich, flavor. Almonds are available whole, sliced, slivered, and chopped.

■ **Brazil nuts.** Brazil nuts (elephant toes to some) are a large nut with a thin, brown skin and an oily, rich flavor.

■ **Cashews.** Crescent-shaped cashews, with their rich, buttery flavor, are a favorite of bakers and snackers. Buy them raw or roasted, salted or plain. Choose roasted cashews for baking unless specified otherwise.

■ **Hazelnuts.** Hazelnuts, also called filberts, are a small, round nut with a mild, sweet flavor. The nut meat is covered with a thin, brown skin that needs to be removed before you use them in baking (see tip, above left).

■ **Hickory nuts.** Hickory nuts resemble walnuts but have a rich, oily flavor similar to that of toasted pecans.

■ **Macadamia nuts.** These tropical nuts taste rich, sweet, and buttery. You can use these small, round nuts wherever you would use cashews.

■ **Peanuts.** America's favorite nut, the peanut, is technically not a nut at all but a legume. Roasting intensifies a peanut's rich, buttery flavor. For baking, it's best to use peanuts that have had their skins removed. Selecting between salted or unsalted peanuts is strictly a personal choice.

■ **Pecans.** Pecans are rich and buttery and have the highest fat content of any nut. Pecans often are substituted for walnuts and vice-versa.

■ **Pine nuts.** Also known as pignolia or piñon, pine nuts actually are seeds from a variety of pine trees. This gives the small, creamy white nut a sweet, faint pine flavor. Pine nuts can be slender and pellet-shaped or more triangular.

■ **Pistachios.** The small pistachio has a pale green meat covered with a paper-thin, brown skin. Their thin, smooth shells, which are split at one end, are often dyed red or green. Their mild,

---

FRUIT MATH

You're making your favorite banana bread, and the recipe calls for 2 cups of mashed bananas. What does that mean in terms of whole bananas? Rest easy. We've done the culinary calculations to answer that question and a few others, too:

1 pound bananas = 3 medium or 4 small = 2 cups sliced = 1 cup mashed

1 pound apples = 4 small, 3 medium, or 2 large = 2¾ cups sliced = 2 cups chopped

1 pound apricots = 8 to 12 whole = 2½ cups sliced

1 pound pears = 3 medium = 3½ cups sliced = 3 cups chopped

1 medium lemon = 3 tablespoons juice = 2 teaspoons shredded peel

---

sweet flavor is similar to that of almonds.

■ **Walnuts.** Black walnuts are rich and oily with an intense flavor. Walnuts, other than the black walnut, are called English walnuts. They have a mild flavor that makes them popular in baking.

FRUITS

Dried fruits add flavor, texture, and color to baked goods.

■ **Berries and cherries.** Dried cranberries, blueberries, and cherries are available in larger supermarkets or through catalogs. They have a very sweet taste and chewy texture. These small, flavor-packed gems can be used in breads, desserts, and pies—anywhere you might expect to find raisins.

■ **Apples, etc.** Dried apples, apricots, pears, and peaches can be used whole or chopped. They're readily available at your supermarket.

■ **Dates and figs.** Dates and figs come in lots of forms. Just remember, when a recipe calls for "snipped dates," use cut-up whole dates, not the sugar-coated dates. You can find figs in light or dark varieties.

■ **Candied fruits.** During the holiday season, supermarkets stock up on candied fruits. They add color and flavor to fruit cakes, quick breads, and cookies. Candied fruits are available as citron, peels, mixed fruit, cherries, pineapple, apricots, mango, and papaya.

■ **Raisins and currants.** In terms of baking, the main point of difference between raisins and currants is their size (currants are smaller than raisins). Both have dark brown, wrinkly skin and are very sweet.

SECTIONING CITRUS FRUIT

Eating all of an orange—including the white membrane that surrounds each segment—may be all right at lunchtime, but when you're baking something special with citrus, the recipe often calls for fruit that has been sectioned or had its segments separated from each other and the white membrane removed. To section a citrus fruit, use a sharp paring knife to remove the peel and white rind. Working over a bowl to catch the juice, cut into the center of the fruit between one section and the membrane. Turn the knife and slide it along the other side of the section, next to the membrane, cutting outward.

CHOCOLATE

Considered to be "food of the gods" to many, chocolate comes in a passel of products on the market. Because chocolate differs in flavor and consistency when it's melted, be sure to use only the type of chocolate called for in a recipe using melted chocolate.

■ **Unsweetened chocolate.** Unsweetened chocolate is the basic type of chocolate from which all others are made. Sometimes called baking or bitter chocolate, unsweetened chocolate is pure chocolate with no sugar or flavoring added.

■ **Semisweet chocolate.** Semisweet chocolate is pure chocolate with cocoa butter and sugar added to it.

■ **Sweet baking chocolate.** Sweet baking chocolate is similar to semisweet chocolate but has a higher sugar content.

■ **Milk chocolate.** Milk chocolate is made of pure chocolate, extra cocoa butter, sugar, and milk solids. Milk chocolate is used mostly for candy bars and other confections. You won't see it called for in too many recipes.

■ **White baking bars.** White baking bars and pieces are often referred to as "white chocolate." But white chocolate isn't really chocolate at all because it lacks pure chocolate (and therefore can't be labeled chocolate in the United States). These products are a blend of sugar, cocoa butter, dry milk solids, and vanilla or vanillin.

■ **Candy coating.** Candy coating is a chocolatelike product with most of the cocoa butter removed and replaced with vegetable fat. You can find it in assorted colors and flavors.

■ **Mexican chocolate.** From our neighbors south of the border comes Mexican-style sweet chocolate. This chocolate starts with roasted cocoa beans ground together with cinnamon and sugar. Ground almonds may also be added. You'll find it in Mexican markets.

■ **Unsweetened cocoa powder.** Unsweetened cocoa powder is made by pressing most of the cocoa butter from pure chocolate, then grinding the remaining chocolate solids into a powder. Dutch-process cocoa powder, also called European-style cocoa powder, is unsweetened cocoa powder that has been treated with alkali to neutralize the naturally occurring acids; its flavor is more mellow and the color redder than unsweetened cocoa powder. These two cocoa powders can be used interchangeably.

■ **Storing chocolate.** Keep your chocolate in a tightly covered container or sealed plastic bag in a cool, dry place. If stored in a too-warm place (higher than 78 degrees), your chocolate may "bloom" or develop a harmless gray film. Keep cocoa powder in a tightly covered container in that same cool, dry place.

■ **Melting chocolate.** Place cut-up chocolate or chocolate pieces in a heavy saucepan. Melt over low heat, stirring often to avoid scorching. When it's necessary that the chocolate set up when it cools, such as when dipping fruits or making chocolate garnishes, before heating, add 1 teaspoon shortening for each ½ cup (3 ounces) of chocolate.

Microwave method: To melt chocolate in your microwave oven, place ½ cup of pieces or 3 ounces cut-up chocolate in a microwave-safe measuring cup or custard cup. Microwave, uncovered, on high for 60 to 90 seconds or until softened enough to stir smooth, stirring after 1 minute. (Chocolate won't seem melted until stirred.)

■ **Quick-tempering chocolate.** Tempering chocolate is a method of slowly melting chocolate followed by carefully cooling it. This procedure stabilizes the cocoa butter so the chocolate holds its shape. Since tempering chocolate is a lengthy process, we use a method of melting chocolate that produces the same results in less time. We call this method "quick-tempering." Quick-temper chocolate when you will be using it for decorations that must hold their shape at room temperature, such as chocolate leaves or chocolate lace (see photos and instructions on page 17) or when dipping dried fruit or nuts. Follow these step-by-step directions for quick-tempering, and your chocolate will set up crisp and glossy every time.

Step 1: Chop up to 1 pound of bars, squares, or large pieces of chocolate into small pieces. In a 4-cup glass measure or a 1½-quart glass mixing bowl, combine the amount of chocolate and shortening called for in the recipe. (Or, use 1 tablespoon of shortening for every 6 ounces of chocolate.)

Step 2: Pour very warm tap water (100° to 110°) into a large glass casserole or bowl to a depth of 1 inch. Place the measure or

CHOCOLATE GARNISHES

Sweet, seductive, and smooth—chocolate makes the ultimate garnish. Here's everything you need to know to craft simple trims as well as stunning chocolate ornaments.

■ **Grated:** Rub a solid piece of chocolate across the grating section—either fine or large—of a handheld grater.

■ **Shaved:** Using a vegetable peeler, make short, quick strokes across the surface of a solid piece of chocolate.

■ **Lace:** Pipe tempered chocolate from a pastry bag onto a chilled, waxed-paper-lined baking sheet; let dry.

■ **Small curls**: Draw a peeler across the narrow side of a chocolate bar (milk chocolate may be easier for small curls).

■ **Leaves:** Brush tempered chocolate on the underside of nontoxic leaves such as mint, rose, lemon, and strawberry.

■ **Large curls:** Carefully draw a vegetable peeler across the broad surface of a bar of chocolate.

bowl containing the chocolate inside the casserole. Water should cover the bottom half of the measure or bowl containing the chocolate. Adjust the water level as necessary. (Do not splash any water into the chocolate.)

Step 3: Stir the chocolate mixture constantly with a rubber spatula until completely melted and smooth. This takes about 15 to 20 minutes. (Don't rush.)

Step 4: If the water begins to cool, remove the measure or bowl containing the chocolate.

Discard the cool water and add warm water. Return the measure or bowl containing the chocolate to the bowl containing water.

Step 5: Do not allow any water or moisture to touch the chocolate. Just one drop can cause the chocolate to become thick and grainy. If water should get into the chocolate, stir in additional shortening, 1 teaspoon at a time, until the mixture becomes shiny and smooth.

Step 6: When melted and smooth, the chocolate is ready for dipping or shaping. If the chocolate becomes too thick during handling, repeat Step 4. Stir the chocolate constantly until it again reaches dipping consistency.

Step 7: Let your finished product set up in a cool, dry place. Do not chill your finished product, or the chocolate will lose temper and become soft at room temperature.

DECORATING

Decorations and garnishes turn a simply delicious dessert into a work of art. Here's how to create some classic embellishments.

■ **Piping.** With a pastry bag fitted with a variety of tips and a little practice, you have almost unlimited options for making beautiful designs on your desserts with whipped cream or frosting. A round tip is used for writing and making dots and lines (a). A star tip can be used to make stars, shells, and zigzags (b). Leaf tips are great for making leaves of all shapes and sizes (c).

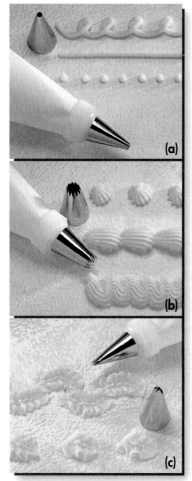

■ **Two-Tone piping.** Fill your decorating bag with two different colors of frosting or whipped cream to pipe marbled decorations or decorations with tinted edges. For these, use a decorating bag fitted with a

medium or large star tip (about ¼- to ½-inch opening). To make marbled stars, shells, or zigzags, carefully fill each side of the bag with a different color frosting or whipped cream (see photo above, top row). To give tinted edges to stars, shells, or zigzags, use a long metal spatula to spread a thin layer of one color frosting or whipped cream onto the inside of the entire decorating bag. Carefully spoon another color frosting or cream into the bag (see photo above, bottom row).

■ **Edible flowers.** Top almost any dessert with naturally colorful, edible flowers. Scatter small flowers over cakes or tortes, or break off some petals and sprinkle them over desserts.

Choose any edible flower to decorate your dessert. If you plan to eat the flower, select one with a flavor that is compatible with sweets. Some good choices are pansies, violets, rose petals, and dianthus.

Be sure to use only edible flowers around food even if you don't plan to eat them. To be edible, the flower must be free of both naturally occurring and man-made toxins. To find edible flowers, look no farther than your own garden, provided that neither you nor your neighbors use chemical fertilizers or pesticides. Pick the flowers just before using, rinse, and gently

pat dry. Or, look for edible flowers in the produce section of your supermarket. Flowers that come from a florist are usually treated with chemicals and should never be used with food.

■ **Dusting.** Dusting is one of the easiest decorating techniques to master. You can dust over cakes, tortes, cheesecakes, cookies, and even puddings. For toppings, try ground nuts, unsweetened cocoa powder, ground spices, coarse-grain or crystal sugar, extra-fine-grain sugar, cinnamon-sugar, powdered sugar, or powdered sugar mixed with spices, unsweetened cocoa powder, or powdered food coloring. Sift the topping through a sieve or sifter onto the top of the dessert. When selecting the utensil to use, consider the fineness of your topping. A sifter works well for powdered sugar or unsweetened cocoa powder. Ground nuts will require a sieve with a coarser mesh.

To dust a dessert top, spoon the topping of your choice into a sieve or sifter. Hold the utensil over the dessert. With your free hand, gently tap the utensil so a little of the topping comes out. Dust lightly, moving the sieve over the dessert to cover the whole surface. For a heavier coating, dust again.

■ **Stenciling.** Personalize your dessert by stenciling a unique design. It works best on cakes, tortes, and pastries with flat surfaces.

For a stencil, use a purchased doily or a purchased stencil, or make your own stencil from lightweight cardboard. A doily can be cut into small pieces to use part of the design.

To make your own stencil, draw a design on a piece of cardboard (a gift box or a manila folder works well). Then use a crafts knife to cut out the design.

Place the stencil on top of the dessert surface. Sift the desired topping over the stencil, as directed for Dusting (see page 18 and photo below). If your stencil has large designs, use a

clean, dry brush to brush any topping left on the stencil into the holes. This keeps the edges of your design sharp and clean. Carefully lift off the stencil. If you like, brush any remaining topping off your stencil and save the stencil to use another time.

To stencil a design on a plate, choose a stencil with large holes. Place the stencil on the plate and lightly brush melted butter or shortening in the holes (or spray the holes with nonstick spray coating). Sprinkle the desired topping over the stencil as directed for Dusting. Carefully lift off the stencil.

■ **Marzipan.** Marzipan, a creamy almond confection, can be formed into a variety of fanciful shapes and decorations. Marzipan can be found in your

grocery store or a gourmet or specialty store. To tint marzipan, break off a small portion and knead in a little liquid or paste food coloring. Add a tiny bit of food coloring at a time until the marzipan becomes a shade you like. Shape the tinted marzipan into tiny fruits; paint (see Painting, below) or roll out and cut with small cookie cutters into hearts, stars, etc.

■ **Painting.** Paint a colorful design on desserts, such as cookies, pastries, and frosted cakes. For paint, use powdered food coloring or petal dust. (Petal dust is a fine dusting powder that is available in many colors, including gold and silver. Use gold and silver petal dust to give a shimmery, glistening highlight to foods. Petal dust is available through mail-order sources or specialty stores.) You can use powdered food coloring or petal dust either diluted with a little alcohol or in its dry form. If you want a smooth finish, mix a little powdered food coloring or petal dust with a few drops of 90- or 100-proof alcohol. (Do not use rubbing alcohol.) The alcohol will evaporate quickly, so you may need to add a few more drops of alcohol to the coloring while painting. With a clean, small paintbrush, paint designs on your desserts. To give soft highlights to decorations made from marzipan, paint with the dry powdered coloring or petal dust. Use a dry, clean, small paintbrush to brush the coloring on the decoration. You may want to try brushing the powdered coloring or petal dust along the edges of the decorations.

CANDIED FLOWERS

With a luster all their own, candied flowers create a glistening garnish. To make candied flowers, gently wash fresh edible flowers in water. Place them on white paper towels and let them air-dry or gently blot them dry. For large flowers or flowers with petals that are closed tightly, break off the petals and candy the individual petals.

In a small bowl stir together 2 tablespoons water and 1 tablespoon thawed frozen egg substitute. Using a small, clean paintbrush, brush the egg mixture on each side of each petal in a thin, even layer. Sprinkle each flower evenly with superfine-grain sugar. To give the flowers a hint of gold color, mix 1/8 teaspoon gold petal dust with the sugar before sprinkling it over the flowers. Shake each flower or petal to remove the excess sugar. Let the flowers dry on waxed paper for 2 to 4 hours.

Store candied flowers in an airtight container between layers of waxed paper for up to 4 weeks. For longer storage, freeze the candied flowers in the airtight container for up to 6 months.

BAKING GLOSSARY

■ **Almond paste.** A creamy mixture made of ground blanched almonds and sugar. For the best baking results, use an almond paste without syrup or liquid glucose. Almond paste is used as a filling in pastries, cakes, and confections.

■ **Baker's ammonia.** A compound also known as hartshorn powder that was once used commonly as a leavening agent. It's most often used in Scandinavian baking and is available at pharmacies.

■ **Baking dish.** A coverless glass or ceramic vessel used for cooking in the oven. A baking dish can be substituted for a metal baking pan of the same size. For baked items, such as breads and cakes, the oven temperature will need to be lowered 25 degrees to prevent overbrowning of the food.

■ **Baking pan.** A coverless metal vessel used for cooking in the oven. Baking pans vary in size and may be round, square, rectangular, or a special shape, such as a heart. The sides of the pan are ¾ inch high or more.

■ **Baking stone.** A heavy, thick plate of beige or brown stone that can be placed in the oven to replicate the baking qualities of brick-floored commercial bread ovens. Baking stones can be round or rectangular and can be left in the oven when not in use.

■ **Batter.** A mixture usually made with flour and a liquid, such as milk or fruit juice. It also may include egg, sugar, butter, shortening, cooking oil, leavening, or flavorings. Batters can vary in consistency from thin enough to pour to thick enough to drop from a spoon.

■ **Beat.** To make a mixture smooth by briskly whipping or stirring it with a spoon, fork, wire whisk, rotary beater, or electric mixer.

■ **Blend.** To combine two or more ingredients until smooth and uniform in texture, flavor, and color; done by hand or with an electric blender or mixer.

■ **Boil.** To cook food in liquid at a temperature that causes bubbles to form in the liquid and rise in a steady pattern, breaking on the surface. A rolling boil is when liquid is boiling so vigorously the bubbles can't be stirred down.

■ **Caramelize.** To heat and stir sugar until it melts and browns. Caramelized, or burnt, sugar is used in dessert recipes such as flan, candy-coated nuts, and burnt sugar cake and frosting.

■ **Chill.** To cool a food to below room temperature in the refrigerator or freezer, or over ice.

■ **Chop.** To cut foods with a knife, cleaver, or food processor into smaller pieces.

■ **Coconut.** The large, oval, husk-covered fruit of the coconut palm. Its market forms include canned and packaged coconut that is processed and sold shredded, flaked, and grated in sweetened and unsweetened forms. Flaked coconut is finer than shredded. Fresh and dried coconut pieces also are available.

■ **Cream.** To beat a fat, such as butter or shortening, either alone or with sugar to a light, fluffy consistency. This process incorporates air into the fat so baked products have a lighter texture and better volume.

■ **Créme fraîche.** A dairy product made from whipping cream and a bacterial culture. The culture causes the whipping cream to thicken and develop a sharp, tangy flavor. Créme fraîche is similar to sour cream but is softer and has a milder flavor. Popular in French cooking, créme fraîche is often spooned over fresh fruit or used in recipes as you would sour cream. It is available at specialty food stores. If you can't find it in your area, you can make a substitute by combining ½ cup whipping cream and ½ cup dairy sour cream. Cover the mixture and let it stand at room temperature for 2 to 5 hours or until it thickens. Refrigerate for up to 1 week.

■ **Crimp.** To pinch or press pastry dough together using your fingers, or a fork or another utensil. Usually done for a piecrust edge.

■ **Cut in.** To work a solid fat, such as shortening or butter, into dry ingredients, usually with a pastry blender or two knives.

■ **Dash.** A measure equal to ¹⁄₁₆ teaspoon. Can be measured by filling a ¼-teaspoon measure one-fourth full.

■ **Devonshire cream.** A specialty of Devonshire, England, this extra-thick cream is made by heating whole, unpasteurized milk until a semisolid layer of cream forms on the surface. After cooling, the Devonshire, or clotted, cream traditionally is served atop scones with jam (see recipe, page 258 steps 1–3).

■ **Dissolve.** To stir a solid food and a liquid food together to form a mixture in which none of the solid remains.

■ **Dough.** A mixture of flour and liquid to which other ingredients, such as sweeteners, shortening, butter, egg, or a leavening agent, may be added. A dough is thick and nonpourable; some doughs can be kneaded. Soft doughs have more liquid and generally are used for biscuits, breads, and drop cookies. Stiff doughs are firm enough to be rolled out easily and are used to make items such as piecrusts and cutout cookies.

■ **Dried egg whites.** Dried egg whites can be used where egg white is needed, but not meringue powder, which has added sugar. Dried egg whites also are safer than raw egg whites. One handy use for them is in making egg white glazes for baked goods (no yolk is wasted). Dried egg whites are found in powdered form in the baking aisle of many grocery stores.

■ **Dried fruit.** Fruit that has been depleted of more than half its water content by exposure to the sun or by mechanical heating methods. Dried fruit is chewy and very sweet due to the concentration of sugars during the drying process.

■ **Drizzle.** To randomly pour a liquid, such as powdered sugar icing, in a thin stream over food.

■ **Dust.** To lightly coat or sprinkle a food with a dry ingredient, such as flour or powdered sugar, either before or after cooking.

■ **Extract and oil.** Products based on the aromatic essential oils of plant materials that are distilled by various means. In extracts, the highly concentrated oils usually are suspended in alcohol to make them easier to combine with other foods in cooking and baking. Almond, anise, lemon, mint, orange, peppermint, and vanilla are some of the extracts sold.

■ **Flavoring.** An imitation extract made of chemical compounds. Unlike an extract or oil, a flavoring often does not contain any of the original food it resembles. Some common imitation flavorings available are banana, black walnut, brandy, cherry, chocolate, coconut, maple, pineapple, raspberry, rum, strawberry, and vanilla.

■ **Flute.** To make a scalloped, decorative pattern or impression in food, usually a piecrust.

■ **Fold.** A method of gently mixing ingredients—usually delicate or whipped ingredients that cannot withstand stirring or beating. To fold, use a rubber spatula to cut down through the mixture, move across the bottom of the bowl, and come back up, folding some of the mixture from the bottom over close to the surface.

■ **Food coloring.** Either liquid, paste, or powdered edible dyes used to tint foods.

■ **Frost.** To apply a sweet cooked or uncooked topping to cakes, cupcakes, or cookies that is soft enough to spread but stiff enough to hold its shape.

■ **Ganache.** A rich chocolate icing made of bittersweet chocolate and whipping cream heated and stirred together until the chocolate melts. The mixture is cooled until lukewarm and poured over a cake or torte for a satiny, glossy finish.

■ **Garnish.** To add visual appeal to a finished dish by decorating it with small pieces of food or edible flowers. The term also refers to the items used for decoration.

■ **Ginger.** A semitropical plant whose root is used as a pungent spice. Ginger has a slightly hot flavor and nippy aroma. Ginger comes fresh as gingerroot, powdered, and in candied or crystallized form.

■ **Glaze.** A thin, glossy coating on a food. There are numerous types of glazes. A mixture of powdered sugar and milk can be drizzled on cookies, cakes, or breads for a glaze.

■ **Gluten.** An elastic protein present in flour, especially wheat flour, that provides most of the structure of baked products.

■ **Grate.** To rub food—especially hard cheeses, vegetables, and whole nutmeg and ginger—across a grating surface to make very fine pieces. A food processor may also be used.

■ **Grease.** To coat a utensil, such as a baking pan or skillet, with a thin layer of fat or oil.

■ **Grind.** To mechanically cut a food into small pieces, usually with a food grinder or a food processor.

■ **Ice.** To drizzle or spread baked goods with a thin frosting.

■ **Juice.** To extract the natural liquid contained in fruits and vegetables. This can be done with a juicer or—in the case of citrus fruits—simply by squeezing wedges of fruit over a measuring cup to catch the juice.

■ **Knead.** To work dough with the heels of your hands in a pressing and folding motion until it becomes smooth and elastic; an essential step in developing the gluten in many yeast breads.

■ **Marble.** To gently swirl one food into another; usually done with light and dark batters for cakes or cookies.

■ **Marscapone cheese.** A very rich cream cheese made primarily of cream. Marscapone cheese most often is used in Italian desserts. Cream cheese may be substituted for marscapone.

■ **Mash.** To press or beat a food to remove lumps and make a smooth mixture. This can be done with a fork, potato masher, food mill, food ricer, or an electric mixer.

■ **Meringue.** Sweetened, stiffly beaten egg whites used for desserts. There are two basic types of meringues. Soft meringues are moist and tender and are used for topping pies and other desserts. Hard meringues are sweeter than soft meringues and are baked to form crisp, dry dessert shells or cookies, such as macaroons. Meringue shells often are filled with fresh fruit or puddings.

■ **Peel.** The skin or outer covering of a vegetable or fruit; also called the rind. Also refers to removing the covering.

■ **Pipe.** To force a semisoft food, such as whipped cream, frosting, or mashed potatoes, through a bag to decorate a food.

■ **Plump.** To allow a food, such as raisins or dried cherries, to soak in a liquid.

■ **Proof.** To allow a yeast dough to rise before baking. Also a term that indicates the amount of alcohol in a distilled liquor.

■ **Puree.** To change a solid food into a liquid or heavy paste, usually by using a food processor, blender, or food mill. Also refers to the resulting mixture.

■ **Ricotta.** A fresh, moist, white cheese that is very mild and semisweet. It has a soft, slightly grainy texture. It is available in whole milk, part-skim milk, or fat-free varieties, with the whole milk cheese having a creamier consistency and fuller flavor than the part-skim types.

■ **Roll.** To form a food into a shape. Dough, for instance, can be rolled into ropes or balls. The phrase "roll out" refers to mechanically flattening a food— usually a dough or pastry—with a rolling pin.

■ **Scald.** To heat a liquid, often milk, to a temperature below the boiling point, when tiny bubbles begin to appear around the edge of the liquid.

■ **Section.** A pulpy segment of citrus fruit with the membrane removed. The phrase also refers to the process of removing those segments (see "Sectioning Citrus Fruits" tip on page 15).

■ **Shred.** To push food across a fine or coarse shredding surface to make long, narrow strips. A food processor may be used.

■ **Sift.** To put one or more dry ingredients, especially flour or powdered sugar, through a sifter or sieve to remove lumps and incorporate air.

■ **Simmer.** To cook a food in liquid that is kept below the boiling point; a few bubbles will form slowly and burst before they reach the surface.

■ **Snip.** To cut food, often fresh herbs or dried fruit, with kitchen scissors into very small, uniform pieces, using short, quick strokes.

■ **Sponge.** A batterlike mixture of yeast, flour, and liquid used in some bread recipes. The mixture is set aside until it bubbles and becomes foamy, which can be several hours or overnight. During this time, the sponge develops a tangy flavor; the remaining ingredients are added to the sponge, and the dough is kneaded and baked as usual.

■ **Steam.** To cook a food in the vapor given off by boiling water.

■ **Vanilla bean.** The pod of an orchid plant that is dried and cured. During curing, the pod turns a dark chocolate color and shrivels to the size of a pencil.

■ **Weeping.** A condition in which liquid separates out of a solid food, such as jellies, custards, and meringues.

■ **Whip.** To beat a food lightly and rapidly using a wire whisk, rotary beater, or electric mixer to incorporate air into the mixture and increase its volume.

■ **Whisk.** A kitchen utensil made of a group of looped wires held together by a long handle. Whisks are used in baking for whipping ingredients such as eggs and cream to incorporate air into them.

■ **Zest.** The colored outer portion of a citrus fruit peel. It is rich in fruit oils and often used as a seasoning. To remove the zest, use a grater, a fruit zester, or a vegetable peeler; be careful to avoid the bitter white membrane beneath the peel.

old-fashioned
desserts

Peach Cobbler with Cinnamon-Swirl Biscuits,
recipe page 29

OLD-FASHIONED
DESSERTS

BRANDIED APRICOT-PEAR DUMPLINGS

BEST-LOVED

Prep: 1 hour   Bake: 40 minutes
Makes: 4 servings   Oven: 400°

- **2 tablespoons snipped dried apricots**
- **2 tablespoons cream cheese**
- **4 small pears (about 4 to 5 ounces each)**
- **1 recipe Single-Crust Pastry (see page 47) or ½ of a 15-ounce package folded refrigerated unbaked piecrust (1 crust)**
- **4 whole cloves (optional)**
- **1 slightly beaten egg white**
- **1 tablespoon water**
- **1 tablespoon sugar**
- **1¼ cups pear or apricot nectar**
- **¼ cup dark-colored corn syrup**
- **¼ cup apricot brandy, brandy, or pear or apricot nectar**

1 **For filling,** in a small mixing bowl combine apricots and cream cheese. Peel and core pears. Spoon some filling into the center of each pear.

2 **On a lightly floured surface flatten** pastry dough. (Or, unwrap refrigerated crust according to package directions.) Roll dough into a 13-inch circle. Trim to form a 12-inch square (leave trim pieces uncut). Using a fluted pastry wheel or long sharp knife, cut dough into twelve 12x¾-inch strips. Pat pears with paper towels.

3 **Using 1 of the pastry strips** and starting ½ inch above the base of a pear (do not cover bottom of pear), wrap pastry strip around pear. Moisten end of strip; seal to the end of a second pastry strip and continue wrapping. Seal to the end of a third pastry strip; finish wrapping pear, covering hole and filling. Moisten end to seal. Press gently, if necessary, to shape pastry around pear. Repeat for each pear.

4 **Cut leaf shapes** (similar to diamonds) from remaining pastry using a knife; mark veins on leaves. Attach leaves to tops of pears, moistening as necessary to attach. Top pears with whole cloves for stems. In a small bowl beat together egg white and water; brush onto pastry. Sprinkle with sugar.

5 **Using a wide spatula,** transfer pears to an ungreased 2-quart square baking dish. Stir together pear or apricot nectar, corn syrup, and brandy; pour around pears in dish. Bake, uncovered, in a 400° oven for 40 to 45 minutes or until golden. Serve dumplings and sauce while warm.

Nutrition Facts per serving: 553 cal., 20 g total fat (6 g sat. fat), 8 mg chol., 187 mg sodium, 84 g carbo., 4 g fiber, 6 g pro. Daily Values: 6% vit. A, 9% vit. C, 3% calcium, 21% iron

Brandied Apricot-Pear Dumplings: Dress apricot-cream-stuffed pears in pastry wraps and bake until golden in a brandy-pear nectar sauce. This soul-soothing dessert is as impressive tasting as it looks.

PICKING FRUITS FOR BAKING

Q What kinds of apples and pears are best for baking?

A The best varieties for baking and filling are those that hold their shape and retain their flavor when baked. Apple varieties that work well for baking include Cortland, Golden Delicious, Granny Smith, Jonathan, McIntosh, Newtown Pippin, Rome Beauty, and Winesap. In the pear department, try Anjou, Bartlett, and Bosc, though most pear varieties work fine. Keep in mind that firmer pears hold their shape better than soft, very ripe ones, as do whole pears and apples left unpeeled or just partially peeled.

BEST-EVER BAKED APPLES

LOW-FAT

Prep: 15 minutes   **Bake:** 45 minutes
Makes: 4 servings   **Oven:** 350°

To keep the apples from turning brown while you work, brush cut areas with lemon juice.

1 recipe desired filling: choose from Dried Fruit, Ginger-Almond, Orange-Macaroon, Peanut Butter, and Apple-Walnut (right)
4 large baking apples (7 ounces each)
⅓ cup apple juice, apple cider, or sweet white wine
Sweetened whipped cream, vanilla yogurt, light cream, or frozen vanilla yogurt (optional)
Ground nutmeg (optional)

1 **Prepare desired filling;** set aside. To core apples, use an apple corer or the rounded tip of a vegetable peeler. Push corer or peeler most of the way through the apple center, but do not cut through the other end; turn corer or peeler to loosen the upper part of the core. Remove and discard core. Enlarge hole slightly at top of the apple for filling.

2 **Using a vegetable peeler or paring knife,** remove the peel from the top half of each apple. If desired, use tines of a fork to score peeled apple.

3 **Place apples** in an ungreased 2-quart square baking dish. Spoon filling into center of each apple. Add apple juice, cider, or wine to dish. Bake, covered, in a 350° oven about 45 minutes or until fork-tender. Transfer apples to dessert dishes; spoon liquid in dish over apples. If desired, serve warm with whipped cream, yogurt, cream, or frozen yogurt and sprinkle with nutmeg.

Nutrition Facts per serving (with Dried Fruit Filling): 215 cal., 1 g total fat (0 g sat. fat), 0 mg chol., 8 mg sodium, 56 g carbo., 6 g fiber, 1 g pro. Daily Values: 0% vit. A, 16% vit. C, 2% calcium, 7% iron

Dried Fruit Filling: Combine ⅔ cup raisins, currants, or mixed dried fruit bits; 2 tablespoons brown sugar; and ½ teaspoon ground cinnamon.

Ginger-Almond Filling: Stir together ¼ cup slivered almonds, 2 tablespoons apricot preserves, and 1 tablespoon chopped crystallized ginger.

Orange-Macaroon Filling: Toss ⅔ cup crumbled soft coconut macaroon cookies with 2 tablespoons orange marmalade.

Peanut Butter Filling: Stir together ⅓ cup coconut with ⅓ cup chunky peanut butter.

Apple-Walnut Filling: Stir together ⅓ cup apple butter with ¼ cup chopped walnuts.

Best-Ever Baked Apples:
Savor America's favorite fruit
in one of America's most
cherished recipes—baked
apples. With this versatile
recipe, choose a new filling
every time you make it.

APPLE-CHERRY
PANDOWDY

Prep: 30 minutes   **Bake:** 50 minutes
Makes: 6 servings   **Oven:** 350°

Tart cherries add color and flavor to this traditional apple deep-dish dessert.

    4 cups sliced, peeled cooking apples
1½ cups fresh or frozen unsweetened
        pitted tart red cherries, thawed
    ¾ cup sugar
    3 tablespoons all-purpose flour
    ¼ teaspoon ground nutmeg
        Dash ground cloves
    1 cup all-purpose flour
    ¼ teaspoon salt
    ¼ cup butter
    1 egg yolk
    3 tablespoons cold water
        Whipped cream or vanilla ice
        cream (optional)

1 For filling, in a mixing bowl combine apples, cherries, sugar, the 3 tablespoons flour, nutmeg, and cloves. Transfer fruit filling to an ungreased 2-quart rectangular baking dish.

2 For crust, in a medium mixing bowl stir together the 1 cup flour and the salt. With a pastry blender, cut in the butter just until mixture resembles coarse crumbs; make a well in the center. Beat together egg yolk and cold water. Add to flour mixture all at once. Using a fork, stir just until the dough forms a ball.

3 On a lightly floured surface roll dough into a 12×8-inch rectangle; place on fruit filling in baking dish. Fold under edge of crust to fit dish; crimp to sides of dish. Cut a 3-inch slit in crust to allow steam to escape.

4 Bake in a 350° oven about 50 minutes or until golden. Use a sharp knife to cut a lattice pattern in the crust. Cool on a wire rack for 30 minutes. If desired, serve with whipped cream or ice cream.

Nutrition Facts per serving: 323 cal., 9 g total fat
(5 g sat. fat), 56 mg chol., 169 mg sodium,
59 g carbo., 2 g fiber, 3 g pro. Daily Values:
16% vit. A, 6% vit. C, 1% calcium, 9% iron

CHERRY-BLUEBERRY
COBBLER SUPREME

Prep: 20 minutes   **Bake:** 40 minutes
Makes: 12 servings   **Oven:** 350°

The batter starts out on the bottom and ends up on top of this unique cobbler.

    2 cups fresh or frozen unsweetened
        pitted tart red cherries
    1 cup fresh or frozen unsweetened
        blueberries
        Cherry juice or water (about 2 cups)
    1 cup all-purpose flour
    1 cup whole wheat flour
    2 teaspoons baking powder
    ¼ teaspoon salt
    ½ cup butter, softened
    1 cup granulated sugar
    ¾ cup milk
    ½ to ¾ cup granulated sugar
        Powdered sugar (optional)
        Ice cream or light cream (optional)

1 Thaw fruit, if frozen; drain, reserving juice. Add enough cherry juice or water to fruit liquid to equal 2 cups. If using fresh fruit, measure 2 cups cherry juice or water. Set aside. Grease a 3-quart oval baking dish or 13×9×2-inch baking pan; set aside.

2 In a medium bowl combine flours, baking powder, and salt; set aside. In a large mixing bowl beat butter and the 1 cup sugar with an electric mixer until fluffy; add flour mixture alternately with milk. Beat until smooth. Spread batter evenly over the bottom of prepared dish or pan.

3 Sprinkle batter with cherries and blueberries. Sprinkle with remaining ½ to ¾ cup sugar, depending on sweetness of fruit. Pour the 2 cups of fruit juice or water mixture over fruit.

4 Bake in a 350° oven for 40 to 45 minutes or until a wooden toothpick inserted in cake comes out clean. (Some of the fruit should sink toward bottom as the cake rises to top.) Cool about 45 minutes. If desired, sprinkle lightly with powdered sugar; serve warm with ice cream or cream.

Nutrition Facts per serving: 280 cal., 9 g total fat
(5 g sat. fat), 22 mg chol., 195 mg sodium,
50 g carbo., 2 g fiber, 4 g pro. Daily Values:
11% vit. A, 8% vit. C, 8% calcium, 7% iron

WHAT'S IN A NAME?

Cobbler: A distant cousin of the deep-dish pie, cobbler gets its name from its biscuit topping, which resembles cobblestones. For a traditional cobbler, be sure the fruit filling is very hot when you drop the biscuit dough on it or the bottom of the topping might not cook properly.

Betty: Betties are topped with soft bread cubes, rather than dry cubes as in bread pudding. The bread is easier to cut if it's frozen; use a serrated knife and a sawing motion to cut the bread into ½-inch cubes.

Crisp: Crisps are topped with a crunchy oatmeal mixture. The topping stores well, so try mixing a double batch and put the extra batch in a freezer bag, seal, label, and freeze it for up to a month.

Pandowdy: A funny name for a delicious dish, this baked apple or fruit dessert has a pastrylike biscuit topping and is usually served with light cream or a sauce. Traditionally, the topping is broken up with a spoon and stirred into the fruit filling (the "dowdying" of the dish) before it is served.

PEACH COBBLER WITH CINNAMON-SWIRL BISCUITS

Prep: 30 minutes   Bake: 25 minutes
Makes: 6 servings   Oven: 375°

Many cobbler recipes have a drop biscuit topping, but this one has biscuit slices filled with a nut-and-spice mixture (see photo, page 23).

  1 **cup all-purpose flour**
  1 **tablespoon brown sugar**
1½ **teaspoons baking powder**
  ⅛ **teaspoon baking soda**
  ¼ **cup butter**
  ⅓ **cup milk**
  ½ **cup finely chopped walnuts**
  3 **tablespoons brown sugar**
  ¼ **teaspoon ground cinnamon**
  1 **tablespoon butter, melted**
  ⅔ **cup packed brown sugar**
  4 **teaspoons cornstarch**
  ½ **teaspoon finely shredded**
       lemon peel
  6 **cups sliced, peeled peaches or**
       6 cups frozen unsweetened
       peach slices

1 **For biscuits,** in a medium mixing bowl stir together flour, the 1 tablespoon brown sugar, the baking powder, baking soda, and ¼ teaspoon salt.

With a pastry blender, cut in the ¼ cup butter until the mixture resembles coarse crumbs; make a well in the center. Add milk all at once. Using a fork, stir just until dough forms a ball.

2 **On a lightly floured surface knead** dough gently for 10 to 12 strokes. Roll or pat dough into a 12×6-inch rectangle. Combine walnuts, the 3 tablespoons brown sugar, and the cinnamon; brush dough with the melted butter and sprinkle with nut mixture. Roll up jelly-roll style, starting from one of the short sides. Seal edge. Use a sharp knife to cut into six 1-inch-thick slices; set aside.

3 **For peach filling,** in a large saucepan stir together the ⅔ cup brown sugar, the cornstarch, and lemon peel. Add peaches and ⅔ cup water. Cook and stir until bubbly. Carefully pour hot filling into an ungreased 2-quart rectangular baking dish. Arrange biscuit slices, cut side down, on hot filling. Bake in a 375° oven about 25 minutes or until biscuit slices are golden.

Nutrition Facts per serving: 436 cal., 17 g total fat (3 g sat. fat), 13 mg chol., 315 mg sodium, 71 g carbo., 4 g fiber, 5 g pro. Daily Values: 19% vit. A, 19% vit. C, 12% calcium, 14% iron

Apple Cobbler: Substitute 6 cups sliced, peeled cooking apples for the peaches and add 1 teaspoon apple pie spice to the fruit filling.

Rhubarb Cobbler: Substitute 6 cups sliced rhubarb for peaches; use 1¼ cups packed brown sugar in filling.

BLACKBERRY COBBLER

Prep: 25 minutes   Bake: 20 minutes
Makes: 8 servings   Oven: 400°

1½ cups all-purpose flour
 ¼ cup granulated sugar
 2 teaspoons baking powder
 ¼ teaspoon salt
 ¼ teaspoon ground cinnamon
 ⅛ teaspoon ground nutmeg
 ⅓ cup shortening
 ¾ cup packed brown sugar or
      granulated sugar
 4 teaspoons cornstarch
 5 cups fresh or frozen unsweetened
      blackberries
 ¾ cup water
 2 teaspoons finely shredded orange
      peel (optional)
 ½ teaspoon vanilla
 1 egg
 ½ cup milk
    Coarse sugar or granulated sugar
    Whipped cream or vanilla ice
      cream (optional)

1 **For topping,** in a large mixing bowl combine flour, the ¼ cup granulated sugar, the baking powder, salt, cinnamon, and nutmeg. With a pastry blender, cut in shortening until mixture resembles coarse crumbs; make a well in the center. Set aside.

2 **For filling,** in a medium saucepan stir together the brown sugar and cornstarch. Stir in fresh or frozen blackberries, water, and orange peel (if using). Cook and stir until thickened and bubbly. Stir in vanilla. Keep filling hot.

3 **In a small bowl use** a fork to beat egg and milk together. Add egg mixture all at once to the dry ingredients; stir just until moistened. Transfer hot filling to an ungreased 2-quart rectangular baking dish. Immediately drop topping into 8 mounds on the hot filling. Sprinkle topping with coarse or granulated sugar.

4 **Bake in a 400° oven** for 20 to 25 minutes or until a wooden toothpick inserted into topping comes out clean. If desired, serve warm with whipped cream or ice cream.

Nutrition Facts per serving: 317 cal., 10 g total fat
(3 g sat. fat), 28 mg chol., 179 mg sodium,
54 g carbo., 6 g fiber, 4 g pro. Daily Values: 3% vit. A,
31% vit. C, 12% calcium, 14% iron

STRAWBERRY-RHUBARB BETTY

Prep: 25 minutes   Bake: 25 minutes
Makes: 6 servings   Oven: 375°

Use the larger measure of sugar with fruit that is extra tart and the smaller amount with fruit that is not quite so tart.

 3 cups sliced fresh or frozen
      unsweetened strawberries
 2 cups thinly sliced fresh or frozen
      unsweetened rhubarb
 ¾ to 1 cup sugar
 2 tablespoons all-purpose flour
 ¼ teaspoon salt
 4 cups soft bread cubes
      (about 5 slices)
 ¼ cup butter, melted

1 **Thaw strawberries and rhubarb,** if frozen. Do not drain. For filling, in a large mixing bowl stir together sugar, flour, and salt. Add strawberries, rhubarb, and their juices; gently toss until coated.

2 **For topping,** place the bread cubes in a medium mixing bowl. Drizzle with the melted butter; toss until mixed. Transfer half the buttered bread cubes to an ungreased 1½-quart casserole. Pour fruit mixture over bread cubes. Sprinkle the remaining bread cubes over the fruit filling.

3 **Bake in a 375° oven** for 25 to 30 minutes or until fruit is tender and the bread-cube topping is golden. Serve warm.

Nutrition Facts per serving: 256 cal., 9 g total fat
(5 g sat. fat), 20 mg chol., 272 mg sodium,
44 g carbo., 3 g fiber, 3 g pro. Daily Values: 7% vit. A,
75% vit. C, 6% calcium, 7% iron

Country Pear and Cherry Crisp: The topping stays extra-crunchy, and the best part is that it's a simple combination of granola and melted butter.

COUNTRY PEAR
AND CHERRY CRISP

EASY

Prep: 20 minutes   Bake: 30 minutes
Makes: 6 servings   Oven: 375°

- 1 16-ounce package frozen unsweetened pitted tart red cherries, thawed, or one 16-ounce can pitted tart red cherries (water pack)
- ⅓ to ½ cup sugar
- 2 tablespoons all-purpose flour
- 1 teaspoon finely shredded orange peel
- ½ teaspoon ground cinnamon
- 3 to 4 medium pears (1 pound), peeled, cored, and thinly sliced (3 cups)
- 1½ cups granola
- 2 tablespoons butter, melted
- Vanilla ice cream (optional)

1 **If using canned cherries,** drain cherries, reserving ½ cup juice. In a large mixing bowl combine frozen or canned cherries and reserved juice; add sugar and toss to coat. Let stand for 5 minutes.

2 **In a small bowl combine** flour, peel, and cinnamon; sprinkle over cherries. Toss to mix. Add pears; toss to mix. Transfer to an ungreased 2-quart square baking dish. Combine granola and butter; sprinkle over filling. Bake in a 375° oven about 30 minutes or until pears are tender. If necessary, to prevent overbrowning, cover with foil the last 5 to 10 minutes. If desired, serve warm with ice cream.

Nutrition Facts per serving: 318 cal., 10 g total fat (4 g sat. fat), 5 mg chol., 94 mg sodium, 58 g carbo., 6 g fiber, 4 g pro. Daily Values: 10% vit. A, 10% vit. C, 3% calcium, 12% iron

IN CASE OF LEFTOVERS ...

Baked fruit desserts and bread puddings are good keepers because leftovers can taste nearly fresh baked if they're stored and reheated the right way.

On the slim chance you have any leftover dessert, transfer it to a smaller casserole or ovenproof dish; cover and store in the refrigerator for up to 2 days. (Be sure to refrigerate desserts that contain dairy products, such as bread pudding, right away.) To reheat, simply cover with a casserole lid or foil and bake in a 350° oven until the dessert is warmed through.

TOOL BOX: COBBLERS AND CRISPS

True to their homey nature, cobblers and crisps bake well in either metal baking pans or casseroles of any kind: glass, pottery, or ceramic baking dishes. Remember these tips:

- Size is more important than shape. Always use the size dish called for in the recipe. The dish needs to be deep enough to allow for the fruit filling to bubble up during baking. It's best to place a baking sheet beneath the dish to catch any spills.
- If the fruit filling is acidic (pineapple, citrus fruits, and cranberries contain acid, for instance), the cobbler or crisp can be baked in a metal pan but shouldn't be stored in one because the acid can react with the metal. However, any leftovers can be stored in a glass baking dish.

A few helpful gadgets to keep on hand when preparing cobblers and crisps include:

- An apple corer for removing the core and seeds from apples and pears.
- A vegetable peeler for removing cores and peeling fruits.
- A pastry blender for easily cutting in cold butter for biscuit toppings and crumbly crisp toppings.

CHOOSE-A-FRUIT CRISP

Prep: 30 minutes   Bake: 30 minutes
Makes: 6 servings   Oven: 375°

5 cups sliced, peeled apples, pears, peaches, or apricots; or frozen unsweetened peach slices
2 to 4 tablespoons granulated sugar
½ cup regular rolled oats
½ cup packed brown sugar
¼ cup all-purpose flour
¼ teaspoon ground nutmeg, ginger, or cinnamon
¼ cup butter
¼ cup chopped nuts or coconut
Vanilla ice cream or light cream (optional)

1 **For filling,** thaw fruit, if frozen. Do not drain. Place fruit in an ungreased 2-quart square baking dish. Stir in the granulated sugar.

2 **For topping,** in a mixing bowl combine oats; brown sugar; flour; and nutmeg, ginger, or cinnamon. With a pastry blender, cut in butter until mixture resembles coarse crumbs. Stir in nuts or coconut. Sprinkle topping over filling.

3 **Bake in a 375° oven** for 30 to 35 minutes (40 minutes for thawed fruit) or until fruit is tender and topping is golden. If desired, serve warm with ice cream or light cream.

Microwave directions: Prepare filling as at left, making sure you use a microwave-safe baking dish. Microwave filling, covered with vented plastic wrap, on 100% power (high) for 4 to 7 minutes or until fruit is tender, stirring twice. (Additional cooking time may be needed if using thawed fruit.) Prepare topping. Sprinkle over filling. Microwave, uncovered, on high for 2 to 3 minutes or until topping is heated, giving the dish a half-turn once.

Nutrition Facts per serving with apple filling: 275 cal., 12 g total fat (5 g sat. fat), 20 mg chol., 83 mg sodium, 43 g carbo., 3 g fiber, 3 g pro.
Daily Values: 7% vit. A, 7% vit. C, 2% calcium, 7% iron

Blueberry Crisp: Prepare as in recipe, except for filling, increase granulated sugar to ¼ cup and combine with 3 tablespoons all-purpose flour. Toss with 5 cups fresh or frozen* unsweetened blueberries.

Cherry Crisp: Prepare as in recipe, except for filling, increase granulated sugar to ½ cup and combine with 3 tablespoons all-purpose flour. Toss the sugar-flour mixture with 5 cups fresh or frozen* unsweetened pitted tart red cherries.

Rhubarb Crisp: Prepare as in recipe, except for filling, increase granulated sugar to ¾ cup and combine with 3 tablespoons all-purpose flour. Toss with 5 cups fresh or frozen* unsweetened sliced rhubarb.

*Note: If fruit is frozen, thaw but do not drain.

HAWAIIAN PINEAPPLE CRISP

Prep: 25 minutes   **Bake:** 45 minutes
Makes: 6 to 8 servings   **Oven:** 375°

- ⅔ **cup granulated sugar**
- 1 **tablespoon cornstarch**
- 1 **teaspoon finely shredded lemon peel**
- ¾ **teaspoon ground cinnamon**
- ¼ **teaspoon ground nutmeg**
- 4 **medium baking apples, peeled, cored, and sliced (4 cups)**
- 1 **20-ounce can pineapple chunks, drained**
- ¾ **cup rolled oats**
- ¼ **cup all-purpose flour**
- ¼ **cup packed brown sugar**
- ¼ **cup butter**
- ¾ **cup chopped macadamia nuts (3.5-ounce jar) or almonds**

1 **In an ungreased 1½-quart casserole** stir together granulated sugar, cornstarch, lemon peel, cinnamon, and nutmeg. Add apples and pineapple; toss to coat.

2 **For topping,** in a medium mixing bowl stir together oats, flour, and brown sugar. With a pastry blender, cut in butter until thoroughly combined (the mixture should be dry). Stir in nuts. Sprinkle nut topping over fruit mixture.

3 **Bake in a 375° oven** for 30 minutes. Cover the casserole loosely with foil to prevent overbrowning. Bake about 15 minutes more or until apples are tender. Serve warm.

Nutrition Facts per serving: 459 cal., 22 g total fat (4 g sat. fat), 10 mg chol., 120 mg sodium, 69 g carbo., 4 g fiber, 3 g pro. Daily Values: 8% vit. A, 21% vit. C, 3% calcium, 9% iron

Hawaiian Pineapple Crisp: Weave a little island dreaming into dessert tonight. This pineapple-macadamia nut crisp, with its tropical flavors, redefines an old-fashioned treat.

Peach and Almond Crisp: Several years ago this ginger-spiced fruit crisp made its debut in *Better Homes and Gardens*® magazine. It's been a real favorite ever since.

PEACH AND ALMOND CRISP

Prep: 30 minutes   **Bake:** 30 minutes
Makes: 12 servings   **Oven:** 400°

Select peaches that have a healthy golden yellow skin without tinges of green. The ripe fruit should yield slightly to gentle pressure.

  8 **cups sliced, peeled peaches or nectarines or frozen unsweetened peach slices**
⅔ **cup packed brown sugar**
½ **cup rolled oats**
½ **cup toasted sliced almonds**
¾ **cup all-purpose flour**
  3 **tablespoons granulated sugar**
½ **cup butter**
⅓ **cup granulated sugar**
½ **teaspoon ground cinnamon**
¼ **teaspoon ground nutmeg**
⅛ **teaspoon ground ginger**
¼ **cup peach nectar or orange juice**
    Vanilla ice cream (optional)

1 Thaw frozen peaches, if using. Do not drain. For topping, in a medium mixing bowl stir together brown sugar, oats, almonds, ½ cup of the flour, and the 3 tablespoons granulated sugar. Using a pastry blender, cut in butter until the mixture resembles coarse crumbs.

2 For filling, in a large mixing bowl stir together remaining flour, the ⅓ cup granulated sugar, the cinnamon, nutmeg, and ginger. Add the peach or nectarine slices with their juices and peach nectar or orange juice. Toss gently to coat. Transfer filling to an ungreased 3-quart rectangular baking dish. Sprinkle topping over the filling.

3 Bake in a 400° oven for 30 to 35 minutes or until peaches or nectarine slices are tender and the topping is golden. If desired, serve warm or at room temperature with ice cream.

Nutrition Facts per serving: 258 cal., 11 g total fat (5 g sat. fat), 20 mg chol., 94 mg sodium, 40 g carbo., 3 g fiber, 3 g pro. Daily Values: 15% vit. A, 13% vit. C, 2% calcium, 6% iron

WHISKEY-SAUCED BREAD PUDDING

Prep: 30 minutes   **Bake:** 35 minutes
Makes: 8 or 9 servings   **Oven:** 325°

Cubes of cinnamon-raisin bread sandwiched together with cream cheese give bread pudding a lovable update.

  6 **slices dry cinnamon-raisin bread**
½ **of an 8-ounce tub cream cheese (about ½ cup)**
  4 **beaten eggs**

2 cups milk
⅓ cup sugar
1 teaspoon finely shredded lemon
    peel (optional)
1 recipe Whiskey Sauce (see below)
    or whipped cream

1 Generously spread 3 slices of the dry bread with cream cheese. Top with remaining bread slices. Cut bread "sandwiches" into cubes and place in an ungreased 2-quart square baking dish. In a mixing bowl beat together eggs, milk, sugar, and lemon peel. Pour over bread cubes in dish.

2 Bake in a 325° oven for 35 to 40 minutes or until center is nearly set. Cool slightly. Serve warm with Whiskey Sauce or whipped cream.

Whiskey Sauce: In a small saucepan melt ¼ cup butter. Stir in ½ cup sugar, 1 beaten egg yolk, and 2 tablespoons water. Cook, stirring constantly, over medium heat for 5 to 6 minutes or until sugar dissolves and mixture boils. Remove from heat. Stir in 1 tablespoon bourbon and 1 tablespoon lemon juice. Serve warm. Makes about ¾ cup.

Nutrition Facts per serving: 316 cal., 16 g total fat (7 g sat. fat), 161 mg chol., 234 mg sodium, 35 g carbo., 0 g fiber, 8 g pro. Daily Values: 24% vit. A, 2% vit. C, 9% calcium, 8% iron

ORANGE BREAD PUDDING WITH WARM MAPLE SAUCE

LOW-FAT

Prep: 30 minutes   Bake: 55 minutes
Makes: 6 servings   Oven: 325°

So much flavor, so little fat—this bread pudding seemingly has it all.

4 slices white or whole wheat bread
⅓ cup raisins
3 eggs
2 egg whites
1¾ cups milk
⅓ cup orange marmalade
¼ cup sugar
½ teaspoon ground cinnamon

½ teaspoon vanilla
1 recipe Maple Sauce (see below)
    Orange slices, halved

1 Cut bread into 2-inch strips; spread strips in an ungreased 14×10×2-inch baking pan. Bake in a 325° oven for 10 to 15 minutes or until dry, stirring twice. Transfer strips to an ungreased 8×1½-inch round baking pan. Sprinkle with raisins. Set aside.

2 In a medium mixing bowl use a wire whisk, fork, or rotary beater to combine eggs, egg whites, milk, marmalade, sugar, cinnamon, and vanilla. Pour over bread and raisins in pan.

3 Bake in a 325° oven about 55 minutes or until a knife inserted near the center comes out clean. Cool slightly on a wire rack. Serve warm with warm Maple Sauce and garnish with orange slices.

Maple Sauce: In a small saucepan combine 1 tablespoon cornstarch and ¼ teaspoon finely shredded orange peel. Stir in ¾ cup orange juice and ⅓ cup maple syrup. Cook and stir until thickened and bubbly; cook 2 minutes more. Remove from heat; stir in 1 teaspoon butter. Makes about 1 cup sauce.

Nutrition Facts per serving: 299 cal., 5 g total fat (2 g sat. fat), 113 mg chol., 187 mg sodium, 56 g carbo., 2 g fiber, 9 g pro. Daily Values: 10% vit. A, 39% vit. C, 12% calcium, 10% iron

Orange Bread Pudding with Warm Maple Sauce: Bread puddings have a long history, dating to the 1800s, as a common way to use up stale bread. Today we consider it a delicious treat.

LEMON-POPPY SEED STRAWBERRY SHORTCAKE

Prep: 35 minutes **Bake:** 15 minutes
Makes: 8 to 10 servings **Oven:** 450°

  2 **cups all-purpose flour**
  2 **tablespoons granulated sugar**
  2 **tablespoons poppy seed**
  2 **teaspoons baking powder**
  ⅛ **teaspoon salt**
  ½ **cup butter**
  ¾ **cup buttermilk or sour milk**
      (see sour milk tip, page 138)
  1 **teaspoon finely shredded lemon peel**
  6 **cups sliced fresh strawberries**
  ¼ **cup granulated sugar (optional)**
  ⅔ **cup whipping cream**
  8 **ounces mascarpone cheese or one**
      8-ounce tub plain cream cheese
  ⅔ **cup sifted powdered sugar**
  1 **teaspoon finely shredded lemon peel**

1 **For shortcake,** in a medium mixing bowl combine flour, the 2 tablespoons granulated sugar, poppy seed, baking powder, and salt. With a pastry blender, cut in butter until mixture resembles coarse crumbs. Make a well in the center; add buttermilk or sour milk and the 1 teaspoon lemon peel all at once. Stir just until dough clings together.

2 **On a lightly floured surface knead** dough gently for 10 to 12 strokes. Pat dough into an 8-inch circle on an ungreased baking sheet. Bake

in a 450° oven for 15 to 18 minutes or until golden. Cool on a wire rack for 10 to 15 minutes.

3 **In medium bowl stir** together strawberries and, if desired, ¼ cup granulated sugar; set aside.

4 **In a chilled bowl beat** cream until soft peaks form. Add cheese, powdered sugar, and 1 teaspoon lemon peel; beat until fluffy (mixture will thicken as it is beaten). Split shortcake into 2 layers. Place bottom layer on serving platter. Spoon half of the cheese mixture over bottom layer. Spoon some of the strawberries onto cheese layer. Add top cake layer. Repeat cheese and strawberry layers. Cut into wedges. Pass remaining strawberries. Serve at once.

Nutrition Facts per serving: 502 cal., 34 g total fat (15 g sat. fat), 79 mg chol., 279 mg sodium, 45 g carbo., 3 g fiber, 11 g pro. Daily Values: 20% vit. A, 107% vit. C, 14% calcium, 14% iron

PECAN STRAWBERRY SHORTCAKE

BEST-LOVED

Prep: 35 minutes **Bake:** 10 minutes
Makes: 8 to 10 servings **Oven:** 450°

  2 **cups all-purpose flour**
  ½ **cup finely ground pecans**
  ¼ **cup sugar**
  2 **teaspoons baking powder**
  ¼ **teaspoon salt**
  ½ **cup butter**
  1 **beaten egg**
  ⅔ **cup milk**
  1 **tablespoon finely shredded**
      orange peel
  1 **teaspoon vanilla**
  6 **cups sliced fresh strawberries**
  ¼ **cup sugar**
  1 **cup whipping cream**
  2 **tablespoons sugar**
  ½ **teaspoon vanilla**
      Whole strawberries (optional)
      Chopped pecans (optional)

1 **For shortcake,** in a large bowl combine flour, ground pecans, ¼ cup sugar, baking powder, and salt. Cut in butter until mixture resembles coarse crumbs. In small bowl combine egg, milk, 2 teaspoons of the peel, and 1 teaspoon vanilla; add all at once to dry ingredients. Stir just until moistened.

STRAWBERRY TIPS

Although the peak season for strawberries is March through August, they're generally available in the supermarket year-round. When buying strawberries, select plump, fresh-looking berries with bright green caps, avoiding those that are bruised, wet, or mushy. Store strawberries in the refrigerator, loosely covered. Don't wash or remove the hulls from the fresh berries until you're ready to use them.

Pecan Strawberry Shortcake: Count on the flaky, biscuitlike texture that you would expect from this American springtime classic, with a bonus of toasted nuts and orange peel in the shortcake.

2 Drop dough into 8 or 10 mounds on an ungreased baking sheet; flatten each mound with back of a spoon until about ¾ inch thick. Bake in a 450° oven about 10 minutes or until golden. Cool shortcakes on wire rack about 10 minutes.

3 Meanwhile, in a bowl stir together strawberries, the second ¼ cup sugar, and 1 teaspoon orange peel; let stand about 20 minutes.

4 In a chilled medium bowl combine cream, the 2 tablespoons sugar, and the ½ teaspoon vanilla. Beat on medium speed until soft peaks form.

5 Using a sharp serrated knife, cut shortcakes in half horizontally. Lift off top layers. Spoon half of the strawberry mixture and half of the whipped cream over bottom layers. Replace shortcake tops. Top with remaining strawberry mixture; spoon remaining cream onto berries. If desired, garnish with whole strawberries and pecans. Serve at once.

Nutrition Facts per serving: 475 cal., 29 g total fat (11 g sat. fat), 84 mg chol., 294 mg sodium, 49 g carbo., 3 g fiber, 6 g pro. Daily Values: 27% vit. A, 108% vit. C, 13% calcium, 14% iron

For a large shortcake: Grease an 8×1½-inch round baking pan; set aside. Prepare shortcake dough as directed; spread in pan. Build up edges slightly. Bake in 450° oven for 15 to 18 minutes or until top is golden and wooden toothpick inserted in center comes out clean (do not overbake). Cool in pan on rack 10 minutes; remove. Split into 2 layers. Place bottom layer on serving platter. Spoon half of the strawberry mixture over bottom layer; top with about half of the whipped cream. Add top. Add remaining strawberry mixture; spoon remaining cream onto berries. Garnish and serve as above.

PUDDING CAKE MAGIC

Mention pudding cake to nearly anyone, and undoubtedly they have memories of a grandmother, father, aunt, or uncle who loved it—maybe gilded with a little vanilla ice cream or whipped cream. Popular in the 1930s, this simple, homey dessert belies the magic that happens when pudding cake batter is put in the oven: The cake rises to the top of the pan, leaving a creamy pudding on the bottom. There's no need for frosting, and one of the best features of this nostalgic two-layer wonder is it's fairly easy to make so it's right in step with modern times.

BROWNIE PUDDING CAKE

Prep: 15 minutes **Bake:** 30 minutes
Makes: 4 servings **Oven:** 350°

This cake makes its own chocolaty sauce.

- ½ **cup all-purpose flour**
- ¼ **cup sugar**
- 3 **tablespoons unsweetened cocoa powder**
- ¾ **teaspoon baking powder**
- ¼ **cup milk**
- 1 **tablespoon cooking oil**
- ½ **teaspoon vanilla**
- ¼ **cup chopped walnuts or pecans**
- ⅓ **cup sugar**
- ¾ **cup boiling water**

1 **In a medium mixing bowl stir** together flour, the ¼ cup sugar, 1 tablespoon of the cocoa powder, and the baking powder. Add milk, oil, and vanilla. Stir until smooth. Stir in nuts. Transfer batter to an ungreased 1-quart casserole.

2 **In a small bowl stir** together ⅓ cup sugar and the remaining 2 tablespoons cocoa powder. Gradually stir in the boiling water. Pour the mixture evenly over batter in casserole.

3 **Bake in a 350° oven** about 30 minutes or until a wooden toothpick inserted near the center of cake comes out clean. Serve warm.

Nutrition Facts per serving: 270 cal., 9 g total fat (1 g sat. fat), 1 mg chol., 78 mg sodium, 44 g carbo., 1 g fiber, 4 g pro. Daily Values: 1% vit. A, 0% vit. C, 11% calcium, 9% iron

Mocha Pudding Cake: Prepare as directed at left, except add 2 teaspoons instant coffee crystals with the boiling water.

LEMON PUDDING CAKE

Prep: 20 minutes **Bake:** 40 minutes
Makes: 4 servings **Oven:** 350°

The egg whites that are folded in give the cake a light texture. Be sure to spoon some of the tasty pudding over the cake layer when serving.

- ½ **cup sugar**
- 3 **tablespoons all-purpose flour**
- 1 **teaspoon finely shredded lemon peel**
- 3 **tablespoons lemon juice**
- 2 **tablespoons butter, melted**
- 2 **slightly beaten egg yolks**
- 1 **cup milk**
- 2 **egg whites**

1 **In a medium mixing bowl stir** together sugar and flour. Stir in lemon peel, lemon juice, and melted butter. Combine egg yolks and milk. Add to flour mixture; stir just until combined.

2 **In a mixing bowl beat** egg whites until stiff peaks form (tips stand straight). Gently fold egg whites into lemon batter. Transfer batter to an ungreased 1-quart casserole. Place the casserole in a large pan on an oven rack. Pour hot water into the large pan around the casserole to a depth of 1 inch.

3 Bake in a 350° oven about 40 minutes or until golden and top springs back when lightly touched near the center. Serve warm.

Nutrition Facts per serving: 237 cal., 9 g total fat (5 g sat. fat), 126 mg chol., 120 mg sodium, 33 g carbo., 0 g fiber, 6 g pro. Daily Values: 25% vit. A, 10% vit. C, 7% calcium, 4% iron

PEANUT BUTTER AND HOT FUDGE PUDDING CAKE

Prep: 15 minutes   Bake: 30 minutes
Makes: 4 servings   Oven: 400°

Brownie pudding cake takes on an irresistible partner—peanut butter. Together these flavors make this fudgy dessert a winner with kids.

½ **cup all-purpose flour**
¼ **cup sugar**
¾ **teaspoon baking powder**
⅓ **cup milk**
1 **tablespoon cooking oil**
½ **teaspoon vanilla**
¼ **cup peanut butter**

½ **cup sugar**
3 **tablespoons unsweetened cocoa powder**
1 **cup boiling water**
   Vanilla ice cream
   Fudge ice-cream topping (optional)
⅓ **cup chopped peanuts**

1 In a medium mixing bowl stir together flour, the ¼ cup sugar, and the baking powder. Add milk, oil, and vanilla. Stir until smooth. Stir in peanut butter. Transfer batter to an ungreased 1½-quart casserole.

2 In the same mixing bowl stir together the ½ cup sugar and the cocoa powder. Gradually stir in the boiling water. Pour the mixture evenly over batter in casserole.

3 Bake in a 400° oven about 30 minutes or until a wooden toothpick inserted near the center of cake comes out clean. Serve warm with vanilla ice cream. If desired, top with fudge ice-cream topping. Sprinkle with chopped peanuts.

Nutrition Facts per serving: 421 cal., 18 g total fat (3 g sat. fat), 1 mg chol., 211 mg sodium, 57 g carbo., 2 g fiber, 10 g pro. Daily Values: 1% vit. A, 0% vit. C, 12% calcium, 12% iron

Peanut Butter and Hot Fudge Pudding Cake: Top the warm pudding cake with a scoop of vanilla ice cream and a drizzle of fudge topping. Your family will love the sprinkling of peanuts that gives this dessert tin-roof sundae appeal.

BAKED RICE **PUDDING**

Prep: 15 minutes **Bake:** 50 minutes
Makes: 8 servings **Oven:** 325°

Surprise! You thought you were overindulging when actually rice pudding is fairly low in fat.

- 4 **beaten eggs**
- 2 **cups milk, half-and-half, or light cream**
- ½ **cup sugar**
- 1 **teaspoon vanilla**
- 1½ **cups cooked rice, cooled***
- ½ to ¾ **cup raisins**
- ⅛ **teaspoon ground nutmeg**
- ⅛ **teaspoon ground cinnamon**

1 In ungreased 2-quart casserole combine eggs, milk, sugar, vanilla, and ¼ teaspoon salt. Beat until combined but not foamy. Stir in cooked rice and raisins. Place casserole in a 13×9×2-inch baking dish on an oven rack. Pour boiling water into baking dish around the casserole to a depth of 1 inch.

2 Bake in a 325° oven for 30 minutes. Stir well; sprinkle with nutmeg and cinnamon. Bake for 20 to 30 minutes more or until a knife inserted near the center comes out clean. Serve warm or cold. To serve cold, cover and chill pudding for up to 3 days.

Nutrition Facts per serving: 184 cal., 4 g total fat (2 g sat. fat), 111 mg chol., 130 mg sodium, 31 g carbo., 0 g fiber, 6 g pro. Daily Values: 8% vit. A, 1% vit. C, 7% calcium, 6% iron

*****Note:** Leftover rice works well in rice pudding.

COOKING RICE

When a recipe calls for cooked rice, keep in mind these proportions: 1 cup of rice (cooked in 2 cups of water) yields about 3 cups cooked rice. Follow package directions, or here's a general guide: Measure water into a saucepan; bring to a full boil. Slowly add rice and return to boiling. Cover; simmer for time specified on package or until rice is tender and most of the water is absorbed. Remove from heat and let stand, covered, about 5 minutes.

SWEDISH RICE **PUDDING**

Prep: 35 minutes **Bake:** 15 minutes
Makes: 8 servings **Oven:** 350°

The Swedes have a delicious way with rice pudding. It's cooked in a saucepan, topped with meringue, and baked until golden.

- 4 **cups milk**
- ½ **cup uncooked long-grain rice**
- ½ **teaspoon salt**
- 4 **egg yolks**
- ½ **cup sugar**
- 2 **tablespoons butter, softened**
- 1 **teaspoon vanilla**
- 4 **egg whites**
- 3 **tablespoons sugar**

1 In a large heavy saucepan bring milk just to boiling (watch carefully to prevent milk from foaming); stir in rice and salt. Reduce heat to medium-low. Cook rice, uncovered, about 18 minutes or until tender, stirring frequently. Grease a 2-quart casserole; set aside.

2 In a medium mixing bowl combine egg yolks, the ½ cup sugar, the butter, and vanilla. Beat until combined but not foamy. Stir 1 cup of the hot rice mixture into egg mixture. While stirring, pour all of the egg-rice mixture into rice mixture in saucepan. Bring mixture to boiling, stirring constantly. Cook and stir 1 minute more or until thickened. Pour pudding mixture into prepared casserole.

3 Meanwhile, in large mixing bowl beat egg whites with electric mixer on medium speed about 1 minute or until soft peaks form (tips curl). Gradually add the 3 tablespoons sugar, 1 tablespoon at a time, beating on high speed about 4 minutes more or until mixture forms stiff, glossy peaks (tips stand straight) and sugar dissolves.

4 Immediately spread the egg white meringue over rice pudding mixture, carefully sealing to the edge of the casserole.

5 Bake in a 350° oven for 15 minutes or until meringue edges are golden. Serve warm or cold. To serve cold, cover and chill.

Nutrition Facts per serving: 234 cal., 8 g total fat (4 g sat. fat), 123 mg chol., 255 mg sodium, 33 g carbo., 0 g fiber, 8 g pro. Daily Values: 26% vit. A, 1% vit. C, 13% calcium, 5% iron

Swedish Rice Pudding:
According to a tradition
that goes along with this
pudding, whoever gets the
whole, unblanched almond
that's stirred into the
pudding before the
meringue is added will
marry within a year.

BAKED CUSTARDS

Prep: 20 minutes   Bake: 30 minutes
Makes: 4 servings   Oven: 325°

Bake this time-honored, smooth-as-silk dessert in individual cups or in one larger dish.

   3 **beaten eggs**
1½ **cups milk**
   ⅓ **cup sugar**
   1 **teaspoon vanilla**
      Ground nutmeg or cinnamon
      (optional)

1 **In a medium mixing bowl combine** eggs, milk, sugar, and vanilla. Beat until well combined but not foamy. Place four ungreased 6-ounce custard cups or one 3½-cup soufflé dish in a 2-quart square baking dish.

2 **Pour egg mixture** into custard cups or soufflé dish. If desired, sprinkle with nutmeg or cinnamon. Place baking dish on oven rack. Pour boiling water into the baking dish around custard cups or soufflé dish to a depth of about 1 inch (see top photo, right).

3 **Bake in a 325° oven** for 30 to 45 minutes for custard cups (50 to 60 minutes for soufflé dish) or until a knife inserted near the centers or center comes out clean (see bottom photo, right). Remove cups or dish from water. Cool slightly on wire rack before serving. Or, cool completely; cover and chill.

4 **To unmold individual custards,** loosen edges with a knife, slipping point of knife down sides to let in air. Invert a dessert plate over each custard; turn custard cup and plate over together.

Carefully pour boiling water into the baking dish around custard cups, making sure no water gets into the custard mixture. Add water to a depth of 1 inch.

Insert tip of a knife into the center of each custard to test for doneness. The knife will come out clean when the custard is done. If any clings to knife, bake a little longer and test again.

Microwave directions: In a 4-cup microwave-safe measure microwave milk, sugar, and vanilla, uncovered, on 100% power (high) for 2½ to 5 minutes or until steaming but not boiling, stirring once or twice. Stir milk mixture into beaten eggs. Pour into the custard cups in the baking dish. (Do not use the soufflé dish version.) Pour boiling water into the baking dish around the custard cups to a depth of about 1 inch (about 2½ cups). Microwave, uncovered, on high for 3 minutes, giving dish a quarter-turn every minute. Rotate custard cups. Microwave for 1 to 3 minutes more or until edges are set but centers still quiver. (After the first minute, check for doneness every 15 seconds, turning cups as necessary.) Remove each cup from dish when it is done.

Nutrition Facts per serving: 170 cal., 6 g total fat (2 g sat. fat), 167 mg chol., 93 mg sodium, 22 g carbo., 0 g fiber, 8 g pro. Daily Values: 12% vit. A, 1% vit. C, 10% calcium, 3% iron

FLAN

LOW-FAT

Prep: 20 minutes **Bake:** 40 minutes
Chill: 4 hours **Makes:** 12 servings **Oven:** 325°

The caramelized sugar becomes the sauce when the custard is inverted.

1¾ cups sugar
8 eggs
4 cups milk
3 inches stick cinnamon
1½ teaspoons vanilla
    Orange sections (optional)
    Peeled papaya slices (optional)
    Strawberry slices (optional)
    Lime slices (optional)

1 **To caramelize sugar,** in a heavy medium skillet melt ¾ cup of the sugar over medium-high heat. Do not stir sugar; shake the skillet occasionally. When the sugar starts to melt, reduce heat to low. Cook, stirring frequently with a wooden spoon, until the sugar is golden brown.

2 **Remove skillet from heat;** immediately pour caramelized sugar into an ungreased shallow 3-quart oval casserole (approximately 13×9-inch oval dish). Holding dish with pot holders, quickly rotate dish to coat bottom and sides evenly. Cool.

3 **In a large mixing bowl beat** eggs with a rotary beater, gradually adding the remaining 1 cup sugar. In a saucepan heat milk and stick cinnamon over medium heat until mixture bubbles. Remove stick cinnamon. Slowly add milk to egg mixture, stirring constantly. Stir in vanilla.

4 **Place caramel-coated** dish in a 14×10×2-inch or 15×11×2-inch baking pan on an oven rack. Pour egg mixture into dish. Pour very hot water into the baking pan around the dish to a depth of 1 inch.

5 **Bake in a 325° oven** about 40 minutes or until a knife inserted halfway between the center and edge comes out clean.

6 **Carefully remove dish** from hot water. Cool flan on a wire rack. Cover and place in the refrigerator. Chill for 4 to 24 hours.

7 **To unmold flan,** loosen edges with a spatula. Slip point of spatula down sides to let in air. Invert a large platter over flan; turn flan and platter over together. Spoon caramelized sugar that remains in dish on top. If desired, garnish with orange sections and papaya, strawberry, and lime slices.

Nutrition Facts per serving: 205 cal., 5 g total fat (2 g sat. fat), 148 mg chol., 83 mg sodium, 34 g carbo., 0 g fiber, 7 g pro. Daily Values: 11% vit. A, 1% vit. C, 9% calcium, 3% iron

---

A SHORT COURSE ON CUSTARD

Flan is a relative of that creamy, silky, soothing family of sweets called custard. A flan is simply a custard of Spanish origin that is baked in a caramel-coated dish. When the baked custard is inverted, the caramel forms a layer on top. Here are a few hints to create custards:

- For the smoothest custard, beat the eggs just until the yolks and whites are blended. If the eggs are beaten until they're foamy, the custard will have bubbles on its surface.
- Don't skip the hot-water bath when baking a custard. It may seem superfluous, but it helps even out the heat so the custard cooks slowly, without overcooking (and drying out) the edges. An overbaked custard will separate and have a curdled appearance.
- Once the custard tests done, remove it from the bath immediately or it will continue to cook. Be careful not to drip hot water on yourself as you lift the mold from the water.
- To unmold a custard, run a knife around the edges; slip the point of the knife down the side of the mold to let in air. Invert a plate over the custard; turn the mold and plate over together. Lift off the mold.
- As soon as the custard is cooled, cover it and place in the refrigerator until serving time.

Citrus-Pumpkin Flans: When you want a pumpkin dessert for the holidays, but pumpkin pie with a crust is too heavy, give these spice- and orange-flavored pumpkin treats a try.

CITRUS-PUMPKIN FLANS

Prep: 20 minutes   **Bake:** 40 minutes
Chill: 4 hours   **Makes:** 4 servings   **Oven:** 325°

  ⅔ **cup sugar**
  3 **beaten eggs**
  ¾ **cup canned pumpkin**
  1 **5-ounce can (⅔ cup) evaporated milk**
  ¼ **cup sugar**
  1 **teaspoon pumpkin pie spice***
  1 **teaspoon finely shredded orange peel**
  1 **teaspoon vanilla**
    Pomegranate seeds (optional)

1 **To caramelize sugar,** in a heavy medium skillet melt the ⅔ cup sugar over medium-high heat. Do not stir sugar; shake the skillet occasionally. When the sugar starts to melt, reduce heat to low. Cook, stirring frequently with a wooden spoon, until sugar is golden brown.

2 **Remove skillet from heat** and immediately pour the caramelized sugar into four ungreased 6-ounce custard cups. Holding cups with pot holders, quickly tilt to evenly coat bottoms of the cups.

3 **Place cups** in a 2-quart square baking dish. In a mixing bowl stir together eggs, pumpkin, milk, the ¼ cup sugar, pumpkin pie spice, orange peel, and vanilla. Pour the pumpkin mixture over caramelized sugar in cups. Place the pan on the oven rack. Pour boiling water into the baking dish around cups to a depth of 1 inch.

4 **Bake in a 325° oven** for 40 to 45 minutes or until a knife inserted near the centers comes out clean. Remove cups from water. Cool slightly on wire rack. Cover and chill for 4 to 24 hours.

5 **To serve,** loosen edges of flans with a knife, slipping the point of the knife down the sides to let in air. Invert a dessert plate over each flan; turn custard cup and plate over together. Scrape the caramelized sugar that remains in cup onto the flan. If desired, garnish with pomegranate seeds.

*Note: To make your own pumpkin pie spice, stir together ½ teaspoon ground cinnamon, ¼ teaspoon ground ginger, ⅛ teaspoon ground nutmeg, and ⅛ teaspoon ground allspice.

Nutrition Facts per serving: 317 cal., 8 g total fat (3 g sat. fat), 174 mg chol., 100 mg sodium, 55 g carbo., 1 g fiber, 8 g pro. Daily Values: 111% vit. A, 6% vit. C, 13% calcium, 9% iron

pies and tarts

Tarte Tatin, recipe page 77

PIES AND TARTS

PASTRY FOR
SINGLE-CRUST PIE

Prep: 10 minutes   **Makes:** 8 servings

1¼ cups all-purpose flour
 ¼ teaspoon salt
 ⅓ cup shortening
 4 or 5 tablespoons cold water

1 **In a medium mixing bowl** stir together flour and salt. Using a pastry blender, cut in shortening until pieces are pea-size.

2 **Sprinkle 1 tablespoon** of the water over part of the mixture; gently toss with a fork. Push moistened dough to the side of the bowl. Repeat, using 1 tablespoon of the water at a time, until all the dough is moistened. Form dough into a ball.

3 **On a lightly** floured surface, use your hands to slightly flatten dough. Roll dough from center to edge into a 12-inch circle.

4 **To transfer pastry,** wrap it around rolling pin. Unroll pastry into 9-inch pie plate. Ease pastry into pie plate, being careful not to stretch pastry.

5 **Trim pastry** to ½ inch beyond edge of pie plate (see photo, top right). Fold under extra pastry. Crimp edge as desired. Do not prick pastry. Fill and bake as directed in individual recipes.

Food processor directions: Prepare as above, except place steel blade in food processor bowl. Add flour, salt, and shortening. Cover and process with on/off turns until most of mixture resembles cornmeal, but with a few larger pieces. With processor running, add 3 tablespoons water through feed tube. Stop processor when all water is added; scrape down side. Process with 2 on/off turns (mixture may not all be moistened). Remove from bowl; shape into a ball.

Baked Pastry Shell: Prepare as above, except generously prick bottom and side of pastry in pie plate with a fork. Prick all around where bottom and side meet. Line pastry with a double thickness of foil (see bottom photo, above right). Bake in a 450° oven for 8 minutes. Remove foil. Bake for 5 to 6 minutes more or until golden. Cool on wire rack.

Nutrition Facts per serving: 141 cal., 9 g total fat (2 g sat. fat), 0 mg chol., 67 mg sodium, 14 g carbo., 0 g fiber, 2 g pro. Daily Values: 0% vit. A, 0% vit. C, 0% calcium, 5% iron

Trim pastry to ½ inch beyond the edge of the pie plate. Fold the extra pastry under, even with the plate's rim, to build up the edge.

To prevent pastry from shrinking during baking, line it with a double thickness of regular foil or one layer of heavy-duty foil.

OIL PASTRY

Prep: 15 minutes   **Makes:** 8 servings

2¼ cups all-purpose flour
 ¼ teaspoon salt
 ½ cup cooking oil
 ⅓ cup cold milk

1 **In a large mixing bowl** combine flour and salt. Pour oil and milk into a measuring cup (do not stir); add all at once to flour mixture. Stir lightly with a fork. Form into 2 balls; flatten each slightly with your hands.

2 **Cut waxed paper** into four 12-inch squares. Place each ball of dough between 2 squares of paper. Roll each ball of dough into a circle to edges of paper. (Dampen work surface with a little water to prevent paper from slipping.)

3 **Peel off top** papers and fit dough, paper side up, into 9-inch pie plates. (Or, reserve one portion for use as a top crust.) Remove paper. Continue as directed for Pastry for Single-Crust or Double-Crust Pie (see left and page 48).

Nutrition Facts per serving: 243 cal., 14 g total fat (2 g sat. fat), 1 mg chol., 72 mg sodium, 25 g carbo., 1 g fiber, 4 g pro. Daily Values: 0% vit. A, 0% vit. C, 1% calcium, 10% iron

PASTRY FOR DOUBLE-CRUST PIE

Prep: 15 minutes   Makes: 8 servings

  2 cups all-purpose flour
  ½ teaspoon salt
  ⅔ cup shortening
  6 or 7 tablespoons cold water

1 In a large mixing bowl stir together flour and salt. Using a pastry blender, cut in shortening until pieces are pea-size.

2 Sprinkle 1 tablespoon of the water over part of the mixture; gently toss with a fork. Push moistened dough to side of bowl. Repeat, using 1 tablespoon water at a time, until all the dough is moistened. Divide in half. Form each half into ball.

3 On a lightly floured surface, use your hands to slightly flatten 1 ball of dough. Roll from the center to the edge into a 12-inch circle.

4 To transfer pastry, wrap it around the rolling pin. Unroll into a 9-inch pie plate. Ease pastry into pie plate, being careful not to stretch pastry. Transfer filling to pastry-lined pie plate. Trim pastry even with rim of pie plate.

5 Roll remaining dough into a 12-inch circle. Cut slits to allow steam to escape. Place remaining pastry on filling; trim ½ inch beyond edge of plate. Fold top pastry under bottom pastry. Crimp edge as desired. Bake as directed in individual recipes.

Pastry for Lattice-Top Pie: Prepare as above, except trim bottom pastry to ½ inch beyond edge of pie plate. Fill pastry-lined pie plate with desired filling. Roll out remaining pastry and cut into ½-inch-wide strips. Weave strips over filling. Press ends of strips into crust rim. Fold bottom pastry over strips; seal and crimp edge as desired. (For a quick lattice, roll out top pastry. Use a mini cookie or canapé cutter to make cutouts an equal distance apart from pastry center to edge. Place pastry on filling; seal and crimp edge.) Bake as directed in individual recipes.

Nutrition Facts per serving: 256 cal., 17 g total fat (4 g sat. fat), 0 mg chol., 134 mg sodium, 22 g carbo., 1 g fiber, 3 g pro. Daily Values: 0% vit. A, 0% vit. C, 0% calcium, 8% iron

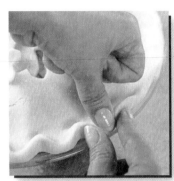

For a fluted edge, place your thumb against the inside of the pastry; press dough around your thumb with your other hand's thumb and index finger.

For a petal edge, flute the pastry as directed in photo above. Press the tines of a fork lightly into the center of each flute.

APPLE-CRANBERRY DEEP-DISH PIE

Prep: 50 minutes   Bake: 50 minutes
Makes: 8 servings   Oven: 375°

  ¼ cup sugar
  3 tablespoons all-purpose flour
  1 teaspoon apple pie spice or
    ¼ teaspoon ground nutmeg
  1 teaspoon finely shredded orange peel
  1½ cups canned whole cranberry sauce
  7 cups thinly sliced, peeled cooking apples (about 2¼ pounds)
  1 recipe Pastry for Single-Crust Pie (see page 47)
  1 egg yolk
  1 tablespoon water
  1 tablespoon sugar
    Vanilla ice cream (optional)

1 In a large bowl combine the ¼ cup sugar, the flour, spice, and orange peel. Stir in cranberry sauce. Add apples. Gently toss to coat. Transfer to a 10-inch deep-dish pie plate or a 1½-quart casserole.

FOOLPROOF PASTRY

You can make perfect pastry every time with these few pointers:

- Measure your ingredients accurately. Too much flour makes for tough pastry; too much shortening makes it crumble; and too much water makes it tough.
- Stir together the flour and salt, then cut in the shortening until the mixture resembles small peas.
- Add water gradually to the mixture, then gently toss it together just until it's evenly moistened.
- Flour the rolling surface just enough to keep the dough from sticking.
- Roll the pastry to an even thickness. Try not to stretch it as you're transferring it to the pie plate.
- Use a glass pie plate or dull metal pie pan so the pastry browns evenly.
- If you're making a double-crust pie, trim the edge of the bottom pastry after you pour in the filling so it doesn't pull the pastry down into the pie plate.
- Patch any cracks with a pastry scrap before adding the filling. Moisten the underside of the scrap with a little water so it stays in place.
- Check that your oven temperature is accurate. If it is too low, the bottom crust will be soggy.
- To prevent pastry edges from overbrowning, tear off a 12-inch square of foil. Fold it in quarters and cut a quarter circle off the folded corner (about 3 inches from the tip). Unfold the foil and place it on the pie, slightly molding the foil over the edge.
- After baking, cool your pie on a wire rack. Allowing the air to circulate under the pie prevents the crust from becoming soggy.

2 Prepare pastry. On a lightly floured surface, flatten pastry dough. Roll dough from center to edge into a 14-inch circle. Using cookie cutters, cut desired shapes from pastry, rerolling and cutting trimmings as necessary. Arrange cutouts on apple mixture so just the edges overlap (see photo, below).

3 In small bowl stir together egg yolk and water; brush onto pastry cutouts. Sprinkle with the 1 tablespoon sugar. To prevent overbrowning, cover edge of pie with foil. Place on baking sheet. Bake in a 375° oven for 25 minutes. Remove foil. Bake for 25 to 30 minutes more or until top is golden and apples are tender. Cool slightly on a wire rack; serve warm. If desired, serve with vanilla ice cream.

Nutrition Facts per serving: 347 cal., 10 g total fat (2 g sat. fat), 27 mg chol., 85 mg sodium, 65 g carbo., 5 g fiber, 3 g pro. Daily Values: 4% vit. A, 4% vit. C, 1% calcium, 10% iron

Apple-Cranberry Deep-Dish Pie: For comfort food at its best, spoon this two-fruit pastry combo into dessert dishes and top it off with some big scoops of vanilla ice cream.

APPLE PIE

Prep: 50 minutes **Bake:** 50 minutes
Makes: 8 servings **Oven:** 375°

> 1 recipe Pastry for Double-Crust Pie
>   (see page 48)
> 6 cups thinly sliced, peeled cooking
>   apples (about 2¼ pounds)
> 1 tablespoon lemon juice (optional)
> ¾ cup sugar
> 2 tablespoons all-purpose flour
> ½ teaspoon ground cinnamon
> ⅛ teaspoon ground nutmeg
> ½ cup raisins or chopped walnuts
>   (optional)

1 Prepare and roll out pastry. Line a 9-inch pie plate with half of the pastry; set aside.

2 If desired, sprinkle apples with lemon juice. In a large mixing bowl stir together sugar, flour, cinnamon, and nutmeg. Add apple slices and, if desired, raisins or walnuts. Gently toss to coat.

3 Transfer apple mixture to the pastry-lined pie plate. Trim pastry to edge of pie plate. Cut slits in remaining pastry; place on filling and seal. Crimp edge as desired.

4 To prevent overbrowning, cover edge of pie with foil. Bake in 375° oven for 25 minutes. Remove foil. Bake for 25 to 30 minutes more or until top is golden. Cool completely on a wire rack.

Nutrition Facts per serving: 380 cal., 18 g total fat (4 g sat. fat), 0 mg chol., 135 mg sodium, 54 g carbo., 3 g fiber, 3 g pro. Daily Values: 0% vit. A, 0% vit. C, 0% calcium, 11% iron

---

AMERICAN PIE

Baseball and hot dogs are as American as, well, you know the rest. Apple pie may be America's favorite, but its origins date back to 14th-century England when apple filling was substituted in traditional meat pies.

The Pilgrims brought apples to America and served apple pie for breakfast (a tradition that should definitely be resurrected). In colonial America, apple pie was served with— not after—the main course at lunch or dinner.

NO-PEEL APPLE PIE

EASY

Prep: 35 minutes **Bake:** 1 hour
Makes: 8 servings **Oven:** 375°

The expression "easy-as-pie" surely applies to this treat. Pick a thin-skinned apple, such as Golden Delicious, Jonagold, or Jonathan, to make it.

> 1 15-ounce package (2 crusts) folded
>   refrigerated unbaked piecrust
> 6 large cooking apples
> ½ cup water
> 2 tablespoons lemon juice
> ½ cup granulated sugar
> 2 tablespoons all-purpose flour
> 1½ teaspoons apple pie spice
>   Whipping cream or milk
>   Coarse and/or granulated sugar

1 Let piecrust stand according to package directions. Line a 9-inch pie plate with half of the pastry; set aside.

2 For filling, core and slice unpeeled apples (you should have 8 cups). In a large mixing bowl combine apples with water and lemon juice. Gently toss to coat. In another large bowl stir together the ½ cup sugar, flour, and spice. Drain apples well; add to sugar mixture. Gently toss to coat.

3 Spoon the apple mixture into the pastry-lined pie plate. Trim pastry to edge of pie plate. Moisten edge with water. Cut out desired shapes from center of remaining crust; set shapes aside. Center top crust on filling and seal. Crimp edge as desired. Brush the top crust with whipping cream or milk. If desired, top with reserved pastry cutouts; brush cutouts with cream or milk. Sprinkle the pie with coarse and/or granulated sugar.

4 To prevent overbrowning, cover the edge of pie with foil. Bake in a 375° oven for 30 minutes. Remove foil. Bake about 30 minutes more or until the top is golden. Cool slightly on a wire rack; serve warm.

Nutrition Facts per serving: 373 cal., 16 g total fat (1 g sat. fat), 18 mg chol., 211 mg sodium, 58 g carbo., 3 g fiber, 2 g pro. Daily Values: 1% vit. A, 13% vit. C, 1% calcium, 3% iron

No-Peel Apple Pie: This juicy pie works perfectly, and you don't even have to use a paring knife. Ready-made refrigerated piecrust saves time, too.

APPLE-CRANBERRY STREUSEL PIE

Prep: 40 minutes **Bake:** 55 minutes
Makes: 8 servings **Oven:** 375°

> 1 **recipe Baked Pastry Shell,
    unpricked (see page 47)**
> ½ **cup dried cranberries or dried tart
    cherries**
> 6 **large cooking apples, peeled,
    cored, and sliced (6 cups)**
> ⅔ **cup granulated sugar**
> 3 **tablespoons all-purpose flour**
> 1 **teaspoon apple pie spice**
> 1 **teaspoon finely shredded lemon peel**
> ¼ **teaspoon salt**
> ⅓ **cup half-and-half or light cream**
> ⅓ **cup all-purpose flour**
> ⅓ **cup toasted finely chopped pecans
    or walnuts (see tip, page 247)**
> ⅓ **cup packed brown sugar**
> ¼ **teaspoon ground nutmeg**
> 3 **tablespoons butter**

1 Prepare Baked Pastry Shell as directed, except do not prick the pastry.

2 For filling, pour boiling water over cranberries or cherries. Let stand for 5 minutes; drain. Mix cranberries or cherries and apples; place in the Baked Pastry Shell. Combine granulated sugar, the 3 tablespoons flour, spice, lemon peel, and salt. Stir in half-and-half. Pour over fruit.

3 For topping, combine the ⅓ cup flour, the nuts, brown sugar, and nutmeg. Using a pastry blender, cut in butter until the pieces are pea-size. Sprinkle over filling.

4 To prevent overbrowning, cover edge of pie with foil. Bake in a 375° oven for 45 minutes. Remove foil. Bake for 10 to 15 minutes more or until topping is golden and fruit is tender. Cool for 45 minutes on a wire rack; serve warm. (Or, cool completely on wire rack.) Store any leftover pie, covered, in the refrigerator.

Nutrition Facts per serving: 415 cal., 18 g total fat
(6 g sat. fat), 15 mg chol., 185 mg sodium,
64 g carbo., 3 g fiber, 4 g pro. Daily Values: 5% vit. A,
8% vit. C, 3% calcium, 12% iron

Apple-Cranberry Streusel Pie: A whisper of cream gives the filling of this streusel-crowned creation a touch of richness. Dried cranberries provide lively bursts of flavor.

THE APPLE OF YOUR PIE

The sweet and crisp Red Delicious has won the affection of the lunchbox set, but bake it in a pie and it turns to mush. Unlike the old adage about the rose, "an apple is an apple is an apple" doesn't hold true. When you bake a pie, you need to choose an apple variety that can stand up to the heat. Try one of these to find your heart's delight:

- **Rome Beauty:** Called the Queen of Bakers, cooking accentuates the rich but mellow flavor of this medium-tart, deep red apple.
- **Golden Delicious:** The way this sweet apple keeps its shape when cooked makes it a natural in pies.
- **Granny Smith:** For the tart-and-tangy lovers out there, this bright green fruit has found legions of fans.
- **Cortland:** A balanced apple, the Cortland is slightly sweet, slightly tart.
- **Newtown Pippin:** Benjamin Franklin and Thomas Jefferson sang the praises of this green-gold fruit. Its highly perfumed flesh is crisp and juicy and has a sweet-tart flavor.
- **Stayman:** This winter apple has a rich, mildly tart taste.
- **Winesap:** As suggested by its name, this delicious all-purpose apple has a tangy, winelike taste.
- **York Imperial:** A good apple for those who like their fruit a little bit tart, but not too much.

MIXED BERRY PIE

Prep: 30 minutes   Bake: 45 minutes
Makes: 8 servings   Oven: 375°

Showcase the summer's best berries in this cream-of-the-crop pie.

1 recipe Pastry for Double-Crust Pie (see page 48)
1 cup sugar
3 tablespoons cornstarch
1 teaspoon finely shredded orange peel
½ teaspoon ground cinnamon
¼ teaspoon ground nutmeg
⅛ teaspoon ground ginger
2 cups sliced fresh strawberries
2 cups fresh blackberries or raspberries
1 cup fresh blueberries
   Milk
   Sugar

1 **Prepare and roll** out pastry. Line a 9-inch pie plate with half of the pastry; set aside.

2 **In a large** mixing bowl combine the 1 cup sugar, the cornstarch, orange peel, cinnamon, nutmeg, and ginger. Add strawberries, blackberries or raspberries, and blueberries. Gently toss to coat. Transfer berry mixture to the pastry-lined pie plate. Trim pastry to the edge of the pie plate. Cut slits in remaining pastry; place on filling and seal. Crimp edge as desired. Brush top crust with milk and sprinkle with sugar.

3 **To prevent** overbrowning, cover edge of pie with foil. Bake in a 375° oven for 25 minutes. Remove foil. Bake for 20 to 25 minutes more or until top is golden and filling is bubbly. Cool completely on a wire rack.

Nutrition Facts per serving: 411 cal., 18 g total fat (4 g sat. fat), 0 mg chol., 137 mg sodium, 61 g carbo., 4 g fiber, 4 g pro. Daily Values: 1% vit. A, 52% vit. C, 2% calcium, 12% iron

BLUEBERRY PIE

Prep: 30 minutes   Bake: 45 minutes
Makes: 8 servings   Oven: 375°

Bring a smile to blueberry-stained lips by baking this timeless pie any time of year with berries fresh-from-the-patch or from the freezer.

    1 recipe Pastry for Double-Crust Pie
        (see page 48)
    ¾ cup sugar
    ⅓ cup all-purpose flour
    2 teaspoons finely shredded lemon
        peel
    1 tablespoon lemon juice
    5 cups fresh or frozen blueberries
        Milk (optional)
        Sugar (optional)

1 Prepare and roll out pastry. Line a 9-inch pie plate with half of the pastry; set aside.

2 In a large mixing bowl stir together the ¾ cup sugar, the flour, lemon peel, and lemon juice. Add blueberries. Gently toss to coat. (If using frozen fruit, let mixture stand for 15 to 30 minutes or until fruit is partially thawed, but still icy.)

3 Transfer berry mixture to pastry-lined pie plate. Trim pastry to edge of pie plate. Cut slits in remaining pastry; place on filling and seal. Crimp edge as desired. If desired, brush top with milk and sprinkle with sugar.

4 To prevent overbrowning, cover edge of the pie with foil. Bake in a 375° oven for 25 minutes for fresh fruit (50 minutes for frozen fruit). Remove foil. Bake for 20 to 25 minutes more for fresh fruit (20 to 30 minutes more for frozen fruit) or until top is golden. Cool completely on a wire rack.

Nutrition Facts per serving: 397 cal., 18 g total fat (4 g sat. fat), 0 mg chol., 140 mg sodium, 57 g carbo., 3 g fiber, 4 g pro. Daily Values: 0% vit. A, 22% vit. C, 1% calcium, 11% iron

RASPBERRY PIE

Prep: 25 minutes   Bake: 50 minutes
Makes: 8 servings   Oven: 375°

Be sure to stir the tender raspberries with a light hand to avoid crushing them.

    1 recipe Pastry for Double-Crust Pie
        (see page 48)
    ½ to ¾ cup sugar
    3 tablespoons all-purpose flour
    5 cups fresh or frozen unsweetened
        red raspberries

1 Prepare and roll out pastry. Line a 9-inch pie plate with half of the pastry; set aside.

2 In a large mixing bowl stir together sugar and flour. Add raspberries. Gently toss to coat. (If using frozen fruit, let mixture stand for 15 to 30 minutes or until fruit is partially thawed, but still icy.)

3 Transfer berry mixture to the pastry-lined pie plate. Trim pastry to edge of pie plate. Cut slits in remaining pastry; place on filling and seal. Crimp edge as desired.

BLUEBERRY LORE

Blueberries—and picking them in the wild—have an undeniable romance about them. In Northern Europe, families trek into the woods in late summer, to jealously guarded locations, in search of wild blueberries they take home and eat with sugar and cream or turn into compotes, cold soups, preserves, and tarts.

Blueberries have a history on this side of the Atlantic, too. When the pilgrims arrived here they found Native Americans gathering blueberries in the wild and using them—both fresh and dried—in dishes both sweet and savory. By the mid-19th century, blueberries were being cultivated on a large scale in the woods of the northern states.

THE PROPER PLATE

If you want your pie perfectly shaped and as nicely browned and flaky on the bottom crust as it is on the top (and who wouldn't?), you need to choose the pie plate you use with some forethought. Here are the qualities to look for:

■ **Surface:** Always use a standard glass or dull metal pie plate. Shiny metal pie pans—which work fine for crumb-crust pies—can cause a bottom pastry crust to turn out soggy.

■ **Size:** Although they may be pretty to look at, ceramic or pottery pie plates aren't necessarily standard size (a standard-size plate holds about 3¾ cups liquid). You can simply adjust the amount of filling and baking time.

■ **When Using Foil:** Disposable foil pans are usually smaller than standard pie plates; deep-dish foil pie pans are closer to standard size.

4 **To prevent** overbrowning, cover edge of the pie with foil. Bake in a 375° oven for 25 minutes for fresh fruit (50 minutes for frozen fruit). Remove foil. Bake for 25 to 30 minutes more for fresh fruit (about 30 minutes more for frozen fruit) or until top is golden. Cool completely on a wire rack.

Nutrition Facts per serving: 351 cal., 18 g total fat (4 g sat. fat), 0 mg chol., 134 mg sodium, 45 g carbo., 4 g fiber, 4 g pro. Daily Values: 1% vit. A, 32% vit. C, 1% calcium, 12% iron

STRAWBERRY PIE

Prep: 40 minutes **Chill:** 2 hours
Makes: 8 servings

A glaze which uses pureed berries makes the whole berries in this beautiful pie glisten and shine—and adds fresh berry flavor, too.

    8 cups fresh strawberries (2 quarts)
      Water
    ⅔ cup granulated sugar
    2 tablespoons cornstarch
    1 recipe Baked Pastry Shell
        (see page 47)
    1 cup whipping cream
    2 tablespoons powdered sugar
    2 tablespoons amaretto or
      ¼ teaspoon almond extract

1 **Remove stems** from strawberries. In blender container or food processor bowl process 1 cup of the berries and ⅔ cup water until smooth. Sieve, if desired. Add water to make 1½ cups mixture.

2 **In a medium** saucepan combine granulated sugar and cornstarch. Stir in berry mixture. Cook and stir over medium heat until mixture is thickened and bubbly. Reduce heat. Cook and stir for 2 minutes more. Remove from heat. Cool 10 minutes without stirring.

3 **Spread about** ¼ cup of the berry mixture over bottom of Baked Pastry Shell. Arrange half of the remaining berries in pastry shell, stem ends down, cutting larger berries in half lengthwise, if necessary. Spoon half of the remaining berry mixture over berries, being careful to cover all of the fruit. Repeat layers. Chill in the refrigerator 2 hours or until set.

4 **To serve,** in a small mixing bowl beat whipping cream and powdered sugar until stiff peaks form. Beat in amaretto or almond extract. Serve with pie.

Nutrition Facts per serving: 382 cal., 20 g total fat (9 g sat. fat), 41 mg chol., 81 mg sodium, 47 g carbo., 3 g fiber, 3 g pro. Daily Values: 13% vit. A, 141% vit. C, 3% calcium, 9% iron

Cherry-Pear Pie: An afternoon coffee break with a slice of homemade pie is an old-time ritual worth resurrecting—especially if you're serving this delicious double-fruit creation.

CHERRY-PEAR **PIE**

Prep: 40 minutes **Bake:** 55 minutes
Makes: 8 servings **Oven:** 375°

The surprise ingredient in this pie is a subtle hint of rosemary that enhances the fresh fruit flavors of the ripe pears and red cherries.

- ⅔ **cup granulated sugar**
- 3 **tablespoons cornstarch**
- ¼ **teaspoon ground nutmeg**
- ¼ **teaspoon dried rosemary, crushed (optional)**
- 4 **cups thinly sliced, peeled pears**
- 3 **cups frozen pitted tart red cherries**
- 1 **recipe Pastry for Double-Crust Pie (see page 48)**
- 1 **beaten egg white**
- 1 **tablespoon water**
  Coarse sugar
  Vanilla ice cream (optional)

1 **In a large** mixing bowl stir together the ¾ cup granulated sugar, the cornstarch, nutmeg, and, if desired, rosemary. Add pears and cherries. Gently toss to coat. Let mixture stand at room temperature for 20 minutes.

2 **Meanwhile,** prepare and roll out pastry. Line a 9-inch pie plate with half of the pastry; set aside.

3 **Transfer fruit** mixture to the pastry-lined pie plate. Trim pastry to edge of pie plate. Using a miniature cookie cutter, cut out hearts from the center of the remaining pastry; set cutouts aside. Place pastry on filling and seal. Crimp edge as desired. Combine egg white and water; brush onto pastry. Top with heart cutouts. Brush again. Sprinkle with coarse sugar.

4 **To prevent** overbrowning, cover edge of pie with foil. Bake in a 375° oven for 25 minutes. Remove foil. Bake for 30 to 35 minutes more or until the top is golden. Cool slightly on a wire rack; serve warm. (Or, cool completely on wire rack.) If desired, serve with ice cream.

Nutrition Facts per serving: 418 cal., 18 g total fat (4 g sat. fat), 0 mg chol., 143 mg sodium, 62 g carbo., 4 g fiber, 4 g pro. Daily Values: 7% vit. A, 15% vit. C, 1% calcium, 11% iron

CHERRY PIE

Prep: 50 minutes **Bake:** 50 minutes
Makes: 8 servings **Oven:** 375°

*Celebrate the Fourth of July with a cherry pie.
Montmorency, Early Richmond, and English
Morello cherries are good pie choices.*

  1¼ to 1½ **cups sugar**
    2 **tablespoons quick-cooking tapioca**
    5 **cups fresh or frozen unsweetened
       pitted tart red cherries**
  ¼ **teaspoon almond extract**
    1 **recipe Pastry for Double-Crust Pie
       (see page 48)**

1 In a large mixing bowl stir together sugar and
tapioca. Add cherries and almond extract. Gently
toss to coat. Let mixture stand about 15 minutes or
until a syrup forms, stirring occasionally. (If using
frozen fruit, let mixture stand about 1 hour.)

2 Meanwhile, prepare and roll out pastry. Line a
9-inch pie plate with half of the pastry; set aside.

3 Stir cherry mixture. Transfer cherry mixture to
pastry-lined pie plate. Trim pastry to edge of pie
plate. Cut slits in remaining pastry; place on filling
and seal. Crimp edge as desired.

4 To prevent overbrowning, cover edge of the pie
with foil. Bake in a 375° oven for 25 minutes for
fresh fruit (50 minutes for frozen fruit). Remove
foil. Bake for 25 to 35 minutes more for fresh fruit
(about 30 minutes more for frozen fruit) or until
top is golden. Cool completely on a wire rack.

Lattice Cherry Pie: Prepare as above, except
substitute 1 recipe Pastry for Lattice-Top Pie (see
page 48) for Pastry for Double-Crust Pie.

Nutrition Facts per serving: 417 cal., 18 g total fat
(4 g sat. fat), 0 mg chol., 135 mg sodium, 63 g carbo.,
2 g fiber, 4 g pro. Daily Values: 6% vit. A, 2% vit. C,
1% calcium, 11% iron

FRUIT PIES 101

A sweet fruit filling paired with a plain
pastry makes for a delicious pie. No
matter the fruit used, here are a few tips for
making each one of your creations a
winning combination:

- Be sure to use either a double-crust or lattice-
top as the recipe specifies. It won't work to
substitute one for the other because some
fillings require the venting of the lattice;
others, such as apples, benefit from steaming
under a top crust.

- You can use either fresh or frozen fruit in
your pie. Be sure to mix frozen fruit with the
sugar-flour mixture; let it thaw for 15 to
30 minutes—until the fruit is partially
thawed but still icy—before transferring it to
a pastry-lined plate. Pies made with frozen
fruit will take a little longer to bake. Before
the foil is removed, bake a pie made with
frozen fruit in a 375° oven about 50 minutes
(rather than 25). Remove the foil and

continue baking until the pie is done (usually
20 to 30 minutes longer).

- Make several cuts in the top of a double-crust
pie before baking to allow the steam to escape
and prevent excessive bubbling.

- For an attractive glazed crust, brush the top
crust with milk, then sprinkle with granulated
sugar before baking.

- Place a pizza pan or baking sheet under a
double-crust fruit pie when you put it in the
oven to catch any filling that bubbles over.

- Fruit pies need to bubble in the center to be
properly cooked—otherwise, the thickener
(flour, cornstarch, or tapioca) won't be clear.
To see if the pie is done, make a small hole in
the top crust and spoon out some of the juice.
If the juice is clear, the pie is done. If it's
cloudy, bake the pie a little longer.

- To serve the pie at its flavorful best—and so
the pieces don't fall apart when you cut it—let
a pie cool for 3 to 4 hours before serving.

RHUBARB PIE

Prep: 25 minutes Bake: 45 minutes
Makes: 8 servings Oven: 375°

To prepare fresh rhubarb, wash it well, trim off the dry ends of the stalks, and slice.

     1 recipe Pastry for Single-Crust Pie*
           (see page 47)
     1 recipe Crumb Topping (below)
     ¾ cup granulated sugar
     ¼ cup all-purpose flour
     ½ teaspoon ground cinnamon
           (optional)
     4 cups fresh or frozen unsweetened
           sliced rhubarb

1 Prepare and roll out pastry. Line a 9-inch pie plate with the pastry. Trim and crimp edge as desired; set aside. Prepare Crumb Topping; set aside.

2 In a large mixing bowl stir together granulated sugar, flour, and, if desired, cinnamon. Add rhubarb. Gently toss to coat. (If using frozen rhubarb, let mixture stand for 15 to 30 minutes or until fruit is partially thawed, but still icy.)

3 Transfer rhubarb mixture to the pastry-lined pie plate. Sprinkle Crumb Topping over filling.

4 To prevent overbrowning, cover edge of the pie with foil. Bake in a 375° oven for 25 minutes for fresh fruit (50 minutes for frozen fruit). Remove foil. Bake for 20 to 25 minutes more for fresh fruit (20 to 30 minutes more for frozen fruit) or until topping is golden. Cool completely on a wire rack.

Crumb Topping: In a small bowl, stir together ½ cup all-purpose flour and ½ cup packed brown sugar. Using a pastry blender, cut in 3 tablespoons butter until mixture resembles coarse crumbs.

*Note: A double-crust pastry works equally well for this pie. Simply prepare the Pastry for Double-Crust Pie (see page 48), omit the Crumb Topping, and bake as directed in step 4.

Nutrition Facts per serving: 345 cal., 13 g total fat (5 g sat. fat), 12 mg chol., 117 mg sodium, 54 g carbo., 2 g fiber, 4 g pro. Daily Values: 4% vit. A, 8% vit. C, 5% calcium, 11% iron

CONCORD GRAPE PIE

Prep: 1 hour Bake: 45 minutes
Makes: 8 servings Oven: 375°

Look for deep-purple Concord grapes in the grocery store during September and October.

     1 recipe Pastry for Single-Crust Pie
           (see page 47)
   1½ pounds Concord grapes (4 cups)
     ¾ cup sugar
     ⅓ cup all-purpose flour
     ¼ teaspoon salt
     2 tablespoons butter, melted
     1 tablespoon lemon juice
     ½ cup all-purpose flour
     ½ cup sugar
     ¼ cup butter

1 Prepare and roll out pastry. Line a 9-inch pie plate with the pastry. Trim and crimp edge as desired; set aside.

2 Remove skins from grapes by gently pressing each grape between your fingers. (The skins will slip off easily.) Set skins aside. In a large saucepan bring grape pulp to boiling. Reduce heat and simmer, uncovered, for 5 minutes. Sieve the pulp to remove the seeds. Add the grape skins to the pulp.

3 In a large mixing bowl stir together the ¾ cup sugar, the ⅓ cup flour, and the salt. Stir in the grape mixture, the 2 tablespoons melted butter, and the lemon juice. Pour into the pastry-lined pie plate.

4 To prevent overbrowning, cover the edge of pie with foil. Bake in a 375° oven for 20 minutes.

5 Meanwhile, stir together the ½ cup flour and the ½ cup sugar. Cut in the ¼ cup butter until mixture resembles coarse crumbs. Remove foil from pie. Sprinkle crumb mixture over pie. Bake about 25 minutes more or until topping is golden. Cool completely on a wire rack.

Nutrition Facts per serving: 402 cal., 18 g total fat (8 g sat. fat), 23 mg chol., 223 mg sodium, 61 g carbo., 2 g fiber, 4 g pro. Daily Values: 11% vit. A, 4% vit. C, 0% calcium, 10% iron

Concord Grape Pie:
A Concord, Massachusetts, man planted the first Concord grapes in 1849. Little did he know that his ultra-juicy, sweet grapes would make such spectacular royal-purple pies.

CHRISTMAS PIE

Mincemeat pie has been a steadfast Christmas tradition since the 13th century when it was baked in a rectangular crust to symbolize the manger. The spices were symbolic of the wise men's gifts. It was the custom to eat a mincemeat pie each day for the 12 days between Christmas and Twelfth Night for good luck in the coming year.

MINCE-PEAR PIE

Prep: 30 minutes **Bake:** 45 minutes
Makes: 8 servings **Oven:** 375°

Although mincemeat was traditionally made with minced meat and suet, these days you can rely on prepared all-fruit mincemeat in jars.

1 recipe Pastry for Double-Crust Pie
   (see page 48)
1 27-ounce jar (2⅔ cups) mincemeat
3 tablespoons orange juice
2 cups thinly sliced, peeled pears
   (about 1 pound)
  Milk (optional)
  Granulated sugar (optional)
  Vanilla ice cream or one recipe
    Hard Sauce (see page 268)
    (optional)

1 **Prepare and roll** out pastry. Line a 9-inch pie plate with half of the pastry; set aside.

2 **In a large** mixing bowl stir together mincemeat and orange juice. Gently stir in pears.

3 **Transfer mincemeat** mixture to the pastry-lined pie plate.* Trim pastry to edge of pie plate. Cut slits in remaining pastry; place on filling and seal. Crimp edge as desired. If desired, brush pastry with milk and sprinkle with granulated sugar.

4 **To prevent** overbrowning, cover edge of pie with foil. Bake in a 375° oven for 25 minutes. Remove foil. Bake for 20 to 25 minutes more or until pastry is golden. Cool completely on a wire rack. If desired, serve with ice cream or Hard Sauce.

*Note: If desired, substitute pastry stars for the top crust. After adding filling to pastry-lined pie plate, trim pastry and crimp as desired. Bake as directed in step 4. Meanwhile, on a lightly floured surface, use a knife or cookie cutter to cut remaining pastry into stars or other decorative shapes. Place pastry cutouts on an ungreased baking sheet. If desired, brush with milk and sprinkle with granulated or coarse sugar. Bake cutouts alongside pie about 10 minutes or until golden. Transfer cutouts to a wire rack; cool completely. To serve, arrange cutouts on pie.

Nutrition Facts per serving: 492 cal., 19 g total fat (4 g sat. fat), 0 mg chol., 414 mg sodium, 79 g carbo., 2 g fiber, 4 g pro. Daily Values: 0% vit. A, 8% vit. C, 3% calcium, 19% iron

Mince-Apple Pie: Prepare as at left, except omit orange juice and substitute 3 cups thinly sliced, peeled cooking apples (about 1 pound) for pears.

Mince-Orange Pie: Prepare as at left, except substitute 3 oranges for the pears. Peel and section the oranges; halve the sections.

Mince-Peach Pie: Prepare as at left, except substitute one 29-ounce can peach slices, drained and cut up, for the pears. Omit the orange juice.

RAISIN PIE

Prep: 30 minutes   **Bake:** 45 minutes
Makes: 10 servings   **Oven:** 375°

*For an elegant, golden version of this lemon-
accented fruit pie, use golden raisins.*

**1 recipe Pastry for Double-Crust Pie
    (see page 48)**
½ **cup sugar**
2 tablespoons all-purpose flour
2 cups raisins
1⅓ **cups water**
½ **teaspoon finely shredded lemon
    peel**
3 tablespoons lemon juice
½ **cup chopped walnuts**

1 Prepare and roll out pastry. Line a 9-inch pie
plate with half of the pastry; set aside.

2 In a saucepan stir together sugar and flour. Stir
in raisins, water, lemon peel, and lemon juice.
Cook and stir until thickened and bubbly. Cook
and stir for 1 minute more. Remove from heat; stir
in the walnuts.

3 Transfer raisin mixture to the pastry-lined pie
plate. Trim pastry to edge of pie plate. Cut slits
in remaining pastry; place on filling and seal. Crimp
edge as desired.

4 To prevent overbrowning, cover edge of the pie
with foil. Bake in a 375° oven for 25 minutes.
Remove foil. Bake for 20 to 25 minutes more or
until top is golden. Cool completely on a wire rack.

Nutrition Facts per serving: 375 cal., 18 g total fat
(4 g sat. fat), 0 mg chol., 112 mg sodium, 53 g carbo.,
2 g fiber, 4 g pro. Daily Values: 0% vit. A, 5% vit. C,
2% calcium, 12% iron

Mince-Peach Pie: Peaches lighten up the spicy richness of the mincemeat in this holiday pie. Serve it with a scoop or two of vanilla ice cream.

Banana Streusel Pie:
A banana lover's delight!
This macadamia-nut
streusel is a touch of
pure decadence.

BANANA STREUSEL PIE

Prep: 35 minutes **Bake:** 40 minutes
Makes: 8 servings **Oven:** 450°/375°

*When you buy bananas to make this pie, select
ones that are firm but not green.*

- 1 **recipe Pastry for Single-Crust Pie
  (see page 47)**
- 4 **cups sliced ripe bananas
  (about 5 medium)**
- ⅔ **cup unsweetened pineapple juice**
- ¼ **cup granulated sugar**
- 1½ **teaspoons finely shredded lemon
  peel**
- ½ **teaspoon ground cinnamon**
- 1 **teaspoon cornstarch**
- ½ **cup all-purpose flour**
- ½ **cup packed brown sugar**
- ⅓ **cup chopped macadamia nuts
  or almonds**
- 1 **teaspoon ground cinnamon**
- ¼ **cup butter**

1 Prepare and roll out pastry. Line a 9-inch pie
plate with the pastry. Trim and crimp edge as
desired. Line pastry with a double thickness of foil
(see photo, page 47). Bake in a 450° oven for
8 minutes. Remove foil. Bake 4 to 5 minutes more
or until pastry is set and dry. Cool in pie plate on a
wire rack. Reduce oven temperature to 375°.

2 Meanwhile, in a bowl gently toss together
bananas and pineapple juice. Drain, reserving
juices. Gently toss bananas with granulated sugar,
lemon peel, and the ½ teaspoon cinnamon. Spoon
banana mixture into partially baked pastry shell. In
saucepan stir together the reserved juice and
cornstarch. Cook and stir over medium heat until
thickened and bubbly. Pour over banana mixture.

3 For topping, combine the flour, brown sugar,
nuts, and the 1 teaspoon cinnamon. Using a
pastry blender, cut in butter until mixture resembles
coarse crumbs. Sprinkle over banana mixture.

4 To prevent overbrowning, cover edge of pie with
foil. Bake in the 375° oven for 40 minutes or
until topping is golden and edge is bubbly. Cool
completely on a wire rack.

Nutrition Facts per serving: 402 cal., 19 g total fat
(6 g sat. fat), 15 mg chol., 130 mg sodium,
57 g carbo., 2 g fiber, 4 g pro. Daily Values: 5% vit. A,
15% vit. C, 2% calcium, 13% iron

CUSTARD PIE

Prep: 30 minutes   **Bake:** 40 minutes
Makes: 8 servings   **Oven:** 450°/350°

Though it's perfect plain, you can dress up this much-loved old-fashioned pie with a drizzle of caramel ice-cream topping.

> **1 recipe Pastry for Single-Crust Pie
>   (see page 47)**
> **4 eggs**
> **½ cup sugar**
> **1 teaspoon vanilla**
> **⅛ teaspoon salt**
> **2½ cups milk**
>   **Ground nutmeg**

1 Prepare and roll out pastry. Line a 9-inch pie plate with pastry. Trim; crimp edge as desired. Line pastry with a double thickness of foil (see photo, page 47). Bake in a 450° oven for 8 minutes. Remove foil. Bake 4 to 5 minutes more or until the pastry is set and dry. Reduce the oven temperature to 350°.

2 Meanwhile, for filling, in a mixing bowl beat eggs slightly with a rotary beater or fork. Stir in sugar, vanilla, and salt. Gradually stir in milk.

3 Place the partially baked pastry shell on the oven rack. Carefully pour filling into the pastry shell. Sprinkle with nutmeg.

4 To prevent overbrowning, cover edge of pie with foil. Bake in the 350° for 25 minutes. Remove foil. Bake for 15 to 20 minutes more or until a knife inserted near the center comes out clean. Cool for 1 to 2 hours on a wire rack. Refrigerate within 2 hours; cover for longer storage.

Nutrition Facts per serving: 266 cal., 13 g total fat (4 g sat. fat), 112 mg chol., 170 mg sodium, 30 g carbo., 0 g fiber, 8 g pro. Daily Values: 9% vit. A, 1% vit. C, 9% calcium, 8% iron

Coconut Custard Pie: Prepare as above, except stir in ½ cup toasted coconut (see tip, page 247) with the milk.

CUSTARD CUES

A custard pie is the embodiment of simplicity—creamy white, slightly sweet, and velvety textured. Here's how to create a smooth custard pie:

■ When you've mixed the filling, place the prepared pastry shell on the oven rack, then pour in the custard filling. It reduces the chance you might spill.

■ A custard pie is done if the liquid area in the center of the pie is smaller than a quarter. (The filling continues to set after you remove the pie from the oven.) Or, insert a knife near the pie's center. If it comes out clean, the pie is done. The knife test can cause the filling to crack, though—so for a prettier pie, use the first test.

■ Let the pie cool for 1 hour on a wire rack; cover and refrigerate it until serving time. Cover and chill any leftovers, too.

EGGNOG CUSTARD PIE

Prep: 30 minutes **Bake:** 40 minutes
Makes: 8 servings **Oven:** 450°/350°

Ring in the holidays with this smooth, spiced pie made with a time-honored yuletide treat.

    1 recipe Pastry for Single-Crust Pie
        (see page 47)
    4 eggs
 2¼ cups dairy or canned eggnog*
    ½ cup sugar
    2 tablespoons light rum
    1 teaspoon vanilla
    ¼ teaspoon salt
      Ground nutmeg

1 Prepare and roll out pastry. Line 9-inch pie plate with the pastry. Trim and crimp edge as desired. Line pastry with a double thickness of foil. Bake in a 450° oven for 8 minutes. Remove foil. Bake for 4 to 5 minutes more or until pastry is set and dry. Reduce the oven temperature to 350°.

2 Meanwhile, for filling, in a large mixing bowl beat eggs slightly with a rotary beater or fork. Stir in eggnog, sugar, rum, vanilla, and salt.

3 Place the partially baked pastry shell on the oven rack. Carefully pour filling into the pastry shell. Sprinkle with nutmeg.

4 To prevent overbrowning, cover edge of pie with foil. Bake in the 350° oven for 25 minutes. Remove foil. Bake for 15 to 20 minutes more or until a knife inserted near the center comes out clean. Cool for 1 to 2 hours on wire rack. Refrigerate within 2 hours; cover for longer storage.

*Note: When eggnog appears on your dairy's shelves, buy an extra quart to freeze for an off-season dessert treat.

Nutrition Facts per serving: 327 cal., 16 g total fat (3 g sat. fat), 107 mg chol., 210 mg sodium, 36 g carbo., 0 g fiber, 7 g pro. Daily Values: 7% vit. A, 0% vit. C, 5% calcium, 8% iron

RHUBARB CUSTARD PIE

Prep: 35 minutes **Bake:** 50 minutes
Makes: 8 servings **Oven:** 375°

Though this homey, lattice-topped pie was crowded out of recent versions of the Better Homes and Gardens® New Cook Book, *fans have held fast to the recipe for this favorite.*

 1½ cups sugar
    ¼ cup all-purpose flour
    ¼ teaspoon ground nutmeg
        or ground cinnamon
      Dash salt
    3 slightly beaten eggs
    4 cups sliced fresh rhubarb*
    1 recipe Pastry for Lattice-Top Pie
        (see page 48)
    2 tablespoons butter

1 In a large mixing bowl stir together sugar, flour, nutmeg, and salt. Add eggs, stirring until smooth. Stir in rhubarb.

2 Prepare and roll out pastry. Line pie plate with half of pastry. Fill with rhubarb mixture. Dot with butter. Weave lattice top; seal and flute edge.

3 To prevent overbrowning, cover edge of pie with foil. Bake in a 375° oven for 25 minutes. Remove foil. Bake for 25 to 30 minutes more or until knife inserted near the center comes out clean. Cool for 1 to 2 hours on wire rack. Refrigerate within 2 hours; cover for longer storage.

*Note: You can substitute one 16-ounce package frozen unsweetened sliced rhubarb for the fresh rhubarb. Thaw frozen rhubarb, but do not drain. Add thawed fruit and its liquid to egg mixture.

Nutrition Facts per serving: 480 cal., 22 g total fat (7 g sat. fat), 88 mg chol., 207 mg sodium, 65 g carbo., 2 g fiber, 6 g pro. Daily Values: 6% vit. A, 8% vit. C, 5% calcium, 12% iron

PECAN PIE

Prep: 25 minutes   Bake: 45 minutes
Makes: 8 servings   Oven: 350°

- 1 recipe Pastry for Single-Crust Pie (see page 47)
- 3 slightly beaten eggs
- 1 cup corn syrup
- ⅔ cup sugar
- ⅓ cup butter, melted
- 1 teaspoon vanilla
- 1¼ cups pecan halves or chopped macadamia nuts

1 Prepare and roll out pastry. Line a 9-inch pie plate with the pastry. Trim and crimp edge as desired; set aside.

2 For filling, in a bowl combine eggs, corn syrup, sugar, butter, and vanilla. Stir in pecans. Place pastry-lined pie plate on oven rack. Carefully pour filling into pastry shell.

3 To prevent overbrowning, cover edge of pie with foil. Bake in a 350° oven 25 minutes. Remove foil. Bake 20 to 25 minutes more or until a knife inserted near center comes out clean. Cool for 1 to 2 hours on a wire rack. Refrigerate within 2 hours.

Nutrition Facts per serving: 541 cal., 30 g total fat (8 g sat. fat), 100 mg chol., 197 mg sodium, 67 g carbo., 2 g fiber, 6 g pro. Daily Values: 10% vit. A, 0% vit. C, 2% calcium, 11% iron

BUTTERMILK CHESS PIE

Prep: 25 minutes   Bake: 35 minutes
Makes: 8 servings   Oven: 450°/350°

The thin top "crust" that rises to the surface of the lemony filling is characteristic of chess pie.

- 1 recipe Pastry for Single-Crust Pie (see page 47)
- 1½ cups sugar
- 2 tablespoons cornmeal
- 4 eggs
- ½ cup buttermilk or sour milk (see tip, page 329)
- ¼ cup butter, melted and cooled
- 1 tablespoon finely shredded lemon peel
- ¼ cup lemon juice
- 1 teaspoon vanilla

1 Prepare and roll out pastry. Line a 9-inch pie plate with pastry. Trim and crimp edge as desired. Line pastry with a double thickness of foil. Bake in a 450° oven 8 minutes. Remove foil; bake for 4 to 5 minutes more or until pastry is set and dry. Reduce the oven temperature to 350°.

2 Meanwhile, for filling, in a small mixing bowl stir together sugar and cornmeal. In a large mixing bowl beat the eggs with an electric mixer on high speed about 5 minutes or until thick and light colored. Add the sugar mixture; mix well. Gradually stir in buttermilk, melted butter, lemon peel, lemon juice, and vanilla.

3 Place partially baked pastry shell on oven rack. Carefully pour the filling into the pastry shell.

4 To prevent overbrowning, cover edge of pie with foil. Bake in the 350° oven for 25 minutes. Remove foil. Bake for 10 to 15 minutes more or until a knife inserted near the center comes out clean. Cool for 1 to 2 hours on a wire rack. Refrigerate within 2 hours; cover for longer storage.

Nutrition Facts per serving: 390 cal., 17 g total fat (7 g sat. fat), 122 mg chol., 173 mg sodium, 55 g carbo., 1 g fiber, 6 g pro. Daily Values: 10% vit. A, 7% vit. C, 3% calcium, 8% iron

PUMPKIN PIE

Prep: 25 minutes **Bake:** 50 minutes
Makes: 8 servings **Oven:** 375°

Instead of measuring three different spices, you can use 1½ teaspoons of pumpkin pie spice.

  1 **recipe Pastry for Single-Crust Pie**
      (see page 47)
  1 **16-ounce can pumpkin**
⅔ **cup sugar**
  1 **teaspoon ground cinnamon**
½ **teaspoon ground ginger**
½ **teaspoon ground nutmeg**
  3 **slightly beaten eggs**
  1 **5-ounce can (⅔ cup) evaporated**
      milk
½ **cup milk**

1 **Prepare and roll** out pastry. Line a 9-inch pie plate with the pastry. Trim and crimp edge as desired; set aside.

2 **For filling,** in a mixing bowl combine pumpkin, sugar, cinnamon, ginger, and nutmeg. Add eggs. Beat lightly with a rotary beater or fork just until combined. Gradually stir in evaporated milk and milk; mix well.

3 **Place the** pastry-lined pie plate on the oven rack. Carefully pour filling into pastry shell.

4 **To prevent** overbrowning, cover edge of the pie with foil. Bake in a 375° oven for 25 minutes.

Remove foil. Bake about 25 minutes more or until a knife inserted near the center comes out clean. Cool for 1 to 2 hours on a wire rack. Refrigerate within 2 hours; cover for longer storage.

Nutrition Facts per serving: 286 cal., 13 g total fat (4 g sat. fat), 86 mg chol., 120 mg sodium, 38 g carbo., 2 g fiber, 7 g pro. Daily Values: 130% vit. A, 9% vit. C, 7% calcium, 13% iron

PUMPKIN-CREAM CHEESE PIE

BEST-LOVED

Prep: 20 minutes **Bake:** 1 hour
Makes: 8 servings **Oven:** 350°

  1 **recipe Pastry for Single-Crust Pie**
      (see page 47)
  1 **8-ounce package cream cheese,**
      softened
¼ **cup granulated sugar**
½ **teaspoon vanilla**
  1 **slightly beaten egg**
1¼ **cups canned pumpkin**
  1 **cup evaporated milk**
  2 **beaten eggs**
¼ **cup granulated sugar**
¼ **cup packed brown sugar**
  1 **teaspoon ground cinnamon**
¼ **teaspoon salt**
¼ **teaspoon ground nutmeg**
½ **cup chopped pecans**

THE GREAT PUMPKIN

C anned pumpkin is definitely convenient, but if time allows, here's how you can make your own pumpkin puree:

Choose a medium (about 6 pounds) pie pumpkin (pumpkins that make happy jack-o'-lanterns don't make the best pie). Cut the pumpkin into 5-inch-square pieces. Remove the seeds and fibrous strings. Arrange the pieces in a single layer, skin side up, in a large shallow baking pan. Cover with foil. Bake in a 375° oven for 1 to 1½ hours or until tender. Scoop the pulp from the rind. Working with part of the pulp at a time, place pulp in a food processor bowl or blender container. Cover and blend or process until smooth. Place pumpkin in a cheesecloth-lined strainer and press out any liquid. Makes about 2 cups pumpkin puree.

Pumpkin-Cream Cheese Pie: This special pie—with its rich creamy base, spicy pumpkin layer, and nutty topping—catapults the Thanksgiving standard into pumpkin-pie paradise. Top it off with whipped cream and nutmeg.

2 tablespoons all-purpose flour
2 tablespoons brown sugar
1 tablespoon butter, softened

1 Prepare and roll out pastry. Line a 9-inch pie plate with the pastry. Trim and crimp edge as desired; set aside.

2 In small mixing bowl beat cream cheese, ¼ cup granulated sugar, the vanilla, and the 1 slightly beaten egg with electric mixer on low to medium speed until smooth. Chill in refrigerator for 30 minutes. Spoon into pastry-lined pie plate.

3 In a medium mixing bowl combine pumpkin, evaporated milk, the 2 eggs, ¼ cup granulated sugar, ¼ cup brown sugar, cinnamon, salt, and nutmeg. Carefully pour over cream-cheese mixture.

4 To prevent overbrowning, cover edge of the pie with foil. Bake in a 350° oven for 25 minutes. Remove foil. Bake for 25 minutes more.

5 Meanwhile, combine the pecans, flour, the 2 tablespoons brown sugar, and butter. Sprinkle over the pie. Bake for 10 to 15 minutes more or until a knife inserted near the center comes out clean. Cool for 1 to 2 hours on a wire rack. Refrigerate within 2 hours; cover for longer storage.

Nutrition Facts per serving: 477 cal., 29 g total fat (11 g sat. fat), 122 mg chol., 295 mg sodium, 46 g carbo., 2 g fiber, 10 g pro. Daily Values: 103% vit. A, 4% vit. C, 12% calcium, 17% iron

SWEET POTATO PIE

Prep: 1 hour   Bake: 50 minutes
Makes: 8 servings   Oven: 375°

  1 **pound sweet potatoes**
  ¼ **cup butter, cut up**
  1 **recipe Cornmeal Pastry (see below)**
  ½ **cup packed brown sugar**
  1 **tablespoon finely shredded orange peel**
  1 **teaspoon ground cinnamon**
  ½ **teaspoon ground nutmeg**
  ½ **teaspoon ground ginger**
  3 **slightly beaten eggs**
  1 **cup half-and-half or light cream**
  1 **recipe Hazelnut Streusel Topping (see above right)**

1 **Peel sweet potatoes.** Cut off woody portions and ends. Cut into quarters. In a covered saucepan cook sweet potatoes in enough boiling salted water to cover for 25 to 35 minutes or until tender. Drain sweet potatoes; mash. (You should have 1½ cups mashed sweet potatoes.) Add butter to hot sweet potatoes, stirring until melted.

2 **Meanwhile,** prepare Cornmeal Pastry. Roll dough into a 12-inch circle. Ease pastry into a 9-inch pie plate, being careful not to stretch pastry. Trim pastry to ½ inch beyond edge of plate. Fold under the extra pastry. Crimp the edge high. Do not prick the pastry.

3 **For filling,** stir brown sugar, orange peel, cinnamon, nutmeg, and ginger into sweet potato mixture. Stir in eggs and half-and-half. Place pastry shell on oven rack. Carefully pour filling into pastry-lined pie plate.

4 **To prevent** overbrowning, cover edge of the pie with foil. Bake in a 375° oven for 30 minutes. Remove foil. Sprinkle with Hazelnut Streusel Topping. Bake for 20 to 25 minutes more or until a knife inserted near the center comes out clean. Cool for 1 to 2 hours on a wire rack. Refrigerate within 2 hours; cover for longer storage.

Cornmeal Pastry: In a medium mixing bowl stir together ¾ cup all-purpose flour, ½ cup yellow cornmeal, 1 tablespoon granulated sugar, and ¼ teaspoon salt. Using a pastry blender, cut in ⅓ cup shortening until pieces are pea-size. Sprinkle 3 to 5 tablespoons cold water, 1 tablespoon at a time, over mixture, tossing with a fork after each addition until all is moistened. Form into a ball.

Hazelnut Streusel Topping: Mix ¼ cup all-purpose flour, ¼ cup packed brown sugar, ⅛ teaspoon ground cinnamon, and ⅛ teaspoon ground nutmeg. Cut in 2 tablespoons butter until mixture resembles coarse crumbs. Stir in ¼ cup chopped toasted hazelnuts or almonds (see tip, page 247).

Nutrition Facts per serving: 457 cal., 25 g total fat (10 g sat. fat), 114 mg chol., 216 mg sodium, 53 g carbo., 3 g fiber, 7 g pro. Daily Values: 114% vit. A, 20% vit. C, 7% calcium, 14% iron

MERINGUE FOR PIE

Prep: 20 minutes   Stand: 30 minutes
Makes: 8 servings

  3 **egg whites**
  ½ **teaspoon vanilla**
  ¼ **teaspoon cream of tartar**
  6 **tablespoons sugar**

1 **Allow egg whites** to stand at room temperature for 30 minutes. In a large mixing bowl combine egg whites, vanilla, and cream of tartar. Beat with an electric mixer on medium speed about 1 minute or until soft peaks form (tips curl).

2 **Gradually add** sugar, 1 tablespoon at a time, beating on high speed about 4 minutes more or until mixture forms stiff, glossy peaks (tips stand straight) and sugar dissolves.

3 **Immediately** spread meringue over warm pie filling, carefully sealing meringue to edge of pastry to prevent shrinkage. Bake as directed in individual recipes.

Nutrition Facts per serving: 44 cal., 0 g total fat, 0 mg chol., 21 mg sodium, 10 g carbo., 0 g fiber, 1 g pro.

Four-Egg-White Meringue: Prepare as above, except use 4 egg whites, 1 teaspoon vanilla, ½ teaspoon cream of tartar, and ½ cup sugar. Beat about 5 minutes or until stiff, glossy peaks form.

CROWNING GLORY

golden, textured, melt-in-your-mouth meringue is a regal topping for any cream pie. To ensure that your meringue is the crown jewel of your pie, heed these suggestions:

- Let egg whites stand at room temperature for 30 minutes, and use a clean bowl.
- Add sugar gradually as soon as soft peaks form (the tips bend over slightly).
- After adding the sugar, continue beating the egg whites until stiff peaks form, the sugar is dissolved, and whites feel completely smooth beneath your fingers. Underbeaten whites may cause your meringue to shrink as it bakes.

- Spread meringue over the hot filling, sealing it well by pushing it into the edge of the pastry.
- To store a meringue-topped cream pie, first let it cool 1 hour, then refrigerate. Chill it for 3 to 6 hours before serving—there's no need to cover it unless you're going to store it longer.
- If you need to cover a meringue-capped pie, insert wooden toothpicks halfway between the centers and edges of the pie and drape loosely with clear plastic wrap.
- An easy way to cut a meringue-topped cream pie is to dip the knife in water (don't dry it off) before cutting each slice of pie. This prevents the meringue from clinging to the knife.

VANILLA CREAM PIE

Prep: 1 hour **Bake:** 25 minutes **Cool:** 1 hour
Chill: 3 to 6 hours **Makes:** 8 servings **Oven:** 325°

If you wish, skip the meringue and crown the chilled pie with whipped cream instead.

> **1 recipe Baked Pastry Shell**
>   **(see page 47)**
> **4 eggs**
> **¾ cup sugar**
> **¼ cup cornstarch or ½ cup**
>   **all-purpose flour**
> **3 cups milk**
> **1 tablespoon butter**
> **1½ teaspoons vanilla**
> **1 recipe Four-Egg-White Meringue**
>   **(see page 68)**

1 Prepare Baked Pastry Shell; set aside. Separate egg yolks from whites; set the egg whites aside for meringue.

2 For filling, in a medium saucepan combine sugar and cornstarch or flour. Gradually stir in milk. Cook and stir over medium-high heat until thickened and bubbly. Cook and stir for 2 minutes more. Remove from heat. Slightly beat egg yolks with a rotary beater or fork. Gradually stir about 1 cup of the hot filling into yolks. Pour egg yolk mixture into hot filling in saucepan. Bring to gentle boil. Cook and stir for 2 minutes more. Remove from heat. Stir in butter and vanilla. Keep filling warm while preparing meringue.

3 Pour warm filling into pastry shell. Spread meringue over warm filling; seal to edge. Bake in a 325° oven for 25 to 30 minutes or until lightly browned. Cool for 1 hour on a wire rack. Chill in the refrigerator for 3 to 6 hours before serving.

Nutrition Facts per serving: 377 cal., 14 g total fat (4 g sat. fat), 113 mg chol., 161 mg sodium, 54 g carbo., 1 g fiber, 8 g pro. Daily Values: 23% vit. A, 1% vit. C, 10% calcium, 8% iron

Coconut Cream Pie: Prepare as above, except stir in 1 cup flaked coconut with butter and vanilla.

Banana Cream Pie: Prepare as above, except before adding filling, arrange 3 medium bananas, sliced (about 2¼ cups), over bottom of pastry shell.

Dark Chocolate Cream Pie: Prepare as above, except increase the sugar to 1 cup. Stir in 3 ounces unsweetened chocolate, cut up, with the milk.

Milk Chocolate Cream Pie: Prepare as above, except stir in 3 ounces semisweet chocolate, cut up, with the milk.

BUTTERSCOTCH PIE

Prep: 1 hour   **Bake:** 15 minutes
Cool and Chill: 4 to 7 hours
Makes: 8 servings   **Oven:** 350°

So what is butterscotch, anyway? The flavor of butter and brown sugar—and for many, a nostalgic taste of the past. This much-beloved recipe is frequently requested by Better Homes and Gardens® readers.

 1 **recipe Baked Pastry Shell**
     (see page 47)
 3 **eggs**
1½ **cups packed brown sugar**
 ⅓ **cup all-purpose flour**
2¼ **cups milk**
 2 **tablespoons butter**
 1 **teaspoon vanilla**
 1 **recipe Meringue for Pie**
     (see page 68)

1 Prepare Baked Pastry Shell; set aside. Separate egg yolks from egg whites; set the egg whites aside for meringue.

2 For filling, in a medium saucepan stir together brown sugar and flour. Gradually stir in milk. Cook and stir over medium heat until thickened and bubbly. Cook and stir for 1 minute more. Remove from heat. Slightly beat egg yolks with a rotary beater or fork. Gradually stir about 1 cup of the hot filling into egg yolks. Pour egg yolk mixture into hot filling in saucepan. Bring to gentle boil. Cook and stir for 2 minutes more. Remove from heat. Stir in butter and vanilla. Keep filling warm while preparing meringue.

3 Pour warm filling into pastry shell. Spread meringue over warm filling; seal to edge. Bake in a 350° oven for 15 minutes. Cool for 1 hour on a wire rack. Chill in the refrigerator for 3 to 6 hours before serving; cover for longer storage.

Nutrition Facts per serving: 410 cal., 15 g total fat (5 g sat. fat), 93 mg chol., 164 mg sodium, 63 g carbo., 1 g fiber, 7 g pro. Daily Values: 18% vit. A, 1% vit. C, 10% calcium, 13% iron

DOUBLE-COCONUT CREAM PIE

Prep: 1 hour   **Bake:** 15 minutes
Cool and Chill: 4 to 7 hours
Makes: 8 servings   **Oven:** 350°

Cream of coconut boosts the nutty flavor of the coconut in this dreamy pie.

 1 **recipe Baked Pastry Shell**
     (see page 47)
 3 **beaten eggs**
 ⅓ **cup sugar**
 ¼ **cup cornstarch**
 ¼ **teaspoon salt**
 2 **cups milk**
 1 **8-ounce can (¾ cup) cream**
     of coconut
 2 **tablespoons butter**
 1 **cup coconut**
 2 **teaspoons vanilla**
 1 **recipe Meringue for Pie**
     (see page 68)
 2 **tablespoons coconut**

1 Prepare Baked Pastry Shell. Separate egg yolks from egg whites; set whites aside for meringue.

2 For filling, in a medium saucepan combine sugar, cornstarch, and salt. Gradually stir in milk and cream of coconut. Cook and stir over medium heat until thickened and bubbly. Cook and stir 2 minutes more. Remove from heat. Slightly beat egg yolks with a rotary beater or fork. Gradually stir about 1 cup of the hot filling into egg yolks. Pour egg yolk mixture into hot filling in saucepan. Bring to a gentle boil. Cook and stir 2 minutes more. Remove from heat. Stir in butter until melted. Stir in the 1 cup coconut and vanilla. Keep filling warm while preparing meringue.

3 Pour warm filling into pastry shell. Spread meringue over warm filling; seal to edge. Sprinkle with the 2 tablespoons coconut. Bake in a 350° oven for 15 minutes. Cool for 1 hour on a wire rack. Chill in refrigerator for 3 to 6 hours before serving; cover for longer storage.

Nutrition Facts per serving: 565 cal., 38 g total fat (13 g sat. fat), 92 mg chol., 229 mg sodium, 50 g carbo., 1 g fiber, 7 g pro. Daily Values: 18% vit. A, 0% vit. C, 7% calcium, 10% iron

Lemon Meringue Pie:
Cool, creamy, and with the refreshing taste of lemon in every bite, here's the perfect pie for catching up with the neighbors over coffee on a summer evening.

LEMON MERINGUE PIE

Prep: 45 minutes **Bake:** 15 minutes
Cool and Chill: 4 to 7 hours
Makes: 8 servings **Oven:** 350°

　1 **recipe Baked Pastry Shell**
　　(see page 47)
　3 **eggs**
1½ **cups sugar**
　3 **tablespoons all-purpose flour**
　3 **tablespoons cornstarch**
1½ **cups water**
　2 **tablespoons butter**
　1 **to 2 teaspoons finely shredded**
　　lemon peel
　⅓ **cup lemon juice**
　1 **recipe Meringue for Pie**
　　(see page 68)

1 Prepare Baked Pastry Shell; set aside. Separate egg yolks from the egg whites; set whites aside for meringue.

2 For filling, in a medium saucepan combine the sugar, flour, cornstarch, and dash salt. Gradually stir in the water. Cook and stir over medium-high heat until thickened and bubbly. Reduce heat. Cook and stir 2 minutes more. Remove from heat. Slightly beat egg yolks with a rotary beater or fork. Gradually stir about 1 cup of the hot filling into yolks. Pour egg yolk mixture into hot filling in saucepan. Bring to a gentle boil. Cook and stir 2 minutes more. Remove from heat. Stir in butter and lemon peel. Gently stir in lemon juice. Keep filling warm while preparing meringue.

3 Pour warm filling into pastry shell. Spread meringue over warm filling; seal to edge. Bake in a 350° oven for 15 minutes. Cool for 1 hour on wire rack. Chill in refrigerator for 3 to 6 hours before serving; cover for longer storage.

Nutrition Facts per serving: 395 cal., 14 g total fat (6 g sat. fat), 96 mg chol., 139 mg sodium, 65 g carbo., 1 g fiber, 5 g pro. Daily Values: 14% vit. A, 8% vit. C, 1% calcium, 8% iron

KEY LIME **PIE**

Prep: 35 minutes **Bake:** 45 minutes
Cool and Chill: 4 to 7 hours
Makes: 8 servings **Oven:** 325°/350°

Tiny Key limes grow only in Florida and the Caribbean, but Persian limes grow in many places and are available in most markets.

> **1 recipe Pastry for Single-Crust Pie (see page 47)**
> **3 eggs**
> **1 14-ounce can (1¼ cups) sweetened condensed milk**
> **½ to ¾ teaspoon finely shredded Key lime peel or 1½ teaspoons finely shredded Persian lime peel**
> **½ cup water**
> **⅓ cup lime juice (8 to 10 Key limes or 2 to 3 Persian limes)**
> **Several drops green food coloring (optional)**
> **1 recipe Meringue for Pie (page 68)**

1 Prepare and roll out pastry. Line a 9-inch pie plate with pastry. Trim and crimp edge as desired; set aside.

2 Separate egg yolks from whites; set whites aside for meringue. For filling, in a medium mixing bowl beat egg yolks with a rotary beater or fork. Gradually stir in sweetened condensed milk and lime peel. Add water, lime juice, and, if desired, food coloring. Mix well (mixture will thicken).

3 Spoon thickened filling into pastry-lined pie plate. Bake in a 325° oven for 30 minutes.

4 Meanwhile, prepare meringue. Remove pie from oven. Increase the oven temperature to 350°. Spread meringue over hot filling; seal to edge. Bake in the 350° oven for 15 minutes. Cool for 1 hour on a wire rack. Chill in the refrigerator for 3 to 6 hours before serving; cover for longer storage.

Nutrition Facts per serving: 370 cal., 15 g total fat (6 g sat. fat), 97 mg chol., 157 mg sodium, 51 g carbo., 0 g fiber, 8 g pro. Daily Values: 8% vit. A, 7% vit. C, 13% calcium, 8% iron

SHAKER LEMON PIE

Prep: 40 minutes **Chill:** 8 to 24 hours
Bake: 45 minutes **Makes:** 8 servings
Oven: 375°

This zingy, custardy pie owes its bold flavor to lemon slices instead of lemon juice.

> **3 medium lemons**
> **1¾ cups sugar**
> **1 recipe Pastry for Double-Crust Pie (see page 48)**
> **4 beaten eggs**
> **1 beaten egg yolk**

1 Peel lemons; halve lengthwise and thinly slice. Stir sugar into lemon slices. Cover; refrigerate 8 hours or overnight, stirring occasionally.

2 Divide pastry in half. Roll each half into 12-inch circle. Use 1 pastry circle to line a 9-inch pie plate; trim to ½ inch beyond edge. Stir beaten whole eggs into lemon mixture; mix well. Turn into pastry-lined pie plate, arranging lemon slices evenly.

3 To make the shortcut lattice top, cut the remaining pastry circle into 10 strips. Lay half of the pastry strips in 1 direction across the filling; lay the other half of the strips in the other direction. Turn under edge; flute with the tines of a fork.

4 Combine beaten egg yolk and 1 tablespoon water. Brush lattice with egg yolk mixture. Cover edge with foil. Bake in 375° oven 25 minutes. Remove foil. Bake 20 to 25 minutes more or until pastry is golden and a knife inserted near center comes out clean. Cool 1 to 2 hours on a wire rack. Refrigerate within 2 hours; cover for longer storage.

Nutrition Facts per serving: 477 cal., 21 g total fat (5 g sat. fat), 133 mg chol., 168 mg sodium, 68 g carbo., 1 g fiber, 7 g pro. Daily Values: 8% vit. A, 19% vit. C, 2% calcium, 12% iron

To form a shortcut lattice crust, space half of the strips evenly over pie. Give pie a quarter turn; arrange remaining strips perpendicular to the first series of strips.

PIE SAFE

Whether you're making a pie or tart ahead of time, or storing a few extra pieces, here are a few golden rules of pastry storage:

- Fruit pies may stand at room temperature for 24 hours. Cover and refrigerate for longer storage.
- Custard and cream pies should be served as soon as they are cool, or covered lightly with plastic wrap and refrigerated for up to 2 days. Don't freeze cream or custard pies.
- To freeze unbaked fruit pies, treat any light-colored fruit with an ascorbic-acid color keeper. Assemble the pie in a metal or freezer-to-oven pie plate. Place it in a freezer bag; seal, label,

and freeze. Frozen pies should be used within 2 to 4 months. To bake a frozen pie, unwrap it and cover with foil. Bake in a 450° oven for 15 minutes; reduce the temperature to 375° and bake another 15 minutes. Uncover and continue baking for 55 to 60 minutes more or until crust is golden and filling is bubbly.

- To freeze baked fruit pies, bake and cool the pie completely. Place it in a freezer bag, seal, label, and freeze for up to 8 months. To use it, thaw, covered, at room temperature. If desired, reheat it by baking it, covered, in a 325° oven until warm.

FRENCH SILK PIE

Prep: 35 minutes   Chill: 5 to 24 hours
Makes: 10 servings

For the chocoholic, this pie is pure bliss. Make it pretty with Double-Chocolate Whipped Cream.

  1 recipe Baked Pastry Shell
      (see page 47)
  1 6-ounce package (1 cup) semisweet
      chocolate pieces
  ¾ cup sugar
  ¾ cup butter
  1 teaspoon vanilla
  ¾ cup refrigerated or frozen egg
      product, thawed
  1 recipe Double-Chocolate Whipped
      Cream (optional) (see right)

1 **Prepare** the Baked Pastry Shell. Heat chocolate pieces over low heat until melted. Cool.

To pipe large swirls on pie, hold pastry bag at 45° angle above center of pie. Squeeze bag gently while guiding the tip to edge to make a swirl. Stop pressure, then lift tip. Repeat.

2 **For filling,** in a large bowl beat sugar and butter with an electric mixer on medium speed about 4 minutes or until fluffy. Stir in chocolate and vanilla. Gradually add egg product, beating on high speed until light and fluffy (scrape bowl constantly).

3 **Transfer filling** to pastry shell. Cover and chill in the refrigerator for 5 to 24 hours. If desired, top with Double-Chocolate Whipped Cream.

Nutrition Facts per serving: 392 cal., 26 g total fat (5 g sat. fat), 18 mg chol., 225 mg sodium, 38 g carbo., 0 g fiber, 5 g pro. Daily Values: 17% vit. A, 0% vit. C, 3% calcium, 9% iron

Double-Chocolate Whipped Cream: For semisweet chocolate portion, in a heavy, small saucepan combine ¼ cup whipping cream and 3 ounces chopped semisweet chocolate. Heat over low heat, stirring constantly, until the chocolate begins to melt. Immediately remove from the heat and stir until smooth. Cool. In a small mixing bowl beat ¾ cup whipping cream with an electric mixer on low speed until soft peaks form. Add the cooled chocolate mixture. Continue beating on low speed just until stiff peaks form; set aside.

For white chocolate portion, repeat as above, except substitute 3 ounces white chocolate or white baking bar for the semisweet chocolate.

Fit pastry bag with large star tip. Spoon the semisweet chocolate portion down 1 side of bag and the white chocolate portion down the other side; close bag. Pipe swirls on pie (see photo, left).

SOUR CREAM, RAISIN, AND PEAR PIE

Prep: 40 minutes   Bake: 40 minutes
Makes: 8 servings   Oven: 375°

Wrapped in Cinnamon Pastry and beneath a layer of fresh pears lies the traditional sour cream-raisin pie. If you like a traditional topping, try the meringue version (see lower right).

    1 recipe Cinnamon Pastry
        (see lower right)
    ¾ cup light raisins
    3 beaten egg yolks
    1½ cups dairy sour cream
    1 cup granulated sugar
    ½ cup milk
    3 tablespoons all-purpose flour
    1 teaspoon ground cinnamon
    ¼ teaspoon ground nutmeg
    ⅛ teaspoon ground cloves
        Milk
        Granulated sugar
    1½ cups water
    ⅔ cup packed brown sugar
    2 tablespoons dark-colored corn
        syrup
    1 tablespoon lemon juice
    2 small pears, peeled and thinly
        sliced (2 cups)
    1 tablespoon cold water
    1 teaspoon cornstarch
        Pomegranate seeds (optional)

1 **Prepare pastry.** On a lightly floured surface, roll pastry to a 12-inch circle. Line a 9-inch pie plate with pastry. Trim to ¼ inch beyond edge of pie plate. Fold under extra pastry.

2 **To decorate** pastry edge with a leaf pattern, use a small, sharp knife to cut pastry scraps into small leaf shapes, about 1 inch long. Use the back side of the knife to score a vein down the middle of each leaf. Brush pastry edge with water. Gently press leaves along pastry edge, overlapping leaves. Do not prick pastry. Set aside.

3 **In a** small mixing bowl pour enough hot water over raisins to cover. Let stand for 5 minutes; drain well.

4 **In a** medium mixing bowl stir together raisins, egg yolks, sour cream, the 1 cup granulated sugar, the ½ cup milk, the flour, cinnamon, nutmeg, and cloves. Pour the raisin mixture into pastry-lined pie plate. Brush pastry edge with additional milk and sprinkle with additional granulated sugar.

5 **To prevent** overbrowning, cover the edge of the pie with foil. Bake in a 375° oven for 20 minutes. Remove foil. Bake for 20 to 25 minutes more or until pie appears nearly set in center when gently shaken. Cool pie for 1 hour on a wire rack.

6 **Meanwhile,** in a large saucepan, combine the 1½ cups water, the brown sugar, corn syrup, and lemon juice; bring to boiling. Stir in pears. Reduce heat. Simmer, covered, about 5 minutes or until pears are tender. Drain pears, reserving ⅓ cup of the poaching liquid. Let pears cool slightly.

7 **Combine** the 1 tablespoon water and the cornstarch; stir into reserved poaching liquid. Cook and stir until thickened and bubbly. Cook and stir 1 minute. Remove from heat; cool slightly.

8 **Arrange pear** slices in a circle on cooled sour-cream filling, overlapping pears slightly. Brush with the thickened poaching mixture. Cool for 1 to 2 hours on a wire rack. Refrigerate within 2 hours; cover for longer storage. If desired, garnish with pomegranate seeds.

Cinnamon Pastry: In a mixing bowl stir together 1¼ cups all-purpose flour, ½ teaspoon ground cinnamon, and ¼ teaspoon salt. Cut in ⅓ cup shortening until pieces are pea-size. Sprinkle 1 tablespoon cold water over part of the mixture; gently toss with a fork. Push moistened dough to side of bowl. Repeat with 3 to 4 tablespoons additional cold water, using 1 tablespoon water at a time, until all the dough is moistened. Form the dough into a ball.

Nutrition Facts per serving: 519 cal., 20 g total fat (9 g sat. fat), 100 mg chol., 113 mg sodium, 82 g carbo., 2 g fiber, 6 g pro. Daily Values: 23% vit. A, 6% vit. C, 9% calcium, 15% iron

Meringue-Topped Sour Cream-Raisin Pie: Prepare as above, except omit pear topping. Prepare 1 recipe Meringue for Pie (see page 68). Spread meringue over warm filling; seal to edge. Bake in a 350° oven 15 minutes. Cool 1 hour on a wire rack. Chill 3 to 6 hours before serving; cover for longer storage.

Sour Cream, Raisin and Pear Pie: If you love sour cream-raisin pie, try this pear-topped version with a cinnamon crust.

APPLE-NUT TART

Prep: 45 minutes   Bake: 1 hour
Makes: 12 servings   Oven: 325°

For an all-almond tart, use sliced almonds in place of the chopped walnuts.

   3 tart cooking apples, cored, peeled, and thinly sliced
   ¼ **cup water**
   ½ **cup all-purpose flour**
   ½ **cup ground toasted almonds (see tip, page 247)**
   ¾ **teaspoon baking powder**
   5 tablespoons butter
   ⅓ **cup sugar**
   3½ **ounces almond paste made without syrup or glucose (about ⅓ cup)**
   1 teaspoon ground cinnamon
   1 teaspoon vanilla
   2 eggs
   2 egg yolks
   2 egg whites
   1 recipe Lemon Butter Pastry (see right)
   ½ **cup apricot jam, melted**
   1 tablespoon butter, melted
   1 tablespoon sugar
   ½ **cup chopped walnuts**

1 Place apples in a large skillet. Add the water. Bring to boiling; reduce heat. Simmer, covered, about 5 minutes or until tender. Drain apples well; set aside.

2 For the filling, stir together flour, almonds, and baking powder; set aside. In a medium mixing bowl beat the 5 tablespoons butter and the ⅓ cup sugar with an electric mixer on medium speed. Slowly beat in almond paste, a small piece at a time, until smooth. Add cinnamon and vanilla; beat until a paste forms. Add whole eggs, 1 at a time, beating well after each. Beat in egg yolks. Stir in flour mixture. In a medium mixing bowl beat egg whites until soft peaks form; fold into batter.

3 Press Lemon Butter Pastry dough onto bottom and 2 inches up side of an ungreased 9-inch springform pan. Snip large fruit pieces in jam. Spread half of the melted jam over pastry. Pour filling into pan. Evenly arrange cooked apples over filling. Drizzle with the 1 tablespoon melted butter; sprinkle with the 1 tablespoon sugar. Sprinkle with walnuts.

4 Bake in a 325° oven for 60 to 65 minutes or until a toothpick inserted near center comes out clean. Cool tart for 1½ hours in pan on a wire rack. Remove side of springform pan; transfer tart to a serving platter. Drizzle remaining melted apricot jam over the tart.

Lemon Butter Pastry: In medium bowl beat ½ cup butter with electric mixer on medium speed for 30 seconds or until softened. Add ½ cup sugar; beat on medium speed 4 minutes or until fluffy. Add 1 egg yolk; beat for 1 minute on low speed. Add 1¼ cups all-purpose flour, 1 teaspoon vanilla, ½ teaspoon finely shredded lemon peel, and dash salt; beat until combined (mixture will be crumbly).

Nutrition Facts per serving: 421 cal., 24 g total fat (16 g sat. fat), 158 mg chol., 195 mg sodium, 48 g carbo., 2 g fiber, 7 g pro. Daily Values: 18% vit. A, 2% vit. C, 6% calcium, 12% iron

IT IS A BIG FAT DEAL

Basic pastry, such as piecrust, is usually made using shortening. However, butter is the best option for making the richer pastries commonly used for tarts. If a pastry recipe calls for butter, do not substitute margarine. Today's margarine is mostly low-fat or reduced-fat. These products will produce a crust that is tough and not the least bit flaky or crisp.

TROUBLESHOOTING PASTRY

If your pastry didn't turn out perfectly, look for one of the following problems (and its solution, too!):

If your pastry is crumbly and hard to roll:
- Add more water, 1 teaspoon at a time.
- Toss the flour mixture and water together just a little more, or until evenly moistened.

If your pastry is tough:
- Use a pastry blender to cut in the shortening or lard until well mixed and all of the mixture resembles small peas.
- Use less water to moisten the flour mixture.
- Toss the flour mixture and water together only until all of the flour mixture is moistened.

- Use less flour when rolling out your pastry.

If your crust shrinks excessively:
- Mix in the water only until evenly moistened.
- Let pastry rest for 5 minutes if it is hard to roll.
- Don't stretch pastry when transferring it.

If the bottom crust is soggy:
- Use a dull metal or glass pie plate rather than a shiny metal pan.
- Patch any cracks in the pastry with a pastry scrap before adding the filling.
- Make sure your oven temperature is accurate. If the temperature is too low, the bottom crust won't bake properly.

TARTE TATIN

Prep: 45 minutes   Bake: 30 minutes
Makes: 8 servings   Oven: 375°

This French upside-down apple tart, baked in an ovenproof skillet, bears the name of the Tatin sisters, who first served it in their restaurant in the early 1900s (see photo, page 45).

⅔ **cup granulated sugar**
½ **cup butter**
2 **pounds (about 6) tart cooking apples, peeled, cored, and quartered**
1 **recipe Egg Tart Pastry (see right)**
1 **recipe Sweetened Whipped Cream (optional) (see lower right)**
Orange peel curls (optional)

1 **In a** 10-inch ovenproof skillet combine granulated sugar and butter. Cook over medium heat, stirring occasionally, until boiling. Cook, without stirring, over medium-low heat for 9 to 10 minutes more or until mixture just begins to turn brown. (Mixture may appear separated.) Remove from heat.

2 **Arrange the apples,** cored sides up, in a single layer on top of the sugar mixture, overlapping them if necessary. Cover and cook over low heat about 10 minutes or until apples are tender.

3 **On a lightly** floured surface, use your hands to slightly flatten Egg Tart Pastry dough. Roll dough from center to edge, forming a 10-inch circle. Cut slits in the pastry. Wrap pastry around rolling pin. Unroll pastry over the apples in the skillet, being careful not to stretch the pastry.

4 **Bake in a** 375° oven about 30 minutes or until the pastry is golden. Cool dessert in skillet for 5 minutes on a wire rack. Invert onto a large serving plate. Lift off the skillet. Serve warm. If desired, serve with Sweetened Whipped Cream and garnish with orange peel curls.

Egg Tart Pastry: In a medium mixing bowl stir together 2 cups all-purpose flour and ¼ cup granulated sugar. Cut in ⅔ cup butter until pieces are pea-size. Using a fork, stir in 1 slightly beaten egg until all dough is moistened. Form into a ball.

Nutrition Facts per serving: 502 cal., 28 g total fat (17 g sat. fat), 72 mg chol., 323 mg sodium, 61 g carbo., 3 g fiber, 4 g pro. Daily Values: 34% vit. A, 0% vit. C, 1% calcium, 11% iron

Sweetened Whipped Cream: Chill a medium mixing bowl and the beaters of an electric mixer in the refrigerator. In the chilled bowl combine ½ cup whipping cream, 1 tablespoon powdered sugar, and ¼ teaspoon vanilla. Beat with the chilled beaters on low speed until soft peaks form. Makes 1 cup.

Mixed Fruit Tart with Amaretto Creme: Ideal for warm-weather get-togethers, this appealing almond tart boasts an array of fresh melon, grapes, tiny champagne grapes, strawberries, raspberries, and peaches.

MIXED FRUIT TART WITH AMARETTO CREME

Prep: 45 minutes   Bake: 12 minutes
Makes: 8 servings   Oven: 450°

Use your 9-inch springform pan for this luscious almond and fruit tart.

  1 recipe Pastry for Single-Crust Pie
      (see page 47)
    Milk
  1 tablespoon granulated sugar
  1 8-ounce package cream cheese,
      softened
  1 3-ounce package cream cheese,
      softened
  ½ cup amaretto*
  3 tablespoons brown sugar

  ½ cup finely chopped almonds, toasted
      (see tip, page 247)
  3 to 4 cups chilled assorted fresh fruit
  1 tablespoon granulated sugar

1 Prepare pastry. On a lightly floured surface, roll piecrust to an 11-inch circle. Wrap piecrust around rolling pin. Unroll into a 9-inch springform pan. Ease piecrust into pan. Press piecrust evenly

Line the piecrust shell in the springform pan with a double thickness of heavy foil. This prevents the piecrust from puffing while baking.

onto the bottom and 1 inch up the side of the pan. If desired, flute edge of piecrust. Generously prick bottom and side. Line with a double thickness of foil (see photo, page 78).

2 **Bake in a** 450° oven for 5 minutes. Remove the foil. Brush the edge of the piecrust with milk. Sprinkle piecrust with 1 tablespoon granulated sugar. Bake for 7 to 9 minutes more or until piecrust is golden. Cool completely in pan on a wire rack.

3 **In a small** mixing bowl beat the cream cheese, amaretto, and brown sugar with an electric mixer on medium speed until smooth. Stir in the almonds. Spread the almond mixture evenly over the cooled piecrust. Serve immediately or chill in the refrigerator for up to 4 hours.

4 **To serve,** top almond mixture with desired fruits. Remove side of pan. If desired, remove bottom of pan. Sprinkle the fruit with 1 tablespoon granulated sugar.

*Note: If desired, substitute ¼ cup milk and ¼ teaspoon almond extract for the amaretto.

Nutrition Facts per serving: 398 cal., 26 g total fat (9 g sat. fat), 51 mg chol., 226 mg sodium, 35 g carbo., 2 g fiber, 6 g pro. Daily Values: 35% vit. A, 14% vit. C, 8% calcium, 7% iron

BROWN BUTTER
TART

Prep: 40 minutes   **Bake:** 35 minutes
Makes: 12 to 16 servings   **Oven:** 350°

A generous spoonful of honeyed fresh fruit brings out the best in each wedge of buttery tart.

    1 recipe Sweet Tart Pastry (see right)
    3 eggs
1¼ cups sugar
    ½ cup all-purpose flour
    1 vanilla bean, split lengthwise,
        or 1 teaspoon vanilla
    ¾ cup butter
    ⅓ cup orange juice
    2 tablespoons honey
    1 tablespoon orange liqueur
    3 cups assorted mixed berries or
        assorted cut-up fresh fruit

1 **On a lightly** floured surface, use your hands to slightly flatten Sweet Tart Pastry dough. Roll dough from center to edge into a 12-inch circle. Wrap pastry around rolling pin. Unroll into an ungreased 10-inch tart pan with a removable bottom. Ease pastry into tart pan, being careful not to stretch pastry. Press pastry into the fluted side of tart pan. Trim edge; set aside.

2 **In a large** mixing bowl use a rotary beater or a wire whisk to beat eggs just until mixed. Stir in sugar, flour, and, if using, liquid vanilla; set aside.

3 **In a heavy,** medium saucepan combine the butter and, if using, vanilla bean. Cook over medium-high heat until the butter turns the color of light brown sugar. Remove from heat. Remove and discard vanilla bean. Slowly add the browned butter to the egg mixture, stirring until mixed. Pour into the pastry-lined tart pan.

4 **Bake in a** 350° oven about 35 minutes or until the top is crisp and golden. Cool 1 to 2 hours in pan on a wire rack. Refrigerate within 2 hours; cover for longer storage.

5 **In a medium mixing bowl** stir together the orange juice, honey, and orange liqueur. Stir in the fruit. Let fruit mixture stand up to 1 hour.

6 **To serve,** remove side of the tart pan. Cut tart into wedges. Place wedges on individual dessert plates. Using a slotted spoon, spoon some of the fruit mixture beside each wedge of tart.

Sweet Tart Pastry: In a medium mixing bowl stir together 1¼ cups all-purpose flour and ¼ cup sugar. Using a pastry blender, cut in ½ cup cold butter until pieces are pea-size. In a small mixing bowl stir together 2 beaten egg yolks and 1 tablespoon water. Gradually stir egg yolk mixture into dry mixture. Using your fingers, gently knead dough just until a ball forms. If necessary, cover with plastic wrap and chill in refrigerator for 30 to 60 minutes or until dough is easy to handle.

Nutrition Facts per serving: 387 cal., 21 g total fat (12 g sat. fat), 140 mg chol., 212 mg sodium, 46 g carbo., 2 g fiber, 4 g pro. Daily Values: 25% vit. A, 24% vit. C, 2% calcium, 8% iron

COUNTRY CHERRY AND
APRICOT TART

Prep: 40 minutes   Bake: 45 minutes
Makes: 8 servings   Oven: 375°

- ¾ **cup granulated sugar**
- 3 **tablespoons cornstarch**
- ¾ **cup apricot nectar**
- 3 **tablespoons cherry brandy, apricot brandy, or orange juice**
- 2 **tablespoons butter**
- 3 **cups sliced fresh apricots**
- 2 **cups pitted fresh sweet cherries**
- 1 **recipe Tart Pastry (see page 84)**
  Milk
  Powdered sugar

Using your fingers, fold the pastry border up and over the apricot-cherry filling, pleating the pastry to fit.

1 **For filling,** in a medium saucepan combine granulated sugar and cornstarch. Stir in nectar. Cook and stir over medium heat until thickened and bubbly. Cook and stir 2 minutes more. Remove from heat. Stir in the brandy or orange juice and butter. Stir in apricots and cherries; set aside.

2 **For pastry,** on a lightly floured surface, use your hands to slightly flatten Tart Pastry dough. Roll dough from center to the edge into a 14-inch circle. Wrap pastry around rolling pin. Unroll into a 10-inch pie plate or quiche dish. Ease pastry into the plate or dish, being careful not to stretch pastry. Trim pastry to 1½ inches beyond the edge.

Country Cherry and Apricot Tart: The "country" in this beautiful tart featuring plump cherries and ripe apricots comes from the rustic form of its classic flaky pastry.

HOMEMADE PIE FROM THE PANTRY

To get a jump-start on your next pastry project, prepare your pastry as directed, but don't roll it out. Instead, flatten the pastry into a patty, place it in a freezer bag, and freeze for up to 2 months. When you're in a pie-baking mood, thaw the pastry overnight in the refrigerator.

You also can roll pastry out and fit it into a pie plate or tart pan. Place the pastry in a freezer bag and freeze as above. Frozen pastry shells can be baked without thawing, but you will need to use a freezer-to-oven pie plate and may need to add 5 or 10 minutes to the baking time.

3 Pour filling into the pastry-lined pie plate or dish. Fold the pastry border up and over the filling (see photo, page 80). Lightly brush pastry with milk.

4 Bake in a 375° oven for 45 to 50 minutes or until pastry is golden. Cool completely in pan on wire rack. Before serving, sift powdered sugar over pastry edges.

Nutrition Facts per serving: 350 cal., 16 g total fat (4 g sat. fat), 0 mg chol., 102 mg sodium, 47 g carbo., 2 g fiber, 3 g pro. Daily Values: 18% vit. A, 9% vit. C, 2% calcium, 8% iron

FRESH BLUEBERRY **TART**

Prep: 30 minutes   Bake: 15 minutes
Chill: 1 hour   Makes: 10 servings   Oven: 375°

Glazed blueberries crown lemony cream cheese in a beautifully speckled Poppy-Seed Pastry.

  1 recipe Poppy-Seed Pastry
     (see right)
  1 8-ounce package cream cheese,
     softened
  ½ cup marshmallow creme
  ½ teaspoon finely shredded lemon peel
  3 cups fresh blueberries
  ¼ cup grape jelly
     Lemon peel curls (optional)

1 Grease a 10- to 11-inch tart pan with a removable bottom (use vegetable shortening, not nonstick spray coating). On lightly floured surface, use your hands to slightly flatten Poppy-Seed Pastry dough. Roll dough from center to edge into a circle 2 inches larger than tart pan. Wrap pastry around rolling pin. Unroll into prepared tart pan. Ease pastry into pan, being careful not to stretch pastry. Press pastry into fluted side of tart pan. Trim edges. Prick pastry. Line pastry in pan with a double thickness of foil (see photo, page 47).

2 Bake in a 375° oven for 10 minutes. Remove foil. Bake for 5 to 10 minutes more or until golden. Cool completely in pan on a wire rack.

3 For filling, in a medium mixing bowl beat cream cheese with an electric mixer on medium speed until light. Fold in marshmallow creme and lemon peel. Spread filling in the cooled pastry shell. Arrange blueberries on filling. In a small saucepan heat and stir jelly over medium heat until jelly is melted. Brush jelly over berries. Chill in the refrigerator for 1 hour or until jelly is set.

4 To serve, remove side of the tart pan. If desired, garnish with lemon peel curls. Cover and refrigerate any leftovers.

Poppy-Seed Pastry: In a medium mixing bowl stir together 1¼ cups all-purpose flour and ¼ cup sugar. Using a pastry blender, cut in ½ cup cold butter until pieces are pea-size. In a small mixing bowl combine 2 beaten egg yolks, 1 tablespoon water, and 1 teaspoon poppy seed. Gradually stir egg yolk mixture into flour mixture. (Dough will not be completely moistened.) Using your fingers, gently knead the dough just until a ball forms. If necessary, cover dough with plastic wrap and chill for 30 to 60 minutes or until dough is easy to handle.

Nutrition Facts per serving: 320 cal., 19 g total fat (8 g sat. fat), 80 mg chol., 162 sodium, 35 g carbo., 2 g fiber, 4 g pro. Daily Values: 25% vit. A, 10% vit. C, 37% calcium, 8% iron

Mango Cream Tart: Treat family and friends to a taste of the tropics with this magnificent mango dessert. Garnishing with fresh raspberries or other fresh fruit makes the tart as eye-catching as it is delicious.

MANGO CREAM TART

Prep: 40 minutes **Bake:** 13 minutes
Chill: 4 hours **Makes:** 8 servings **Oven:** 450°

You can use fresh mangoes or refrigerated mango slices (found in your supermarket produce section) to make this creamy tart.

  1 **recipe Pastry for Single-Crust Pie**
       (see page 47)
  1 **cup sugar**
  ¼ **cup cornstarch**
  ¼ **teaspoon salt**
2½ **cups sliced ripe mango**
       (about 1½ mangoes)
1½ **cups plain yogurt or dairy sour**
       cream
  3 **egg yolks**
  1 **tablespoon lime juice**
       Fresh fruit (optional)

1 **Prepare** pastry. Roll dough into 13-inch circle. Ease pastry into an ungreased 11-inch tart pan with a removable bottom. Press pastry into pan; trim edges. Prick bottom and side of pastry. Line with a double thickness of foil (see photo, page 47). Bake in a 450° oven for 8 minutes. Remove foil. Bake 5 to 6 minutes more or until lightly browned. Cool completely in pan on a wire rack.

2 **For filling,** in a heavy, medium saucepan stir together sugar, cornstarch, and salt. Place mango in blender container or food processor bowl. Cover; blend or process until smooth (should have

1½ cups). Stir mango and yogurt into sugar mixture. Cook and stir over medium heat until thickened and bubbly. Cook and stir 2 minutes more. Remove from heat. Slightly beat egg yolks. Gradually, stir about 1 cup of the hot filling into egg yolks. Pour egg yolk mixture into hot filling in saucepan. Bring to gentle boil. Cook and stir for 2 minutes more. Remove from heat. Stir in lime juice.

3 **Pour warm filling** into pastry shell. Cool for 1 hour on wire rack. Chill in refrigerator for at least 4 hours before serving; cover for longer storage. If desired, garnish with fresh fruit.

Nutrition Facts per serving: 327 cal., 11 g total fat (3 g sat. fat), 83 mg chol., 168 mg sodium, 52 g carbo., 1 g fiber, 5 g pro. Daily Values: 28% vit. A, 19% vit. C, 7% calcium, 7% iron

LINZER TORTE

Prep: 50 minutes **Bake:** 35 minutes **Chill:** 1 hour
Makes: 8 servings **Oven:** 325°

  ⅔ **cup butter**
  ⅔ **cup granulated sugar**
  1 **egg**
  2 **hard-cooked egg yolks, sieved**
  1 **tablespoon kirsch (cherry brandy)**
       or water
  1 **teaspoon finely shredded lemon peel**
  ½ **teaspoon ground cinnamon**
  ¼ **teaspoon ground cloves**
1½ **cups all-purpose flour**
1¼ **cups ground almonds or hazelnuts**

1 12-ounce jar seedless red
   raspberry jam
   Powdered sugar

1 **In a medium** mixing bowl beat the butter with an electric mixer on medium to high speed about 30 seconds or until softened. Add the granulated sugar, whole egg, hard-cooked egg yolks, kirsch or water, lemon peel, cinnamon, and cloves. Beat until thoroughly combined, scraping side of bowl occasionally. Stir in the flour and almonds. Form dough into a ball. Wrap dough in plastic wrap; chill in the refrigerator for 1 hour.

2 **On a lightly** floured surface, use your hands to slightly flatten two-thirds of the dough. (Refrigerate remaining dough until ready to use.) Roll dough from the center to edge into an 11-inch circle. Wrap pastry around rolling pin. Unroll onto an ungreased 10-inch tart pan with removable bottom or into 10-inch springform pan. Ease pastry into pan, pressing dough about ½ inch up the side. Spread the raspberry jam over the bottom of pastry in pan.

3 **Roll the** remaining pastry to form a 10×6-inch rectangle. Cut six 1-inch-wide strips. Carefully weave strips on top of jam to make a lattice. Press ends of strips into rim of bottom crust, trimming ends as necessary.

4 **Bake in a** 325° oven for 35 to 40 minutes or until crust is golden. Cool completely in pan on wire rack. To serve, remove side of pan. Sift powdered sugar over torte.

Nutrition Facts per serving: 558 cal., 29 g total fat (6 g sat. fat), 100 mg chol., 158 mg sodium, 70 g carbo., 3 g fiber, 8 g pro. Daily Values: 24% vit. A, 0% vit. C, 6% calcium, 16% iron

PEACHES-AND-CREAM
TART

Prep: 25 minutes   **Bake:** 15 minutes
Makes: 10 to 12 servings   **Oven:** 350°

9 soft coconut macaroon cookies,
   crumbled (2 cups)
1 cup (4 ounces) ground pecans*
3 tablespoons margarine or butter
½ cup whipping cream

1 8-ounce package cream cheese,
   softened
⅓ cup sugar
2 teaspoons dark rum or orange
   juice
1 teaspoon vanilla
¼ teaspoon almond extract
2 to 4 medium peaches, peeled, pitted,
   and thinly sliced (1½ to 3 cups)
2 tablespoons lemon juice
½ cup fresh raspberries
¼ cup apricot preserves
2 teaspoons honey

1 **For crust,** in a large mixing bowl stir together macaroon crumbs, pecans, and butter. Press mixture onto bottom and up side of a 10- to 11-inch tart pan with a removable bottom, or into a 12-inch pizza pan. Bake in a 350° oven until golden, allowing 15 to 18 minutes for tart pan and 12 to 15 minutes for pizza pan. Cool on a wire rack.

2 **For filling,** chill a medium mixing bowl and beaters of an electric mixer. In the chilled bowl beat whipping cream with a mixer on medium speed until soft peaks form; set aside.

3 **In a small** mixing bowl beat cream cheese and sugar with an electric mixer on medium speed until fluffy. Add rum or orange juice, vanilla, and almond extract; beat until smooth. Gently fold in whipped cream. Turn mixture into cooled crust; spread evenly. Cover and chill for 2 to 4 hours.

4 **Before serving,** toss peach slices with lemon juice. Place peaches and raspberries over filling.

5 **For glaze,** in small saucepan combine preserves and honey; heat and stir just until melted. Snip any large pieces of fruit in the glaze. Strain glaze, if desired. Carefully brush or spoon the glaze over the fruit.

6 **To serve,** remove side of pan (if using tart pan). Transfer tart to serving platter. Cut into wedges.

*Note: To grind pecans, process or blend the nuts, ½ cup at a time, in your food processor or blender. Cover and process or blend until very finely chopped. Be careful not to overprocess or the nuts will form a paste.

Nutrition Facts per serving: 388 cal., 28 g total fat (11 g sat. fat), 51 mg chol., 115 mg sodium, 33 g carbo., 2 g fiber, 4 g pro. Daily Values: 19% vit. A, 8% vit. C, 3% calcium, 5% iron

WARM PEACH AND NUTMEG TART

Prep: 1 hour   Bake: 30 minutes
Makes: 8 servings   Oven: 400°

Peach season is fleeting but sweet. Showcase summer's best in this irresistible tart.

  1 **recipe Tart Pastry (see lower right)**
  1 **beaten egg**
      Sugar
²/₃ **cup sugar**
  3 **tablespoons all-purpose flour**
1½ **teaspoons finely shredded orange peel**
  ¼ **teaspoon ground nutmeg**
  4 **cups sliced, peeled peaches (7 to 8 medium)**
  1 **recipe Orange Whipped Cream (see lower right)**
      Coarsely shredded orange peel

1 **For the crust,** on a lightly floured surface, roll three-fourths of the Tart Pastry into a 13×10-inch rectangle. (Refrigerate remaining pastry until ready to use.) Ease pastry into an ungreased 11×8×1-inch rectangular tart pan with a removable bottom. (Or, roll pastry into a 12-inch circle. Ease pastry into a 10-inch round tart pan with a removable bottom.) Use your fingers to trim pastry from pan edge or roll a rolling pin across the pan edge to remove excess pastry; reserve trimmings. Line pastry with a double thickness of foil (see photo, page 78); set aside.

Use the dull edge of a table knife to make decorative marks, such as veins in leaves and indents in peaches, in the pastry shapes.
.

2 **On a lightly** floured surface, roll remaining pastry and any pastry trimmings to ⅛-inch thickness. Using a small knife, cookie cutters, or your hands, cut or shape pastry into desired shapes, such as a bunch of grapes, peaches, cherries, branches, and leaves. Transfer shapes to an ungreased baking sheet. Make decorative marks in pastry shapes (see photo, lower left). Brush with beaten egg; sprinkle with a little sugar.

3 **Bake crust** and pastry shapes in a 400° oven for 10 to 12 minutes or until pastry shapes are golden (if sizes of pastry shapes vary, smaller shapes may brown more quickly). Transfer pastry shapes to a wire rack. Carefully remove foil from crust; place crust in the pan on a wire rack.

4 **For filling,** in a large mixing bowl stir together the ⅔ cup sugar, the flour, the 1½ teaspoons orange peel, and the nutmeg. Add peaches; toss gently to coat. Spoon mixture into pastry.

5 **Bake in a** 400° oven for 30 to 40 minutes or until pastry is golden. Cool slightly on a wire rack.

6 **Top tart** with pastry shapes. Serve warm, or cover and store at room temperature for up to 1 day. For longer storage, cover and chill in the refrigerator for up to 3 days.

7 **To serve,** transfer Orange Whipped Cream to a serving bowl; top with coarsely shredded orange peel. Serve with tart.

Tart Pastry: In a medium mixing bowl combine 1½ cups all-purpose flour and ¼ teaspoon salt. Using a pastry blender, cut in ½ cup shortening until pieces are pea-size. Sprinkle 1 tablespoon cold water over part of the mixture; gently toss with a fork. Push the moistened dough to side of bowl. Repeat with 3 to 4 tablespoons additional cold water, using 1 tablespoon water at a time, until all the dough is moistened. Form dough into a ball.

Orange Whipped Cream: Chill a medium mixing bowl and the beaters of an electric mixer in refrigerator. In chilled bowl beat ½ cup whipping cream, 1 tablespoon sugar, and ½ teaspoon finely shredded orange peel with electric mixer on medium-high speed just until soft peaks form.

Nutrition Facts per serving: 348 cal., 19 g total fat (7 g sat. fat), 47 mg chol., 81 mg sodium, 42 g carbo., 2 g fiber, 4 g pro. Daily Values: 15% vit. A, 0% vit. C, 0% calcium, 0% iron

Warm Peach and Nutmeg Tart: Pure and simple in its flavors, this peach of a tart—embellished with exquisite pastry shapes—is absolutely beautiful.

Raspberry-Lemon Tartlets: Sharing is nice, but having your own tart isn't too bad, either. During the height of raspberry season, top these diminutive desserts with a combination of red, yellow, and black raspberries.

RASPBERRY-LEMON
TARTLETS

Prep: 1 hour   **Bake:** 16 minutes
Chill: 1 hour   **Makes:** 8 servings   **Oven:** 375°

- ½ **cup sugar**
- 1 **tablespoon cornstarch**
- 1½ **teaspoons finely shredded lemon peel**
- 3 **tablespoons lemon juice**
- 3 **beaten egg yolks**
- ¼ **cup unsalted butter**
   Nonstick spray coating
- 1 **recipe Poppy-Seed Pastry**
   (see page 81)
- ¼ **cup apple jelly**
- 2 to 2½ **cups fresh raspberries**

Use your fingers to press the Poppy-Seed Pastry onto the bottom and up the side of each tart pan.

1 **For lemon** curd filling, in a small saucepan stir together sugar and cornstarch. Stir in the lemon peel, lemon juice, and 3 tablespoons water. Cook and stir over medium heat until thickened and bubbly.

2 **Gradually stir** half of the hot filling into yolks. Pour yolk mixture into hot filling in saucepan. Bring to gentle boil. Cook and stir for 2 minutes more. Remove from heat. Stir in butter. Cover surface with plastic wrap. Chill in refrigerator at least 1 hour or for up to 48 hours.

3 **Spray nonstick** coating onto four 4- to 4¼-inch tart pans with removable bottoms. Divide Poppy-Seed Pastry into 4 equal portions. Press 1 portion of pastry onto bottom and up the side of each tart pan. Generously prick bottom and side of pastry in each tart pan. Line pastry shells with a double thickness of foil (see photo, page 78).

4 **Bake in a** 375° oven for 7 minutes. Remove foil. Bake for 9 to 10 minutes more or until golden. Cool completely in pan on a wire rack.

5 **Heat and** stir jelly and 2 teaspoons water until melted; cool slightly. Spread filling into pastry shells. Top with berries; brush gently with jelly. Cover and chill in refrigerator for up to 4 hours.

Nutrition Facts per serving: 374 cal., 21 g total fat (12 g sat. fat), 179 mg chol., 124 mg sodium, 45 g carbo., 2 g fiber, 4 g pro. Daily Values: 36% vit. A, 18% vit. C, 3% calcium, 10% iron

pastries and
crackers

PASTRIES AND CRACKERS

QUICK-METHOD
CROISSANT DOUGH

Prep: 1 hour   Chill: 5 hours

This method doesn't require the frequent attention that the classic recipe demands. Use the dough for plain or filled croissants, or try one of the other pastries (see pages 90–93).

1½ **cups cold butter**
4½ **cups all-purpose flour**
  1 **package active dry yeast**
1¼ **cups milk**
  ¼ **cup sugar**
  ¼ **teaspoon salt**
  1 **egg**
  ¼ **to** ½ **cup all-purpose flour**

Completely coat the butter pieces with flour. The butter will make layers in the baked dough, producing flaky croissants.

Roll out dough on a well-floured surface or pastry cloth using a floured rolling pin. After the first rolling, the dough will be bumpy from the pieces of butter.

Fold the rolled out dough crosswise into thirds. Repeat the rolling and folding steps. The folding helps to make flaky croissants.

1 Cut butter into ½-inch-thick slices. In a medium bowl stir slices into 3 cups of the flour until slices are coated and separated (see top photo, right). Chill butter mixture while preparing the dough.

2 For dough, in a large mixing bowl combine remaining 1½ cups flour and the yeast; set aside. In a medium saucepan heat and stir milk, sugar, and salt just until warm (120° to 130°). Add to flour-yeast mixture. Add egg. Beat with an electric mixer on low to medium speed 30 seconds, scraping sides of bowl. Beat on high speed 3 minutes.

3 Using a wooden spoon, stir chilled flour-butter mixture into dough until flour is moistened (butter will remain in large pieces).

4 Sprinkle a pastry cloth or surface with ¼ cup of the remaining flour. Turn dough out onto surface. With floured hands, gently knead dough for 8 strokes. Using a well-floured rolling pin, roll dough into a 21×12-inch rectangle (if necessary, sprinkle surface of dough with enough remaining flour to prevent sticking) (see middle photo, right). Fold dough crosswise into thirds to form a 7×12-inch rectangle. Loosely wrap in plastic wrap; chill 1 to 1½ hours in refrigerator or 20 to 30 minutes in freezer or until firm but not excessively stiff.

5 On a well-floured surface roll dough into a 21×12-inch rectangle. Fold dough crosswise into thirds again (see bottom photo, above) and give dough a quarter-turn. Then roll, fold, and turn twice more, flouring surface as needed (it is not necessary to chill dough between each rolling). Place dough in a plastic bag. Seal bag, leaving room for dough to expand. Chill dough for 4 to 24 hours. Use as directed in recipes on pages 90–93.

FREEZING DOUGH FOR FUTURE TREATS

Croissant and puff pastry doughs can be frozen for future pastry making, shifting some of the preparation time to another day. To freeze, wrap the dough portions tightly in foil or place in freezer bags. Label with contents and date; freeze up to 3 months. Thaw in the refrigerator overnight.

Baked Croissants: Enjoy a morning cup of java coffeehouse-style—with a buttery, homemade croissant and jelly. Or, opt for a filled variety, choosing from the fillings offered on page 91.

BAKED CROISSANTS

Prep: 20 minutes plus dough   **Rise:** 1 hour
Bake: 15 minutes   **Makes:** 16   **Oven:** 375°

1 recipe Quick-Method Croissant Dough (see page 89)
1 egg
1 tablespoon water or milk

1 Prepare and chill Quick-Method Croissant Dough as directed. Cut dough crosswise into 4 portions. Wrap and return 3 portions to refrigerator until ready to use.

2 To shape croissants, on a lightly floured surface, roll 1 portion of dough into a 16×8-inch rectangle. Cut rectangle crosswise in half to form 2 squares. Cut each square diagonally in half to form 2 triangles. (You will have 4 triangles from each rectangle.) Loosely roll up each triangle from an 8-inch side, rolling toward opposite point.

3 Repeat cutting and shaping with remaining 3 portions. Place croissants, points down, 4 inches apart on ungreased baking sheets. Curve ends. Cover and let rise in a warm place until double (about 1 hour).

4 Beat egg and the water or milk using a fork. Lightly brush croissants with egg mixture. Bake in a 375° oven for 15 minutes or until golden. Remove from baking sheets. Cool slightly on wire racks. Serve warm or cool.

Nutrition Facts per croissant: 308 cal., 18 g total fat (11 g sat. fat), 74 mg chol., 225 mg sodium, 30 g carbo., 1 g fiber, 5 g pro. Daily Values: 18% vit. A, 0% vit. C, 3% calcium, 12% iron

FILLED CROISSANTS

Prep: 30 minutes plus dough   **Rise:** 1 hour
Bake: 15 minutes   **Makes:** 16   **Oven:** 375°

1 recipe Quick-Method Croissant Dough (see page 89)
1 recipe Blueberry Filling, Cheese Filling, Almond Filling, or Dilled Ham Filling (see page 91)
1 egg
1 tablespoon water

1 Prepare and chill Quick-Method Croissant Dough as directed. Prepare desired filling. Cut dough crosswise into 4 portions. Wrap and return 3 portions to refrigerator until ready to use.

2 On a lightly floured surface roll 1 portion of dough into a 16×8-inch rectangle. Cut rectangle into four 8×4-inch rectangles. Spoon filling onto center of each smaller rectangle. In a small mixing bowl beat egg and water using a fork. Brush edges of dough with egg mixture. Fold short sides of the rectangles over the filling to overlap in center, forming bundles. Pinch edges together to seal. Place 4 inches apart, seam sides down, on ungreased baking sheets. Repeat with remaining 3 portions.

3 Cover and let rise until nearly double (about 1 hour). Brush again with egg mixture. Bake in a 375° oven about 15 minutes or until golden. Remove from baking sheets. Cool on wire racks.

Nutrition Facts per croissant with blueberry filling: 343 cal., 19 g total fat (11 g sat. fat), 87 mg chol., 231 mg sodium, 39 g carbo., 1 g fiber, 6 g pro. Daily Values: 18% vit. A, 2% vit. C, 3% calcium, 13% iron

Blueberry Filling: Using ½ cup blueberry preserves and 1 cup fresh or frozen blueberries, spoon 2 teaspoons of the preserves in the center of each rectangle. Add 3 or 4 blueberries.

Cheese Filling: In a bowl beat together one 8-ounce package cream cheese, softened; ¼ cup sugar; and 2 teaspoons finely shredded orange peel. Spoon 1 tablespoon in the center of each rectangle.

Almond Filling: In a mixing bowl stir together 1 egg white, one 8-ounce can almond paste*, ½ cup granulated sugar, and ½ cup packed brown sugar. Spoon 1 tablespoon in center of each rectangle.

Dilled Ham Filling: In a mixing bowl combine one 8-ounce package cream cheese, softened; ⅓ cup finely chopped cooked ham; 2 tablespoons sliced green onion; and ½ teaspoon dried dillweed. Spoon 1 tablespoon in center of each rectangle.

*Note: For best results, use an almond paste made without syrup or liquid glucose.

CHEESE AND LEMON DANISH

Prep: 50 minutes plus dough   **Rise:** 30 minutes
Bake: 18 minutes   **Makes:** 20   **Oven:** 375°

Traditionally made from a buttery yeast-bread dough with a sweet filling, Danishes have long been a favorite of their namesake country.

  1 recipe Quick-Method Croissant
      Dough (see page 89)
  1 8-ounce package cream cheese,
      softened

  ⅓ cup sugar
  1 tablespoon all-purpose flour
  1 tablespoon dairy sour cream
  1 egg yolk
  1 teaspoon butter
  1 teaspoon finely shredded lemon peel
  ½ teaspoon vanilla
  1 egg
  1 tablespoon water

1 Prepare and chill Quick-Method Croissant Dough as directed.

2 For filling, in a medium mixing bowl beat cream cheese, sugar, flour, sour cream, egg yolk, butter, lemon peel, and vanilla with an electric mixer on medium speed for 3 minutes or until well mixed. Set aside.

3 To shape pastries, on a lightly floured surface roll the chilled dough into a 20×12-inch rectangle. Cut rectangle into twenty 12×1-inch strips. Twist ends of each strip in opposite directions 3 or 4 times. Place 1 twisted strip on an ungreased baking sheet; form it into a wide U-shape. Then coil 1 end of the strip to the center to form a snail shape. Coil the opposite end of the U-shape strip to the center so the 2 coils nearly touch. Repeat with remaining strips, placing them 4 inches apart on baking sheets. Spoon 1 teaspoon of the filling onto the center of each coil (2 teaspoons per roll). Cover and let rise until nearly double (30 to 45 minutes).

4 In a small mixing bowl beat egg and water using a fork. Lightly brush dough portions of pastries with egg mixture. Bake in a 375° oven for 18 to 20 minutes or until golden. Remove from baking sheets. Cool slightly on wire racks.

Nutrition Facts per pastry: 305 cal., 19 g total fat (12 g sat. fat), 83 mg chol., 217 mg sodium, 28 g carbo., 1 g fiber, 5 g pro. Daily Values: 21% vit. A, 0% vit. C, 3% calcium, 10% iron

---

TOOL BOX: PASTRIES

As for any project, the right tools for pastry-making will help your pastry turn out right every time. Consider these:
- **Rolling pin:** A good, all-purpose wooden rolling pin that fits your hands comfortably.
- **Pastry cloth:** A cloth for rolling dough thin.
- **Pastry bag:** A reusable pastry bag with decorative tips for piping pastry dough.
- **Pastry brush:** A fine-bristled pastry brush for brushing on butter, milk, and egg glazes.

APPLE-MAPLE CLAWS

Prep: 50 minutes plus dough   Rise: 45 minutes
Bake: 15 minutes   Makes: 18   Oven: 375°

Glaze with maple icing and serve warm for breakfast, dessert, or as a midday snack.

1 recipe Quick-Method Croissant
   Dough (see page 89)
1½ cups chopped, peeled apples
2 tablespoons granulated sugar
½ teaspoon ground cinnamon
¼ cup butter
½ cup powdered sugar
2 tablespoons all-purpose flour
2 teaspoons vanilla
1 teaspoon maple flavoring
1 egg
1 tablespoon water
1 recipe Maple Glaze (see right)

1 **Prepare and chill** Quick-Method Croissant Dough as directed.

2 **For filling,** in a medium saucepan combine apples and granulated sugar. Heat slowly until liquid accumulates. Bring mixture to boiling. Reduce heat; cover and simmer for 8 to 10 minutes or until apples are tender. Uncover and simmer for 2 to 3 minutes more or until most of the liquid evaporates. Stir in cinnamon. Mash apples slightly, leaving some chunks; set aside.

To make the "claws," cutting from the sealed edge, make 4 or 5 evenly spaced cuts in each filled pastry. Cut almost to the folded edge.

3 **In a medium mixing bowl beat** butter, powdered sugar, flour, vanilla, and maple flavoring with an electric mixer on medium speed for 2 to 3 minutes or until light and fluffy; set aside.

4 **To shape claws,** cut chilled dough crosswise in half. On a lightly floured surface, roll each half into a 12-inch square. Cut each square into three 4-inch-wide strips (6 strips total).

5 **Spread about 1 tablespoon** of the maple mixture down the center of each strip. Spoon about 2 tablespoons of the apple mixture on top of the maple mixture. Fold the strips lengthwise in half to cover the filling. Pinch the edges to seal.

6 **Cut each strip** into three 4-inch-long pieces. Make 4 or 5 evenly spaced cuts in each piece, snipping from the sealed edge almost to the folded edge (see photo, above). Place 2 inches apart on ungreased baking sheets, curving slightly to separate slits. Cover and let rise in a warm place until nearly double (45 to 60 minutes).

7 **In a small mixing bowl beat** egg and water using a fork. Lightly brush dough with egg mixture. Bake in a 375° oven about 15 minutes or until pastries are golden. Remove pastries from baking sheets. Cool slightly on wire racks. Drizzle with Maple Glaze. Serve warm.

Maple Glaze: In a small mixing bowl combine 1 cup sifted powdered sugar, ¼ teaspoon maple flavoring, and enough milk (1 to 2 tablespoons) to make a glaze that is easy to drizzle.

Nutrition Facts per pastry: 345 cal., 19 g total fat (11 g sat. fat), 73 mg chol., 227 mg sodium, 39 g carbo., 1 g fiber, 5 g pro. Daily Values: 18% vit. A, 0% vit. C, 2% calcium, 11% iron

STORING PASTRIES

To store croissants and Danish to enjoy for another time, place the baked pastries in an airtight container or bag and keep them in the refrigerator for up to 3 days. (Storage at room temperature is not recommended because of their high butter content.) Let the pastries stand at room temperature about 25 minutes before serving.

   To freeze golden baked croissants and Danish, place them in a freezer container or bag and freeze up to 2 months. To serve, wrap frozen croissants or Danish in foil and bake in a 400° oven for 5 to 8 minutes or until warm.

Strawberry Turnovers: Stuffed inside these golden pastries discover a simple filling of fresh strawberries mixed with strawberry preserves. Fork marks make the decorative trim on the edges.

STRAWBERRY TURNOVERS

Prep: 25 minutes plus dough   Rise: 45 minutes
Bake: 15 minutes   Makes: 18   Oven: 375°

1 recipe Quick-Method Croissant Dough (see page 89)
½ cup strawberry preserves or peach preserves
½ cup chopped strawberries
1 egg
1 tablespoon water
Sifted powdered sugar (optional)

1 **Prepare and chill** Quick-Method Croissant Dough as directed.

2 **To shape turnovers,** cut the chilled dough crosswise in half. On a lightly floured surface roll each half of dough into a 12-inch square. Cut each square into nine 4-inch squares (18 squares total). Spoon about 2 teaspoons of the preserves onto the center of each square. Top with several pieces of the chopped strawberries.

3 **In a small mixing bowl beat** egg and water using a fork. Lightly brush edges of dough with some of the egg mixture. Fold squares in half to form triangles; seal edges with tines of a fork. Place the triangles 4 inches apart on ungreased baking sheets. Cover and let rise in a warm place until nearly double (45 to 60 minutes).

4 **Brush turnovers** with additional egg mixture. Bake in a 375° oven about 15 minutes or until golden. Remove turnovers from baking sheets. Cool slightly on wire racks. If desired, sprinkle powdered sugar over warm turnovers. Serve warm or cool.

Nutrition Facts per turnover: 298 cal., 16 g total fat (10 g sat. fat), 66 mg chol., 201 mg sodium, 33 g carbo., 1 g fiber, 5 g pro. Daily Values: 16% vit. A, 4% vit. C, 2% calcium, 11% iron

SOUR CREAM DANISH DOUGH

Prep: 25 minutes   **Chill:** 1 hour

This dough is flaky and rich, like the croissant dough recipe, but it's substantially quicker to make and requires less chilling time.

 2 **cups all-purpose flour**
¼ **teaspoon salt**
 1 **cup cold butter, cut up**
½ **cup dairy sour cream**
 1 **to 2 tablespoons cold water**

1 **In a medium bowl stir** together flour and salt. Add butter. Using a pastry blender, cut cold butter into flour until mixture resembles coarse meal, leaving some pieces of butter the size of small peas.

2 **In a small bowl stir** together the sour cream and 1 tablespoon of the water. Add to the flour mixture and stir with a fork until the mixture starts to clump together. Add the remaining water, if necessary, to moisten. Form into a ball. Shape the dough into a rectangle. Place between 2 pieces of waxed paper or plastic wrap. Roll to 18×9-inch rectangle.

3 **Peel off the top sheet** of waxed paper or plastic wrap. Turn the dough over onto a lightly floured surface and peel off remaining paper or wrap. Fold the dough crosswise into thirds, forming a 6×9-inch rectangle. Fold dough in thirds again, forming a thick piece about 3×6 inches. Wrap dough and chill in the refrigerator 1 hour or until firm. (Dough may be chilled up to 24 hours; let stand at room temperature until easily rolled.) For longer storage, wrap in heavy foil. Seal, label, and freeze up to 3 months. Thaw the dough, covered, in the refrigerator overnight before using. Use the dough as directed in Sunrise Apple Tartlets (see right) and Apricot-Almond Breakfast Pastries (see page 95).

SUNRISE APPLE TARTLETS

Prep: 30 minutes plus dough   **Bake:** 25 minutes
Makes: 4   **Oven:** 400°

Don't be surprised if these pastries pop open a bit during baking, unveiling the buttery apple filling.

½ **recipe Sour Cream Danish Dough**
   (see left)
⅓ **cup sugar**
 1 **teaspoon cornstarch**
 3 **large baking apples, peeled, cored,**
   and sliced ⅛ inch thick
   (about 4 cups)
 2 **tablespoons butter**
 1 **tablespoon lemon juice**

1 **Prepare and chill** the Sour Cream Danish Dough as directed. Line a baking sheet with parchment paper or foil; set aside.

2 **For filling,** in a large skillet stir together sugar and cornstarch. Add apple slices, butter, and lemon juice. Cook over medium heat about 8 minutes or until apples are tender, stirring occasionally. Place in bowl to cool completely.

3 **On a lightly floured surface roll** dough to a 12-inch square and cut into four 6-inch squares. Place pastry squares on prepared baking sheet.

4 **Divide apple mixture** among the pastry squares, spooning about ½ cup in the center of each square. Fold corners up over the apple mixture to center of tarts (they should just meet).

5 **Bake in a 400° oven** about 25 minutes or until golden brown. Remove tartlets from baking sheet. Cool slightly on wire rack. Serve warm.

Nutrition Facts per tartlet: 518 cal., 32 g total fat (20 g sat. fat), 83 mg chol., 365 mg sodium, 57 g carbo., 3 g fiber, 4 g pro. Daily Values: 30% vit. A, 13% vit. C, 3% calcium, 10% iron

APRICOT-ALMOND
BREAKFAST PASTRIES

Prep: 50 minutes plus dough   **Bake:** 25 minutes
Makes: 8   **Oven:** 375°

Prepare both the dough and almond filling a day ahead and store them in the refrigerator.

>   1 **recipe Sour Cream Danish Dough**
>   **(see page 94)**
>   1 **cup sliced almonds**
>   3 **tablespoons sugar**
>   3 **tablespoons honey**
>   1 **egg**
>   1 **tablespoon water**
>   1 **8-ounce package cream cheese,**
>   **softened**
>   ½ **cup snipped dried apricots**
>   ½ **cup apricot preserves**
>   4 **teaspoons sugar**
>   ¼ **cup sliced almonds**

1 **Prepare and chill** the Sour Cream Danish Dough as directed.

2 **For filling,** in a food processor bowl combine the almonds, the 3 tablespoons sugar, and the honey. Cover and process until the almonds are ground and the mixture begins to form a ball. (If mixture seems dry, add 1 teaspoon water.) Divide into 8 equal portions and roll each on lightly floured surface to a 3½-inch circle. Cover and set aside.

3 **On a lightly floured surface roll** the dough about ⅛ inch thick. Cut eight 4½-inch circles. Cut the pastry scraps into ½-inch-wide strips. Beat egg and water using a fork; use to brush top edges of pastry circles. Arrange the pastry strips around the top edge of each pastry circle, trimming as needed. Place pastry circles on an ungreased baking sheet. Place almond circle in center of each pastry circle.

4 **Place the softened cream cheese** in a small plastic food storage bag. Snip off one corner of the bag and pipe cream cheese in dots over almond mixture. In a small bowl combine dried apricots and preserves. Spoon over the cream cheese. Brush the pastry-strip edges of the circles with egg mixture and sprinkle lightly with the 4 teaspoons sugar. Sprinkle the preserves with almonds.

5 **Bake in a 375° oven** about 25 minutes or until golden. Remove from baking sheets; cool on wire rack. Serve warm or at room temperature.

Nutrition Facts per pastry: 689 cal., 47 g total fat (24 g sat. fat), 126 mg chol., 406 mg sodium, 60 g carbo., 3 g fiber, 11 g pro. Daily Values: 43% vit. A, 1% vit. C, 9% calcium, 21% iron

Apricot-Almond Breakfast Pastries: Treat your overnight company to the best bed and breakfast pastries in town. Filled with a homemade almond-paste layer, cream cheese dollops, and apricot glaze, these a.m. delights are incredibly memorable.

QUICK-METHOD
PUFF PASTRY DOUGH

Prep: 40 minutes   Chill: 40 minutes

Save preparation steps with this shortcut method by tossing the butter with the flour instead of making a rolled-out butter layer.

    4 cups all-purpose flour
    1 teaspoon salt
    2 cups cold butter (1 pound)
1¼ cups ice water

1 **In a large mixing bowl stir** together flour and salt. Cut the cold butter into ½-inch-thick slices (not cubes). Add butter slices to the flour mixture and toss until slices are coated and separated.

2 **Pour ice water** over flour mixture. Using a spoon, quickly mix (butter will remain in large pieces and flour will not be completely moistened).

3 **Turn the dough out** onto a lightly floured pastry cloth. Knead dough 10 times by pressing and pushing dough together to form a rough-looking ball, lifting the pastry cloth if necessary to press dough together. Shape dough into a rectangle (dough still will have some dry-looking areas). Make corners as square as possible. Slightly flatten dough.

4 **Working on a well-floured pastry cloth,** roll the dough into a 15×12-inch rectangle. Fold dough crosswise into thirds to form a 5×12-inch rectangle. Give dough a quarter turn; fold crosswise into thirds to form a 4×5-inch rectangle.

5 **Repeat the rolling** and folding process once more, forming a 4×5-inch rectangle. Wrap the dough with plastic wrap. Chill dough in the refrigerator for 20 minutes. Repeat rolling and folding process 2 more times. Chill dough in the refrigerator for 20 minutes more before using.

6 **Using a sharp knife,** cut the dough in half crosswise into 2 equal portions. To store the dough, wrap each portion in plastic wrap and refrigerate until ready to use or for up to 3 days. For longer storage, wrap each dough portion in heavy foil. Seal, label, and freeze up to 3 months. Thaw the dough, covered, in the refrigerator about 24 hours before using. Use the dough as directed in recipes on pages 96–98.

BANANA CREAM
NAPOLEONS

Prep: 40 minutes plus dough
Bake: 18 minutes   Makes: 8   Oven: 425°

Some believe that pastries similar to these are named after the French emperor Napoleon Bonaparte. Others think that Napoleons got their name from an elaborately decorated cake called a napolitain. So what are the similarities between the cake and the pastries? Both are rectangles and are made of many layers glossed with a rich cream filling.

    1 portion Quick-Method Puff Pastry
        Dough (see left) or ½ of a
        17¼-ounce package (1 sheet)
        frozen puff pastry, thawed
    1 recipe Cream Filling (see page 97)
    1 cup sifted powdered sugar
    1 to 2 tablespoons milk
    2 ripe medium bananas or 1 cup
        fresh raspberries or strawberries
    2 tablespoons orange juice
    1 ounce semisweet chocolate,
        chopped, melted, and cooled

1 **Prepare and chill** Quick-Method Puff Pastry Dough. Line a baking sheet with parchment paper or plain brown paper; set aside.

2 **On a lightly floured surface roll** the Quick-Method pastry into a 9×8-inch rectangle. Using a sharp knife, cut off ½ inch on all 4 sides to make an 8×7-inch rectangle. (Or, if using purchased puff pastry, unfold the thawed sheet and trim to an 8×7-inch rectangle.) Cut the pastry rectangle into eight 3½×2-inch rectangles. Transfer pastry rectangles to the prepared baking sheet. Using the tines of a fork, prick pastry rectangles.

3 **Bake in a 425° oven** for 18 to 23 minutes or until golden. Carefully remove pastry rectangles and cool on a wire rack.

4 **Meanwhile, prepare Cream Filling;** set aside to chill in the refrigerator. For glaze, in a bowl combine powdered sugar and 1 tablespoon of the milk. If necessary, stir in enough additional milk until glaze is of spreading consistency; set aside. Thinly slice the bananas or strawberries (if using). Sprinkle with orange juice.

5 To assemble, use the tines of a fork to separate each pastry rectangle horizontally into 3 layers. Spread about 1 tablespoon of Cream Filling on each bottom layer. Arrange about half of the fruit on filling. Top with middle pastry layers; spread each with another 1 tablespoon Cream Filling and top with remaining fruit. Finally, top with remaining pastry layers. Spoon glaze over each pastry, spreading as necessary to glaze tops. Drizzle with the melted chocolate. Serve immediately or cover and keep at room temperature up to 30 minutes.

Cream Filling: In a heavy saucepan stir together ¼ cup sugar, 2 tablespoons all-purpose flour, and ⅛ teaspoon salt. Gradually stir in 1 cup half-and-half or light cream. Cook and stir over medium heat until thickened and bubbly. Cook and stir for 1 minute more. Gradually stir about half of the hot mixture into 2 beaten egg yolks. Return all of the yolk mixture to the saucepan. Bring to a gentle boil; reduce heat. Cook and stir for 2 minutes. Remove from heat and stir in ½ teaspoon finely shredded orange peel or lemon peel and ½ teaspoon vanilla. Transfer to a bowl. Cover surface with plastic wrap. Chill until serving time (do not stir).

Nutrition Facts per pastry: 487 cal., 29 g total fat (18 g sat. fat), 127 mg chol., 418 mg sodium, 53 g carbo., 2 g fiber, 6 g pro. Daily Values: 33% vit. A, 8% vit. C, 4% calcium, 12% iron

MOCHA-FILLED CREAM HORNS

Prep: 40 minutes plus dough Bake: 15 minutes
Chill: 2 hours Makes: 12 Oven: 425°

Fill sugared puff pastry tubes with a chocolate-coffee cream filling (see photo, page 87).

1 portion Quick-Method Puff Pastry Dough (see page 96) or one 17¼-ounce package (2 sheets) frozen puff pastry, thawed
1 egg white
1 tablespoon water
1 tablespoon sugar
1 recipe Mocha Pastry Cream (see right)

1 Prepare and chill Quick-Method Puff Pastry Dough. Line a baking sheet with parchment paper or plain brown paper.

2 On a lightly floured surface roll the puff pastry dough into a 16×12-inch rectangle. Using a sharp knife, cut pastry lengthwise into twelve 16×1-inch strips. (If using purchased pastry, unfold and roll each sheet into a 12×10-inch rectangle. Cut each sheet into twelve 10×1-inch strips. Press 2 strips of purchased pastry together at ends to make a long strip; repeat with remaining strips.)

3 Wrap each strip of dough around a well-greased cream horn mold or ¾-inch-wide cannoli tube. Overlap layers slightly and press gently. Place 1 inch apart on the prepared baking sheet. In a small bowl beat egg white and water using a fork; use to brush over pastry. Sprinkle with the sugar.

4 Bake in a 425° oven for 15 to 20 minutes or until golden for Quick-Method pastry (12 to 15 minutes for purchased pastry). Transfer to a wire rack. While still warm, slightly twist the molds and remove from pastry horns. Cool on a wire rack.

5 Prepare Mocha Pastry Cream; chill. Spoon cream mixture into a pastry bag fitted with a large star tip (about 1-inch opening). Pipe cream into each horn. If desired, chill up to 1 hour.

Mocha Pastry Cream: In a heavy saucepan stir together ½ cup sugar, ¼ cup all-purpose flour, and ¼ teaspoon salt. Gradually stir in 1½ cups half-and-half or light cream; 4 ounces semisweet chocolate, chopped; and 1 tablespoon instant coffee crystals. Cook and stir over medium heat until thickened and bubbly. Cook and stir 1 minute more. Gradually stir about half of the hot mixture into 4 beaten egg yolks. Return all of the yolk mixture to the saucepan. Bring to a gentle boil; reduce heat. Cook and stir for 2 minutes. Remove from heat; stir in 1 teaspoon vanilla. Transfer to a bowl. Cover surface with plastic wrap. Cool slightly. Chill 2 to 3 hours or until cold (do not stir). In a chilled small mixing bowl beat ½ cup whipping cream until soft peaks form. Gradually fold whipped cream into cooled pastry cream; chill well before using.

Nutrition Facts per cream horn: 433 cal., 30 g total fat (16 g sat. fat), 142 mg chol., 273 mg sodium, 37 g carbo., 1 g fiber, 6 g pro. Daily Values: 35% vit. A, 0% vit. C, 5% calcium, 11% iron

CINNAMON PALMIERS

Prep: 30 minutes plus dough   Bake: 15 minutes
Makes: about 60   Oven: 375°

When you don't have time to make puff pastry dough, use the directions for purchased.

1 portion Quick-Method Puff Pastry
    Dough (see page 96) or one
    17¼-ounce package (2 sheets)
    frozen puff pastry, thawed
½ cup sugar
1 teaspoon ground cinnamon

1 **Prepare and chill** Quick-Method Puff Pastry Dough or unfold thawed puff pastry. Line baking sheets with parchment paper or plain brown paper; set aside.

2 **If using Quick-Method Puff Pastry,** cut the portion of dough crosswise in half. Cover and return 1 piece of the dough to the refrigerator. On a lightly floured surface roll the remaining piece of dough or 1 sheet of the purchased pastry into a 14×10-inch rectangle.

3 **Sprinkle the rectangle** with a mixture of ¼ cup of the sugar and ½ teaspoon of the cinnamon. Lightly press sugar into the dough. Roll 2 short sides, jelly-roll style, to meet in center.

Use a thin, sharp knife to cut the filled and shaped puff pastry dough.

4 **Cut the pastry roll crosswise** into about ¼-inch-thick slices (see photo, above). If the roll is too soft to slice easily, chill the rolled dough for a few minutes. Place the slices 2 inches apart on the prepared baking sheets.

5 **Bake in a 375° oven** for 15 to 18 minutes or until golden and crisp. Remove from baking sheet and cool on a wire rack. Repeat with remaining piece of dough or sheet of purchased pastry and remaining cinnamon and sugar.

Nutrition Facts per pastry: 49 cal., 3 g total fat (1 g sat. fat), 4 mg chol., 46 mg sodium, 5 g carbo., 0 g fiber, 0 g pro. Daily Values: 3% vit. A, 0% vit. C, 0% calcium, 1% iron

RASPBERRY DANISH

Prep: 15 minutes   Bake: 15 minutes
Makes: 12   Oven: 400°

In 30 minutes from start to finish, you can have fresh, showy pastries to serve for dessert or as a breakfast treat. These pastries are at their best when baked and served on the same day.

½ of a 17¼-ounce package (1 sheet)
    frozen puff pastry, thawed
⅓ cup seedless raspberry preserves
    Pressurized whipped dessert
      topping
    Chopped pistachio nuts or almonds

1 **On a lightly floured surface,** unfold the thawed puff pastry sheet. If necessary, use a rolling pin to flatten and smooth the pastry.

PUFF PASTRY PERFECTION

Heed these tips to assure flaky, tender puff pastry every time:

- Use only butter; don't try substituting margarine for the butter.
- Be sure to use *ice* water when making the puff pastry dough.
- Keep pastry dough in the refrigerator until you're ready to roll it out. That way, the butter won't soften and melt into the dough when you roll it.
- Be sure pastries are fully baked. They'll look golden when done.

2 Cut the pastry into 12 equal strips. Coil each strip, wrapping loosely, into a circle or spiral. Moisten the outside end of each strip with a little water and secure it to the pastry to prevent pastry from uncoiling during baking. Place pastries on an ungreased baking sheet.

3 Bake in a 400° oven about 15 minutes or until golden. Cool on a wire rack. To serve, in a small saucepan heat preserves until melted, stirring often; drizzle over baked pastries. Let the preserves cool slightly. Top with whipped topping. Sprinkle pastries with chopped nuts. Serve immediately.

Nutrition Facts per pastry: 142 cal., 9 g total fat (0 g sat. fat), 0 mg chol., 81 mg sodium, 15 g carbo., 0 g fiber, 1 g pro. Daily Values: 1% vit. A, 0% vit. C, 0% calcium, 1% iron

DUTCH LETTERS
BEST-LOVED

Prep: 1 hour Chill: 40 minutes
Bake: 20 minutes Makes: 20 Oven: 375°

To shortcut preparations, substitute two 17¼-ounce packages (4 sheets) frozen puff pastry instead of preparing dough. Roll each unfolded sheet into a 12½×10-inch rectangle. Cut, fill, and shape. Bake for 15 to 20 minutes.

  4½ **cups all-purpose flour**
   1 **teaspoon salt**
   2 **cups cold butter (1 pound)**
   1 **beaten egg**
   1 **cup ice water**
   1 **egg white**
   1 **8-ounce can almond paste***
  ½ **cup granulated sugar**
  ½ **cup packed brown sugar**
    Granulated sugar

1 In a large mixing bowl stir together flour and salt. Cut cold butter into ½-inch-thick slices (not cubes). Add butter slices to flour mixture and toss until slices are coated and are separated.

2 In a small mixing bowl stir together egg and ice water. Add all at once to flour mixture. Using a spoon, quickly mix (butter will remain in large pieces and flour will not be completely moistened).

3 Turn the dough out onto a lightly floured pastry cloth. Knead the dough 10 times by pressing and pushing dough together to form a rough-looking ball, lifting pastry cloth if necessary to press the dough together. Shape the dough into a rectangle (dough still will have some dry-looking areas). Make corners as square as possible. Slightly flatten dough. Working on a well-floured pastry cloth, roll dough into a 15×10-inch rectangle. Fold 2 short sides to meet in center; fold in half like a book to form 4 layers each measuring 7½×5 inches.

4 Repeat the rolling and folding process once more. Wrap dough with plastic wrap. Chill dough for 20 minutes in refrigerator. Repeat rolling and folding process 2 more times. Chill dough for 20 minutes before using.

5 For filling, in a bowl stir together egg white, almond paste, ½ cup granulated sugar, and the brown sugar. Set aside.

6 Using a sharp knife, cut dough crosswise into 4 equal parts. Wrap 3 portions in plastic wrap and return to the refrigerator. On a well-floured surface, roll 1 portion into a 12½×10-inch rectangle. Cut rectangle into five 10×2½-inch strips.

7 Shape a slightly rounded tablespoon of filling into a 9-inch rope and place it down the center third of one strip. Roll up the strip lengthwise. Brush edge and ends with water; pinch to seal. Place, seam side down, on an ungreased baking sheet, shaping strip into a letter (traditionally the letter "S"). Brush with water and sprinkle with additional granulated sugar. Repeat with remaining dough strips and filling. Repeat with remaining 3 dough portions and filling. Bake in a 375° oven for 20 to 25 minutes or until golden. Remove from baking sheet; cool on racks.

***Note:** For best results, use an almond paste made without syrup or liquid glucose.

Nutrition Facts per pastry: 362 cal., 23 g total fat (5 g sat. fat), 35 mg chol., 285 mg sodium, 36 g carbo., 1 g fiber, 5 g pro. Daily Values: 18% vit. A, 0% vit. C, 3% calcium, 11% iron

CREAM PUFF (CHOUX) PASTRY

Prep: 30 minutes   Bake: 30 minutes
Makes: 12   Oven: 400°

Cream puffs are so versatile! Fill regular-size puffs with savory salads for a main dish and stuff miniature ones for appetizers. Or, add pudding, ice cream, or whipped cream and serve as a spectacular dessert for any meal.

 1 **cup water**
 ½ **cup butter**
 ⅛ **teaspoon salt**
 1 **cup all-purpose flour**
 4 **eggs**

1 **In a medium saucepan combine** water, butter, and salt. Bring to boiling. Add flour all at once, stirring vigorously. Cook and stir until mixture forms a ball (see top photo, right). Remove from heat. Cool 10 minutes. Add eggs, one at a time, beating well with a wooden spoon after each. Bake as directed below or use as directed in recipes on pages 101–103.

Baked Cream Puffs: Drop Cream Puff Pastry dough by heaping tablespoons into 12 mounds 3 inches apart onto a greased baking sheet (see middle photo, right). Bake in a 400° oven for 30 to 35 minutes or until golden. Remove from baking sheet; cool on a wire rack. Cut off the tops of each puff; remove any soft dough from inside (see bottom photo, right). Fill each with ¼ cup whipped cream, pudding, ice cream, or as desired. Replace cream puff tops. If desired, sift powdered sugar over tops of the filled puffs.

After adding flour to the water and butter, stir vigorously until the mixture forms a ball that does not separate. Remove the pan from the heat before adding eggs.

Drop cream puff pastry using 2 spoons. For evenly shaped puffs, if possible, avoid going back to add more dough to the mounds.

After baking and cooling puffs, cut off the top fourth of each puff and remove any soft dough inside, using a fork or a spoon.

Nutrition Facts per cream puff (with whipped cream): 229 cal., 20 g total fat (12 g sat. fat), 132 mg chol., 132 mg sodium, 8 g carbo., 0 g fiber, 4 g pro.
Daily Values: 23% vit. A, 0% vit. C, 2% calcium, 4% iron

Chocolate Cream Puff Pastry: Prepare Cream Puff Pastry as directed, except in a small bowl combine flour with 3 tablespoons unsweetened cocoa powder and 2 tablespoons granulated sugar. Add flour mixture all at once to boiling water-butter mixture. Continue as directed.

DOUBLE-CHOCOLATE
CREAM PUFFS

Prep: 20 minutes plus pastry   **Bake:** 30 minutes
Chill: 2 hours   **Makes:** 12   **Oven:** 400°

If you really love chocolate, here's a dessert idea. Serve chocolate cream puffs filled with a creamy rich and chocolate filling.

  1 **recipe Chocolate Cream Puff**
       Pastry (see page 100)
 ⅔ **cup granulated sugar**
 ⅓ **cup all-purpose flour**
 ⅛ **teaspoon salt**
1½ **cups milk**
  1 **ounce unsweetened chocolate,**
       chopped
  2 **slightly beaten egg yolks**
 ⅓ **cup butter, softened**
  1 **teaspoon vanilla**
       Powdered sugar

1 Grease a baking sheet; set aside. Prepare Chocolate Cream Puff Pastry as directed. Drop dough by heaping tablespoons into 12 mounds about 3 inches apart onto the prepared baking sheet. Bake in a 400° oven about 30 minutes or until firm. Remove puffs from baking sheet; cool the puffs on a wire rack.

2 For chocolate filling, in a heavy medium saucepan stir together granulated sugar, flour, and salt. Gradually stir in milk. Add chopped chocolate. Cook and stir over medium heat until thickened and bubbly. Reduce heat. Cook and stir for 2 minutes more. Remove from heat. Gradually stir about 1 cup of the hot filling into the beaten egg yolks. Return egg yolk mixture to saucepan. Bring to a gentle boil. Cook and stir for 2 minutes more. Remove from heat. Cover surface of filling with plastic wrap. Refrigerate about 2 hours or until cold.

3 In a medium mixing bowl beat butter until creamy. Continue beating and gradually add chilled filling, beating until the mixture is light and creamy. Beat in vanilla.

4 To assemble, cut off the top fourth of each puff. Remove any soft dough from inside. Spoon a scant ¼ cup chocolate filling into each puff. Replace tops of the puffs. If desired, chill for up to 2 hours. Before serving, sift powdered sugar over the tops.

Nutrition Facts per cream puff: 279 cal., 17 g total fat (10 g sat. fat), 143 mg chol., 234 mg sodium, 27 g carbo., 1 g fiber, 6 g pro. Daily values: 22% vit. A, 0% vit. C, 6% calcium, 8% iron

Chocolate-Filled Cream Puffs: Prepare Double Chocolate Cream Puffs as directed, except substitute Cream Puff Pastry for the Chocolate Cream Puff Pastry. Bake, cool, and fill with chocolate filling.

CREAM PUFFS 101

The perfect cream puff is crisp, tender, and, well, puffy. If your cream puffs or éclairs fall short of your expectations, try again with these hints in mind:
- Use large eggs; add them one at a time.
- Be sure to measure the water carefully.
- Add the flour as soon as the butter is melted and the water boils so that the water doesn't boil away in the saucepan.

- Set a timer so the pastry dough cools for 10 minutes—then beat in the first egg.
- Be sure the puffs are golden brown, firm, and dry before you remove them from the oven.
- For mini appetizer puffs, drop dough by rounded teaspoons. Bake at 400° about 18 minutes.
- Fill the shells just before serving, or fill and chill the puffs up to 2 hours to keep the bottoms from getting soggy.

STORING CREAM PUFFS

Cream puff shells can be made ahead and won't lose their crisp freshness if you store them properly.

- For short-term storage, let the cream puffs cool completely; place the unfilled puffs in a plastic bag so they won't dry out. Store in the refrigerator for up to 24 hours.
- For long-term storage, place cooled, unfilled shells in an airtight container; seal, label, and freeze for up to 2 months. To thaw the shells, let them stand at room temperature about 15 minutes.
- For savory appetizers that you want to serve warm, make the puffs ahead, chill or freeze, and reheat them at the last minute. To warm for serving, transfer the chilled or frozen puffs to an ungreased baking sheet. Heat in a 350° oven for 5 to 10 minutes until warm.

STRAWBERRY-FILLED ALMOND PUFFS

Prep: 20 minutes plus pastry **Bake:** 25 minutes **Makes:** 12 **Oven:** 400°

Almond paste gives the cream puffs a nutty flavor while the amaretto or almond extract flavors the whipped cream.

- 1 recipe Cream Puff Pastry (see page 100)
- ½ cup almond paste* (about ½ of an 8-ounce can)
- 1 cup whipping cream
- 2 tablespoons powdered sugar
- 2 tablespoons amaretto or ¼ teaspoon almond extract
- ½ cup dairy sour cream
- 3 cups strawberries, sliced Powdered sugar

1 Grease a baking sheet; set aside. Prepare Cream Puff Pastry as directed except heat almond paste with butter and water. Drop dough by heaping tablespoons into 12 mounds 3 inches apart onto the prepared baking sheet. Bake in a 400° oven for 25 to 30 minutes or until golden and firm. Remove puffs from baking sheet; cool on wire rack.

2 For filling, in a medium mixing bowl combine whipping cream, 2 tablespoons powdered sugar, and amaretto. Beat just until stiff peaks form. Fold in sour cream. Cover and refrigerate.

3 To assemble, cut off the top fourth of each puff. Remove any soft dough from inside. Spoon a heaping tablespoon of whipped cream filling into each puff. Top with about ¼ cup strawberries. Replace tops of the puffs. If desired, cover and chill for up to 2 hours. Before serving, sift powdered sugar over the tops.

*Note: For best results, use an almond paste made without syrup or liquid glucose.

Nutrition Facts per cream puff: 285 cal., 21 g total fat (11 g sat. fat), 123 mg chol., 158 mg sodium, 18 g carbo., 1 g fiber, 5 g pro. Daily Values: 21% vit. A, 35% vit. C, 5% calcium, 7% iron

Peach-Filled Almond Puffs: Prepare Strawberry-Filled Almond Puffs as directed, except substitute sliced fresh peaches for the strawberries.

CANNOLI-STYLE ÉCLAIRS

Prep: 20 minutes **Bake:** 35 minutes
Makes: 12 **Oven:** 400°

**1 recipe Cream Puff Pastry
    (see page 100)**
1½ cups ricotta cheese
 ½ cup sugar
 2 teaspoons amaretto (optional)
 1 teaspoon vanilla
 **⅔ cup miniature semisweet chocolate
    pieces**
 1 cup whipping cream
 1 tablespoon shortening
 1 teaspoon light-colored corn syrup
    Chopped pistachio nuts

1 Grease a baking sheet; set aside. Prepare Cream Puff Pastry as directed, except spoon batter into a pastry bag fitted with a large plain round tip (½- to 1-inch opening).

2 Slowly pipe strips of batter onto prepared baking sheet 3 inches apart, making each éclair about 4 inches long, 1 inch wide, and ¾ inch high. Bake in a 400° oven for 35 to 40 minutes or until golden brown and puffy. Remove from baking sheet and cool on a wire rack.

3 For filling, in a mixing bowl stir together ricotta cheese, sugar, amaretto (if desired), and vanilla. Stir in ⅓ cup of the chocolate pieces. Cover and chill the filling.

4 Up to 1 hour before serving beat the whipping cream until soft peaks form (tips curl). Fold into ricotta mixture. Cut off top of each éclair. Remove any soft dough from inside. Fill éclairs with ricotta filling. Replace tops.

5 In a small saucepan melt remaining chocolate pieces, shortening, and corn syrup over low heat. Drizzle over éclairs and sprinkle with nuts. Chill up to 2 hours.

Nutrition Facts per éclair: 334 cal., 24 g total fat (12 g sat. fat), 128 mg chol., 168 mg sodium, 25 g carbo., 0 g fiber, 8 g pro. Daily Values: 23% vit. A, 0% vit. C, 9% calcium, 8% iron

GRUYÈRE PUFFS

Prep: 25 minutes **Bake:** 30 minutes
Stand: 10 minutes **Makes:** 18 **Oven:** 400°

Serve these cheese puffs filled with chicken salad for a tasty luncheon dish or serve them warm with the salad course when entertaining.

1 cup water
½ cup butter
¾ teaspoon dried basil, crushed
¼ teaspoon garlic salt
⅛ teaspoon ground red pepper
1 cup all-purpose flour
4 eggs
**½ cup shredded Gruyère or Swiss
    cheese (2 ounces)**
**2 tablespoons grated Parmesan
    cheese**

1 Grease a baking sheet; set aside. In a medium saucepan combine water and butter. Add basil, garlic salt, and red pepper. Bring to boiling. Add flour all at once, stirring vigorously. Cook and stir until mixture forms a ball that doesn't separate. Remove from heat. Cool for 5 minutes.

2 Add eggs, one at a time, beating well with a wooden spoon after each addition until smooth. Stir in Gruyère or Swiss cheese.

3 Drop dough by rounded tablespoons into 18 mounds 2 inches apart onto the prepared baking sheet. Sprinkle with Parmesan cheese.

4 Bake in a 400° oven for 30 to 35 minutes or until golden. Turn off oven; let puffs stand in oven 10 minutes. Serve hot. (To make ahead, bake and cool puffs completely. Place in airtight container and refrigerate for up to 2 days or freeze up to 1 month. To reheat for serving, place the chilled or frozen puffs on an ungreased baking sheet. Heat in a 350° oven for 5 to 10 minutes or until warm.)

Nutrition Facts per puff: 101 cal., 7 g total fat (4 g sat. fat), 65 mg chol., 118 mg sodium, 5 g carbo., 0 g fiber, 3 g pro. Daily Values: 8% vit. A, 0% vit. C, 4% calcium, 3% iron

STRUDEL DOUGH

Prep: 1 hour   Rest: 1½ hours

1½ to 1¾ cups all-purpose flour
¼ teaspoon salt
¼ cup butter
1 beaten egg yolk
⅓ cup warm water (110° to 115°)
½ cup butter, melted

1 **In a large mixing bowl stir** together 1½ cups of the flour and the salt. Cut in ¼ cup butter until pieces are the size of small peas. In a small bowl stir together egg yolk and the water. Add egg yolk mixture to flour mixture. Stir until combined.

2 **Turn dough out** onto a lightly floured surface. Knead dough for 5 minutes. If necessary, knead in some or all of the remaining flour if dough is sticky. Cover with plastic wrap; let dough stand at room temperature for 1 hour.

3 **Cover a large surface** (at least 4×3 feet) with a cloth or sheet. Lightly flour cloth. On the cloth roll the dough into a 15-inch square. Brush with 2 tablespoons of the melted butter. Cover dough with plastic wrap. Let dough rest for 30 minutes.

4 **To stretch dough,** use palms of your hands and work underneath dough (see top photo, right). Starting from the middle and working toward edges, gently lift and pull your hands apart. At the same time, pull dough away from middle toward yourself. Continue stretching until dough is paper thin, forming a 40×20-inch rectangle. Use scissors to trim uneven edges. Brush with remaining melted butter. Fill; shape as directed in recipes on page 105.

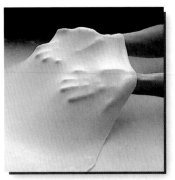

Gently lift and stretch the strudel dough with the palms of your hands, pulling your hands apart and away from middle of dough.

Use the cloth under the strudel dough to lift and roll the pastry over the filling and then to roll up the dough.

Shortcut Phyllo Strudel: To substitute frozen phyllo dough for Strudel Dough, thaw 12 sheets of frozen phyllo dough. Cover a large surface with a cloth. Lightly flour the cloth. Unfold sheets of phyllo dough. Remove 6 sheets, keeping rest covered with plastic wrap. Arrange the 6 sheets of phyllo on floured cloth, overlapping the stacks as necessary to form a rectangle about 40×20 inches. Brush each sheet of phyllo with some of the melted butter; press to seal the seams. Top with 6 more sheets of phyllo dough, brushing each sheet with remaining butter and overlapping as necessary (but do not overlap in the same places where the bottom layer overlaps). Fill and shape as for homemade dough.

STRUDEL 101

Ultra-flaky strudel starts with a large, paper-thin sheet of pulled dough that is filled and rolled into multiple layers. It can be a bit challenging, but it's worth the effort. Follow these tips for success:

- Prepare filling while the dough is resting.
- A fabric sheet makes a good pastry cloth.
- Keep strudel dough covered with a lightly damp cloth when you're not working on it.

- Remove any jewelry before stretching your dough—the thin dough tears easily.
- If you're stretching strudel dough with a friend, work on opposite sides of the dough so you are stretching across from each other. The stretching should take about 5 minutes. If you are working alone, place a heavy rolling pin on one edge of the dough and pull from the opposite side; it will take about 15 minutes.

APPLE STRUDEL

Prep: 20 minutes plus dough **Bake:** 30 minutes
Makes: 12 to 16 **Oven:** 350°

Apple is one of the most traditional fillings for this German-Austrian favorite.

> 1 recipe Strudel Dough or phyllo
>   dough (see page 104)
> 3 cups thinly sliced, peeled tart
>   apples
> ⅓ cup packed brown sugar
> ⅓ cup raisins
> ¼ cup chopped walnuts or pecans
> ¾ teaspoon ground cinnamon
> 1 slightly beaten egg white
> 1 tablespoon water
>   Powdered sugar

1 Prepare Strudel Dough as directed. For filling, in a large mixing bowl toss together apples, brown sugar, raisins, nuts, and cinnamon; set aside. Lightly grease a large baking sheet; set aside.

2 To assemble strudel, prepare dough as directed in recipe. Beginning 4 inches from one of the 20-inch sides of dough, spoon filling across the dough in a 4-inch-wide band.

3 Using the cloth beneath dough as a guide, gently lift 4-inch section of dough and lay it over filling (see bottom photo, page 104). Slowly and evenly lift cloth and tightly roll up dough and filling, jelly-roll style. If needed, cut excess dough from ends to within 1 inch of the filling. Fold ends under to seal.

4 Carefully transfer the strudel roll to the prepared baking sheet. Curve the ends to form a crescent shape. Combine egg white and water; brush over top of strudel. (If using phyllo dough, roll up and seal but do not curve into a crescent shape on baking sheet. Brush with 2 tablespoons melted butter instead of egg mixture.)

5 Bake in a 350° oven for 30 to 35 minutes or until golden. Carefully remove strudel from pan and cool on a wire rack. Just before serving, sift powdered sugar over strudel.

Nutrition Facts per serving: 235 cal., 14 g total fat (7 g sat. fat), 48 mg chol., 170 mg sodium, 27 g carbo., 1 g fiber, 3 g pro. Daily Values: 13% vit. A, 0% vit. C, 1% calcium, 7% iron

SAVORY TOMATO-OLIVE STRUDEL

Prep: 25 minutes plus dough **Bake:** 30 minutes
Makes: 40 appetizers **Oven:** 350°

> 1 recipe Strudel Dough or phyllo
>   dough (see page 104)
> ½ cup oil-packed dried tomatoes
> 1 8-ounce package cream cheese,
>   softened
> ½ cup finely chopped pitted ripe
>   olives
> ¼ cup sliced green onions
> 1 egg yolk
> ½ teaspoon dried basil, crushed
> 1 slightly beaten egg white
>   Grated Parmesan cheese

1 Prepare Strudel Dough as directed. For filling, drain tomatoes, reserving oil. Chop tomatoes. In a medium bowl combine tomatoes, cream cheese, olives, onions, egg yolk, basil, and ½ teaspoon pepper. If necessary, stir in enough reserved tomato oil (about 1 tablespoon) to make of spreading consistency. Lightly grease a large baking sheet; set aside.

2 To assemble strudel, prepare dough as directed in recipe. Beginning 4 inches from one of the 20-inch sides of dough, spread filling across the dough in a 4-inch-wide band.

3 Using the cloth beneath dough as a guide, gently lift 4-inch section of dough and lay it over filling (see bottom photo, page 104). Slowly and evenly lift cloth and tightly roll up dough and filling, jelly-roll style. If needed, cut excess dough from ends to within 1 inch of the filling. Fold ends under to seal.

4 Transfer to prepared baking sheet. Curve the ends to form a crescent shape. Combine egg white and 1 tablespoon water; brush over top. (If using phyllo dough, roll up and seal but do not curve. Brush with 2 tablespoons melted butter instead of egg mixture.) Sprinkle with Parmesan.

5 Bake in a 350° oven for 30 to 35 minutes or until golden. Carefully remove strudel from pan and cool on a wire rack. Serve warm or at room temperature. Cut into 1-inch-wide appetizer slices.

Nutrition Facts per appetizer: 78 cal., 7 g total fat (4 g sat. fat), 26 mg chol., 92 mg sodium, 4 g carbo., 0 g fiber, 1 g pro. Daily Values: 7% vit. A, 2% vit. C, 1% calcium, 2% iron

BAKLAVA

Prep: 50 minutes **Bake:** 35 minutes
Makes: 60 **Oven:** 325°

To cut diamond shapes, make several cuts the length of the baking pan, then make diagonal crosswise cuts. The corners and end pieces will yield odd-shaped pieces.

　 4 **cups walnuts, finely chopped
　　　 (1 pound)**
　 2 **cups sugar**
　 1 **teaspoon ground cinnamon**
1¼ **cups butter, melted**
　 1 **16-ounce package frozen phyllo
　　　 dough, thawed**
　 1 **cup water**
　 ¼ **cup honey**
　 ½ **teaspoon finely shredded lemon
　　　 peel**
　 2 **tablespoons lemon juice**
　 2 **inches stick cinnamon
　　　 Grape leaves (optional)**

1 **For filling,** in a large mixing bowl stir together chopped walnuts, ½ cup of the sugar, and the ground cinnamon. Set aside.

2 **Brush the bottom** of a 15×10×1-inch baking pan with some of the melted butter. Unfold phyllo dough. Keep phyllo covered with plastic wrap, removing sheets as you need them. Layer one-fourth (about 5) of the phyllo sheets in the pan, generously brushing each sheet with melted butter as you layer, and allowing phyllo to extend up the sides of the pan. Sprinkle about 1½ cups of the filling on top of the phyllo. Repeat layering the phyllo sheets and filling 2 more times.

3 **Layer remaining phyllo sheets** on the third layer of filling, brushing each sheet with butter before adding the next phyllo sheet. Drizzle any remaining butter over the top layers. Trim edges of phyllo to fit the pan. Using a sharp knife, cut through all the layers to make 60 diamond-, triangle-, or square-shaped pieces.

4 **Bake in a 325° oven** for 35 to 45 minutes or until golden. Slightly cool in pan on a wire rack.

5 **Meanwhile, for syrup,** in a medium saucepan stir together the remaining 1½ cups sugar, the water, honey, lemon peel, lemon juice, and stick cinnamon. Bring to boiling; reduce heat. Simmer, uncovered, for 20 minutes. Remove cinnamon. Pour honey mixture over slightly cooled baklava in the pan. Cool completely. If desired, serve pieces on a grape-leaf-lined patter.

Nutrition Facts per piece: 138 cal., 9 g total fat (3 g sat. fat), 10 mg chol., 76 mg sodium, 13 g carbo., 0 g fiber, 2 g pro. Daily Values: 4% vit. A, 1% vit. C, 1% calcium, 3% iron

---

PHYLLO-DOUGH KNOW-HOW

Frozen phyllo dough is not as difficult to work with as its delicate nature suggests. Follow these techniques for success:

- Allow frozen phyllo dough to thaw while it is still wrapped and sealed.
- Once unwrapped, sheets of phyllo dough can dry out quickly and crumble. To preserve, keep the opened stack of dough covered with a moist cloth or plastic wrap until needed.
- Brush each sheet you lay down with melted butter, margarine, or—in the case of a savory dish—olive oil.
- Rewrap tightly any remaining sheets of the dough and return them to the freezer.

Baklava: Layers of paper-thin phyllo dough, walnut filling, and a glistening honey-lemon syrup make up this traditional Greek sweet.

PEACH-FILLED PHYLLO BUNDLES

Prep: 35 minutes Bake: 20 minutes
Cool: 5 minutes Makes: 4 servings Oven: 375°

If using thawed, frozen peaches, remove the excess moisture by blotting with paper towels before chopping.

Butter-flavored nonstick spray coating
3 **medium peaches, peeled, pitted, and coarsely chopped, or 2¼ cups frozen unsweetened peach slices, thawed and coarsely chopped**
2 **tablespoons granulated sugar**
4 **teaspoons miniature semisweet chocolate pieces**
1 **tablespoon all-purpose flour**
1 **teaspoon lemon juice**
4 **sheets frozen phyllo dough (17×12-inch rectangles), thawed**
2 **teaspoons powdered sugar**
Fresh raspberries (optional)
Fresh peach slices (optional)

1 **Spray four** 6-ounce custard cups with nonstick coating; set aside. In a medium mixing bowl combine peaches, granulated sugar, miniature chocolate pieces, flour, and lemon juice. Toss to mix; set filling aside.

2 **Unfold phyllo dough.** Spray 1 phyllo sheet with nonstick coating. Keep remaining phyllo sheets covered with plastic wrap to keep them from drying out. Place another sheet of phyllo on top of the first sheet; spray with nonstick coating. Repeat twice. Cut stack in half lengthwise and then in half crosswise to form 4 rectangles.

3 **Using one stack of phyllo,** gently ease center of phyllo into bottom and up sides of 1 custard cup (phyllo will hang over edge). Spoon about ½ cup of the peach filling into center. Bring phyllo up over filling, pinching together to form a ruffled edge. Spray again with nonstick coating. Repeat with remaining phyllo and filling. Place custard cups in a 15×10×1-inch baking pan.

4 **Bake in a 375° oven** for 20 minutes. Cool 5 minutes in custard cups on a wire rack. Remove from cups. Cool slightly or completely. Sift powdered sugar over pastry tops before serving. If desired, garnish with a few fresh raspberries and fresh peach slices.

Nutrition Facts per serving: 164 cal., 2 g total fat (0 g sat. fat), 0 mg chol., 92 mg sodium, 35 g carbo., 2 g fiber, 3 g pro. Daily Values: 6% vit. A, 14% vit. C, 0% calcium, 6% iron

CUMIN-CARAWAY ROUNDS

Prep: 20 minutes Bake: 15 minutes
Makes: 40 Oven: 350°

These crispy crackers with caraway seed taste as wonderful as rye bread.

¾ **cup all-purpose flour**
¾ **cup rye flour**
1 **tablespoon caraway seed**
½ **teaspoon baking powder**
½ **teaspoon salt**
½ **teaspoon ground cumin**
¼ **teaspoon ground coriander**
¼ **cup butter, cut into 4 pieces**
⅓ **cup milk**
1 **beaten egg white**

1 **In a food processor bowl** combine all-purpose flour, rye flour, caraway seed, baking powder, salt, cumin, and coriander in food processor bowl. Add butter; cover and process until blended. Add milk and process just until mixture forms a dough (if necessary, add an additional 1 tablespoon milk).

2 **Transfer dough** to a floured surface and let stand 5 minutes. Roll to ⅛-inch thickness and cut with a 2-inch round cutter or knife into desired shapes. Transfer cutouts to an ungreased baking sheet. Brush lightly with egg white. Using a fork, prick crackers all over.

Cumin-Caraway Rounds, Herbed Crackers: Set out a bowl of crispy crackers along with an assortment of tangy cheeses for your next party. Or, tuck away a container of crackers for everyday snacking or impromptu gatherings.

3 **Bake in a 350° oven** for 15 to 17 minutes or until crisp. Cool completely on wire racks and store in an airtight container.

Nutrition Facts per cracker: 27 cal., 1 g total fat (1 g sat. fat), 3 mg chol., 45 mg sodium, 3 g carbo., 0 g fiber, 1 g pro. Daily Values: 1% vit. A, 0% vit. C, 0% calcium, 1% iron

HERBED CRACKERS ~LOW-FAT~

Prep: 25 minutes   **Bake:** 18 minutes
Makes: 24   **Oven:** 325°

The green flecks in these homemade crisps come from the parsley and green onion.

>   1 **cup all-purpose flour**
> ¾ **teaspoon ground sage**
> ½ **teaspoon salt**
> ⅛ **to ¼ teaspoon pepper**
>   3 **tablespoons milk**
>   3 **tablespoons finely snipped fresh parsley**
>   2 **tablespoons olive oil**
>   2 **tablespoons finely chopped green onion**
>   **Kosher salt**

1 **In a food processor bowl combine** flour, sage, salt, and pepper; cover and process briefly, just until combined. Add milk, parsley, oil, and green onion. Cover and process just until combined (dough will look crumbly). Form dough into a ball.

2 **Transfer dough** to floured surface and flatten to a rectangle. Roll to a 12×9-inch rectangle, about ¹⁄₁₆ inch thick (trim uneven edges, if necessary). Using a fork, prick dough all over. Using a pastry wheel, cut into 3×1½-inch rectangles. Transfer rectangles to an ungreased baking sheet and sprinkle tops with kosher salt.

3 **Bake in a 325° oven** for 18 to 20 minutes or just until crackers start to brown and are firm to the touch. Cool completely on wire racks and store in an airtight container.

Nutrition Facts per cracker: 29 cal., 1 g total fat (0 g sat. fat), 0 mg chol., 68 mg sodium, 4 g carbo., 0 g fiber, 1 g pro. Daily Values: 0% vit. A, 1% vit. C, 0% calcium, 1% iron

SCANDINAVIAN OATMEAL CRACKERS

Prep: 45 minutes **Bake:** 15 minutes
Makes: 84 **Oven:** 350°

You'll love the crispness of these lightly sweetened crackers. Start them off by making your own oat flour in a food processor or blender.

    2 cups rolled oats
    1 cup all-purpose flour
    ¼ cup packed brown sugar
    1 teaspoon baking powder
    ⅓ cup butter
    ½ cup cold water

1 For oat flour, in a food processor bowl or blender container place ½ cup of the oats. Cover and process or blend until reduced to a powder. Transfer to a large bowl. Repeat with the remaining oats, ½ cup at a time. (You should have about 1½ cups of oat flour.)

2 Add all-purpose flour, brown sugar, and baking powder to the oat flour. Stir until thoroughly combined. Using a pastry blender, cut in the butter until the mixture resembles coarse crumbs.

3 Make a well in the center of the flour mixture. Add cold water all at once. Using a fork, stir until the mixture can be gathered into a ball. Divide dough in half.

4 On a lightly floured surface roll each half of dough to ⅛-inch thickness. Using a 2-inch round cookie cutter, cut dough into rounds. Place on an ungreased baking sheet. Using a fork, prick crackers all over.

5 Bake in a 350° oven for 15 to 18 minutes or until firm. Cool crackers on a wire rack.

Nutrition Facts per cracker: 21 cal., 1 g total fat
(0 g sat. fat), 2 mg chol., 12 mg sodium, 3 g carbo.,
0 g fiber, 0 g pro. Daily Values: 0% vit. A, 0% vit. C,
0% calcium, 1% iron

SPICY DOUBLE-CHEESE STRAWS

Prep: 35 minutes **Bake:** 10 minutes
Makes: 40 **Oven:** 400°

Two cheeses—cheddar and Parmesan—add flavor to these crackers. For a stronger cheese taste, use an aged cheddar cheese.

    1 cup all-purpose flour
    ¼ teaspoon ground red pepper
    ⅛ teaspoon salt
    1 cup finely shredded cheddar
        cheese (4 ounces)
    ¼ cup butter
    3 to 5 tablespoons cold water
    1 beaten egg
    2 tablespoons grated Parmesan
        cheese

1 In a large mixing bowl combine flour, red pepper, and salt. Using a pastry blender, cut in cheddar cheese and butter until pieces are the size of small peas. Sprinkle 1 tablespoon of the water over part of the mixture. Gently toss with a fork. Push to side of bowl. Repeat until all of the flour mixture is moistened. Shape dough into a ball.

2 On a lightly floured surface flatten dough with your hands. Roll out dough from center to edges forming a 10-inch square. Brush with egg; sprinkle with Parmesan cheese. Cut dough into 5×½-inch strips. Place the strips ½ inch apart on a lightly greased baking sheet.

3 Bake in a 400° oven for 10 to 12 minutes or until golden brown. Cool crackers on wire rack.

Nutrition Facts per cracker: 35 cal., 2 g total fat
(1 g sat. fat), 12 mg chol., 43 mg sodium, 2 g carbo.,
0 g fiber, 1 g pro. Daily Values: 2% vit. A, 0% vit. C,
2% calcium, 1% iron

cakes

Triple-Layer Lemon
Cake, recipe page 150

CAKES

Numbers in *italics* indicate photo pages.

YELLOW CAKE

Prep: 20 minutes   **Bake:** 30 minutes
Cool: 1 hour   **Makes:** 12 servings   **Oven:** 375°

Your grandmother may have served this cake—a version of this classic has appeared in every edition of the Better Homes and Gardens® Cook Book since it was published in 1930.

    2½ **cups all-purpose flour**
    2½ **teaspoons baking powder**
     ½ **teaspoon salt**
     ⅔ **cup butter**
    1¾ **cups sugar**
    1½ **teaspoons vanilla**
     2 **eggs**
    1¼ **cups milk**

1 Grease and lightly flour two 8×1½-inch or 9×1½-inch round baking pans or grease one 13×9×2-inch baking pan; set pan(s) aside. Stir together flour, baking powder, and salt; set aside.

2 In a mixing bowl beat butter with an electric mixer on medium to high speed for 30 seconds. Add sugar and vanilla; beat until well combined. Add eggs, 1 at a time, beating 1 minute after each. Add flour mixture and milk alternately to beaten mixture, beating on low speed after each addition just until combined. Pour batter into pan(s).

3 Bake in a 375° oven for 30 to 35 minutes or until a wooden toothpick comes out clean. Cool layer cakes in pans on wire racks for 10 minutes. Remove from pans. Cool thoroughly on wire racks. Or, place 13×9-inch cake in pan on a wire rack; cool thoroughly. Frost with desired frosting.

Nutrition Facts per serving (cake only): 316 cal., 12 g total fat (7 g sat. fat), 65 mg chol., 292 mg sodium, 49 g carbo., 1 g fiber, 4 g pro. Daily Values: 12% vit. A, 0% vit. C, 9% calcium, 9% iron

Citrus Yellow Cake: Prepare as above, except stir 2 teaspoons finely shredded orange peel or lemon peel into batter.

WHITE CAKE

Prep: 20 minutes   **Bake:** 30 minutes
Cool: 1 hour   **Makes:** 12 servings   **Oven:** 350°

Frost it green on St. Patrick's Day or pink for Valentine's Day, or top it with candles for a birthday. With the right decoration and frosting, this traditional cake fits any occasion.

    2 **cups all-purpose flour**
    1 **teaspoon baking powder**
     ½ **teaspoon baking soda**
     ⅛ **teaspoon salt**
     ½ **cup shortening or butter**
    1¾ **cups sugar**
    1 **teaspoon vanilla**
    4 **egg whites**
    1⅓ **cups buttermilk or sour milk**
        (see tip, page 138)

1 Grease and lightly flour two 8×1½-inch or 9×1½-inch round baking pans or grease one 13×9×2-inch baking pan; set aside. Combine flour, baking powder, baking soda, and salt; set aside.

2 In a large mixing bowl beat shortening or butter with an electric mixer on medium to high speed for 30 seconds. Add sugar and vanilla; beat until well combined. Add egg whites, 1 at a time, beating well after each. Add flour mixture and buttermilk or sour milk alternately to beaten mixture, beating on low speed after each addition just until combined. Pour batter into the prepared pan(s).

3 Bake in a 350° oven for 30 to 35 minutes or until a wooden toothpick comes out clean. Cool layer cakes in pans on wire racks for 10 minutes. Remove from pans. Cool thoroughly on racks. Or, place 13×9-inch cake in pan on a wire rack; cool thoroughly. Frost with desired frosting.

Nutrition Facts per serving (cake only): 275 cal., 9 g total fat (2 g sat. fat), 1 mg chol., 149 mg sodium, 45 g carbo., 1 g fiber, 4 g pro. Daily Values: 0% vit. A, 0% vit. C, 5% calcium, 6% iron

DEVIL'S FOOD CAKE

Prep: 20 minutes Bake: 35 minutes
Cool: 1 hour Makes: 12 servings Oven: 350°

The first devil's food recipe appeared almost a century ago and was named so because of its chocolaty richness. This cake fits the name, too.

2¼ **cups all-purpose flour**
 ½ **cup unsweetened cocoa powder**
1½ **teaspoons baking soda**
 ¼ **teaspoon salt**
 ½ **cup shortening**
1¾ **cups sugar**
 1 **teaspoon vanilla**
 3 **eggs**
1⅓ **cups cold water**

1 **Grease and lightly flour** two 9×1½-inch round baking pans or grease one 13×9×2-inch baking pan; set pan(s) aside. Stir together flour, cocoa powder, baking soda, and salt; set aside.

2 **In a large mixing bowl beat** shortening with an electric mixer on medium to high speed for 30 seconds. Add sugar and vanilla; beat until well combined. Add eggs, 1 at a time, beating well after each. Add flour mixture and water alternately to beaten mixture, beating on low speed after each addition just until combined. Pour batter into the prepared pan(s).

3 **Bake in a 350° oven** for 35 to 40 minutes or until a wooden toothpick comes out clean. Cool layer cakes in pans on wire racks for 10 minutes. Remove from pans. Cool thoroughly on wire racks. Or, place 13×9-inch cake in pan on a wire rack; cool thoroughly. Frost with desired frosting.

Nutrition Facts per serving (cake only): 302 cal., 11 g total fat (3 g sat. fat), 53 mg chol., 219 mg sodium, 48 g carbo., 1 g fiber, 5 g pro. Daily Values: 2% vit. A, 0% vit. C, 4% calcium, 11% iron

CLASSIC CHOCOLATE CAKE

Prep: 25 minutes Bake: 30 minutes
Cool: 1 hour Makes: 12 servings Oven: 350°

2¼ **cups all-purpose flour**
 1 **teaspoon baking powder**
 ¾ **teaspoon baking soda**
 ¼ **teaspoon salt**
 ⅔ **cup butter**
1¾ **cups sugar**
 2 **eggs**
 3 **ounces unsweetened chocolate,
    melted and cooled**
 1 **teaspoon vanilla**
1¼ **cups water**

1 **Grease and lightly flour** two 9×1½-inch round baking pans or grease one 13×9×2-inch baking pan; set pan(s) aside. Stir together flour, baking powder, baking soda, and salt; set aside.

2 **In a large mixing bowl beat** the butter with an electric mixer on medium to high speed for 30 seconds. Add sugar; beat until well combined. Add eggs, 1 at a time, beating well after each. Beat in chocolate and vanilla. Add flour mixture and water alternately to beaten mixture, beating on low speed after each addition just until combined. Pour batter into the prepared pan(s).

3 **Bake in a 350° oven** for 30 to 35 minutes or until a wooden toothpick comes out clean. Cool layer cakes in pans on wire racks for 10 minutes. Remove from pans. Cool thoroughly on wire racks. Or, place 13×9-inch cake in pan on a wire rack; cool thoroughly. Frost with desired frosting.

Nutrition Facts per serving (cake only): 329 cal., 15 g total fat (8 g sat. fat), 63 mg chol., 269 mg sodium, 48 g carbo., 1 g fiber, 4 g pro. Daily Values: 11% vit. A, 0% vit. C, 3% calcium, 11% iron

---

A CAKE OF YOUR OWN

Almost any creamed cake (one that starts with beating the sugar and butter or shortening until fluffy) can be made into cupcakes. Just grease and flour a muffin pan (or line the cups with paper bake cups) and fill cups half full. Bake at the same temperature called for in the cake recipe, but reduce baking time by one-third to one-half. A two-layer cake recipe usually yields 24 to 30 cupcakes.

German Chocolate Cake: All the rage in the 1950s, this layered beauty, with its sweet chocolate flavor and a gooey pecan-coconut topping, has been satisfying sweet tooths ever since.

GERMAN CHOCOLATE
CAKE

Prep: 50 minutes **Bake:** 30 minutes
Cool: 1 hour **Makes:** 12 servings **Oven:** 350°

1½ **cups all-purpose flour**
¾ **teaspoon baking soda**
¼ **teaspoon salt**
1 **4-ounce package sweet baking chocolate**
1 **cup sugar**
¾ **cup shortening**
3 **eggs**
1 **teaspoon vanilla**
¾ **cup buttermilk or sour milk (see tip, page 138)**
1 **recipe Coconut-Pecan Frosting (see right)**
1 **recipe Chocolate Butter Frosting (optional) (see page 158)**

1 **Grease and lightly flour** two 8×1½-inch or 9×1½-inch round baking pans; set pans aside. Stir together flour, baking soda, and salt; set aside.

2 **In a saucepan combine** chocolate and ½ cup water. Cook and stir over low heat until melted; cool.

3 **Beat sugar and shortening** with an electric mixer on medium speed until fluffy. Add eggs and vanilla; beat on low speed until combined. Beat on medium speed 1 minute. Beat in chocolate mixture. Add the flour mixture and buttermilk alternately to beaten mixture; beat on low speed after each addition just until combined. Pour batter into prepared pans.

4 **Bake in a 350° oven** for 30 minutes for 9-inch layers, 35 to 40 minutes for 8-inch layers or until a wooden toothpick comes out clean. Cool layers on wire racks for 10 minutes. Remove from pans. Cool thoroughly. Spread Coconut-Pecan Frosting over top of layers; stack. If desired, frost the sides with Chocolate Butter Frosting (see photo, below).

Coconut-Pecan Frosting: In a saucepan slightly beat 1 egg. Stir in one 5-ounce can (⅔ cup) evaporated milk, ⅔ cup sugar, and ¼ cup butter. Cook and stir over medium heat about 12 minutes or until thickened and bubbly. Remove from heat; stir in 1⅓ cups flaked coconut and ½ cup chopped pecans. Cover and cool thoroughly.

Nutrition Facts per serving (with Coconut-Pecan Frosting only): 470 cal., 29 g total fat (11 g sat. fat), 85 mg chol., 214 mg sodium, 51 g carbo., 2 g fiber, 6 g pro. Daily Values: 7% vit. A, 3% vit. C, 5% calcium, 9% iron

Dress up the sides of this classic cake by using a narrow spatula to evenly spread the chocolate frosting. Use smooth, up-and-down strokes.

SPICE CAKE

Prep: 20 minutes **Bake:** 35 minutes
Cool: 1 hour **Makes:** 12 servings **Oven:** 350°

Here's another heirloom recipe. Though it's been updated over the years, it's as homey and satisfying as the 1930s version. Try it with the Penuche Frosting, page 161.

    2 cups all-purpose flour
1½ teaspoons baking powder
    1 teaspoon ground cinnamon
½ teaspoon baking soda
¼ teaspoon ground nutmeg
¼ teaspoon ground cloves
¼ teaspoon ground ginger
¼ cup butter
¼ cup shortening
1½ cups sugar
½ teaspoon vanilla
    2 eggs
1¼ cups buttermilk or sour milk
        (see tip, page 138)

1 **Grease a** 13×9×2-inch baking pan or grease and lightly flour two 8×1½-inch round baking pans; set pan(s) aside. Combine flour, baking powder, cinnamon, soda, nutmeg, cloves, and ginger; set aside.

2 **In a large mixing bowl beat** butter and shortening with an electric mixer on medium to high speed for 30 seconds. Add sugar and vanilla; beat until well combined. Add eggs, 1 at a time, beating well after each. Add flour mixture and buttermilk or sour milk alternately to beaten mixture, beating on low speed after each addition just until combined. Pour into prepared pan(s).

3 **Bake in a 350° oven** for 35 to 40 minutes for 13×9-inch pan or 30 to 35 minutes for round pans or until a wooden toothpick comes out clean. Place 13×9-inch cake in pan on a wire rack; cool thoroughly. Or, cool layer cakes on wire racks for 10 minutes. Remove layer cakes from pans. Cool thoroughly on racks. Frost with desired frosting.

Nutrition Facts per serving (cake only): 263 cal., 9 g total fat (4 g sat. fat), 47 mg chol., 181 mg sodium, 41 g carbo., 1 g fiber, 4 g pro. Daily Values: 6% vit. A, 0% vit. C, 6% calcium, 7% iron

Applesauce Spice Cake: Prepare as above, except reduce buttermilk or sour milk to ¼ cup and combine it with 1 cup applesauce. Add this mixture to cake alternately with flour mixture.

Pumpkin Spice Cake: Prepare as above, except reduce buttermilk or sour milk to 1 cup and combine it with ½ cup canned pumpkin. Add this mixture to cake alternately with flour mixture.

THE CREAMED CAKE DEFINED—AND MASTERED

That luscious, old-fashioned layer cake your grandmother baked to serve on the front porch with coffee or lemonade was probably a creamed cake. A creamed cake is simply one with a recipe that involves beating fat (shortening or butter) and sugar together until the mixture is fluffy. The process traps air, which helps leaven the cake and give it a tender texture.

Here's how to make a creamed cake that's the cream of the crop:

- Beat the fat and sugar until they're well combined or the cake's texture may be coarse. If you have a freestanding mixer, use a lower speed in the recommended range; if you have a portable mixer, use a higher speed.

- Unless specified otherwise, add the eggs one at a time and beat well after each addition.

- Use the oven temperature listed with the recipe. If the oven temperature is too hot, the cake could develop tunnels and cracks; if it's too cool, the texture may become too coarse.

- Don't overbake your cake. Check it at the lower end of the baking time range. Creamed cakes are done when a wooden toothpick inserted near the center comes out clean. If it's not done, return it to the oven for more baking.

READY, SET, BAKE

Embarking on a cake-baking adventure is great fun—and the process will go more smoothly if you're prepared. Take these steps:

- Buy large eggs and allow them to stand at room temperature 30 minutes before using. If the eggs are to be separated, do so immediately after removing them from the refrigerator.
- For the recipes in this book we recommend using butter. If you use margarine, use one that contains no less than 80% vegetable oil. Do not use whipped butter, low-calorie spreads, or soft spreadable margarines or butter blends sold in tubs.
- Give your oven 10 minutes to preheat to the recommended baking temperature.

- Unless specified otherwise, grease and lightly flour baking pans for creamed layer cakes that will be removed from their pans. Use a paper towel or pastry brush to evenly spread the shortening in the pan. Add a tablespoon or two of flour, tilt the pan, and tap it so the flour covers all the greased surfaces, then tap out the excess flour.
- For creamed cakes that will be left in their pans, grease only the bottom of the baking pan and do not coat it with flour.
- Do not grease pans for angel, sponge, and chiffon cakes unless specified otherwise in a particular recipe.

BEST-EVER CARROT
CAKE

Prep: 30 minutes Bake: 30 minutes
Cool: 1 hour Makes: 12 servings Oven: 350°

The appeal of this thoroughly American cake hasn't waned since it became popular in the 1960s. Here's our favorite version.

    2 cups all-purpose flour
    2 cups sugar
    2 teaspoons baking powder
    ½ teaspoon baking soda
    4 beaten eggs
    3 cups finely shredded carrots*
    ¾ cup cooking oil
    1 recipe Cream Cheese Frosting
        (see page 160)
    1 cup toasted, finely chopped pecans
        (optional) (see tip, page 247)

1 **Grease and flour** two 9×1½-inch round baking pans. Line bottoms with parchment or waxed paper. Grease paper; set pans aside. In a large mixing bowl combine flour, sugar, baking powder, and baking soda.

2 **In another mixing bowl combine** eggs, carrots, and oil. Add egg mixture to flour mixture. With a spoon, stir until combined. Pour batter into the prepared pans.

3 **Bake in a 350° oven** for 30 to 35 minutes or until a toothpick inserted near the centers comes out clean. Cool on wire racks for 10 minutes. Remove from pans; remove paper. Cool thoroughly on racks.

4 **Frost tops and sides** with Cream Cheese Frosting. To add texture to frosting, use a cake comb. If desired, press nuts onto sides of the cake. Store cake in the refrigerator for up to 3 days.

*Note: The carrots need to be finely shredded or they may sink to the bottom of pan during baking.

Nutrition Facts per serving: 620 cal., 28 g total fat (10 g sat. fat), 107 mg chol., 265 mg sodium, 89 g carbo., 1 g fiber, 6 g pro. Daily Values: 93% vit. A, 4% vit. C, 7% calcium, 10% iron

Gingered Carrot Cake: Prepare as above, except add ¾ cup dried fruit bits and 2 teaspoons grated gingerroot or ¾ teaspoon ground ginger to egg mixture. Frost with 1 recipe Orange Cream Cheese Frosting (see page 160).

BUTTERMILK-PINEAPPLE CARROT CAKE

Prep: 30 minutes Bake: 40 minutes
Cool: 1 hour Makes: 16 servings Oven: 350°

  2 cups all-purpose flour
  2 cups sugar
  2 teaspoons baking soda
1½ teaspoons ground cinnamon
  1 teaspoon baking powder
  ¼ teaspoon salt
  2 cups finely shredded carrots*
  ¼ cup buttermilk or sour milk
      (see tip, page 138)
  ¼ cup cooking oil
  1 8¼-ounce can crushed pineapple,
      drained
  1 cup chopped walnuts
  3 eggs
  ½ cup coconut
  1 teaspoon vanilla
  1 recipe Buttermilk Glaze (see right)
  1 recipe Cream Cheese Frosting
      (see page 160)
  ½ cup chopped walnuts

1 **Grease a** 13×9×2-inch baking pan or grease and lightly flour two 9×1½-inch round baking pans; set aside.

2 **In a large mixing bowl combine** flour, sugar, baking soda, cinnamon, baking powder, and salt. Add shredded carrots, buttermilk or sour milk, cooking oil, drained pineapple, the 1 cup nuts, eggs, coconut, and vanilla. Stir until combined. Spread batter in prepared pan(s).

3 **Bake in a 350° oven** for 40 to 45 minutes or until cake(s) spring back when touched lightly. Pour Buttermilk Glaze evenly over top(s) of cake(s). Cool layer cakes in pans on wire racks for 15 minutes. Remove from pans. Cool thoroughly on racks. Or, place 13×9-inch pan on wire rack; cool thoroughly. Frost with Cream Cheese Frosting. Sprinkle with the ½ cup nuts.

Buttermilk Glaze: In a medium saucepan combine ½ cup sugar, ¼ cup buttermilk or sour milk, ¼ cup butter, and 2 teaspoons light-colored corn syrup. Bring to boiling; reduce heat. Cook and stir for 4 minutes. Remove saucepan from heat and stir in ½ teaspoon vanilla.

*Note: The carrots need to be finely shredded or they may sink to the bottom of pan during baking.

Nutrition Facts per serving: 544 cal., 25 g total fat (10 g sat. fat), 75 mg chol., 360 mg sodium, 79 g carbo., 2 g fiber, 6 g pro. Daily Values: 53% vit. A, 4% vit. C, 5% calcium, 10% iron

Buttermilk-Pineapple Carrot Cake: A decadent version of the classic, this cake adds pineapple, coconut, and a luscious buttermilk glaze layer. Consider the 13×9-inch size cake when toting.

TOOLBOX: CAKE PANS

All cake pans are not created equal. For even baking, we suggest sturdy, single-wall aluminum pans. When choosing cake pans, also consider both the pan's depth and surface finish:

Depth: When a recipe calls for 8×1½-inch round pans, make sure the pans you choose are truly 1½ inches deep. Some pans can be as much as ¼ inch shallower than others—cakes may run over these pans.

Surface finish: Bakeware is made in a range of materials that have different effects on a cake. Shiny bakeware, including aluminum, tin, and stainless steel, reflects heat and will result in a thinner cake crust. Dark or dull-finish bakeware, including tin, glass, and many nonstick pans, absorbs more heat, increasing the amount of browning and resulting in a thicker crust.

GINGERBREAD CAKE

Prep: 15 minutes **Bake:** 35 minutes
Cool: 30 minutes **Makes:** 9 servings
Oven: 350°

Talk about traditional. This molasses-sweetened specialty has been around for centuries.

  1½ **cups all-purpose flour**
  ¾ **teaspoon ground cinnamon**
  ¾ **teaspoon ground ginger**
  ½ **teaspoon baking powder**
  ½ **teaspoon baking soda**
  ½ **cup shortening**
  ¼ **cup packed brown sugar**
  1 **egg**
  ½ **cup light-flavored molasses**
  1 **recipe Autumn Fruit Caramel**
      (optional) (see right)
      Sweetened whipped cream
      (optional)

1 Grease a 9×1½-inch round baking pan; set aside. Combine flour, cinnamon, ginger, baking powder, and baking soda; set aside.

2 In a large mixing bowl beat shortening with an electric mixer on medium speed for 30 seconds. Add brown sugar; beat until fluffy. Add egg and molasses; beat 1 minute. Add flour mixture and ½ cup water alternately to egg mixture, beating on low speed after each addition until combined. Pour batter into pan.

3 Bake in a 350° oven for 35 to 40 minutes or until a wooden toothpick inserted near center comes out clean. Cool for 30 minutes in pan on wire rack. If desired, serve warm with Autumn Fruit Caramel and sweetened whipped cream.

Nutrition Facts per serving: 243 cal., 12 g total fat (3 g sat. fat), 24 mg chol., 102 mg sodium, 31 g carbo., 1 g fiber, 3 g pro. Daily Values: 1% vit. A, 0% vit. C, 5% calcium, 13% iron

Autumn Fruit Caramel: In a medium saucepan melt 2 tablespoons butter over medium-low heat. Stir in 2 small cooking apples, peeled, cored, and sliced; ⅓ cup dried apricots, cut into slivers; and 2 tablespoons dried cranberries. Cover; cook over medium-low heat about 5 minutes or until apples are just tender, stirring occasionally. Remove from heat; set aside.

In a medium saucepan stir together 1 cup packed brown sugar and 2 tablespoons cornstarch. Stir in ⅔ cup half-and-half or light cream, ½ cup water, and ¼ cup light-colored corn syrup. Cook, stirring constantly, until slightly thickened and bubbly (mixture may appear curdled). Cook and stir for 2 minutes more. Remove saucepan from heat. Stir fruit mixture and 1 teaspoon vanilla into brown sugar mixture. Serve warm spooned over cake.

BANANA LAYER CAKE

Prep: 30 minutes   Bake: 30 minutes
Cool: 1 hour   Makes: 12 servings   Oven: 350°

  2 cups all-purpose flour
1½ teaspoons baking powder
  ¾ teaspoon baking soda
  ½ cup shortening
1½ cups sugar
  1 teaspoon vanilla
  2 eggs
  1 cup mashed ripe bananas (3 medium)
  ½ cup buttermilk or sour milk
       (see tip, page 138)

1 **Grease and flour** two 9×1½-inch round baking pans; set aside. Stir together flour, baking powder, baking soda, and ½ teaspoon salt; set aside.

2 **In a large mixing bowl beat** shortening with an electric mixer on medium to high speed for 30 seconds. Add sugar and vanilla; beat until well combined. Add eggs, 1 at a time, beating well after each. Combine bananas and buttermilk. Add flour mixture and buttermilk mixture alternately to egg mixture, beating on low speed after each addition just until combined. Pour into prepared pans.

3 **Bake in 350° oven** 30 minutes or until wooden toothpick inserted near centers comes out clean. Cool on wire racks 10 minutes. Remove from pans; cool thoroughly on racks. Frost with desired frosting.

Nutrition Facts per serving (cake only): 286 cal., 10 g total fat (3 g sat. fat), 36 mg chol., 235 mg sodium, 47 g carbo., 1 g fiber, 4 g pro. Daily Values: 1% vit. A, 4% vit. C, 5% calcium, 7% iron

---

COOL IT!

Before removing a creamed layer cake from its baking pan, let it cool about 10 minutes on a wire rack. To remove, loosen the cake edges from the pan and place an inverted wire rack over the top of the pan. Turn cake and rack over and lift off pan. Place a second rack on cake layer and turn it over again so the baked cake is upright; let it cool completely.

BANANA SPLIT CAKE

Prep: 30 minutes (plus cake)
Makes: 12 servings

  1 recipe Banana Layer Cake
       (see left) or one 2-layer-size
       banana cake mix
  1 recipe Sweetened Whipped Cream
       (see page 160) or 6 ounces frozen
       whipped dessert topping, thawed
  1 cup sliced fresh strawberries
  1 8¼-ounce can crushed pineapple,
       well drained
  1 11- to 12-ounce jar fudge
       ice-cream topping
  ½ cup chopped peanuts
       Banana slices (optional)

1 **Prepare the** Banana Layer Cake or, if using banana cake mix, prepare according to package directions for a two-layer cake.

2 **For fillings,** divide whipped cream or dessert topping in half. Fold berries into half of the whipped cream. Fold drained pineapple into the other half of the whipped cream. In a small saucepan, heat and stir fudge ice-cream topping over low heat just until warm (not hot).

3 **To assemble,** using a serrated knife, split each cake layer in half horizontally. Place bottom of 1 split layer on serving plate. Top with the strawberry-cream mixture, spreading to edge of the cake layer. Place another split cake layer atop. Spread with half of the warm fudge topping, letting it drizzle down the sides. Sprinkle with half of the nuts.

4 **Top with another** split cake layer. Spread with pineapple-cream mixture. Top with remaining split cake layer. Spread remaining warm fudge topping atop cake, letting some drizzle down sides of cake. Sprinkle top of cake with remaining nuts. Serve immediately. (Or, cover loosely with plastic wrap, placing a few toothpicks in top of the cake so the wrap doesn't stick to the topping, and chill up to 2 hours.) If desired, garnish with banana slices.

Nutrition Facts per serving: 494 cal., 24 g total fat (10 g sat. fat), 63 mg chol., 222 mg sodium, 67 g carbo., 2 g fiber, 7 g pro. Daily Values: 11% vit. A, 19% vit. C, 9% calcium, 11% iron

Banana Split Cake:
Looking for a star dessert for your next social gathering? This one wins rave reviews for its soda fountain flavors.

ANGEL FOOD CAKE

Prep: 50 minutes **Bake:** 40 minutes
Cool: 2 hours **Makes:** 12 servings **Oven:** 350°

*Loosen the cooled cake from the pan by sliding a
long metal spatula between the pan and cake.
Constantly pressing the spatula against the pan,
draw it around the pan in a continuous, not
sawing, motion so you don't cut into the cake.
For help with techniques, see photos, right.*

1½ **cups egg whites (10 to 12 large)**
1½ **cups sifted powdered sugar**
 1 **cup sifted cake flour or sifted
     all-purpose flour**
1½ **teaspoons cream of tartar**
 1 **teaspoon vanilla**
 1 **cup granulated sugar**

1 **In an extra-large mixing bowl allow** egg
whites to stand at room temperature for 30 minutes. Meanwhile, sift powdered sugar and flour
together 3 times; set aside.

2 **Add cream of tartar** and vanilla to egg whites.
Beat with an electric mixer on medium speed
until soft peaks form (tips curl). Gradually add granulated sugar, about 2 tablespoons at a time, beating
until stiff peaks form (tips stand straight).

3 **Sift about one-fourth** of the flour mixture over
beaten egg whites; fold in gently. Repeat, folding
in remaining flour mixture by fourths. Pour into an
ungreased 10-inch tube pan. Gently cut through
batter with a narrow metal spatula or knife to
remove large air pockets.

4 **Bake on the lowest rack** in a 350° oven for
40 to 45 minutes or until top springs back when
lightly touched. Immediately invert cake (leave in
pan); cool thoroughly. Using a narrow metal spatula, loosen sides of cake from pan; remove cake.

Nutrition Facts per serving: 161 cal., 0 g total fat,
0 mg chol., 46 mg sodium, 37 g carbo., 0 g fiber,
4 g pro. Daily Values: 0% vit. A, 0% vit. C, 0% calcium,
4% iron

Honey Angel Food Cake: Prepare as above, except
after beating egg whites to soft peaks, gradually pour
¼ cup honey in a thin stream over the egg white
mixture. Continue as above, except beat only ½ cup
granulated sugar into the egg whites.

Initially, beat the egg whites, cream of tartar, and vanilla until soft peaks form. This means that the tips will curl when beaters are lifted.

As the granulated sugar is gradually added, continue beating until stiff peaks form. This means that the peaks will stand straight when beaters are lifted.

Sift flour mixture over the stiffly beaten egg white mixture. If you don't have a sifter, you can press the flour mixture through a sieve.

To fold in, cut down through the mixture with a rubber spatula; scrape across the bottom of the bowl and bring spatula up and over, close to surface.

Gently cutting through the cake batter with a narrow metal spatula or table knife helps eliminate any air pockets.

CHOCOLATE ANGEL CAKE WITH COFFEE LIQUEUR GLAZE

LOW-FAT

Prep: 1 hour **Bake:** 40 minutes
Cool: 2 hours **Makes:** 12 servings
Oven: 350°

Here's luscious proof that chocolate can fit into a low-fat diet.

1½ **cups egg whites (10 to 12 large)**
1½ **cups sifted powdered sugar**
  1 **cup sifted cake flour or sifted**
     all-purpose flour
 ¼ **cup unsweetened cocoa powder**
1½ **teaspoons cream of tartar**
  1 **teaspoon vanilla**
  1 **cup granulated sugar**
  1 **cup sifted powdered sugar**
 ¼ **teaspoon vanilla**
   Coffee liqueur

1 **In an extra-large mixing bowl allow** egg whites to stand at room temperature for 30 minutes. Meanwhile, sift the 1½ cups powdered sugar, flour, and cocoa powder together 3 times; set aside.

2 **Add cream of tartar** and the 1 teaspoon vanilla to egg whites. Beat with an electric mixer on medium to high speed until soft peaks form (tips curl). Gradually add granulated sugar, about 2 tablespoons at a time, beating on medium to high speed until stiff peaks form (tips stand straight).

3 **Sift about one-fourth** of flour mixture over the beaten egg whites; fold in gently. Repeat, folding in remaining flour mixture by fourths. Pour into an ungreased 10-inch tube pan. Gently cut through the cake batter with a narrow metal spatula or knife.

4 **Bake on the lowest rack** in a 350° oven for 40 to 45 minutes or until top springs back when lightly touched. Immediately invert cake (leave in the pan); cool thoroughly. Using a narrow metal spatula, loosen the sides of the cake from the pan. Remove cake from the pan.

5 **For glaze,** combine the 1 cup powdered sugar, the ¼ teaspoon vanilla, and enough of the coffee liqueur (about 2 tablespoons), 1 teaspoon at a time, to make of drizzling consistency. Drizzle over top of the cake.

Nutrition Facts per serving: 211 cal., 0 g total fat, 0 mg chol., 47 mg sodium, 47 g carbo., 0 g fiber, 4 g pro. Daily Values: 0% vit. A, 0% vit. C, 1% calcium, 5% iron

---

ANGEL, SPONGE, AND CHIFFON CAKES MASTERED

For an angel, sponge, or chiffon cake that rises above the rest, keep these tips in mind:

- Be sure when you separate your eggs that not a speck of egg yolk or any other fat gets into the whites—it can ruin their beating quality. To safeguard against that, separate the whites into a small bowl, then transfer them to a clean glass or metal bowl that is wide enough to keep the beaters from being buried in the egg white as they fluff. Plastic bowls are not recommended for beating egg whites, as even after washing, they can hold an oily film on the interior, minimizing egg white volume.

- Separate eggs as soon as you take them out of the refrigerator. Let them stand at room temperature for 30 minutes along with other ingredients.

- Don't over- or under-beat egg whites. They should be stiff but not dry, or your cake may fall.

- Measure the flour accurately using a dry measuring cup. Sift dry ingredients three times to ensure thorough blending of dry ingredients.

- Fold dry ingredients into egg white mixture gently with a rubber spatula. Keep the spatula under surface of batter while folding. If you add too much flour or overmix the batter, the volume drops and your cake will be tough.

- When making a chiffon cake, add egg yolks to flour mixture after the cooking oil. Otherwise, they might bind with the flour and form streaks.

- When making a sponge cake, beat the egg yolks until they're thick and the color of lemons, or an eggy bottom layer may form.

- Cool angel, sponge, and chiffon cakes upside down to set their structures.

MARBLE ANGEL FOOD
CAKE

LOW-FAT

Prep: 50 minutes   Bake: 40 minutes
Cool: 2 hours   Makes: 12 servings   Oven: 350°

*To keep this classic low in fat, top with fruit
instead of the whipped cream.*

1½ **cups egg whites (10 to 12 large)**
1½ **cups sifted powdered sugar**
   1 **cup sifted cake flour or sifted
       all-purpose flour**
   2 **tablespoons unsweetened cocoa
       powder**
1½ **teaspoons cream of tartar**
   1 **teaspoon vanilla**
   1 **cup granulated sugar**
   1 **recipe Chocolate Powdered Sugar
       Icing (optional) (see page 159)**
   **Sweetened whipped cream
       (optional)**
   Fresh fruit (optional)

1 **In an extra-large mixing bowl allow** egg whites
  to stand at room temperature for 30 minutes.
Meanwhile, sift powdered sugar and flour together

To marble batter, using a folding motion, bring a narrow spatula down through batter and up other side. Go completely around pan, turning pan as you fold. Do not overfold.

3 times. Measure 1 cup of the flour mixture; sift
together with the cocoa powder. Set mixtures aside.

2 **Add cream of tartar** and vanilla to the egg
  whites. Beat with an electric mixer on medium
speed until soft peaks form (tips curl). Gradually
add the granulated sugar, about 2 tablespoons at a
time, beating until stiff peaks form (tips stand
straight). Transfer one-third of the mixture to
another bowl.

3 **Sift about one-fourth** of the plain flour mixture
  over the larger portion of beaten egg whites;
gently fold in. Repeat folding in the remaining plain
flour mixture, using one-fourth of the flour mixture
each time. Sift flour-cocoa mixture, one-third at a
time, over smaller portion of beaten egg whites,
folding in as above.

Marble Angel Food Cake:
The best-kept secret about
this impressive angel cake is
that the marbling of the
layers is simple to do (see
photo, above).

4 **Gently spoon one-third** of the white batter evenly into an ungreased 10-inch tube pan. Spoon half of the chocolate batter over white batter in pan. Repeat. Top with remaining white batter. Marble the batter (see top photo, page 124).

5 **Bake on the lowest rack** in a 350° oven for 40 to 45 minutes or until top springs back when lightly touched. Immediately invert cake (leave in pan). Cool completely. Using a narrow metal spatula, loosen sides of cake from pan. Remove cake from pan. If desired, drizzle with Chocolate Powdered Sugar Icing and serve with sweetened whipped cream or fresh fruit.

Nutrition Facts per serving: 165 cal., 0 g total fat, 0 mg chol., 46 mg sodium, 37 g carbo., 0 g fiber, 4 g pro. Daily Values: 0% vit. A, 0% vit. C, 1% calcium, 5% iron

SPONGE CAKE *LOW-FAT*

Prep: 40 minutes **Bake:** 55 minutes
Cool: 2 hours **Makes:** 12 servings **Oven:** 325°

A simple drizzle of Powdered Sugar Icing (page 159) is all it takes to dress up this golden yellow ring.

  6 egg yolks
  1 tablespoon finely shredded
      orange peel
  ½ cup orange juice or pineapple juice
  1 teaspoon vanilla
  1 cup sugar
1¼ cups all-purpose flour
  6 egg whites
  ½ teaspoon cream of tartar
  ½ cup sugar

1 **In a mixing bowl beat** egg yolks with an electric mixer on high speed about 5 minutes or until thick and lemon colored. Add orange peel, orange or pineapple juice, and vanilla; beat on low speed until combined. Gradually beat in the 1 cup sugar at low speed. Increase to medium speed; beat until mixture thickens slightly and doubles in volume (about 5 minutes total).

2 **Sprinkle** ¼ cup of the flour over egg yolk mixture; fold in until combined. Repeat with remaining flour, ¼ cup at a time. Set egg yolk mixture aside.

ANGEL, SPONGE, AND CHIFFON CAKES— THE EGGS HAVE IT

Q What's the difference in angel, sponge, and chiffon cakes? They seem pretty similar in that they all have beaten eggs.

A Eggs are indeed the common denominator in these airy cakes. They all rely on the power of the beaten egg to make them light as a feather. The main difference in them is that each contains elements of the egg in different measures.

- Angel food cakes—the lightest of the three—contain just beaten egg whites, no yolks. They also do not contain oil.
- Sponge cakes are richer than angel food cakes because they feature egg yolks as well as whites.
- Chiffon cakes are the richest of the three; they contain whole eggs, beaten separately, as well as cooking oil.

3 **Thoroughly wash beaters.** In a mixing bowl beat egg whites and cream of tartar on medium speed until soft peaks form (tips curl). Gradually add the ½ cup sugar, beating on high speed until stiff peaks form (tips stand straight). Fold 1 cup of the beaten egg white mixture into the egg yolk mixture; fold yolk mixture into remaining egg white mixture. Pour into an ungreased 10-inch tube pan.

4 **Bake on lowest rack** in a 325° oven 60 minutes or until cake springs back when lightly touched. Immediately invert cake (leave in pan); cool thoroughly. Loosen sides from pan; remove from pan.

Nutrition Facts per serving: 184 cal., 3 g total fat (1 g sat. fat), 107 mg chol., 32 mg sodium, 36 g carbo., 0 g fiber, 4 g pro. Daily Values: 16% vit. A, 9% vit. C, 1% calcium, 6% iron

Lemon Sponge Cake: Prepare as above, except substitute 2 teaspoons finely shredded lemon peel for the orange peel and ¼ cup lemon juice plus ¼ cup water for the orange juice or pineapple juice.

Chocolate Sponge Cake: Prepare as above, except omit orange peel. Reduce flour to 1 cup. Stir ⅓ cup unsweetened cocoa powder into flour.

SHERRY-ALMOND SPONGE CAKE

Prep: 1 hour   Bake: 25 minutes   Cool: 1 hour
Chill: 2 hours   Makes: 12 servings   Oven: 325°

    4 egg yolks
    ⅓ cup dry or cream sherry
    ⅔ cup sugar
    ⅔ cup all-purpose flour
    ¼ cup ground toasted almonds
        (see tip, page 247)
    4 egg whites
    ½ teaspoon cream of tartar
    ⅓ cup sugar
    1 cup whipping cream
    1 tablespoon sugar
    2 to 3 teaspoons dry or cream
        sherry
    ½ cup strawberry or seedless
        raspberry preserves
    2 tablespoons coarsely chopped toasted
        almonds (see tip, page 247)
        Edible flowers (optional)
        (see tip, page 175)

1 **Beat egg yolks** with electric mixer on high speed about 5 minutes or until thick and lemon colored. Add the ⅓ cup sherry. Beat on low speed until combined. Gradually beat in the ⅔ cup sugar. Increase speed to medium; beat until mixture thickens slightly and doubles in volume (about 5 minutes total).

2 **Sprinkle ⅓ cup of flour** over yolk mixture; gently fold in until combined. Repeat with remaining flour. Gently fold in ground almonds. Set aside.

3 **Thoroughly wash beaters.** In a large mixing bowl beat egg whites and cream of tartar on medium speed until soft peaks form (tips curl). Gradually add the ⅓ cup sugar, beating on high speed until stiff peaks form (tips stand straight). Fold about 1 cup beaten egg white mixture into yolk mixture.

4 **Gently fold the yolk mixture** into the remaining white mixture. Pour batter into 2 ungreased 8×1½-inch round cake pans.

5 **Bake in a 325° oven** about 25 minutes or until top springs back when lightly touched. Invert onto racks (leave in pans); cool. Remove from pans.

6 **In a chilled medium mixing bowl combine** whipping cream, the 1 tablespoon sugar, and the 2 to 3 teaspoons sherry; beat until soft peaks form.

Remove cooled cake from pans. Spread preserves between cake layers. Spread whipped cream on top and sides of cake. Pat almonds onto sides. Cover and chill up to 2 hours. If desired, garnish the top with edible flowers.

Nutrition Facts per serving: 256 cal., 11 g total fat (5 g sat. fat), 98 mg chol., 31 mg sodium, 34 g carbo., 1 g fiber, 4 g pro. Daily Values: 19% vit. A, 0% vit. C, 3% calcium, 5% iron

CHIFFON CAKE

Prep: 30 minutes   Bake: 1 hour 5 minutes
Cool: 2 hours   Makes: 12 servings   Oven: 325°

    2¼ cups sifted cake flour or 2 cups
        sifted all-purpose flour
    1½ cups sugar
    1 tablespoon baking powder
    ½ cup cooking oil
    7 egg yolks
    2 teaspoons finely shredded
        orange peel
    1 teaspoon finely shredded
        lemon peel
    1 teaspoon vanilla
    7 egg whites
    ½ teaspoon cream of tartar

1 **In a large mixing bowl** mix flour, sugar, baking powder, and ¼ teaspoon salt. Make well in center of flour mixture. Add oil, egg yolks, orange and lemon peels, vanilla, and ¾ cup cold water. Beat with electric mixer on low speed until combined. Beat on high speed for 5 minutes more or until satin smooth.

2 **Thoroughly wash beaters.** In an extra-large mixing bowl beat egg whites and cream of tartar on medium speed until stiff peaks form (tips stand straight). Pour batter in a thin stream over beaten egg whites; fold in gently. Pour into an ungreased 10-inch tube pan.

3 **Bake on lowest rack** in a 325° oven for 65 to 70 minutes or until top springs back when lightly touched. Immediately invert cake (in pan); cool thoroughly. Loosen sides of cake from pan; remove cake.

Nutrition Facts per serving: 298 cal., 12 g total fat (2 g sat. fat), 124 mg chol., 173 mg sodium, 42 g carbo., 0 g fiber, 5 g pro. Daily Values: 18% vit. A, 1% vit. C, 8% calcium, 11% iron

Sherry-Almond Sponge Cake: A colorful berry filling nestles between light sponge cake layers. Add to that an infusion of sherry and a sprinkling of almonds, and this cake becomes reminiscent of an elegant Victorian trifle.

GÉNOISE

Prep: 30 minutes   Bake: 25 minutes
Cool: 1 hour   Makes: 12 servings   Oven: 350°

This fine-crumbed, buttery French sponge cake provides the foundation for many elegant desserts, such as the one at right. It's also lovely served with a fruity sorbet or fresh fruit and whipped cream.

  1 cup sugar
  6 slightly beaten eggs
  2 teaspoons vanilla
  1 cup all-purpose flour
  ½ cup unsalted butter, melted
    and cooled

1 Grease two 9×1½-inch or 8×1½-inch round baking pans. Line bottoms with waxed paper or parchment paper; grease paper. Set aside.

2 Place sugar and eggs in a 3- to 4-quart heat-proof mixing bowl.* Place bowl over 1 to 2 inches hot water in a large saucepan (bowl should not touch water). Heat over low heat, stirring occasionally, for 5 to 10 minutes or until egg mixture is lukewarm (105° to 110°). Remove bowl from saucepan. Stir in vanilla.

3 Beat egg mixture with an electric mixer on high speed for 10 minutes. Sift about one-third of the flour over egg mixture. Gently fold in flour. Repeat sifting and folding in one-third of the flour at a time. Gently fold in melted butter. Spread batter into prepared pans.

4 Bake in a 350° oven for 25 to 30 minutes or until a wooden toothpick inserted near the center of each cake comes out clean. Cool cakes in pans on wire racks for 10 minutes. Remove cakes and peel off paper. Cool cakes thoroughly on racks.

*Note: The sugar and egg mixture is heated to help maximize volume while beating.

Nutrition Facts per serving: 207 cal., 10 g total fat
(6 g sat. fat), 127 mg chol., 33 mg sodium,
25 g carbo., 0 g fiber, 4 g pro. Daily Values:
11% vit. A, 0% vit. C, 1% calcium, 5% iron

Chocolate Génoise: Prepare Génoise as directed, except melt 3 ounces semisweet chocolate; cool chocolate. Fold the chocolate into the batter with the melted butter.

LEMON TEA CAKES

Prep: 3 hours   Bake: 25 minutes   Cool: 1 hour
Makes: 35 to 40 cakes   Oven: 350°

  1 recipe Génoise (see left)
  1 tablespoon finely shredded
    lemon peel
  1 tablespoon lemon juice
  1 recipe Lemon Satin Icing (see below)
    Melted chocolate, candied violets,
    edible flowers, and/or small
    decorative candies (optional)

1 Grease a 13×9×2-inch baking pan. Line bottom of pan with waxed paper or parchment paper; grease paper. Set aside.

2 Prepare the Génoise batter as directed, except stir in lemon juice with vanilla and fold in lemon peel with melted butter. Spread batter in prepared pan. Bake in a 350° oven about 25 minutes or until a wooden toothpick inserted near the center of the cake comes out clean. Cool cake in pan on a wire rack for 10 minutes. Remove cake from pan; peel off paper. Cool thoroughly on the rack.

3 With a serrated knife, trim sides and top of cake to make the edges smooth and straight. Cut cake into 1½-inch squares, diamonds, hearts, and/or circles. Brush off crumbs. Place the cake pieces on wire racks with waxed paper underneath racks.

4 Insert a 2- or 3-pronged, long-handled fork into the side of 1 cake piece. Holding the cake over the saucepan of Lemon Satin Icing, spoon on enough icing to cover sides and top (see bottom photo, page 129). Place frosted cake piece back on the wire rack, making sure it doesn't touch other cake pieces. Repeat with remaining pieces. Let cakes dry 15 minutes. Repeat with a second layer of icing, except set cake pieces on top of the fork prongs (do not spear them). Repeat with a third layer of icing. If necessary, reuse the icing that has dripped onto the waxed paper, straining it to remove crumbs. Tint any remaining icing with food coloring as desired and pipe or drizzle atop cakes. If desired, garnish with piped melted chocolate, candied violets, edible flowers, and/or decorative candies. (Do not eat silver candies, if using.)

Lemon Satin Icing: In a 3-quart saucepan combine 4½ cups granulated sugar, 2¼ cups water, and

Lemon Tea Cakes: Sweet and petite, these teatime gems can be made even more elegant with candied violets and edible flowers. You also can color the Lemon Satin Icing as desired and drizzle or pipe it onto the cakes.

¼ teaspoon cream of tartar. Bring mixture to boiling over medium-high heat, stirring constantly for 5 to 9 minutes or until the sugar dissolves. Reduce heat to medium-low. Clip a candy thermometer to side of the saucepan. Cook until thermometer registers 226°, stirring only when necessary to prevent sticking. Mixture should boil at a moderate, steady rate over the entire surface (this should take about 15 minutes). Remove saucepan from heat. Cool sugar mixture at room temperature, without stirring, to 110° (allow about 1 hour).

Stir 1 tablespoon lemon juice or ¼ teaspoon almond extract and 1½ teaspoons clear vanilla into sugar mixture. Stir in 6 to 6¾ cups sifted powdered sugar until icing is easy to drizzle. If necessary, beat the icing with a rotary beater or a wire whisk to remove any lumps. If desired, stir in enough food coloring to make color you want. (If icing gets too thick to drizzle, beat in a few drops hot water.) Makes 5 cups.

Nutrition Facts per cake: 237 cal., 4 g total fat (2 g sat. fat), 44 mg chol., 12 mg sodium, 51 g carbo., 0 g fiber, 1 g pro. Daily Values: 4% vit. A, 1% vit. C, 0% calcium, 2% iron

To ice cakes, spear 1 cake piece with a fork and hold it over the pan of icing. Spoon icing over cake piece, covering sides and top. Repeat with remaining cakes.

JELLY ROLL

Prep: 30 minutes **Bake:** 12 minutes
Cool: 1 hour **Makes:** 10 servings **Oven:** 375°

*Can a Victorian dessert actually be low in fat?
Sure, when it's a light, spongy jelly roll. This
basic recipe, filled with jelly, has only 2 grams
of fat per serving.*

  ½ **cup all-purpose flour**
  1 **teaspoon baking powder**
  4 **egg yolks**
  ½ **teaspoon vanilla**
  ⅓ **cup granulated sugar**
  4 **egg whites**
  ½ **cup granulated sugar**
    Sifted powdered sugar
  ½ **cup jelly or jam**

1 Grease and lightly flour a 15×10×1-inch jelly-
roll pan; set aside. Combine flour and baking
powder; set aside. In a medium mixing bowl beat egg
yolks and vanilla with an electric mixer on high
speed for 5 minutes or until thick and lemon colored. Gradually add the ⅓ cup granulated sugar,
beating on high speed until sugar is almost dissolved.

2 Thoroughly wash the beaters. In a mixing
bowl beat egg whites on medium speed until
soft peaks form (tips curl). Gradually add the ½ cup
granulated sugar, beating until stiff peaks form (tips
stand straight). Fold egg yolk mixture into beaten
egg whites. Sprinkle flour mixture over egg mixture;
fold in gently just until combined. Spread batter
evenly in the prepared pan.

3 Bake in a 375° oven for 12 to 15 minutes or
until top springs back when lightly touched.
Immediately loosen edges of cake from pan; turn cake
out onto a towel sprinkled with powdered sugar.
Roll up towel and cake, jelly-roll style, starting from
a short side (see photos, above right). Cool on a wire
rack. Unroll cake; remove towel. Spread cake with
jelly or jam to within 1 inch of edges. Roll up cake.

Nutrition Facts per serving: 162 cal., 2 g total fat
(1 g sat. fat), 85 mg chol., 64 mg sodium, 33 g carbo.,
0 g fiber, 3 g pro. Daily Values: 12% vit. A, 1% vit. C,
3% calcium, 5% iron

Chocolate Cake Roll: Prepare as above, except reduce
flour to ⅓ cup and omit baking powder. Add ¼ cup

Starting from a
short side of the
warm cake, roll it
up with the
powdered sugar-
coated towel. Let the
cake cool.

After carefully
unrolling the cooled
cake and towel,
spread the desired
filling over the cake.
Leave a 1-inch
border around
the edges.

Roll up the cake
and filling (without
the towel), again
starting from a
short side.

unsweetened cocoa powder and ¼ teaspoon baking
soda to flour. Substitute 2 cups whipped cream or
cooled chocolate pudding for the jelly. Roll up cake;
chill up to 2 hours.

Pumpkin Cake Roll: Prepare as at left, except add
2 teaspoons pumpkin pie spice to flour mixture and
stir ½ cup canned pumpkin into egg yolk mixture.
Substitute 1 recipe Cream Cheese Frosting (see page
160) for the jelly. Sprinkle cake roll with additional
sifted powdered sugar; chill.

Lemon Cake Roll: Prepare as at left, except substitute 1 recipe Lemon Curd (see page 159) for the
jelly. Sprinkle cake roll with additional sifted powdered sugar; chill up to 2 hours.

Ice-Cream Cake Roll: Prepare as at left, except substitute 2 cups of your choice of ice cream, softened,
for the jelly. Store in the freezer.

APRICOT-HAZELNUT
CAKE ROLL

Prep: 1 hour   Bake: 10 minutes   Cool: 1 hour
Chill: 2 hours   Makes: 10 servings   Oven: 375°

Apricots make it sweet and rich; hazelnuts make it glamorous—and you can make it up to 24 hours before your next dinner gathering. To serve, drizzle with zigzag lines of jelly.

  1 **cup all-purpose flour**
  1 **teaspoon baking powder**
  ½ **teaspoon salt**
  ½ **teaspoon apple pie spice**
  1 **15¼-ounce can unpeeled apricot**
      halves (in syrup)
  2 **tablespoons granulated sugar**
  3 **eggs**
  ½ **cup granulated sugar**
  ¾ **cup finely chopped hazelnuts**
      or pecans
      Sifted powdered sugar
  1 **recipe Apricot Cream Cheese**
      Filling (see right)
  ¼ **cup cherry or currant jelly**
      (optional)
      Fresh cranberries (optional)
      Fresh mint (optional)

1 **Grease and flour** a 15×10×1-inch jelly-roll pan. Set aside. Stir together the flour, baking powder, salt, and apple pie spice; set aside.

2 **Drain apricots,** reserving ⅓ cup of the syrup. Finely chop the apricots. Reserve ½ cup of the chopped apricots for the filling. In a small saucepan combine remaining chopped apricots, reserved apricot syrup, and the 2 tablespoons granulated sugar. Bring apricot mixture to boiling; reduce heat. Cook and stir over low heat about 4 minutes or until thickened, stirring and mashing with a spoon. Remove from heat; cool to room temperature.

3 **In a medium mixing bowl beat** eggs with an electric mixer on high speed for 5 minutes. Gradually beat in the ½ cup granulated sugar and the apricot mixture. Gently fold flour mixture into egg mixture. Spread batter into prepared pan. Sprinkle with nuts.

4 **Bake in a 375° oven** for 10 to 12 minutes or until wooden toothpick inserted near center comes out clean. Turn out onto a towel sprinkled with powdered sugar. Starting at a short side, roll up cake and towel together; cool. Unroll cake and spread with Apricot Cream Cheese Filling. Reroll without towel; cover and chill for at least 2 hours or up to 24 hours.

5 **Before serving,** if desired, heat cherry or currant jelly over medium heat until melted, stirring constantly; cool. Spoon jelly into a small plastic bag. Snip a small hole at a corner of the bag. Pipe the jelly atop the cake roll in 2 zigzag lines (see photo, below). If desired, garnish with cranberries and mint.

Apricot Cream Cheese Filling: In a small mixing bowl combine two 3-ounce packages cream cheese, softened; ¼ cup butter, softened; and ½ teaspoon vanilla. Beat mixture with an electric mixer on medium-high speed until fluffy. Beat in 1 cup sifted powdered sugar. Stir in the reserved ½ cup chopped apricots. Makes 2 cups.

Nutrition Facts per serving: 345 cal., 18 g total fat (7 g sat. fat), 95 mg chol., 264 mg sodium, 43 g carbo., 2 g fiber, 6 g pro. Daily Values: 19% vit. A, 2% vit. C, 6% calcium, 10% iron

For a decorative touch, drizzle jelly over the cake roll. Fill a small plastic bag with melted and cooled jelly, snip off corner, and squeeze bag to pipe zigzag lines atop cake.

AMAZING BANANA NUT ROLL

BEST-LOVED

Prep: 30 minutes   Bake: 15 minutes
Cool: 1 hour   Makes: 10 servings   Oven: 375°

½ cup all-purpose flour
½ teaspoon baking powder
¼ teaspoon baking soda
1 8-ounce package cream cheese, softened
1 3-ounce package cream cheese, softened
½ cup granulated sugar
1 egg
3 tablespoons milk
4 egg yolks
½ teaspoon vanilla
⅓ cup granulated sugar
1 large banana, mashed (about ½ cup)
½ cup finely chopped walnuts or pecans
4 egg whites
½ cup granulated sugar
Sifted powdered sugar
1 recipe Vanilla Cream Cheese Frosting (see right)
Chocolate-flavored syrup (optional)

1 Lightly grease a 15×10×1-inch baking pan. Line bottom with waxed paper; grease paper. Set aside. In a medium mixing bowl stir together flour, baking powder, and baking soda; set aside.

2 For filling, in a small mixing bowl combine cream cheese and the ½ cup granulated sugar; beat with an electric mixer on medium speed until smooth. Add whole egg and milk; beat until combined. Spread in the prepared pan; set aside.

3 In a medium mixing bowl beat egg yolks and vanilla on medium speed about 5 minutes or until thick and lemon colored. Gradually add the ⅓ cup granulated sugar, beating until sugar is dissolved. Stir in banana and nuts.

4 Thoroughly wash the beaters. In a large mixing bowl beat the egg whites on medium speed until soft peaks form (tips curl). Gradually add the ½ cup granulated sugar, beating on high speed until stiff peaks form (tips stand straight). Fold yolk mixture into egg whites. Sprinkle the flour mixture evenly over egg mixture; fold in just until blended.

5 Carefully spread the batter evenly over the filling in the pan. Bake in a 375° oven for 15 to 20 minutes or until the top springs back when lightly touched.

6 Immediately loosen cake from sides of pan and turn out onto a towel sprinkled with powdered sugar. Carefully peel off paper. Starting with a short side, roll up cake, using towel as a guide but not rolling towel into cake. Cool completely on rack.

7 Spread top with Vanilla Cream Cheese Frosting. If desired, drizzle with chocolate-flavored syrup.

Vanilla Cream Cheese Frosting: In a small mixing bowl combine half of a 3-ounce package cream cheese, softened, and ½ teaspoon vanilla; beat with an electric mixer on medium speed until light and fluffy. Gradually beat in 1 cup unsifted powdered sugar. Beat in enough milk (1 to 2 tablespoons) to make a frosting of spreading consistency. Makes about ½ cup frosting.

Nutrition Facts per serving: 400 cal., 19 g total fat (9 g sat. fat), 146 mg chol., 162 mg sodium, 51 g carbo., 1 g fiber, 8 g pro. Daily Values: 29% vit. A, 2% vit. C, 4% calcium, 9% iron

THE RISE OF CAKES

The first cakes can be traced back thousands of years to the Middle East, where they were flat baked mixtures of coarsely ground grain and water. Later, honey and sugar became standard ingredients, then sweet spices such as cinnamon, cloves, and nutmeg. When cakes made their way to Europe, they evolved to the status of sweetened breads, leavened with yeast. It wasn't until the 17th century, though, that cakes took on the rich, delicate qualities we've come to know and love.

Amazing Banana Nut Roll:
Some jelly-roll cakes require rolling twice. Not this one! The layers bake together creating a wonderful banana cake and cream cheese filling, which are easily rolled into one memorable dessert.

SOUR CREAM
POUND CAKE

Prep: 40 minutes   Bake: 1 hour
Cool: 2 hours   Makes: 10 servings   Oven: 325°

Once upon a time, the pound cake was so named because it combined a pound each of butter, sugar, eggs, and flour. This updated version includes sour cream for additional richness.

½ cup butter
3 eggs
½ cup dairy sour cream
1½ cups all-purpose flour
¼ teaspoon baking powder
⅛ teaspoon baking soda
1 cup sugar
½ teaspoon vanilla

1 **Allow butter, eggs, and sour cream** to stand at room temperature for 30 minutes. Meanwhile, grease and lightly flour an 8×4×2-inch or 9×5×3-inch loaf pan; set aside. Combine flour, baking powder, and baking soda; set aside.

2 **In a mixing bowl beat** butter with an electric mixer on medium to high speed for 30 seconds. Gradually add sugar, beating about 10 minutes or until very light and fluffy. Beat in vanilla. Add eggs, 1 at a time, beating 1 minute after each addition and scraping bowl frequently. Add flour mixture and sour cream alternately to egg mixture, beating on low to medium speed after each addition just until combined. Pour batter into prepared pan.

3 **Bake in a 325° oven** for 60 to 75 minutes or until a wooden toothpick inserted near center comes out clean. Cool in pan on wire rack 10 minutes. Remove from pan; cool thoroughly on rack.

Nutrition Facts per serving: 260 cal., 12 g total fat (7 g sat. fat), 93 mg chol., 141 mg sodium, 34 g carbo., 0 g fiber, 4 g pro. Daily Values: 12% vit. A, 0% vit. C, 2% calcium, 7% iron

Orange-Rosemary Pound Cake: Prepare as above, except stir 1¼ teaspoons finely shredded orange peel and 1 teaspoon snipped fresh rosemary into batter.

POPPY SEED POUND CAKE
WITH LEMON ICING

Prep: 40 minutes   Bake: 1¼ hours
Cool: 2 hours   Makes: 16 servings   Oven: 325°

1 cup butter
1 8-ounce package cream cheese
6 eggs
3 cups all-purpose flour
1 teaspoon baking powder
¼ teaspoon salt
2¼ cups sugar
¼ cup poppy seed
2 teaspoons vanilla
1 recipe Lemon Icing (see below)

1 **Allow butter,** cream cheese, and eggs to stand at room temperature for 30 minutes. Meanwhile, grease and lightly flour a 10-inch tube pan; set aside. Combine flour, baking powder, and salt. Set aside.

2 **In a large mixing bowl beat** butter and cream cheese with an electric mixer on medium to high speed about 30 seconds or until softened. Gradually add sugar, 2 tablespoons at a time, beating on medium speed about 5 minutes or until very light and fluffy. Add poppy seed and vanilla. Add eggs, 1 at a time, beating on low to medium speed 1 minute after each addition and scraping bowl frequently. Gradually add flour mixture, beating on low speed just until combined. Pour batter into prepared pan.

3 **Bake in a 325° oven** about 75 minutes or until a wooden toothpick inserted near center comes out clean. Cool in pan on wire rack 15 minutes. Remove from pan. Cool thoroughly on wire rack. Drizzle Lemon Icing over cake.

Lemon Icing: In a small mixing bowl stir together 1½ cups sifted powdered sugar, ½ teaspoon finely shredded lemon peel, and 1 to 2 tablespoons lemon juice to make icing of a drizzling consistency.

Nutrition Facts per serving: 415 cal., 19 g total fat (11 g sat. fat), 126 mg chol., 239 mg sodium, 55 g carbo., 1 g fiber, 6 g pro. Daily Values: 20% vit. A, 0% vit. C, 6% calcium, 11% iron

Pumpkin-Pear Cake: No frosting needed! When you invert this upside-down-style cake, a smooth, caramel syrup oozes over the pears and warm pumpkin cake.

PUMPKIN-PEAR CAKE

Prep: 20 minutes **Bake:** 35 minutes
Cool: 5 minutes **Makes:** 10 servings **Oven:** 350°

- ⅓ **cup packed brown sugar**
- 2 **tablespoons butter, melted**
- 1 **tablespoon water**
- 2 **medium pears, cored, peeled, and sliced**
- 1¼ **cups all-purpose flour**
- 1¼ **teaspoons baking powder**
- 1 **teaspoon pumpkin pie spice***
- ¼ **teaspoon baking soda**
- 3 **egg whites**
- ¾ **cup granulated sugar**
- ¾ **cup canned pumpkin**
- ⅓ **cup cooking oil**
- 2 **tablespoons water**
- 1 **teaspoon vanilla**
  Orange peel curls (optional)

1 In a small bowl combine brown sugar, melted butter, and the 1 tablespoon water. Pour into an ungreased 9×1½-inch round baking pan. Arrange pear slices in pan. Set pan aside.

2 In a small bowl combine flour, baking powder, pumpkin pie spice, and baking soda; set aside. In another mixing bowl beat egg whites with electric mixer on medium speed until soft peaks form (tips curl). Gradually add granulated sugar, beating until stiff peaks form (tips stand straight). Using low speed, blend in pumpkin, oil, the 2 tablespoons water, and vanilla. Fold flour mixture into pumpkin mixture just until moistened; carefully spoon over pears. Spread mixture evenly with back of spoon.

3 Bake in a 350° oven about 35 minutes or until a wooden toothpick inserted near center comes out clean. Cool in pan on wire rack for 5 minutes. Loosen from sides of pan; invert onto serving plate. Serve warm. If desired, garnish with orange peel curls.

*Note: Pumpkin pie spice is available at most grocery stores in the spice aisle. If you prefer to make your own, see the Emergency Baking Substitutions chart inside the front cover.

Nutrition Facts per serving: 250 cal., 10 g total fat (3 g sat. fat), 6 mg chol., 120 mg sodium, 39 g carbo., 2 g fiber, 3 g pro. Daily Values: 42% vit. A, 3% vit. C, 5% calcium, 8% iron

Granny Cake: Also known as the "hummingbird cake," this old-fashioned, church-social-style goody is one of those recipes that's been traded over backyard fences for years.

GRANNY CAKE

Prep: 20 minutes **Bake:** 70 minutes
Cool: 2 hours **Makes:** 12 servings **Oven:** 325°

3 cups all-purpose flour
2 cups granulated sugar
1 teaspoon baking soda
1 teaspoon ground nutmeg
½ teaspoon salt
½ teaspoon ground cloves
¾ cup butter
2 cups mashed ripe bananas
1 8-ounce can crushed pineapple
3 eggs
2 teaspoons vanilla
1 cup finely chopped pecans
   Paper doily (optional)
   Powdered sugar (optional)

1 **Grease and flour** a 10-inch fluted tube pan; set aside. In a medium mixing bowl stir together flour, granulated sugar, baking soda, nutmeg, salt, and cloves; set aside.

2 **In large mixing bowl beat** butter with an electric mixer on medium speed for 30 seconds. Add bananas, undrained pineapple, eggs, and vanilla. Beat until combined. Add flour mixture. Beat on low speed until combined. Beat on medium speed 1 minute. Fold in pecans. Spread in prepared pan.

3 **Bake in a 325° oven** for 70 to 75 minutes or until a wooden toothpick inserted near the center comes out clean. Cool cake in pan on a wire rack for 10 minutes. Remove cake from pan. Cool thoroughly on wire rack.

4 **If desired, decorate cake** with a powdered-sugar design. Place doily on top of cake. Sift powdered sugar over the doily to fill cutout designs. Carefully remove and discard the doily.

Nutrition Facts per serving: 481 cal., 19 g total fat (8 g sat. fat), 84 mg chol., 328 mg sodium, 74 g carbo., 2 g fiber, 6 g pro. Daily Values: 13% vit. A, 12% vit. C, 2% calcium, 13% iron

CHOCOLATE COOKIE CAKE

Prep: 50 minutes **Bake:** 40 minutes
Cool: 1 hour **Makes:** 16 servings **Oven:** 350°

2⅔ cups all-purpose flour
2¼ cups sugar
1¼ teaspoons baking soda
¾ teaspoon salt
½ teaspoon baking powder
1⅓ cups milk
1 8-ounce carton dairy sour cream
5 ounces unsweetened chocolate,
   melted and cooled

⅓ cup butter, softened

3 eggs

2 teaspoons vanilla

1 recipe Cookie Filling (see right)

1 recipe Chocolate-Sour Cream
   Frosting (see page 162)

4 chocolate sandwich cookies, crushed

1 Grease and lightly flour two 8×1½-inch or 9×1½-inch round cake pans. Set pans aside.

2 In an extra-large mixing bowl combine flour, sugar, baking soda, salt, and baking powder. Add milk, sour cream, melted chocolate, butter, eggs, and vanilla. Beat with an electric mixer on low speed about 1 minute or until mixture is combined. Beat on high speed 3 minutes, scraping sides of bowl occasionally.

3 Place half of the batter in a medium bowl; cover and chill. Divide remaining half of batter evenly between the prepared pans. Bake in a 350° oven for 20 to 25 minutes for 9-inch layers and 25 to 30 minutes for 8-inch layers or until a wooden toothpick inserted near centers comes out clean. Cool cakes in pans on wire racks for 10 minutes. Remove cakes from pans. Cool layers thoroughly on wire racks.

4 Wash the 2 cake pans. Grease and lightly flour pans. Divide reserved, chilled batter evenly between pans. Bake and cool as directed above.

5 Prepare Cookie Filling, reserving the ¾ cup filling (without crumbs) for the cake garnish.

6 To assemble the cake, put a cake layer on a serving plate and top with one-third of the remaining cookie filling, spreading filling evenly over layer. Add a second layer of cake and spread with another one-third portion of the cookie filling. Add another cake layer and spread with remaining cookie filling. Top with remaining cake layer.

7 Prepare the Chocolate-Sour Cream Frosting. Spread top and sides of cake with frosting. Stir reserved Cookie Filling and enough milk (about 2 to 3 teaspoons) to make it a drizzling consistency. Spoon onto center top of cake. Carefully spread filling to force some down sides of cake. Garnish top of cake with the 4 crushed chocolate sandwich cookies.

Cookie Filling: In large mixing bowl combine 4 cups sifted powdered sugar; ⅓ cup butter, softened; 2 tablespoons milk; and 1 teaspoon vanilla. Beat with electric mixer on low speed until combined; beat on medium speed until very smooth. Beat in enough additional milk (1 to 2 tablespoons) until frosting is easy to spread. Set aside ¾ cup of mixture. Crush 10 chocolate sandwich cookies; stir into remaining mixture.

Nutrition Facts per serving: 638 cal., 26 g total fat (12 g sat. fat), 79 mg chol., 408 mg sodium, 102 g carbo., 1 g fiber, 7 g pro. Daily Values: 18% vit. A, 0% vit. C, 7% calcium, 14% iron

Chocolate Cookie Cake: Definitely an indulgence, this chocolate-and-cream cake is perfect for a birthday party or any other special occasion.

VANILLA-FUDGE
MARBLE CAKE

Prep: 30 minutes   Bake: 50 minutes
Cool: 2 hours   Makes: 12 servings   Oven: 350°

2¾ cups sifted flour
1½ teaspoons baking powder
½ teaspoon baking soda
½ teaspoon salt
¾ cup butter
1½ cups sugar
2 teaspoons vanilla
2 eggs
1¼ cups buttermilk or sour milk
(see tip, lower right)
⅔ cup chocolate-flavored syrup
1 recipe Semisweet Icing (see below)

1 **Grease and lightly flour** a 10-inch fluted tube pan; set aside. Combine flour, baking powder, baking soda, and salt. Set aside.

2 **Beat butter** on low to medium speed with an electric mixer about 30 seconds. Add sugar and vanilla; beat until fluffy. Add eggs, 1 at a time, beating on low to medium speed 1 minute after each addition and scraping bowl frequently. Alternately add flour mixture and buttermilk, beating on low speed after each addition just until combined. Reserve 2 cups batter. Spread remaining batter in the prepared pan.

3 **In a mixing bowl combine** chocolate-flavored syrup and reserved batter. Beat on low speed until well combined. Pour chocolate batter over vanilla batter in pan. Do not mix.

4 **Bake in a 350° oven** about 50 minutes or until wooden toothpick inserted near center comes out clean. Cool in pan on wire rack for 15 minutes. Remove from pan; cool thoroughly on wire rack. Drizzle cake with Semisweet Icing.

Semisweet Icing: In small saucepan heat ½ cup semisweet chocolate pieces, 2 tablespoons butter, and 1 tablespoon light-colored corn syrup over low heat, stirring until chocolate melts and mixture is smooth. Stir in ¼ teaspoon vanilla. Use immediately.

Nutrition Facts per serving: 412 cal., 17 g total fat (9 g sat. fat), 71 mg chol., 391 mg sodium, 63 g carbo., 1 g fiber, 5 g pro. Daily Values: 18% vit. A, 0% vit. C, 7% calcium, 13% iron

NUT TORTE   *EASY*

Prep: 15 minutes   Bake: 20 minutes
Cool: 1 hour   Makes: 12 servings   Oven: 350°

2 tablespoons all-purpose flour
1 teaspoon baking powder
1 teaspoon finely shredded orange peel
4 eggs
¾ cup sugar
2½ cups walnuts or almonds
1 recipe Chocolate Butter Frosting (see page 158)

1 **Grease and lightly flour** two 8×1½-inch round baking pans; set pans aside. Stir together the flour, baking powder, and orange peel; set aside.

2 **Place eggs and sugar** in a blender container or food processor bowl. Cover and blend or process until smooth. Add nuts. Blend or process about 1 minute or until nearly smooth. Add flour mixture; blend or process just until combined. Spread batter evenly in the prepared pans.

3 **Bake in a 350° oven** about 20 minutes or until lightly browned. Cool cakes in pans on wire racks for 10 minutes. Remove cakes from pans. Cool thoroughly on wire racks. Frost with Chocolate Butter Frosting.

Nutrition Facts per serving: 430 cal., 23 g total fat (5 g sat. fat), 85 mg chol., 108 mg sodium, 54 g carbo., 1 g fiber, 7 g pro. Daily Values: 8% vit. A, 1% vit. C, 9% calcium, 10% iron

MAKING SOUR MILK

If you wish to substitute sour milk for the buttermilk in a recipe, here's how to make the sour milk: For each cup of sour milk needed, place 1 tablespoon lemon juice or vinegar in a glass measuring cup, then add enough milk to make 1 cup total liquid. (Increase or decrease measures proportionately to get the amount called for in the recipe.) Let the mixture stand for 5 minutes before using it in your recipe.

Pistachio Cake with White Chocolate Buttercream: It's a beauty. Tender cake layers slathered with a sumptuous buttercream frosting and studded with rich pistachios— it all stacks up to an unforgettable dessert.

PISTACHIO CAKE WITH WHITE CHOCOLATE BUTTERCREAM

Prep: 40 minutes   Bake: 30 minutes
Cool: 1 hour   Makes: 12 servings   Oven: 350°

1⅔ cups all-purpose flour
  4 teaspoons baking powder
  ½ teaspoon baking soda
  ¾ cup butter
  2 cups sugar
  1 teaspoon vanilla
  1 teaspoon almond extract
  1 cup buttermilk or sour milk
  6 egg whites (reserve yolks for White
     Chocolate Buttercream)
1½ cups toasted chopped pistachio
     nuts (see tip, page 247)
  2 teaspoons finely shredded orange peel
  1 recipe White Chocolate
     Buttercream (see page 161)
  1 cup toasted chopped pistachio nuts
     (see tip, page 247)

1 Grease and lightly flour three 8×1½-inch round baking pans (see tip, page 141); set aside.

Stir together flour, baking powder, and baking soda; set aside. Beat butter with an electric mixer on medium to high speed 30 seconds. Add sugar, vanilla, and almond extract to butter; beat until fluffy. Alternately add flour mixture and buttermilk, beating on low to medium speed just until combined.

2 Thoroughly wash beaters. In a medium mixing bowl beat egg whites until stiff peaks form (tips stand straight). Gently fold beaten egg whites into batter. Fold in the 1½ cups pistachio nuts and the orange peel. Pour batter into prepared pans.

3 Bake in a 350° oven 30 to 35 minutes or until a wooden toothpick inserted near the center of each cake comes out clean. Cool in pans on wire racks for 10 minutes. Remove cakes from pans and cool thoroughly on wire racks. Frost with White Chocolate Buttercream. If desired, using a decorating bag fitted with a star tip, pipe a scalloped edge around the top of the cake. Press the 1 cup pistachio nuts onto sides of cake. Cover and store cake in the refrigerator for up to 3 days. Let stand at room temperature for 30 minutes before serving.

Nutrition Facts per serving: 753 cal., 47 g total fat (22 g sat. fat), 182 mg chol., 466 mg sodium, 74 g carbo., 3 g fiber, 13 g pro. Daily Values: 43% vit. A, 4% vit. C, 17% calcium, 20% iron

CARAMEL-ALMOND TORTE

Prep: 25 minutes Bake: 25 minutes
Cool: 1 hour Makes: 12 servings Oven: 325°

  6 **egg yolks**
1½ **cups sugar**
  ½ **cup apple cider or apple juice**
  1 **teaspoon baking powder**
  1 **teaspoon vanilla**
  ½ **teaspoon ground cinnamon**
  6 **egg whites**
  2 **cups graham cracker crumbs**
  1 **cup ground almonds**
  1 **recipe Caramel Sauce**
       (see page 141) (reserve ½ cup
       for Caramel Cream Filling)
  1 **recipe Caramel Cream Filling**
       (see page 141)
  1 **recipe Sweetened Whipped Cream**
       (see page 160)

1 **Generously grease and flour** three 8×1½-inch round baking pans (see tip, page 141); set aside. In a medium mixing bowl combine egg yolks, 1 cup of the sugar, the apple cider or juice, baking powder, vanilla, and cinnamon. Beat with an electric mixer on medium speed about 3 minutes or until thickened and light.

2 **Thoroughly wash the beaters.** In an extra-large mixing bowl beat egg whites on medium speed until soft peaks form (tips curl). Gradually add the remaining sugar, beating on high speed until stiff peaks form (tips stand straight).

3 **Fold the egg yolk mixture** into the egg white mixture. Fold cracker crumbs and almonds into egg mixture, one-fourth at a time. Divide batter evenly among the prepared pans.

4 **Bake in a 325° oven** for 25 to 30 minutes or until top springs back when lightly touched near the center. Cool on wire racks for 10 minutes. Loosen sides; remove cake layers from pans. Cool thoroughly on wire racks.

Caramel-Almond Torte: Love caramel? This torte gets a triple dose of this smooth, sweet ingredient—in the filling, the frosting, and with its drizzled finish.

TWO PANS—THREE LAYERS

The high and mighty Caramel-Almond Torte on page 140 has three layers and calls for three baking pans. However, if you only have two pans, don't let that stop you from making this exquisite dessert. Simply chill one-third of the batter while two of the three layers bake. For the third layer, bake the remaining chilled batter as directed.

HICKORY NUT CAKE

Prep: 25 minutes **Bake:** 35 minutes
Cool: 1 hour **Makes:** 12 servings **Oven:** 375°

Find hickory nuts at farmers' markets or through mail-order catalogs.

- 2¾ cups all-purpose flour
- 1 cup ground hickory nuts or pecans
- 2½ teaspoons baking powder
- ¼ teaspoon salt
- ½ cup butter
- 1¾ cups sugar
- 1½ teaspoons vanilla
- 2 eggs
- 1¼ cups half-and-half, light cream, or milk
- 1 recipe Cream Cheese Frosting (see page 160) or 1 recipe Browned Butter Frosting (see page 160)
- ½ cup finely chopped hickory nuts or pecans

1 **Grease and lightly flour** two 8×1½-inch round baking pans; set aside. In a mixing bowl stir together flour, the 1 cup ground nuts, baking powder, and salt; set aside.

2 **In a large mixing bowl beat** butter with an electric mixer on medium to high speed about 30 seconds or until softened. Add sugar and vanilla; beat until combined. Add eggs, 1 at a time, beating on medium speed until combined. Alternately add flour mixture and half-and-half, beating on low to medium speed after each addition just until combined. Spread batter in the prepared pans.

3 **Bake in a 375° oven** for 35 to 40 minutes or until a wooden toothpick comes out clean. Cool cakes in pans on wire racks for 10 minutes. Remove cakes from pans. Cool thoroughly on the racks.

4 **To assemble,** place a layer on serving plate. Spread with some of the frosting. Sprinkle with half of the finely chopped nuts. Top with second layer. Spread top and sides with remaining frosting; sprinkle top with remaining chopped nuts. Store in the refrigerator.

5 **Place a cake layer** on a cake plate; spread with half of the Caramel Cream Filling. Top with second layer; spread with the remaining filling. Top with third layer. Frost the top and sides with the Sweetened Whipped Cream. Drizzle with the remaining Caramel Sauce.

Caramel Sauce: In a small saucepan combine ⅔ cup packed brown sugar and 1 tablespoon cornstarch. Add ¼ cup apple cider or apple juice and ¼ cup butter. Cook and stir over medium heat until thickened and bubbly. Cook and stir for 2 minutes more. Remove from heat. In a small bowl beat 1 egg yolk; gradually stir in ½ cup of the hot brown sugar mixture. Add the egg mixture to the saucepan. Cook and stir until bubbly; reduce heat. Cook and stir for 2 minutes more. Remove from heat; cover and cool. Use ½ cup of the Caramel Sauce for the Caramel Cream Filling. Use remaining sauce to drizzle atop the Sweetened Whipped Cream. If necessary, thin the remaining Caramel Sauce with 1 to 2 teaspoons apple cider or apple juice to make a topping of drizzling consistency. Makes ¾ cup.

Caramel Cream Filling: In a bowl beat one 8-ounce package cream cheese until fluffy. Gradually beat in ½ cup of the Caramel Sauce.

Nutrition Facts per serving: 490 cal., 28 g total fat (13 g sat. fat), 183 mg chol., 247 mg sodium, 54 g carbo., 2 g fiber, 9 g pro. Daily Values: 39% vit. A, 0% vit. C, 9% calcium, 13% iron

Nutrition Facts per serving: 680 cal., 33 g total fat (16 g sat. fat), 101 mg chol., 339 mg sodium, 92 g carbo., 2 g fiber, 8 g pro. Daily Values: 25% vit. A, 0% vit. C, 10% calcium, 13% iron

Pecan Cake with Tangerine Cream Filling: It's hard to believe a cake this stunning is mixed together easily in the blender. Finishing touches include a sweet and simple filling and a luscious whipped cream frosting.

PECAN CAKE WITH TANGERINE CREAM FILLING

Prep: 35 minutes   Bake: 25 minutes
Cool: 1 hour   Makes: 12 servings   Oven: 350°

2½ cups broken pecans, toasted
        (see tip, page 247)
  3 tablespoons all-purpose flour
  4 teaspoons baking powder
  6 eggs
  1 cup granulated sugar
  1 8-ounce package cream cheese,
        softened
¼ cup butter
½ cup packed brown sugar
  1 teaspoon finely shredded tangerine
        peel or orange peel
  1 teaspoon vanilla

  1 recipe Tangerine Whipped Cream
        Frosting (see page 160)
      Edible roses (optional)
      (see tip, page 175)

1 Grease two 8×1½-inch round baking pans. Line the bottoms with waxed paper or parchment paper. Grease the paper. Lightly flour pans; set aside. Place half the pecans in a blender container or food processor bowl. Cover; blend or process until coarsely ground. Repeat with remaining nuts.

2 In a mixing bowl combine pecans, flour, and baking powder. Place eggs and granulated sugar in blender container or food processor bowl. Cover; blend or process until smooth. Add nut mixture. Cover; blend or process until smooth, stopping and scraping sides as needed to mix evenly (mixture may be foamy). Spread evenly in prepared pans.

3 Bake in a 350° oven for 25 to 30 minutes or until light brown and tops spring back when lightly touched (centers may dip slightly). Cool in pans on wire racks for 10 minutes. Remove from pans; cool thoroughly on racks.

4 **For tangerine filling,** in a small mixing bowl beat cream cheese and butter with an electric mixer on medium to high speed until fluffy. Gradually add brown sugar, beating for 3 to 4 minutes or until smooth. Stir in citrus peel and vanilla.

5 **To assemble,** with a serrated knife, cut cakes in half horizontally. Place 1 split cake layer, cut side up, on a platter. Spread one-third of the filling atop cake. Place another split cake layer, cut side down, atop filling. Spread top with another one-third of the filling. Repeat with remaining cake layers and filling, ending with a cake layer on top.

6 **Frost top and sides** of cake with Tangerine Whipped Cream Frosting, reserving some of the frosting for piping, if desired. To decorate top of cake with piped frosting, place reserved frosting in a decorating bag fitted with a large star tip. Pipe frosting atop cake in a ring. If desired, decorate with edible roses. Refrigerate frosted cake for up to 4 hours.

Nutrition Facts per serving: 533 cal., 43 g total fat (18 g sat. fat), 192 mg chol., 265 mg sodium, 34 g carbo., 2 g fiber, 7 g pro. Daily Values: 34% vit. A, 1% vit. C, 15% calcium, 10% iron

BLACK FOREST CHERRY CAKE

Prep: 1¾ hours   Bake: 22 minutes
Cool: 1 hour   Makes: 16 servings   Oven: 350°

As if this favorite chocolate-and-cherry treat weren't already exquisite enough, we've made it even more so with two luscious frostings.

2¼ **cups all-purpose flour**
1 **teaspoon baking powder**
¾ **teaspoon baking soda**
¼ **teaspoon salt**
⅔ **cup butter**
1¾ **cups sugar**
2 **eggs**
3 **ounces unsweetened chocolate, melted and cooled**
1 **teaspoon vanilla**
1½ **recipes Chocolate Butter Frosting (see page 158)**
1 **recipe Tart Cherry Filling (see below)**
1 **recipe Sweetened Whipped Cream (see page 160)**

1 **Grease and lightly flour** three 8×1½-inch round baking pans (see tip, page 141); set aside. Stir together flour, baking powder, baking soda, and salt; set aside.

2 **In a large mixing bowl beat** butter on medium to high speed for 30 seconds. Add sugar; beat until well combined. Add eggs, 1 at a time, beating well after each. Beat in chocolate and vanilla. Add flour mixture and 1¼ cups water alternately to egg mixture, beating on low speed after each addition just until combined. Pour into prepared pans.

3 **Bake in a 350° oven** for 22 minutes or until a wooden toothpick inserted near centers of the cakes comes out clean. Cool the cakes in pans on wire racks for 10 minutes. Remove cakes from pans. Cool thoroughly on wire racks.

4 **To assemble,** place a cake layer on a large serving plate. Using about ⅔ cup of the Chocolate Butter Frosting, spread a ½-inch-wide and ¾-inch-high border around the top edge. Spread half of the Tart Cherry Filling in the center (about ¾ cup). Top with the second cake layer. Using ⅔ cup Chocolate Butter Frosting, repeat spreading a border on top edge of cake and spread remaining filling in center. Top with remaining cake layer. Frost sides with remaining butter frosting; frost top with the Sweetened Whipped Cream. Refrigerate up to 2 hours. Let stand at room temperature 30 minutes before serving.

Tart Cherry Filling: In a medium saucepan stir together ½ cup sugar and 2 tablespoons cornstarch. Stir in ¼ cup water. Add 2 cups fresh or frozen pitted tart red cherries. Cook and stir over medium heat until thickened and bubbly. Cook and stir for 2 minutes more. Remove from heat. Stir in 1 tablespoon cherry liqueur or cherry brandy. Cover surface with plastic wrap; cool. Makes about 1¾ cups.

Nutrition Facts per serving: 486 cal., 21 g total fat (12 g sat. fat), 78 mg chol., 249 mg sodium, 74 g carbo., 1 g fiber, 4 g pro. Daily Values: 21% vit. A, 3% vit. C, 6% calcium, 11% iron

DOUBLE CHOCOLATE-
ORANGE TORTE

Prep: 40 minutes **Bake:** 35 minutes
Cool: 1 hour **Makes:** 10 servings **Oven:** 350°

*For a nonalcoholic version, replace the liqueur
with orange juice.*

    3 squares (3 ounces) unsweetened
         chocolate, coarsely chopped
    ¾ cup all-purpose flour
    1½ teaspoons baking powder
    ½ teaspoon baking soda
    ½ teaspoon salt
    ½ cup butter
    1 cup sugar
    4 eggs
    2 tablespoons orange liqueur
    ½ cup water
    1 tablespoon finely shredded
         orange peel
    1 tablespoon orange liqueur
    1 tablespoon orange juice
    ½ cup orange marmalade
    1 recipe Bittersweet Chocolate Icing
         (see right)
         Chocolate curls (optional)
         (see tip, below)

1 **Grease and flour** an 8×8×2-inch baking pan; set
aside. In a heavy saucepan place chopped
unsweetened chocolate over low heat, stirring constantly, until chocolate just starts to melt. Remove
from heat. Stir until smooth; cool. Stir together the
flour, baking powder, baking soda, and salt; set aside.

2 **In a large mixing bowl beat** the butter with an
electric mixer on medium to high speed for
30 seconds. Add sugar; beat until well combined.
Add eggs, 1 at a time, beating well after each. Beat

in chocolate and the 2 tablespoons liqueur. Add
flour mixture and water alternately to egg mixture,
beating on low speed after each addition just until
combined. Stir in orange peel. Pour batter into the
prepared pan.

3 **Bake in a 350° oven** about 35 minutes or until
a wooden toothpick inserted near the center
comes out clean. Cool cake on a wire rack for
10 minutes. Loosen edges of cake with a spatula.
Invert onto wire rack. Remove the pan. Cool cake
thoroughly on wire rack.

4 **Combine the 1 tablespoon liqueur** and orange
juice. Split cake in half horizontally. Sprinkle each
cut side with half of the liqueur mixture. Place bottom half of cake, cut side up, on a platter; spread the
marmalade evenly on top. Top with remaining cake
layer, cut side down.

5 **Frost the cake** with Bittersweet Chocolate
Icing. (You can frost the cake several hours
before serving.) If desired, decorate the sides of the
frosted cake with chocolate curls pressed into icing.

Bittersweet Chocolate Icing: In a heavy small
saucepan combine ⅓ cup whipping cream and
1 tablespoon light-colored corn syrup. Bring just to
boiling, stirring constantly. Remove from heat. Stir
in 6 ounces semisweet chocolate, finely chopped, or
1 cup semisweet chocolate pieces, stirring until
chocolate is melted and mixture is smooth. Cool to
room temperature. Stir before using.

Nutrition Facts per serving: 429 cal., 24 g total fat
(13 g sat. fat), 121 mg chol., 350 mg sodium,
54 g carbo., 3 g fiber, 6 g pro. Daily Values:
16% vit. A, 4% vit. C, 7% calcium, 14% iron

Chocolate-Raspberry Torte: Prepare as above,
except substitute raspberry liqueur for the orange
liqueur and seedless raspberry preserves for the
orange marmalade.

CHOCOLATE CURLS

Chocolate curls—whether used as a smattering on top of a cream pie or as a border around a
cake—make exquisite dessert decorations. To make curls, carefully draw a vegetable peeler
across a bar of chocolate (milk chocolate works best). For narrow curls, use the short side of the bar;
for wide curls, use the broad surface. See page 15 for chocolate curl photos and more information.

Double Chocolate-Orange Torte: This incredibly rich, bittersweet torte is equally dazzling with orange or raspberry flavorings.

RASPBERRY TRUFFLE CAKE

Prep: 25 minutes **Bake:** 25 minutes
Cool: 2 hours **Chill:** 4 hours
Makes: 12 servings **Oven:** 350°

Don't worry if this nearly flourless cake seems soft after baking; it firms up when chilled.

16 ounces semisweet or bittersweet chocolate, cut up
½ cup butter
1 tablespoon sugar
1½ teaspoons all-purpose flour
1 teaspoon raspberry liqueur (optional)
4 eggs, separated
1 12-ounce jar seedless raspberry jam (1 cup)
Sweetened whipped cream (optional)
Fresh raspberries (optional)

1 **Grease an** 8-inch springform pan; set aside. In a large heavy saucepan, combine chocolate and butter. Cook and stir over low heat until chocolate melts. Remove from heat. Stir in sugar, flour, and, if desired, liqueur. Using a spoon, beat in egg yolks, 1 at a time, until combined. Set aside.

2 **In a medium mixing bowl beat** egg whites with an electric mixer on high speed until stiff peaks form. Fold into chocolate mixture. Pour batter into prepared pan.

3 **Bake in a 350° oven** 25 to 30 minutes or until edges puff. Cool in pan on a wire rack for 30 minutes. Remove sides of pan; cool thoroughly. Chill, covered, for 4 to 24 hours.

4 **To serve, allow cake** to come to room temperature (about 45 minutes). Heat jam just until melted. Drizzle jam on each dessert plate; top with cake slice. If desired, top with sweetened whipped cream and fresh raspberries.

Nutrition Facts per serving: 358 cal., 22 g total fat (10 g sat. fat), 81 mg chol., 95 mg sodium, 44 g carbo., 3 g fiber, 5 g pro. Daily Values: 10% vit. A, 0% vit. C, 2% calcium, 12% iron

Raspberry Truffle Cake: Nothing like a traditional, fine-textured crumb cake, this is a very rich, dense dessert—almost like a fudge brownie but much more elegant. It's also surprisingly easy to make.

IS IT DONE YET?

A cake baking in the oven can cause trepidation when it comes time to test its doneness. (Remember those warnings from your mother about not opening the oven door or jumping around the house too much when she had a cake in the oven lest it fall?) But now you can relax. The doneness tests for creamed and foam cakes (angel, sponge, and chiffon), though different, are easy:

- To test whether a foam cake is done, touch the top lightly. The cake is finished baking if the top springs back.
- To test a creamed cake for doneness, insert a wooden toothpick into the cake near the center. If it comes out clean, it's done. If it comes out wet, bake the cake a few minutes longer; test in another spot near the center.

LADY BALTIMORE CAKE

Prep: 45 minutes   Bake: 30 minutes
Cool: 1 hour   Makes: 12 servings   Oven: 350°

One of the South's most famous desserts, this candied-fruit-studded treat is truly a charmer.

    1 cup raisins
    8 dried figs, snipped (½ cup)
  ¼ cup brandy
2½ cups all-purpose flour
    2 cups sugar
    1 teaspoon baking powder
    1 teaspoon finely shredded
          orange peel
  ½ teaspoon baking soda
  ⅛ teaspoon salt
1⅓ cups buttermilk or sour milk
          (see tip, page 138)
  ½ cup shortening or butter, softened
    1 teaspoon vanilla
    4 egg whites
    1 cup toasted chopped pecans
          (see tip, page 247)
  ⅓ cup finely chopped candied red
          or green cherries
  ⅓ cup finely chopped candied
          pineapple or mixed candied
          fruits and peels
    1 recipe Seven-Minute Frosting
          (see page 159)

1 **In a medium bowl combine** raisins, figs, and brandy; let stand at room temperature 2 hours or until brandy is absorbed, stirring occasionally.

2 **Meanwhile, grease and flour** three 8×1½-inch round baking pans (see tip, page 141); set aside. Combine flour, sugar, baking powder, orange peel, baking soda, and salt. Add the buttermilk or sour milk, shortening or butter, and vanilla. Beat with an electric mixer on low speed for 30 seconds, scraping sides of bowl. Beat on medium to high speed for 2 minutes, scraping bowl often. Add egg whites; beat 2 minutes more, scraping bowl. Pour batter into prepared pans.

3 **Bake in a 350° oven** about 30 minutes or until a wooden toothpick inserted near center comes out clean. Cool in pans on wire racks for 10 minutes. Loosen from sides; remove from pans. Cool thoroughly on wire racks. (At this point, you may cover and freeze the cake for up to 6 months.)

4 **For filling,** stir pecans, fruits, and about one-third (1½ cups) of the Seven-Minute Frosting into the raisin mixture.

5 **To assemble,** place a cake layer on a platter; spread half of the filling on top. Add another cake layer and the remaining filling. Top with the remaining cake layer. Frost tops and sides with the remaining Seven-Minute Frosting.

Nutrition Facts per serving: 569 cal., 15 g total fat (3 g sat. fat), 1 mg chol., 165 mg sodium, 103 g carbo., 3 g fiber, 7 g pro. Daily Values: 0% vit. A, 1% vit. C, 7% calcium, 12% iron

ITALIAN CRÈME CAKE

Prep: 40 minutes **Bake:** 25 minutes
Cool: 1 hour **Makes:** 14 servings **Oven:** 350°

Cakes infused or showered with coconut are a southern Italian favorite.

1¾ cups all-purpose flour
1½ teaspoons baking powder
 ¼ teaspoon baking soda
 ½ cup butter
 ⅓ cup shortening
1¾ cups sugar
 4 egg yolks
 1 teaspoon vanilla
 ¾ cup buttermilk or sour milk
     (see tip, page 138)
 1 3½-ounce can flaked coconut
 1 cup chopped pecans
 4 egg whites
 1 recipe Pecan Frosting (see right)
     Pecan halves (optional)

1 Grease and flour three 8×1½-inch round baking pans (see tip, page 141); set aside. Combine flour, baking powder, and baking soda; set aside.

2 In a large mixing bowl beat butter and shortening with an electric mixer on medium to high speed for 30 seconds. Add sugar; beat until fluffy. Add egg yolks and vanilla; beat on medium speed until combined. Add flour mixture and buttermilk alternately to egg yolk mixture, beating on low speed after each addition just until combined. Fold in coconut and chopped pecans.

3 Thoroughly wash the beaters. In a small mixing bowl beat egg whites until stiff peaks form (tips stand straight). Fold about one-third of the egg whites into cake batter to lighten. Fold in remaining whites. Spread batter evenly into prepared pans.

4 Bake in a 350° oven for 25 to 30 minutes or until a wooden toothpick inserted near centers comes out clean. Cool in pans on wire racks 10 minutes; remove from pans. Cool thoroughly on racks.

5 When cool, spread the top of a cake layer with frosting. Top with another layer, frost, and top with the third layer. Frost top and sides of cake with remaining frosting. If desired, decorate cake with pecan halves. Chill cake until serving time. Store any leftover cake, covered, in the refrigerator up to 2 days.

Pecan Frosting: In a bowl beat 12 ounces cream cheese, softened; 6 tablespoons butter, softened; and 1½ teaspoons vanilla until smooth. Gradually add 6 cups sifted powdered sugar, beating until smooth. Stir in ½ cup chopped pecans. Makes 4 cups.

Nutrition Facts per serving: 682 cal., 37 g total fat (17 g sat. fat), 119 mg chol., 284 mg sodium, 86 g carbo., 2 g fiber, 7 g pro. Daily Values: 30% vit. A, 0% vit. C, 7% calcium, 11% iron

MINIATURE AMARETTO CAKES

Prep: 45 minutes **Bake:** 20 minutes
Cool: 1 hour **Makes:** 24 servings **Oven:** 325°

 ¾ cup butter
 3 eggs
1½ cups all-purpose flour
 1 teaspoon baking powder
 ¼ teaspoon ground nutmeg
 ¾ cup granulated sugar
 ¼ cup amaretto
 1 teaspoon finely shredded lemon
     peel
 ½ teaspoon vanilla
 ⅓ cup granulated sugar
 ¼ cup water
 2 tablespoons brown sugar
 2 tablespoons light-colored corn
     syrup
 ½ cup amaretto

1 Allow butter and eggs to stand at room temperature 30 minutes. Generously grease and flour six 4-inch fluted tube pans or one 6-cup fluted tube pan. Combine flour, baking powder, and nutmeg; set aside.

2 In a large mixing bowl beat butter with electric mixer on medium speed for 30 seconds. Beat on medium-high speed, adding the ¾ cup granulated sugar, 2 tablespoons at a time, about 6 minutes or until mixture is very light and fluffy.

3 Stir in the ¼ cup amaretto, lemon peel, and vanilla. Add eggs, 1 at a time, beating for 1 minute after each addition and scraping bowl often. Gradually add flour mixture to egg mixture, beating on medium-low speed just until combined. Pour into prepared pans.

Miniature Amaretto Cakes: When holiday gift-giving season rolls around, remember these amaretto-soaked cakes. They make luscious gifts, and the recipients can enjoy them for weeks to come.

4 **Bake in a 325° oven** for 20 to 25 minutes for the 4-inch pans (40 to 45 minutes for the 6-cup fluted pan) or until a wooden toothpick inserted near the center(s) comes out clean. Cool in pans on wire racks for 10 minutes. Remove from pans. Cool thoroughly on rack(s). Prick fluted top and sides of each cake generously with tines of a fork.

5 **For syrup,** in a medium saucepan combine the ⅓ cup granulated sugar, the water, brown sugar, and corn syrup. Cook and stir over medium heat until bubbly and most of the sugar is dissolved; remove from heat. Stir in ½ cup amaretto. Cool for 5 minutes.

6 **Dip fluted top and sides** of each cooled 4-inch cake into syrup. Place cakes on wire racks above a large tray or baking sheet. Spoon or brush any remaining syrup over tops of cakes. (If using 6-cup

pan, do not dip cake into syrup. Place cake on wire rack over tray or baking sheet; spoon or brush syrup over top and sides of cake, reusing syrup on tray.) Cool cake(s).

7 **Wrap cakes individually** in plastic wrap or cellophane; chill, fluted side up, for up to 3 weeks. (Or, transfer to a tightly covered container and chill for up to 3 weeks.)

Nutrition Facts per serving: 157 cal., 7 g total fat (2 g sat. fat), 34 mg chol., 78 mg sodium, 20 g carbo., 0 g fiber, 2 g pro. Daily Values: 6% vit. A, 0% vit. C, 1% calcium, 3% iron

LET THEM CUT CAKE

Once it is frosted and decorated, your cake becomes a feast for the eyes. But the best is yet to come: sharing your masterpiece with your guests. To do so as neatly as possible, let the frosted cake stand for at least 1 hour before cutting it (unless otherwise specified). When cutting a cake with a fluffy icing, a creamed cake, or a cheesecake, it will be considerably easier if you dip the knife in hot water and shake it to remove excess water (don't dry it completely) between cuts.

TRIPLE-LAYER LEMON CAKE

BEST-LOVED

Prep: 35 minutes **Bake:** 25 minutes
Cool: 1 hour **Makes:** 12 servings **Oven:** 350°

Tart lemon curd fills this showy cake. Make your own or look for it with jams at the supermarket (see photo, page 111).

2⅓ cups all-purpose flour
1½ teaspoons baking powder
½ teaspoon baking soda
¼ teaspoon salt
1 cup butter
2 cups sugar
2 teaspoons finely shredded lemon peel
2 tablespoons lemon juice
4 eggs
1 cup buttermilk or sour milk (see tip, page 138)
1 recipe Lemon Curd (see recipe, page 159) or 1 cup purchased lemon curd
1 recipe Lemon Cream Cheese Frosting (see right)
Lemon peel curls (optional)

1 **Grease and lightly flour** three 9×1½-inch round baking pans (see tip, page 141). Combine flour, baking powder, soda, and salt. Set aside.

2 **In a large mixing bowl beat** butter with an electric mixer on medium to high speed for 30 seconds. Add sugar, lemon peel, and lemon juice; beat until well combined. Add eggs, 1 at a time, beating well after each. Add flour mixture and buttermilk or sour milk alternately to beaten mixture,

beating on low speed after each addition just until combined. Pour into prepared pans.

3 **Bake in a 350° oven** for 25 to 30 minutes or until a wooden toothpick inserted near the center of each cake layer comes out clean. Cool cakes in pans on wire racks for 10 minutes. Remove cakes from pans. Cool thoroughly on wire racks.

4 **To assemble,** place a cake layer on a cake plate. Spread with half of the Lemon Curd. Top with second layer; spread with the remaining Lemon Curd. Top with third layer. Frost top and sides with Lemon Cream Cheese Frosting. (If desired, pipe frosting on sides of cake as shown in photo on page 111 using a decorating bag fitted with a star tip). Cover and store cake in the refrigerator for up to 3 days. Let stand at room temperature for 30 minutes before serving. If desired, garnish with lemon peel curls.

Lemon Cream Cheese Frosting: Finely shred 1 teaspoon lemon peel; set aside. In a medium mixing bowl combine two 3-ounce packages cream cheese, softened; ½ cup butter, softened; and 1 teaspoon lemon juice; beat with electric mixer on low to medium speed until light and fluffy. Gradually add 2 cups sifted powdered sugar, beating well. Gradually beat in 2½ to 2¾ cups additional powdered sugar to make frosting that is easy to spread. Stir in the lemon peel.

Nutrition Facts per serving: 721 cal., 36 g total fat (11 g sat. fat), 158 mg chol., 484 mg sodium, 96 g carbo., 1 g fiber, 7 g pro. Daily Values: 37% vit. A, 8% vit. C, 8% calcium, 11% iron

Wedding Cake: What a grand gift for the bride and groom—a home-baked wedding cake made for their special day (see recipe, page 152).

WEDDING CAKE

Prep: 8 hours **Bake:** 35 minutes per batch
Cool: 1 hour per batch **Makes:** 45 servings
Oven: 350° or 375°

*Tall and traditional, this beauty befits that
happiest of occasions (see photo, page 151).*

  **4 recipes White Cake (see page 113),
       Classic Chocolate Cake
       (see page 114), or Citrus Yellow
       Cake (see page 113)
  4 recipes Raspberry Filling*
       (see page 159) or 3 recipes
       Lemon Curd (see page 159)
  5 recipes Butter Frosting
       (see page 158)**

Using a metal spatula, quickly spread thick layer of Butter Frosting (at least ¼ inch thick) over entire cake tier. Use short, slightly curved strokes to spread the frosting.

To insert dowels, place a dowel about 2 inches from edge of cake; gently push it into cake until flush with cake top. Repeat with other dowels, spacing evenly apart.

Holding tip at 45-degree angle almost touching cake, squeeze gently to make leaf base. Continue squeezing but ease up on pressure as you pull tip away. Stop pressure; lift off.

Equipment for making cake:
   **Round wedding cake pans
      (6×2-, 8×2-, and 10×2-inch)
   Cardboard cake circles covered
      with foil (6-, 8-, and 10-inch)
   Long serrated knife
   Wooden dowel (¼-inch diameter)
   Small saw (to cut dowel)
   Metal spatula**
Equipment for assembling cake:
   **Large round cake plate
      (12- to 16-inch diameter)
   Decorating bag, coupler, medium
      leaf tip, and medium round tip
   Assorted fresh edible flowers and
      greenery (such as roses, tulips,
      carnations, and grape ivy)
      (see tip, page 175)
   Ribbon
   Scissors
   Metal spatula**

1 To make cake, grease and flour cake pans. Line bottoms with parchment or waxed paper; grease paper. Prepare 1 recipe cake batter; spoon into a prepared 10-inch pan, filling pan half full. Bake in a 350° or 375° oven (as specified in cake recipe) for 35 to 45 minutes or until a wooden toothpick inserted near center comes out clean. Cool cake in pan on wire rack for 10 minutes. Remove cake from pan; remove paper. Cool, right side up, on wire rack. Repeat to make 2 cake layers of each pan size. (Each recipe of cake batter makes one 10-inch cake layer or one 6-inch and one 8-inch cake layer.) Using a long serrated knife, trim off rounded tops of cooled cakes. Prepare desired filling; chill.

2 To make cake tiers, place a 6-inch cake layer, right side up, on the foil-covered 6-inch cake circle. Place cake and cake circle on a piece of waxed paper. Spread ⅓ cup filling over top of cake. Place remaining 6-inch cake, top side down, on filling. Repeat with 8- and 10-inch cake layers to make 3 tiers total, using ½ cup filling between 8-inch cake layers and ¾ cup filling between 10-inch cake layers.

3 To frost cake tiers, prepare Butter Frosting as directed, adding just enough milk to make of spreading consistency. (The frosting should be creamy enough to spread easily but firm enough to stay in place on sides of cakes.) (You can make a

NOW OR LATER? STORING AND FREEZING CAKES

How far in advance can you make a cake? Once made, should the cake be stored in the refrigerator? Can it be frozen? The answers depend on the cake. Here are some guidelines.

- Cakes filled or frosted with whipped cream should be assembled no more than 2 hours before serving to prevent them from getting soggy.
- If your cake filling or frosting contains whipped cream, cream cheese, yogurt, or eggs, store it in the refrigerator. If you don't have a cake cover, invert a bowl over the cake.

- To freeze an unfrosted layer cake, place the cooled cake on a baking sheet and freeze just until firm. Wrap and seal the frozen cake in freezer wrap or seal it in a freezer bag or airtight freezer container and freeze for up to 4 months.
- Angel food, sponge, and chiffon cakes are best frozen unfrosted. Place them in a large freezer bag and freeze for up to 3 months. Don't store them any longer than that or the delicate sponge texture may deteriorate. Thaw at room temperature for several hours before serving.

double recipe at a time. Avoid beating too much air into frosting.) Place 3 cups of the frosting in a bowl; stir in enough milk (about 1 tablespoon) to thin slightly. Using a metal spatula, spread some of the thinned frosting on the side of each cake tier for a crumb coating.** Let stand at least 15 minutes or until surface is firm to touch. Frost 1 cake tier (see top photo, page 152). Clean spatula; quickly smooth side and top of freshly frosted cake tier, using spatula to remove any excess frosting so surface is smooth and flat. Repeat with other 2 cake tiers. Let frosted cake tiers dry for 1 hour. Measure height of 10-inch tier; using a small saw, cut 4 dowels this height, making sure all 4 dowels are exactly the same length. Repeat for the 8-inch tier. Insert the dowels into the cakes to provide support (see middle photo, page 152). At this point, you can loosely cover cakes and tightly cover remaining frosting and refrigerate for up to 1 day. (The cake should not be moved after decorating, so assemble and decorate it at the site of the wedding reception.)

4 **To assemble cake,** transfer 10-inch cake tier to cake plate. Place on table where cake will be displayed. Place 8-inch cake tier on top of 10-inch tier, centering on bottom cake and resting the cake circle on the dowels of bottom cake. Repeat to position 6-inch tier on 8-inch tier.

5 **Fit decorating bag** with coupler and leaf tip. Fill bag with frosting. Pipe a row of leaves around bottom edge of each cake tier (see bottom photo, page 152). Replace leaf tip with round tip. Pipe a vine design randomly on sides of cake tiers. Using leaf tip, pipe a few leaves on vine design. For cake top, gather a few of the fresh flowers together with ribbon. Tie ribbon into bow; trim ends of flower stems. Place flowers on top of cake. Cut remaining flowers and greenery to desired lengths; arrange on edges of cake and on cake plate. (Flowers will stay fresh-looking for 2 to 3 hours in a cool room.) Remove the flowers and wooden dowels as needed when cutting cake tiers.

*Note: If using raspberry filling, chill several hours or overnight for maximum stiffness.

**Note: The crumb coating prevents loose crumbs from getting into the final layer of frosting. For the crumb coating, spread a thin layer of frosting on cake, allowing cake to show through frosting and making sure sides of cakes are straight. Be careful not to get crumbs into frosting in bowl.

Nutrition Facts per serving: 582 cal., 17 g total fat (7 g sat. fat), 20 mg chol., 236 mg sodium, 107 g carbo., 2 g fiber, 5 g pro. Daily Values: 7% vit. A, 7% vit. C, 6% calcium, 8% iron

CASTLE **CAKE**

Prep: 2 hours   **Bake:** 30 minutes per batch (cakes)
Cool: 1 hour   **Makes:** 28 servings   **Oven:** 350°

2 **recipes White Cake (see page 113)***
2 **recipes Creamy White Frosting**
   (see page 160)
   Paste food coloring (purple, green,
   orange, and yellow)

Fruit-flavored candy corn
2 **white chocolate candy bars**
   Small gumdrops
5 **to 8 pointed ice-cream cones**
   (sugar cones)
   Pull-apart string licorice
Equipment:
   2 **8×8×2-inch baking pans**
   2 **6×1½-inch round baking pans**
   Muffin pan with 2½-inch cups

Castle Cake: Serve this fanciful fortress at your next children's birthday party. The excited smiles from all the little princes and princesses will make your effort worthwhile.

Foil bake cups
Large cutting board (about 16
    inches square) or piece of heavy
    cardboard covered with foil
4 decorating bags, couplers, and tips
Foil and blue plastic wrap
    (optional for moat)
8 plastic drinking straws
1 6-inch cardboard cake circle
    Ribbon, toothpicks, and clear tape
    (for flags)

1 Grease and flour baking pans; line muffin cups with bake cups. Prepare 1 recipe cake batter; divide evenly between prepared square pans. Bake in 350° oven about 30 minutes or until wooden toothpick inserted near centers comes out clean. Prepare second recipe cake batter; fill prepared round pans and muffin cups half full. (You need 5 cupcakes for the castle cake. You will have enough batter to make a few extra cupcakes.) Bake in the 350° oven about 20 minutes for cupcakes and about 30 minutes for round cakes or until wooden toothpick comes out clean. Cool in pans on wire racks 10 minutes; remove from pans. Cool cakes and cupcakes.

2 Prepare Creamy White Frosting as directed. Tint about 4 cups frosting purple, ½ cup frosting green, ½ cup frosting orange, and ½ cup frosting yellow. (You should have about 1 cup white frosting remaining.) For square cake, spread about ½ cup white frosting on top of 1 square layer; top with other square layer. For round cake, spread remaining white frosting on 1 round layer; top with remaining round layer. Place about 1 cup of the purple frosting in a decorating bag that has been fitted with coupler; set aside. Place each of the other colored frostings in decorating bag fitted with a coupler.

3 To assemble, place square cake on the cutting board. If desired, make a moat around cake with foil and plastic wrap.** Place round cake on cardboard cake circle. Cut 8 drinking straws to same height as square cake. Insert 4 of the straws near middle of square cake (see photo, above). Insert the remaining 4 straws on the outside corners of the square cake. (Straws add support for top of cake and cupcakes.) Place round cake on top of square cake, centering on bottom cake and resting cake circle on straws. Frost both round and square cakes by spreading with remaining purple frosting.

Turn cakes, cones, and candy into a colorful castle cake that is sure to enchant any youngster.

4 To decorate, fit decorating bag filled with purple frosting with medium star tip; pipe swirls around edge of 5 cupcakes, top edge of round cake, and top edge of square cake. Gently press candy corn, points up, into frosting swirls on round and square cakes, leaving space on corners of square cake for cupcakes to stand. Using more purple frosting, attach pieces of white candy bar to castle for door and windows. Pipe another row of frosting around base of square cake; press gumdrops into frosting.

5 To finish cupcakes, press an ice-cream cone, point up, into the frosting piped on each cupcake. Fit decorating bags filled with green, orange, and yellow frosting with small round or star tips; pipe windows and other designs onto cones. Use ribbon, toothpicks, and tape to make flags. Attach flags to points of cones using a little frosting. Place 4 cupcakes on corners of square cake and 1 cupcake on top of round cake. (If desired, decorate any remaining cupcakes for additional servings.)

6 If desired, make trees by decorating additional cones; arrange around castle. For drawbridge, position large piece of white candy bar over moat; arrange gumdrops around moat. Attach string licorice to drawbridge with some piped frosting. To serve, remove straws as needed when cutting cake.

*Note: Cakes can be prepared in advance and frozen (see tip, page 153). The frosting can be made in advance and refrigerated up to 3 days. Bring to room temperature before using.

**Note: To make moat, place 2-inch-wide strips of foil around square cake, tucking 1 edge of foil under cake edge; place strips of blue plastic wrap over foil.

Nutrition Facts per serving: 557 cal., 24 g total fat (7 g sat. fat), 63 mg chol., 149 mg sodium, 82 g carbo., 0 g fiber, 5 g pro. Daily Values: 3% vit. A, 0% vit. C, 5% calcium, 7% iron

Ark Cake:
Anchors Aweigh! This whimsical cake requires no special equipment or decorative piping.

ARK CAKE

Prep: 2 hours **Bake:** 37 minutes **Cool:** 1 hour
Stand: 2 hours **Makes:** 16 servings **Oven:** 350°

1 recipe Classic Chocolate Cake
   (see page 114)
½ recipe Sugar Cookie Cutouts
   (see page 201)
   Assorted cookie cutters
   (animals and man)
1 6-ounce package white baking bar,
   cut up
2 tablespoons shortening
   Decorative candies and sprinkles
   About 20 pretzel rods
   Blue plastic wrap or cellophane
   (optional)
1 recipe Chocolate Butter Frosting
   (see page 158)
½ recipe Creamy White Frosting
   (see page 160)
   Blue paste food coloring
4 to 6 whole graham cracker
   rectangles

1 **Prepare and bake cake** as directed in a greased and floured 13×9×2-inch baking pan. Cool in pan 10 minutes. Remove from pan; cool on wire rack.

2 **For animal cookies,** prepare cookie dough and roll out as directed. Cut out several pairs of animals and 1 Noah. If desired, cut out a dove, using a paper pattern and knife. Bake as directed; cool on wire racks. In medium skillet melt white baking bar and shortening over low heat. Remove from heat. Holding a cookie over the skillet, carefully spoon and spread melted baking bar mixture over cookie in a thin, even layer. Place on waxed paper. Sprinkle cookie with candies and sprinkles. Repeat with remaining cookies.* Let stand until coating sets up.

3 **To make walls** for cabin of the ark, cut eight 4-inch lengths of pretzel and eight 2½-inch lengths of pretzel. Roll cut pretzels in melted baking bar mixture; place on waxed paper.* For each wall, lay 4 pretzels of the same length side by side (form 2 long walls and 2 short walls). Let walls stand until coating sets up.

4 **If desired,** cover serving platter with blue plastic wrap or cellophane, crinkling it to resemble water; set aside. Using a long serrated knife, cut the cake in half crosswise. Stack cake pieces; working from top to bottom, cut wedge shape from each short end of stacked cake, creating an ark-shaped cake. Place bottom cake piece on serving platter;

spread with about ½ cup of the Chocolate Butter Frosting. Top with other cake piece. Frost with remaining Chocolate Butter Frosting. Arrange uncut pretzel logs around top edge of ark, cutting to fit and leaving space for boarding ramp on front side. Let stand about 2 hours or until frosting is set. Set aside ½ cup Creamy White Frosting. Tint remaining white frosting blue. Using a small metal spatula or table knife, carefully swirl waves of blue frosting onto bottom edge of frosted cake.

5 **For cabin,** carefully arrange the cabin walls on top of cake in shape of a box. Spread some of the reserved Creamy White Frosting on inside corners of box to hold cabin together. For roof supports, cut two 3-inch lengths of pretzel. Place the roof supports straight up on the inside of cabin so each touches the center of a short wall; secure with some white frosting. For cabin roof, spread some frosting along 1 long edge of each of 2 graham crackers; position on top of cabin, pressing frosting-covered

edges onto top of long cabin walls and leaning crackers together so that they meet at roof peak and rest on roof supports. Use some frosting to secure crackers at roof peak, if needed. For ramp, lay 3 additional pretzels at angle against front of cake.

6 **To make animals stand up,** cut remaining graham crackers into small triangles. Using dabs of frosting, secure 1 or 2 small triangles to the back of each animal and Noah. Arrange animals around ark and Noah and dove on ark. To serve, cut cake into small pieces and serve with cookies.

*Note: If coating thickens while working, reheat, stirring constantly, just until smooth.

Nutrition Facts per serving: 729 cal., 32 g total fat (15 g sat. fat), 73 mg chol., 463 mg sodium, 107 g carbo., 1 g fiber, 7 g pro. Daily Values: 14% vit. A, 0% vit. C, 8% calcium, 17% iron

THE ICING ON THE CAKE

Decorating a cake can be as simple as swirling creamy frosting over its layers. For best results, take these steps to make your finished product a work of art:

- Get rid of loose crumbs. Brushing the layers with a pastry brush or your hand works great.
- To keep the serving plate clean, tuck strips of waxed paper under the edge of the cake before you frost it. Spread about ½ cup frosting on the top of the first cake layer.
- Place the second cake layer, top side up, on top of the frosted layer. Spread a thin coating of frosting on the sides of the cake to seal in any crumbs. Let stand 15 minutes.
- Add a thicker coating of frosting to the sides of the cake. Then frost the sides again, swirling and building up the top edge of the frosting about ¼ inch above the cake.
- Spread the remaining frosting on top of the cake, blending it with the frosting at the edge. Remove the strips of waxed paper once you've finished.
- Let the cake stand—if time allows—for about an hour before you slice it to let the frosting set up.

To help frosting spread more smoothly, get rid of loose crumbs with a pastry brush.

Spreading a thin coating of frosting on the sides helps seal in any crumbs, allowing for a smoother overall look.

Use smooth, up-and-down strokes to decoratively swirl the frosting.

BUTTER FROSTING

Start to finish: 15 minutes   Frosts: tops and sides of two 8- or 9-inch cake layers, top of one 13x9-inch cake, or 24 cupcakes

One creamy, sweet master recipe provides the base for seven festive frosting variations.

⅓ **cup butter**
4½ **cups sifted powdered sugar**
¼ **cup milk**
1½ **teaspoons vanilla**
   Additional milk
   Food coloring (optional)

1 **In a large mixing bowl beat** butter until fluffy. Gradually add 2 cups of the powdered sugar, beating well. Slowly beat in ¼ cup milk and vanilla.

2 **Gradually add remaining** powdered sugar, beating until combined. If necessary, beat in a little additional milk to make frosting that is easy to spread. Tint with food coloring as desired, or use as a base for any of the variations below. Transfer unused frosting to a storage container and chill for up to 1 week.

Nutrition Facts per serving (1/12 of a recipe): 97 cal., 3 g total fat (2 g sat. fat), 7 mg chol., 27 mg sodium, 19 g carbo., 0 g fiber, 0 g pro. Daily Values: 2% vit. A, 0% vit. C, 0% calcium, 0% iron

Peanut Butter Crunch
Substitute creamy peanut butter for the butter. Sprinkle chopped candy-coated peanut butter pieces or chopped peanuts over frosting.

Mocha Cocoa
Reduce powdered sugar to 4 cups and add ½ cup unsweetened cocoa powder along with the first 2 cups powdered sugar. Add 1 tablespoon instant coffee crystals to the ¼ cup milk. Let stand 3 minutes; stir until dissolved.

Maraschino Cherry
Substitute 3 tablespoons maraschino cherry juice for the milk; add ⅓ cup chopped maraschino cherries with the cherry juice.

Vanilla Polka Dot
Stir 2 to 3 tablespoons candy sprinkles in the Butter Frosting before using. (Pictured in center.)

Mini Mint Chip
Add ¼ teaspoon mint extract and a few drops green food coloring with the milk. Stir in ⅓ cup miniature semisweet chocolate pieces before using.

Double Orange
Substitute fresh orange juice for the milk; add 1 teaspoon finely shredded orange peel after all the powdered sugar is added. If desired, top with thin strips of orange peel.

Chocolate Butter Frosting Reduce powdered sugar to 4 cups and add ½ cup unsweetened cocoa powder along with the first 2 cups powdered sugar. If desired, top with chocolate curls.

LEMON CURD

Prep: 5 minutes   **Cook:** 8 minutes
Cool: 45 minutes   **Makes:** about 1 cup

Translucent, tart, and tangy, this makes a great filling for almost any cake.

  ⅓ **cup sugar**
  2 **teaspoons cornstarch**
  2 **teaspoons finely shredded lemon**
    peel
  ¼ **cup lemon juice**
  ¼ **cup butter**
  2 **beaten eggs**

1 In saucepan combine sugar and cornstarch. Stir in peel and juice. Add butter. Cook and stir until thickened and bubbly. Stir half lemon mixture into eggs. Pour egg mixture into the pan. Cook and stir 2 minutes more. Cover with waxed paper; cool.

Nutrition Facts per serving (1/12 of a recipe): 53 cal., 3 g total fat (3 g sat. fat), 42 mg chol., 41 mg sodium, 5 g carbo., 0 g fiber, 1 g pro. Daily Values: 4% vit. A, 3% vit. C, 0% calcium, 0% iron

RASPBERRY FILLING

Prep: 10 minutes   **Cool:** 30 minutes
Chill: 2 hours   **Makes:** ⅔ cup

Use this to add a lovely red ribbon between white cake layers.

  1 **10-ounce package frozen**
    raspberries in syrup, thawed
  4 **teaspoons cornstarch**

1 In small saucepan combine berries and syrup with cornstarch. Cook and stir until thickened and bubbly. Reduce heat; cook and stir 2 minutes more. Remove from heat. Immediately press through sieve; discard seeds. Transfer to bowl. Cover surface of filling with plastic wrap. Cool without stirring. Chill at least 2 hours; for maximum stiffness, chill overnight.

Nutrition Facts per serving (1/12 of a recipe): 33 cal., 0 g total fat, 0 mg chol., 0 mg sodium, 8 g carbo., 1 g fiber, 0 g pro. Daily Values: 0% vit. A, 7% vit. C, 0% calcium, 1% iron

POWDERED SUGAR ICING

Start to finish: 5 minutes   **Makes:** ½ cup (enough to drizzle over 10-inch tube cake)

This simple drizzle adds dazzle to angel, sponge, and chiffon cakes.

  1 **cup sifted powdered sugar**
  ¼ **teaspoon vanilla**
  1 **tablespoon milk or orange juice**

1 Combine powdered sugar, vanilla, and milk or juice. Stir in additional milk or juice, 1 teaspoon at a time, until icing is easy to drizzle.

Nutrition Facts per serving (1/12 of a recipe): 33 cal., 0 g total fat, 0 mg chol., 1 mg sodium, 8 g carbo., 0 g fiber, 0 g pro.

Chocolate Powdered Sugar Icing: Prepare as above, except add 2 tablespoons unsweetened cocoa powder to powdered sugar. Do not use orange juice.

SEVEN-MINUTE FROSTING

Start to finish: 25 minutes   **Frosts:** tops and sides of two 8- or 9-inch layers or one 10-inch tube cake

Beat well for a fluffy, marshmallowlike topper.

  1½ **cups sugar**
  2 **egg whites**
  ¼ **teaspoon cream of tartar or**
    2 **teaspoons light-colored corn**
    syrup
  1 **teaspoon vanilla**

1 In top of double boiler combine sugar, ⅓ cup cold water, egg whites, and cream of tartar or syrup. Beat with portable electric mixer on low speed for 30 seconds. Place over boiling water (upper pan should not touch water). Cook, beating constantly with mixer on high speed, about 7 minutes or until stiff peaks form. Remove from heat; add vanilla. Beat 2 to 3 minutes more or until easy to spread.

Nutrition Facts per serving (1/12 of a recipe) 100 cal., 0 g total fat, 0 mg chol., 10 mg sodium, 25 g carbo., 0 g fiber, 1 g pro.

CREAMY WHITE FROSTING

Start to finish: 25 minutes   Frosts: tops and sides of two 8- or 9-inch cake layers

  1 cup shortening
1½ teaspoons vanilla
  ½ teaspoon lemon extract, orange
       extract, or almond extract
4½ cups sifted powdered sugar
  3 to 4 tablespoons milk

1 Beat shortening, vanilla, and extract with an electric mixer on medium speed for 30 seconds. Slowly add half of the sugar, beating well. Add 2 tablespoons of the milk. Gradually beat in remaining sugar and enough milk to make frosting that is easy to spread.

Nutrition Facts per serving (1/12 of a recipe): 300 cal., 17 g total fat (4 g sat. fat), 0 mg chol., 2 mg sodium, 38 g carbo., 0 g fiber, 0 g pro.

CREAM CHEESE FROSTING

Start to finish: 20 minutes   Frosts: tops and sides of two 8- or 9-inch cake layers

  2 3-ounce packages cream cheese,
       softened
  ½ cup butter, softened
  2 teaspoons vanilla
4½ to 4¾ cups sifted powdered sugar

1 Beat cream cheese, butter, and vanilla with an electric mixer until light and fluffy. Gradually add 2 cups sifted powdered sugar, beating well. Gradually beat in enough of the remaining sifted powdered sugar to make frosting that is easy to spread. (Cover and store cake in refrigerator.)

Nutrition Facts per serving (1/12 of a recipe): 263 cal., 13 g total fat (8 g sat. fat), 36 mg chol., 120 mg sodium, 38 g carbo., 0 g fiber, 1 g pro. Daily Values: 13% vit. A, 0% vit. C, 1% calcium, 1% iron

Orange Cream Cheese Frosting: Prepare as above, except omit vanilla; beat in 1 tablespoon apricot brandy or orange juice with the cream cheese mixture. After frosting is of spreading consistency, stir in ½ teaspoon finely shredded orange peel.

SWEETENED WHIPPED CREAM

Start to finish: 10 minutes   Makes: 2 cups

As a frosting or topping, this provides a smooth, rich contrast to lighter cakes, such as angel, chiffon, and sponge cakes.

1 cup whipping cream
1 to 2 tablespoons sugar
1 teaspoon vanilla (optional)

1 In a small chilled mixing bowl combine whipping cream, sugar, and vanilla. Beat with chilled beaters of an electric mixer on medium speed until soft peaks form. Do not overbeat.

Nutrition Facts per tablespoon: 28 cal., 3 g total fat (2 g sat. fat), 10 mg chol., 3 mg sodium, 1 g carbo., 0 g fiber, 0 g pro. Daily Values: 3% vit. A, 0% vit. C, 0% calcium, 0% iron

Tangerine Whipped Cream Frosting: Prepare as above, except increase whipping cream to 2 cups and sugar to 2 tablespoons. Omit vanilla and add ¾ teaspoon finely shredded tangerine or orange peel with sugar. Use frosting immediately.

BROWNED BUTTER FROSTING

Start to finish: 20 minutes   Frosts: tops and sides of two 8- or 9-inch cake layers

½ cup butter
4 cups sifted powdered sugar
2 tablespoons milk
1 teaspoon vanilla

1 In a small saucepan heat butter over low heat until melted. Continue heating until butter turns a delicate brown. Remove from heat; pour into small bowl. Add powdered sugar, milk, and vanilla. Beat with an electric mixer on low speed until combined. Beat on medium to high speed, adding more milk, if necessary, to make frosting that is easy to spread.

Nutrition Facts per serving (1/12 of a recipe): 197 cal., 8 g total fat (5 g sat. fat), 21 mg chol., 79 mg sodium, 34 g carbo., 0 g fiber, 0 g pro. Daily Values: 9% vit. A, 0% vit. C, 0% calcium, 0% iron

PENUCHE **FROSTING**

Start to finish: 15 minutes   Frosts: top of one 13×9-inch cake

This caramel-flavored frosting works well for a 13×9-inch cake because it sets up so quickly.

½ **cup butter**
1 **cup packed brown sugar**
¼ **cup milk**
3½ **cups sifted powdered sugar**

1 In a medium saucepan melt butter; stir in brown sugar. Cook and stir until bubbly. Remove from heat. Add milk; beat vigorously with a wooden spoon until smooth. Add sifted powdered sugar; beat by hand until frosting is easy to spread. Use frosting immediately.

Nutrition Facts per serving (1⁄12 of a recipe): 251 cal., 8 g total fat (5 g sat. fat), 21 mg chol., 87 mg sodium, 47 g carbo., 0 g fiber, 0 g pro. Daily Values: 7% vit. A, 0% vit. C, 2% calcium, 2% iron

BUTTERCREAM

Prep: 30 minutes   Cool: 30 minutes   Frosts: tops and sides of two 8- or 9-inch cake layers

Just as you might expect, this pastry-shop favorite is lusciously buttery and creamy— perfect for frosting and decorating cakes.

⅔ **cup sugar**
¼ **cup water***
4 **slightly beaten egg yolks**
1 **teaspoon vanilla**
1 **cup unsalted butter, softened**

1 In a heavy medium saucepan combine sugar and water. Bring to boiling; remove from heat. Gradually stir about half of the sugar mixture into the egg yolks. Return all of egg yolk mixture to saucepan. Bring to a gentle boil; reduce heat. Cook and stir for 2 minutes. Remove from heat. Stir in vanilla. Cool to room temperature. In a large mixing bowl beat butter with an electric mixer on high speed until fluffy. Add cooled sugar mixture, beating until combined. If necessary, chill until easy to spread.

***Note:** If desired, flavor Buttercream with 1 tablespoon liqueur, decreasing water to 3 tablespoons. Stir in liqueur with vanilla.

Nutrition Facts per serving (1⁄12 of a recipe): 200 cal., 17 g total fat (10 g sat. fat), 113 mg chol., 5 mg sodium, 12 g carbo., 0 g fiber, 1 g pro. Daily Values: 25% vit. A, 0% vit. C, 1% calcium, 1% iron

WHITE CHOCOLATE **BUTTERCREAM**

Prep: 30 minutes   Cool: 30 minutes   Frosts: tops and sides of two 8- or 9-inch cake layers

½ **cup sugar**
2 **tablespoons all-purpose flour**
6 **egg yolks**
1½ **cups milk**
1 **6-ounce package white baking bar, chopped**
1½ **teaspoons vanilla**
½ **teaspoon almond extract**
1 **cup butter, softened**

1 In a medium mixing bowl combine sugar and flour; add the egg yolks. Beat mixture with a wire whisk until combined; set aside. In a heavy medium saucepan heat milk over medium heat just to boiling. Remove from heat. Gradually beat hot milk into egg mixture with the wire whisk; return entire mixture to saucepan. Cook over medium heat until bubbly, whisking constantly. Cook for 2 minutes more. Remove from heat. Add white baking bar, vanilla, and almond extract. Let stand 1 minute; stir until smooth.

2 Transfer mixture to a bowl. Cover surface with plastic wrap to prevent skin from forming; cool to room temperature. In a medium mixing bowl beat butter on medium to high speed until fluffy. Add cooled baking bar mixture, one-fourth at a time, beating on low speed after each addition until combined.

Nutrition Facts per serving (1⁄12 of a recipe): 298 cal., 23 g total fat (14 g sat. fat), 155 mg chol., 189 mg sodium, 19 g carbo., 0 g fiber, 4 g pro. Daily Values: 32% vit. A, 0% vit. C, 5% calcium, 2% iron

NO-COOK FUDGE FROSTING

Start to finish: 30 minutes   **Frosts:** tops and sides of two 8- or 9-inch cake layers

4¾ cups sifted powdered sugar
½ cup unsweetened cocoa powder
½ cup butter softened
⅓ cup boiling water
1 teaspoon vanilla

1 **Combine powdered sugar** and cocoa powder. Add butter, boiling water, and vanilla. Beat with an electric mixer on low speed until combined. Beat for 1 minute on medium speed. Cool 20 to 30 minutes or until frosting is easy to spread.

Nutrition Facts per serving (¹⁄₁₂ of a recipe): 235 cal., 8 g fat (5 g sat. fat), 20 mg chol., 78 mg sodium, 41 g carbo., 0 g fiber, 1 g pro. Daily Values: 7% vit. A, 0% vit. C, 3% calcium, 3% iron

BLENDER CHOCOLATE FROSTING

Start to finish: 10 minutes   **Frosts:** tops of two 8-inch cake layers

A Better Homes and Gardens® magazine reader told us that the appeal of this easy frosting had outlasted two blenders. It's been a family favorite since she spotted it in the magazine decades ago.

1 cup sugar
3 1-ounce squares unsweetened chocolate, cut into small pieces
1 5-ounce can (⅔ cup) evaporated milk

1 **Place sugar in blender container;** cover and blend at high speed for 1 minute. Add cut-up chocolate, evaporated milk, and dash salt. Cover and blend at high speed about 3 minutes or until thick, using rubber spatula to scrape sides, if necessary. (If firmer frosting is desired, chill frosted cake.)

Nutrition Facts per serving (¹⁄₁₂ of a recipe): 115 cal., 5 g total fat (2 g sat. fat), 3 mg chol., 13 mg sodium, 20 g carbo., 0 g fiber, 2 g pro. Daily Values: 0% vit. A, 0% vit. C, 3% calcium, 3% iron

CHOCOLATE-SOUR CREAM FROSTING

Start to finish: 25 minutes   **Frosts:** tops and sides of two 8- or 9-inch cake layers

1 6-ounce package (1 cup) semisweet chocolate pieces
¼ cup butter
½ cup dairy sour cream
2½ cups sifted powdered sugar

1 **In a saucepan melt** chocolate and butter over low heat, stirring frequently. Cool about 5 minutes. Stir in sour cream. Gradually add powdered sugar, beating until smooth and easy to spread. (Cover and store in the refrigerator.)

Nutrition Facts per serving (¹⁄₁₂ of a recipe): 211 cal., 8 g total fat (3 g sat. fat), 14 mg chol., 53 mg sodium, 35 g carbo., 0 g fiber, 1 g pro. Daily Values: 4% vit. A, 0% vit. C, 2% calcium, 2% iron

TRUFFLE FROSTING

Prep: 15 minutes   **Chill:** 1½ hours   **Frosts:** tops and sides of two 8- or 9-inch cake layers

For a devilishly rich combination, spread the Devil's Food Cake on page 114 with this fluffy yet intensely chocolate frosting.

1½ cups whipping cream
¼ cup light-colored corn syrup
1 12-ounce package (2 cups) semisweet chocolate pieces
1 teaspoon vanilla

1 **In a medium heavy saucepan bring** whipping cream and corn syrup to a simmer. Remove from heat. Stir in chocolate pieces and vanilla; let stand for 2 minutes. Whisk mixture until smooth and melted. Cover and chill about 1½ hours or until mixture is easy to spread, stirring occasionally. Beat with an electric mixer until fluffy.

Nutrition Facts per serving (¹⁄₁₂ of a recipe): 255 cal., 19 g total fat (7 g sat. fat), 41 mg chol., 16 mg sodium, 25 g carbo., 0 g fiber, 0 g pro. Daily Values: 13% vit. A, 0% vit. C, 29% calcium, 6% iron

cheesecakes

Very Berry Cheesecake, recipe page 167

CHEESECAKES

CHEESECAKE SUPREME

Prep: 30 minutes   Bake: 45 minutes
Cool: 1¾ hours   Chill: 4 hours
Makes: 12 servings   Oven: 375°

This is it—the rich, creamy, and traditional choice for the cheesecake purist.

1¾ **cups finely crushed graham crackers (24 squares)**
¼ **cup finely chopped walnuts**
½ **teaspoon ground cinnamon**
½ **cup butter, melted**
3 **8-ounce packages cream cheese, softened**
1 **cup sugar**
2 **tablespoons all-purpose flour**
1 **teaspoon vanilla**
½ **teaspoon finely shredded lemon peel (optional)**
2 **eggs**
1 **egg yolk**
¼ **cup milk**

1 **For crust,** combine crushed crackers, walnuts, and cinnamon. Stir in butter. If desired, reserve ¼ cup of the crumb mixture for topping. Press remaining mixture onto bottom and about 2 inches up sides of an ungreased 8- or 9-inch springform pan (see photo, top right). Set crust aside.

2 **For filling,** in a large mixing bowl beat cream cheese, sugar, flour, vanilla, and, if desired, lemon peel with an electric mixer until combined. Add eggs and egg yolk all at once, beating on low speed just until combined. Stir in milk.

3 **Pour filling** into crust-lined pan. If desired, sprinkle with reserved crumbs. Place in a shallow baking pan in oven. Bake in a 375° oven for 45 to 50 minutes for the 8-inch pan, 35 to 40 minutes for the 9-inch pan, or until center appears nearly set when gently shaken.

4 **Cool in pan** on a wire rack 15 minutes. Loosen crust from sides of pan (see photo, above right); cool 30 minutes more. Remove sides of pan; cool 1 hour. Cover and chill at least 4 hours.

Nutrition Facts per serving: 429 cal., 32 g total fat (21 g sat. fat), 157 mg chol., 329 mg sodium, 30 g carbo., 1 g fiber, 7 g pro. Daily Values: 35% vit. A, 0% vit. C, 5% calcium, 10% iron

Use a small measuring cup to press the graham cracker crumb mixture firmly into the bottom of a springform pan.

Using a small spatula, loosen the cheesecake from the sides of the pan. Cool for 30 minutes; remove the pan sides from the cheesecake.

Sour Cream Cheesecake: Prepare as at left, except reduce cream cheese to 2 packages and omit the milk. Add three 8-ounce cartons dairy sour cream with the eggs. Bake about 55 minutes for 8-inch pan (about 50 minutes for 9-inch pan).

Chocolate-Swirl Cheesecake: Prepare cheesecake as at left, except omit lemon peel. Melt 2 ounces semi-sweet chocolate. Stir the melted chocolate into half of the filling. Pour chocolate filling into the crust-lined pan; carefully pour plain filling on top of chocolate filling. Use a spatula to gently swirl fillings.

Low-Fat Cheesecake: Prepare as at left, except reduce crushed crackers to ⅓ cup and omit walnuts, cinnamon, and butter. Sprinkle crackers on bottom and sides of a well-buttered 8- or 9-inch springform pan. Substitute three 8-ounce packages fat-free cream cheese for the regular cream cheese and ½ cup refrigerated or frozen egg product (thawed) for the eggs and egg yolk. Bake as directed. If desired, serve with fresh fruit such as strawberries, raspberries, blueberries, and/or sliced kiwifruit.

Nutrition Facts per serving (Low-Fat Cheesecake): 158 cal., 1 g total fat (0 g sat. fat), 11 mg chol.

Classic Ricotta Cheesecake: The ricotta cheese, plump golden raisins, and tart candied citrus peel are the hallmarks of this Italian tradition.

CLASSIC RICOTTA CHEESECAKE

Prep: 50 minutes   **Bake:** 45 minutes
Cool: 1¾ hours   **Chill:** 4 hours
Makes: 12 servings   **Oven:** 350°

    ¾ **cup all-purpose flour**
    3 **tablespoons sugar**
    ½ **teaspoon finely shredded lemon
        peel**
    ⅓ **cup butter**
    1 **beaten egg yolk**
    3 **cups ricotta cheese**
    ½ **cup sugar**
    ¼ **cup milk**
    2 **tablespoons all-purpose flour**
    3 **eggs**
    ¼ **cup golden raisins**
    2 **tablespoons diced candied orange
        or lemon peel**
    1 **teaspoon finely shredded lemon
        peel**
       Orange peel strips (optional)

1 **For crust,** in a medium mixing bowl combine ¾ cup flour, 3 tablespoons sugar, and ½ teaspoon lemon peel. Cut in ⅓ cup butter until pieces are the size of small peas. Using a fork, stir in egg yolk until all of the dough is moistened.

2 **Remove the sides** from an ungreased 8-inch springform pan. Press one-third of the dough onto the bottom of pan. Bake in a 350° oven for 7 to 10 minutes or until golden. Cool on wire rack.

3 **Grease the sides** of the springform pan with the additional butter. Attach the pan sides to the bottom. Press remaining dough 1½ inches up the sides of the pan. Set the pan aside.

4 **For filling,** in a large mixing bowl beat the ricotta cheese, ½ cup sugar, milk, and 2 tablespoons flour with an electric mixer on medium to high speed until smooth. Add whole eggs all at once. Beat on low speed just until combined. Stir in raisins, candied peel, and 1 teaspoon lemon peel.

5 **Pour filling** into the crust-lined pan. Place in a shallow baking pan in oven. Bake in a 350° oven about 45 minutes or until center appears nearly set when gently shaken.

6 **Cool in springform pan** on a wire rack for 15 minutes. Loosen crust from sides of pan and cool for 30 minutes more. Remove sides of the springform pan; cool 1 hour. Cover and chill in the refrigerator at least 4 hours. If desired, garnish with orange peel.

Nutrition Facts per serving: 247 cal., 12 g total fat (7 g sat. fat), 104 mg chol., 148 mg sodium, 26 g carbo., 0 g fiber, 10 g pro. Daily Values: 18% vit. A, 0% vit. C, 15% calcium, 6% iron

VERY BERRY CHEESECAKE

BEST-LOVED

Prep: 35 minutes   Bake: 40 minutes
Cool: 1¾ hours   Chill: 4 hours
Makes: 12 servings   Oven: 375°

Pick your favorite summer berry or use several types. The juicy gems add sparkle to this brandied beauty (see photo, page 163).

1½ **cups finely crushed vanilla wafers**
6 **tablespoons butter, melted**
2 **8-ounce packages reduced-fat cream cheese (Neufchâtel) or regular cream cheese, softened**
¾ **cup sugar**
2 **tablespoons all-purpose flour**
2 **teaspoons vanilla**
1 **cup cream-style cottage cheese**
¼ **cup blackberry or cherry brandy or orange juice**
3 **eggs**
3½ **cups fresh raspberries, blueberries, blackberries, boysenberries, and/or chopped, pitted cherries**
1 **tablespoon blackberry or cherry brandy or orange juice**
1 **tablespoon sugar**

1 **For crust,** combine crushed vanilla wafers and butter. Press onto the bottom and 1¾ inches up sides of an ungreased 8-inch springform pan. Set pan aside.

2 **For filling,** beat cream cheese, ¾ cup sugar, flour, and vanilla until smooth. Set aside.

3 **Place cottage cheese** in a blender container or food processor bowl. Cover; blend or process until smooth. Stir into cream cheese mixture. Stir in the ¼ cup brandy or juice. Add eggs all at once; beat on low speed just until combined.

4 **Pour half of the cheese mixture** into the crust-lined pan. Spread 1 cup of the fruit atop. Top with remaining cream cheese mixture and ½ cup of the fruit. Place in a shallow baking pan in oven. Bake in a 375° oven for 40 to 45 minutes or until center appears nearly set when gently shaken.

5 **Cool in springform pan** on a wire rack for 15 minutes. Loosen crust from sides of pan; cool 30 minutes more. Remove sides of pan; cool 1 hour. Cover and chill at least 4 hours before serving.

6 **For topping,** combine remaining 2 cups fruit, the 1 tablespoon brandy or juice, and the 1 tablespoon sugar. Cover and chill up to 2 hours. To serve, top cheesecake with fruit topping.

Nutrition Facts per serving: 344 cal., 20 g total fat (9 g sat. fat), 92 mg chol., 345 mg sodium, 29 g carbo., 2 g fiber, 8 g pro. Daily Values: 21% vit. A, 14% vit. C, 4% calcium, 5% iron

DID YOU KNOW? CHEESECAKE THROUGH THE AGES

Cheesecake lovers are legion, and, it turns out, they have been so for centuries. Despite the creamy sweet's association with Manhattan, its true roots go back much further—to ancient Greece.

The Greeks and Romans had a variety of cheesecakes, many of which were served at wedding feasts. At the end of the second century, a Greek writer living in Rome offered a basic recipe for cheesecake that called for pounding and straining cheese, adding honey and flour, and cooking.

Cheesecakes are an early-American tradition, too. It is said that George Washington so loved cheesecake that Martha kept several recipes in her cookbook. It wasn't until years later, however, that Lindy's, a Manhattan restaurant, firmed up the notion of the classic, New York-style cheesecake so enjoyed today. Dense and rich, the common denominators are often cream cheese, eggs, and vanilla (and perhaps a touch of lemon)—all tucked into a crumb or pastry crust. As you can see in this chapter, many variations on this theme exist.

TOFFEE-APPLE CHEESECAKE

Prep: 45 minutes   Bake: 45 minutes
Cool: 1¾ hours   Chill: 4 hours
Makes: 12 servings   Oven: 375°

1¼ cups finely chopped toasted
     walnuts (see tip, page 247)
⅔ cup all-purpose flour
⅓ cup butter, melted
 2 8-ounce packages cream cheese,
     softened
 1 14-ounce can (1¼ cups) sweetened
     condensed milk

½ cup frozen apple juice concentrate,
     thawed; or ¼ cup frozen apple
     juice concentrate, thawed, plus
     ¼ cup apple brandy
 3 eggs
½ cup finely chopped, peeled apple
 1 or 2 medium apples, such as
     Jonathan or Golden Delicious,
     cored and cut into thin slices
¼ cup caramel ice-cream topping
    White Chocolate Leaves (optional)
    (see page 169)
    Apple Rose (optional)
    (see page 169)

Toffee-Apple Cheesecake: Reminiscent of another harvesttime treat—the caramel apple—this all-out-decadent creamy dessert gets its dazzle from the autumn flavors of walnuts, apples, and warm caramel drizzle.

BAKE THE PERFECT CHEESECAKE

There is a misconception surrounding the cheesecake—that it's tricky and temperamental. Here are a few tips to dispel those rumors and ensure success:

- Let your ingredients stand at room temperature for 30 minutes. This eases the mixing process.
- Blend cheese and sugar thoroughly before adding anything else; once the batter thins, it is difficult to smooth out the lumps.
- Avoid overbeating, especially after adding the eggs. Overbeating incorporates too much air, causing the cake to puff, then fall and crack.
- Don't overbake. An overbaked cheesecake is a dry and cracked cheesecake, so check it at the minimum baking time. The cheesecake is done when the center appears nearly set. A 1-inch area at its center will jiggle slightly when the cheesecake is done (it will firm up as the cake cools). Don't do a knife or toothpick test in the cake's center—it makes a crack. And if there is sour cream in the batter, the knife won't come out clean even when the cheesecake is done.
- Set a timer for the exact cooling time given in the recipe. When it rings, carefully loosen the crust of the cheesecake from the pan. If you wait, the cheesecake may begin pulling away from the sides and crack.

1 **For crust,** combine chopped walnuts and flour. Stir in melted butter. Press onto the bottom and 2 inches up the sides of an ungreased 8- or 9-inch springform pan. Set pan aside.

2 **For filling,** in large mixing bowl beat cream cheese with an electric mixer on low speed until fluffy. Gradually beat in sweetened condensed milk. Add juice concentrate and eggs; beat on low speed just until combined. Stir in finely chopped apple.

3 **Pour filling** into crust-lined pan. Place in a shallow baking pan in oven. Bake in a 375° oven 45 to 50 minutes for the 8-inch pan, 35 to 40 minutes for 9-inch pan, or until center appears nearly set when gently shaken.

4 **Cool in pan** on a wire rack for 15 minutes. Loosen crust from sides of pan and cool for 30 minutes more. Remove sides of pan; cool 1 hour.

5 **In a medium skillet poach** apple slices in a small amount of boiling water for 1 minute or until softened; drain. Cover; chill cheesecake and apples separately at least 4 hours.

6 **To serve,** arrange apple slices atop cheesecake. Drizzle with warm caramel topping. If desired, garnish with White Chocolate Leaves and an Apple Rose.

White Chocolate Leaves: Melt 6 ounces vanilla-flavored candy coating over low heat, stirring constantly; cool. Stir in 3 tablespoons light-colored corn syrup. Turn mixture out onto a large sheet of waxed paper. Let stand at room temperature for 3 to 24 hours or until dry to the touch. Gently knead for 10 to 15 strokes or until mixture is smooth and pliable. If mixture is too soft, chill in the refrigerator about 15 minutes or until easy to handle (or knead in enough powdered sugar to stiffen the mixture). Store any unused mixture in a sealed plastic bag at room temperature for 3 to 4 weeks (mixture will stiffen with storage; before using, knead mixture until it is pliable). Flatten mixture slightly; place between 2 sheets of waxed paper dusted with powdered sugar. Roll to ⅛-inch thickness. Using leaf-shaped cutters or a knife, cut into shapes. Use a wooden toothpick to draw veins on leaves. Curve leaves as desired.

Apple Rose: Starting at the tip of an unpeeled, extra-thin fresh apple slice, roll up diagonally to form a cone shape for the rose center. Press on additional slices, curving around center to make thin petals. Add enough of these thin petals to make a rose.

Nutrition Facts per serving: 451 cal., 30 g total fat (14 g sat. fat), 120 mg chol., 251 mg sodium, 38 g carbo., 1 g fiber, 10 g pro. Daily Values: 26% vit. A, 2% vit. C, 12% calcium, 9% iron

RIBBON-OF-CRANBERRY CHEESECAKE

Prep: 40 minutes **Bake:** 45 minutes **Cool:** 1¾ hours
Chill: 4 hours **Makes:** 16 servings **Oven:** 375°

With its festive ruby-red band, this makes an eye-catching addition to a holiday table.

1½ cups finely crushed vanilla wafers
  6 tablespoons butter, melted
  1 cup sugar
  2 tablespoons cornstarch
  2 cups cranberries
  1 cup orange juice
  1 cup cottage cheese
  2 8-ounce packages cream cheese, softened
  1 cup sugar
  2 tablespoons all-purpose flour
  2 teaspoons vanilla
  3 eggs
  2 teaspoons finely shredded orange peel

1 **For crust,** combine vanilla wafers and butter. Press mixture onto bottom and 1 inch up sides of an ungreased 9-inch springform pan. Set aside.

2 **For sauce,** in a medium saucepan stir together 1 cup sugar and the cornstarch. Stir in cranberries and orange juice. Cook and stir over medium heat until thickened and bubbly. Cook and stir for 2 minutes more. Remove ¾ cup of the sauce; cool slightly. Meanwhile, cover and chill remaining sauce in the refrigerator until serving time.

3 **Place the ¾ cup sauce** in a blender container or food processor bowl. Cover and blend or process until smooth. Set the pureed sauce aside. Wash the blender container or food processor bowl.

4 **For filling,** place cottage cheese in the blender container or food processor bowl. Cover and blend or process until smooth. Transfer cottage cheese to a large mixing bowl. Add cream cheese, 1 cup sugar, flour, and vanilla. Beat with an electric mixer until smooth. Add eggs all at once. Beat on low speed just until combined. Stir in orange peel.

5 **Pour half of the filling** (about 2 cups) into the crust-lined pan. Drizzle pureed sauce over the filling in the pan. Carefully spoon on the remaining filling, covering sauce as much as possible. Place in a shallow baking pan in oven. Bake in a 375° oven for 45 to 50 minutes or until center appears nearly set when gently shaken.

6 **Cool in springform pan** on a wire rack for 15 minutes. Loosen crust from sides of the pan and cool for 30 minutes more. Remove sides of pan; cool 1 hour. Cover and chill at least 4 hours.

7 **To serve,** top cheesecake with some of the chilled cranberry sauce. Pass remaining sauce.

Nutrition Facts per serving: 431 cal., 23 g total fat (13 g sat. fat), 120 mg chol., 286 mg sodium, 50 g carbo., 1 g fiber, 8 g pro. Daily Values: 25% vit. A, 23% vit. C, 4% calcium, 6% iron

---

TOOLBOX: SPRINGFORM PANS

A good springform pan will greatly enhance the pleasure (and success) of baking the perfect cheesecake. Springform pans are available in 8-, 9-, 10-, and 11-inch sizes, though an 8- or 9-inch springform is what you will need for most recipes. If your pan is not marked, measure its diameter from inside edge to inside edge.

Don't try to use a regular cake pan, it simply can't hold the volume of a springform pan and would make removing the cheesecake from the pan nearly impossible. A nonstick springform can make it easier to remove the sides of the pan but is certainly not necessary for success.

Assembling a springform is easy: Place the side piece on a flat surface and open the clasp. Place the bottom inside the side piece and close the clasp, making sure the lip of the bottom is firmly in place in the groove that runs along the bottom of the side piece. Even with a firm seal, it's possible a springform pan may leak, so it's always a good idea to place a filled springform pan in a shallow baking pan before placing it in the oven.

TROPICAL LIME
CHEESECAKE

Prep: 45 minutes   Bake: 45 minutes
Cool: 1¾ hours   Chill: 4 hours
Makes: 12 to 16 servings   Oven: 375°

1¾ cups finely crushed graham
    crackers (24 squares)
1 teaspoon ground cinnamon
¼ teaspoon ground allspice
½ cup butter, melted
3 8-ounce packages cream cheese,
    softened
1 cup sugar
2 tablespoons lime juice
1 tablespoon grated fresh gingerroot
1 teaspoon vanilla
2 eggs
1 egg yolk
½ cup dairy sour cream
1½ teaspoons finely shredded lime peel
1½ cups fresh fruit, such as cut-up kiwi-
    fruit, mango, and/or pineapple
2 tablespoons toasted coconut
    (see tip, page 247)
¼ cup lime or orange marmalade

1 For crust, combine crushed crackers, cinnamon, and allspice. Stir in butter. Press onto bottom and 1½ to 2 inches up the sides of an ungreased 9-inch springform pan. Chill while preparing filling.

2 For filling, in a large bowl, beat cream cheese until smooth. Add sugar, lime juice, gingerroot, and vanilla; beat well. Add eggs, yolk, and sour cream; beat at low speed just until smooth. Stir in lime peel.

3 Pour filling into crust-lined pan. Place in a shallow baking pan in oven. Bake in 375° oven 45 to 50 minutes or until center appears nearly set when gently shaken. Cool in pan on wire rack for 15 minutes. Loosen crust from sides of pan and cool 30 minutes more. Remove sides of pan; cool 1 hour. Cover and chill at least 4 hours.

4 To serve, top cheesecake with fruit and toasted coconut. Melt marmalade in small saucepan; spoon over fruit. Serve immediately.

Nutrition Facts per serving: 468 cal., 32 g total fat (19 g sat. fat), 141 mg chol., 335 mg sodium, 39 g carbo., 1 g fiber, 7 g pro. Daily Values: 44% vit. A, 23% vit. C, 6% calcium, 10% iron

ORANGE DELIGHT
CHEESECAKE

LOW-FAT

Prep: 35 minutes   Bake: 45 minutes
Cool: 1¾ hours   Chill: 4 hours
Makes: 16 servings   Oven: 350°

1½ cups crushed chocolate graham
    crackers (about 20 squares)
1¼ cups sugar
2 tablespoons all-purpose flour
¼ cup butter, melted
3 8-ounce packages fat-free cream
    cheese or reduced-fat cream
    cheese (Neufchâtel)
2 tablespoons all-purpose flour
1 cup refrigerated or frozen egg
    product, thawed, or 4 eggs
1 teaspoon vanilla
1½ teaspoons finely shredded orange
    peel
⅓ cup orange marmalade or apricot
    or peach preserves,* melted
¼ cup semisweet chocolate pieces
½ teaspoon shortening

1 Combine crushed crackers, ¼ cup of the sugar, and 2 tablespoons flour. Stir in butter. Press onto bottom and 1½ inches up sides of ungreased 9-inch springform pan. Bake in 350° oven 8 minutes; set aside.

2 For filling, beat the cream cheese for 30 seconds. Add the remaining sugar and 2 tablespoons flour; beat well. Add egg product or eggs and vanilla. Beat on low speed just until combined. Stir in peel.

3 Pour filling into crust. Place in a shallow baking pan. Bake in 350° oven 45 to 50 minutes or until center appears nearly set when shaken. Cool in springform pan on wire rack for 15 minutes. Loosen crust from sides of pan; cool for 30 minutes. Remove sides of pan; cool 1 hour. Cover and chill at least 4 hours.

4 To serve, drizzle melted marmalade over cheesecake. In a heavy small saucepan cook and stir the chocolate pieces and shortening over low heat until melted. Drizzle chocolate over cheesecake.

*Note: Snip any large pieces of fruit in preserves.

Nutrition Facts per serving: 221 cal., 5 g total fat (1 g sat. fat), 12 mg chol., 402 mg sodium, 32 g carbo., 1 g fiber, 12 g pro. Daily Values: 19% vit. A, 1% vit. C, 26% calcium, 5% iron

DOUBLE RASPBERRY CHEESECAKE

Prep: 1 hour   Bake: 35 minutes
Cool: 1¾ hours   Chill: 4 hours
Makes: 12 servings   Oven: 375°

- **2 cups packaged chocolate wafer crumbs**
- **⅓ cup butter, melted**
- **3 tablespoons sugar**
- **2½ cups fresh or lightly sweetened, frozen red raspberries, thawed**
- **⅔ cup sugar**
- **2 tablespoons cornstarch**
- **2 teaspoons lemon juice**
- **3 8-ounce packages cream cheese, softened**
- **½ cup sugar**
- **2 tablespoons all-purpose flour**
- **1 teaspoon vanilla**
- **2 egg whites**
- **1 cup whipping cream**
- **1 cup fresh or lightly sweetened frozen red raspberries, thawed**
- **2 tablespoons raspberry liqueur or orange juice**

1 **For crust,** combine wafer crumbs, butter, and 3 tablespoons sugar. Press onto the bottom and 1 inch up the sides of an ungreased 8- or 9-inch springform pan. Chill while preparing filling.

2 **For raspberry sauce,** in a blender container blend the 2½ cups raspberries until smooth. Press through a sieve to remove seeds. Add water to sieved raspberries if necessary to equal 1 cup. Combine ⅔ cup sugar and cornstarch in a small saucepan; stir in sieved raspberries. Cook and stir over medium heat until thickened and bubbly. Reduce heat; cook and stir 2 minutes more. Stir in lemon juice. Remove ¾ cup sauce; cool slightly without stirring. Cover remaining sauce and chill until serving time.

3 **For filling,** in a large bowl combine cream cheese, ½ cup sugar, flour, and vanilla. Beat with an electric mixer until fluffy. Add egg whites, beating on low speed just until combined. Stir in cream.

4 **Pour half the mixture** into crust-lined pan. Drizzle the ¾ cup raspberry sauce over cheese mixture in pan. Carefully spoon on remaining cheese mixture, covering sauce. Place in a shallow baking pan. Bake in a 375° oven for 35 to 40 minutes or until center appears nearly set when shaken.

5 **Cool in springform pan** on wire rack for 15 minutes. Loosen crust from sides of pan and

Double Raspberry Cheesecake: A jewel of a dessert—the chocolate crust pairs perfectly with the raspberry in the filling and topping.

HAVE YOUR CHEESECAKE TODAY AND TOMORROW, TOO

No doubt about it—because of the richness of cheesecake, one cake serves a crowd. What to do when you've got a cheesecake that's bigger than your dinner party (or when you'd like to make it ahead of time)? Store it. Here's how:

- **To refrigerate cheesecake,** cover it thoroughly with plastic wrap. It will stay fresh in the refrigerator for up to 3 days.

- **To freeze cheesecake,** seal a whole cheesecake or pieces in a freezer bag, in an airtight container, or wrapped in heavy foil. Freeze a whole cheesecake for up to a month and pieces for up to 2 weeks.

- **To thaw frozen cheesecake,** loosen the covering slightly. Thaw a whole cheesecake in the refrigerator for 24 hours. Thaw individual pieces at room temperature about 30 minutes.

---

cool 30 minutes more. Remove sides of pan; cool 1 hour. Cover and chill at least 4 hours.

6 **To serve,** top cheesecake with 1 cup raspberries. Stir liqueur or juice into remaining raspberry sauce and spoon over berries.

Nutrition Facts per serving: 556 cal., 35 g total fat (19 g sat. fat), 96 mg chol., 333 mg sodium, 55 g carbo., 3 g fiber, 7 g pro. Daily Values: 38% vit. A, 19% vit. C, 6% calcium, 12% iron

PUMPKIN CHEESECAKE

Prep: 35 minutes   Bake: 1 hour 5 minutes
Cool: 1¾ hours   Chill: 4 hours
Makes: 16 servings   Oven: 325°

This special dessert first appeared in Better Homes and Gardens® magazine in 1971 and is still a big favorite.

1½ **cups zwieback crumbs (about 17 crackers) or 1½ cups graham cracker crumbs (about 20)**
⅓ **cup sugar**
3 **tablespoons butter, melted**
2 **8-ounce packages cream cheese, softened**
1 **cup half-and-half or light cream**
1 **cup canned pumpkin**
¾ **cup sugar**
3 **tablespoons all-purpose flour**
1½ **teaspoons vanilla**

1 **teaspoon ground cinnamon**
½ **teaspoon ground ginger**
½ **teaspoon ground nutmeg**
¼ **teaspoon salt**
4 **eggs**
1 **8-ounce carton dairy sour cream**
2 **tablespoons sugar**
½ **teaspoon vanilla**

1 **For crust,** combine zwieback crumbs, ⅓ cup sugar, and melted butter. Press onto bottom and about 2 inches up sides of an ungreased 9-inch springform pan. Bake in a 325° oven for 5 minutes.

2 **For filling,** beat cream cheese, half-and-half, pumpkin, ¾ cup sugar, flour, 1½ teaspoons vanilla, the cinnamon, ginger, nutmeg, and salt with an electric mixer until smooth. Add eggs, beating on low speed just until combined.

3 **Spoon filling** into crust-lined pan. Place in a shallow baking pan in oven. Bake in a 325° oven for 1 hour or until center appears nearly set when gently shaken. Combine sour cream, 2 tablespoons sugar, and ½ teaspoon vanilla; spread over cheesecake. Bake 5 minutes more.

4 **Cool in springform pan** on a wire rack for 15 minutes. Loosen crust from sides of pan and cool 30 minutes more. Remove sides of pan; cool 1 hour. Cover and chill at least 4 hours.

Nutrition Facts per serving: 297 cal., 19 g total fat (11 g sat. fat), 103 mg chol., 194 mg sodium, 27 g carbo., 1 g fiber, 6 g pro. Daily Values: 55% vit. A, 2% vit. C, 5% calcium, 6% iron

Chocolate-Hazelnut Cheesecake: Name your pleasure—this generously nutty version, a white chocolate cake, or the triple-chocolate original. All are variations on a rich theme that will take you straight to chocolate heaven.

CHOCOLATE CHEESECAKE

BEST-LOVED

Prep: 35 minutes   Bake: 45 minutes
Cool: 1¾ hours   Chill: 4 hours
Makes: 12 servings   Oven: 350°

1¾ **cups finely crushed chocolate wafers (about 30 cookies)**
⅓ **cup butter, melted**
4 **ounces semisweet chocolate, chopped**
1 **ounce unsweetened chocolate or semisweet chocolate, chopped**
3 **8-ounce packages cream cheese, softened**
1¼ **cups sugar**

2 **tablespoons all-purpose flour**
1 **teaspoon vanilla**
4 **eggs**
¼ **cup milk**

1 **For crust,** in a mixing bowl combine crushed wafers and butter. Press mixture evenly onto the bottom and 1¾ inches up the sides of an ungreased 9-inch springform pan. Chill while preparing filling.

2 **In a small heavy saucepan combine** the semisweet chocolate and the unsweetened chocolate; melt over low heat, stirring occasionally. Cool slightly.

3 **In a large mixing bowl beat** cream cheese, sugar, flour, and vanilla with an electric mixer on medium speed until smooth. With mixer running, slowly add melted chocolate, beating on low speed until combined (see photo, page 175). Add eggs all at once. Beat on low speed just until combined. Stir in milk.

4 **Pour filling** into crust-lined pan. Place in a shallow baking pan in oven. Bake in a 350° oven for 45 to 50 minutes or until the center appears nearly set when gently shaken.

5 **Cool in springform pan** on a wire rack for 15 minutes. Loosen crust from sides of pan and cool for 30 minutes more. Remove sides of pan; cool 1 hour. Cover and chill at least 4 hours.

Nutrition Facts per serving: 480 cal., 33 g total fat (19 g sat. fat), 148 mg chol., 341 mg sodium, 41 g carbo., 1 g fiber, 9 g pro. Daily Values: 34% vit. A, 0% vit. C, 6% calcium, 13% iron

Chocolate-Hazelnut Cheesecake: Prepare Chocolate Cheesecake as directed, except, for hazelnut crust, omit chocolate wafers and butter. Using 2 teaspoons butter, grease bottom and 1¾ inches up the sides of a 9-inch springform pan. Press 1 cup toasted, finely ground hazelnuts or almonds onto the bottom and 1¾ inches up the sides of the greased springform pan. Cover; chill. For filling, prepare as

With the mixer running, slowly add melted chocolate in a steady stream, beating just until combined. This prevents the chocolate from forming little chips.

directed, except decrease milk to 1 tablespoon and stir in 3 tablespoons hazelnut liqueur with the milk at the end. If desired, top the cooled cheesecake with fresh strawberries.

White Chocolate Cheesecake: Prepare Chocolate Cheesecake as directed, except substitute one 6-ounce package white baking bars, melted and cooled, for all of the semisweet and unsweetened chocolate squares. (To melt white baking bars, heat and stir constantly over extra-low heat.)

MAKE IT PRETTY, PLEASE

Cheesecake is one kind of cake that isn't frosted or iced. Its smooth top is like a blank canvas that calls for garnishing, limited only by your imagination. Consider these:
- **Chocolate:** To make chocolate garnishes (such as the coffee cup shown on page 177), place melted chocolate—thinned with a little melted shortening, if needed—into a clean, small plastic bag. Snip a small hole in one corner of the bag; pipe desired shapes onto wax paper. Let stand until dry; peel from waxed paper.
- **Glazed Nuts:** In a heavy 10-inch skillet, combine 1½ cups blanched whole almonds, hazelnuts, macadamia nuts, walnut or pecan halves; ½ cup sugar; 2 tablespoons butter; and ½ teaspoon vanilla. Cook over medium-high heat, shaking skillet occasionally (don't stir!)

until sugar begins to melt. Reduce heat to low; cook until sugar is melted and golden brown, stirring often. Remove from heat. With a well-buttered spoon, remove a few nuts at a time from the skillet and place on a well-buttered piece of foil laid on a baking sheet. Cool completely and store in a cool, dry place up to 1 month. Makes 2 cups.
- **Edible Flowers:** Some favorites include the rose, violet, pansy, calendula, Johnny jump-ups, and pineapple sage. Use only edible flowers that have not been sprayed or treated with chemicals in any way. They can come from your garden or from the produce section of your grocery store—but not from a florist. Rinse and gently pat dry before using.

CAFÉ AU LAIT CHEESECAKE

Prep: 45 minutes   Bake: 50 minutes
Cool: 1¾ hours   Chill: 4 hours
Makes: 12 servings   Oven: 350°

1¾ **cups finely crushed chocolate
    wafers (about 30 cookies)**
⅓ **cup butter, melted**
2 **ounces semisweet chocolate,
    chopped**
2 **tablespoons water**
1 **tablespoon instant espresso coffee
    powder or instant coffee crystals**
2 **tablespoons coffee liqueur or water**
3 **8-ounce packages cream cheese,
    softened**
1 **cup sugar**
2 **tablespoons all-purpose flour**
1 **teaspoon vanilla**
3 **eggs**
    **Coffee-cup garnishes (optional)
    (see chocolate tip, page 175)**

1 **For crust,** combine crushed wafers and butter. Press onto the bottom and 2 inches up the sides of an ungreased 8-inch springform pan. Chill crust while preparing filling.

Carefully pour the reserved cream cheese mixture in a ring over the outside edge of the partially baked chocolate filling.

2 **In a small saucepan combine** the chocolate, 2 tablespoons water, and the instant espresso. Cook and stir over low heat until chocolate starts to melt. Remove from heat. Stir until smooth. Stir in liqueur or 2 tablespoons water; cool.

3 **For filling,** in a large mixing bowl beat cream cheese, sugar, flour, and vanilla with an electric mixer on medium speed until smooth. Add eggs all at once, beating on low speed just until mixed. Do not overbeat.

4 **Reserve 2 cups** of the cream cheese mixture; cover and set aside. Stir cooled chocolate-coffee mixture into the remaining cream cheese mixture, stirring just until combined.

5 **Pour chocolate mixture** into the crust-lined pan. Place in a shallow baking pan in oven. Bake in a 350° oven for 30 minutes or until edge is set (center will be soft set). Carefully pour reserved mixture in a ring over the outside edge of the chocolate mixture (where chocolate mixture is set), allowing it to flow into center, spreading if necessary. Bake cheesecake about 25 minutes more or until center appears nearly set when gently shaken.

6 **Cool in springform pan** on wire rack for 10 minutes. Loosen crust from sides of pan and cool for 30 minutes more. Remove sides of pan; cool completely. Cover and chill cheesecake at least 4 hours before serving. If desired, top each slice with a coffee-cup garnish.

Nutrition Facts per serving: 429 cal., 30 g total fat (18 g sat. fat), 130 mg chol., 326 mg sodium, 34 g carbo., 0 g fiber, 7 g pro. Daily Values: 31% vit. A, 0% vit. C, 5% calcium, 11% iron

---

CUTTING A CHEESECAKE

Q What's the best way to cut a cheesecake and avoid clumps of the filling sticking to the knife?

A First of all, it helps to choose the right tool—a straight-edged, thin-bladed knife works best. Don't use a serrated knife, as clumps can form around the ridged edges. Also, to avoid dragging the filling down as you slice, dip the knife into hot water and wipe it dry after each cut.

Café au Lait Cheesecake:
Indulge in mocha madness
with this incredible coffee-
and-cream dessert patterned
after café au lait, a French
blend of brewed coffee
and warm milk.

CHOCOLATE-IRISH
CREAM CHEESECAKE

Prep: 35 minutes   **Bake:** 50 minutes
Cool: 1¾ hours   **Chill:** 4 hours
Makes: 12 to 16 servings   **Oven:** 325°

Impress your guests with this home-baked version of a favorite often found on dessert carts in fine restaurants.

    1 **cup finely crushed chocolate wafers (about 17 cookies)***
    ¼ **cup butter, melted**
    ½ **teaspoon ground cinnamon**
    3 **8-ounce packages cream cheese, softened**
    1 **8-ounce carton dairy sour cream**
    1 **cup sugar**
    1 **8-ounce package semisweet chocolate, melted and cooled**
    3 **eggs**
    ½ **cup Irish cream liqueur****
    2 **tablespoons whipping cream or milk**
    2 **teaspoons vanilla**
    ⅓ **cup semisweet chocolate pieces, melted (optional)**

1 **For crust,** combine crushed wafers, butter, and cinnamon. Press mixture onto bottom of an ungreased 9- or 10-inch* springform pan. Set aside.

2 **For filling,** in a large mixing bowl beat cream cheese, sour cream, sugar, and the 8 ounces melted chocolate with an electric mixer on medium to high speed until smooth. Add eggs all at once. Beat on low speed just until combined. Stir in liqueur, whipping cream, and vanilla.

3 **Pour** into crust-lined pan. Place in shallow baking pan in oven. Bake in a 325° oven 50 to 60 minutes or until center appears nearly set when shaken.

4 **Cool in springform pan** on a wire rack for 15 minutes. Loosen crust from sides of pan; cool for 30 minutes more. Remove sides of pan; cool 1 hour. Cover; chill at least 4 hours before serving.

5 **To serve,** if desired, drizzle with the ⅓ cup melted chocolate.

***Note:** If using a 10-inch springform pan, use 1¼ cups crushed chocolate wafers for the crust.

****Note:** If you prefer to use less liqueur, substitute whipping cream or milk for some of the liqueur.

Nutrition Facts per serving: 525 cal., 37 g total fat (20 g sat. fat), 134 mg chol., 295 mg sodium, 34 g carbo., 3 g fiber, 7 g pro. Daily Values: 36% vit. A, 0% vit. C, 6% calcium, 7% iron

---

THE CHEESE IN CHEESECAKE

The most common cheese found in cheesecake is cream cheese, but that variety certainly doesn't stand alone! Cheesecake can be made from a variety of soft cheeses. Here's a sampling:

- **Cream Cheese:** A white, fresh cheese that has a smooth, dense, spreadable consistency and a mild flavor. It's made from a blend of cow's milk and cream and makes for the traditional dense, rich cheesecake.

  A perfect cream cheese cheesecake is smooth and creamy. To ensure a silky, lump-free texture, allow cream cheese to soften before preparing the filling. To speed the process, unwrap the cream cheese and cut each block into 10 cubes. Let the cubes stand at room temperature for 30 minutes.

- **Neufchâtel:** A less-firm cream cheese with fewer calories and less fat. It makes a slightly lighter, softer cheesecake than regular cream cheese.
- **Mascarpone:** The crème de la crème of cream cheeses, mascarpone is made with a higher percentage of cream than cream cheese. It makes for a very rich, extra-special cheesecake.
- **Ricotta:** A fresh, soft, white cheese with a very mild, semisweet taste and a slightly grainy texture. It puts the "Italian" in cheesecake and makes for a fluffier, airier texture.
- **Yogurt Cheese:** A cheese made from nonfat yogurt from which the whey has been drained. It makes a soft cheesecake with lower calorie and fat-gram counts per slice.

Black Forest Cheesecake: Chocolate, cherries, and kirsch—the cornerstones of an old-fashioned German torte—get a cheesecake update in this luscious creation piled high with whipped cream and shaved chocolate curls.

BLACK FOREST
CHEESECAKE

Prep: 40 minutes   **Bake:** 55 minutes
Cool: 1¾ hours   **Chill:** 4 hours
Makes: 16 servings   **Oven:** 350°

1½ **cups finely crushed chocolate**
   wafers (about 25 cookies)
⅓ **cup butter, melted**
1 **tablespoon butter**
¼ **cup sliced almonds**
2 **8-ounce packages cream cheese,**
   softened
¾ **cup sugar**
2 **tablespoons all-purpose flour**
1 **teaspoon vanilla**
½ **teaspoon almond extract**
3 **8-ounce cartons dairy sour cream**
3 **eggs**
2 **tablespoons kirsch* or cherry juice**
¾ **cup dried tart or sweet cherries,**
   coarsely chopped
1 **cup whipping cream**
   Chocolate curls (optional)

1 **For crust,** combine crushed wafers and ⅓ cup melted butter. Press onto the bottom (only) of an ungreased 9-inch springform pan. Generously grease sides of pan using the 1 tablespoon butter; press sliced almonds onto sides of pan. Set aside.

2 **For filling,** in a large mixing bowl beat cream cheese, sugar, flour, vanilla, and almond extract with an electric mixer on medium to high speed until smooth. Add sour cream, eggs, and kirsch or cherry juice. Beat on low speed just until combined.

3 **Pour half of the filling** into the crust-lined pan. Layer dried tart cherries over filling. Carefully spoon the remaining filling over the dried cherries. Place in a shallow baking pan in oven. Bake in a 350° oven about 55 minutes or until center appears nearly set when gently shaken.

4 **Cool in springform pan** on a wire rack for 15 minutes. Loosen crust from sides of pan and cool 30 minutes more. Remove sides of pan; cool for 1 hour. Cover and chill at least 4 hours before serving.

5 **To serve,** whip cream to soft peaks. Spoon whipped cream onto cheesecake. If desired, top with chocolate curls.

*Note: Kirsch is a clear cherry brandy. To purchase a small amount for this recipe, check to see if half-pint bottles are available at your liquor store.

Nutrition Facts per serving: 416 cal., 33 g total fat (17 g sat. fat), 116 mg chol., 221 mg sodium, 26 g carbo., 0 g fiber, 6 g pro. Daily Values: 38% vit. A, 0% vit. C, 8% calcium, 6% iron

TIRAMISU CHEESECAKE

Prep: 45 minutes **Bake:** 45 minutes
Cool: 1¾ hours **Chill:** 4 hours
Makes: 12 to 16 servings **Oven:** 350°

Like the popular Italian dessert it's named for, this treat is made extra dreamy with mascarpone—an extra-rich cream cheese.

¾ **cup finely crushed chocolate wafers (about 13 cookies)**
2 **tablespoons butter, melted**
6 **ladyfingers, split lengthwise**
1 **teaspoon instant espresso coffee powder or instant coffee crystals**
2 **tablespoons rum, brandy, or milk**
2 **8-ounce packages cream cheese, softened**
1 **8-ounce carton mascarpone cheese, softened, or one 8-ounce package cream cheese, softened**
1 **cup sugar**
1 **tablespoon cornstarch**
1 **teaspoon vanilla**
3 **eggs**
1 **8-ounce carton dairy sour cream**
½ **teaspoon unsweetened cocoa powder**
   Shaved semisweet chocolate (optional)

If ladyfingers are purchased in strips, do not separate them into individual cookies. By keeping the strips intact, they will stand up against the side of the pan more easily.

1 **For crust,** combine wafers and butter. Press onto the bottom of an ungreased 9-inch springform pan. Cut the split ladyfingers in half crosswise; line side of pan with ladyfinger pieces, rounded side out and cut side down (see photo, above). Set aside.

2 **For filling,** dissolve coffee powder or crystals in rum, brandy, or milk (there's no need to heat liquid to dissolve powder or crystals); set aside. Beat cream cheese and mascarpone until combined. Gradually add sugar, beating on medium to high speed until smooth. Beat in cornstarch and vanilla. Add eggs all at once. Beat on low speed just until combined. Stir coffee mixture into cheese mixture.

3 **Pour filling** into crust-lined pan. Place in a shallow baking pan in oven. Bake in a 350° oven for 45 to 50 minutes or until center appears nearly set when gently shaken. Remove from oven. Immediately stir sour cream; gently spoon sour cream on top of hot cheesecake; carefully spread to within about 1 inch of edge.

A SKINNY CHEESECAKE?

Q Cheesecakes are truly an indulgence. Is there any way to make them lower in fat and calories? Can fat-free or reduced-fat cream cheese be substituted for regular cream cheese?

A In some of the recipes, such as the Orange Delight Cheesecake, page 171, we have offered options for using reduced-fat cream cheese (Neufchâtel) or fat-free cream cheese. These recipes were tested with the lower-fat options and were found to meet our standards of taste appeal.

If you wish to experiment with lower-fat cheeses in other recipes, be sure to use the block varieties of cream cheese—not those found in a tub, which are generally not for baking purposes (unless specified in recipe). Be advised, however, that the lower-fat cream cheeses may make your cheesecake softer or cause it to crack more easily.

Another way to reduce the fat in cheesecake is to reduce the graham cracker or cookie crust ingredients by half and line only the bottom of the cheesecake with the mixture (not the sides).

4 **Cool in springform pan** on wire rack for 15 minutes. Use a narrow metal spatula to carefully loosen ladyfingers from side of pan. Cool 30 minutes more. Remove sides of pan; cool 1 hour. Cover and chill at least 4 hours before serving. To serve, sift cocoa powder over top and, if desired, sprinkle with shaved chocolate.

Nutrition Facts per serving: 416 cal., 30 g total fat (18 g sat. fat), 153 mg chol., 225 mg sodium, 29 g carbo., 0 g fiber, 10 g pro. Daily Values: 25% vit. A, 0% vit. C, 5% calcium, 6% iron

YOGURT CHEESE CHEESECAKE

Prep: 30 minutes   (plus preparation of Yogurt Cheese)   Bake: 35 minutes   Cool: 1¾ hours
Chill: 4 hours   Makes: 12 servings   Oven: 350°

In this creamy cheesecake, yogurt cheese adds tang while reducing fat and calories.

1¼ cups finely crushed graham crackers (about 18 squares)
¼ cup sugar
¼ cup butter, melted
1 recipe Yogurt Cheese (see right)
3 ounces cream cheese or reduced-fat cream cheese (Neufchâtel), softened
¾ cup sugar
1 tablespoon all-purpose flour
1½ teaspoons lemon juice
1 teaspoon vanilla
2 eggs
⅓ cup orange marmalade
1 cup sliced strawberries

1 **For crust,** combine crushed crackers, ¼ cup sugar, and butter. Press crumb mixture onto the bottom and 1 inch up sides of an ungreased 8-inch springform pan. Set pan aside.

2 **For filling,** beat Yogurt Cheese, cream cheese, ¾ cup sugar, flour, lemon juice, and vanilla until smooth. Add eggs and beat at low speed just until combined.

3 **Pour filling** into crust-lined pan. Place in a shallow baking pan in oven. Bake in a 350° oven about 35 minutes or until cheesecake jiggles evenly

YOGURT CHEESE

In this cheesecake, yogurt cheese provides a healthful alternative to cream cheese, as it is much lower in fat and calories. To make yogurt cheese, consider these pointers:
■ Start early: Remember to make the cheese a day or two before preparing the cheesecake.
■ Use only gelatin-free yogurt (check the label) so the yogurt will separate into curds (the

cheese) and whey (the liquid).
■ Expect the resulting cheese to be soft in texture, as shown.

over entire surface when gently shaken. Cool in springform pan on a wire rack for 15 minutes. Loosen the crust from sides of pan and cool for 30 minutes more. Remove the sides of the pan; cool 1 hour. Cover and chill at least 4 hours before serving.

4 **To serve,** in saucepan melt marmalade over low heat. Remove from heat; stir in strawberries. Let stand 10 minutes. Spoon over cheesecake. (If you anticipate leftovers, spoon the topping over individual servings. When the cake is refrigerated with the berry topping, the crust gets soggy.).

Yogurt Cheese: Line a sieve with a double layer of 100-percent cotton cheesecloth. Place sieve over a large bowl (bottom of sieve should be a few inches from bottom of bowl). Spoon 32 ounces plain nonfat yogurt (containing no gelatin) into sieve; cover. Place in the refrigerator to drain about 15 hours or overnight to separate the curd from the whey. The cheese will be soft. Place cheese in a bowl; cover and chill up to 2 weeks, if desired. Use as directed in Yogurt Cheese Cheesecake.

Nutrition Facts per serving: 253 cal., 9 g total fat (5 g sat. fat), 58 mg chol., 173 mg sodium, 37 g carbo., 1 g fiber, 7 g pro. Daily Values: 9% vit. A, 14% vit. C, 13% calcium, 1% iron

HONEY-NUT CHEESECAKE

Prep: 50 minutes   **Bake:** 50 minutes
Cool: 1¾ hours   **Chill:** 4 hours
Makes: 12 to 16 servings   **Oven:** 425°/350°

- ¾ **cup ground hazelnuts, pecans, or walnuts***
- 8 **sheets frozen phyllo dough (about 17×12-inch rectangles), thawed**
- ¼ **cup butter, melted**
- 2 **tablespoons sugar**
- 2 **8-ounce packages cream cheese, softened**
- 1 **cup mascarpone cheese, softened, or ricotta cheese (8 ounces)**
- ⅔ **cup honey**
- 2 **tablespoons all-purpose flour**
- 3 **eggs**
- ¼ **cup milk**

1 **For crust,** generously grease the bottom and sides of a 9-inch springform pan. Sprinkle ¼ cup of the ground nuts evenly over the bottom of the pan. Set pan aside.

2 **Unfold phyllo.** Cover the stack of phyllo with plastic wrap to prevent drying; remove sheets as needed. Brush one phyllo sheet with some of the butter. Top with another sheet, overlapping to create a 17×14-inch rectangle; brush with a little more butter. Repeat with remaining phyllo and butter to make 8 layers in a 17×14-inch rectangle.

3 **Using kitchen shears** trim phyllo to a 14-inch circle, reserving trimmings. Ease the phyllo into the prepared pan, creasing as necessary and being careful not to tear dough (see photo, page 183). Trim even with top of pan, reserving trimmings.

4 **Combine remaining nuts and sugar;** reserve 1 tablespoon for topping. Sprinkle remaining nut mixture over phyllo in pan. Cut reserved phyllo trimmings into ½- to 1-inch pieces; place on a greased baking sheet.

5 **Bake crust and trimmings** in a 425° oven until golden, allowing 4 to 6 minutes for trimmings and 6 to 8 minutes for crust. Cool slightly on a wire rack. Reduce oven temperature to 350°.

6 **For filling,** in a large mixing bowl beat cream cheese, mascarpone or ricotta cheese, honey, and flour with an electric mixer on low speed until smooth. Add eggs all at once; beat on low speed just until combined. Stir in milk.

Honey-Nut Cheesecake: If you like baklava, a traditional Greek dessert, you will enjoy this pairing of a honey-sweetened filling with a nutty phyllo crust.

Gently ease the buttered, stacked, and trimmed layers of phyllo into the springform pan, creasing and folding as necessary.

7 **Pour filling** into phyllo crust. Place in a shallow baking pan in oven. Bake, uncovered, in a 350° oven for 50 to 55 minutes or until the center appears nearly set when gently shaken. If necessary, to prevent overbrowning, carefully cover the crust with foil the last 20 minutes.

8 **Cool in springform pan** on a wire rack for 15 minutes. Loosen crust from sides of pan and cool for 30 minutes more. Remove sides of pan; cool 1 hour. Cover and chill at least 4 hours before serving. Store trimmings in a tightly covered container in a cool, dry place.

9 **To serve** top cheesecake with phyllo trimmings and reserved sugar-nut mixture.

*Note: Use a grinder, blender, or food processor to grind nuts. Because nuts can form a paste if ground too much, grind in small batches at a time.

Nutrition Facts per serving: 439 cal., 34 g total fat (17 g sat. fat), 130 mg chol., 319 mg sodium, 30 g carbo., 1 g fiber, 10 g pro. Daily Values: 23% vit. A, 0% vit. C, 5% calcium, 9% iron

MAPLE-PRALINE CHEESECAKE

Prep: 45 minutes   Bake: 45 minutes
Cool: 1¾ hours   Chill: 4 hours
Makes: 16 servings   Oven: 375°

With a distinct maple taste and buttery glazed-nut garnish, the legendary flavors of a Southern-style praline make an appearance here.

⅓ **cup butter**
¼ **cup packed brown sugar**
¼ **teaspoon vanilla**
1 **cup all-purpose flour**

¼ **cup finely chopped pecans**
2 **8-ounce packages cream cheese, softened**
1 **cup granulated sugar**
2 **tablespoons all-purpose flour**
4 **eggs**
1 **cup half-and-half or light cream**
⅓ **cup maple or maple-flavored syrup**
⅓ **cup finely chopped pecans**
   Glazed Pecans (optional)
   (see glazed nuts tip, page 175)

1 **For crust,** in a medium mixing bowl beat butter with an electric mixer on medium to high speed about 30 seconds or until softened. Add brown sugar and vanilla; beat until fluffy. Add 1 cup flour and ¼ cup pecans. Beat on low to medium speed just until combined. Press dough onto bottom and 1½ inches up sides of an ungreased 9-inch springform pan. Bake the crust in a 375° oven about 10 minutes or until lightly browned. Cool on a wire rack while preparing filling.

2 **For filling,** in a large mixing bowl beat cream cheese, granulated sugar, and 2 tablespoons flour with an electric mixer on medium to high speed until smooth. Add eggs all at once. Beat on low speed just until combined. Stir in half-and-half or light cream, syrup, and ⅓ cup pecans.

3 **Pour filling** into crust-lined pan. Place in a shallow baking pan in oven. Bake in a 375° oven for 45 to 50 minutes or until center appears nearly set when gently shaken.

4 **Cool in springform pan** on a wire rack for 15 minutes. Loosen the crust from the sides of pan and cool for 30 minutes more. Remove the sides of pan; cool 1 hour. Cover and chill for at least 4 hours before serving. If desired, garnish with Glazed Pecans.

Nutrition Facts per serving: 304 cal., 20 g total fat (10 g sat. fat), 100 mg chol., 153 mg sodium, 28 g carbo., 0 g fiber, 5 g pro. Daily Values: 21% vit. A, 0% vit. C, 4% calcium, 7% iron

MACADAMIA CHEESECAKE

Prep: 45 minutes **Bake:** 45 minutes
Cool: 1¾ hours **Chill:** 4 hours
Makes: 12 servings **Oven:** 350°

1⅓ cups finely crushed vanilla wafers
½ cup flaked coconut
½ cup finely chopped, toasted
    macadamia nuts (see tip, page 247)
⅓ cup butter, melted
2 8-ounce packages cream cheese,
    softened
1 8-ounce tub cream cheese with
    pineapple
1 cup sugar
2 eggs
1 egg yolk
2 teaspoons vanilla
1 teaspoon lemon juice
⅓ cup finely chopped, toasted
    macadamia nuts (see tip, page 247)
2 tablespoons toasted coconut (see
    tip, page 247)
    Sliced carambola (star fruit)
    (optional)

1 **For crust,** combine crushed wafers, coconut, and ½ cup nuts. Stir in melted butter. Press mixture onto bottom and 1 inch up sides of an ungreased 9-inch springform pan. Set pan aside.

2 **For filling,** in a large mixing bowl beat cream cheeses until smooth. Add sugar, beating on medium to high speed until smooth. Add whole eggs and egg yolk all at once. Beat on low speed just until combined. Stir in vanilla, lemon juice, and ⅓ cup nuts.

3 **Pour filling** into crust-lined pan. Place in a shallow baking pan in oven. Bake in a 350° oven for 45 to 50 minutes or until the center appears nearly set when gently shaken.

4 **Cool in pan** on a wire rack for 15 minutes. Loosen crust from sides of pan and cool 30 minutes more. Remove sides of pan; cool 1 hour. Cover and chill at least 4 hours.

5 **To serve,** sprinkle with toasted coconut. If desired, top with several carambola slices.

Nutrition Facts per serving: 467 cal., 37 g total fat (16 g sat. fat), 119 mg chol., 300 mg sodium, 31 g carbo., 1 g fiber, 6 g pro. Daily Values: 29% vit. A, 0% vit. C, 4% calcium, 7% iron

Macadamia Cheesecake:
Tropical tastes star, thanks to the pineapple in the filling, the coconut in the crust—and those rich, sweet Hawaiian nuts throughout.

Pistachio Nut Stars of India,
recipe page 206

COOKIES

CHOCOLATE CHIP
COOKIES

Prep: 25 minutes **Bake:** 8 minutes per batch
Makes: 60 cookies **Oven:** 375°

The Toll House restaurant added chopped chocolate to a basic dough in the 1930s. The result? The most popular cookie in the country.

- ½ **cup shortening**
- ½ **cup butter**
- 1 **cup packed brown sugar**
- ½ **cup granulated sugar**
- ½ **teaspoon baking soda**
- 2 **eggs**
- 1 **teaspoon vanilla**
- 2½ **cups all-purpose flour**
- 1 **12-ounce package (2 cups) semisweet chocolate pieces**
- 1½ **cups chopped walnuts, pecans, or hazelnuts (optional)**

1 In a large mixing bowl beat the shortening and butter with an electric mixer on medium to high speed for 30 seconds. Add the brown sugar, granulated sugar, and baking soda. Beat mixture until combined, scraping sides of bowl occasionally. Beat in the eggs and vanilla until combined. Beat in as much of the flour as you can with the mixer. Using a wooden spoon, stir in any remaining flour. Stir in chocolate pieces and, if desired, nuts. Drop the dough by rounded teaspoons 2 inches apart on an ungreased cookie sheet.

2 Bake in a 375° oven for 8 to 10 minutes or until edges are lightly browned. Transfer cookies to a wire rack and let cool.

Nutrition Facts per cookie: 93 cal., 5 g total fat (1 g sat. fat), 11 mg chol., 29 mg sodium, 12 g carbo., 0 g fiber, 1 g pro. Daily Values: 1% vit. A, 0% vit. C, 0% calcium, 3% iron

Giant Chocolate Chip Cookies: Prepare as at left, except use a ¼-cup dry measure or scoop to drop mounds of dough about 4 inches apart on an ungreased cookie sheet. Bake in a 375° oven for 11 to 13 minutes or until edges are lightly browned. Makes about 20 cookies.

Macadamia Nut and White Chocolate Cookies: Prepare as at left, except substitute chopped white baking bars or white chocolate baking squares for the semisweet chocolate pieces. Stir in one 3½-ounce jar macadamia nuts, chopped, with the white chocolate.

Chocolate Chip Cookie Bars: Prepare as at left, except press dough into an ungreased 15×10×1-inch baking pan. Bake in a 375° oven for 15 to 20 minutes or until golden. Cool in pan on a wire rack. Cut into bars. Makes 48 bars.

DROP EVERYTHING!

Drop cookies are so easy to make, the time they take out of your day is a drop in the bucket. These tips will help make homemade cookies a staple at your house:
- If a recipe calls for greased cookie sheets, use only a very light coating or your cookies may spread too far when baking. If a recipe specifies ungreased cookie sheets, use regular or nonstick sheets—but don't grease them.
- If your electric mixer begins to strain while mixing dough, stir the last bit of flour in with a wooden spoon.
- Drop the dough using spoons from your flatware—not measuring spoons—to get the right number of cookies from each batch. Make sure the mounds are rounded and about the same size so they'll bake evenly.
- Let cookie sheets cool between batches so the dough doesn't spread too much.
- Bake on only one oven rack at a time for even browning.
- Drop cookies are done when the dough looks set and the edges and bottoms of the baked cookies are lightly browned.

Browned Butter Cookies (front) and Pecan Drops: Each of these simple cookies is dressed up with a pretty topping that tastes good. Browned Butter Cookies get a nutty nuance from frosting flavored with lightly browned butter. Pecan Drops get a flavor and texture boost from the real thing.

BROWNED BUTTER
COOKIES

Prep: 25 minutes   Bake: 10 minutes per batch
Makes: 56 cookies   Oven: 350°

The French term for browned butter is "beurre noisette," referring to butter cooked to a light hazelnut color. Browned butter has a nutty flavor, too.

½ **cup butter**
1½ **cups packed brown sugar**
1 **teaspoon baking soda**
½ **teaspoon baking powder**
¼ **teaspoon salt**
2 **eggs**
1 **teaspoon vanilla**
2½ **cups all-purpose flour**
1 **8-ounce carton dairy sour cream**
1 **cup coarsely chopped walnuts**
1 **recipe Browned Butter Icing (see right)**

1 **Grease a cookie sheet;** set aside. In a large mixing bowl beat butter with an electric mixer on medium speed for 30 seconds. Beat in brown sugar, baking soda, baking powder, and salt until combined. Beat in eggs and vanilla until fluffy. Add flour to beaten mixture along with the sour cream, mixing well. Stir in walnuts. Drop dough by rounded teaspoons 2 inches apart on prepared cookie sheet.

2 **Bake in a 350° oven** about 10 minutes or until set. Transfer cookies to a wire rack and let cool. Frost with Browned Butter Icing.

Browned Butter Icing: In a small saucepan heat ¼ cup butter over medium heat until butter turns the color of light brown sugar. Remove saucepan from heat. Stir in 2 cups sifted powdered sugar and enough boiling water (1 to 2 tablespoons) to make icing smooth and easy to spread. Frost the cooled cookies immediately after preparing frosting. If the frosting becomes grainy, soften with a few more drops of hot water.

Nutrition Facts per cookie: 97 cal., 5 g total fat (2 g sat. fat), 16 mg chol., 66 mg sodium, 13 g carbo., 0 g fiber, 1 g pro. Daily Values: 3% vit. A, 0% vit. C, 1% calcium, 2% iron

PECAN DROPS

Prep: 30 minutes   Bake: 8 minutes per batch
Makes: 36 cookies   Oven: 375°

Pick out the nicest pecan halves to use for the cookie tops and chop the rest to stir into the dough (see photo, page 188).

　½ **cup butter**
　2 cups sifted powdered sugar
1¾ **cups all-purpose flour**
　⅓ **cup milk**
　1 egg
　1 teaspoon baking powder
　1 teaspoon vanilla
　1 cup coarsely chopped pecans
　　Granulated sugar
　　Pecan halves (optional)

1 Lightly grease a cookie sheet; set aside. In a large mixing bowl beat butter with an electric mixer on medium to high speed for 30 seconds. Add powdered sugar, about half of the flour, half of the milk, the egg, baking powder, and vanilla. Beat until thoroughly combined, scraping sides of bowl occasionally. Beat or stir in remaining flour and milk. Stir in chopped pecans.

2 Drop dough by rounded teaspoons 2 inches apart on the prepared cookie sheet. Sprinkle with granulated sugar. If desired, lightly press a pecan half in the center of each cookie.

3 Bake in a 375° oven for 8 to 10 minutes or until edges are slightly golden. Transfer cookies to a wire rack and let cool.

Nutrition Facts per cookie: 90 cal., 5 g total fat (1 g sat. fat), 9 mg chol., 36 mg sodium, 11 g carbo., 0 g fiber, 1 g pro. Daily Values: 2% vit. A, 0% vit. C, 1% calcium, 2% iron

TRIPLE-CHOCOLATE CHUNK COOKIES

BEST-LOVED

Prep: 25 minutes   Bake: 12 minutes per batch
Makes: 22 cookies   Oven: 350°

For the true chocophile, there is no such thing as too much chocolate. These chunky, oversize treats contain a trio of chocolates.

　1 cup butter
　¾ **cup granulated sugar**
　¾ **cup packed brown sugar**
　1 teaspoon baking soda
　2 eggs
　1 teaspoon vanilla
　3 ounces unsweetened chocolate, melted and cooled
　2 cups all-purpose flour
　8 ounces semisweet chocolate, cut into ½-inch pieces, or 1⅓ cups large semisweet chocolate pieces
　6 ounces white baking bar, cut into ½-inch pieces, or 1 cup white baking pieces
　1 cup chopped black walnuts or pecans (optional)

1 Lightly grease a cookie sheet; set aside. In a large mixing bowl beat butter with an electric mixer on medium to high speed for 30 seconds. Beat in granulated sugar, brown sugar, and baking soda until combined. Beat in eggs and vanilla until combined. Stir in melted chocolate. Beat in as much of the flour as you can with the mixer. Stir in any remaining flour. Stir in chocolate and white baking pieces and, if desired, nuts.

2 Using a ¼-cup dry measure or scoop, drop mounds of dough about 4 inches apart on the prepared cookie sheet.

3 Bake in a 350° oven for 12 to 14 minutes or until edges are firm. Cool on cookie sheet for 1 minute. Transfer cookies to a wire rack; let cool.

Nutrition Facts per cookie: 280 cal., 17 g total fat (10 g sat. fat), 44 mg chol., 158 mg sodium, 33 g carbo., 1 g fiber, 3 g pro. Daily Values: 8% vit. A, 0% vit. C, 2% calcium, 8% iron

APRICOT-OATMEAL COOKIES

Prep: 30 minutes   **Bake:** 10 minutes per batch
Makes: 48 cookies   **Oven:** 375°

Homey oatmeal cookies take on an elegant air with the addition of sweet and chewy dried apricots and hazelnuts.

¾ **cup snipped dried apricots**
¾ **cup butter**
1 **cup packed brown sugar**
½ **cup granulated sugar**
1 **teaspoon baking powder**
½ **teaspoon ground cinnamon**
¼ **teaspoon baking soda**
1 **egg**
1 **teaspoon vanilla**
1¾ **cups all-purpose flour**
2 **cups rolled oats**
½ **cup chopped hazelnuts or walnuts**
1 **recipe Powdered Sugar Icing (optional) (see page 201)**

1 In a small mixing bowl combine apricots and enough boiling water to cover. Let stand for 5 minutes. Drain.

2 In a large mixing bowl beat the butter with an electric mixer on medium to high speed for 30 seconds. Add brown sugar, granulated sugar, baking powder, cinnamon, and baking soda; beat until combined. Beat in egg and vanilla until combined. Beat in as much flour as you can with the mixer. Using a wooden spoon, stir in drained apricots, rolled oats, nuts, and any remaining flour.

3 Drop dough by rounded teaspoons 2 inches apart on an ungreased cookie sheet.

4 Bake in a 375° oven about 10 minutes or until edges are golden. Transfer cookies to a wire rack and let cool. If desired, drizzle cooled cookies with Powdered Sugar Icing.

Nutrition Facts per cookie: 90 cal., 4 g total fat (2 g sat. fat), 12 mg chol., 46 mg sodium, 13 g carbo., 1 g fiber, 1 g pro. Daily Values: 4% vit. A, 0% vit. C, 1% calcium, 3% iron

---

SHEET SMARTS

All cookie sheets are not created equal. Here's what to look for when you go shopping for your next cookie sheet:

- Heavy-gauge aluminum with low sides or no sides at all.
- Lighter-colored cookie sheets. If they are too dark, cookies can overbrown.
- A dull finish so cookie bottoms brown evenly. (For cookies that should not brown on the bottoms—such as shortbread—choose a shiny cookie sheet.)

- If you don't want to grease your sheets, use a nonstick cookie sheet. The dough won't spread as much, though, so you'll get thicker cookies.
- Insulated cookie sheets are fine if you want pale drop cookies with soft centers. You might have trouble using them for cookies high in butter, shaped cookies, and some drop cookies because the butter may start to melt and leak out before the dough is set. Because dough spreads before it sets, you're also likely to have cookies with thin edges.

COOKIES BY POST

The safe arrival of gift cookies starts with selecting good travelers. Crisp cookies such as slice-and-bake cookies, most drop cookies, uncut bars, and cutouts are good choices. (Frosted and filled cookies are not.) So, brighten someone's day with a perfectly posted box of homemade sweets.

- Bake cookies just before packing and shipping so they're as fresh as possible; ship early in the week so delivery won't be delayed over a weekend.
- Package cookies in plastic- or foil-lined heavy boxes. Tuck generous cushions of bubble wrap, foam packing pieces, crumpled tissue paper, paper towels, or waxed paper around cookies.
- Wrap cookies with plastic wrap, singly or in back-to-back pairs. Make layers with the sturdiest cookies on the bottom then a layer of filler. Continue layering and end with plenty of filler to prevent shifting. Cookies should not shift when the box is shaken.
- Insert a card with the recipient's address. Tape the box shut securely with strapping tape and mark it "perishable." Cover the outside address with transparent tape.

SAUCEPAN OATMEAL COOKIES *EASY*

Prep: 15 minutes
Bake: 6 minutes per batch
Makes: 48 cookies   Oven: 375°

Dress up these super-simple cookies: Heat ½ cup semisweet chocolate pieces with 1 tablespoon shortening over low heat just until melted, stirring occasionally. Drizzle over cooled cookies.

     1 cup butter
     1 cup granulated sugar
     1 cup packed brown sugar
     3 cups quick-cooking rolled oats
  1¼ cups all-purpose flour
     1 teaspoon baking powder
     1 teaspoon baking soda
   ¼ teaspoon salt
     2 well-beaten eggs
   ½ cup coconut, chopped (optional)

1 **Grease a cookie sheet;** set aside. In a medium saucepan combine butter, granulated sugar, and brown sugar. Cook and stir over medium heat until melted. Remove from heat. Add oats, flour, baking powder, baking soda, and salt. Stir until combined. Add eggs; mix well. If desired, stir in coconut.

2 **Drop batter** by rounded teaspoons 3 inches apart on the prepared cookie sheet, stirring the batter often.

3 **Bake in a 375° oven** for 6 to 7 minutes or until edges are firm. Cool on cookie sheet for 1 minute. Transfer cookies to a wire rack and cool.

Nutrition Facts per cookie: 102 cal., 5 g total fat (1 g sat. fat), 14 mg chol., 85 mg sodium, 14 g carbo., 0 g fiber, 1 g pro. Daily Values: 4% vit. A, 0% vit. C, 1% calcium, 3% iron

Giant Cherry-Oatmeal Cookies: Tart dried cherries stand in for more traditional raisins in these super-size, spicy drop cookies. They're perfect with a cup of rich, full-flavored coffee.

GIANT CHERRY-
OATMEAL COOKIES

Prep: 30 minutes   Bake: 8 minutes per batch
Makes: 14 large cookies   Oven: 375°

½ **cup shortening**
½ **cup butter**
¾ **cup packed brown sugar**
½ **cup granulated sugar**
2 **teaspoons apple pie spice or**
      pumpkin pie spice
½ **teaspoon baking powder**
¼ **teaspoon baking soda**
¼ **teaspoon salt**
2 **eggs**
1 **teaspoon vanilla**
1⅓ **cups all-purpose flour**
2½ **cups regular rolled oats**
1½ **cups snipped dried tart cherries**
      or raisins
1 **teaspoon finely shredded**
      orange peel

1 **Grease a cookie sheet;** set aside. In a large mixing bowl beat shortening and butter for 30 seconds. Add brown sugar, granulated sugar, pie spice, baking powder, baking soda, and salt. Beat until fluffy. Add eggs and vanilla; beat thoroughly. Beat in flour. Using a wooden spoon, stir in oats, dried cherries or raisins, and orange peel.

2 **Generously fill** a ⅓-cup dry measure with dough and drop onto a greased cookie sheet. Press into a 4-inch circle. Repeat with the remaining dough, placing cookies 3 inches apart.

3 **Bake in a 375° oven** for 8 to 10 minutes or until edges are golden. Let stand 1 minute. Transfer cookies to a wire rack and let cool.

Nutrition Facts per cookie: 345 cal., 16 g total fat (6 g sat. fat), 48 mg chol., 141 mg sodium, 47 g carbo., 2 g fiber, 5 g pro. Daily Values: 15% vit. A, 0% vit. C, 2% calcium, 0% iron

HICKORY NUT MACAROONS

BEST-LOVED

Prep: 20 minutes **Bake:** 15 minutes per batch
Makes: 36 cookies **Oven:** 325°

This recipe was first published in Better Homes and Gardens® magazine in 1925, and it has been an all-time favorite ever since.

- **4 egg whites**
- **4 cups sifted powdered sugar**
- **2 cups chopped hickory nuts, black walnuts, or toasted pecans**

1 Grease a cookie sheet; set aside. In a large mixing bowl beat egg whites with an electric mixer on high speed until stiff, but not dry, peaks form. Gradually add powdered sugar, about ¼ cup at a time, beating at medium speed just until combined. Beat for 1 to 2 minutes more or until combined. Using a wooden spoon, fold in nuts. Drop mixture by rounded teaspoons 2 inches apart on the prepared cookie sheet.

2 Bake in a 325° oven about 15 minutes or until edges are very lightly browned. Transfer cookies to a wire rack and let cool.

Note: It is normal for these cookies to split around the edges as they bake.

Nutrition Facts per cookie: 86 cal., 4 g total fat (0 g sat. fat), 0 mg chol., 6 mg sodium, 12 g carbo., 1 g fiber, 1 g pro.

SANDIES

Prep: 25 minutes **Bake:** 20 minutes per batch
Makes: 36 cookies **Oven:** 325°

Sometimes called wedding cakes or snowballs, these powdered sugar cookies are always a hit.

- **1 cup butter**
- **⅓ cup granulated sugar**
- **1 tablespoon water**
- **1 teaspoon vanilla**
- **2¼ cups all-purpose flour**
- **1 cup chopped pecans**
- **1 cup sifted powdered sugar**

1 In a large mixing bowl beat butter with an electric mixer on medium to high speed for 30 seconds. Add granulated sugar. Beat until combined, scraping sides of bowl occasionally. Beat in the water and vanilla until combined. Beat in as much flour as you can with mixer. Using a wooden spoon, stir in any remaining flour and the pecans.

2 Shape dough into 1-inch balls or 2×½-inch logs. Place the balls or logs about 1 inch apart on an ungreased cookie sheet.

3 Bake in a 325° oven for 20 minutes or until bottoms are lightly browned. Transfer cookies to a wire rack and let cool. Gently shake cooled cookies in a plastic bag with the powdered sugar.

Nutrition Facts per cookie: 109 cal., 7 g total fat (3 g sat. fat), 14 mg chol., 52 mg sodium, 11 g carbo., 0 g fiber, 1 g pro. Daily Values: 4% vit. A, 0% vit. C, 0% calcium, 2% iron

MARVELOUS MACAROONS

The classic macaroon is the essence of simplicity—ground nuts (usually almonds) mixed with sugar and egg whites. Though our Depression-era macaroons often called for cornflakes instead of nuts, we've returned to the real McCoy. Perhaps macaroons have remained so popular because there's something in them for everyone: They're crisp around the edges and chewy in the center. Some are made with coconut, or flavored with chocolate, maraschino cherries, orange peel, or pistachios. The French like their macaroons on the double—two cookies held together with a rich chocolate filling.

SNICKERDOODLES

Prep: 30 minutes   **Chill:** 1 hour
Bake: 10 minutes per batch
Makes: 36 cookies   **Oven:** 375°

The whimsical name of these cookies that originated in 19th-century New England seems to have no purpose other than fun.

  ½ **cup butter**
  1 **cup sugar**
  ¼ **teaspoon baking soda**
  ¼ **teaspoon cream of tartar**
  1 **egg**
  ½ **teaspoon vanilla**
1½ **cups all-purpose flour**
  2 **tablespoons sugar**
  1 **teaspoon ground cinnamon**

1 **In a medium mixing bowl beat** the butter with an electric mixer on medium to high speed for 30 seconds. Add the 1 cup sugar, baking soda, and cream of tartar. Beat until combined, scraping sides of bowl occasionally. Beat in the egg and vanilla until combined. Beat in as much of the flour as you can with the mixer. Using a wooden spoon, stir in any remaining flour. Cover and chill for 1 hour.

2 **Combine the** 2 tablespoons sugar and the cinnamon. Shape dough into 1-inch balls. Roll balls in sugar-cinnamon mixture to coat. Place balls 2 inches apart on an ungreased cookie sheet.

3 **Bake in a 375° oven** for 10 to 11 minutes or until edges are golden. Transfer cookies to a wire rack and let cool.

Nutrition Facts per cookie: 66 cal., 3 g total fat (2 g sat. fat), 13 mg chol., 36 mg sodium, 10 g carbo., 0 g fiber, 1 g pro. Daily Values: 2% vit. A, 0% vit. C, 0% calcium, 1% iron

PEANUT BUTTER COOKIES

Prep: 30 minutes   **Bake:** 7 minutes per batch
Makes: 36 cookies   **Oven:** 375°

  ½ **cup butter**
  ½ **cup peanut butter**
  ½ **cup granulated sugar**
  ½ **cup packed brown sugar or**
      ¼ **cup honey**
  ½ **teaspoon baking soda**
  ½ **teaspoon baking powder**
  1 **egg**
  ½ **teaspoon vanilla**
1¼ **cups all-purpose flour**
    Granulated sugar

1 **In a large mixing bowl beat** the butter and peanut butter with an electric mixer on medium to high speed for 30 seconds. Add the granulated sugar, brown sugar or honey, baking soda, and baking powder. Beat until combined, scraping sides of

---

IT'S A MATTER OF DEGREES

For all kinds of baking—cookies included—it's important that your oven temperature is accurate. If you've noticed that your cookies brown too fast or that they seem to take forever to bake and are pale, coarsely textured, and dry when they finally do come out of the oven, your oven might be a little bit off.

To be certain, set your oven at 350° and let it heat for at least 10 minutes. Place an oven thermometer (available at hardware stores) in the oven and close the door for at least 5 minutes.

If the thermometer reads higher than 350°, reduce the oven setting specified in the recipe by the number of degrees between 350° and the thermometer reading. If it's lower, increase the temperature.

If it's off more than 50 degrees in either direction, have your thermostat adjusted.

MIX NOW, BAKE LATER

Forget those tubes of cookie dough in the grocery store—you can do the same thing, only better! Most cookie doughs (except bar cookie batters and meringues) can be mixed then refrigerated or frozen for baking later.

Just pack your favorite dough into freezer containers or shape slice-and-bake dough into rolls and wrap. Store in a tightly covered container in the refrigerator for up to one week or freeze for up to six months.

Before baking, thaw the frozen dough in the container in the refrigerator. If it's too stiff to work with, let the dough stand at room temperature to soften.

---

bowl occasionally. Beat in the egg and vanilla until combined. Beat in as much of the flour as you can with the mixer. Using a wooden spoon, stir in any remaining flour. If necessary, cover and chill dough until easy to handle.

2 **Shape dough** into 1-inch balls. Roll in additional granulated sugar to coat. Place balls 2 inches apart on an ungreased cookie sheet. Flatten by making crisscross marks with the tines of a fork.

3 **Bake in a 375° oven** for 7 to 9 minutes or until bottoms are lightly browned. Transfer cookies to a wire rack and let cool.

Nutrition Facts per cookie: 83 cal., 4 g total fat (2 g sat. fat), 13 mg chol., 68 mg sodium, 10 g carbo., 0 g fiber, 1 g pro. Daily Values: 2% vit. A, 0% vit. C, 0% calcium, 2% iron

PEANUT BUTTER BLOSSOMS

Prep: 30 minutes   Bake: 10 minutes per batch
Makes: 54 cookies   Oven: 350°

Do kid-pleasing peanut butter cookies one better with the addition of a milk chocolate star or kiss in the center of each rich, nutty round.

½ cup shortening
½ cup peanut butter
½ cup granulated sugar
½ cup packed brown sugar
1 teaspoon baking powder
⅛ teaspoon baking soda

1 egg
2 tablespoons milk
1 teaspoon vanilla
1¾ cups all-purpose flour
¼ cup granulated sugar
   Milk chocolate stars or kisses

1 **In a large mixing bowl beat** the shortening and peanut butter with an electric mixer on medium speed for 30 seconds. Add the ½ cup granulated sugar, the brown sugar, baking powder, and baking soda. Beat until combined, scraping sides of bowl. Beat in egg, milk, and vanilla until combined. Beat in as much of the flour as you can with the mixer. Using a wooden spoon, stir in any remaining flour.

2 **Shape dough** into 1-inch balls. Roll balls in the ¼ cup granulated sugar. Place balls 2 inches apart on an ungreased cookie sheet.

3 **Bake in a 350° oven** for 10 to 12 minutes or until edges are firm and bottoms are lightly browned. Immediately press a chocolate star or kiss into the center of each cookie. Transfer cookies to a wire rack and let cool.

Nutrition Facts per cookie: 83 cal., 4 g total fat (2 g sat. fat), 4 mg chol., 27 mg sodium, 10 g carbo., 0 g fiber, 1 g pro. Daily Values: 0% vit. A, 0% vit. C, 1% calcium, 2% iron

Jam Thumbprints: A variety of jewel-toned jams and preserves—in apricot, strawberry, or cherry—lend their beautiful hues to these nut-encrusted treats.

JAM THUMBPRINTS

Prep: 30 minutes **Chill:** 1 hour
Bake: 10 minutes per batch
Makes: 42 cookies **Oven:** 375°

Have these thumbprint cookies baked, cooled, and on hand for drop-in company during the holidays. Fill them right before serving.

⅔ **cup butter**
½ **cup sugar**
2 **egg yolks**
1 **teaspoon vanilla**
1½ **cups all-purpose flour**
2 **slightly beaten egg whites**
1 **cup finely chopped walnuts**
⅓ to ½ **cup strawberry, cherry, or apricot jam or preserves**

1 **Grease a cookie sheet;** set aside. In a large mixing bowl beat butter with an electric mixer on medium to high speed for 30 seconds. Add the sugar and beat until combined, scraping sides of bowl occasionally. Beat in egg yolks and vanilla until combined. Beat in as much of the flour as you can with mixer. Stir in any remaining flour. Cover and chill dough about 1 hour or until easy to handle.

2 **Shape dough** into 1-inch balls. Roll balls in egg whites; roll in walnuts. Place balls 1 inch apart on the prepared cookie sheet. Press your thumb into the center of each ball.

3 **Bake in a 375° oven** for 10 to 12 minutes or until edges are lightly browned. Transfer to a wire rack; cool. Before serving, fill centers with jam.

Nutrition Facts per cookie: 79 cal., 5 g total fat (2 g sat. fat), 18 mg chol., 33 mg sodium, 8 g carbo., 0 g fiber, 1 g pro. Daily Values: 4% vit. A, 0% vit. C, 0% calcium, 2% iron

LEMON-POPPY SEED COOKIES

EASY

Prep: 20 minutes   Chill: 1 hour
Bake: 8 minutes per batch
Makes: 50 cookies   Oven: 375°

Sugaring the bottom of a glass helps keep the dough from sticking to the glass when pressing the dough to flatten. Try a little colored sugar to brighten the tops of these delicate tea cookies.

    1 **cup butter**
    1 **cup granulated sugar**
    1 **egg**
    1 **teaspoon vanilla**
    2 **teaspoons poppy seed**
    1 **teaspoon finely shredded lemon
        peel**
   ¼ **teaspoon salt**
    2 **cups all-purpose flour**
       Granulated sugar
       Powdered sugar (optional)

1 In a large mixing bowl beat the butter with an electric mixer on medium to high speed for 30 seconds. Add the 1 cup granulated sugar; beat until combined. Beat in egg and vanilla until combined. Beat in poppy seed, lemon peel, salt, and as much of the flour as you can with the mixer. Using a wooden spoon, stir in any remaining flour. Cover and chill for 1 to 2 hours or until easy to handle.

2 Shape dough into 1-inch balls. Place balls 2 inches apart on an ungreased cookie sheet. Using the bottom of a glass dipped in granulated sugar, slightly flatten balls to ½-inch thickness.

3 Bake in a 375° oven for 8 to 10 minutes or until edges are firm and bottoms are lightly browned. Cool on cookie sheet for 1 minute. Transfer cookies to a wire rack and let cool. If desired, sprinkle cookies with powdered sugar.

Nutrition Facts per cookie: 67 cal., 4 g total fat (2 g sat. fat), 14 mg chol., 39 mg sodium, 8 g carbo., 0 g fiber, 1 g pro. Daily Values: 3% vit. A, 0% vit. C, 0% calcium, 1% iron

OLD-FASHIONED SUGAR COOKIES

Prep: 30 minutes   Chill: 2 hours
Bake: 7 minutes per batch
Makes: 60 cookies   Oven: 375°

For round sugar cookies without making cutouts, this recipe calls for shaping the cookie dough into balls. They flatten into rounds as they bake.

    1 **cup butter, softened**
   1½ **cups sugar**
    2 **eggs**
    2 **teaspoons cream of tartar**
    1 **teaspoon baking soda**
    1 **teaspoon vanilla**
   ¼ **teaspoon salt**
   2¾ **cups all-purpose flour**
   ¼ to ⅓ **cup sugar**

1 In a large mixing bowl beat the butter with an electric mixer on medium to high speed for 30 seconds. Add the 1½ cups sugar; beat until combined. Beat in eggs, cream of tartar, baking soda, vanilla, and salt until combined. Beat in as much of the flour as you can with the mixer. Using a wooden spoon, stir in any remaining flour. Cover and chill for 2 to 3 hours.

2 Shape dough into 1-inch balls. Roll balls in the ¼ to ⅓ cup sugar. Place balls 2 inches apart on an ungreased cookie sheet.

3 Bake in a 375° oven for 7 to 8 minutes or until lightly browned. Transfer cookies to a wire rack and let cool.

Nutrition Facts per cookie: 71 cal., 3 g total fat (2 g sat. fat), 15 mg chol., 63 mg sodium, 10 g carbo., 0 g fiber, 1 g pro. Daily Values: 3% vit. A, 0% vit. C, 0% calcium, 1% iron

WHERE DID COOKIES COME FROM?

One of the world's best-loved treats was a bit of serendipity that took on a life of its own. The word "cookie" comes from the Dutch word for cake, "koekje." The first cookies were actually tiny cakes baked as a test to make sure the oven temperature was right for baking a large cake. Someone obviously liked the results of the test.

CHOCOLATE CRINKLES

Prep: 30 minutes   Chill: 1 hour
Bake: 8 minutes per batch
Makes: 48 cookies   Oven: 375°

Snow white powdered sugar on these chocolate cookies gives them a crackly appearance.

    3 eggs
1½ cups granulated sugar
    4 ounces unsweetened chocolate, melted
½ cup cooking oil
    2 teaspoons baking powder
    2 teaspoons vanilla
    2 cups all-purpose flour
        Sifted powdered sugar

1 **In a mixing bowl beat** eggs, granulated sugar, melted chocolate, cooking oil, baking powder, and vanilla with an electric mixer until combined. Beat in as much flour as you can with the mixer. Using a wooden spoon, stir in any remaining flour. Cover and chill 1 to 2 hours or until easy to handle.

2 **Shape dough** into 1-inch balls. Roll balls in powdered sugar to coat generously. Place balls 1 inch apart on an ungreased cookie sheet.

3 **Bake in a 375° oven** for 8 to 10 minutes or until edges are set and tops are crackled. Transfer cookies to a wire rack and let cool. If desired, sprinkle with additional powdered sugar.

Nutrition Facts per cookie: 80 cal., 4 g total fat (1 g sat. fat), 13 mg chol., 19 mg sodium, 11 g carbo., 0 g fiber, 1 g pro. Daily Values: 0% vit. A, 0% vit. C, 1% calcium, 3% iron

FAIRY DROPS

Prep: 30 minutes   Chill: 30 minutes
Bake: 10 minutes per batch
Makes: 84 cookies   Oven: 350°

    1 cup butter
    1 cup sifted powdered sugar
    1 cup granulated sugar
    1 teaspoon baking soda
    1 teaspoon cream of tartar
    1 teaspoon salt
    1 cup cooking oil
    2 eggs
    2 teaspoons almond extract
4½ cups all-purpose flour
        Plain or colored granulated sugar
        or one recipe Almond Frosting
        (see page 199)
        Crushed hard candies (optional)

1 **In a large mixing bowl beat** the butter with an electric mixer on medium to high speed for 30 seconds. Add powdered sugar, granulated sugar, baking soda, cream of tartar, and salt; beat on medium-high speed until fluffy. Add cooking oil, eggs, and almond extract; beat just until combined. Gradually beat in as much of the flour as you can with the mixer. Stir in any remaining flour. Cover and chill dough about 30 minutes or until needed.

2 **Working with one-fourth** of the dough at a time, shape dough into 1¼-inch balls. (The dough will be soft; keep it chilled as you work with a portion.) Arrange balls 2 inches apart on an ungreased cookie sheet. With the palm of your hand or, if desired, the bottom of a glass or a patterned cookie stamp dipped in granulated sugar, gently flatten balls to about ¼ inch thick (see photo, page

One way to flatten balls of dough when making Fairy Drops is to use a cookie stamp that has been dipped into granulated sugar between each stamping.

Fairy Drops: These cookies sparkle like magic when spread with Almond Frosting and sprinkled with crushed candy or trimmed with a simple sprinkling of plain or colored sugar.

198). Sprinkle with sugar (unless flattened with sugared glass or stamp) or leave plain for frosting.

3 Bake in a 350° oven for 10 to 12 minutes or until edges just begin to brown. Transfer cookies to a wire rack and let cool. If desired, frost with Almond Frosting and sprinkle with crushed candy.

Almond Frosting: In a small mixing bowl beat ½ cup butter with an electric mixer on medium speed until fluffy. Beat in ½ teaspoon almond extract and ½ teaspoon vanilla. Alternately add 2½ to 3½ cups sifted powdered sugar and 3 tablespoon light cream or milk, beating until smooth and easy to spread. To tint, if desired, stir in a few drops food coloring. Makes about 2 cups.

Nutrition Facts per cookie: 77 cal., 5 g total fat (2 g sat. fat), 10 mg chol., 61 mg sodium, 8 g carbo., 0 g fiber, 1 g pro. Daily Values: 2% vit. A, 0% vit. C, 0% calcium, 1% iron

BEYOND THE COOKIE JAR

An heirloom cookie jar or pretty tin may be the most aesthetic way to store homemade cookies, but there are better ways to ensure they retain their just-baked freshness.

- **To store cookies short-term,** cool them completely. In an airtight container, arrange unfrosted cookies in single layers separated by sheets of waxed paper. If frosted, store cookies in a single layer or place waxed paper between layers. (Don't mix soft and crisp cookies in the same container or the crisp cookies will soften.) Store them at room temperature for up to three days. If they are frosted with a cream cheese or yogurt icing, you'll need to refrigerate them.

- **To store cookies long-term,** let them cool completely, then package them in freezer bags or containers and freeze for up to three months. Before serving, thaw them in the container for about 15 minutes. If the cookies are to be frosted, glazed, or sprinkled with sugar, wait until they have thawed to decorate them.

GINGERSNAPS

Prep: 30 minutes   Bake: 8 minutes per batch
Makes: 48 cookies   Oven: 375°

¾ **cup shortening**
1 **cup packed brown sugar**
1 **teaspoon baking soda**
1 **teaspoon ground ginger**
1 **teaspoon ground cinnamon**
½ **teaspoon ground cloves**
¼ **cup molasses**
1 **egg**
2¼ **cups all-purpose flour**
¼ **cup granulated sugar**

1 **In a large mixing bowl beat** shortening with an electric mixer on medium to high speed for 30 seconds. Add brown sugar, baking soda, ginger, cinnamon, and cloves. Beat until combined. Beat in molasses and egg. Beat in as much of the flour as you can with the mixer. Stir in any remaining flour.

2 **Shape dough** into 1-inch balls. Roll balls in the granulated sugar to coat. Place balls 2 inches apart on an ungreased cookie sheet.

3 **Bake in a 375° oven** for 8 to 10 minutes or until edges are set and tops are crackled. Cool cookies on cookie sheet for 1 minute. Transfer cookies to a wire rack and let cool.

Nutrition Facts per cookie: 72 cal., 3 g total fat
(1 g sat. fat), 4 mg chol., 29 mg sodium, 10 g carbo.,
0 g fiber, 1 g pro. Daily Values: 0% vit. A, 0% vit. C,
0% calcium, 2% iron

BIG SOFT GINGER COOKIES

Prep: 25 minutes   Bake: 10 minutes per batch
Makes: 24 large cookies   Oven: 350°

This recipe shared by a Better Homes and Gardens® reader first appeared in a holiday sweets story called "With Love From Grandma's Kitchen" in the magazine's December 1989 issue.

2¼ **cups all-purpose flour**
2 **teaspoons ground ginger**
1 **teaspoon baking soda**
¾ **teaspoon ground cinnamon**
½ **teaspoon ground cloves**
¾ **cup butter**
1 **cup sugar**
1 **egg**
¼ **cup molasses**
2 **tablespoons sugar**

1 **In a medium bowl combine** the flour, ginger, baking soda, cinnamon, and cloves; set aside.

2 **In a large mixing bowl beat** butter with an electric mixer on medium speed for 30 seconds. Beat in the 1 cup sugar. Add egg and molasses; beat well. Stir flour mixture into egg mixture.

3 **Shape dough** into 1½–inch balls, using about 1 heaping tablespoon dough for each. Roll balls in the 2 tablespoons sugar to coat. Place balls about 2½ inches apart on an ungreased cookie sheet.

4 **Bake in a 350° oven** about 10 minutes or until light brown and still puffed. (Do not overbake.) Cool cookies on cookie sheet for 2 minutes. Transfer cookies to a wire rack and let cool.

Nutrition Facts per cookie: 138 cal., 6 g total fat (4 g sat. fat), 24 mg chol., 114 mg sodium, 20 g carbo., 0 g fiber, 1 g pro. Daily Values: 5% vit. A, 0% vit. C, 0% calcium, 4% iron

SUGAR COOKIE
CUTOUTS

Prep: 45 minutes   **Chill:** 3 hours (if necessary)
Bake: 7 minutes per batch
Makes: 36 to 48 cookies   **Oven:** 375°

⅓ **cup butter**
⅓ **cup shortening**
¾ **cup sugar**
1 **teaspoon baking powder**
 Dash salt
1 **egg**
1 **teaspoon vanilla**
2 **cups all-purpose flour**
1 **recipe Powdered Sugar Icing (optional) (see right)**

1 **In a medium mixer bowl beat** butter and shortening with an electric mixer on medium to high speed for 30 seconds. Add sugar, baking powder, and salt. Beat until combined, scraping sides of bowl occasionally. Beat in egg and vanilla. Beat in as much of the flour as you can with the mixer. Using a wooden spoon, stir in any remaining flour. Divide dough in half. If necessary, cover and chill the dough for 3 hours or until it is easy to handle.

2 **On a lightly floured surface roll** half of the dough at a time to ⅛-inch thickness. Using a 2½-inch cookie or biscuit cutter, cut into desired shapes. Place on ungreased cookie sheet.

3 **Bake in a 375° oven** for 7 to 8 minutes or until edges are firm and bottoms are very lightly browned. Transfer cookies to a wire rack and let cool. If desired, frost with Powdered Sugar Icing.

Powdered Sugar Icing: In a mixing bowl combine 1 cup sifted powdered sugar, ¼ teaspoon vanilla, and 1 tablespoon milk. Stir in additional milk, 1 teaspoon at a time, until icing is easy to drizzle. Makes ½ cup.

Nutrition Facts per cookie: 74 cal., 4 g total fat (2 g sat. fat), 10 mg chol., 33 mg sodium, 9 g carbo., 0 g fiber, 1 g pro. Daily Values: 1% vit. A, 0% vit. C, 1% calcium, 2% iron

CUTOUT COOKIE KNOW-HOW

There's no end to the versatility and fun of cutout cookies. Here are a few ways to ensure their success:

- When rolling and cutting, work with half of the cookie dough at a time. Keep the other half of the dough refrigerated until you're ready to roll it out.
- Keep the cookie dough from sticking to the countertop by lightly sprinkling the surface with all-purpose flour. A pastry stocking and pastry cloth also can help prevent the dough from sticking.

- Dip the cutter in flour between uses to keep dough from sticking to it.
- Leave little space between cutouts to get the greatest number of cookies from the dough.
- After you've cut out your cookies, combine any scraps and reroll on a very lightly floured surface. Handle and roll the dough as little as possible to keep the cookies tender.
- Cutout cookies are done when the bottoms are very lightly browned and edges are firm.
- Cool cookies completely before storing them so they don't lose their shape.

EGGNOG COOKIES

Prep: 30 minutes   Chill: 2 hours
Bake: 10 minutes per batch
Makes: 24 cookies   Oven: 375°

2 cups all-purpose flour
1 cup sugar
¾ teaspoon baking powder
¼ teaspoon salt
¼ teaspoon ground nutmeg
⅔ cup butter
1 slightly beaten egg
¼ cup eggnog
½ cup finely crushed butterscotch-
or rum-flavored hard candies
(about twenty-five 1-inch candies)
1 recipe Eggnog Glaze
(see above right)
Yellow colored sugar (optional)

1 **In a large mixing bowl combine** flour, sugar, baking powder, salt, and nutmeg. Using a pastry blender, cut in butter until pieces are size of small peas. Make a well in center. Mix egg and eggnog; add all at once to dry mixture. Stir until moistened. Cover and chill for 2 hours or until easy to handle.

2 **Line a cookie sheet** with foil; set aside. On a well-floured surface roll dough to ¼-inch thickness. Using cookie cutters, cut into desired shapes, rerolling trimmings as necessary. Cut smaller shapes out of the centers of the larger shapes, rerolling the trimmings. Place cookies with holes in center about 1 inch apart on the prepared cookie sheet. Sprinkle crushed candies into the holes.

3 **Bake in a 375° oven** for 10 to 12 minutes or until edges are firm and lightly browned. Cool on the cookie sheet 5 minutes. Carefully transfer the cookies on the foil to a wire rack and let cool.

4 **When cookies are cool,** carefully peel foil from bottoms. Spread the cookie tops with Eggnog Glaze. If desired, sprinkle with colored sugar.

Eggnog Glaze: In a small mixing bowl stir together 3 cups sifted powdered sugar, ¼ teaspoon rum extract, and enough eggnog (2 to 3 tablespoons) to make a glaze that is easy to spread.

Nutrition Facts per cookie: 177 cal., 5 g total fat (3 g sat. fat), 22 mg chol., 91 mg sodium, 31 g carbo., 0 g fiber, 1 g pro. Daily Values: 5% vit. A, 0% vit. C, 1% calcium, 3% iron

PAINTED SOUR CREAM-SUGAR COOKIES

Prep: 40 minutes   Chill: 1 hour
Bake: 7 minutes per batch
Makes: 48 cookies   Oven: 375°

½ cup butter
1 cup sugar
1 teaspoon baking powder
¼ teaspoon baking soda
Dash salt
½ cup dairy sour cream
1 egg
1 teaspoon vanilla
1 teaspoon finely shredded lemon peel
2½ cups all-purpose flour

SLICE 'N' BAKE

Once called icebox cookies because they could be at the ready in that new-fangled invention, melt-in-your-mouth sliced cookies are still the ultimate in convenience. These tips will make them easy and delicious:

■ Give cookies a pretty coat by rolling the dough in finely chopped nuts, colored sugar, or flaked coconut; press to make coating stick; chill.

■ If a recipe makes more than one roll of dough, take only one roll at a time from the refrigerator to slice. Keep the other one chilled until you're ready for it.

■ To make your cookies nice and round, keep your dough in a perfect cylinder while it's chilling by sliding the roll into a tall drinking glass. While you're slicing, rotate the roll frequently to avoid flattening one side.

Painted Sour Cream-Sugar Cookies: Let loose the Michelangelo in you. Pure white frosting is your canvas, food coloring your paint. Use a small, clean brush to make your edible frescoes.

1 recipe Meringue Powder Icing (see below right)
Food coloring

1 **In a large mixing bowl beat** butter with an electric mixer on medium to high speed for 30 seconds. Add sugar, baking powder, baking soda, and salt; beat until combined. Beat in sour cream, egg, vanilla, and lemon peel. Beat in as much flour as you can with the mixer. Using a wooden spoon, stir in any remaining flour. Divide dough in half. Cover and chill 1 to 2 hours or until easy to handle.

2 **On a well-floured surface roll** half of the dough at a time to ⅛- to ¼-inch thickness. Using cookie cutters, cut into desired shapes. Place cookies 1 inch apart on an ungreased cookie sheet.

3 **Bake in a 375° oven** for 7 to 8 minutes or until edges are firm and bottoms are very lightly browned. Transfer cookies to a wire rack; let cool.

4 **When cookies are cool,** spread the cookie tops with Meringue Powder Icing. Allow icing to dry completely. Using a small paintbrush, paint designs on each cookie with food coloring.

Meringue Powder Icing: Beat together 2 tablespoons meringue powder and ¼ cup water until combined. Beat in 2¾ cups sifted powdered sugar.

Nutrition Facts per cookie: 84 cal., 3 g total fat (2 g sat. fat), 11 mg chol., 39 mg sodium, 15 g carbo., 0 g fiber, 1 g pro. Daily Values: 2% vit. A, 0% vit. C, 0% calcium, 2% iron

GINGERBREAD CUTOUTS

Prep: 40 minutes Chill: 3 hours
Bake: 5 minutes per batch
Makes: 36 to 48 cookies Oven: 375°

½ **cup shortening**
½ **cup sugar**
1 **teaspoon baking powder**
1 **teaspoon ground ginger**
½ **teaspoon baking soda**
½ **teaspoon ground cinnamon**
½ **teaspoon ground cloves**
½ **cup molasses**
1 **egg**
1 **tablespoon vinegar**
2½ **cups all-purpose flour**
1 **recipe Powdered Sugar Icing (optional) (see page 201)**
  Decorative candies (optional)

1 **In a large mixing bowl beat** shortening with an electric mixer on medium to high speed for 30 seconds. Add sugar, baking powder, ginger, baking soda, cinnamon, and cloves. Beat until combined, scraping bowl. Beat in molasses, egg, and vinegar until combined. Beat in as much of the flour as you can with the mixer. Using a wooden spoon, stir in any remaining flour. Divide dough in half. Cover and chill for 3 hours or until easy to handle.

2 **Grease a cookie sheet;** set aside. On a lightly floured surface, roll half of the dough at a time to ⅛-inch thickness. Using a 2½-inch cookie cutter, cut into desired shapes. Place 1 inch apart on the prepared cookie sheet.

3 **Bake in a 375° oven** for 5 to 6 minutes or until edges are lightly browned. Cool on cookie sheet 1 minute. Transfer cookies to a wire rack and let cool. If desired, decorate with icing and candies.

Nutrition Facts per cookie: 79 cal., 3 g total fat (1 g sat. fat), 6 mg chol., 30 mg sodium, 12 g carbo., 0 g fiber, 1 g pro. Daily Values: 0% vit. A, 0% vit. C, 1% calcium, 4% iron

Gingerbread People Cutouts: Prepare as at left, except roll dough to ¼-inch thickness. Cut with 4½- to 6-inch people-shaped cookie cutters. Bake in a 375° oven for 6 to 8 minutes or until edges are lightly browned. Makes about 18 large cookies.

LIME ZINGERS

Prep: 40 minutes Bake: 8 minutes per batch
Makes: 72 cookies Oven: 350°

These tangy treats became an immediate hit when they were prizewinners in a Better Homes and Gardens® magazine cookie contest in 1994.

1 **cup butter**
½ **cup granulated sugar**
2 **teaspoons finely shredded lime peel**
¼ **cup lime juice (2 limes)**

FROSTING TIPS

Fanciful frosting can make your cutouts miniature works of art. Here's how:

- Cool cookies completely before frosting, allowing about 15 minutes.
- For easy cleanup, use disposable decorating bags.
- Have on hand just a few basic decorating tips—a small writing tip, a star tip, and perhaps a small rose tip for special touches.
- Make the consistency of your frosting thick enough to hold the piping shape but thin enough to squeeze easily from the bag.
- For the brightest colors, use a frosting made with shortening instead of butter.
- Use either liquid or paste food coloring; paste gives more intense color without thinning the frosting.
- Squeeze frosting from the end of the decorating bag and use steady pressure to keep the frosting flowing evenly.
- Let frosted cookies stand on a rack until frosting is firm. Store in a single layer in cool, dry place. Decorated cookies can be frozen, just be sure frosting is dry first to prevent color from bleeding when cookies are thawed.

1 teaspoon vanilla
2¼ cups all-purpose flour
¾ cup finely chopped Brazil nuts or hazelnuts
½ of an 8-ounce package cream cheese, softened
1 cup sifted powdered sugar
1 tablespoon lemon or lime juice
1 teaspoon vanilla
Food coloring

1 **In a large mixing bowl beat** butter with an electric mixer on medium speed for 30 seconds. Beat in granulated sugar until combined. Beat in lime peel, the ¼ cup lime juice, and 1 teaspoon vanilla. Beat in as much flour as you can with the mixer. Using a wooden spoon, stir in any remaining flour. Stir in nuts. Divide dough in half.

2 **On a lightly floured surface roll** half of the dough at a time to about ¼-inch thickness. Using 1- or 2-inch cookie cutters, cut into desired shapes. Place on an ungreased cookie sheet.

3 **Bake in a 350° oven** for 8 to 10 minutes or until edges are lightly browned. Transfer cookies to a wire rack and let cool.

4 **For frosting,** beat cream cheese, powdered sugar, the 1 tablespoon lemon or lime juice, and 1 teaspoon vanilla with an electric mixer on medium speed until smooth. Tint frosting as desired with food coloring. Frost cooled cookies.

Nutrition Facts per cookie: 62 cal., 4 g total fat (2 g sat. fat), 9 mg chol., 31 mg sodium, 6 g carbo., 0 g fiber, 1 g pro. Daily Values: 3% vit. A, 0% vit. C, 0% calcium, 1% iron

MORMOR'S SYLTKAKOR

Prep: 40 minutes **Bake:** 7 minutes per batch
Makes: 36 to 42 cookies **Oven:** 375°

These buttery cutouts, pronounced "MOR-morz soolt-KAH-kor," are of Swedish origin. The name simply means Grandmother's jelly cookies.

1 cup butter, softened
¾ cup granulated sugar
1 egg
3 cups all-purpose flour
1 slightly beaten egg white

To assemble Mormor's Syltkakor, center a dot of jelly on a large cookie and top with a smaller cookie that has the center cut out, allowing jelly to peek through.

⅓ cup finely chopped almonds and/or 1 tablespoon pearl sugar or granulated sugar
¼ to ½ cup currant jelly

1 **Lightly grease a cookie sheet;** set aside. In a large mixing bowl combine butter and the ¾ cup granulated sugar; beat on medium speed until fluffy. Add egg; beat well. Beat in as much of the flour as you can with the mixer. Stir in any remaining flour. Divide dough in half.

2 **On a lightly floured surface roll** half of the dough to ⅛-inch thickness. Using a star- or round-shaped cookie cutter, cut into 2½-inch stars or rounds. Roll out second portion to ⅛-inch thickness; cut with a 2-inch star- or round-shaped cookie cutter. Using a ¾- or 1-inch cutter, cut a circle from center of smaller stars or rounds. Reroll the dough trimmings.

3 **Brush tops** of 2-inch shapes with egg white; sprinkle with almonds and/or the 1 tablespoon pearl sugar or granulated sugar. Arrange shapes on prepared cookie sheet.

4 **Bake in a 375° oven** for 7 to 9 minutes or until bottoms are lightly browned. Transfer cookies to a wire rack and let cool.

5 **Place a small amount** of jelly in centers of 2½-inch cookies; top with 2-inch cookies, nut and/or sugar side up, and press together, showing jelly in center of top cookie (see photo, above).

Nutrition Facts per cookie: 112 cal., 6 g total fat (3 g sat. fat), 20 mg chol., 56 mg sodium, 13 g carbo., 0 g fiber, 2 g pro. Daily Values: 5% vit. A, 0% vit. C, 0% calcium, 3% iron

PISTACHIO NUT
STARS OF INDIA

Prep: 40 minutes   Chill: 2 hours
Bake: 6 minutes per batch
Makes: 36 cookies   Oven: 375°

Indian cooks spice rice with cinnamon and cardamom. Here, the flavors infuse after-dinner treats with warmth (see photo, page 185).

    1 cup butter, softened
   ½ cup granulated sugar
   ¼ cup packed brown sugar
    2 tablespoons vanilla yogurt
    1 egg
 2½ cups all-purpose flour
    1 teaspoon ground cinnamon
   ¼ to ½ teaspoon ground cardamom
   ¼ teaspoon salt
    2 cups finely chopped pistachio nuts
      or almonds
    1 slightly beaten egg white
   ½ cup orange marmalade
    2 tablespoons powdered sugar

1 **In a large mixing bowl beat** butter, granulated sugar, brown sugar, and yogurt with an electric mixer on medium to high speed until creamy. Add egg; beat well. Beat in flour, cinnamon, cardamom, and salt. Using a wooden spoon, stir in nuts. Divide dough in half. Cover and chill for 2 hours.

2 **Lightly grease a cookie sheet;** set aside. On a floured surface, roll half of dough at a time to ⅛-inch thickness. Using a 3-inch star cookie cutter, cut out 36 stars from each half of dough, rerolling trimmings as needed. Place on prepared cookie sheet. With a small star-shaped cutter, cut stars from centers of half of stars. Brush all cookies with egg white.

3 **Bake in a 375° oven** for 6 to 8 minutes or until lightly browned. Transfer cookies to a wire rack and let cool.

4 **To assemble cookies,** spread dull side of each whole star with ½ teaspoon marmalade. Top each with a cutout cookie, shiny side up. Press cookies together gently. Sift powdered sugar lightly over tops of filled cookies.

Nutrition Facts per cookie: 146 cal., 9 g total fat (4 g sat. fat), 20 mg chol., 72 mg sodium, 16 g carbo., 1 g fiber, 3 g pro. Daily Values: 5% vit. A, 1% vit. C, 1% calcium, 6% iron

CASHEW-SUGAR
COOKIES

Prep: 35 minutes   Bake: 8 minutes per batch
Makes: 42 cookies   Oven: 375°

These shortbread-style sweets are perfect with a cup of afternoon tea.

 1¼ cups all-purpose flour
   ½ cup ground lightly salted cashews
      or ground almonds
   ¼ cup granulated sugar
   ¼ cup packed brown sugar
   ½ cup butter
      Granulated sugar
      Whole cashews or toasted blanched
      whole almonds
      (see tip, page 247)

1 **In a medium mixing bowl combine** flour, ground nuts, granulated sugar, and brown sugar. Using a pastry blender, cut in butter until mixture resembles fine crumbs. Form mixture into a ball and knead gently until smooth.

2 **On a lightly floured surface roll** dough to ¼-inch thickness. Cut into 1½-inch circles. Place 1 inch apart on an ungreased cookie sheet. Lightly sprinkle with the granulated sugar. Lightly press a whole nut in the center of each cookie.

3 **Bake in a 375° oven** for 8 to 10 minutes or until lightly browned. Transfer cookies to a wire rack and let cool.

Nutrition Facts per cookie: 62 cal., 4 g total fat (1 g sat. fat), 3 mg chol., 41 mg sodium, 6 g carbo., 0 g fiber, 1 g pro. Daily Values: 2% vit. A, 0% vit. C, 0% calcium, 2% iron

DECORATING 101

Cookies are wonderful because they satisfy that craving for just a bite of something sweet; you can have one (or more) all to yourself; and with
a few simple tools and techniques, they become miniature works of art. Apply one of these fun effects to the next batch of cookies you bake.

Stenciling
A condiment bottle filled with colored sugar is handy for applying stencils. It's easy to control the flow of sugar and have precise aim.

Stenciling
Sift powdered sugar over a waxed-paper snowflake pattern. Or, use a tiny cookie cutter and spoon colored sugar inside the cutter.

Chocolate Trims To make chocolate-mint curls, draw a vegetable peeler at an angle across room-temperature, layered mint candies. To make marble cutouts, swirl melted chocolate and white candy coating together, let chill 10 minutes, and cut into diamonds.

Painting Paint with cocoa paint (equal parts unsweetened cocoa powder and water) on glazed baked cookies. Or, brush egg paint (1 egg yolk, 1 teaspoon water, and food coloring) on unbaked cookies and bake.

Candy Trims
Nothing's easier—and sweeter—than a quick candy trim. Try sliced gumdrops and red cinnamon candy to make bells or holly and berries, or crushed peppermint for a cool and colorful finish.

Two-Color Glaze
Spoon one color of icing evenly over the cookie. While the first color is still wet, apply a small amount of a second color, then use a toothpick to pull the icing and make a design.

Candlewicking
To get this embroidered French-knot effect, fit a decorating tube with a small writing tip. Pipe dots in a pattern, using a swirl action so each dot looks like a thread knot.

Dips and Drizzles
Start by melting 6 ounces chocolate with 2 teaspoons shortening. Dip half or all of each cooled cookie in the melted mixture or drizzle it over the tops of the cookies.

LEMON-ALMOND TEA
COOKIES

LOW-FAT

Prep: 20 minutes **Chill:** 4 hours
Bake: 8 minutes per batch
Makes: 64 cookies **Oven:** 375°

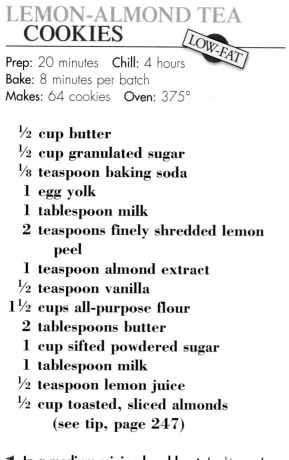

½ cup butter
½ cup granulated sugar
⅛ teaspoon baking soda
1 egg yolk
1 tablespoon milk
2 teaspoons finely shredded lemon peel
1 teaspoon almond extract
½ teaspoon vanilla
1½ cups all-purpose flour
2 tablespoons butter
1 cup sifted powdered sugar
1 tablespoon milk
½ teaspoon lemon juice
½ cup toasted, sliced almonds
(see tip, page 247)

1 **In a medium mixing bowl beat** the ½ cup butter with an electric mixer on medium to high speed for 30 seconds. Add the granulated sugar and baking soda. Beat until combined. Beat in the egg yolk, 1 tablespoon milk, lemon peel, almond extract, and vanilla. Beat in as much of the flour as you can with the mixer. Stir in any remaining flour.

2 **Shape dough** into an 8-inch-long roll. Wrap in waxed paper or plastic wrap. Chill the dough at least 4 hours.

3 **Cut dough** into ¼-inch-thick slices. Place slices 2 inches apart on an ungreased cookie sheet.

4 **Bake in a 375° oven** 8 to 10 minutes or until edges are firm and bottoms are lightly browned. Transfer cookies to a wire rack and let cool.

5 **For frosting,** in a small bowl beat 2 tablespoons butter with an electric mixer on medium to high speed for 30 seconds. Beat in half the powdered sugar. Beat in the 1 tablespoon milk and the lemon juice. Mix thoroughly. Gradually beat in the remaining powdered sugar. Spread about 1 teaspoon of frosting atop each cookie. Sprinkle with almonds.

Nutrition Facts per cookie: 45 cal., 2 g total fat (1 g sat. fat), 8 mg chol., 21 mg sodium, 5 g carbo., 0 g fiber, 1 g pro. Daily Values: 2% vit. A, 0% vit. C, 0% calcium, 1% iron

RED RASPBERRY
TWIRLS

LOW-FAT

Prep: 30 minutes **Chill:** 5 hours
Bake: 9 minutes per batch
Makes: 60 cookies **Oven:** 375°

½ cup butter
1 cup sugar
½ teaspoon baking powder
1 egg
3 tablespoons milk
¼ teaspoon almond extract (optional)
2¾ cups all-purpose flour
½ cup seedless red raspberry jam
1½ teaspoons cornstarch
½ cup toasted almonds, ground
(see tip, page 247)

1 **In a large mixing bowl beat** the butter with an electric mixer on medium to high speed for 30 seconds. Add sugar and baking powder. Beat until combined, scraping sides of bowl occasionally. Beat in egg, milk, and, if desired, almond extract. Beat in as much flour as you can with the mixer. Using a wooden spoon, stir in any remaining flour. Cover; chill 1 hour or until dough is easy to handle.

2 **Meanwhile, for filling,** in a saucepan combine jam and cornstarch. Cook and stir until thickened and bubbly. Cook and stir for 1 minute more. Stir in almonds. Cover and set aside to cool.

3 **Divide dough** in half. On waxed paper use a floured rolling pin to roll each portion into a 12×8-inch rectangle. Spread with filling. From short side, roll up each, jelly-roll style, removing waxed paper as you roll. Moisten edges and pinch to seal. Wrap in waxed paper or clear plastic wrap. Chill for 4 to 24 hours.

4 **Line a cookie sheet** with foil. Grease foil; set aside. Using a thin-bladed knife, cut dough into ¼-inch-thick slices. Place 2 inches apart on the prepared cookie sheet.

5 **Bake in a 375° oven** for 9 to 11 minutes or until edges are firm and bottoms are lightly browned. Transfer cookies to a wire rack; let cool.

Nutrition Facts per cookie: 62 cal., 2 g total fat (0 g sat. fat), 6 mg chol., 19 mg sodium, 10 g carbo., 0 g fiber, 1 g pro. Daily Values: 1% vit. A, 0% vit. C, 0% calcium, 2% iron

Red Raspberry Twirls: These pretty, swirled cookies have the flavors of the classic Austrian dessert, linzertorte (raspberry and almonds) all wrapped up in a sweet you can eat with your fingers.

BROWN SUGAR-HAZELNUT ROUNDS

Prep: 40 minutes   Chill: 4 hours
Bake: 10 minutes per batch
Makes: 60 cookies   Oven: 375°

These nutty sweets are one of our top picks from 75 years of publishing recipes. If you like, roll the log of dough in chopped toasted nuts before chilling, or dip half of each baked, cooled cookie in melted chocolate and sprinkle with chopped toasted nuts.

½ **cup shortening**
½ **cup butter**
1¼ **cups packed brown sugar**
½ **teaspoon baking soda**
¼ **teaspoon salt**
1 **egg**
1 **teaspoon vanilla**
2½ **cups all-purpose flour**
¾ **cup toasted ground hazelnuts or pecans**

1 **In a large mixing bowl beat** shortening and butter with an electric mixer on medium to high speed for 30 seconds. Add the brown sugar, baking soda, and salt. Beat until combined. Beat in egg and vanilla until combined. Beat in as much of the flour as you can with the mixer. Using a wooden spoon, stir in any remaining flour and ¾ cup ground nuts.

2 **On waxed paper** shape dough into two 10-inch rolls. Wrap each in waxed paper or plastic wrap. Chill for 4 to 48 hours or until firm enough to slice.

3 **Using a thin-bladed knife,** cut dough into ¼-inch-thick slices. Place slices 1 inch apart on ungreased cookie sheets.

4 **Bake in a 375° oven** for 10 minutes or until edges are firm. Transfer the cookies to a wire rack and let cool.

Nutrition Facts per cookie: 70 cal., 4 g total fat (1 g sat. fat), 8 mg chol., 37 mg sodium, 7 g carbo., 0 g fiber, 1 g pro. Daily Values: 1% vit. A, 0% vit. C, 0% calcium, 2% iron

SPUMONI SLICES

Prep: 30 minutes   Chill: 2 hours
Bake: 10 minutes per batch
Makes: 60 cookies   Oven: 350°

2½ **cups all-purpose flour**
1½ **teaspoons baking powder**
½ **teaspoon salt**
1 **cup butter, softened**
1½ **cups sugar**
1 **egg**
1 **teaspoon vanilla**
¼ **teaspoon peppermint extract**
5 **drops red food coloring**
¼ **cup ground pistachio nuts or almonds**
5 **drops green food coloring**
1 **ounce unsweetened chocolate, melted and cooled**
Sugar (optional)

1 **In a medium mixing bowl stir** together flour, baking powder, and salt; set aside.

2 **In a large mixing bowl** beat butter with an electric mixer on medium speed for 30 seconds. Add the 1½ cups sugar and beat until fluffy. Add the egg and vanilla; beat just until combined. Slowly add the flour mixture, beating on medium speed until combined.

3 **Divide dough** into 3 equal portions. To 1 portion of the dough, stir in peppermint extract and red food coloring. To another portion of the dough, stir in the pistachio nuts and green food coloring. To remaining dough, stir in melted chocolate.

For a tricolored effect, line rolls of 3 different colored and flavored doughs side by side, taking care not to flatten the roll during assembling and slicing.

4 **Divide each portion** of dough in half (you should have 6 portions total). On waxed paper shape each portion into a 10-inch roll. Lift and smooth the waxed paper to help shape the roll. Gently press 1 roll of pistachio dough and 1 roll of chocolate dough together, lengthwise, keeping the round shapes intact (see photo, page 210). Gently press 1 roll peppermint dough atop, lengthwise, making a shape similar to a triangle. Repeat with remaining 3 rolls.

5 **Wrap each tricolored roll** in waxed paper or plastic wrap. Chill for 2 to 48 hours or until firm enough to slice.

6 **Using a thin-bladed knife,** cut a tricolored roll of the dough into ¼-inch-thick slices. Rotate the roll as you slice to avoid flattening the roll. Place cutouts 1 inch apart on an ungreased cookie sheet. Sprinkle with sugar, if desired.

7 **Bake in a 350° oven** for 10 to 12 minutes or until edges are firm and lightly browned. Cool on cookie sheet for 1 minute. Transfer cookies to a wire rack and let cool.

Nutrition Facts per cookie: 70 cal., 4 g total fat (2 g sat. fat), 12 mg chol., 59 mg sodium, 9 g carbo., 0 g fiber, 1 g pro. Daily Values: 2% vit. A, 0% vit. C, 0% calcium, 2% iron

MOCHA MOSAIC COOKIES

Prep: 30 minutes   Chill: 5 hours
Bake: 9 minutes per batch
Makes: about 40 cookies   Oven: 375°

These fun, funky treats are like a mocha latte in a cookie: Dark, chocolate-coffee dough is topped off with dough made with light cream or milk.

　1 **tablespoon coffee liqueur or milk**
　2 **teaspoons instant espresso powder or instant coffee crystals**
　½ **cup butter**
　¾ **cup sugar**
　½ **teaspoon baking powder**
　1 **egg**
　1 **ounce semisweet chocolate, melted and cooled**
1¾ **cups all-purpose flour**
　1 **recipe Cream Dough (see right)**

For a mosaic pattern, place the light-colored Cream Dough in a pastry bag with a round tip and pipe dough in a coiled design over the cookie slices.

1 **In a small bowl stir** together coffee liqueur or milk and espresso powder or coffee crystals; set aside a few minutes until coffee is dissolved.

2 **In a large mixing bowl beat** butter with an electric mixer on medium to high speed for 30 seconds. Add sugar and baking powder; beat until combined. Beat in egg, chocolate, and liqueur mixture until combined. Beat in as much of the flour as you can with the mixer. Using a wooden spoon, stir in any remaining flour.

3 **Cover and chill dough** about 1 hour or until easy to handle. Shape dough into a 1¾-inch square log 10 inches long. Wrap in waxed paper or plastic wrap. Chill for 4 to 24 hours or until firm enough to slice. Shortly before baking, prepare Cream Dough. Place Cream Dough in a pastry bag with a round tip or in a heavy clear plastic bag.

4 **Using a thin-bladed knife,** cut dough into ¼-inch-thick slices. Place about 2 inches apart on an ungreased cookie sheet. Carefully pipe Cream Dough in a square coil pattern over cookie slices (see photo, above). If using a plastic bag, use scissors to snip a small corner from bag with Cream Dough and pipe dough onto the cookie slices.

5 **Bake in a 375° oven** for 9 to 11 minutes or until edges are firm. Cool on cookie sheet for 1 minute. Transfer cookies to wire rack and let cool.

Cream Dough: In a small mixing bowl beat 2 tablespoons butter on medium speed for 30 seconds. Add 2 tablespoons sugar and beat until combined. Add 3 tablespoons light cream or milk. Beat in ½ cup all-purpose flour until dough is smooth.

Nutrition Facts per cookie: 74 cal., 3 g total fat (2 g sat. fat), 13 mg chol., 36 mg sodium, 10 g carbo., 0 g fiber, 1 g pro. Daily Values: 3% vit. A, 0% vit. C, 0% calcium, 2% iron

Apricot-Hazelnut Biscotti:
After the first baking of the biscotti logs, use a serrated knife to cut the logs into slices. Reduce the oven temperature and continue baking the cookie slices until they are dry and crisp. For a shiny surface, mix an egg yolk with a little water and brush over the top of the biscotti logs before the first baking.

APRICOT-HAZELNUT
BISCOTTI

Prep: 35 minutes   **Chill:** 1 hour (if necessary)
Bake: 41 minutes per batch   **Cool:** 1 hour
Makes: 32 cookies   **Oven:** 375°/325°

- ⅓ **cup butter**
- ⅔ **cup sugar**
- 2 **teaspoon baking powder**
- ½ **teaspoon ground cardamom or cinnamon**
- 2 **eggs**
- 1 **teaspoon vanilla**
- 2 **cups all-purpose flour**
- ¾ **cup toasted chopped hazelnuts or almonds**
- ¾ **cup finely snipped dried apricots**

1 **In a large bowl beat** butter with an electric mixer on medium speed for 30 seconds. Add sugar, baking powder, and cardamom; beat until combined. Beat in eggs and vanilla. Beat in as much flour as you can with mixer. Stir in any remaining flour, the nuts, and apricots. Divide dough in half. If necessary, cover and chill until easy to handle.

2 **Lightly grease a cookie sheet;** set aside. Shape each portion of dough into a 9-inch log. Place 4 inches apart on the prepared cookie sheet. Flatten logs slightly until about 2 inches wide.

3 **Bake in a 375° oven** for 25 to 30 minutes or until a wooden toothpick inserted near the centers comes out clean. Cool logs on the cookie sheet on a wire rack for 1 hour. With a serrated knife, cut each log diagonally into ½-inch-thick slices (see photo, above). Lay slices, cut side down, on an ungreased cookie sheet.

4 **Bake in a 325° oven** for 8 minutes. Turn slices over; bake for 8 to 10 minutes more or until dry and crisp (do not underbake). Transfer cookies to a wire rack and let cool.

Nutrition Facts per cookie: 96 cal., 5 g total fat (1 g sat. fat), 18 mg chol., 51 mg sodium, 13 g carbo., 1 g fiber, 2 g pro. Daily Values: 5% vit. A, 0% vit. C, 1% calcium, 4% iron

ONE BISCOTTO, PLEASE

In Italy, "biscotti" refers to all kinds of cookies—not just the crunchy, twice-baked variety it implies on this side of the Atlantic. Biscotti is the plural of "biscotto," or biscuit. Try serving biscotti the Tuscan way: Dip them into coffee, tea, or a dessert wine, such as Vin Santo.

BISCOTTI D'ANICI

Prep: 30 minutes **Bake:** 40 minutes per batch
Cool: 1 hour **Makes:** 36 cookies
Oven: 375°/325°

These anise-flavored sweet biscuits are the most beloved and traditional kind of Italian cookie.

½ **cup butter**
1 **cup sugar**
1 **tablespoon anise seed, crushed, or**
   1 **teaspoon anise extract**
2½ **teaspoons baking powder**
3 **eggs**
3¼ **cups all-purpose flour**
1 **tablespoon finely shredded lemon**
   or orange peel

1 In a large mixing bowl beat butter with an electric mixer on medium to high speed for 30 seconds. Add the sugar, anise seed or anise extract, and baking powder. Beat until combined, scraping sides of bowl occasionally. Beat in eggs until combined. Beat in as much flour as you can with the mixer. Using a wooden spoon, stir in any remaining flour and the peel. Divide dough in half.

2 Lightly grease a cookie sheet; set aside. Shape each portion of dough into an 11-inch log. Place about 5 inches apart on the prepared cookie sheet. Flatten logs slightly until about 2 inches wide.

3 Bake in a 375° oven for 20 to 25 minutes or until lightly browned. Cool logs on cookie sheet on a wire rack for 1 hour. With a serrated knife, cut each log diagonally into ½-inch-thick slices. Lay slices, cut side down, on an ungreased cookie sheet.

4 Bake in a 325° oven for 10 minutes. Turn slices over; bake 10 to 15 minutes more or until dry and crisp. Transfer cookies to a wire rack; cool.

Nutrition Facts per cookie: 89 cal., 3 g total fat (2 g sat. fat), 25 mg chol., 57 mg sodium, 14 g carbo., 0 g fiber, 2 g pro. Daily Values: 3% vit. A, 0% vit. C, 2% calcium, 4% iron

Sesame Seed Biscotti: Prepare Biscotti d'Anici as directed above, except omit anise seed or anise extract and use the orange peel option. Shape dough into logs as directed above, then roll logs in ⅓ cup (2 ounces) toasted sesame seed. Place on cookie sheet; bake and cool as directed above.

ALMOND BISCOTTI

Prep: 35 minutes **Bake:** 36 minutes per batch
Cool: 1 hour **Makes:** 36 cookies
Oven: 375°/325°

⅓ **cup butter**
2 **cups all-purpose flour**
⅔ **cup sugar**
2 **eggs**
2 **teaspoons baking powder**
1 **teaspoon vanilla**
1½ **cups slivered almonds or hazelnuts,**
   finely chopped
1 **egg yolk (optional)**
1 **tablespoon milk or water (optional)**
1 **cup milk chocolate or semisweet**
   chocolate pieces
1 **tablespoon shortening**

1 In a large mixing bowl beat butter with an electric mixer on medium speed for 30 seconds. Add 1 cup of the flour, the sugar, 2 eggs, baking powder, and vanilla; beat until combined. Using a wooden spoon, stir in remaining flour and nuts. Divide dough in half.

2 Lightly grease a cookie sheet; set aside. Shape each portion into a 9-inch log. Place about 4 inches apart on prepared cookie sheet. Flatten logs slightly until about 2 inches wide. (For a shiny surface, if desired, combine egg yolk and milk; brush onto logs.)

3 Bake in a 375° oven for 20 to 25 minutes or until a wooden toothpick inserted near centers comes out clean. Cool on cookie sheet on wire rack for 1 hour. With a serrated knife, cut each log diagonally into ½-inch-thick slices. Lay slices, cut side down, on an ungreased cookie sheet.

4 Bake in a 325° oven for 8 minutes. Turn slices over; bake for 8 to 10 minutes more or until dry and crisp. Transfer to a wire rack and let cool.

5 In a heavy small saucepan heat chocolate and shortening over low heat until melted; stir occasionally. Place cooled cookies, flat side up, on waxed paper. Drizzle chocolate atop cookies or dip into melted chocolate. Let chocolate set up.

Nutrition Facts per cookie: 110 cal., 6 g total fat (1 g sat. fat), 15 mg chol., 43 mg sodium, 13 g carbo., 1 g fiber, 3 g pro. Daily Values: 2% vit. A, 0% vit. C, 3% calcium, 4% iron

SHORTBREAD EASY

Prep: 15 minutes
Bake: 25 minutes per batch
Makes: 16 cookie wedges   Oven: 325°

1¼ **cups all-purpose flour**
  3 **tablespoons granulated sugar**
½ **cup butter**

1 **In a medium mixing bowl combine** flour and sugar. Using a pastry blender, cut in butter until mixture resembles fine crumbs and starts to cling. Form mixture into a ball and knead until smooth.

To make shortbread wedges: On an ungreased cookie sheet pat or roll the dough into an 8-inch circle. Make a scalloped edge (see photo, top right). Cut circle into 16 wedges (see middle photo, right). Leave wedges in the circle. Bake in a 325° oven for 25 to 30 minutes or until bottom just starts to brown and center is set. Cut circle into wedges again while warm. Cool on the cookie sheet for 5 minutes. Transfer to a wire rack and let cool.

To make shortbread rounds: On a lightly floured surface roll the dough to ½-inch thickness. Use a 1½-inch cookie cutter to cut 24 rounds. Place them 1 inch apart on an ungreased cookie sheet and bake in the 325° oven for 20 to 25 minutes.

To make shortbread strips: On a lightly floured surface roll dough into an 8×6-inch rectangle about ½ inch thick. Using a knife, cut into twenty-four 2×1-inch strips (see bottom photo, right). Place 1 inch apart on an ungreased cookie sheet. Bake in the 325° oven for 20 to 25 minutes.

Nutrition Facts per cookie wedge: 92 cal., 6 g total fat (4 g sat. fat), 15 mg chol., 58 mg sodium, 9 g carbo., 0 g fiber, 1 g pro. Daily Values: 5% vit. A, 0% vit. C, 0% calcium, 2% iron

Butter-Pecan Shortbread: Prepare Shortbread as above, except substitute brown sugar for the granulated sugar. After cutting in butter, stir in 2 tablespoons finely chopped pecans. Sprinkle mixture with ½ teaspoon vanilla before kneading.

For a scalloped edge, use your thumb on the inside hand and thumb and index finger on the other and carefully crimp a scalloped edge around dough.

To cut shortbread into wedges, use a long, sharp knife to carefully cut dough circle into pie-shaped wedges of equal size.

For shortbread strips, mark the long sides of the rectangle at 1-inch intervals and mark the short sides at 2-inch intervals. Cut with a sharp knife or pizza cutter.

Lemon-Poppy Seed Shortbread: Prepare Shortbread as at left, except stir 1 tablespoon poppy seed into flour mixture and add 1 teaspoon finely shredded lemon peel with the butter.

Oatmeal Shortbread: Prepare Shortbread as at left, except reduce flour to 1 cup. After cutting in butter, stir in ⅓ cup quick-cooking rolled oats.

Spiced Shortbread: Prepare Shortbread as at left, except substitute brown sugar for the granulated sugar and stir ½ teaspoon ground cinnamon, ¼ teaspoon ground ginger, and ⅛ teaspoon ground cloves into the flour mixture.

BLACK WALNUT SHORTBREAD

Prep: 20 minutes **Bake:** 8 minutes per batch
Makes: 36 to 48 cookies **Oven:** 375°

    1 cup butter, softened
    1 cup sugar
1½ cups chopped black walnuts or
        English walnuts, toasted
        (see tip, page 247)
    2 cups all-purpose flour
    ½ teaspoon baking powder
    ¼ teaspoon salt
    1 cup semisweet chocolate pieces
    2 tablespoons shortening

1 In a large mixing bowl beat butter with an electric mixer on medium speed to high speed for 30 seconds. Add ¾ cup of the sugar. Beat on medium speed until light. Stir in 1 cup of the walnuts and mix well; set aside. In another bowl combine flour, baking powder, and salt. Stir flour mixture into butter mixture. Mix thoroughly to form a dough.

2 On a lightly floured surface roll dough to ½-inch thickness. Mix together the remaining sugar and nuts; sprinkle evenly atop dough. Roll dough to ¼-inch thickness. Using a 2½-inch cookie cutter dipped in flour, cut into desired shapes. Place cookies 1 inch apart on an ungreased cookie sheet.

3 Bake in a 375° oven for 8 to 10 minutes or until edges just begin to brown. Transfer cookies to a wire rack and let cool.

4 In a small saucepan melt chocolate and shortening over low heat; stir occasionally. Drizzle over cookies (see photo, below); let chocolate set.

Nutrition Facts per cookie: 121 cal., 8 g total fat (3 g sat. fat), 14 mg chol., 72 mg sodium, 11 g carbo., 0 g fiber, 2 g pro. Daily Values: 4% vit. A, 0% vit. C, 0% calcium, 3% iron

When using a chocolate drizzle, to eliminate big drips, hold chocolate-filled spoon briefly over saucepan, carry it over edge of pan, and drizzle over cookie.

SPRITZ

Prep: 25 minutes **Bake:** 8 minutes per batch
Makes: about 84 cookies **Oven:** 375°

Use a cookie press to shape these classic Christmas cookies.

1½ cups butter
    1 cup sugar
    1 teaspoon baking powder
    1 egg
    1 teaspoon vanilla
    ¼ teaspoon almond extract (optional)
3½ cups all-purpose flour
    1 recipe Powdered Sugar Icing
        (optional) (see page 201)

1 In a large mixing bowl beat butter with an electric mixer on medium to high speed for 30 seconds. Add sugar and baking powder. Beat until combined, scraping sides of bowl occasionally. Beat in egg, vanilla, and, if desired, almond extract until combined. Beat in as much flour as you can with the mixer. Using a wooden spoon, stir in any remaining flour.

2 Force unchilled dough through a cookie press onto an ungreased cookie sheet.

3 Bake in a 375° oven for 8 to 10 minutes or until edges are firm but not browned. Transfer cookies to a wire rack and let cool. If desired, dip tops into icing.

Nutrition Facts per cookie: 56 cal., 3 g total fat (2 g sat. fat), 11 mg chol., 38 mg sodium, 6 g carbo., 0 g fiber, 1 g pro. Daily Values: 3% vit. A, 0% vit. C, 0% calcium, 1% iron

Chocolate Spritz: Prepare as above, except reduce all-purpose flour to 3¼ cups and add ¼ cup unsweetened cocoa powder with the sugar.

Nutty Spritz: Prepare as above, except reduce sugar to ⅔ cup and flour to 3¼ cups. After adding flour, stir in 1 cup finely ground toasted almonds or hazelnuts (see tip, page 247).

BRANDY SNAPS *LOW-FAT*

Prep: 40 minutes
Bake: 5 minutes per batch
Makes: 20 to 24 cookies   Oven: 350°

¼ cup packed brown sugar
3 tablespoons butter, melted
1 tablespoon light-flavored molasses
2 teaspoons brandy
⅓ cup all-purpose flour
¼ teaspoon ground ginger
¼ teaspoon ground nutmeg

1 **Line a cookie sheet** with foil. Grease foil; set aside. Combine brown sugar, butter, molasses, and brandy. Stir in flour and spices until combined.

2 **Drop batter** by slightly rounded teaspoons 5 inches apart on prepared cookie sheet (bake 3 or 4 at a time); spread each to about 2 inches in diameter.

3 **Bake in a 350° oven** for 5 to 7 minutes or until bubbly and deep golden brown. Let stand for 1 to 2 minutes or until set. Quickly shape cookies, one at a time (see photo, top right); cool. (If cookies harden before you can shape them, return them to the hot oven for 1 minute or until softened.)

Nutrition Facts per serving: 34 cal., 2 g total fat (1 g sat. fat), 5 mg chol., 18 mg sodium, 4 g carbo., 0 g fiber, 0 g pro. Daily Values: 1% vit. A, 0% vit. C, 0% calcium, 1% iron

DATE AND ORANGE POCKETS

Prep: 25 minutes   Chill: 1 hour
Bake: 7 minutes per batch
Makes: about 48 cookies   Oven: 375°

½ cup butter
⅔ cup packed brown sugar
1 teaspoon baking powder
½ teaspoon ground cinnamon
⅛ teaspoon salt
1 egg
½ teaspoon vanilla
1 cup all-purpose flour
⅔ cup whole wheat flour
1 8-ounce package chopped pitted dates (sugar-coated)
⅓ cup orange juice

Work quickly to shape Brandy Snaps. Roll warm cookie around a metal cone (for cone shapes) or the greased handle of a wooden spoon (for cigar shapes).

¼ cup granulated sugar
¼ cup chopped pecans or walnuts
1 recipe Golden Icing (see below)

1 **In a large mixing bowl beat** butter with an electric mixer on medium to high speed for 30 seconds. Add the brown sugar, baking powder, cinnamon, and salt. Beat mixture until combined, scraping sides of bowl occasionally. Beat in the egg and vanilla until combined. Beat in as much of the flours as you can with the mixer. Using a wooden spoon, stir in any remaining flours. Cover and chill dough about 1 hour or until firm enough to handle.

2 **Meanwhile, for filling,** in a food processor bowl or blender container, combine dates, orange juice, granulated sugar, and nuts. Cover; process or blend until smooth, stopping to scrape sides.

3 **On a lightly floured surface roll** dough to ⅛-inch thickness. Cut into rounds using a 2½-inch cookie cutter. Place rounds ½ inch apart on an ungreased cookie sheet. Spoon 1 level teaspoon date filling into center of each round. Fold half of the round over filling, creating a half-moon shape. Seal cut edges of each round with tines of a fork.

4 **Bake in a 375° oven** for 7 to 9 minutes or until edges are firm and bottoms are light brown. Cool on a wire rack. Drizzle with Golden Icing.

Golden Icing: In a saucepan heat 2 tablespoons butter over medium-low heat for 10 to 12 minutes or until light brown. Remove from heat. Gradually stir in ¾ cup sifted powdered sugar and ¼ teaspoon vanilla (mixture will be crumbly). Gradually stir in enough milk (2 to 3 teaspoons) to make icing that is easy to drizzle. If icing sets up, add milk.

Nutrition Facts per cookie: 74 cal., 3 g total fat (2 g sat. fat), 11 mg chol., 40 mg sodium, 12 g carbo., 1 g fiber, 1 g pro. Daily Values: 2% vit. A, 1% vit. C, 1% calcium, 2% iron

brownies
and bars

Ultimate Bar Cookies, recipe page 230
Creamy, Fudgy, Nutty Brownies, recipe page 221

BROWNIES AND BARS

Brickle Bars: Give the traditional fudgy brownie treat a crunchy topping by sprinkling almond brickle and chocolate pieces over the batter before baking.

EASY FUDGE BROWNIES

Prep: 30 minutes   Bake: 30 minutes
Makes: 24 brownies   Oven: 350°

These no-mixing-bowl brownies are a breeze to make. Mix them in a saucepan, pour them in a baking pan, and enjoy them in no time.

    ½ **cup butter**
    2 **ounces unsweetened chocolate,**
         chopped
    1 **cup sugar**
    2 **eggs**
    1 **teaspoon vanilla**
    ¾ **cup all-purpose flour**
    ½ **cup chopped nuts**

1 **Grease an** 8×8×2-inch baking pan; set aside. In a medium saucepan melt butter and chocolate over low heat. Remove from heat. Stir in sugar, eggs, and vanilla. Using a wooden spoon, lightly beat the mixture just until combined (don't overbeat or brownies will rise too high then fall). Stir in flour and chopped nuts. Spread batter in prepared pan.

2 **Bake in a 350° oven** for 30 minutes. Cool in pan on a wire rack. Cut into bars.

Nutrition Facts per brownie: 113 cal., 7 g total fat (3 g sat. fat), 28 mg chol., 44 mg sodium, 12 g carbo., 0 g fiber, 2 g pro. Daily Values: 4% vit. A, 0% vit. C, 0% calcium, 3% iron

Brickle Bars: Prepare as above, except omit the nuts. Spread the batter in the prepared pan and sprinkle ¾ cup almond brickle pieces and ½ cup miniature semisweet chocolate pieces evenly over top of batter. Bake. Cool in pan on a wire rack. Cut into bars.

WHEN IN SYDNEY ...

I s there anything better than a soft, chewy brownie and a glass of milk? Those nutty, much-beloved cookies that are claimed to be as American as apple pie actually evolved from cocoa scones, a variation of Scottish tea cakes. In Australia if you ask for a brownie, you'll be served raisin bread traditionally eaten on cattle ranches at a "smoke oh," or morning break.

IRISH CREAM BROWNIES

Prep: 25 minutes **Bake:** 15 minutes
Cool: 2 hours **Makes:** 36 brownies **Oven:** 350°

Your family and friends will feel they have the luck of the Irish when you make these extra-special, Irish cream-infused brownies.

1¼ cups sugar
¾ cup butter
½ cup unsweetened cocoa powder
2 eggs
1 teaspoon vanilla
1½ cups all-purpose flour
1 teaspoon baking powder
¼ teaspoon baking soda
1 cup milk
1 cup chopped walnuts or pecans
¼ cup Irish cream liqueur or crème de cacao
1 recipe Liqueur Glaze (see above right)
1 recipe Powdered Sugar Frosting (optional) (see above right)

1 Grease a 15×10×1-inch baking pan; set aside. In a large saucepan heat sugar, butter, and cocoa powder over medium heat until butter melts, stirring constantly. Remove from heat; cool slightly. Add eggs, one at a time, and vanilla. Using a wooden spoon, lightly beat mixture just until combined. In a bowl combine flour, baking powder, and baking soda. Add flour mixture and milk alternately to chocolate mixture, beating by hand after each addition. Stir in nuts. Pour into the prepared pan.

2 Bake in a 350° oven for 15 to 20 minutes or until a wooden toothpick inserted near center comes out clean. Place pan on a wire rack. While brownies are still hot, use a pastry brush to brush liqueur or crème de cacao evenly over top. Cool. Spread with Liqueur Glaze. If desired, pipe with Powdered Sugar Frosting. Cut into bars.

Liqueur Glaze: In a medium bowl combine 2½ cups sifted powdered sugar, 2 tablespoons unsweetened cocoa powder, and ¼ teaspoon vanilla. Stir in 1 tablespoon Irish cream liqueur or crème de cacao. Stir in 3 to 4 teaspoons milk, 1 teaspoon at a time, until of drizzling consistency.

Powdered Sugar Frosting: Stir together ½ cup sifted powdered sugar and enough milk (about 1½ teaspoons) to make of piping consistency.

Nutrition Facts per brownie: 149 cal., 7 g total fat (1 g sat. fat), 17 mg chol., 62 mg sodium, 20 g carbo., 0 g fiber, 2 g pro. Daily Values: 4% vit. A, 0% vit. C, 3% calcium, 3% iron

FUDGE BROWNIE TARTS

Prep: 25 minutes **Bake:** 10 minutes
Makes: 30 tarts **Oven:** 350°

5 ounces unsweetened chocolate, chopped
⅓ cup butter
1 cup sugar
2 beaten eggs
1 teaspoon vanilla
½ cup all-purpose flour
Pecan halves (optional)

1 Line 1¾-inch muffin cups with 1¾-inch paper bake cups or grease the muffin cups; set aside. In a heavy medium saucepan melt unsweetened chocolate and butter over low heat until smooth, stirring constantly. Remove from heat.

2 Stir in sugar, eggs, and vanilla. Using a wooden spoon, lightly beat the mixture just until combined. Stir in flour. Spoon about 1 tablespoon batter into each prepared muffin cup. If desired, top with a pecan half.

3 Bake in a 350° oven for 10 to 12 minutes or until edges appear set (centers should be soft). Cool in pan on a wire rack for 5 minutes. Transfer tarts, in the paper bake cups, to a wire rack to cool.

Nutrition Facts per tart: 80 cal., 5 g total fat (2 g sat. fat), 17 mg chol., 23 mg sodium, 10 g carbo., 0 g fiber, 1 g pro. Daily Values: 2% vit. A, 0% vit. C, 0% calcium, 3% iron

CREAMY, FUDGY, NUTTY BROWNIES

Prep: 25 minutes Bake: 50 minutes
Chill: 2 hours Makes: 12 brownies Oven: 350°

The creamy crown on these brownies is essentially a chocolate cheesecake mixture, so store them in the refrigerator (see photo on page 217).

Use a flexible rubber spatula to easily spread the chocolate-cheese topping on the hot brownies. Continue baking until topping is set.

    4 ounces unsweetened chocolate, chopped
½ cup butter
    1 cup all-purpose flour
½ cup chopped walnuts or pecans, toasted (see tip, page **247**)
¼ teaspoon baking powder
1½ cups sugar
    3 eggs
    1 teaspoon vanilla
    3 ounces semisweet chocolate, chopped
    2 3-ounce packages cream cheese, softened
    1 egg
¼ cup sugar
    1 tablespoon milk
½ teaspoon vanilla

1 **Grease and lightly flour** an 8×8×2-inch baking pan; set aside. In a small saucepan melt unsweetened chocolate and butter. Remove from heat; set aside to cool slightly. In a medium bowl stir together flour, nuts, and baking powder; set aside.

2 **In a large mixing bowl stir** together the melted chocolate mixture and the 1½ cups sugar. Add the 3 eggs and 1 teaspoon vanilla. Using a wooden spoon, lightly beat mixture just until combined (don't overbeat or brownies will rise too high then fall). Stir in flour mixture. Spread batter in the prepared pan. Bake in a 350° oven for 40 minutes.

3 **Meanwhile, for topping,** in a heavy small saucepan melt semisweet chocolate over low heat; cool slightly. In a medium mixing bowl beat the softened cream cheese with melted semisweet chocolate, 1 egg, ¼ cup sugar, 1 tablespoon milk, and ½ teaspoon vanilla until combined.

4 **Carefully spread topping** evenly over hot brownies (see photo, above). Bake in the 350° oven about 10 minutes more or until topping appears set. Cool thoroughly in pan on a wire rack. Cover and chill in the refrigerator at least 2 hours before serving. Cut into bars. Cover and refrigerate to store.

Nutrition Facts per brownie: 409 cal., 27 g total fat (9 g sat. fat), 97 mg chol., 143 mg sodium, 43 g carbo., 2 g fiber, 7 g pro. Daily Values: 17% vit. A, 0% vit. C, 4% calcium, 14% iron

MAKE 'EM MELT

Melting chocolate for drizzling over cookies can be done in one of two ways:
- To melt chocolate on top of the stove, place chocolate pieces or cut-up chocolate in a heavy saucepan. Add 1 teaspoon shortening for each ½ cup (3 ounces) chocolate. (The shortening helps the chocolate set up.) Melt chocolate over low heat; stir often to avoid scorching.

- To melt chocolate in a microwave oven, place ½ cup pieces (3 ounces cut-up chocolate) in a microwave-safe measuring cup or custard cup. Microwave, uncovered, on 100% power (high) 60 to 90 seconds or until soft enough to stir smoothly; stir after 60 seconds (makes about ¼ cup melted chocolate). Pieces or squares of chocolate won't seem melted until stirred.

THINK OUTSIDE THE SQUARE

Bar cookies—including brownies—are called that because they're generally served in the shape of a bar of gold, a square, or a rectangle. You'll get the most equally sized pieces if you use a ruler to measure and toothpicks to mark the lines. Also, it's easier to get the cookies out of the pan if you remove a corner piece first.

But there's certainly more than one way to cut bars and brownies into the proper pieces:

- To make triangles, cut bars into 2- or 2½-inch squares. Cut each square in half diagonally. Or, cut bars into rectangles; cut each diagonally for triangles.
- To make diamonds, first cut parallel lines 1 or 1½ inches apart down the length of the pan. Then cut diagonal lines 1 or 1½ inches apart across the pan, forming a diamond pattern.

TRILEVEL BROWNIES

Prep: 40 minutes   Bake: 35 minutes
Makes: 32 brownies   Oven: 350°

A favorite that first appeared in Better Homes and Gardens® cookbooks during the days of bell-bottoms and the Beach Boys, these triple-layered treats are always a hit.

　　1　cup quick-cooking rolled oats
　½　cup all-purpose flour
　½　cup packed brown sugar
　¼　teaspoon baking soda
　½　cup butter, melted
　　1　egg
　¾　cup granulated sugar
　⅔　cup all-purpose flour
　¼　cup milk
　¼　cup butter, melted
　　1　ounce unsweetened chocolate,
　　　　melted and cooled
　　1　teaspoon vanilla
　¼　teaspoon baking powder
　½　cup chopped walnuts
　　1　ounce unsweetened chocolate
　　2　tablespoons butter
1½　cups sifted powdered sugar
　½　teaspoon vanilla
　　　Walnut halves (optional)

1 **For bottom layer,** stir together oats, the ½ cup flour, the brown sugar, and baking soda. Stir in the ½ cup melted butter. Press mixture into bottom of an ungreased 11×7×1½-inch baking pan. Bake in a 350° oven for 10 minutes.

2 **Meanwhile, for middle layer,** stir together egg, granulated sugar, the ⅔ cup flour, milk, the ¼ cup melted butter, 1 ounce melted chocolate, the 1 teaspoon vanilla, and baking powder until smooth. Fold in chopped walnuts. Spread batter over baked layer in pan. Bake in the 350° oven about 25 minutes more or until a wooden toothpick inserted near the center comes out clean. Place the pan on a wire rack while preparing top layer.

3 **For top layer,** in a medium saucepan heat and stir the 1 ounce chocolate and the 2 tablespoons butter until melted. Stir in the powdered sugar and the ½ teaspoon vanilla. Stir in enough hot water (1 to 2 tablespoons) to make a mixture that is almost pourable. Spread over brownies. If desired, garnish with walnut halves. Cool in pan on a wire rack. Cut into bars.

Nutrition Facts per brownie: 140 cal., 7 g total fat (4 g sat. fat), 20 mg chol., 68 mg sodium, 18 g carbo., 1 g fiber, 2 g pro. Daily Values: 5% vit. A, 0% vit. C, 1% calcium, 3% iron

PEANUT BUTTER-SWIRL
BROWNIES

Prep: 25 minutes   **Bake:** 20 minutes
Makes: 16 brownies   **Oven:** 350°

½ **cup butter**
1 **cup sugar**
2 **eggs**
1 **cup all-purpose flour**
2 **ounces unsweetened chocolate,**
   melted and cooled
⅓ **cup chunky-style peanut butter**
¼ **cup miniature semisweet chocolate**
   pieces or chopped peanuts

1 Grease a 9×9×2-inch baking pan; set aside. In a medium saucepan heat butter until melted. Remove from heat. Stir in the sugar and eggs. Using a wooden spoon, lightly beat the mixture just until combined. Stir in the flour. Remove ¾ cup of the batter; set aside.

2 Stir the melted unsweetened chocolate into the remaining batter in the saucepan. Spread chocolate batter in the prepared pan. Set aside.

3 Stir peanut butter into the reserved ¾ cup batter. Dot peanut butter batter atop the chocolate batter. Sprinkle with chocolate pieces or peanuts. Using a knife, swirl the batter.

4 Bake in a 350° oven for 20 to 25 minutes or until the brownies appear set on the surface. Do not overbake. Cool the brownies in pan on a wire rack. Cut into squares.

Nutrition Facts per brownie: 194 cal., 12 g total fat (5 g sat. fat), 42 mg chol., 101 mg sodium, 22 g carbo., 1 g fiber, 3 g pro. Daily Values: 8% vit. A, 0% vit. C, 1% calcium, 5% iron

CHEWY GINGER BARS

Prep: 20 minutes   **Bake:** 20 minutes
Makes: 32 bars   **Oven:** 350°

All the warm, spicy flavor of gingerbread is in this easy-to-make bar—just right with a cup of coffee on a crisp fall afternoon.

2 **cups all-purpose flour**
2 **teaspoons baking powder**
1 **teaspoon ground ginger**
1 **teaspoon ground cinnamon**
⅛ **teaspoon ground cloves**
½ **cup butter**
1¾ **cups packed brown sugar**
2 **eggs**
¼ **cup molasses**
1 **teaspoon vanilla**
   Powdered sugar

1 Grease a 13×9×2-inch baking pan; set aside. In a bowl combine flour, baking powder, ginger, cinnamon, and cloves; set aside.

2 In a saucepan melt butter. Remove from heat. Stir in brown sugar. Add eggs, one at a time, stirring until combined. Stir in the molasses and vanilla. Gradually add flour mixture, stirring until combined. Spread batter in the prepared pan.

3 Bake in a 350° oven for 20 to 25 minutes or until center appears set (center will sink slightly). Cool in pan on a wire rack. Sift powdered sugar over top. Cut into bars.

Nutrition Facts per bar: 111 cal., 3 g total fat (1 g sat. fat), 17 mg chol., 58 mg sodium, 19 g carbo., 0 g fiber, 1 g pro. Daily Values: 3% vit. A, 0% vit. C, 3% calcium, 5% iron

---

THE SKINNY ON REDUCED-FAT PEANUT BUTTER

So many peanut butters, so little clarity. First there was just creamy or chunky. Now there are natural and no-preservative renditions of each of those—and there are reduced-fat peanut butters, too. But let's get to the heart of the matter: Can you make your favorite peanut butter bars with reduced-fat PB? You bet. Substitute the same amount of reduced-fat peanut butter for the regular stuff. The lower-fat cookies might be slightly chewier. That shouldn't bother true stick-to-the-roof-of-your-mouth peanut butter fans one bit.

CHOCOLATE MALT BARS

Prep: 25 minutes **Bake:** 25 minutes
Cool: 2 hours **Makes:** 16 bars **Oven:** 350°

⅓ **cup butter, softened**
½ **cup sugar**
1 **egg**
½ **cup chocolate-flavored instant malted milk powder**
¼ **cup milk**
1 **teaspoon baking powder**
1 **teaspoon vanilla**
1¼ **cups all-purpose flour**
1 **cup malted milk balls, coarsely chopped**
1 **recipe Quick Fudge Frosting (see below)**

1 Grease a 9×9×2-inch baking pan; set aside. In a large mixing bowl beat butter and sugar with an electric mixer on medium speed until combined. Add egg, malted milk powder, milk, baking powder, and vanilla. Beat 2 minutes more or until combined.

2 With mixer on low speed, gradually add flour to the sugar mixture, beating just until combined. Fold in the 1 cup malted milk balls. Spread batter in the prepared pan.

3 Bake in a 350° oven about 25 minutes or until a wooden toothpick inserted near center comes out clean. Cool in pan on a wire rack. Frost cooled bars with Quick Fudge Frosting.

Quick Fudge Frosting: In a mixing bowl combine 2½ cups sifted powdered sugar, ¼ cup unsweetened cocoa powder, and 2 tablespoons chocolate-flavored instant malted milk powder. Add ¼ cup softened butter, 3 tablespoons boiling water, and ½ teaspoon vanilla. Beat with an electric mixer on low speed until combined. Beat 1 minute on medium speed. Cool 20 to 30 minutes or until spreadable.

Nutrition Facts per bar: 259 cal., 9 g total fat
(4 g sat. fat), 32 mg chol., 131 mg sodium,
44 g carbo., 0 g fiber, 3 g pro. Daily Values: 7% vit. A,
0% vit. C, 4% calcium, 6% iron

SPICED SESAME BARS

Prep: 20 minutes **Bake:** 15 minutes
Makes: 24 bars **Oven:** 350°

Toasted sesame seeds impart a rich, nutty flavor to these sophisticated spice bars. Serve them with a steaming cup of espresso.

½ **cup all-purpose flour**
½ **teaspoon ground cinnamon**
¼ **teaspoon baking soda**
¼ **teaspoon ground allspice**
¼ **teaspoon ground mace**
1 **egg**
¾ **cup packed brown sugar**
3 **tablespoons butter, melted**
¼ **cup sesame seed, toasted (see tip, page 247)**

1 Lightly grease an 8×8×2-inch baking pan; set aside. Stir together flour, cinnamon, baking soda, allspice, mace, and ¼ teaspoon salt; set aside.

2 In a bowl combine egg, brown sugar, and melted butter. Stir in flour mixture until combined. Fold in half of the sesame seed. Spread batter evenly in prepared pan; sprinkle with remaining seed. Bake in a 350° oven for 15 to 20 minutes or until a wooden toothpick inserted near center comes out clean. Cool in pan on wire rack. Cut into bars.

Nutrition Facts per bar: 60 cal., 2 g total fat
(1 g sat. fat), 11 mg chol., 54 mg sodium, 9 g carbo.,
0 g fiber, 1 g pro. Daily Values: 1% vit. A, 0% vit. C,
1% calcium, 3% iron

Chocolate Malt Bars: The nostalgic taste of malt infuses these sweet treats that call for a glass of cold milk.

Toffee Triangles: A bar cookie is not always cut in its namesake shape. For a change of pace and a fanciful touch, these easy and elegant treats are cut into triangles.

TOFFEE TRIANGLES

BEST-LOVED

Prep: 25 minutes   Bake: 33 minutes
Makes: 36 bars   Oven: 350°

    ¾ **cup butter**
    ¾ **cup packed brown sugar**
    1 **egg yolk**
    1½ **cups all-purpose flour**
    1 **14-ounce can (1¼ cups) sweetened**
       condensed milk
    2 **tablespoons butter**
    2 **teaspoons vanilla**
    1 **12-ounce package (2 cups)**
       semisweet chocolate pieces
    1 **cup almond brickle pieces or**
       toasted chopped pecans
       (see tip, page 247)

1 **Grease a** 13×9×2-inch baking pan; set aside. In a large mixing bowl beat ¾ cup butter and brown sugar with an electric mixer on medium to high speed until combined. Add egg yolk; beat well. Stir in flour and ¼ teaspoon salt; mix well. With floured hands, press dough into prepared pan.

2 **Bake in a 350° oven** about 20 minutes or until light brown. Transfer pan to a wire rack.

3 **For filling,** in a heavy medium saucepan heat condensed milk and 2 tablespoons butter over medium heat until bubbly, stirring constantly. Cook and stir for 5 minutes more. (Mixture will thicken and become smooth.) Stir in vanilla. Spread filling over baked layer. Bake in the 350° oven for 12 to 15 minutes more or until top layer is golden.

4 **Sprinkle baked layers** evenly with chocolate pieces. Bake 1 to 2 minutes more or until pieces are shiny and melted. Remove from oven; transfer to a wire rack. Immediately spread chocolate evenly over baked layer. Sprinkle with brickle pieces or pecans. Cool. Cover and chill until chocolate is set. Cut into 3×2-inch rectangles; cut diagonally into triangles. Store, covered, in the refrigerator.

Nutrition Facts per bar: 180 cal., 9 g total fat
(3 g sat. fat), 23 mg chol., 109 mg sodium,
24 g carbo., 0 g fiber, 2 g pro. Daily Values: 6% vit. A,
0% vit. C, 4% calcium, 3% iron

PAN SIZE COUNTS

As easy as bar cookies are to make, you can't be too casual about the pan in which they bake if you want them to turn out just right. Here are a couple of alternatives:

- If you don't have a 15×10×1-inch pan, use two 9×9×2-inch baking pans.

- If you don't have a 13×9×2-inch pan, use two 8×8×2-inch baking pans.

  In both substitutions, use the same oven temperature but check the bars for doneness 5 minutes before the minimum baking time given in the recipe is reached.

LAYERED CHOCOLATE-PEANUT BARS

Prep: 30 minutes   Bake: 32 minutes
Makes: 42 bars   Oven: 350°

A peanut-buttery crust, a cheesecake-like center, and a chocolate topping add up to the promise of a kid-pleasing favorite.

⅓ cup butter
¼ cup peanut butter
¾ cup packed brown sugar
1¼ cups all-purpose flour
1 8-ounce package cream cheese, softened
¼ cup honey
2 tablespoons all-purpose flour
2 tablespoons brown sugar
2 eggs
1½ cups finely chopped peanuts
1 6-ounce package (1 cup) semisweet chocolate pieces

1 **In a medium mixing bowl beat** the butter and peanut butter with an electric mixer on medium to high speed for 30 seconds. Add the ¾ cup brown sugar and beat until combined. Add the 1¼ cups flour and beat until combined. Press mixture into the bottom of an ungreased 13×9×2-inch baking pan. Bake in a 350° oven about 15 minutes or until lightly browned.

2 **Meanwhile, in a medium mixing bowl** combine cream cheese, honey, the 2 tablespoons flour, and the 2 tablespoons brown sugar. Beat on medium speed until smooth. Add eggs and beat on low speed just until combined. Stir in 1 cup of the peanuts. Pour over partially baked crust. Bake in the 350° oven about 15 minutes more or until set.

3 **Sprinkle the baked layers** evenly with chocolate pieces. Bake in the 350° oven about 2 minutes more or until chocolate is softened. Remove from oven; transfer to wire rack. Spread softened chocolate evenly over the baked layers. Sprinkle with remaining peanuts. Cool completely. Cut into bars or squares. Store, covered, in the refrigerator.

Nutrition Facts per bar: 132 cal., 8 g total fat (3 g sat. fat), 18 mg chol., 42 mg sodium, 12 g carbo., 1 g fiber, 3 g pro. Daily Values: 4% vit. A, 0% vit. C, 1% calcium, 3% iron

BLONDIES *(EASY)*

Prep: 25 minutes   **Bake:** 25 minutes
Makes: 36 bars   **Oven:** 350°

A saucepan and a spoon are all you need to mix up these butterscotch bars.

  2 **cups packed brown sugar**
⅔ **cup butter**
  2 **eggs**
  2 **teaspoons vanilla**
  2 **cups all-purpose flour**
  1 **teaspoon baking powder**
¼ **teaspoon baking soda**
  1 **6-ounce package (1 cup) semisweet**
       chocolate pieces
  1 **cup chopped nuts**

1 Grease a 13×9×2-inch baking pan; set aside. In a medium saucepan heat brown sugar and butter over medium heat until sugar dissolves, stirring constantly. Cool slightly. Using a wooden spoon, stir in eggs, one at a time, and vanilla. Stir in flour, baking powder, and baking soda. Spread batter in the prepared pan. Sprinkle with chocolate and nuts.

2 Bake in a 350° oven for 25 to 30 minutes or until done. Cool slightly in pan on a wire rack. Cut into bars while warm; cool completely in pan.

Nutrition Facts per bar: 138 cal., 7 g total fat (2 g sat. fat), 21 mg chol., 61 mg sodium, 18 g carbo., 0 g fiber, 2 g pro. Daily Values: 3% vit. A, 0% vit. C, 2% calcium, 5% iron

THE SOFT TOUCH

Most recipes that call for cream cheese call for it to be softened. There are two ways to do this.

If you have the time, simply let it stand at room temperature for about 30 minutes. If not, place 3 ounces of cream cheese in a microwave-safe container. Microwave, uncovered, on 100% power (high) for 15 to 30 seconds (30 to 60 seconds for 8 ounces) or until the cheese is softened.

OATMEAL-CARAMEL BARS

Prep: 25 minutes   **Bake:** 22 minutes
Makes: 60 bars   **Oven:** 350°

Enlist help from the kids to unwrap the caramels needed to make the topping (just be sure enough candies go in the bowl).

     1 **cup butter**
     2 **cups packed brown sugar**
     2 **eggs**
     2 **teaspoons vanilla**
     1 **teaspoon baking soda**
2½ **cups all-purpose flour**
     3 **cups quick-cooking rolled oats**
     1 **cup semisweet chocolate pieces**
½ **cup chopped walnuts or pecans**
   30 **vanilla caramels (8 ounces)**
     3 **tablespoons milk**

1 In a large mixing bowl beat butter with an electric mixer on medium to high speed for 30 seconds. Add the brown sugar. Beat until well combined. Add eggs, vanilla, and baking soda. Beat mixture until combined. Beat or stir in the flour. Stir in the oats.

2 Press two-thirds (about 3⅓ cups) of the rolled oats mixture into the bottom of an ungreased 15×10×1-inch baking pan. Sprinkle with chocolate pieces and nuts.

3 In a medium saucepan combine caramels and milk. Cook over low heat until caramels are melted. Drizzle caramel mixture over chocolate and nuts. Drop remaining one-third of the rolled-oat mixture by teaspoons over the top.

4 Bake in a 350° oven for 22 to 25 minutes or until top is light brown. Cool in pan on a wire rack. Cut into bars.

Nutrition Facts per bar: 120 cal., 5 g total fat (2 g sat. fat), 15 mg chol., 66 mg sodium, 17 g carbo., 1 g fiber, 2 g pro. Daily Values: 3% vit. A, 0% vit. C, 1% calcium, 4% iron

CHOCOLATE REVEL BARS

Prep: 30 minutes   Bake: 25 minutes
Makes: 60 bars   Oven: 350°

These fudgy bars have been the all-time favorite of the Better Homes and Gardens® Test Kitchen since they first appeared in 1968.

　　1　**cup butter**
　　2　**cups packed brown sugar**
　　1　**teaspoon baking soda**
　　2　**eggs**
　　2　**teaspoons vanilla**
2½　**cups all-purpose flour**
　　3　**cups quick-cooking rolled oats**
1½　**cups semisweet chocolate pieces**
　　1　**14-ounce can (1¼ cups) sweetened
　　　　condensed milk or low-fat
　　　　sweetened condensed milk**
　½　**cup chopped walnuts or pecans**
　　2　**teaspoons vanilla**

1 **Set aside** 2 tablespoons of the butter. In a large mixing bowl beat the remaining butter with an electric mixer on medium to high speed for 30 seconds. Add brown sugar and baking soda. Beat until combined, scraping sides of bowl occasionally. Beat in eggs and 2 teaspoons vanilla until combined.

Beat in as much of the flour as you can with the mixer. Stir in remaining flour. Stir in the oats.

2 **For filling,** in a medium saucepan combine the reserved 2 tablespoons butter, chocolate pieces, and sweetened condensed milk. Cook over low heat until chocolate melts, stirring occasionally. Remove from heat. Stir in the nuts and 2 teaspoons vanilla.

3 **Press two-thirds** (about 3⅓ cups) of the rolled oats mixture into the bottom of an ungreased 15×10×1-inch baking pan. Spread filling evenly over the oat mixture. Dot remaining rolled oats mixture on filling (see photo, below).

4 **Bake in a 350° oven** about 25 minutes or until top is light brown (chocolate filling will look moist). Cool in pan on a wire rack. Cut into bars.

Nutrition Facts per bar: 148 cal., 6 g total fat (2 g sat. fat), 17 mg chol., 79 mg sodium, 21 g carbo., 1 g fiber, 3 g pro. Daily Values: 3% vit. A, 0% vit. C, 3% calcium, 4% iron

Break up the reserved oat mixture with your hands, making small clumps of dough. Scatter the dough pieces evenly over the fudgy chocolate filling.

OATS—MORE THAN A MEAL

O atmeal—that wintertime breakfast favorite dressed up with butter, brown sugar, and milk—might not have gained its legions of fans among the ranks of American mothers had it not been for the German and Scottish immigrants who brought oats to American shores. Besides being cooked into hot cereal, oats were used to make bread and scones, and to thicken soups.

In your own baking, use either quick- or old-fashioned rolled oats. Because they're thicker, old-fashioned oats impart a more rugged texture than quick-cooking oats.

At opposite ends of the spectrum, neither instant (almost powdery) or steel-cut (also called Irish or Scottish; they are sliced whole oat grains) oats should be used for baking.

Cranberry-Macadamia Bars: Bake up a batch of these bars for the holidays when fresh cranberries are in season. Like tiny slices of a special tart, they add a different shape and beautiful color to any holiday cookie tray.

CRANBERRY-
MACADAMIA BARS

Prep: 40 minutes Bake: 40 minutes
Makes: 48 bars Oven: 350°

1¼ **cups all-purpose flour**
 ¾ **cup sugar**
 ½ **cup butter**
 ½ **cup finely chopped macadamia**
     nuts, hazelnuts (filberts),
     or pecans
1¼ **cups sugar**
 2 **beaten eggs**
 2 **tablespoons milk**
 1 **teaspoon finely shredded**
     orange peel
 1 **teaspoon vanilla**
 ½ **cup finely chopped macadamia**
     nuts, hazelnuts (filberts),
     or pecans
 1 **cup finely chopped cranberries**
 ½ **cup coconut**

1 **In a mixing bowl stir** together the flour and the ¾ cup sugar. Using a pastry blender, cut in butter until mixture resembles coarse crumbs. Stir in the ½ cup nuts. Press flour mixture into the bottom of an ungreased 13×9×2-inch baking pan. Bake in a 350° oven for 10 to 15 minutes or until the crust is light brown around the edges.

2 **Meanwhile, in a mixing bowl** combine the 1¼ cups sugar, eggs, milk, orange peel, and vanilla. Beat until combined. Pour over the hot crust. Sprinkle with the ½ cup nuts, the cranberries, and coconut.

3 **Bake in the 350° oven** for 30 minutes more or until golden. Cool slightly in pan on a wire rack. Cut into 24 bars and cut bars in half diagonally while warm. Cool completely in pan.

Nutrition Facts per bar: 88 cal., 4 g total fat (2 g sat. fat), 14 mg chol., 23 mg sodium, 12 g carbo., 0 g fiber, 1 g pro. Daily Values: 2% vit. A, 0% vit. C, 0% calcium, 1% iron

BARS IN THE BAG

Bake a batch of bars and stash them in the freezer for the future; you'll be glad you had such discipline when the craving for something sweet hits. Here's how to bake and store bars:

Before spreading the batter in the pan, line it with foil (see tip, page 231). Follow the recipe for baking and cooling. Lift the bars out of the pan on the foil. Place the uncut and unfrosted bars in freezer bags or airtight containers. Seal, label, date, and freeze. Thaw the bars at room temperature for about 15 minutes. Once thawed, the bars can be frosted and cut.

ULTIMATE BAR COOKIES

Prep: 30 minutes   Bake: 30 minutes
Makes: 36 bars   Oven: 350°

Crush any leftover bars and sprinkle over ice cream as a topping (see photo, page 217).

  2 cups all-purpose flour
  ½ cup packed brown sugar
  ½ cup butter, softened
  1 cup coarsely chopped walnuts
  1 3½-ounce jar macadamia nuts,
       coarsely chopped (1 cup)
  1 6-ounce package white baking
       bars, coarsely chopped (1 cup)
  1 cup milk chocolate pieces
  ¾ cup butter
  ½ cup packed brown sugar

1 **In a medium mixing bowl beat** flour, ½ cup brown sugar, and ½ cup butter with an electric mixer on medium speed until mixture forms fine crumbs. Press mixture firmly into the bottom of an ungreased 13×9×2-inch baking pan.

2 **Bake in a 350° oven** 15 minutes or until lightly browned. Transfer pan to a rack. Sprinkle nuts, baking bars, and milk chocolate pieces over hot crust.

3 **Heat and stir** the ¾ cup butter and ½ cup brown sugar over medium heat until bubbly. Cook and stir for 1 minute more. Pour evenly over layers in pan. Bake in the 350° oven for 15 minutes more or until just bubbly around edges. Cool in pan on a wire rack. Cut into desired shapes.

Nutrition Facts per bar: 188 cal., 13 g total fat (6 g sat. fat), 18 mg chol., 12 mg sodium, 16 g carbo., 1 g fiber, 2 g pro. Daily Values: 6% vit. A, 0% vit. C, 2% calcium, 4% iron

HAZELNUT BARS

Prep: 20 minutes   Bake: 50 minutes
Makes: 48 bars   Oven: 350°

  2 cups all-purpose flour
  2 3-ounce packages cream cheese,
       softened
  ½ cup butter, softened
  ½ cup packed brown sugar
  4 eggs
  2 cups granulated sugar
  1½ cups buttermilk or sour milk
       (see tip, page 329)
  ½ cup butter, melted
  ⅓ cup all-purpose flour
  2 teaspoons vanilla
  ¼ teaspoon salt
  2 cups chopped hazelnuts, toasted
       (see tip, page 247)

1 **For crust,** beat the 2 cups flour, cream cheese, the ½ cup softened butter, and brown sugar with an electric mixer until well combined. With lightly floured hands, press mixture into bottom and up sides of an ungreased 15×10×1-inch baking pan. Bake in a 350° oven for 15 minutes.

2 **Meanwhile, for filling,** in a large mixing bowl beat the eggs, granulated sugar, buttermilk, the ½ cup melted butter, the ⅓ cup flour, vanilla, and salt with an electric mixer until combined. Stir in nuts. Pour mixture into prebaked crust. Bake about 35 minutes more or until golden. Cool on a wire rack. Cut into bars. Cover and store in refrigerator.

Nutrition Facts per bar: 146 cal., 9 g total fat (4 g sat. fat), 32 mg chol., 75 mg sodium, 16 g carbo., 1 g fiber, 2 g pro. Daily Values: 5% vit. A, 0% vit. C, 2% calcium, 3% iron

Apricot-Cardamom Bars: Applesauce fills in for some of the fat in these bars to make them moist and flavorful.

APRICOT-CARDAMOM BARS

LOW-FAT

Prep: 25 minutes **Bake:** 25 minutes
Cool: 2 hours **Makes:** 24 bars
Oven: 350°

  1 **cup all-purpose flour**
  ½ **teaspoon baking powder**
  ¼ **teaspoon baking soda**
  ¼ **teaspoon ground cardamom or**
      ⅛ **teaspoon ground cloves**
  1 **slightly beaten egg**
  ½ **cup packed brown sugar**
  ½ **cup apricot nectar or orange juice**
  ¼ **cup unsweetened applesauce**
  2 **tablespoons cooking oil**
  ½ **cup finely snipped dried apricots**
  1 **recipe Apricot Icing (see right)**

1 **In a medium bowl stir** together flour, baking powder, soda, and cardamom; set aside. In another bowl stir together egg, brown sugar, apricot nectar, applesauce, and oil until combined. Add to flour mixture; stir until combined. Stir in apricots.

2 **Spread batter** in an ungreased 11×7×1½-inch baking pan. Bake in a 350° oven about 25 minutes or until a wooden toothpick inserted near the center comes out clean. Cool in pan on a wire rack. Drizzle with Apricot Icing. Cut into bars.

Apricot Icing: Stir together ½ cup sifted powdered sugar and enough apricot nectar or orange juice (2 to 3 teaspoons) to make icing that is easy to drizzle.

Nutrition Facts per bar: 63 cal., 1 g total fat (0 g sat. fat), 9 mg chol., 25 mg sodium, 12 g carbo., 0 g fiber, 1 g pro. Daily Values: 3% vit. A, 3% vit. C, 1% calcium, 3% iron

QUICK CLEANUP

Lining your baking pan with foil not only makes it easier to get the bars or brownies out of the pan when they have finished baking, it makes it easier to clean up, too.

Simply line the pan with foil, slightly extending the foil over the edges of the pan. If the recipe calls for a greased pan, grease the foil instead. Spread the cookie dough evenly in the pan. Bake and cool the bars in the pan; then pull the foil edges down to the counter and lift the bars out. Cut into whatever shapes you wish (see tip, page 222).

MOCHA CHEESECAKE
DREAMS

Prep: 30 minutes Bake: 35 minutes
Makes: 32 bars Oven: 350°

1¼ **cups all-purpose flour**
  1 **cup sifted powdered sugar**
  ½ **cup unsweetened cocoa powder**
  ¼ **teaspoon baking soda**
  ¾ **cup butter**
  1 **tablespoon instant coffee crystals**
  1 **tablespoon hot water**
  1 **8-ounce package cream cheese, softened**
  1 **14-ounce can (1¼ cups) sweetened condensed milk**
  2 **eggs**
    Chocolate-flavored syrup (optional)

1 **For crust,** in a large mixing bowl stir together flour, powdered sugar, cocoa powder, and baking soda. Using a pastry blender or fork, cut in butter until crumbly; press flour mixture into the bottom of an ungreased 13×9×2-inch baking pan. Bake in a 350° oven for 15 minutes.

2 **Meanwhile, dissolve** instant coffee crystals in hot water. Set aside. In a large mixing bowl beat cream cheese with an electric mixer until fluffy. Gradually beat in the sweetened condensed milk. Add the coffee mixture and eggs; beat until combined. Pour over the hot baked crust.

3 **Bake in the 350° oven** for 20 minutes or until set. Cool in pan on a wire rack. Cut into bars. Store, covered, in the refrigerator. If desired, drizzle bars with chocolate-flavored syrup.

Nutrition Facts per bar: 143 cal., 8 g total fat (7 g sat. fat), 49 mg chol., 94 mg sodium, 14 g carbo., 0 g fiber, 3 g pro. Daily Values: 8% vit. A, 0% vit. C, 4% calcium, 3% iron

Mocha Cheesecake Dreams: These mocha-flavored treats are easy-to-make bar cookies masquerading as cheesecake. Drizzle extra chocolate on your serving plates for a sophisticated presentation.

CHERRY CHEESECAKE BARS

Prep: 30 minutes **Bake:** 25 minutes
Cool: 2 hours **Makes:** 32 bars **Oven:** 350°

A chocolate cookie crust and cherry pie filling make these bars an easy dessert.

> **2 cups finely crushed chocolate wafers (about 44 wafers)**
> **⅓ cup butter, melted**
> **1 8-ounce package cream cheese, softened**
> **1 3-ounce package cream cheese, softened**
> **¾ cup sugar**
> **½ teaspoon almond extract or vanilla**
> **4 eggs**
> **¼ cup milk**
> **1 21-ounce can cherry pie filling**
> **½ cup sliced almonds**

1 Grease a 13×9×2-inch baking pan; set aside. For crust, in a mixing bowl combine crushed wafers and melted butter. Press crumb mixture evenly into bottom of the prepared pan; set aside.

2 For filling, in a mixing bowl beat cream cheese, sugar, and almond extract or vanilla with an electric mixer on medium to high speed until combined. Add eggs all at once. Beat on low speed just until combined. Stir in milk. Spread cream cheese filling evenly over the crust.

3 Bake in a 350° oven for 25 to 30 minutes or until center appears set. Cool on wire rack.

4 For topping, in a bowl stir together pie filling and almonds. Spread over cream cheese filling. Cover and chill thoroughly. Cut into bars.

Nutrition Facts per bar: 146 cal., 8 g total fat
(4 g sat. fat), 43 mg chol., 107 mg sodium,
17 g carbo., 0 g fiber, 3 g pro. Daily Values: 7% vit. A,
0% vit. C, 2% calcium, 4% iron

FRUIT CRUMB BARS

Prep: 30 minutes **Bake:** 32 minutes
Makes: 50 bars **Oven:** 350°

Dress up these pielike bars with a drizzle of powdered sugar icing.

> **2½ cups all-purpose flour**
> **2½ cups quick-cooking rolled oats**
> **1½ cups packed brown sugar**
> **¼ teaspoon baking soda**
> **1½ cups butter, melted**
> **1 21- to 24-ounce can apple, apricot, blueberry, cherry, peach, or raisin pie filling or 2 cups prepared mincemeat**
> **1 teaspoon finely shredded lemon or orange peel**

1 In a mixing bowl stir together flour, oats, brown sugar, and baking soda. Stir in melted butter until combined. Set 2 cups of the rolled oats mixture aside for topping. Press the remaining rolled oats mixture into the bottom of an ungreased 15×10×1-inch baking pan. Bake in a 350° oven for 12 minutes.

2 Snip large pieces of fruit in pie filling. Stir lemon or orange peel into pie filling or mincemeat. Carefully spread on top of baked crust. Sprinkle with remaining rolled oats mixture. Slightly pat mixture into filling.

3 Bake in the 350° oven for 20 to 25 minutes more or until top is golden. Cool in pan on a wire rack. Cut into bars.

Nutrition Facts per bar: 124 cal., 6 g total fat
(1 g saturated fat), 7 mg chol., 65 mg sodium,
17 g carbo., 0 g fiber, 1 g pro. Daily Values: 6% vit. A,
2% vit. C, 0% calcium, 4% iron

MIXED NUT BARS

Prep: 20 minutes   **Bake:** 25 minutes
Makes: 20 bars   **Oven:** 350°

*Though there's not a trace of chocolate in these
nutty bars, they have a rich, fudgy texture.*

1 cup packed brown sugar
⅓ cup butter
1 beaten egg
½ teaspoon vanilla
1 cup all-purpose flour
½ teaspoon baking powder
1 cup mixed nuts, Brazil nuts, or
    cashews, coarsely chopped

1 Grease an 8×8×2-inch baking pan; set aside. In
a medium saucepan heat brown sugar and butter
over medium heat until sugar dissolves, stirring constantly. Remove from heat. Cool slightly.

2 Stir in egg and vanilla. Stir in flour and baking
powder just until combined. Stir in nuts. Spread
batter in the prepared pan.

3 Bake in a 350° oven about 25 minutes or until
a wooden toothpick inserted near center comes
out clean. Cool slightly in pan on a wire rack. Cut
into bars while warm; cool completely in pan.

Nutrition Facts per bar: 138 cal., 7 g total fat (1 g sat.
fat), 15 mg chol., 45 mg sodium, 17 g carbo.,
1 g fiber, 2 g pro. Daily Values: 3% vit. A, 0% vit. C,
2% calcium, 5% iron

BEAUTIFUL BARS

Besides their great taste, much of the
beauty of bar cookies is their ease: just
stir, bake, and eat. If you'd like to dress them
up a bit, try one of these simple garnishes:

■ For unfrosted bars, lay waxed-paper strips
across top in a pattern. Sprinkle with a
mixture of powdered sugar and a spice
that's called for in the recipe.

■ For frosted bars, sprinkle with grated
chocolate or chocolate curls, miniature
chocolate chips, chopped nuts, or dried or
candied fruit.

CARROT-PUMPKIN BARS WITH ORANGE ICING

Prep: 40 minutes   **Bake:** 20 minutes
Cool: 2 hours   **Makes:** 36 bars   **Oven:** 350°

2 cups all-purpose flour
2 teaspoons baking powder
1 teaspoon finely shredded orange
    peel
½ teaspoon baking soda
¼ teaspoon salt
3 beaten eggs
1½ cups packed brown sugar
1 cup canned pumpkin
⅔ cup cooking oil
¼ cup milk
1 teaspoon vanilla
1 cup finely shredded carrots
1 cup chopped walnuts
1 recipe Orange Icing (see below)
    Walnut halves (optional)

1 Grease a 15×10×1-inch baking pan; set aside.
In a large mixing bowl stir together flour, baking powder, orange peel, baking soda, and salt. Set
mixture aside.

2 In a medium bowl combine eggs and brown
sugar. Stir in pumpkin, cooking oil, milk, and
vanilla. Stir in carrots and walnuts. Add egg mixture
to flour mixture, stirring with a wooden spoon until
combined. Spread batter in the prepared pan.

3 Bake in a 350° oven for 20 to 25 minutes or
until a wooden toothpick inserted near the center comes out clean. Cool in pan on a wire rack.
Spread with Orange Icing and cut into triangles or
squares. If desired, garnish each with a walnut half.
Store, covered, in the refrigerator.

Orange Icing: In a mixing bowl combine 1½ cups
sifted powdered sugar and enough orange liqueur or
orange juice (1 to 2 tablespoons) to make an icing
that is easy to drizzle.

Nutrition Facts per bar: 137 cal., 7 g total fat
(1 g sat. fat), 18 mg chol., 63 mg sodium, 18 g carbo.,
1 g fiber, 2 g pro. Daily Values: 24% vit. A, 1% vit. C,
3% calcium, 4% iron

Carrot-Pumpkin Bars with Orange Icing: Chunky walnut halves make an attractive addition atop these autumnal treats.

Raspberry-Citrus Bars:
Raspberry and lemon are classically compatible flavors. The tang of the lemon heightens the sweetness of the fresh raspberries that are baked right into the bars.

LEMON BARS DELUXE

Prep: 25 minutes **Bake:** 45 minutes
Cool: 2 hours **Makes:** 30 bars
Oven: 350°

Who says you can't freshen up a classic? One version of this longtime favorite lemon bar recipe gets a sprinkling of fresh raspberries and orange peel (see lower right).

  1 cup butter
½ cup sifted powdered sugar
2 cups all-purpose flour
4 beaten eggs
1½ cups granulated sugar
2 teaspoons finely shredded lemon peel (set aside)
⅓ cup lemon juice
¼ cup all-purpose flour
½ teaspoon baking powder
  Sifted powdered sugar
  Citrus peel strips (optional)

1 **In a large mixing bowl beat** the butter with an electric mixer on medium to high speed for 30 seconds. Add the ½ cup powdered sugar and beat until combined. Beat in the 2 cups flour until crumbly. Press mixture into the bottom of an ungreased 13×9×2-inch baking pan. Bake in a 350° oven for 20 to 25 minutes or until lightly browned.

2 **Meanwhile, beat together** eggs, granulated sugar, and lemon juice. Combine the ¼ cup flour and the baking powder; stir into egg mixture along with the lemon peel. Pour over baked crust.

3 **Bake in the 350° oven** for 25 minutes more or until lightly browned around edges and center appears set. Cool in pan on a wire rack. Sprinkle with additional powdered sugar. Cut into squares or diamonds. If desired, garnish with strips of citrus peel. Store, covered, in the refrigerator.

Nutrition Facts per bar: 142 cal., 7 g total fat (4 g sat. fat), 45 mg chol., 77 mg sodium, 19 g carbo., 0 g fiber, 2 g pro. Daily Values: 6% vit. A, 2% vit. C, 1% calcium, 3% iron

Raspberry-Citrus Bars: Prepare as above, except substitute 2 tablespoons finely shredded orange peel for the lemon peel in the filling. After crust is baked, sprinkle 1½ cups fresh raspberries over crust. Pour filling over berries, arranging berries evenly with a spoon. Bake for 25 to 30 minutes or until set.

CITRUS-HAZELNUT BARS

Prep: 30 minutes   Bake: 30 minutes
Makes: 20 bars   Oven: 350°

⅓ **cup butter, softened**
¼ **cup granulated sugar**
1 **cup all-purpose flour**
⅓ **cup finely chopped hazelnuts,**
   toasted* (see tip, page 247)
2 **eggs**
¾ **cup granulated sugar**
2 **tablespoons all-purpose flour**
1 **teaspoon finely shredded orange**
   peel
1 **teaspoon finely shredded lemon**
   peel
2 **tablespoons orange juice**
1 **tablespoon lemon juice**
½ **teaspoon baking powder**
   Powdered sugar (optional)

1 **In a medium mixing bowl beat** the butter with an electric mixer on medium to high speed for 30 seconds. Add the ¼ cup granulated sugar. Beat until combined. Beat in 1 cup flour and about half of the nuts until crumbly. Press mixture into the bottom of an ungreased 8×8×2-inch baking pan. Bake in a 350° oven for 10 minutes or until lightly browned.

2 **Meanwhile, in a mixing bowl** combine eggs, the ¾ cup granulated sugar, 2 tablespoons flour, peels, orange juice, lemon juice, and baking powder. Beat for 2 minutes at medium speed or until combined. Pour over hot baked layer. Sprinkle with remaining nuts.

3 **Bake in a 350° oven** about 20 minutes more or until light brown around the edges and the center appears set. Cool in pan on a wire rack. If desired, sift powdered sugar over top. Cut into bars. Store, covered, in the refrigerator.

*Note: Chopped almonds may be substituted for the chopped toasted hazelnuts. Do not toast almonds.

Nutrition facts per bar: 108 cal., 5 g total fat
(2 g sat. fat), 29 mg chol., 43 mg sodium, 15 g carbo.,
0 g fiber, 2 g pro. Daily Values: 4% vit. A, 1% vit. C,
0% calcium, 2% iron

FROSTED FIG BARS

Prep: 35 minutes   Bake: 30 minutes
Cool: 2 hours   Makes: 20 bars   Oven: 350°

Look for dried fig varieties such as Black Mission or Calimyrna (golden in color) on your supermarket shelves or in the produce aisle.

1 **cup all-purpose flour**
1 **cup rolled oats**
⅔ **cup packed brown sugar**
¼ **teaspoon baking soda**
½ **cup butter**
1 **recipe Fig Filling (see below)**
½ **cup sifted powdered sugar**
¼ **teaspoon vanilla**
1 **to 2 teaspoons orange juice**

1 **In a mixing bowl combine** flour, oats, brown sugar, and baking soda. Using a pastry blender, cut in butter until mixture resembles coarse crumbs. Reserve ½ cup of the flour mixture. Press remaining flour mixture into the bottom of an ungreased 9×9×2-inch baking pan. Spread with Fig Filling. Sprinkle with reserved flour mixture.

2 **Bake in a 350° oven** about 30 minutes or until golden. Cool in pan on a wire rack.

3 **For glaze,** mix powdered sugar, vanilla, and enough orange juice to make glaze that is easy to drizzle. Drizzle over top. Cut into bars.

Fig Filling: In a medium saucepan combine 1½ cups finely chopped dried figs, ⅓ cup water, ¼ cup orange juice, 3 tablespoons granulated sugar, and 1 teaspoon finely shredded orange peel. Bring to boiling. Reduce heat and simmer, uncovered, for 5 to 10 minutes or until thick.

Nutrition facts per bar: 161 cal., 5 g total fat
(3 g sat. fat), 12 mg chol., 68 mg sodium, 29 g carbo.,
2 g fiber, 2 g pro. Daily Values: 5% vit. A, 2% vit. C,
2% calcium, 6% iron

BRANDIED CRANBERRY-APRICOT BARS

BEST-LOVED

Prep: 35 minutes **Bake:** 1 hour
Cool: 2 hours **Makes:** 16 bars **Oven:** 350°

Relatively new to our archives, these rich, cakelike bars were the first Better Homes and Gardens® Prize-Tested Recipe Grand Prize Winner.

⅓ **cup golden raisins**
⅓ **cup dark raisins**
⅓ **cup dried cranberries**
⅓ **cup snipped dried apricots**
½ **cup brandy or water**
1 **cup all-purpose flour**
⅓ **cup packed brown sugar**
½ **cup butter**
2 **eggs**
1 **cup packed brown sugar**
½ **cup all-purpose flour**
1 **teaspoon vanilla**
⅓ **cup chopped pecans**
   Powdered sugar

1 **In a saucepan** combine the golden raisins, dark raisins, dried cranberries, apricots, and brandy or water. Bring to boiling. Remove from heat. Let stand for 20 minutes; drain.

2 **In a medium mixing bowl** stir together the 1 cup flour and ⅓ cup brown sugar. Using a pastry blender, cut in butter until mixture resembles coarse crumbs. Press mixture into the bottom of an ungreased 8×8×2-inch baking pan. Bake in a 350° oven about 20 minutes or until golden.

3 **Meanwhile, in a medium mixing bowl** beat the eggs with an electric mixer on low speed for 4 minutes. Stir in 1 cup brown sugar, the ½ cup flour, and the vanilla. Stir in the drained fruit and pecans. Pour fruit mixture over crust; spread evenly.

4 **Bake in the 350° oven** about 40 minutes more or until a toothpick inserted near center comes out clean, covering with foil the last 10 minutes to prevent overbrowning. Cool in pan on a wire rack. Sprinkle powdered sugar over top. Cut into bars.

Nutrition facts per bar: 221 cal., 8 g total fat (6 g sat. fat), 57 mg chol., 72 mg sodium, 32 g carbo., 1 g fiber, 2 g pro. Daily Values: 8% vit. A, 0% vit. C, 2% calcium, 8% iron

Brandied Cranberry-Apricot Bars: These perfect-for-the-holidays bars prove easy and elegant are not mutually exclusive.

PIÑA COLADA SQUARES

Prep: 20 minutes **Bake:** 30 minutes
Makes: 48 bars **Oven:** 350°

Pineapple ice-cream topping makes these island-inspired bar cookies a breeze to bake.

2 **cups all-purpose flour**
2 **cups quick-cooking rolled oats**
1⅓ **cups packed brown sugar**
¼ **teaspoon baking soda**
1 **cup butter**
1 **cup pineapple ice-cream topping**
1 **teaspoon rum extract**
1 **cup coconut**

1 **In a large mixing bowl** combine the flour, oats, brown sugar, and baking soda. Using a pastry blender, cut in butter until mixture resembles coarse crumbs. Reserve 1 cup of the crumb mixture for topping. Press the remaining mixture into the bottom of an ungreased 13×9×2-inch baking pan.

2 **For filling,** in a small mixing bowl combine pineapple topping and rum extract. Spread pineapple mixture evenly over the crust.

3 **For topping,** stir coconut into reserved crumb mixture. Sprinkle topping evenly over the pineapple-rum filling. Bake in a 350° oven about 30 minutes or until golden. Cool. Cut into bars.

Nutrition facts per bar: 108 cal., 5 g total fat (3 g sat. fat), 10 mg chol., 52 mg sodium, 16 g carbo., 1 g fiber, 1 g pro. Daily Values: 3% vit. A, 6% vit. C, 0% calcium, 3% iron

spectacular
desserts

Mini Molten Chocolate Cakes, recipe page 243

SPECTACULAR DESSERTS

BRANDIED PEACH-
PRALINE BASKETS

Prep: 40 minutes   Bake: 8 minutes per batch
Makes: 12 servings   Oven: 350°

½ **cup butter**
1 **cup sugar**
¼ **cup dark-colored corn syrup**
1⅓ **cups toasted, finely chopped
        pecans (see tip, page 247)**
¼ **cup all-purpose flour
    Melted chocolate (optional)**
1½ **quarts butter pecan or other
        desired ice cream or sorbet**
1 **recipe Brandied Peach Sauce
        (see right)**
    **Chocolate Leaves (see right) and/or
    gold paper leaves (optional)**

1 **Line a large** cookie sheet with heavy foil; grease foil. Grease outside bottoms and sides of 4 inverted 6-ounce custard cups. Set sheet and cups aside.

2 **Melt butter** in a medium saucepan; remove from heat. Stir in sugar and corn syrup. Stir in nuts and flour. For each basket, drop 2 tablespoons of the batter 7 inches apart on the prepared cookie sheet; spread batter to 3-inch circles. (Bake only 2 cookies at a time.)

3 **Bake in a 350° oven** 8 to 10 minutes or until a deep golden brown. Cool on cookie sheet 2 minutes or just until cookies are firm enough to hold their shape. Quickly remove cookies from sheet and place each cookie over a prepared custard cup. Using a wooden spoon, gently fold edges down to form ruffles or pleats. (If cookies harden before shaping, reheat them in oven for 1 minute.) Cool completely. Remove baskets from custard cups. Repeat with remaining batter, wiping excess fat from cookie sheet between batches. Tightly cover and store in a cool, dry place up to 1 week or in freezer up to 6 months.

4 **To serve,** if desired, brush basket edges with melted chocolate. Scoop ice cream into baskets. Top with warm Brandied Peach Sauce. If desired, garnish with Chocolate Leaves and/or gold paper leaves.

Brandied Peach Sauce: In small saucepan combine ½ cup packed brown sugar and 1 tablespoon cornstarch. Add ½ cup whipping cream and 2 teaspoons butter. Cook and stir over medium heat until bubbly. Add 1 cup thinly sliced peaches, ¼ cup toasted chopped pecans, and 1 tablespoon brandy. Cook and stir until bubbly. Cool slightly. Makes 1¾ cups.

Nutrition Facts per serving: 467 cal., 29 g total fat (13 g sat. fat), 65 mg chol., 148 mg sodium, 52 g carbo., 1 g fiber, 4 g pro. Daily Values: 20% vit. A, 3% vit. C, 9% calcium, 6% iron

Chocolate Leaves: With a clean, small paintbrush, brush 1 or 2 coats of melted chocolate on the underside of nontoxic leaves such as mint, rose, or lemon. Wipe away any chocolate from top side of leaf. Place the leaves, chocolate side up, on waxed-paper-lined baking sheet until dry. Before using, peel the leaf away from the chocolate.

Brandied Peach-Praline Baskets: Present your guests with an edible basket of goodies as a final course. You can make the nutty, caramelized cups up to six months in advance, freezing until needed. To serve, thaw and fill.

Olive Oil Génoise in Strawberry Champagne Sauce: This airy sponge cake surrounded by a champagne-laced fruit sauce is the definition of simple elegance. The cake is made especially delicate thanks to olive oil.

OLIVE OIL GÉNOISE
IN STRAWBERRY
CHAMPAGNE SAUCE

Prep: 40 minutes Bake: 30 minutes
Makes: 10 to 12 servings Oven: 350°

6 eggs
   Granulated sugar
   Cake flour or all-purpose flour
¾ cup granulated sugar
**⅓ cup extra-light or pure olive oil
      (not extra-virgin olive oil)**
**1⅓ cups sifted cake flour or 1¼ cups
      sifted all-purpose flour**
   Powdered sugar
**1 recipe Strawberry Champagne
      Sauce (see right)**
   Fresh strawberries (optional)
   Fresh mint (optional)

1 Let eggs stand at room temperature for 30 minutes. Grease bottom and sides of a 9-inch springform pan. Line bottom with parchment paper; grease paper. Sprinkle bottom and sides with granulated sugar; dust with flour. Set pan aside.

2 In a large mixing bowl combine eggs and the ¾ cup granulated sugar. Beat with an electric mixer on high speed for 15 minutes. With mixer running, gradually add oil in a thin, steady stream (this will take 1½ to 2 minutes). Turn off mixer immediately after all of the oil has been added.

3 Sift flour over egg mixture; fold until no lumps remain. Pour into the prepared pan; place on a baking sheet.

4 Bake in a 350° oven 30 to 35 minutes or until top springs back when touched. Cool cake completely in the pan on a wire rack.

5 To assemble, remove cake from pan; remove and discard parchment paper. Sift powdered sugar atop cake. Cut cake into wedges. Place wedges on plates or in shallow bowls. If desired, sprinkle rims with powdered sugar. Pour Strawberry Champagne Sauce around cake wedges. If desired, garnish with strawberries and mint.

Strawberry Champagne Sauce: In a blender container combine 4 cups strawberries, ⅔ cup champagne or sparkling white wine, and 3 tablespoons sugar. Cover and blend until smooth. (Or, for food processor, combine half of the ingredients at a time; cover and process until smooth.) Cover and chill until needed, up to 24 hours. Makes about 3½ cups.

Nutrition Facts per serving: 273 cal., 11 g total fat (2 g sat. fat), 128 mg chol., 39 mg sodium, 38 g carbo., 1 g fiber, 5 g pro. Daily Values: 5% vit. A, 56% vit. C, 2% calcium, 11% iron

MINI MOLTEN CHOCOLATE CAKES

EASY

Prep: 20 minutes Bake: 12 minutes
Makes: 6 servings Oven: 400°

*American restaurants made these rich cakes that
ooze with chocolate popular; we made them easy
(pictured on page 239).*

- ¾ **cup butter**
- 6 **ounces semisweet chocolate, chopped**
-   **Granulated sugar**
- 3 **eggs**
- 3 **egg yolks**
- ⅓ **cup sifted powdered sugar**
- 1½ **teaspoons vanilla**
- ¼ **cup all-purpose flour**
- 2 **tablespoons unsweetened cocoa powder**
- 1 **recipe Mocha Cream (see right)**
-   **Chocolate spiral garnishes (optional) (see tip, page 251)**
-   **Fresh raspberries (optional)**

1 In heavy saucepan combine butter and chopped chocolate; melt over low heat, stirring constantly. Remove from heat; cool. Grease six 1-cup soufflé dishes or 6-ounce custard cups. Coat with granulated sugar. Place in shallow baking pan; set aside.

2 Beat eggs, egg yolks, powdered sugar, and vanilla with an electric mixer on high speed about 5 minutes or until thick and pale yellow. Beat in chocolate mixture on medium speed. Sift flour and cocoa over chocolate mixture; beat on low speed just until blended. Spoon into prepared dishes.

3 Bake in a 400° oven 12 to 14 minutes or until cakes rise slightly and feel firm at edges and softer in the center when pressed gently. Cool in dishes 5 minutes. Invert with pot holders onto plates. Cool 15 minutes before serving with Mocha Cream. If desired, sprinkle with additional sifted powdered sugar and top with spiral garnishes and raspberries.

Mocha Cream: In a cup stir 1 teaspoon instant espresso powder or 2 teaspoons instant coffee crystals and 1 teaspoon hot water until dissolved. In chilled bowl combine ½ cup cold whipping cream, 2 tablespoons powdered sugar, 1 teaspoon unsweetened cocoa powder, ½ teaspoon vanilla, and espresso mixture. Beat with chilled beaters of electric mixer on medium-high speed until soft peaks form.

Nutrition Facts per serving: 532 cal., 45 g total fat (26 g sat. fat), 302 mg chol., 276 mg sodium, 31 g carbo., 2 g fiber, 8 g pro. Daily Values: 50% vit. A, 0% vit. C, 6% calcium, 14% iron

CHOCOLATE CHOICES

Chocolate lovers take note of these common chocolates types:

- Unsweetened chocolate is pure chocolate and cocoa butter (no sugar added). Often called baking or bitter chocolate, it is almost used exclusively for baking and cooking.
- Unsweetened cocoa powder is pure chocolate with most of the cocoa butter removed. It is most often used in baking. Those labeled Dutch-process or European-style have been treated to neutralize natural acids, giving the cocoa powder a mellow flavor and darker, redder color.
- Semisweet chocolate is pure chocolate with added cocoa butter and sugar. Although it is sometimes referred to as bittersweet chocolate, the latter is usually darker and less sweet than that labeled semisweet. Some European bittersweet chocolates are labeled dark chocolate. Use dark, semisweet, and bittersweet chocolate interchangeably in recipes.
- Milk chocolate is pure chocolate with added cocoa butter, sugar, and milk or cream. Milk chocolate has a creamier texture, lighter color, and milder flavor than semisweet chocolate.
- White baking bars or pieces and vanilla-flavored candy coatings often are referred to as white chocolate. This is a misnomer. Because none of these products contains pure chocolate (although some contain cocoa butter), legally they can't be labeled as chocolate in the United States.

SACHER TORTE

Prep: 50 minutes   Stand: 30 minutes
Bake: 35 minutes   Makes: 12 servings   Oven: 350°

> **6 egg whites**
> **5 ounces semisweet or bittersweet**
>   **chocolate, chopped**
> **½ cup butter**
> **6 egg yolks**
> **1½ teaspoons vanilla**
> **½ cup sugar**
> **¾ cup all-purpose flour**
> **⅔ cup apricot preserves**
> **1 recipe Chocolate Glaze (see right)**
>   **Sweetened whipped cream (optional)**
>   **Apricot Roses (optional) (see right)**

1 **In a very large mixing bowl allow** egg whites to stand at room temperature 30 minutes. Grease and lightly flour a 9-inch springform pan. Set aside.

2 **In a heavy medium saucepan** melt chocolate and butter; cool. Stir egg yolks and vanilla into the cooled chocolate mixture. Set mixture aside.

3 **Beat egg whites** with an electric mixer on medium to high speed until soft peaks form (tips curl). Gradually add the sugar, about 1 tablespoon at a time, beating about 4 minutes or until stiff peaks form (tips stand straight).

4 **Fold about 1 cup** of the egg white mixture into chocolate mixture. Fold mixture into remaining egg white mixture. Sift about one-third of the flour over the chocolate-egg mixture; gently fold in. Repeat sifting and folding in one-third of the flour mixture at a time. Spread batter into prepared pan.

5 **Bake in a 350° oven** 35 to 40 minutes or until a wooden toothpick inserted near the center of the cake comes out clean. Completely cool cake in pan on a wire rack. Remove sides of springform pan. Brush crumbs from edges of cake. (Top crust will be slightly flaky.) Remove bottom of springform pan from cake.

6 **In a small saucepan heat** preserves until melted. Press preserves through a sieve; cool slightly. To assemble, cut cake horizontally into 2 even layers (see top photo, lower left). Set top layer aside. Spread preserves over bottom layer. Top with second cake layer. Spoon Chocolate Glaze over torte, spreading to glaze top and sides completely (see bottom photo, lower left). Let torte stand at room temperature at least 1 hour before serving.* If desired, serve with whipped cream and garnish with Apricot Roses.

*Note: If desired, after Chocolate Glaze is dry, decorate with piped Powdered Sugar Icing (see recipe, page 159) made to piping consistency. For light brown icing, stir in chocolate syrup until desired shade is achieved. Allow piping to dry before serving.

Chocolate Glaze: In a saucepan heat 4 ounces semisweet chocolate, cut up, and 2 tablespoons butter over low heat just until melted, stirring occasionally; set aside. In a heavy small saucepan bring ½ cup whipping cream and 2 teaspoons light-colored corn syrup to a gentle boil. Reduce heat and simmer for 2 minutes. Remove from heat. Stir in chocolate mixture. Cool to room temperature before using.

Nutrition Facts per serving: 356 cal., 23 g total fat (13 g sat. fat), 146 mg chol., 135 mg sodium, 37 g carbo., 2 g fiber, 6 g pro. Daily Values: 29% vit. A, 0% vit. C, 34% calcium, 10% iron

Apricot Roses: Roll dried apricot halves between waxed paper to ⅛-inch-thick circles. Cut in half. For center of each rose, roll 1 half-circle into a cone shape. For petals, press on as many half-circles around center as desired, curving rounded edges outward and overlapping petals. Trim bottom. Hold together with half a wooden toothpick.

To split cake, mark the halfway point around the cake's side with toothpicks. Use a long, sharp or serrated knife to slice cake with sawing motion. Lift off top with wide spatula.

Place cake on rack over waxed paper to catch glaze drips. Carefully pour cooled glaze over cake and immediately spread to completely cover top and sides.

Sacher Torte: Do as some Viennese pastry chefs do: Pipe the word "Sacher" on the torte to show this is the real thing—a celebrated torte of chocolate layers filled with apricot jam and generously covered with a chocolate glaze.

CHOCOLATE-HAZELNUT COOKIE TORTE

Prep: 40 minutes Bake: 20 minutes
Chill: 2 hours Makes: 12 servings
Oven: 375°

You can bake the large cookies and wedges up to a month ahead of time and freeze. Layer the cooled cookies, with waxed paper between each, in a freezer container. Thaw before using. Or, store at room temperature for up to two days.

    2 cups shelled whole hazelnuts or
         almonds, toasted (see tip, page 247)
    ⅔ cup sugar
    1 cup all-purpose flour
    ¾ cup butter, cut in pieces
    ½ teaspoon salt
    1 egg yolk
       Sugar
    1 recipe Chocolate Mousse
         (see page 247)
    1 cup whipping cream
    1 tablespoon sugar
    1 teaspoon vanilla
    2 cups sliced strawberries
    2 to 3 ounces semisweet chocolate,
         chopped
    1 teaspoon shortening
       Whole strawberries (optional)

1 Chill two medium mixing bowls and the beaters of an electric mixer. Place toasted nuts and the ⅔ cup sugar in a food processor bowl (to use a blender, see note on page 247). Cover and process until nuts are finely ground but not oily. Add flour, butter, and salt. Process until combined. Add egg yolk. Process until combined. Divide dough into 4 equal balls. Cover and chill 2 balls until needed.

Brush off any loose cookie crumbs before dipping the edges of the cookie wedge into the warm chocolate.

2 Grease and lightly flour 2 baking sheets; place each sheet on a towel to prevent slipping while rolling out dough. On each baking sheet, draw an 8-inch circle with your finger using an 8-inch cake pan as a guide. On 1 of the prepared baking sheets, roll out 1 ball of dough to fit the circle, trimming edges of dough with a knife to make an even circle. Repeat with another ball of dough on the second baking sheet. Score 1 round into wedges, keeping circle intact. Sprinkle both rounds with sugar.

3 Bake the dough rounds in a 375° oven for 10 to 12 minutes or until browned around the edges. Cool the cookies on baking sheets for 5 minutes. Cut the warm, scored cookie into wedges. Carefully transfer cookie and wedges to a wire rack; cool completely. Allow baking sheets to cool completely. Grease and flour baking sheets again. Repeat shaping and baking the remaining 2 balls of dough, except do not score either round.

4 Use 1 of the chilled mixing bowls to prepare Chocolate Mousse; chill (for no more than 2 hours). In another chilled mixing bowl, beat whipping cream, the 1 tablespoon sugar, and vanilla on medium speed just until stiff peaks form. Spoon whipped cream into a pastry bag fitted with a large star tip.

5 To assemble torte, place a whole cookie on a serving platter. Spread with half of the Chocolate Mousse and top with half of the sliced strawberries. Place another whole cookie atop. Repeat with remaining Chocolate Mousse and sliced strawberries. Top with remaining whole cookie.

6 Pipe large dollops of the sweetened whipped cream atop torte, covering the whole top. Cover and chill about 2 hours to soften the cookies.

7 Place the chocolate (use the 3 ounces if also dipping berries) and shortening in a heavy small saucepan over low heat, stirring constantly until partially melted. Immediately remove from the heat and stir until smooth. Dip a long side of each cookie wedge into melted chocolate mixture (see photo, left). Set aside on waxed paper until chocolate is set. If desired, dip whole strawberries in remaining melted chocolate. (If your saucepan is not small, you may need additional chocolate to dip.)

8 Just before serving, arrange chocolate-dipped cookie wedges atop the sweetened whipped cream on the torte, placing chocolate-dipped edges

Chocolate-Hazelnut Cookie Torte: With a silky chocolate mousse and piped whipped cream, giant shortbread-style cookies go uptown in this showy layered torte. Chocolate-dipped berries come along for the ride.

up and tilting slightly in a pinwheel pattern. Pipe a large star of whipped cream in the center where the cookie wedges meet. If using chocolate-dipped strawberries, place between wedges and on top of the whipped cream star in the center. Serve immediately, cutting into wedges with a serrated knife.

Note: To use a blender instead of a food processor, place half of the nuts in a blender container. Cover and blend until finely ground but not oily. Transfer nuts to a mixing bowl; repeat with remaining nuts. In a mixing bowl beat butter and the ⅔ cup sugar until combined. Beat in egg yolk. Beat in ground nuts and half of the flour. Beat or stir in remaining flour. Continue as directed.

Chocolate Mousse: In a chilled mixing bowl combine ¼ cup sugar and 3 tablespoons unsweetened cocoa powder. Add 1½ cups whipping cream. Beat with the chilled beaters of an electric mixer on medium speed just until stiff peaks form. Chill until needed. Makes 3 cups.

Nutrition Facts per serving: 536 cal., 45 g total fat (21 g sat. fat), 117 mg chol., 226 mg sodium, 34 g carbo., 3 g fiber, 6 g pro. Daily Values: 35% vit. A, 24% vit. C, 7% calcium, 10% iron

TOASTING NUTS, SEEDS, AND COCONUT

Toasting heightens the flavor of nuts, seeds, and coconut. To toast, spread the nuts, seeds, or coconut in a single layer in a shallow baking pan. Bake in a 350° oven for 5 to 10 minutes or until light golden brown, watching carefully and stirring once or twice to brown evenly.

Battenberg Cake: This was a favorite of Queen Victoria's daughter, Beatrice, whose married name was Battenberg (Anglicized to Mountbatten). Fortunately, you don't need a royal baking staff to enjoy this showpiece—it starts with pound cake mix and finishes with purchased marzipan (see tip, page 249).

BATTENBERG CAKE

Prep: 1¼ hours   **Bake:** according to package
Makes: 8 servings   **Oven:** according to package

- **2 16-ounce packages pound cake mix**
- **Red paste food coloring**
- **2 tablespoons orange juice**
- **½ cup seedless red raspberry jam**
- **2 tablespoons light-colored corn syrup**
- **2 7-ounce packages marzipan**
- **Sifted powdered sugar**
- **Sugared Raspberries and Mint Leaves (optional) (see page 249)**

1 **Grease and flour** two 9×5×3-inch loaf pans; set aside. Prepare pound cake mixes according to package directions (make each package separately). Spread batter from 1 mix into 1 of the prepared pans. Tint second batter pink with food coloring; spread into the second pan. Bake cakes according to package directions or until tops spring back when lightly touched. Cool in pans on a rack 10 minutes; remove from pans; cool completely.

2 **To assemble,** trim crusts from sides, ends, and tops of cakes to make evenly shaped loaves. Trim loaves so each measures 7½×4×1½ inches. Cut the plain loaf into 4 logs measuring 7½×1×¾ inches. Cut pink loaf into 5 logs measuring 7½×1×¾ inches (see top photo, page 249). You will have some cake leftover from each loaf; use for another dessert.

3 **Drizzle the 9 logs** with orange juice; set aside. In a small saucepan combine the raspberry jam and corn syrup; heat and stir over low heat until jam is melted and mixture is smooth; set aside.

4 **In a bowl knead marzipan** with your hands to soften. Sprinkle both sides of marzipan with powdered sugar; roll between 2 sheets of waxed paper to a 12×8-inch rectangle. (If desired, roll marzipan to a 15×8-inch rectangle; trim 3 inches from a short side and use to cut decorative shapes for garnishes.) Brush off excess sugar.

5 **Remove top sheet** of waxed paper. Brush jam mixture on 1 long side of a plain cake log. Place log crosswise in the center of marzipan sheet, jam side down. Brush jam mixture on the other 3 long sides of log. Brush a long side of 2 pink logs with jam mixture. Place, jam side down, on each side of the plain log. Brush exposed long sides with jam mixture. For second layer, place another pink log on top of first plain log. Brush exposed sides with jam. Place 2 plain logs on either side of the second pink log, brushing exposed sides with jam. Repeat layering with remaining cake logs, alternating colors to make checkerboard pattern. Press logs together.

6 **Bring marzipan** up over sides of cake (see bottom photo, right) so edges meet at top of cake, covering long sides but not ends. Crimp marzipan to seal; decorate top with marzipan trimmings as desired. Transfer to a serving plate. Using a serrated knife, trim cake and marzipan to make ends even.

7 **Let cake stand,** covered, for several hours or overnight before serving. If desired, garnish with Sugared Raspberries and Mint Leaves.

A perfectly shaped dessert starts with evenly sized cake logs. Slice the cake with long, even cuts and measure frequently to assure that your cuts are 1 inch apart.

Press the marzipan to the cake logs as you wrap it around the assembled logs.

Nutrition Facts per serving: 450 cal., 17 g total fat (7 g sat. fat), 66 mg chol.,136 mg sodium, 69 g carbo., 2 g fiber, 6 g pro. Daily Values: 10% vit. A, 3% vit. C, 11% calcium, 9% iron

Sugared Raspberries and Mint Leaves: Place 2 teaspoons dried egg whites (available in cake-decorating stores) and ¼ cup water in a 6-ounce custard cup; stir together with a wire whisk or fork. Place superfine or granulated sugar in a shallow dish. Using a pastry brush, brush egg white mixture onto berries and mint leaves; roll in sugar. Allow to dry on a wire rack. Arrange atop marzipan.

SPECTACULAR INGREDIENTS

The desserts in this chapter are made even more spectacular with these inventive basics from several origins:

- **Crème Anglaise:** A rich custard sauce served hot or cold over cake, fresh fruit, and other desserts.
- **Ganache:** Created in Paris around 1850, this exquisitely smooth chocolate icing is made of semisweet or bittersweet chocolate and whipping cream.
- **Marzipan:** A sweet, shapable mixture of almond paste, sugar, and sometimes beaten egg whites, marzipan often is rolled into sheets to cover whole cakes. It also can be tinted and formed into shapes, including miniature fruits or flowers. Marzipan is available in larger supermarkets.
- **Génoise:** Rising out of Genoa, Italy, and adapted by the French, this rich, light, and versatile cake is used in many famous desserts, including petit fours, cake rolls, and baked Alaska.
- **Phyllo:** In Greek, phyllo means "leaf," which is an apt description for these tissue-thin layers of pastry dough. Its most famous use is in baklava.
- **Ladyfingers:** These small, light sponge cakes are used in such desserts as charlottes and tiramisu.

Marjolaine: Bring a French pastry-shop favorite home. Extra-rich mocha ganache nestles between nutty cake layers. The frosting? A smooth, elegant buttercream.

MARJOLAINE

BEST-LOVED

Prep: 50 minutes
Bake: 40 minutes   Chill: 4 hours
Makes: 16 to 20 servings   Oven: 300°

  6 egg whites
1¾ cups hazelnuts
  2 tablespoons all-purpose flour
  1 cup sugar
  1 recipe Mocha Ganache
      (see below right)
  1 recipe Buttercream
      (see recipe, page 161)
  Chocolate lace wedges (optional)
      (see tip, page 251)
  Chocolate-dipped hazelnuts
      (optional)

1 **In a large mixing bowl let** egg whites stand at room temperature for 30 minutes. Meanwhile, grease three 8×1½-inch round baking pans. Line the bottoms with waxed paper; grease paper. Set pans aside.

2 **Place half** of the hazelnuts in a blender container or food processor bowl. Cover; blend or process until finely ground but not oily. Repeat with remaining nuts. In a bowl stir together 2 cups of the ground hazelnuts and the flour. Set nut mixture aside. Reserve remaining ground nuts for garnish.

3 **Beat egg whites** with electric mixer on medium to high speed until soft peaks form (tips curl). Gradually add sugar, 1 tablespoon at a time, beating on high speed about 8 minutes or until stiff peaks form (tips stand straight) and sugar is almost dissolved. By hand, fold hazelnut mixture into egg white mixture. Spread into prepared pans.

4 **Bake in a 300° oven** for 40 to 45 minutes or until very lightly browned and just set when lightly touched. Cool in pans on racks 10 minutes. Carefully loosen sides from pans. Remove from pans. Peel off waxed paper; cool completely on racks.

5 **To assemble,** place a cake layer on a large serving plate. Spread half of the Mocha Ganache on top of cake layer to within ¼ inch of the edge. Chill in the freezer for 5 minutes. Spread ½ cup of the Buttercream on top of the Mocha Ganache. Top with second cake layer. Spread with remaining Mocha Ganache. Top with remaining cake layer. Spread remaining Buttercream on sides and top of cake.

6 **To garnish,** gently press remaining ground nuts into Buttercream two-thirds up sides of torte. Lightly cover; refrigerate 4 to 24 hours. To serve, let stand at room temperature for 10 minutes. If desired, garnish with chocolate lace wedges and whole nuts.

Mocha Ganache: In a heavy medium saucepan combine 8 ounces coarsely chopped semisweet chocolate, 1 cup whipping cream, 3 tablespoons unsalted butter, and 2 teaspoons instant espresso coffee powder or coffee crystals. Heat and stir over low heat until chocolate is melted. Remove from heat. Place the saucepan in a bowl of ice water. Using a rubber spatula, stir almost constantly for 6 to 8 minutes or until mixture thickens and is easy to spread. Remove the saucepan from the bowl of ice water. Makes about 2 cups.

Nutrition Facts per serving: 450 cal., 35 g total fat (16 g sat. fat), 111 mg chol., 154 mg sodium, 34 g carbo., 3 g fiber, 5 g pro. Daily Values: 27% vit. A, 0% vit. C, 4% calcium, 8% iron

LIME PHYLLO NAPOLEONS

Prep: 30 minutes **Bake:** 8 minutes **Chill:** 2 hours
Makes: 8 servings **Oven:** 350°

Lime curd makes it opulent; phyllo makes it easy.

  4 sheets frozen phyllo dough, thawed
  ¼ cup butter, melted
  ¼ cup sugar
  3 tablespoons toasted coconut
      (see tip, page 247)
  3 tablespoons toasted, finely chopped almonds (see tip, page 247)
  1 recipe Lime Curd (see above right)
  1 recipe Tropical Fruit Salsa (see right)

1 **Lightly grease** 2 large baking sheets. Unfold phyllo dough. Remove a sheet, keeping remaining phyllo dough covered with plastic wrap or waxed paper and a damp towel. Place sheet on a large cutting board. Brush with some of the melted butter. Sprinkle with 1 tablespoon each sugar, coconut, and almonds. Repeat layers twice. Top with remaining phyllo sheet; brush with butter. Sprinkle with remaining sugar.

2 **Cut sheets** lengthwise into 4 equal strips and again crosswise into 4 pieces, making 16 rectangles. Transfer to prepared baking sheets.

3 **Bake in a 350° oven** 8 to 10 minutes or until golden. Transfer rectangles to wire rack to cool.

4 **Spread 1 to 2 tablespoons Lime Curd** on 12 of the rectangles. Stack 3 of the 12 filled rectangles; top with 1 of the remaining unfilled rectangles.

Repeat stacking to make 4 layered Napoleons; carefully cut each stack in half crosswise. Serve immediately with Tropical Fruit Salsa.

Lime Curd: Finely shred 1 teaspoon lime peel; set aside. In a medium saucepan stir together ¾ cup sugar and 1 tablespoon cornstarch. Add ¼ cup fresh lime juice and ¼ cup water. Cook and stir over medium heat until thickened and bubbly. Slowly stir about half of the lime mixture into 3 beaten egg yolks. Return all of the egg yolk mixture to saucepan. Bring to a gentle boil. Cook and stir 1 minute. Remove from heat and stir in 3 tablespoons butter until melted. Cover surface with plastic wrap. Chill until set and cold, about 2 hours. In a chilled bowl beat ⅓ cup whipping cream with an electric mixer on medium speed until stiff peaks form. Gently fold whipped cream and the finely shredded lime peel into lime filling.

Tropical Fruit Salsa: Combine 2 cups tropical fruits such as kiwifruit, mango, pineapple, strawberries, and/or oranges cut into ¼-inch pieces; 2 tablespoons light-colored corn syrup; 1 tablespoon rum (if desired); and 1 tablespoon orange or lime juice.

Nutrition Facts per serving: 361 cal., 18 g total fat (6 g sat. fat), 106 mg chol., 154 mg sodium, 49 g carbo., 1 g fiber, 4 g pro. Daily Values: 38% vit. A, 37% vit. C, 3% calcium, 7% iron

CHOCOLATE TOUCHES

Here's how to make the chocolate garnishes in this chapter: Melt 6 ounces chocolate and 1 tablespoon shortening; cool the mixture slightly. Place the mixture in a plastic bag with a small hole snipped in a corner.

■ For the Marjolaine, page 250, pipe about 10 pie-wedge shapes on a waxed-paper-lined baking sheet; drizzle chocolate randomly within outlines.

■ For the Mini Molten Chocolate Cakes, page 243, pipe spiral shapes.

For both garnishes, let designs stand until dry; peel garnishes from waxed paper. For best results, do not chill the garnishes.

PASSION FRUIT TARTS

Prep: 1¼ hours   Bake: 30 minutes
Cool and Chill: 3½ to 6½ hours
Makes: 4 small tarts or 1 large tart   Oven: 350°

Make the fruit puree by blending or processing the fruit pulp in a blender or food processor until smooth. Or, check food specialty shops for frozen puree.

  2 egg whites
  1 recipe Sweet Tart Pastry
      (see tip, page 253)
  ¾ cup sugar
  ½ cup fresh or frozen passion fruit
      puree or mango puree
  ⅓ cup unsalted butter
  3 eggs
  ½ teaspoon vanilla
  ⅛ teaspoon cream of tartar

1 **Let egg whites stand** at room temperature for 30 minutes. Divide the chilled tart pastry into 4 portions. On a lightly floured surface, roll each portion to ⅛-inch thickness. Cut into a 5½-inch round. Fit rounds into 4 ungreased 4-inch tart pans with removable bottoms. (Or, roll pastry to an 11-inch round; fit pastry into a 9-inch tart pan with removable bottom.) Line pastry in pan(s) with a double thickness of foil. Place on a baking sheet.

2 **Bake in a 350° oven** for 15 minutes; remove foil. Bake for 5 to 6 minutes more for small tarts (12 to 15 minutes for large tart) or until golden. Cool in pan(s) on a wire rack.

3 **For filling,** in a saucepan combine ½ cup of the sugar, fruit puree, and butter. Bring just to boiling over medium heat, stirring occasionally. Beat the 3 eggs slightly with a fork. Slowly add fruit mixture, beating continuously. Return to saucepan; heat and stir over medium heat 4 to 5 minutes until slightly thickened (do not boil). Strain; cover. Keep warm.

4 **For meringue,** in a large mixing bowl combine the egg whites, vanilla, and cream of tartar. Beat with an electric mixer on high speed until soft peaks form (tips curl). Gradually add the remaining sugar, beating on high speed until stiff peaks form (tips stand straight).

5 **To assemble,** remove pastry shell(s) from pan(s). Place shell(s) on a baking sheet. Spoon fruit filling into shells. Spoon meringue into a pastry bag fitted with a large star tip. Pipe meringue onto the top of tart(s) in a woven pattern. Bake in a 350° oven for 10 to 12 minutes for small tarts (15 minutes for large tart) or until meringue edges are golden. Cool 30 minutes on a wire rack. Chill in the refrigerator for 3 to 6 hours.

Nutrition Facts per serving: 766 cal., 44 g total fat (25 g sat. fat), 368 mg chol., 316 mg sodium, 83 g carbo., 2 g fiber, 12 g pro. Daily Values: 60% vit. A, 15% vit. C, 4% calcium, 17% iron

Passion Fruit Tarts: End dinner on a passionate note. With their buttery crusts, fragrant fruit fillings, and light pipings of meringue, these little gems are seductive indeed.

PASTRIES FOR SPECTACULAR DESSERTS

Patterned after the rich, buttery French pastries, pâte brisée (short pastry) and pâte sucrée (sweetened short pastry), the following tart pastries result in short, crisp, and buttery crusts (unlike the flaky crust the piecrust pastry on page 256 provides). The key ingredients: butter and egg yolk.

Rich Tart Pastry: In a medium mixing bowl cut ½ cup cold butter into 1¼ cups all-purpose flour until pieces are the size of small peas. In a small mixing bowl, combine 1 beaten egg yolk and 1 tablespoon ice water. Gradually stir egg yolk mixture into flour mixture. Add 1 to 2 tablespoons ice water, 1 tablespoon at a time, until all of the dough is moistened. Using your fingers, gently knead the dough just until a ball forms. If necessary, cover dough with plastic wrap and chill in the refrigerator for 30 to 60 minutes or until dough is easy to handle.

Sweet Tart Pastry: In a medium mixing bowl stir together 1¼ cups all-purpose flour and ¼ cup sugar. Using a pastry blender, cut in ½ cup cold butter until pieces are pea-size. In a small mixing bowl stir together 2 beaten egg yolks and 1 tablespoon water. Gradually stir egg yolk mixture into dry mixture. Using your fingers, gently knead dough just until a ball forms. If necessary, cover with plastic wrap and chill in refrigerator for 30 to 60 minutes or until dough is easy to handle.

RASPBERRY MARZIPAN TART

Prep: 30 minutes **Bake:** 48 minutes
Makes: 12 servings **Oven:** 350°

Decadent chocolate and raspberry jam meet up with a generously nutty marzipan filling—with marvelous results in this company-special dessert.

  1 recipe Sweet Tart Pastry
      (see tip, above)
½ cup slivered almonds
⅔ cup sugar
  3 tablespoons all-purpose flour
⅓ cup butter, softened
  2 eggs
  1 teaspoon vanilla
½ teaspoon almond extract
⅓ cup unsalted pistachio nuts,
      chopped
⅓ cup seedless raspberry jam
  2 ounces semisweet chocolate, cut up
      Raspberries and pistachio nuts for
      garnish (optional)

1 **Prepare pastry.** Grease a 9-inch fluted tart pan with removable bottom. Press dough evenly into bottom and sides of prepared pan. Bake in a 350° oven 18 to 20 minutes or until just lightly browned. Place pan on a wire rack.

2 **In food processor or blender container,** combine almonds, sugar, and flour. Cover; process or blend 1 minute or until almonds are finely ground. Add butter and 1 of the eggs. Process until smooth. Add the remaining egg, vanilla, and almond extract. Process until blended. Add the nuts and process with on-off turns until mixed in. Spread the jam over the bottom of the tart shell. Spoon the filling over the jam and spread evenly to cover. Bake in 350° oven 30 to 35 minutes or until the filling is golden brown and firm when lightly touched. Cool in pan on wire rack. In a small saucepan melt the chocolate over low heat. Spread over the filling. If desired, arrange raspberries and nuts around edge and in center to garnish. Refrigerate tart 10 minutes or until chocolate sets.

Nutrition Facts per serving: 344 cal., 21 g total fat (10 g sat. fat), 105 mg chol., 143 mg sodium, 37 g carbo., 2 g fiber, 5 g pro. Daily Values: 18% vit. A, 0% vit. C, 3% calcium, 10% iron

Della Robbia Fruit Tart:
This artistic pastry ring, with its hand-painted array of fruits, resembles a della Robbia wreath. Originally, in the 15th and 16th centuries, the della Robbias were a family of sculptors. Today, they are known as much for their fruit designs as their sculptures.

DELLA ROBBIA FRUIT TART

BEST-LOVED

Prep: 1 hour   **Bake:** 30 minutes
Makes: 10 servings   **Oven:** 375°

**2 recipes Rich Tart Pastry
   (see tip, page 253)**
**3 ripe medium nectarines, peaches,
   apples, or pears (about 1 pound)**
¼ cup sugar
1 tablespoon all-purpose flour
¼ teaspoon ground nutmeg
¼ cup chopped pecans
¼ cup dried tart cherries or raisins
**1 recipe Pastry Paint (see page 255)
   or 1 slightly beaten egg yolk and
   1 tablespoon water**
**Vanilla ice cream or 1 recipe
   Custard Sauce (optional)
   (see page 263)**

1 Divide pastry dough in half. Shape each half into a ball. For bottom pastry, on a lightly floured surface, use hands to slightly flatten 1 ball.

Roll dough from center to edges, forming an 11-inch circle. Trim circle to 10 inches; reserve scraps. Transfer to an ungreased baking sheet; set aside.

2 If using peaches, apples, or pears, peel. Cut fruit in half. Remove and discard pits or seeds. With cut sides down, cut each fruit half into 16 slices. Do not separate slices. Set fruit aside. Stir together sugar, flour, and nutmeg. Sprinkle about half of the sugar mixture over pastry circle on baking sheet to within ½ inch of edge. Sprinkle with pecans and cherries or raisins. Arrange fruit halves, cut sides down, in a circle about 1 inch from edge of pastry. (Leave center open.) Press down on the fruit halves to slightly fan out slices. Sprinkle with remaining sugar mixture.

3 For top pastry, on lightly floured surface, use hands to slightly flatten remaining ball of dough. Roll from center to edges, forming 12½-inch circle. Trim to 11½ inches; reserve scraps. Moisten edge of bottom pastry. Drape top pastry over fruit, aligning edges. Press pastry around fruit, being careful not to stretch pastry. Fold edges of top pastry under bottom pastry. Seal; make petal edge (see photo, page 48). If desired, cut 1½-inch circle from center of top and bottom pastries to form ring. Seal; crimp inside ring.

4 Roll dough scraps to ⅛-inch thickness. Using a knife or small cookie cutters, cut fruit and leaf shapes from the dough. Brush bottoms of pastry cutouts with a little water. Press cutouts onto the top pastry. Brush cutouts with the Pastry Paint or a mixture of the 1 egg yolk and 1 tablespoon water.

5 Bake in a 375° oven 30 to 40 minutes or until fruit is tender. (If necessary, to prevent overbrowning, cover with foil after 25 minutes.) Cool on baking sheet for 10 minutes. Carefully transfer tart from baking sheet to serving plate. Serve warm. If desired, serve with ice cream or Custard Sauce.

Pastry Paint: Combine 2 slightly beaten egg yolks and 2 teaspoons water; divide mixture among 3 or 4 custard cups. To each cup, stir in a few drops food coloring. Makes about 2 tablespoons.

Nutrition Facts per serving: 359 cal., 23 g total fat (12 g sat. fat), 134 mg chol., 189 mg sodium, 35 g carbo., 2 g fiber, 5 g pro. Daily Values: 34% vit. A, 3% vit. C, 1% calcium, 11% iron

PEANUT BUTTER AND CHOCOLATE SHORTBREAD TART

Prep: 30 minutes **Bake:** 15 minutes
Freeze: 30 minutes **Chill:** 30 minutes
Makes: 20 servings **Oven:** 350°

1 recipe Chocolate Shortbread Crust
   (see right)
1 8-ounce package cream cheese,
   softened
1 cup sifted powdered sugar
¾ cup creamy peanut butter
1½ cups whipping cream
¾ cup chocolate-covered peanuts,
   coarsely chopped
¾ cup semisweet chocolate pieces
3 tablespoons creamy peanut butter
3 tablespoons whipping cream

1 Prepare Chocolate Shortbread Crust. Press dough evenly into bottom and sides of a 10- to 11-inch tart pan with removable bottom. Prick bottom and sides of tart shell with a fork. Bake in a 350° oven for 15 to 18 minutes or until crisp and edges are beginning to brown. Cool on a wire rack.

2 For filling, beat cream cheese, powdered sugar, and the ¾ cup peanut butter with an electric mixer on medium speed until light. Beat in ¼ cup of the cream. In a medium bowl beat ¾ cup of the cream with electric mixer on high speed just until soft peaks form. Gently fold whipped cream into peanut butter mixture. Fold in chopped peanuts. Pour filling into the cooled pastry shell and spread evenly. Freeze the tart 30 minutes or until firm.

3 For glaze, heat remaining ½ cup cream over medium-low heat until hot. Add chocolate pieces; remove from heat. Whisk until melted and smooth. Set glaze aside to cool for 3 to 5 minutes.

4 Meanwhile, beat the 3 tablespoons peanut butter and 3 tablespoons cream until smooth. Place peanut butter mixture in a heavy-duty plastic bag. Spread chocolate glaze in a thin layer over filling. Cut a tiny corner from bag containing peanut butter mixture; squeeze to pipe concentric circles on top of chocolate. Using a wooden toothpick or tip of a sharp knife, pull tip through peanut butter, starting from center and pulling to edge of pan. Repeat to create 8 to 10 evenly-spaced lines in a weblike pattern. Chill 30 minutes or until glaze sets.

Chocolate Shortbread Crust: In a food processor bowl* combine 1 cup all-purpose flour, ½ cup powdered sugar, 3 tablespoons unsweetened cocoa powder, and ⅛ teaspoon salt. Cover and process until combined. Add 6 tablespoons cold butter, cut into 8 pieces. Process until mixture is the texture of cornmeal. In a small bowl beat together 1 egg yolk and 1 teaspoon vanilla. Drizzle egg mixture over flour mixture. Process just until dough begins to pull away from sides of bowl.

***Note:** For hand-mixed method, in a medium bowl, combine 1 cup all-purpose flour, ½ cup powdered sugar, 3 tablespoons unsweetened cocoa powder, and ⅛ teaspoon salt. Using a pastry blender, cut in 6 tablespoons cold butter until mixture resembles fine crumbs and starts to cling. In a small bowl beat together 1 egg yolk and 1 teaspoon vanilla. Drizzle egg mixture over flour mixture. Form the mixture into a ball and knead until smooth.

Nutrition Facts per serving: 325 cal., 25 g total fat (11 g sat. fat), 60 mg chol., 150 mg sodium, 23 g carbo., 1 g fiber, 6 g pro. Daily Values: 18% vit. A, 0% vit. C, 3% calcium, 6% iron

ULTIMATE NUT AND CHOCOLATE CHIP TART

Prep: 35 minutes   Bake: 40 minutes
Makes: 8 to 10 servings   Oven: 350°

  1 recipe Pastry for Single-Crust Pie
        (see page 47)
  3 eggs
  1 cup light-colored corn syrup
  ½ cup packed brown sugar
  ⅓ cup butter, melted and cooled
  1 teaspoon vanilla
  1 cup coarsely chopped salted
        mixed nuts
  ½ cup miniature semisweet
        chocolate pieces
  ⅓ cup miniature semisweet
        chocolate pieces
  1 tablespoon shortening
        Vanilla ice cream (optional)

1 Prepare Pastry for Single-Crust Pie. On a lightly floured surface, flatten dough with your hands. Roll pastry from center to edge, forming a circle about 12 inches in diameter. Ease pastry into 11-inch tart pan with removable bottom. Trim pastry even with the rim of pan. Do not prick pastry.

2 For filling, in a large mixing bowl beat eggs slightly with a rotary beater or a fork. Stir in the corn syrup. Add the brown sugar, butter, and vanilla, stirring until brown sugar is dissolved. Stir in the nuts and the ½ cup chocolate pieces.

3 Place the pastry-lined tart pan on a baking sheet on the oven rack. Carefully pour filling into pan. Bake in a 350° oven for 40 minutes or until a knife inserted near the center comes out clean. Cool on a wire rack.

4 Before serving, place the ⅓ cup chocolate pieces and the shortening in a small heavy saucepan over very low heat, stirring constantly just until it begins to melt. Immediately remove from heat and stir until smooth. Cool slightly. Transfer chocolate mixture to a clean, small, heavy plastic bag. Snip a tiny hole in a corner of the bag. Drizzle the melted chocolate in zigzag lines across individual servings of tart, overlapping onto the plate. If desired, serve with vanilla ice cream.

Nutrition Facts per serving: 616 cal., 34 g total fat (9 g sat. fat), 100 mg chol., 340 mg sodium, 74 g carbo., 1 g fiber, 8 g pro. Daily Values: 10% vit. A, 0% vit. C, 7% calcium, 25% iron

Ultimate Nut and Chocolate Chip Tart: Reminiscent of an all-time favorite—pecan pie—this tart mixes several kinds of nuts and chocolate pieces in a caramel custard filling. Served with a scoop of ice cream, it's heavenly.

ENGLISH TRIFLE

Prep: 40 minutes   Chill: 5 hours
Makes: 8 to 10 servings

The sun never sets on this quintessentially Victorian dessert, for it travels the world in a variety of versions, including this time-honored one.

  1 **recipe Hot Milk Sponge Cake (see lower right)**
1⅓ **cups whipping cream**
  1 **vanilla bean, split lengthwise, or 1 teaspoon vanilla**
  2 **egg yolks**
⅔ **cup sugar**
  2 **tablespoons cream sherry or orange juice**
¼ **cup seedless red raspberry or strawberry preserves**
¼ **cup toasted sliced almonds (see tip, page 247)**
  1 **recipe Sweetened Whipped Cream (see page 160)**
  1 **cup fresh raspberries or 1½ cups small fresh strawberries**

1 Prepare cake; cool completely. To prepare crème anglaise, in a heavy saucepan bring 1⅓ cups whipping cream and vanilla bean, if using, just to boiling, stirring frequently. Remove from heat. In a mixing bowl, combine a small amount of the hot cream, egg yolks, and sugar. Beat with an electric mixer on high speed for 2 to 3 minutes or until thick and lemon-colored. Gradually stir about half of the remaining cream mixture into the egg yolk mixture. Return all of the egg yolk mixture to the saucepan. Cook and stir over medium heat just until mixture returns to boiling. Remove from heat. Remove and discard vanilla bean or stir in liquid vanilla, if using. Cover surface with plastic wrap. Chill for at least 2 hours or overnight.

2 Cut or tear the cake layer into 1-inch pieces. In a 1½-quart clear glass serving bowl with straight sides, a soufflé dish, or a serving bowl, place half of the cake pieces. Sprinkle with half of the sherry or orange juice. Spoon on half of the raspberry or strawberry preserves by small teaspoons. Sprinkle with the almonds. Pour half of the crème anglaise over all. Repeat layers

using the remaining cake pieces, sherry or orange juice, preserves, and crème anglaise. Cover and chill in the refrigerator for 3 to 24 hours before serving.

3 Just before serving, spread about half of the Sweetened Whipped Cream over top. Arrange raspberries or strawberries on top, reserving some berries to garnish. To garnish, spoon the remaining Sweetened Whipped Cream into a pastry bag fitted with a medium star tip (about ¼-inch opening). Pipe stars around the outer edge of the trifle. Place a berry in the center of each star.

Nutrition Facts per serving: 491 cal., 31 g total fat (18 g sat. fat), 179 mg chol., 96 mg sodium, 49 g carbo., 1 g fiber, 5 g pro. Daily Values: 41% vit. A, 7% vit. C, 8% calcium, 6% iron

HOT MILK SPONGE CAKE

Prep: 15 minutes   Bake: 18 minutes
Makes: 8 servings   Oven: 350°

½ **cup all-purpose flour**
½ **teaspoon baking powder**
   Dash salt
  1 **egg**
½ **cup sugar**
¼ **cup milk**
  1 **tablespoon butter**

1 Grease and lightly flour a 9×1½-inch or 8×1½-inch round baking pan; set aside. Stir together flour, baking powder, and salt; set aside.

2 Beat egg with an electric mixer on high speed 3 to 4 minutes or until thick and lemon-colored. Gradually add sugar, beating on medium speed 4 to 5 minutes or until sugar is almost dissolved. Add flour mixture. Beat on low to medium speed just until combined. Heat the milk and butter just until butter melts. Stir warm milk mixture into egg mixture. Pour batter into prepared pan; spread evenly.

3 Bake in a 350° oven 18 minutes or until top springs back when touched. Cool cake in pan on a wire rack for 10 minutes. Remove cake and cool completely on wire rack.

Nutrition Facts per serving: 100 cal., 2 g total fat (1 g sat. fat), 31 mg chol., 66 mg sodium, 18 g carbo., 0 g fiber, 2 g pro. Daily Values: 2% vit. A, 0% vit. C, 2% calcium, 3% iron

DEVONSHIRE CREAM TRIFLE

Prep: 35 minutes   **Cool:** 30 minutes
Chill: 2½ hours   **Makes:** 12 servings

We've matched the effect of England's beloved Devonshire cream—a thick, rich ingredient also known as clotted cream—by combining gelatin, whipping cream, and sour cream. Try this recipe when you're blessed with a bounty of summer fruits.

  1 **teaspoon unflavored gelatin**
  1 **cup whipping cream**
  ¼ **cup sugar**
  2 **teaspoons vanilla**
  1 **8-ounce carton dairy sour cream**
  4 **cups assorted fresh fruit such as raspberries, sliced strawberries, chopped peeled nectarines or peaches,* and cut-up peeled kiwifruit**
  2 **tablespoons sugar**
  1 **recipe Hot Milk Sponge Cake (see page 257) or one 10¾-ounce frozen loaf pound cake, thawed**
  ¼ **cup peach brandy, amaretto, orange liqueur, or orange juice**
    Grated chocolate (optional)

1 **For Devonshire cream,** in a small saucepan combine gelatin and ½ cup cold water; let stand 5 minutes to soften. Heat and stir over medium heat until gelatin dissolves; cool.

2 **In a chilled medium mixing bowl** beat whipping cream, the ¼ cup sugar, and vanilla with an electric mixer on medium-low speed until soft peaks form (tips curl). Do not overbeat.

3 **Combine cooled gelatin mixture** and sour cream; mix well. Fold sour cream mixture into whipped cream. Chill for 30 to 45 minutes or until mixture thickens and will mound on a spoon.

4 **Meanwhile, for fruit filling,** in a large mixing bowl combine the fresh fruit and the 2 tablespoons sugar. Let stand for 10 minutes.

5 **Cut the Hot Milk Sponge Cake** or pound cake into 2×½-inch strips. In a 2½- or 3-quart clear glass serving bowl or a soufflé dish, arrange half of the cake strips on the bottom. Arrange half of the fruit atop the cake strips. Sprinkle with 2 tablespoons of the brandy, liqueur, or juice. Spoon half of the Devonshire cream on top. Repeat layers, piping or spooning remaining Devonshire cream on top.

6 **Cover and chill** for 2 to 24 hours. If desired, sprinkle with chocolate.

*Note: If using peaches or nectarines, dip slices in a mixture of 1 cup water and 1 tablespoon lemon juice to prevent them from discoloring.

Nutrition Facts per serving: 235 cal., 13 g total fat (8 g sat. fat), 56 mg chol., 62 mg sodium, 25 g carbo., 2 g fiber, 3 g pro. Daily Values: 15% vit. A, 17% vit. C, 5% calcium, 3% iron

---

MERINGUE MAGIC

Q Is the kind of meringue that goes on top of a tart or pie the same kind of meringue used to make shells for holding fillings?

A Yes, although the length of time the meringue spends in the oven gives it a different texture. Meringue toppings are baked only until they are cooked and their tops are slightly golden brown. Their interiors are still soft.

   Meringue shells are baked until they are cooked and are left in the oven to cool and dry out until crisp enough to stand up to fruit or custard fillings.

To ensure the success of either kind of meringue:

■ Let the egg whites stand at room temperature for 30 minutes so they'll beat more readily and with heightened volume.

■ Use a clean glass or metal bowl. A plastic bowl will not work, as it may contain a film of oil, which can inhibit beating.

■ Make sure no yolk or other fat gets into the egg whites. Fat can reduce the meringue's volume.

■ Pipe or shape the meringue immediately after beating; then bake so that none of the volume is lost.

Berries in a Cloud:
Ever hear of cloud nine?
With baked meringue,
a generous mound of
creamy cocoa mousse,
and a crown of sweet ripe
strawberries, this is it.

BERRIES IN A CLOUD

Prep: 45 minutes   **Bake:** 45 minutes
Stand: 1 hour   **Makes:** 12 servings   **Oven:** 300°

> **3** egg whites
> **1** teaspoon vanilla
> **¼** teaspoon cream of tartar
> **1** cup granulated sugar
> **½** cup toasted, finely chopped
>   almonds (see tip, page **247**)
> **1** 3-ounce package cream cheese,
>   softened
> **½** cup packed brown sugar
> **½** cup unsweetened cocoa powder
> **2** tablespoons milk
> **½** teaspoon vanilla
> **1** cup whipping cream
> **3** cups fresh whole strawberries,
>   stems and caps removed
> **1** ounce semisweet chocolate, cut up
> **1** teaspoon shortening

1 **Allow egg whites to stand** at room temperature for 30 minutes. Cover a baking sheet with plain brown paper or parchment paper. Draw a 9-inch circle on the paper; set aside.

2 **In a large mixing bowl combine** egg whites, the 1 teaspoon vanilla, and cream of tartar. Beat with an electric mixer on medium speed until soft peaks form (tips curl). Gradually add the granulated sugar, 1 tablespoon at a time, beating on high speed until stiff peaks form (tips stand straight) and sugar is almost dissolved. Fold in the almonds.

3 **Spread meringue mixture** over circle drawn on paper, building sides up taller than the center to form a shell. Bake in a 300° oven 45 minutes. Turn off oven; let meringue dry in oven with door closed at least 1 hour (do not open oven door). Remove baking sheet from oven. Lift meringue and carefully peel off paper; transfer to a flat serving platter. (Or, store shell in a flat, airtight container overnight).

4 **For cocoa mousse,** in a small mixing bowl beat cream cheese and brown sugar until smooth. Add cocoa powder, milk, and the ½ teaspoon vanilla; beat until smooth. In another small chilled mixing bowl beat whipping cream with chilled beaters of an electric mixer on medium speed until soft peaks form; fold into cocoa mixture. Carefully spoon cocoa mousse into meringue shell. Press whole berries, stemmed side down, into the mousse. In a small heavy saucepan melt semisweet chocolate and shortening over low heat, stirring constantly. With a small spoon, lightly drizzle over filling and meringue.

5 **Serve immediately** or cover and chill up to 2 hours. To serve, cut into wedges, dipping knife in water between cuts.

Nutrition Facts per serving: 265 cal., 14 g total fat (7 g sat. fat), 35 mg chol., 47 mg sodium, 32 g carbo., 1 g fiber, 4 g pro. Daily Values: 12% vit. A, 35% vit. C, 7% calcium, 7% iron

Crème Brûlée:
We've simplified the caramelized sugar process; it's now done on top of the stove. But the dessert—with its ever-so-thin glaze of melted sugar atop a smooth, rich custard—is as delectable as ever.

CRÈME BRÛLÉE *EASY*

Prep: 20 minutes   **Bake:** 18 minutes
Cool: 20 minutes   **Chill:** 1 hour   **Stand:** 20 minutes
Makes: 4 servings   **Oven:** 325°

- **2 cups half-and-half or light cream**
- **5 slightly beaten egg yolks**
- **⅓ cup sugar**
- **1 teaspoon vanilla**
- **⅓ cup sugar**

1 **In a small heavy saucepan heat** half-and-half or light cream over medium-low heat just until bubbly. Remove from heat; set aside.

2 **In a medium mixing bowl** combine egg yolks, the ⅓ cup sugar, vanilla, and ¼ teaspoon salt. Beat with a wire whisk or rotary beater just until combined. Slowly whisk or stir the hot cream into the egg mixture.

3 **Place four ungreased 4-inch quiche dishes** or oval or round tart pans without removable bottoms into a 13×9×2-inch baking pan. Set the baking pan on oven rack in a 325° oven. Pour the custard mixture evenly into the 4 dishes. Pour very hot water into the baking pan around the 4 dishes, about halfway up the sides of the dishes.

4 **Bake in the 325° oven** for 18 to 24 minutes or until a knife inserted near the center of each dish comes out clean. Remove dishes from the water bath; let cool on a wire rack. Cover and chill for at least 1 hour or up to 8 hours.

5 **Before serving,** let the custards stand at room temperature for 20 minutes.

6 **Place the ⅓ cup sugar** in a heavy 10-inch skillet. Heat skillet over medium-high heat until sugar begins to melt, shaking skillet occasionally to heat sugar evenly. Do not stir. Once sugar starts to melt, reduce heat to low; cook until sugar is completely melted and golden (3 to 5 minutes more), stirring as needed.

7 **Spoon melted sugar** quickly over custards in a lacy pattern or in a solid piece. If melted sugar starts to harden in pan, return to heat, stirring until it melts. If it starts to form clumps, carefully stir in 1 to 2 teaspoons water. Serve immediately.

Nutrition Facts per serving: 364 cal., 20 g total fat (11 g sat. fat), 311 mg chol., 192 mg sodium, 39 g carbo., 0 g fiber, 7 g pro. Daily Values: 56% vit. A, 1% vit. C, 13% calcium, 5% iron

TIRAMISU

Prep: 30 minutes   **Chill:** 11 hours
Makes: 9 servings

    1 **cup milk**
    ½ **cup granulated sugar**
    2 **tablespoons cornstarch**
    4 **egg yolks**
    2 **tablespoons light rum or brandy**
    2 **tablespoons butter, cut up**
    2 **teaspoons vanilla**
    8 **ounces mascarpone cheese**
    ½ **cup whipping cream**
    1 **tablespoon instant coffee crystals**
    2 **tablespoons coffee liqueur**
    1 **recipe Ladyfingers (see right)***
    2 **ounces semisweet chocolate, grated**
    1 **tablespoon powdered sugar**

1 **Heat ¾ cup of the milk** over low heat. In a saucepan combine granulated sugar and cornstarch. Add remaining ¼ cup milk and the egg yolks. Whisk until smooth. Gradually stir in hot milk. Cook and stir over medium heat until thick and bubbly. Reduce heat. Cook and stir 2 minutes more. Stir in rum or brandy, butter, and vanilla. Cover surface with plastic wrap; cool. Refrigerate until cold, about 3 hours (mixture will be very thick). Allow mascarpone to stand at room temperature for 30 minutes.

2 **Stir mascarpone** until smooth; fold in custard. In a chilled small bowl, beat whipping cream just until stiff peaks form. Fold into custard mixture. In a small bowl dissolve coffee crystals in ¾ cup water; add liqueur. Brush 12 Ladyfingers with half of coffee mixture. Arrange in the bottom of a 2-quart square baking dish. Spread half of custard mixture on top and sprinkle with half of grated chocolate. Repeat with remaining Ladyfingers, coffee, custard, and chocolate. Cover; chill 8 hours or overnight. To serve, sprinkle powdered sugar over top. Cut into squares.

*Note: Commercial ladyfingers are available in some supermarkets and Italian food shops. To substitute for the homemade Ladyfingers, purchase two 3-ounce packages (24 ladyfingers total).

Nutrition Facts per serving: 457 cal., 27 g total fat (14 g sat. fat), 248 mg chol., 151 mg sodium, 44 g carbo., 1 g fiber, 12 g pro. Daily Values: 38% vit. A, 0% vit. C, 6% calcium, 10% iron

LADYFINGERS

Prep: 45 minutes   **Bake:** 12 minutes
Makes: 24 ladyfingers   **Oven:** 350°

These cakelike cookies, resembling a plump finger, often are found in layered desserts. Try them in the Tiramisu at left or the Mocha Java Ice-Cream Bombe on page 262.

    4 **egg yolks**
    ¼ **cup granulated sugar**
    1 **tablespoon hot water**
    1½ **teaspoons vanilla**
    4 **egg whites**
    ¼ **teaspoon salt**
    ¼ **cup granulated sugar**
    1 **cup all-purpose flour**
    2 **tablespoons powdered sugar**

1 **Grease and** flour 2 large baking sheets. In a medium mixing bowl combine egg yolks, the ¼ cup granulated sugar, the water, and vanilla. Beat with an electric mixer on medium speed 2 minutes, until thickened and pale yellow.

2 **Thoroughly wash beaters.** In a large mixing bowl beat egg whites and salt with mixer on medium to high speed until soft peaks form (tips curl). Gradually add the ¼ cup granulated sugar, beating until stiff peaks form (tips stand straight). Add the yolk mixture and fold in by hand just until blended. Sift ⅓ cup of the flour over egg mixture. Fold flour in gently, until just blended. Repeat with remaining flour, ⅓ cup at a time; do not overfold.

3 **Place mixture** in a pastry bag fitted with a ½-inch round tip. Pipe batter into 24 ladyfinger shapes (about 4 inches long and 1 inch wide) on prepared baking sheets, 1 inch apart. Sift powdered sugar over ladyfingers.

4 **Bake in a 350° oven** 12 to 15 minutes or until set and golden brown. Let cool on sheets 10 minutes. Remove with spatula to wire racks to cool completely.

Nutrition Facts per ladyfinger: 49 cal., 1 g total fat (0 g sat. fat), 36 mg chol., 33 mg sodium, 9 g carbo., 0 g fiber, 2 g pro. Daily Values: 5% vit. A, 0% vit. C, 0% calcium, 2% iron

MOCHA JAVA ICE-CREAM BOMBE

Prep: 40 minutes **Freeze:** 9 hours
Stand: 20 minutes **Makes:** 8 to 10 servings

Purchased or homemade ladyfingers will work.

  ¼ **cup hot strong coffee**
  1 **tablespoon coffee liqueur (optional)**
  1 **teaspoon sugar**
18 **to 20 Ladyfingers, split in half**
      horizontally (see page 261)
  1 **8-ounce package cream cheese,**
      softened
  ¼ **cup sugar**
  1 **teaspoon vanilla**
1½ **cups vanilla ice cream**
  ½ **cup miniature semisweet chocolate**
      pieces
  1 **pint coffee ice cream**
  1 **recipe Coffee-Hot Fudge Sauce**
      (see page 263) or 1½ cups fudge
      ice-cream topping (optional)

1 **Chill two medium mixing bowls.** Line a 5-cup round-bottomed bowl or mold with plastic wrap, letting the edges of the wrap hang over the sides of the bowl or mold.

2 **In a shallow bowl** combine the hot coffee, coffee liqueur (if desired), and the 1 teaspoon sugar; stir to dissolve sugar. Brush rounded sides of ladyfingers with the coffee mixture.

3 **Line the bottom and sides** of the bowl or mold with Ladyfingers, placing the rounded side outward. Fill any gaps with ladyfinger trimmings so that the lining is solid. Drizzle with any remaining coffee mixture. Reserve remaining ladyfingers. Cover and chill the lined bowl or mold until needed.

4 **In a medium mixing bowl** beat cream cheese, the ¼ cup sugar, and vanilla with an electric mixer on medium speed until fluffy; set aside.

5 **In 1 of the chilled bowls** stir vanilla ice cream, pressing it against the side of bowl with a spoon, just until softened (do not let ice cream get too soft).

6 **Immediately fold** the softened vanilla ice cream and chocolate pieces into the cream cheese mixture; cover and freeze for 3 to 4 hours or until stiff, stirring mixture occasionally so chips don't sink. Spread cream cheese mixture over the ladyfingers in the bowl or mold, spreading up the sides, to make a lining. Cover with heavy foil and freeze for 2 to 4 hours or until firm.

7 **In the other chilled bowl** soften coffee ice cream as directed for vanilla. Spoon on top of the cream cheese mixture, spreading smoothly. Cover surface of the bombe completely with the remaining ladyfingers.

**Mocha Java Ice-Cream
Bombe:** Make this coffee
and fudge ice-cream dream
a reality at your next dinner
party. Start planning now;
you can make it up to a
month in advance.

Fold excess plastic wrap over surface. Cover tightly with heavy foil. Freeze until firm or up to 1 month.

8 **To serve,** remove foil and invert bombe onto a serving platter; remove bowl or mold and plastic wrap. Let stand at room temperature for 20 to 30 minutes to soften slightly before cutting.

9 **Meanwhile, if desired,** in a small saucepan heat and stir the Coffee-Hot Fudge Sauce or fudge ice-cream topping. Cut the bombe into wedges and transfer to dessert plates. Drizzle each wedge with some of the sauce; pass any remaining sauce.

Nutrition Facts per serving: 387 cal., 22 g total fat (12 g sat. fat), 147 mg chol., 168 mg sodium, 40 g carbo., 2 g fiber, 7 g pro. Daily Values: 22% vit. A, 2% vit. C, 9% calcium, 8% iron

Coffee-Hot Fudge Sauce: Place ¾ cup miniature semisweet chocolate pieces and ¼ cup butter in a small heavy saucepan over very low heat, stirring constantly until smooth. Add ⅔ cup sugar and 4 teaspoons instant coffee crystals. Gradually stir in one 5-ounce can evaporated milk. Bring to boiling; reduce heat. Boil gently over low heat 8 minutes, stirring frequently. Remove from heat. Makes 1½ cups.

ORANGE SOUFFLÉ

Prep: 25 minutes **Bake:** 20 minutes
Makes: 8 servings **Oven:** 350°

This delicate wonder will rise to a special occasion.

Butter
Sugar
¼ cup butter
⅓ cup all-purpose flour
1 cup milk
2 teaspoons finely shredded orange peel
3 tablespoons orange liqueur or orange juice
6 beaten egg yolks
6 egg whites
1 teaspoon vanilla
⅓ cup sugar
1 recipe Custard Sauce (see right)

1 **Butter the sides** of eight 1-cup soufflé dishes or a 2-quart soufflé dish and sprinkle with sugar. To make a collar for each soufflé dish, measure enough foil to wrap around the top of the soufflé dish and add 1 inch for the individual soufflé dishes or 3 inches for the 2-quart dish. Fold the foil in thirds lengthwise. Lightly butter 1 side of the foil and sprinkle with sugar. Attach the foil, sugar side in, around the outside of the dish so the foil extends 2 inches above each dish. Tape or pin the ends of the foil together; set aside. Adjust the oven rack to the lowest position.

2 **In a small saucepan** melt the ¼ cup butter. Stir in the flour. Add milk. Cook and stir over medium heat until thickened and bubbly. Remove from heat. Stir in orange peel and orange liqueur or orange juice. Gradually stir the mixture into the beaten yolks; set aside.

3 **Thoroughly wash beaters.** In a large mixing bowl beat egg whites and vanilla on medium speed until soft peaks form (tips curl). Gradually add the ⅓ cup sugar, about 1 tablespoon at a time, beating on medium-high speed until stiff peaks form (tips stand straight).

4 **Gently fold** the egg yolk mixture into the egg white mixture. Spoon mixture into the prepared soufflé dish(es). Bake in a 350° oven for 20 minutes for individual dishes or 40 to 45 minutes for 2-quart dish or until a knife inserted near center comes out clean. Serve at once with Custard Sauce.

Custard Sauce: In a saucepan stir together ¾ cup milk, 2 tablespoons sugar, ½ teaspoon cornstarch, and ½ teaspoon vanilla until smooth. Cook and stir over medium heat until slightly thickened and bubbly; cook and stir for 2 minutes more. Gradually stir the mixture into 2 beaten egg yolks. Return mixture to saucepan and cook and stir over medium-low heat for 2 minutes more. Stir in 1 teaspoon orange liqueur and ½ teaspoon finely shredded orange peel. (If preparing Cappuccino Soufflé, omit liqueur and peel.) Pour through a sieve into a small bowl; let cool. Cover and refrigerate until cold.

Nutrition Facts per serving: 230 cal., 12 g total fat (6 g sat. fat), 232 mg chol., 133 mg sodium, 21 g carbo., 0 g fiber, 8 g pro. Daily Values: 40% vit. A, 2% vit. C, 7% calcium, 5% iron

Cappuccino Soufflé: Add 1 tablespoon instant coffee crystals to saucepan with milk. Omit orange peel and orange liqueur or orange juice.

THE STRUDEL DEFINED

Q Sometimes a strudel pastry is light and flaky; other times it's a rich, dense pastry. Which is the real strudel?

A They both are. A strudel is defined by the method by which it's made: It's an elongated pastry wrapped around a filling, typically made of fruit or cheese. Its name speaks of its shape—"strudel" means "whirlpool" in German. Traditional strudels are made with layers of tissue-thin dough (making flaky pastry), but the Fall Fruit Strudel also fits the definition. It uses a cream-cheese dough that is simply rolled instead of pulled and offers a heartier pastry, ideal for the mixed-fruit filling.

FALL FRUIT STRUDEL

Prep: 30 minutes   Bake: 35 minutes
Chill: 1 hour   Makes: 8 servings   Oven: 375°

$1\frac{1}{2}$ **cups all-purpose flour**
  2 **tablespoons sugar**
 $\frac{1}{4}$ **teaspoon salt**
 $\frac{1}{4}$ **cup cold butter, cut up**
  1 **3-ounce package cream cheese, chilled and cut into $\frac{1}{2}$-inch pieces**
  3 **to 4 tablespoons cold water**
 $\frac{1}{2}$ **cup golden raisins**
 $\frac{1}{2}$ **cup dried tart cherries**
 $\frac{1}{4}$ **cup snipped dried apricots**
  3 **tablespoons dark rum, cream sherry, or apple juice**
  1 **large firm ripe pear, peeled, cored, and diced**
 $\frac{1}{4}$ **cup chopped walnuts or pecans**
  3 **gingersnaps, coarsely crushed**
  3 **tablespoons sugar**
 $\frac{1}{4}$ **teaspoon ground cinnamon**
  1 **tablespoon sugar**
  1 **recipe Eggnog Custard Sauce (see right) or vanilla ice cream**

1 **Lightly grease a** 15×10×1-inch baking pan. In a large mixing bowl stir together flour, the 2 tablespoons sugar, and the salt. Using a pastry blender, cut in the butter and cream cheese until pieces are the size of small peas. Sprinkle water gradually over dough, tossing with a fork until dough is moistened. Gather dough into a ball. Flatten dough into a disk, wrap in plastic wrap, and refrigerate 1 hour.

2 **Meanwhile, for filling,** in a bowl stir together raisins, cherries, apricots, and rum. Let stand 1 hour. Add pear, walnuts, gingersnaps, the 3 tablespoons sugar, and the cinnamon. Toss until blended.

3 **On a lightly floured surface** roll dough with a floured rolling pin to a 14×8-inch rectangle. Trim rough edges. Place the filling in a lengthwise strip down center of the rectangle to about 2 inches from the ends. Brush the edges of the dough lightly with water. Fold a long side of pastry up over the filling. Brush the edge lightly with water and fold the other side over, overlapping slightly. Press gently to seal. Bring the ends of the pastry up to the top and press gently to seal.

4 **Place the prepared baking pan** next to strudel. Ease the strudel into pan, seam side down. Brush top lightly with water and sprinkle with the 1 tablespoon sugar. Bake in a 375° oven for 35 minutes or until golden. Cool on baking sheet on a wire rack. Cut into slices with a serrated knife. Serve with Eggnog Custard Sauce or ice cream.

Eggnog Custard Sauce: In a small saucepan heat 1 cup milk over medium-low heat. In a small bowl stir together 3 tablespoons sugar, $\frac{1}{2}$ teaspoon cornstarch, and $\frac{1}{8}$ teaspoon ground nutmeg. Add 2 beaten egg yolks and whisk until smooth. Gradually whisk about half of the hot milk into the yolk mixture. Pour all of the yolk mixture into the hot milk. Cook over low heat, stirring constantly until the custard thickens slightly and coats a metal spoon. Remove from heat. Stir in 2 teaspoons dark rum and $\frac{1}{2}$ teaspoon vanilla. Cover surface with plastic wrap. Cool; chill in refrigerator up to 3 days.

Nutrition Facts per serving: 383 cal., 14 g total fat (5 g sat. fat), 75 mg chol., 186 mg sodium, 55 g carbo., 2 g fiber, 6 g pro. Daily Values: 27% vit. A, 2% vit. C, 5% calcium, 13% iron

holiday classics

Rum Babas, recipe page 267

HOLIDAY CLASSICS

RUM BABAS

Prep: 1 hour   Rise: 1⅓ hours
Bake: 15 minutes   Makes: 8 servings   Oven: 350°

From Russia with love—these sweet and light glazed desserts make for a glowing finale to a holiday meal (see photo, page 265).

     2 cups all-purpose flour
     1 package active dry yeast
    ⅓ cup milk
     1 tablespoon sugar
    ½ teaspoon salt
     4 eggs
    ½ cup butter
    ½ cup golden raisins
     1 teaspoon finely shredded
        orange peel
  1½ cups water
    ¾ cup sugar
    ⅓ cup rum
    ½ cup apricot preserves
     1 tablespoon water
    ¾ cup whipping cream (optional)
    ¾ cup dairy sour cream (optional)

1 **In a large bowl stir together** 1½ cups of the flour and the yeast; set aside. In a small saucepan heat and stir milk, the 1 tablespoon sugar, and salt just until warm (120° to 130°).

2 **Add milk mixture** to flour mixture. Add eggs. Beat with an electric mixer on low to medium speed for 30 seconds, scraping sides of the bowl constantly. Beat on high speed for 3 minutes. Using a spoon, stir in the remaining flour. (The batter will be soft and sticky.) Cut butter into small pieces; place atop batter. Cover; let rise in a warm place until double (about 1 hour).

3 **Grease** twelve ½-cup baba molds, twelve 2½-inch muffin cups, or 8 popover pan cups. Set aside.

4 **Stir butter,** raisins, and orange peel into the batter. Divide the batter among molds or cups, filling each ½ to ⅔ full. Cover and let rise in a warm place for 20 to 30 minutes or until batter fills molds or cups. (Or, cover and refrigerate overnight. Let stand at room temperature for 20 minutes before baking.)

5 **Bake in a 350° oven** for 15 to 20 minutes or until golden. Meanwhile, place wire racks over waxed paper. Remove babas from molds or cups onto racks. Cool on wire racks.

6 **For the rum syrup,** in a heavy small saucepan stir together the 1½ cups water and the ¾ cup sugar. Cook and stir over medium heat until the sugar is dissolved. Bring to boiling. Boil, uncovered, without stirring, for 5 minutes. Remove from heat; cool slightly. Stir in the rum.

7 **Using the tines of a large fork,** prick babas all over. Dip babas, top side down, into the rum syrup 2 or 3 times or until moistened. Return to rack. Spoon any remaining syrup over babas.

8 **For glaze,** if necessary, snip any large pieces of apricot in the preserves. In a small saucepan combine the preserves and the 1 tablespoon water. Heat and stir over low heat until preserves are melted. Brush the glaze onto the babas.

9 **If desired, for cream sauce,** in a small mixing bowl stir together whipping cream and sour cream. To serve, spoon cream sauce onto 8 or 12 dessert plates. Place a baba on each plate.

Nutrition Facts per baba baked in a baba mold or muffin pan: 291 cal., 10 g total fat (7 g sat. fat), 103 mg chol., 206 mg sodium, 44 g carbo., 1 g fiber, 5 g pro. Daily Values: 13% vit. A, 1% vit. C, 2% calcium, 9% iron

BAKE AHEAD

Stash a few holiday treats in the freezer now, and you'll have more time to slow down and savor the season. Here are some general guidelines for how long fresh-baked sweets can be stored in the freezer:

Cookies (unfrosted): Up to 3 months
Cheesecakes (whole): Up to 1 month
Layer Cakes (unfrosted): Up to 4 months
Muffins and Quick Breads: Up to 3 months
Yeast Breads: Up to 3 months
Fruitcakes: Up to 12 months
Fruit Pies (unbaked): Up to 3 months
Fruit Pies (baked): Up to 8 months

PLUM PUDDING

Prep: 20 minutes (plus 2 hours soak time)
Steam: 1½ hours   **Cool:** 15 minutes
Makes: 18 servings

Author Charles Dickens made this English holiday dessert world famous, and its appeal has endured since "A Christmas Carol" was written in the 19th century.

1½ cups pitted prunes, snipped
½ cup brandy or orange juice
1 medium apple, peeled and finely
    shredded
¾ cup chopped walnuts
½ cup diced mixed candied fruits
    and peels
1 tablespoon finely shredded
    orange peel
3 cups all-purpose flour
1 teaspoon ground cinnamon
½ teaspoon baking soda
½ teaspoon salt
½ teaspoon ground ginger
½ teaspoon ground nutmeg
½ cup butter
1½ cups packed brown sugar
3 eggs
1¼ cups milk
1 recipe Hard Sauce (optional)
    (see right)

1 **Soak prunes** in brandy or orange juice, covered, in a cool place for 2 hours or overnight or until most of the liquid is absorbed. Do not drain. Stir shredded apple, walnuts, candied fruits and peels, and orange peel into prune mixture; set aside.

2 **Grease and flour** a 12-cup fluted tube mold or pan; set aside. Stir together flour, cinnamon, baking soda, salt, ginger, and nutmeg; set aside.

3 **In a large mixing bowl** beat butter with an electric mixer on medium speed for 30 seconds. Beat in brown sugar until well combined. Add eggs, one at a time, beating on low speed just until combined (do not overbeat). Add flour mixture alternately with milk, beating on low speed after each addition just until combined. Stir in prune mixture.

4 **Spread batter** into prepared mold. Lightly grease a square of foil; cover mold with foil,

greased side down. Press foil tightly against the rim of mold. Place mold on a rack in a deep kettle containing 1 inch of simmering water. Cover kettle; steam pudding over low heat for 1½ to 2 hours or until a toothpick inserted near center comes out clean, adding additional boiling water to kettle if necessary. Remove from kettle. Remove foil. Cool 15 minutes. Carefully invert; remove pudding from mold. Cool slightly on wire rack. If desired, serve warm with Hard Sauce.

Make-ahead directions: Cool completely and wrap in 100-percent cotton cheesecloth moistened with additional brandy or orange juice. Wrap tightly with foil and store in refrigerator for up to 2 weeks. To reheat, unwrap pudding and remove cheesecloth; return pudding to the mold or pan. Cover tightly with foil; place on a rack in kettle containing 1 inch of simmering water. Cover kettle; steam over low heat for 30 to 40 minutes or until heated through.

Nutrition facts per serving: 290 cal., 10 g total fat (4 g sat. fat), 50 mg chol., 171 mg sodium, 44 g carbo., 2 g fiber, 5 g pro. Daily Values: 10% vit. A, 2% vit. C, 4% calcium, 12% iron

Hard Sauce: Beat together ¾ cup butter and 1¼ cups sifted powdered sugar until fluffy. Beat in 3 tablespoons brandy, rum, or orange juice and ½ teaspoon vanilla. Store, covered, in refrigerator for up to 2 weeks. Let stand at room temperature for 30 minutes before serving. Makes 1¼ cups.

CANDIED FRUIT

Like Christmas lights and candy canes, candied fruits are hallmarks of the holiday season. In their colorful variety—whether citron, pineapple, red or green cherries, or orange, grapefruit, and lemon peels—they add a decorative touch and spark of flavor to holiday breads, cakes, and cookies. Candied fruit differs from dried fruit in that it is cooked in a sugar syrup as its means of preservation. For optimum freshness, store candied fruit in a tightly sealed container in the freezer up to 6 months.

White Christmas Cake: This luscious cake, made extra rich with white chocolate and pecans, was a winner in the *Better Homes and Gardens*® monthly Prize Tested Recipe contest in December 1994.

WHITE CHRISTMAS CAKE

Prep: 30 minutes   Bake: 25 minutes
Cool: 1 hour   Makes: 16 servings
Oven: 350°

1½ cups butter
4 ounces white baking bar, chopped
1½ cups buttermilk or sour milk
4 eggs, slightly beaten
¼ teaspoon rum extract
3½ cups all-purpose flour
1 cup toasted chopped pecans
    (see tip, page 247)
2¼ cups sugar
½ cup flaked coconut
1 teaspoon baking soda
1 teaspoon baking powder
1 recipe White Chocolate Frosting
    (see right)
Toasted coconut (optional)
    (see tip, page 247)
Pecan halves (optional)

1 Grease and lightly flour three 9×1½-inch round baking pans; set aside. (If you have only 2 baking pans, see tip, page 141). Bring butter and ¾ cup water to boiling, stirring constantly. Remove from heat. Add baking bar; stir until melted. Stir in

buttermilk, eggs, and rum extract; set aside. Combine ½ cup of the flour and the chopped pecans; set aside.

2 In an extra-large mixing bowl combine the remaining flour, the sugar, the ½ cup coconut, baking soda, and baking powder. Stir in butter mixture. Fold in flour-pecan mixture. Divide evenly into prepared pans. Bake in a 350° oven 25 to 30 minutes or until toothpick inserted near centers comes out clean. Cool in pans on wire racks 10 minutes. Remove from pans; cool completely on racks.

3 To assemble, place a cake layer on a platter. Spread top with ½ cup frosting. Repeat with another cake layer and ½ cup frosting. Top with remaining cake layer. Frost top and sides with remaining frosting. If desired, garnish with toasted coconut and pecan halves.

White Chocolate Frosting: Melt 4 ounces chopped white baking bar. Cool 10 minutes. In a large mixing bowl beat ½ cup butter, softened, and one 8-ounce package and one 3-ounce package cream cheese, softened, with an electric mixer until combined. Beat in melted baking bar. Gradually add 6 cups sifted powdered sugar, beating until smooth.

Nutrition Facts per serving: 776 cal., 41 g total fat (23 g sat. fat), 137 mg chol., 477 mg sodium, 98 g carbo., 1 g fiber, 8 g pro. Daily Values: 39% vit. A, 0 % vit. C, 9% calcium, 12% iron

YULE LOG

Prep: 40 minutes **Bake:** 12 minutes
Cool: 1 hour **Makes:** 10 servings **Oven:** 375°

Reminiscent of a log on a blazing fire, this cake roll symbolizes the warmth and fellowship of the season.

  1 **cup all-purpose flour**
¼ **teaspoon salt**
  5 **egg yolks**
  2 **tablespoons sherry or milk**
  1 **cup granulated sugar**
  5 **egg whites**
¼ **teaspoon cream of tartar**
     Powdered sugar
  1 **recipe Coffee-Cream Filling**
       (see right)
  1 **recipe Rich Chocolate Frosting**
       (see right)

1 **Grease and lightly flour** a 15×10×1-inch jelly-roll pan; set aside. Stir together flour and salt; set aside. Beat egg yolks and sherry with an electric mixer on high speed about 5 minutes or until thick and lemon-colored. Gradually add ½ cup of the granulated sugar, beating until sugar is almost dissolved.

2 **Thoroughly wash beaters.** In a very large bowl beat egg whites and cream of tartar on medium to high speed until soft peaks form (tips curl). Gradually add the remaining granulated sugar, 2 tablespoons at a time, beating on medium to high speed until stiff peaks form (tips stand straight). Fold 1 cup of the egg-white mixture into egg-yolk mixture. Fold egg-yolk mixture into remaining egg-white mixture. Fold in flour mixture; spread in prepared pan.

3 **Bake in a 375° oven** for 12 to 15 minutes or until top springs back when lightly touched. Immediately loosen edges of cake from pan. Turn cake out onto a towel sprinkled with powdered sugar. Roll up warm cake and towel, jelly-roll style, starting from a short side. Cool on a rack.

4 **Gently unroll cake.** Spread Coffee-Cream Filling on cake to within 1 inch of the edges. Roll up cake without towel, jelly-roll style, starting from 1 of the short sides. Cut a 1½-inch slice from 1 end of cake. Frost cake with Rich Chocolate Frosting. Place the slice on side of log to form a branch (see photo, above right). Frost branch. Using the tines of a fork, score the cake lengthwise to resemble tree bark.

To add branch, cut off a 1½-inch slice from end of cake before frosting. Frost cake, put branch slice in place, and frost branch.

Coffee-Cream Filling: Beat 1 cup whipping cream, ¼ cup sifted powdered sugar, and 1½ teaspoons instant coffee crystals in a mixing bowl until soft peaks form. Makes about 2 cups.

Rich Chocolate Frosting: Heat and stir 3 ounces unsweetened chocolate and 3 tablespoons butter in a saucepan until chocolate melts. Remove from heat; stir in 1½ cups sifted powdered sugar, 1 teaspoon vanilla, and ¼ cup milk. Add 1½ cups additional sifted powdered sugar and enough milk to make of spreading consistency (about 1 to 2 tablespoons). Makes about 1½ cups.

Nutrition Facts per serving: 449 cal., 20 g total fat (10 g sat. fat), 149 mg chol., 138 mg sodium, 66 g carbo., 1 g fiber, 6 g pro. Daily Values: 31% vit. A, 0% vit. C, 3% calcium, 10% iron

ROYAL CHRISTMAS CAKE

BEST-LOVED

Prep: 45 minutes **Bake:** 1 hour
Cool: 2 hours **Chill:** 1 week
Stand: 30 minutes **Makes:** 16 servings **Oven:** 300°

  2 **cups all-purpose flour**
  1 **teaspoon ground cinnamon**
½ **teaspoon baking powder**
¼ **teaspoon baking soda**
¼ **teaspoon ground nutmeg**
¼ **teaspoon ground cloves**
1½ **cups currants**
1½ **cups dark or golden raisins**
1½ **cups diced mixed candied fruits**
       and peels
  1 **cup candied red and/or green cherries**
½ **cup almonds, ground***
  4 **eggs**
  1 **cup granulated sugar**
¾ **cup butter, melted**

½ cup rum, brandy, or orange juice
3 tablespoons lemon juice
  Rum, brandy, or orange juice
    (about ⅓ cup)
1 8-ounce can almond paste
    (see tip, page 274)
1 recipe Royal Icing (see lower right)

1 **Grease** bottom and sides of two 9×1½-inch round baking pans. Line bottoms with waxed paper. Grease paper; sprinkle bottom and sides of pans lightly with flour; set aside. Stir together flour, cinnamon, baking powder, baking soda, nutmeg, and cloves. Stir in currants, raisins, fruits and peels, cherries, and almonds. Set aside.

2 **In a medium mixing bowl** beat eggs slightly with a fork. Add granulated sugar, butter, ½ cup rum, and lemon juice; stir until combined. Stir egg mixture into fruit mixture; pour into prepared pans.

3 **Bake in a 300° oven** for 1 to 1¼ hours or until a toothpick inserted near the center comes out clean. (If necessary, cover pans loosely with foil after 1 hour to prevent overbrowning.) Cool in pans on wire racks 20 minutes; loosen edges. Remove cakes from pans. Cool thoroughly on wire racks.

4 **Wrap layers** separately in 100-percent cotton cheesecloth moistened with additional rum, brandy, or juice. Wrap with foil or place in large self-sealing plastic bags. Store in the refrigerator for 1 to 2 weeks. Remoisten cheesecloth with a little additional rum if it becomes dry.

5 **To assemble,** up to 2 hours before serving, unwrap cake layers. Place 1 cake layer, top side down, on a serving plate. Spread with half of the almond paste. (Or, if paste is too thick to spread, divide in half and shape into balls. Place each ball between 2 sheets of waxed paper; flatten slightly. With a rolling pin, roll each portion into a 9½-inch circle; trim to form a 9-inch circle. Remove top sheet of paper from 1 circle; invert onto cake. Remove remaining paper.)

6 **Spread** about ¾ cup of the Royal Icing over almond paste on first cake layer. Add second cake layer, top side up; spread or top with remaining almond paste. Frost top and sides of cake with remaining Royal Icing. If desired, garnish with bay leaves (do not eat). Let stand at least 30 minutes to allow Icing to set. Serve within 2 hours of frosting.

Royal Icing: Combine 4 cups sifted powdered sugar, ½ cup water, ¼ cup meringue powder, and 1 teaspoon vanilla. Beat with an electric mixer on high speed 7 to 10 minutes or until very stiff. Use immediately; cover icing in bowl with damp paper towel or with plastic wrap while working to prevent drying. Makes about 3½ cups.

*Note: Use a grinder, blender, or food processor to grind nuts.

Nutrition Facts per serving: 565 cal., 16 g total fat (6 g sat. fat), 76 mg chol., 139 mg sodium, 98 g carbo., 2 g fiber, 7 g pro. Daily Values: 10% vit. A, 4% vit. C, 7% calcium, 15% iron

Royal Christmas Cake: Generously studded with candied fruits and nuts, then slathered with a snowy-white frosting—here, the colors and flavors of Christmas are rolled into one regal dessert.

FRUITCAKE

Prep: 30 minutes **Bake:** 1¼ hours **Cool:** 2 hours
Store: 2 weeks **Makes:** 16 servings **Oven:** 300°

*Forget all the jokes about fruitcakes getting passed
around. Make it from scratch, and this sweet,
mellow treat won't make it out of the house.*

1½   **cups all-purpose flour**
 1   **teaspoon ground cinnamon**
½   **teaspoon baking powder**
¼   **teaspoon baking soda**
¼   **teaspoon ground nutmeg**
¼   **teaspoon ground allspice**
¼   **teaspoon ground cloves**
¾   **cup diced mixed candied fruits and
      peels or snipped mixed dried fruit**
½   **cup raisins or chopped pitted dates**
½   **cup candied red or green cherries,
      quartered**
½   **cup chopped pecans or walnuts**
 2   **eggs**
½   **cup packed brown sugar**
½   **cup orange juice or apple juice**
⅓   **cup butter, melted**
 2   **tablespoons light-flavored molasses
      Brandy or fruit juice (¼ to ⅓ cup)**

1 Grease an 8×4×2-inch loaf pan. Line bottom
and sides with brown paper to prevent overbrowning; grease paper; set aside. Stir together flour,
cinnamon, baking powder, baking soda, nutmeg,
allspice, and cloves. Add fruits and peels, raisins,
cherries, and nuts. Mix ingredients well; set aside.

2 In mixing bowl beat eggs; stir in brown sugar,
juice, butter, and molasses until combined. Stir
into fruit mixture. Pour batter into prepared pan.

3 Bake in 300° oven for 1¼ to 1½ hours or until a
wooden toothpick comes out clean; cover pan
loosely with foil after 1 hour of baking to prevent overbrowning. Cool cake thoroughly in pan on wire rack.

4 Remove cake from pan. Wrap cake in brandy-
or fruit-juice-moistened 100-percent cotton
cheesecloth. Wrap with foil. Store in the refrigerator
for 2 to 8 weeks to mellow flavors. Remoisten
cheesecloth about once a week or as needed.

Nutrition Facts per serving: 202 cal., 7 g total fat
(3 g sat. fat), 37 mg chol., 80 mg sodium,
32 g carbo., 1 g fiber, 3 g pro. Daily Values:
4% vit. A, 6% vit. C, 2% calcium, 7% iron

Light-Colored Fruitcake: Prepare as above, except
omit nutmeg, allspice, and cloves and substitute
light-colored corn syrup for the molasses. Add 1 teaspoon finely shredded lemon peel and 1 tablespoon
lemon juice with the corn syrup.

DRIED-FRUIT FRUITCAKE

Prep: 25 minutes **Bake:** 1 hour **Cool:** 2 hours
Store: 2 weeks **Makes:** 16 servings **Oven:** 300°

1½   **cups all-purpose flour**
½   **teaspoon baking powder**
¼   **teaspoon baking soda**
½   **cup butter**
¾   **cup packed brown sugar**
 2   **eggs**

TOOLBOX: HOLIDAY DESSERT WARE

Although these holiday dessert classics are
often tied to specific traditions, only a few
require special equipment:
Plum Pudding: This traditional English dessert
must be steamed in a fluted tube mold, a metal
mold that embosses the pudding with a
decorative texture as it steams in a kettle. Fluted
tube molds are available at department stores and
specialty cookware shops.

Rum Babas: Though babas can be made in
muffin cups or popover pan cups, to
get their classic mushroom shape, they're ideally
made in ½-cup baba molds, which can be
found at specialty cookware shops.
Fruitcake: The magic mellowing of fruitcake
takes place as it ages wrapped in brandy-soaked
cheesecloth. Be sure to look for food-grade,
100-percent cotton cheesecloth.

Dried-Fruit Fruitcake: It's mellowed in a brandy-soaked cheesecloth, like a traditional fruitcake, but this updated version gets added spark from dried cherries and apricots. Serve as a dessert or as a coffee cake.

  1 teaspoon finely shredded orange peel
 ½ cup orange juice or apple juice
  2 tablespoons light-colored corn syrup
  1 teaspoon vanilla
 ¾ cup snipped dried apricots
 ½ cup dried tart cherries or raisins
 ½ cup pitted whole dates, chopped
 ½ cup chopped pecans or walnuts
    Brandy or orange juice
      (¼ to ⅓ cup)
    Pearl or coarse sugar (optional)
    Orange-peel curls (optional)

1 **Grease and lightly flour** an 8-inch fluted tube mold. Or, grease an 8×4×2-inch loaf pan; line pan with parchment paper; grease paper. Set aside.

2 **Combine** flour, baking powder, and baking soda; set aside. In a bowl beat butter with an electric mixer on medium speed for 30 seconds. Add the brown sugar; beat until mixture is combined. Add eggs, 1 at a time, beating on medium speed until combined (batter may appear curdled).

3 **Combine** orange peel, juice, corn syrup, and vanilla. Add flour mixture and juice mixture alternately to butter mixture, beating on low speed after each addition just until combined. Combine fruits and nuts. Fold into batter. Spread into prepared pan.

4 **Bake in a 300° oven** about 1 hour in tube pan, about 1½ hours in loaf pan, or until a wooden toothpick comes out clean. If necessary, cover cake with foil the last 15 to 30 minutes to prevent overbrowning.

5 **Cool cake** in tube pan on wire rack 10 minutes. Remove from pan; cool thoroughly on rack. Or, thoroughly cool the cake in loaf pan on wire rack; remove from pan. Wrap cake in brandy- or juice-moistened 100-percent cotton cheesecloth. Overwrap in foil. Store in refrigerator 2 to 8 weeks; remoisten cheesecloth about once a week or as needed. If desired, sprinkle with pearl sugar and garnish with orange-peel curls before slicing.

Nutrition Facts per serving: 218 cal., 9 g total fat (4 g sat. fat), 42 mg chol., 102 mg sodium, 32 g carbo., 2 g fiber, 3 g pro. Daily Values: 13% vit. A, 7% vit. C, 2% calcium, 8% iron

Cake of Kings: Do as the French—honor the visit of the three kings to the holy infant while treating your family and friends to this simple dessert of a flaky puff pastry and sumptuous almond filling.

CAKE OF KINGS

EASY

Prep: 20 minutes   Stand: 20 minutes
Bake: 20 minutes   Cool: 1 hour
Makes: 12 servings   Oven: 375°

  1 17¼-ounce package frozen puff
      pastry (2 sheets)
  4 ounces (½ of an 8-ounce can)
      almond paste (see tip, below)
1¼ cups sifted powdered sugar
1½ teaspoons lemon juice
      Water
      Toasted sliced almonds
        (see tip, page 247)
      Cut-up candied red and green cherries
      Chopped candied pineapple

ALMOND PASTE

Available in the baking aisle of larger supermarkets, almond paste is made from finely ground almonds and sugar. For best results, use an almond paste made without syrup or liquid glucose. When almond paste contains these ingredients, the final results may be softer.

1 **Let folded pastry stand** at room temperature for 20 minutes to thaw. Unfold. Cut out one 9-inch circle from each sheet.

2 **Place almond paste** between 2 sheets of waxed paper; roll into a 9-inch circle, trimming edges with a knife if necessary. Remove top sheet of waxed paper.

3 **On an ungreased baking sheet, place** 1 circle of puff pastry. Invert the circle of almond paste onto pastry; remove waxed paper. Top with remaining circle of puff pastry. If desired, for decoration, score the vertical sides of pastry with a table knife to make a scalloped edge.

4 **Bake in a 375° oven** for 20 to 25 minutes or until golden brown. Remove from baking sheet; cool completely on a wire rack.

5 **For icing,** stir together powdered sugar, lemon juice, and enough water (1 to 2 teaspoons) to make an icing of drizzling consistency. Transfer pastry to a platter. Spoon icing over pastry, allowing icing to drizzle down sides. Top with almonds, cherries, and pineapple. Cut into wedges to serve.

Nutrition Facts per serving: 272 cal., 16 g total fat (0 g sat. fat), 0 mg chol., 154 mg sodium, 30 g carbo., 0 g fiber, 3 g pro. Daily Values: 0% vit. A, 0% vit. C, 2% calcium, 2% iron

PEAR AND MINCEMEAT TART

Prep: 25 minutes   **Bake:** 10 minutes
Makes: 8 servings   **Oven:** 350°

Mincemeat is more fruit than meat. In fact, these days, this chopped apple and raisin filling rarely contains the ground meat and suet our grandmothers may have added. Find mincemeat with the pie fillings in your supermarket.

　　1　recipe Sweet Tart Pastry
　　　　(see page 253)
　　2　medium red or yellow pears
　　　　(such as Bartlett), sliced
　　⅔　cup orange juice
　　½　cup whipping cream
　　1　8-ounce package cream cheese,
　　　　softened
　　½　cup orange marmalade
　　1　cup canned mincemeat
　　1　cup seedless red or green grapes,
　　　　halved
　　¼　cup orange marmalade or apple
　　　　jelly, melted

1 Prepare pastry. On a lightly floured surface slightly flatten the pastry dough. Roll dough from center to edges, forming a 13-inch circle. Wrap pastry around a rolling pin. Unroll pastry onto an 11-inch tart pan with a removable bottom or a 10-inch pie plate or quiche dish. Ease pastry into pan, being careful not to stretch it. Press pastry into the fluted sides of the pan; trim edges. Line pastry shell with a double thickness of foil.

2 Bake in a 350° oven for 10 minutes. Remove foil. Bake for 8 to 10 minutes more or until golden. Completely cool pastry shell in pan on wire rack.

3 If desired, peel pears. In a large skillet combine pear slices and orange juice. Bring to boiling; reduce heat. Cover and simmer for 6 to 8 minutes or just until pears are tender. Drain, discarding liquid. Cover and chill for 2 to 24 hours.

4 For filling, in a chilled mixing bowl beat whipping cream with chilled beaters on medium speed until soft peaks form; set aside. In a medium mixing bowl beat cream cheese and the ½ cup marmalade on medium speed until fluffy. Gently fold in whipped cream. Cover; chill up to 2 hours.

5 To assemble, spread mincemeat atop baked pastry. Top with cream cheese mixture. Cover and chill until ready to serve, up to 2 hours.

6 To serve, arrange pear slices and grapes atop the cream cheese mixture. Brush with the ¼ cup melted orange marmalade.

Nutrition Facts per serving: 556 cal., 29 g total fat (17 g sat. fat), 136 mg chol., 319 mg sodium, 72 g carbo., 4 g fiber, 6 g pro. Daily Values: 38% vit. A, 26% vit. C, 6% calcium, 15% iron

Pear and Mincemeat Tart: With mincemeat on the bottom, an orange-infused cream cheese layer in the middle, and pears on top, you can taste winter's best flavors in every bite.

CROSTATA

Prep: 45 minutes **Bake:** 40 minutes
Makes: 8 servings **Oven:** 375°

Twisting the pastry wedges is made easier by keeping the dough chilled until you're ready to shape it. If dough becomes too warm, just pop it back into the refrigerator for a few minutes.

Twist each pastry twice at the narrow end. Place atop the apples and figs, arranging in a circle with the wide ends toward the edge.

     2 **cups all-purpose flour**
    ⅓ **cup sugar**
  1½ **teaspoons baking powder**
    ⅓ **cup butter**
     1 **slightly beaten egg**
    ⅓ **cup milk**
     1 **teaspoon vanilla**
     4 **cups sliced, peeled apples**
    ½ **cup snipped dried figs**
    ⅔ **cup apricot or peach preserves**
        Milk
        Sugar

1 **Stir together** flour, sugar, and baking powder. Cut in butter until mixture resembles coarse crumbs. Combine egg, milk, and vanilla; add to flour mixture. Mix well. Shape into a ball.

2 **On a lightly floured surface knead** dough gently for 10 to 12 strokes or until smooth. Wrap and chill one-third of the dough. Pat remaining dough onto the bottom and up the sides of a 10- or 11-inch tart pan with removable bottom.

3 **Arrange apple slices** and figs on pastry in tart pan. Stir and spoon preserves evenly over fruit.

4 **On a lightly floured surface roll** chilled pastry into a 9- or 10-inch circle. Cut into 12 wedges. Twist each wedge twice at narrow end; arrange pastry in a circle atop apples (see photo, above). Brush with milk. Sprinkle with sugar.

5 **Bake in a 375° oven** 40 to 45 minutes or until fruit is tender. If necessary, cover loosely with foil the last 10 to 15 minutes of baking to prevent overbrowning. Remove sides of pan before serving. Serve warm.

Nutrition Facts per serving: 364 cal., 9 g total fat (5 g sat. fat), 48 mg chol., 164 mg sodium, 68 g carbo., 3 g fiber, 5 g pro. Daily Values: 9% vit. A, 6% vit. C, 9% calcium, 14% iron

HOLIDAY DESSERT LORE

As you share these holiday desserts with family and friends, share, too, the stories behind these time-honored recipes:

Plum Pudding: In Victorian times, the prettiest sprig of holly was always reserved for garnishing the plum pudding as it made its grand entrance into the dining room. This English dessert got its name from the fact that it indeed once contained plums, which it no longer does.

Rum Babas: Baba means granny in Russia, and it's likely these rum-soaked sponge cakes got their name from their resemblance to a Russian grandmother's old-fashioned skirt.

Yule Log: Called the *bûche de Noël* in France, the country of its origin, this log-shaped cake is meant to represent the great log that's thrown on the blazing fire to warm celebrants on Christmas Eve.

Crostata: The reason this Italian fruit tart is so popular at Christmastime is tied to the season. In winter months of bygone days, bakers filled these tarts with dried fruits and preserves because fresh fruit was scarce.

Cake of Kings: This simple almond pastry reigns in France at Twelfth Night celebrations on January 6 (12 days after Christmas), when the three gift-bearing kings are said to have visited the holy infant. The pastry is often topped with crowns to symbolize the royal visitors.

Crostata: Serve this one warm. The fresh-baked aroma of figs, apricots, apples, and buttery-rich pastry will tempt diners even before this beautiful tart reaches the table.

BERLINER KRANSER

Prep: 45 minutes   **Chill:** 1 hour
Bake: 18 minutes per batch
Makes: 36 cookies   **Oven:** 325°

This buttery treat is one of the many cookies Scandinavians might serve at one of their traditional "coffee tables"—a three-course event often served as part of the Christmas holiday festivities.

  1 **cup butter**
  ½ **cup sifted powdered sugar**
  1 **hard-cooked egg yolk, sieved**
  1 **raw egg yolk**
  1 **teaspoon vanilla**
2¼ **cups all-purpose flour**
  1 **slightly beaten egg white**
  2 **to 3 tablespoons pearl sugar or**
       coarse sugar

1 In a large mixing bowl beat butter with an electric mixer on medium to high speed for 30 seconds. Add powdered sugar; beat until fluffy. Beat in hard-cooked and raw egg yolks and vanilla. Beat in flour until combined. Cover and chill about 1 hour or until firm enough to handle. (Chilling longer may make dough too firm to roll.)

2 Using about 1 tablespoon dough for each cookie, roll into 6-inch-long ropes. On an ungreased cookie sheet shape each into a ring, overlapping about 1 inch from ends (see photo, page 279). Brush with egg white; sprinkle with pearl or coarse sugar.

3 Bake in a 325° oven for 18 to 20 minutes or until edges are lightly browned. Cool on cookie sheet for 1 minute. Transfer cookies to a wire rack and let cool completely.

Nutrition Facts per cookie: 83 cal., 5 g total fat (3 g sat. fat), 25 mg chol., 54 mg sodium, 8 g carbo., 0 g fiber, 1 g pro. Daily Values: 6% vit. A, 0% vit. C, 0% calcium, 2% iron

PEPPARKAKOR

Prep: 30 minutes   **Chill:** 2 hours
Bake: 5 minutes per batch
Cool: 45 minutes   **Makes:** 36 cookies   **Oven:** 375°

Popular shapes for these spicy Swedish cutout cookies include hearts, stars, men, and goats.

  ½ **cup sugar**
  ½ **cup light-flavored molasses**
  ¼ **cup shortening**
  ¼ **cup butter**
  1 **beaten egg**
  1 **teaspoon ground cinnamon**
  ½ **teaspoon finely shredded orange**
       peel
  ½ **teaspoon ground allspice**
  ½ **teaspoon ground nutmeg**
  ¼ **teaspoon salt**
  ¼ **teaspoon baking soda**
  ¼ **teaspoon ground cardamom**
  ¼ **teaspoon ground cloves**
2½ **cups all-purpose flour**
       Finely chopped, slivered, or sliced
          nuts (optional)
       Candied cherries, quartered
          (optional)

1 In a 2-quart saucepan combine sugar, molasses, shortening, and butter. Bring to boiling; reduce heat. Cook and stir over low heat for 2 minutes. Remove from heat; cool for 45 minutes.

2 Add egg, cinnamon, orange peel, allspice, nutmeg, salt, baking soda, cardamom, and cloves to saucepan, stirring well to mix. Add flour, one-third at a time, stirring well after each addition. Divide dough in half. Wrap and chill dough for 2 to 24 hours or until firm enough to handle.

3 Lightly grease a cookie sheet. On a well-floured surface, roll each portion of dough to ⅛-inch thickness. Cut into desired shapes (such as hearts or stars) with a 2½- to 3-inch cookie cutter. Place on prepared cookie sheet. If desired, top with nuts or cherries.

A tray of Scandinavian classics: Molasses-colored Pepparkakor cutouts, sugar-topped Berliner Kranser loops, and saffron-colored St. Lucia Buns (see page 285) are all sure to rekindle the spirit of Christmases past.

4 **Bake in a 375° oven** for 5 to 6 minutes or until edges are lightly browned. Transfer cookies to a wire rack to cool.

Nutrition Facts per cookie: 77 cal., 3 g total fat (1 g sat. fat), 9 mg chol., 39 mg sodium, 12 g carbo., 0 g fiber, 1 g pro. Daily Values: 1% vit. A, 0% vit. C, 0% calcium, 4% iron

KRINGLA

Prep: 40 minutes   **Freeze:** 4 hours
Bake: 7 minutes per batch
Makes: 24 cookies   **Oven:** 425°

Distinct in both flavor and texture, these mildly sweet and tangy Scandinavian treats are almost breadlike.

   3 cups all-purpose flour
   2 teaspoons baking powder
     Dash salt
1⅓ cups sugar
   2 tablespoons shortening
   1 egg yolk
   2 8-ounce cartons dairy sour cream
   1 teaspoon baking soda
  ½ teaspoon vanilla

1 **In a medium mixing bowl stir together** the flour, baking powder, and salt; set aside.

2 **In a large** mixing bowl beat the sugar and shortening with an electric mixer until combined. Beat in the egg yolk.

3 **Combine** the sour cream, baking soda, and vanilla. Mix well. Add the sour cream mixture to the sugar mixture and beat together until combined. Add half of the flour mixture and beat until combined. Beat or stir in remaining flour mixture. Cover and chill overnight or freeze 4 to 6 hours.

4 **On a well-floured pastry cloth,** drop 2 rounded tablespoons of dough for each cookie. With your hands, roll dough into an 8×½-inch rope. Form the rope into a circle, placing 1 end looped under the other end. Place on an ungreased cookie sheet. Bake in a 425° oven about 7 minutes or until bottoms are lightly browned. Remove cookies from cookie sheet and cool slightly on a wire rack. If desired, serve warm. Place in an airtight container and store at room temperature for up to 3 days.

Nutrition Facts per cookie: 148 cal., 5 g total fat (3 g sat. fat), 17 mg chol., 99 mg sodium, 23 g carbo., 0 g fiber, 2 g pro. Daily Values: 5% vit. A, 0% vit. C, 4% calcium, 5% iron

FLORENTINES

Prep: 50 minutes   Bake: 8 minutes per batch
Makes: 24 cookies   Oven: 350°

    6 tablespoons butter
    ⅓ cup milk
    ¼ cup sugar
    2 tablespoons honey
    1 cup sliced almonds
    ½ cup finely chopped candied mixed
        fruits and peels
    ¼ cup all-purpose flour
    ¾ cup semisweet chocolate pieces
    2 tablespoons shortening
    2 ounces white baking bar
    2 teaspoons shortening

1 **Grease and lightly flour** a cookie sheet; set aside. In a medium saucepan combine butter, milk, sugar, and honey. Bring to a full rolling boil, stirring occasionally. Remove from heat (mixture will appear curdled). Stir in almonds and candied fruits and peels. Stir in flour.

2 **Drop batter** by level tablespoons at least 3 inches apart onto prepared sheet. Using the back of a spoon, spread the batter into 3-inch circles.

3 **Bake in a 350° oven** for 8 to 10 minutes or until the edges are lightly browned. Cool on cookie sheet 1 minute. Carefully transfer to waxed paper. Cool thoroughly.

4 **Repeat** with the remaining batter, greasing and flouring the cookie sheet between batches.

5 **In a small heavy saucepan heat** semisweet chocolate pieces and the 2 tablespoons shortening over low heat until melted, stirring occasionally. Spread the bottom of each cookie with about 1 teaspoon of the chocolate mixture.

6 **In another small saucepan melt** white baking bar and the 2 teaspoons shortening; drizzle onto dark chocolate. To marble, draw the tines of a fork through the white drizzle. Store, covered, in the refrigerator.

Nutrition Facts per cookie: 131 cal., 9 g total fat (3 g sat. fat), 8 mg chol., 33 mg sodium, 13 g carbo., 0 g fiber, 2 g pro. Daily Values: 2% vit. A, 0% vit. C, 2% calcium, 3% iron

A TASTE OF TRADITION

Cookies are synonymous with Christmas. Here are a few fun facts to mull over as you munch these classic cookies:

Pepparkakor: There's a tradition in Sweden surrounding the eating of these spicy Christmastime sweets. Hold a cookie flat in the palm of your hand; then tap it in the middle with the knuckle of your pointer finger and make a wish. If it breaks in three pieces, your wish will come true.

Lebkuchen: A specialty of southern Germany, these substantial, ginger-spiced, cakelike cookies with lemon glaze have become favorites throughout Germany. Traditionally, they contain citron and often are baked in decorative molds.

Krumkake: The irons used to make these cone-shaped Norwegian cookies often are engraved with Christmas and nativity scenes, which are then embossed on the cookies themselves.

Kringla: These cake-style, not-too-sweet Norwegian cookies are enjoyed as a treat or with butter and coffee for breakfast.

Florentines: Most likely these crispy fruitcake cookies were invented by an Austrian baker. The reference to Florence may come from the fact that they contain candied fruit, an Italian favorite.

Berliner Kranser: Though their name suggests German heritage, these rich, buttery cookies are served with equally rich coffee all over Scandinavia on Christmas Eve.

Sandbakkelse: These pretty molded Scandinavian "sand tarts" can be filled with jam and a tiny touch of whipped cream.

Jan Hagels: Dutch cooks are known for their outstanding sweets—especially those made with lots of butter, such as these cinnamon-sugar and almond-topped treats.

Florentines: For a twist on tradition, our version adds a swirl of white chocolate to the dark chocolate that usually coats these chewy gems.

Krumkake: Though they're not difficult to make, the quick cooking, rolling, and shaping of these delicate cream-filled cookies is best done with a helper. What a great reason to spend an afternoon with an old friend.

KRUMKAKE

Prep: 25 minutes   **Cook:** 30 seconds per cookie
Makes: 24 cookies

½ **cup butter**
3 **eggs**
½ **cup sugar**
½ **cup all-purpose flour**
1 **teaspoon vanilla or ½ teaspoon
    almond extract**
   Dash ground nutmeg
1 **recipe Sweetened Whipped Cream
    (optional) (see page 160)**
   **Toasted chopped almonds
    (see tip, page 247) or chocolate-
    flavored sprinkles (optional)**
   **Lingonberry, cherry, or strawberry
    preserves (optional)**

1 Melt butter; cool slightly. In a medium mixing bowl beat eggs with an electric mixer on medium speed about 1 minute. Add sugar; beat about

3 minutes or until sugar is almost dissolved. Stir butter into egg mixture. Add flour, vanilla or almond extract, and nutmeg; stir just until smooth.

2 Heat a krumkake iron on the range top over medium-low heat. For a 6-inch iron, spoon about 1 tablespoon of the batter onto the hot, ungreased iron. Close gently but firmly. Cook over medium-low heat about 30 seconds. Open the iron carefully. Loosen cookie with a narrow spatula; invert onto a wire rack. Using a metal form, immediately roll the cookie into a cone or cylinder. Let cool around the cone or cylinder until the cookie holds its shape.

3 Reheat iron and repeat with remaining batter. Cool rolled cookies on a wire rack. If desired, just before serving, pipe or spoon Sweetened Whipped Cream into rolled cookies; top with chopped almonds or chocolate-flavored sprinkles and serve with preserves.

Nutrition Facts per krumkake: 68 cal., 4 g total fat (3 g sat. fat), 37 mg chol., 47 mg sodium, 6 g carbo., 0 g fiber, 1 g pro. Daily Values: 4% vit. A, 0% vit. C, 0% calcium, 1% iron

SANDBAKKELSE

Prep: 40 minutes   **Bake:** 8 minutes per batch
Makes: 24 cookies   **Oven:** 375°

½ **cup butter**
½ **cup sugar**
1 **egg yolk**
¼ **teaspoon almond extract**
1⅓ **cups all-purpose flour**
     Sugar (optional)

1 **In a large mixer bowl beat** the butter with an electric mixer on medium to high speed for 30 seconds. Add ½ cup sugar and beat until well combined. Add egg yolk and almond extract. Beat until thoroughly combined. Beat or stir in the flour.

2 **Season** 2½-inch sandbakkelse molds, if necessary (see tip, below). Place about 2 teaspoons of dough in center of each seasoned mold. Press dough in an even, very thin layer along the bottom and up the sides. Place molds on a cookie sheet. (Or, shape dough into 1-inch balls. Place 2 inches apart on an ungreased cookie sheet. Using a cookie stamp or bottom of a glass dipped in sugar, flatten balls to ¼-inch thickness.)

3 **Bake in a 375° oven** 8 to 9 minutes or until edges are lightly browned. Cool molded cookies in molds on a rack. To remove, invert the molds and tap lightly. If necessary, loosen edges of cookies. Cool completely on a wire rack. For stamped cookies, after baking remove to a wire rack to cool completely.

Nutrition Facts per cookie: 75 cal., 4 g total fat (2 g sat. fat), 19 mg chol., 39 mg sodium, 9 g carbo., 0 g fiber, 1 g pro. Daily Values: 4% vit. A, 0% vit. C, 0% calcium, 2% iron

JAN HAGELS

Prep: 20 minutes   **Bake:** 15 minutes
Makes: 48 cookies   **Oven:** 350°

Cut these brown-sugar cookies into diamonds.

2 **cups all-purpose flour**
⅛ **teaspoon salt**
1 **cup butter**
1 **cup packed brown sugar**
1 **teaspoon vanilla**
1 **egg yolk**
1 **slightly beaten egg white**
¼ **cup granulated sugar**
½ **teaspoon ground cinnamon**
¾ **cup sliced almonds**

1 **Stir together flour and salt.** In a large mixing bowl beat butter with an electric mixer on medium to high speed for seconds. Add brown sugar and vanilla; beat until fluffy. Add egg yolk; beat until well combined. Stir flour mixture into brown sugar mixture, mixing well.

2 **Pat the dough** evenly in an ungreased 15×10×1-inch baking pan. Brush top with beaten egg white. Combine granulated sugar and cinnamon; sprinkle evenly over top. Sprinkle almonds over all.

3 **Bake in a 350° oven** 15 to 18 minutes or until lightly browned. Cut into 1½-inch diamonds while warm. Cool in pan. Remove from pan with spatula.

Nutrition Facts per cookie: 83 cal., 5 g total fat (2 g sat. fat), 15 mg chol., 47 mg sodium, 9 g carbo., 0 g fiber, 1 g pro. Daily Values: 4% vit. A, 0% vit. C, 0% calcium, 2% iron

---

SANDBAKKELSE AND KRUMKAKE WARE

Q Where can I find sandbakkelse molds? How do I season them?

A Resembling tart molds, sandbakkelse molds can be found at Scandinavian import or specialty cookware shops. To season, grease inside of the molds with shortening. Heat them in a 300° oven 30 minutes. Cool. Wipe out the excess shortening. After you use them, just rinse with water and wipe with paper towels. No further seasoning is needed.

Q What equipment do I need to make the unique lacy cone for Krumkake?

A This cream-filled Scandinavian specialty requires a special iron that's heated on the stove top to bake the paper-thin cookies. The cookies are then immediately rolled around a metal cone-shaped form. Both the iron and the form can be found at specialty cookware shops or Scandinavian import shops.

LEBKUCHEN

LOW-FAT

Prep: 30 minutes **Chill:** 2 hours
Bake: 8 minutes per batch
Makes: 48 cookies **Oven:** 350°

These cookies taste best when stored for several days to allow their spicy flavors to mellow.

  1 **egg**
 ¾ **cup packed brown sugar**
 ½ **cup honey**
 ½ **cup dark-flavored molasses**
  3 **cups all-purpose flour**
  1 **teaspoon ground cinnamon**
 ½ **teaspoon baking soda**
 ½ **teaspoon ground cloves**
 ½ **teaspoon ground ginger**
 ¼ **teaspoon ground cardamom**
 ½ **cup chopped almonds**
 ½ **cup finely chopped mixed candied
      fruits and peels**
  1 **recipe Lemon Glaze (see right)
      Chopped mixed candied fruits
      and peels**

1 **In a small bowl beat egg** with electric mixer on high speed about 1 minute. Add brown sugar; beat on medium speed until light and fluffy. Add honey and molasses. Beat well.

2 **Stir together flour,** cinnamon, baking soda, cloves, ginger, and cardamom in a large bowl. Add egg mixture. Stir by hand until combined. (Dough will be stiff.) Stir in almonds and the ½ cup candied fruits and peels. Cover and chill dough for several hours or until easy to handle. Meanwhile, grease cookie sheet(s).

3 **Divide dough** in half. On a lightly floured surface, roll each half to a 12×8-inch rectangle. Cut into 2-inch squares. Place 2 inches apart on prepared sheets.

4 **Bake in a 350° oven** 8 to 10 minutes or until edges are set. Remove from oven. Cool cookies on cookie sheet for 1 minute. Transfer cookies to wire racks. Place waxed paper under racks.

5 **Brush cookies** with Lemon Glaze while warm. Garnish with additional candied fruits and peels. Allow glaze to dry. Store, tightly covered, overnight or up to 7 days to soften.

Lemon Glaze: In a small bowl combine 1½ cups sifted powdered sugar; 1 tablespoon butter, melted; and 1 tablespoon lemon juice. Stir in enough water (about 3 to 4 teaspoons) to make of drizzling consistency.

Nutrition Facts per cookie: 87 cal., 1 g total fat (0 g sat. fat), 5 mg chol., 19 mg sodium, 19 g carbo., 0 g fiber, 1 g pro. Daily Values: 0% vit. A, 0% vit. C, 1% calcium, 4% iron

Lebkuchen: Sometimes called German honey bars, spiced Lebkuchen, a specialty of Nuremberg, has been a holiday favorite for centuries. Coated on top with a snowy-white glaze and topped with candied fruits and peels, they have an unmistakable Christmasy look.

HOLIDAY BREAD LORE

S avor the stories as well as the flavor of these international breads:

St. Lucia Buns: Legend has it that one winter, when Sweden was suffering from famine, a young Sicilian woman named Lucia appeared with food and wearing a white robe and a crown of candles. Each December 13, the eldest girl in each Swedish house dons a white robe and a crown of candles and awakens her family with these saffron-scented buns and coffee.

Three Kings' Ring: Bakers of this sweet, fruit-filled bread from Spain, Portugal, and Mexico traditionally hide symbolic gifts from the three kings inside the ring. The first three—a coin, a bead, and a charm—foretell good luck or prosperity to the finder. Whoever plucks the fourth charm—a doll representing the baby Jesus—becomes king or queen for the day and the host of the next party (see recipe and photo, page 286).

ST. LUCIA BUNS

Prep: 45 minutes **Rise:** 1½ hours **Bake:** 12 minutes
Makes: 24 single buns **Oven:** 350°

These spiced buns are worthy of a place in the bread basket at a holiday breakfast or brunch. Pictured on page 279.

2½ to 3 cups all-purpose flour
  1 package active dry yeast
 ¾ cup milk
 ⅓ cup sugar
 ¼ cup butter
 ½ teaspoon salt
 ¼ teaspoon ground cardamom
 ⅛ teaspoon ground saffron
  1 egg
 ¼ cup golden raisins
 ¼ cup slivered almonds, ground*
   Golden raisins
  1 slightly beaten egg white
  1 tablespoon water
   Sugar

1 **In a large mixing bowl stir together** 1 cup of the flour and the yeast; set aside. In a small saucepan heat and stir milk, the ⅓ cup sugar, butter, salt, cardamom, and saffron just until warm (120° to 130°) and butter almost melts. Add milk mixture to flour mixture. Add whole egg. Beat with electric mixer on low to medium speed for 30 seconds, scraping the sides of the bowl constantly. Beat on high speed for 3 minutes. Using a wooden spoon, stir in the ¼ cup raisins, ground almonds, and as much remaining flour as you can.

2 **Turn dough out** onto a lightly floured surface. Knead in enough of remaining flour to make a moderately soft dough that is smooth and elastic (3 to 5 minutes total). Shape into ball. Place in lightly greased bowl; turn once to grease surface. Cover; let rise in warm place until double (1 to 1¼ hours).

3 **Punch dough down.** Turn dough out onto lightly floured surface. Divide in half. Cover; let rest for 10 minutes. Meanwhile, grease baking sheet(s).

4 **To shape buns,** divide each dough portion into 12 equal pieces. Roll each piece into a 12-inch-long rope. Place 3 inches apart on prepared baking sheets. Form each rope into an S shape, coiling ends snail fashion (see photo, page 279). (If desired, make double buns by pressing the centers of 2 of the S-shaped pieces together to form a cross.) Press 1 raisin into center of each coil. Cover; let rise in warm place until nearly double (30 to 40 minutes). Stir together egg white and water. Lightly brush onto buns. Sprinkle with additional sugar.

5 **Bake in a 350° oven** 12 minutes or until golden. Remove from sheets. Serve warm or cool.

*Note: Use a grinder, blender, or food processor to grind nuts.

Nutrition Facts per single S bun: 97 cal., 3 g total fat (2 g sat. fat), 14 mg chol., 76 mg sodium, 16 g carbo., 1 g fiber, 2 g pro. Daily Values: 3% vit. A, 0% vit. C, 1% calcium, 4% iron

Three Kings' Ring:
Though traditionally served on Epiphany, this sweet yeast-bread ring makes a memorable breakfast any time of year.

THREE KINGS' RING

Prep: 45 minutes **Rise:** 1½ hours **Bake:** 25 minutes
Makes: 12 servings **Oven:** 350°

3¼ to 3¾ cups all-purpose flour
1 package active dry yeast
⅔ cup milk
⅓ cup butter
⅓ cup granulated sugar
½ teaspoon salt
2 eggs
3 tablespoons butter, softened
¼ cup granulated sugar
2 teaspoons ground cinnamon
¾ cup diced mixed candied fruits
   and peels
½ cup toasted chopped almonds
   (see tip, page 247)
1 cup sifted powdered sugar
¼ teaspoon vanilla
1 to 2 tablespoons orange juice
   Ground cinnamon
   Finely shredded orange peel
   (optional)

1 **In a large mixing bowl stir together** 1½ cups of the flour and the yeast; set aside. In a small saucepan heat and stir milk, the ⅓ cup butter, the ⅓ cup granulated sugar, and salt just until warm (120° to 130°) and butter almost melts. Add milk mixture to flour mixture; add eggs.

2 **Beat** with an electric mixer on low to medium speed for 30 seconds, scraping the sides of the bowl constantly. Beat on high speed for 3 minutes. Using a wooden spoon, stir in as much of the remaining flour as you can.

3 **Turn the dough out** onto a lightly floured surface. Knead in enough of the remaining flour to make a moderately soft dough that is smooth and elastic (3 to 5 minutes total).

4 **Shape the dough** into a ball. Place in a lightly greased bowl; turn once to grease the surface. Cover and let rise in a warm place until double in size (1 to 1½ hours).

5 **Punch dough down.** Turn out onto a lightly floured surface. Cover and let rest for 10 minutes. Meanwhile, grease a baking sheet; set aside.

6 **Roll dough** into a 20×12-inch rectangle. Spread with the 3 tablespoons softened butter. For filling, in a small mixing bowl combine the ¼ cup granulated sugar and cinnamon. Add mixed fruits and peels and almonds; toss gently to coat. Sprinkle the mixture onto the surface of the dough.

7 **Beginning at a long side,** loosely roll up the dough jelly-roll style. Moisten edges; pinch firmly to seal. Place roll, seam side down, on a prepared baking sheet. Bring ends together to form a ring. Moisten ends; pinch together to seal ring. Flatten slightly. Using a sharp knife, make 12 cuts around the edge of the dough at 1½-inch intervals, cutting about two-thirds of the way to the center. Cover and let rise in a warm place until nearly double (30 to 40 minutes).

8 **Bake in a 350° oven** for 25 to 30 minutes or until bread sounds hollow when tapped. If necessary, cover with foil after 20 minutes to prevent overbrowning. Remove from baking sheet; cool on a wire rack.

9 **For icing,** combine powdered sugar and vanilla. Stir in enough orange juice to make an icing of drizzling consistency. Spoon icing over ring. Before icing dries, sprinkle with cinnamon and, if desired, orange peel.

Nutrition Facts per serving: 335 cal., 12 g total fat (5 g sat. fat), 58 mg chol., 200 mg sodium, 53 g carbo., 2 g fiber, 6 g pro. Daily Values: 12% vit. A, 1% vit. C, 4% calcium, 13% iron

FESTIVE HOLIDAY BRIOCHES

Prep: 1¼ hours   Rise: 2¾ hours   Chill: 6 hours
Bake: 15 minutes   Makes: 24   Oven: 375°

A French classic with its egg-and-butter richness and quaint nob atop, brioche gets in the holiday spirit with the addition of colorful dried fruits.

  1 package active dry yeast
  ¼ cup warm water (105° to 115°)
  ½ cup butter, softened
  ⅓ cup sugar
  1 teaspoon salt
  4 cups all-purpose flour
  ½ cup milk
  4 eggs
  ½ cup dried cranberries or dried tart cherries
  ½ cup chopped candied citron or miniature chocolate pieces
  ¼ cup currants
  1 tablespoon sugar

1 **In a small bowl stir yeast** into warm water to soften. In a large mixing bowl beat butter, the ⅓ cup sugar, and salt with an electric mixer on medium to high speed until fluffy. Add 1 cup of the flour and the milk to the sugar mixture. Separate one of the eggs. Add the egg yolk and 3 whole eggs to beaten mixture. (Chill remaining egg white to use later.) Add softened yeast to flour mixture; beat well. Stir in cranberries, citron or chocolate pieces, and currants. Stir in remaining flour. Place dough in a greased bowl, turning dough once to grease surface. Cover and let rise in a warm place until double (about 2 hours). Refrigerate dough for 6 hours. (Or, omit 2-hour rise and refrigerate dough overnight.)

2 **Grease twenty-four 2½-inch muffin cups;** set aside. Stir down dough. Turn dough out onto a floured surface. Divide dough into 4 equal portions. Set 1 portion aside. Divide each of the remaining 3 portions into 8 pieces for a total of 24. To shape, pull each piece into a ball, tucking edges beneath to make a smooth top. Place a ball in each prepared muffin cup. Divide reserved dough portion into 24 pieces; shape into small balls. Using your thumb, make an indentation in middle of each large ball with your thumb. Press a small ball into each indentation.

3 **In a small bowl combine** the reserved egg white and the 1 tablespoon sugar. Brush mixture over rolls. Cover and let rise in a warm place until nearly double (about 45 minutes). Bake in a 375° oven about 15 minutes or until tops are golden. Remove rolls from muffin cups and cool on a wire rack.

Nutrition Facts per serving: 155 cal., 5 g total fat (3 g sat. fat), 46 mg chol., 142 mg sodium, 24 g carbo., 1 g fiber, 3 g pro. Daily Values: 5% vit. A, 0% vit. C, 1% calcium, 7% iron

CHRISTOLLEN **BREAD**

Prep: 45 minutes   **Rise:** 2 hours   **Bake:** 20 minutes
Makes: 32 servings   **Oven:** 350°

*Leftovers welcome here—save some for breakfast,
as this bread is particularly good toasted.*

4¾ to 5¼ cups all-purpose flour
  2 packages active dry yeast
  1 teaspoon ground cardamom
1¼ cups milk
  ½ cup sugar
  ½ cup butter
  ¾ teaspoon salt
  1 egg
  1 cup diced mixed candied fruits
    and peels

  1 cup raisins
  ¾ cup chopped walnuts
  1 tablespoon finely shredded
    lemon peel
  Milk

1 In a large mixing bowl stir together 2 cups of the flour, the yeast, and cardamom. In a medium saucepan heat and stir the milk, sugar, butter, and salt until warm (120° to 130°) and butter is almost melted. Add to flour mixture along with egg. Beat with an electric mixer on low speed for 30 seconds, scraping bowl constantly. Beat on high speed for 3 minutes. Using a spoon, stir in candied fruits and peels, raisins, walnuts, and lemon peel; stir in as much of the remaining flour as you can.

Christollen Bread: Bring centuries of tradition to your holiday table with this rich, candied-fruit-studded bread. The Germans have been making it since the Middle Ages.

To braid ropes, start at the middle and work your way to 1 end; braid the other end. Braid the ropes loosely so the bread has room to expand.

2 **Turn out** onto a lightly floured surface. Knead in enough remaining flour to make a moderately soft dough that is smooth and elastic (3 to 5 minutes total). Shape into a ball. Place in a greased bowl; turn once to grease surface. Cover and let rise in a warm place until double (about 1 to 1½ hours).

3 **Punch dough down.** Turn out onto a lightly floured surface. Divide dough in half; divide each half into thirds. Cover and let rest for 10 minutes. Meanwhile, grease 2 baking sheets.

4 **With hands, roll** each piece of dough into a 1-inch-thick rope about 15 inches long. Line up 3 of the ropes, 1 inch apart, on prepared baking sheet. Starting in the middle, loosely braid by bringing the left rope under the center rope. Next, bring the right rope under the new center rope. Repeat to end of loaf (see photo, above).

5 **On the other end,** braid by bringing alternate ropes over center rope from center. Press rope ends on each side together to seal. Repeat braiding with the remaining 3 ropes on other prepared baking sheet. Cover and let rise until nearly double (about 1 hour).

6 **Brush loaves** with milk. Bake in a 350° oven for 20 to 25 minutes or until golden and loaves sound hollow when tapped. (Switch baking sheets to a different oven rack halfway through baking time to ensure even baking.) If necessary, cover with foil the last few minutes to prevent overbrowning. Remove from baking sheets. Cool on wire racks.

Nutrition Facts per serving: 157 cal., 5 g total fat (3 g sat. fat), 22 mg chol., 92 mg sodium, 25 g carbo., 1 g fiber, 3 g pro. Daily Values: 4% vit. A, 0% vit. C, 1% calcium, 6% iron

PANETTONE BREAD

Prep: 15 minutes
Bake: per bread machine directions

In Italy, this fruit-studded sweet bread is often enjoyed at Christmas. Our bread-machine recipe adds American ease to the Italian tradition.

For 1-Pound Loaf (16 servings):
- ⅔ **cup milk**
- 1 **egg**
- 1 **tablespoon butter**
- 2 **cups bread flour**
- 1 **tablespoon honey**
- 1 **teaspoon anise seed, crushed**
- ½ **teaspoon salt**
- 1 **teaspoon active dry yeast**
- ¼ **cup golden raisins**
- ¼ **cup dried currants**
- ¼ **cup chopped candied citron**
- 1 **recipe Powdered Sugar Icing (see page 159)**

For 1½-Pound Loaf (24 servings):
- ¾ **cup milk**
- 1 **egg**
- 3 **tablespoons butter**
- 3 **cups bread flour**
- 2 **tablespoons honey**
- 1½ **teaspoons anise seed, crushed**
- ¾ **teaspoon salt**
- 1 **teaspoon active dry yeast**
- ⅓ **cup golden raisins**
- ⅓ **cup dried currants**
- ⅓ **cup chopped candied citron**
- 1 **recipe Powdered Sugar Icing (see page 159)**

1 **Add ingredients** (except icing) to bread machine according to manufacturer's directions. Bake according to manufacturer's directions, using a light setting, if available. Cool on wire rack; drizzle with Powdered Sugar Icing.

Nutrition Facts per serving: 130 cal., 2 g total fat (1 g sat. fat), 16 mg chol., 84 mg sodium, 26 g carbo., 1 g fiber, 3 g pro. Daily Values: 1% vit. A, 0% vit. C, 1% calcium, 6% iron

Chocolate Challah: This chocolaty version of the well-known Jewish bread is just right for when the Sabbath falls on a holiday—traditionally the time when sweeter versions of the classic are served.

CHOCOLATE CHALLAH

Prep: 40 minutes   **Rise:** 2½ hours
Bake: 35 minutes   **Makes:** 24 servings
Oven: 325°

2¾ **to** 3¼ **cups all-purpose flour**
    ⅓ **cup unsweetened cocoa powder**
    1 **package active dry yeast**
    ¾ **cup water**
    ½ **cup granulated sugar**
    ¼ **cup margarine (pareve)**
    ½ **teaspoon salt**
    1 **egg**
    ½ **cup chopped pecans**
    ¼ **cup chopped pitted dates (not sugared)**
    1 **tablespoon finely shredded orange
       peel**
    1 **recipe Three Glazes (see right)**

1 **In a large mixing bowl stir together** 1 cup of the flour, cocoa powder, and yeast; set aside. Heat water, granulated sugar, margarine, and salt just until warm (120° to 130°) and margarine almost melts. Add margarine mixture to flour mixture; add egg. Beat with an electric mixer on low to medium speed 30 seconds, scraping sides of bowl constantly. Beat on high speed 3 minutes. Using a wooden spoon, stir in pecans, chopped dates, and peel. Stir in as much of the remaining flour as you can.

2 **Turn dough out** onto a lightly floured surface; knead in enough of the remaining flour to make a moderately soft dough that is smooth and elastic (3 to 5 minutes). Shape dough into ball. Place in a lightly greased bowl; turn once to grease the surface. Cover and let dough rise in warm place until double in size (about 1½ hours).

3 **Punch dough down.** Turn dough onto a lightly floured surface. Divide dough into thirds. Cover and let rest for 10 minutes. Meanwhile, lightly grease a baking sheet; set aside.

4 **Shape each portion** of dough into a 16-inch-long rope (3 ropes total). Line up ropes about 1 inch apart on prepared baking sheet. Starting in the middle of ropes, loosely braid by bringing the left rope under the center rope. Next bring right rope under the new center rope. Repeat to the end. On the other end, braid by bringing alternate ropes over center rope from center to end. Press ends together to seal; tuck under. Cover; let rise in a warm place until nearly double (about 1 hour).

5 **Bake in a 325° oven** about 35 minutes or until bread sounds hollow when tapped (if necessary, cover loosely with foil the last 10 to 15 minutes to prevent overbrowning). Remove from baking sheet. Cool on wire rack; drizzle with Three Glazes.

Three Glazes: Stir together 1½ cups sifted powdered sugar and 4 teaspoons softened margarine. Add 1 to 2 tablespoons warm water until icing is of drizzling consistency. Divide evenly into 3 portions. To 1 portion, stir in 1 teaspoon unsweetened cocoa powder, adding more warm water 1 drop at a time, if necessary, until icing is of drizzling consistency. For another portion, combine ¼ teaspoon instant coffee crystals and a few drops of hot water until coffee is dissolved. Add coffee mixture to powdered sugar mixture, adding more warm water a drop at a time, if necessary, until of drizzling consistency. Leave the third portion white. Use to glaze the bread.

Nutrition facts per serving: 140 cal., 5 g total fat (1 g sat. fat), 9 mg chol., 77 mg sodium, 23 g carbo., 1 g fiber, 2 g pro. Daily Values: 3% vit. A, 0% vit. C, 1% calcium, 6% iron

SUFGANYOT

Prep: 40 minutes   Rise: 1 hour   Fry: 2 minutes each
Makes: 24 servings   Fry: 365°

3¼ to 3½ cups all-purpose flour
  2 packages active dry yeast
  ½ teaspoon ground cinnamon
  ⅓ cup granulated sugar
  2 tablespoons cooking oil
  ½ teaspoon salt
  1 egg
  ½ teaspoon vanilla
  ¼ cup fruit preserves (such as raspberry or blueberry) or chocolate-hazelnut spread
  Cooking oil for deep-fat frying
  Sifted powdered sugar

1 Stir together 1¼ cups of the flour, the yeast, and cinnamon; set aside. In a medium saucepan heat and stir 1 cup water, the granulated sugar, cooking oil, and salt just until warm (120° to 130°). Add oil mixture to flour mixture; add egg and vanilla. Beat with an electric mixer on low to medium speed for 30 seconds, scraping the sides of the bowl constantly. Beat on high speed for 3 minutes. Using a wooden spoon, stir in as much of the remaining flour as you can.

2 Turn dough out onto a lightly floured surface. Knead in enough of the remaining flour to make a moderately soft dough that is smooth and elastic (3 to 5 minutes total). Shape dough into a ball. Place in a lightly greased bowl, turning once to grease the surface of the dough. Cover and let rise in a warm place until double in size (about 1 hour).

3 Punch dough down. Turn dough out onto a lightly floured surface. Divide in half. Cover and let rest 10 minutes. Roll dough, 1 portion at a time, to ¼-inch thickness. Cut dough with a floured 2½-inch biscuit cutter, dipping cutter into flour between cuts. Place about ½ teaspoon preserves or chocolate-hazelnut spread onto the centers of half of the circles. Lightly moisten edges of circles; top with remaining circles. Press edges together to seal. Repeat with remaining dough and filling. Reroll and cut trimmings.

4 Fry filled doughnuts, 2 or 3 at a time, in deep hot oil (365°) about 1 minute on each side or until golden, turning once with a slotted spoon. Remove from oil; drain on paper towels. Sprinkle with powdered sugar. Cool on wire racks.

Nutrition Facts per serving: 117 cal., 4 g total fat (1 g sat. fat), 9 mg chol., 48 mg sodium, 19 g carbo., 1 g fiber, 2 g pro. Daily Values: 0% vit. A, 0% vit. C, 0% calcium, 5% iron

Sufganyot: These fruit-filled doughnuts are a traditional Hanukkah treat in Israel, where in some communities, vendors sell them by the basketful.

STRAWBERRY SWEETHEART TART

Prep: 25 minutes **Bake:** 12 minutes **Cool:** 1 hour
Makes: 6 servings **Oven:** 375°

½ of a 17¼-ounce package frozen
    puff pastry, thawed (1 sheet)
1 egg
1 tablespoon water
⅓ cup sliced almonds, coarsely
    chopped
2 tablespoons sugar
2 3-ounce packages cream cheese,
    softened
3 tablespoons sugar
2 tablespoons amaretto or orange
    juice
½ teaspoon vanilla
½ cup whipping cream
2 cups sliced strawberries
¼ cup currant jelly, melted

1 **On a lightly floured surface roll** pastry sheet to a 12-inch square. Cut out an 11-inch heart. Transfer heart to an ungreased baking sheet. Cut excess pastry into ¾-inch-wide strips. In a small cup, beat egg and water. Brush egg mixture in a ¾-inch border around top of heart. Twist pastry strips and arrange around top edge of heart to make a border, brushing ends with egg mixture and overlapping strips slightly. Brush pastry with egg mixture. Prick center of pastry with a fork. Sprinkle pastry with almonds and the 2 tablespoons sugar.

2 **Bake in a 375° oven** 12 to 15 minutes or until pastry is browned, pricking bottom once with fork if necessary to make it puff evenly. Let tart cool on baking sheet on a wire rack.

3 **In a medium mixing bowl beat** cream cheese and the 3 tablespoons sugar with an electric mixer on medium speed about 1 minute or until fluffy. Add amaretto or orange juice and vanilla. Beat until thoroughly combined; set aside. In a chilled mixing bowl beat whipping cream until soft peaks form. Fold into cream cheese mixture. Spoon filling into cooled pastry shell and spread evenly.

4 **Arrange sliced strawberries** over filling, over-lapping to cover filling completely. Brush with melted jelly. Cover; chill up to 2 hours before serving.

Nutrition Facts per serving: 505 cal., 35 g total fat
(11 g sat. fat), 94 mg chol., 259 mg sodium,
42 g carbo., 2 g fiber, 7 g pro. Daily Values:
22% vit. A, 48% vit. C, 5% calcium, 7% iron

Strawberry Sweetheart Tart:
Start with purchased
puff pastry, add an
amaretto-infused creamy
filling, and top with romantic
red berries—what a sweet
and simple way to steal
someone's heart.

WALNUT EASTER BREAD

BEST-LOVED

Prep: 50 minutes **Rise:** 1 ½ hours
Bake: 45 minutes **Makes:** 32 servings **Oven:** 350°

To ease the Easter-brunch crunch, make these rich, nutty loaves in advance. Wrap in freezer wrap or foil and freeze for up to 8 months. Then thaw, covered, overnight in the refrigerator.

5¾ to 6¼ **cups all-purpose flour**
  2 **packages active dry yeast**
1⅔ **cups milk**
  ½ **cup sugar**
  ⅔ **cup butter**
  ½ **teaspoon salt**
  ½ **teaspoon ground nutmeg**
  1 **egg**
  ¾ **cup finely chopped walnuts**
 10 **walnut halves**
  1 **beaten egg yolk**
  1 **tablespoon water**

1 **In a large mixing bowl stir together** 2½ cups of the flour and the yeast. In a saucepan heat and stir milk, sugar, butter, salt, and nutmeg until warm (120° to 130°) and butter is almost melted. Add to flour mixture. Add whole egg. Beat with an electric mixer on low to medium speed for 30 seconds, scraping sides of bowl constantly. Beat on high speed for 3 minutes. Using a wooden spoon, stir in the chopped nuts and as much remaining flour as you can.

2 **Turn dough out** onto a lightly floured surface. Knead in enough of the remaining flour to make a moderately stiff dough that is smooth and elastic (6 to 8 minutes total). Shape into a ball. Place in a lightly greased bowl; turn once to grease surface of dough. Cover; let rise in a warm place until double in size (about 1 hour).

3 **Punch dough down.** Turn out onto a lightly floured surface. Divide into 3 portions. Cover; let rest 10 minutes. Grease 1 or 2 baking sheets; set aside.

4 **Shape 2 dough portions** into balls. Place on prepared baking sheet(s), allowing 4 inches between balls if using 1 baking sheet. Flatten each to a 5½-inch diameter. Divide the remaining portion of dough into 16 pieces. Roll each piece into a

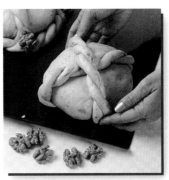

Encircle the loaves entirely with the twisted ropes. Start by placing 2 ropes in a cross atop each flattened ball. Place 2 more ropes around the base, stretching ropes so ends meet.

10-inch-long rope. Loosely twist 2 ropes together; repeat with remaining ropes, making 8 twisted ropes total.

5 **Place 2 of the twisted ropes** in a cross atop each flattened ball of dough (see photo, above); tuck rope ends under balls. Place 2 more twisted ropes around the base of each ball, stretching the ropes if necessary so ends will meet. Brush ends with water; pinch together to seal. Also, brush water onto centers and ends of crossed ropes. Press a walnut half in center and at ends of ropes. Cover and let rise in a warm place until almost double (about 30 minutes). In a small cup stir together yolk and the 1 tablespoon water; brush onto loaves.

6 **Bake in a 350° oven** for 45 minutes, covering loosely with foil after 25 minutes. (If using 2 baking sheets, refrigerate 1 loaf while the other bakes.) Remove from sheet; cool on a wire rack.

Nutrition Facts per serving: 157 cal., 7 g total fat (3 g sat. fat), 25 mg chol., 82 mg sodium, 20 g carbo., 1 g fiber, 4 g pro. Daily Values: 5% vit. A, 0% vit. C, 2% calcium, 7% iron

---

GIVE IT A REST

Q Why do recipes call for letting yeast dough "rest"?

A Recipes often call for letting the dough rest after you've punched it down and before you begin rolling it out. A brief rest lets it relax, which improves its elasticity and makes the dough easier to roll out or shape.

HOT CROSS BUNS

Prep: 35 minutes   Rise: 2¼ hours
Bake: 12 minutes   Makes: 20 servings   Oven: 375°

Perfect for a traditional Easter Sunday dinner, these buns are not only symbolic of the holiday, but fresh and pretty as a spring day.

    4 to 4½ cups all-purpose flour
    1 package active dry yeast
    ¾ teaspoon ground cinnamon
    ¼ teaspoon ground nutmeg
      Dash ground cloves
    ¾ cup milk
    ½ cup butter
    ⅓ cup granulated sugar
    ½ teaspoon salt
    3 eggs
    ⅔ cup dried currants or raisins
    ¼ cup diced candied orange peel
      (optional)
    1 beaten egg white
    1 cup sifted powdered sugar
    ¼ teaspoon vanilla
    1 tablespoon milk or orange juice

1 **In a large mixing bowl combine** 2 cups of the flour, the yeast, cinnamon, nutmeg, and cloves. In a medium saucepan heat and stir milk, butter, granulated sugar, and salt until warm (120° to 130°) and butter almost melts. Add milk mixture to flour mixture. Add eggs. Beat with an electric mixer on low to medium speed 30 seconds, scraping sides of bowl constantly. Beat on high speed 3 minutes. Using a wooden spoon, stir in currants, orange peel (if desired), and as much remaining flour as you can.

2 **Turn out** onto a lightly floured surface. Knead in enough remaining flour to make a moderately soft dough that is smooth and elastic (3 to 5 minutes total). Shape into a ball. Place in a greased bowl, turning once to grease surface. Cover; let rise in a warm place until double (about 1½ hours).

3 **Punch dough down.** Turn onto floured surface. Cover; let rest 10 minutes. Meanwhile, grease baking sheet(s); set aside.

4 **Divide dough** into 20 portions. Shape portions into smooth balls. Place balls 1½ inches apart on prepared baking sheet(s). Cover; let rise until nearly double in size (45 to 60 minutes).

5 **Using a sharp knife, make** a crisscross slash across top of each bun. In a small cup combine beaten egg white and 1 tablespoon water. Brush egg-white mixture over rolls.

6 **Bake in a 375° oven** for 12 to 15 minutes or until golden brown. Cool slightly. For icing, in a mixing bowl combine powdered sugar, vanilla, and milk or juice. Stir in additional milk or juice, 1 teaspoon at a time, until icing is of drizzling consistency. Drizzle icing into slashes atop each bun. Serve warm.

Nutrition Facts per serving: 188 cal., 6 g total fat (3 g sat. fat), 45 mg chol., 118 mg sodium, 30 g carbo., 1 g fiber, 4 g pro. Daily Values: 6% vit. A, 0% vit. C, 2% calcium, 9% iron

HOT CROSS BUNS: EASTER'S BREAD

The recipe for these currant-studded buns was brought to America by English immigrants. Traditionally eaten on Good Friday or Easter Sunday, the yeast rolls get their name from the cross that's slashed in their tops before baking. The cross is then piped full of sweet icing after the buns are baked and cooled.

quick breads

Streusel Banana Bread, recipe page 297

QUICK BREADS

NUT BREAD

Prep: 25 minutes **Bake:** 1 hour
Makes: 1 loaf (18 servings) **Oven:** 350°

One easy batter makes three great breads.
Choose plain nut bread, cranberry, or blueberry.

    3 cups all-purpose flour
    1 cup sugar
    1 tablespoon baking powder
    ½ teaspoon salt
    ¼ teaspoon baking soda
    1 beaten egg
1⅔ cups milk
    ¼ cup cooking oil
    ¾ cup chopped almonds, pecans,
        or walnuts

1 Grease the bottom and ½ inch up the sides of a 9×5×3-inch loaf pan; set aside. In a large mixing bowl combine flour, sugar, baking powder, salt, and baking soda. Make a well in center of dry mixture; set aside.

2 In a medium mixing bowl combine the egg, milk, and oil. Add egg mixture all at once to dry mixture. Stir just until moistened (batter should be lumpy). Fold in nuts.

3 Spoon batter into prepared pan. Bake in a 350° oven for 1 to 1¼ hours or until a wooden toothpick inserted near center comes out clean. Cool in pan on a wire rack for 10 minutes. Remove from pan. Cool completely on the wire rack. Wrap and store overnight before slicing.

Nutrition Facts per serving: 187 cal., 7 g total fat (1 g sat. fat), 14 mg chol., 153 mg sodium, 28 g carbo., 1 g fiber, 4 g pro. Daily Values: 1% vit. A, 0% vit. C, 7% calcium, 7% iron

Cranberry Nut Bread: Prepare as above, except add 2 teaspoons finely shredded orange peel to the dry mixture. Fold 1 cup coarsely chopped cranberries into batter along with nuts.

Blueberry Nut Bread: Prepare as above, except add 1 teaspoon finely shredded lemon peel to the dry mixture. Fold 1 cup fresh or frozen blueberries into batter along with nuts.

BANANA BREAD

Prep: 25 minutes **Bake:** 55 minutes
Makes: 1 loaf (16 servings) **Oven:** 350°

If you have the time or inclination, dress up this familiar favorite with a streusel topping (see photo, page 295).

    2 cups all-purpose flour
1½ teaspoons baking powder
    ½ teaspoon baking soda
    ¼ teaspoon salt
    ¼ teaspoon ground cinnamon
    ⅛ teaspoon ground nutmeg
    2 beaten eggs
1½ cups mashed banana (5 medium)
    1 cup sugar
    ½ cup cooking oil
    1 teaspoon finely shredded lemon
        peel (optional)
    ¼ cup chopped walnuts

1 Grease the bottom and ½ inch up sides of a 9×5×3-inch loaf pan; set aside. Combine flour, baking powder, soda, salt, cinnamon, and nutmeg. Make well in center of dry mixture; set aside.

2 Combine eggs, banana, sugar, oil, and, if desired, lemon peel. Add egg mixture all at once to dry mixture. Stir just until moistened (batter should be lumpy). Fold in nuts.

3 Spoon batter into prepared pan. Bake in 350° oven 55 to 65 minutes or until a wooden toothpick inserted near center comes out clean. (If necessary, cover with foil for the last 15 minutes of baking to prevent overbrowning.) Cool in pan on a wire rack for 10 minutes. Remove from pan. Cool completely on wire rack. Wrap and store overnight before slicing.

Nutrition Facts per serving: 258 cal., 12 g total fat (2 g sat. fat), 30 mg chol., 129 mg sodium, 36 g carbo., 1 g fiber, 3 g pro. Daily Values: 2% vit. A, 4% vit. C, 3% calcium, 7% iron

Streusel Banana Bread: Prepare as above, except combine ⅓ cup packed brown sugar and ¼ cup all-purpose flour. Using a pastry blender, cut in 2 tablespoons butter until mixture resembles coarse crumbs. Stir in ⅓ cup chopped walnuts. Sprinkle over batter before baking.

Blueberry-Orange Loaf: Cut thick slices of this delicate-but-bursting-with-fruit loaf to nibble for breakfast or to snack on for your morning break.

BLUEBERRY-ORANGE LOAF

Prep: 25 minutes   **Bake:** 1 hour
Makes: 1 loaf (16 servings)   **Oven:** 350°

Citrus-lovers, take note: Try serving this bread with orange cream-cheese spread. Just stir 2 teaspoons finely shredded orange peel into 8 ounces of softened cream cheese.

    1 cup fresh or frozen blueberries,
      thawed
  ½ cup chopped pecans
    1 tablespoon all-purpose flour
    1 teaspoon finely shredded orange
      peel
    3 cups all-purpose flour
    1 cup sugar
    1 tablespoon baking powder
  ½ teaspoon baking soda
  ½ teaspoon salt
    1 beaten egg
1⅓ cups milk
  ¼ cup orange juice
  ¼ cup cooking oil
    1 teaspoon vanilla

1 **Grease the bottom** and ½ inch up sides of one 9×5×3-inch loaf pan or two 7½×3½×2-inch loaf pans; set aside.

2 **In a small mixing bowl** combine blueberries, pecans, the 1 tablespoon flour, and orange peel. Toss lightly to mix; set aside.

3 **In a large mixing bowl** combine the 3 cups flour, sugar, baking powder, soda, and salt. Make a well in the center of dry mixture; set aside.

4 **In a medium mixing bowl** combine the egg, milk, orange juice, oil, and vanilla. Add egg mixture all at once to dry mixture. Stir just until moistened (batter should be lumpy). Fold in blueberry mixture.

5 **Spoon batter into prepared** pan(s). Bake in a 350° oven about 1 hour for 9×5×3-inch loaf or 45 to 50 minutes for 7½×3½×2-inch loaves or until a wooden toothpick inserted near center comes out clean. (If necessary, cover with foil for the last 10 to 15 minutes of baking to prevent overbrowning.) Cool in pan(s) on wire rack for 10 minutes. Remove from pan(s) and cool thoroughly on wire rack. Wrap and store overnight before slicing.

Nutrition Facts per serving: 204 cal., 7 g total fat (1 g sat. fat), 15 mg chol., 189 mg sodium, 33 g carbo., 1 g fiber, 4 g pro. Daily Values: 2% vit. A, 5% vit. C, 7% calcium, 8% iron

WHOLE WHEAT BRICK ALLEY BREAD

LOW-FAT

Prep: 20 minutes   **Bake:** 25 minutes
Makes: 1 loaf (16 servings)   **Oven:** 350°

Despite its name, this whole-wheat quick bread—dotted with raisins and lightly sweetened with honey—is light and tender.

    1 cup whole wheat flour
    1 cup all-purpose flour
1½ teaspoons baking powder
  ¾ teaspoon salt
  ½ teaspoon baking soda
    1 beaten egg
    1 cup buttermilk or sour milk
      (see tip, page 329)
    3 tablespoons honey
    1 cup raisins
    1 beaten egg white

1 **Grease a baking sheet;** set aside. In a large mixing bowl combine whole wheat flour, all-purpose flour, baking powder, salt, and baking soda. Make a well in center of dry mixture; set aside.

2 **In a small mixing bowl** combine the egg, buttermilk, and honey. Add egg mixture all at once to dry mixture. Stir just until moistened. Stir in raisins.

3 **Turn dough out** onto prepared baking sheet; pat with wet fingers to an 8-inch round (dough will be wet). Brush with egg white.

4 **Bake in a** 350° oven about 25 minutes or until golden brown and wooden toothpick comes out clean. (If necessary, cover with foil for last 5 minutes of baking to prevent overbrowning.) Serve warm.

Nutrition Facts per serving: 103 cal., 1 g total fat (0 g sat. fat), 14 mg chol., 196 mg sodium, 22 g carbo., 2 g fiber, 3 g pro. Daily Values: 0% vit. A, 0% vit. C, 5% calcium, 6% iron

LEMON TEA BREAD *LOW-FAT*

Prep: 25 minutes   Bake: 45 minutes
Makes: 1 loaf (16 servings)   Oven: 350°

1⅔ **cups all-purpose flour**
¾ **cup granulated sugar**
1½ **teaspoons baking powder**
½ **teaspoon salt**
½ **teaspoon baking soda**
¼ **teaspoon ground nutmeg**
1 **beaten egg**
¾ **cup milk**
¼ **cup cooking oil**
1 **teaspoon finely shredded lemon peel**
1 **tablespoon lemon juice**
2 **teaspoons poppy seed**
1 **recipe Powdered Sugar Glaze (see right)**

1 **Grease bottom** and ½ inch up the sides of one 8×4×2-inch loaf pan or two 5¾×3×2-inch loaf pans. In a medium bowl combine flour, granulated sugar, baking powder, salt, baking soda, and nutmeg. Make a well in center of dry mixture; set aside.

LIKE MONEY IN THE BANK...

Q Do quick breads keep well?

A Absolutely. To store quick breads for the short term, let the loaves cool completely on a wire rack after baking. Wrap them in foil or plastic wrap, or place them in plastic bags. Store them in the refrigerator for up to 1 week.

Or, place completely cooled loaves in freezer containers or bags and freeze for up to 3 months. Thaw the wrapped loaves overnight in the refrigerator.

2 **In another bowl** combine egg, milk, oil, lemon peel, lemon juice, and poppy seed. Add the egg mixture all at once to dry mixture. Stir just until moistened (batter should be lumpy).

3 **Spoon batter into prepared** pan(s). Bake in a 350° oven for 45 to 50 minutes for 8×4×2-inch pan or 30 to 35 minutes for 5¾×3×2-inch pans or until wooden toothpick inserted near the center comes out clean. Cool in pan(s) on wire rack for 10 minutes. Remove from pan(s). Cool completely on wire rack. Wrap and store overnight. Drizzle with Powdered Sugar Glaze before serving.

Powdered Sugar Glaze: In small mixing bowl stir together ½ cup sifted powdered sugar, ½ teaspoon finely shredded lemon peel, and enough lemon juice (2 to 3 teaspoons) to make drizzling consistency.

Nutrition Facts per serving: 135 cal., 4 g total fat (1 g sat. fat), 14 mg chol., 150 mg sodium, 23 g carbo., 0 g fiber, 2 g pro. Daily Values: 1% vit. A, 1% vit. C, 4% calcium, 4% iron

ZUCCHINI BREAD

Prep: 25 minutes   **Bake:** 55 minutes
Makes: 1 loaf (16 servings)   **Oven:** 350°

When your garden is overflowing with zucchini, choose the smallest ones to make this bread. They're young and their skins are extra-tender.

1½ **cups all-purpose flour**
 1 **teaspoon ground cinnamon**
½ **teaspoon baking soda**
¼ **teaspoon baking powder**
¼ **teaspoon salt**
¼ **teaspoon ground nutmeg**
 1 **beaten egg**
 1 **cup sugar**
 1 **cup finely shredded, unpeeled**
      zucchini or apple
¼ **cup cooking oil**
¼ **teaspoon finely shredded lemon peel**
½ **cup chopped walnuts or pecans**

1 **Grease bottom** and ½ inch up sides of an 8×4×2-inch loaf pan; set aside. In a medium mixing bowl combine the flour, cinnamon, baking soda, baking powder, salt, and nutmeg. Make a well in center of dry mixture; set aside.

2 **In another medium mixing bowl** combine egg, sugar, zucchini, oil, and lemon peel. Add zucchini mixture all at once to dry mixture. Stir just until moistened (batter should be lumpy). Fold in the nuts.

3 **Spoon batter into prepared** pan. Bake in a 350° oven 55 to 60 minutes or until wooden toothpick inserted near center comes out clean. Cool in pan on a wire rack for 10 minutes. Remove from pan. Cool completely on wire rack. Wrap and store overnight before slicing.

Nutrition Facts per serving: 148 cal., 6 g total fat (1 g sat. fat), 13 mg chol., 83 mg sodium, 22 g carbo., 1 g fiber, 2 g pro. Daily Values: 0% vit. A, 1% vit. C, 1% calcium, 4% iron

PUMPKIN BREAD

Prep: 25 minutes   **Bake:** 55 minutes
Makes: 3 large loaves (48 servings)   **Oven:** 350°

 3 **cups sugar**
 1 **cup cooking oil**
 4 **eggs**
3⅓ **cups all-purpose flour**
 2 **teaspoons baking soda**
1½ **teaspoons salt**
 1 **teaspoon ground cinnamon**
 1 **teaspoon ground nutmeg**
⅔ **cup water**
 1 **15-ounce can pumpkin**

1 **Grease bottom** and ½ inch up sides of three 8×4×2-inch or four 7½×3½×2-inch loaf pans; set aside. In an extra large mixing bowl beat sugar and oil with an electric mixer on medium speed. Add eggs and beat well; set aside.

QUICK BREADS 101

A s suggested by their name, quick breads are a breeze to make if you adhere to the few golden rules of quick-bread baking:

■ Measure ingredients accurately.

■ Avoid mixing the batter too much. When you add the liquid, stir until the dry ingredients are just moistened; the batter will be lumpy. If you overmix, your bread will be tough.

■ If your bread is soggy and the middle has fallen, it could mean one of several things: There is too much liquid in proportion to the dry ingredients; there is insufficient leavening; the batter stood too long before baking; or it's underdone.

■ If your bread has a coarse texture, it means there's probably too much fat and leavening in it.

■ If your bread has a thick, dark brown crust, there's probably too much sugar in it.

■ If your bread has a bitter or soapy aftertaste, there's probably too much leavening (baking powder or baking soda, respectively) in it.

2 In a large mixing bowl combine flour, soda, salt, cinnamon, and nutmeg. Add dry mixture and water alternately to sugar mixture, beating on low speed after each addition just until combined. Beat in pumpkin.

3 Spoon batter into prepared pans. Bake in a 350° oven 55 to 60 minutes or until wooden toothpick inserted in centers comes out clean. Cool in pans on wire racks for 10 minutes. Remove from pans. Cool completely on wire racks. Wrap and store overnight before slicing.

Nutrition Facts per serving: 127 cal., 5 g total fat (1 g sat. fat), 18 mg chol., 125 mg sodium, 19 g carbo., 0 g fiber, 1 g pro. Daily Values: 20% vit. A, 0% vit. C, 0% calcium, 3% iron

BOSTON BROWN BREAD

Prep: 20 minutes **Steam:** 2 hours
Makes: 1 loaf (14 servings)

  ½ cup cornmeal
  ½ cup whole wheat flour
  ½ cup rye flour
  ½ teaspoon baking powder
  ¼ teaspoon baking soda
  ¼ teaspoon salt
  1 cup buttermilk or sour milk
     (see tip, page 329)
  ⅓ cup light molasses
  2 tablespoons brown sugar
  1 tablespoon cooking oil
  ¼ cup raisins or chopped walnuts

1 Grease the bottom and ½ inch up sides of a 7½×3½×2-inch loaf pan; set aside. In a large mixing bowl combine cornmeal, whole wheat flour, rye flour, baking powder, soda, and salt; set aside.

2 In a medium mixing bowl combine buttermilk, molasses, brown sugar, and oil. Gradually add buttermilk mixture to dry mixture, stirring just until combined. Stir in raisins. Spoon into prepared pan. Grease a piece of foil. Place the foil, greased side down, over the pan. Press foil around edges to seal.

3 Place loaf pan on rack in a Dutch oven. Pour hot water into Dutch oven around loaf pan until water comes 1 inch up side of pan. Bring water to boiling; reduce heat. Cover; simmer 2 to 2½ hours or until a wooden toothpick inserted near center

comes out clean. (Add additional boiling water to the Dutch oven as needed.)

4 Remove loaf pan from pot; let stand for 10 minutes. Remove from pan. Serve warm.

Nutrition Facts per serving: 94 cal., 1 g total fat (0 g sat. fat), 1 mg chol., 94 mg sodium, 19 g carbo., 1 g fiber, 2 g pro. Daily Values: 0% vit. A, 0% vit. C, 4% calcium, 6% iron

IRISH SODA BREAD *EASY*

Prep: 20 minutes **Bake:** 35 minutes
Makes: 1 loaf (8 servings) **Oven:** 375°

  1 cup whole wheat flour
  1 cup all-purpose flour
  1 teaspoon baking powder
  ½ teaspoon baking soda
  ¼ teaspoon salt
  3 tablespoons butter
  2 beaten eggs
  ¾ cup buttermilk or sour milk
     (see tip, page 329)
  2 tablespoons brown sugar
  ⅓ cup dried tart cherries or raisins

1 Grease a baking sheet; set aside. In a medium mixing bowl combine whole wheat flour, all-purpose flour, baking powder, soda, and salt. Using a pastry blender, cut in butter until mixture resembles coarse crumbs. Make a well in center of dry mixture; set aside.

2 In a small mixing bowl stir together 1 of the eggs, buttermilk, brown sugar, and cherries. Add egg mixture all at once to dry mixture. Stir just until moistened.

3 Turn dough out onto a lightly floured surface. Quickly knead dough by folding and gently pressing dough for 10 to 12 strokes or until dough is nearly smooth. Shape into a 6-inch round loaf. Cut a 4-inch cross, ½ inch deep, on the top. Place on prepared baking sheet. Brush with remaining egg. Bake in 375° oven about 35 minutes or until golden. Serve warm.

Nutrition Facts per serving: 196 cal., 6 g total fat (3 g sat. fat), 66 mg chol., 276 mg sodium, 30 g carbo., 3 g fiber, 6 g pro. Daily Values: 9% vit. A, 0% vit. C, 7% calcium, 10% iron

GINGER-DATE PUMPKIN LOAVES

Prep: 25 minutes   **Bake:** 35 minutes
Makes: 5 small loaves (25 servings)   **Oven:** 350°

  2 cups all-purpose flour
  1 cup granulated sugar
  1 tablespoon finely chopped
     crystallized ginger
2½ teaspoons baking powder
  ½ teaspoon baking soda
  ½ teaspoon ground nutmeg
  ¼ teaspoon salt
  1 cup canned pumpkin
  ½ cup milk
  2 eggs
  ⅓ cup shortening
  1 cup coarsely chopped pitted dates
  1 recipe Spiced Glaze (see below)

1 **Grease five** 4½×2½×1½-inch loaf pans or two 8×4×2-inch loaf pans; set aside. In a medium mixing bowl combine 1 cup of the flour, sugar, ginger, baking powder, baking soda, nutmeg, and salt. Add pumpkin, milk, eggs, and shortening. Beat with an electric mixer on low to medium speed for 30 seconds. Beat on high speed for 2 minutes, scraping bowl occasionally. Add the remaining flour; beat until well mixed. Stir in dates.

2 **Spoon the batter** into prepared pans. Bake in a 350° oven 35 to 40 minutes for 4½×2½×1½-inch loaves or 45 minutes for 8×4×2-inch loaves or until a wooden toothpick inserted near centers comes out clean. Cool in pans on wire racks for 10 minutes. Remove from pans. Cool completely. Wrap bread and store overnight. Drizzle with Spiced Glaze before serving.

Spiced Glaze: In a small mixing bowl stir together ½ cup sifted powdered sugar and ⅛ teaspoon ground ginger. Stir in enough water (2 to 3 teaspoons) to make drizzling consistency.

Nutrition Facts per serving: 129 cal., 3 g total fat (1 g sat. fat), 17 mg chol., 70 mg sodium, 24 g carbo., 1 g fiber, 2 g pro. Daily Values: 22% vit. A, 0% vit. C, 4% calcium, 5% iron

SWEET ONION WHEAT BUNS

Prep: 30 minutes   **Bake:** 12 minutes
Makes: 8 to 10 buns   **Oven:** 400°

  2 tablespoons butter
  2 teaspoons brown sugar
  1 large onion, thinly sliced
  1 cup all-purpose flour
  ¾ cup whole wheat flour
1½ teaspoons baking powder
  ¾ teaspoon salt
  ¾ teaspoon dried sage, crushed
  ½ teaspoon baking soda
  1 beaten egg
  1 8-ounce carton plain lowfat yogurt
  2 tablespoons brown sugar

1 **Grease baking sheet;** set aside. In large skillet combine butter and the 2 teaspoons brown sugar. Cook and stir over medium heat about 1 minute or just until combined. Add the onion. Cook, uncovered, over low heat for 10 to 12 minutes or until onion is very tender and light brown, stirring occasionally. Set some of the smaller onion rings aside for a garnish. Don't drain off the butter. Chop the remaining cooked onion.

2 **In a large mixing bowl** combine all-purpose flour, whole wheat flour, baking powder, salt, sage, and baking soda. Make a well in center of dry mixture; set aside.

3 **In small mixing bowl** combine egg, yogurt, and the 2 tablespoons brown sugar. Add egg mixture all at once to dry mixture. Stir just until moistened. Stir in chopped onion and butter mixture. (The dough will be slightly sticky.)

4 **With a ¼- or ⅓-cup** measure, scoop dough into mounds onto prepared baking sheet. With wet hands, form mounds into rounded buns, about 1 inch thick. Top with the reserved onion rings, pressing them gently into buns.

5 **Bake in a** 400° oven about 12 minutes or until the buns are golden and a wooden toothpick inserted in the center comes out clean. Serve warm.

Nutrition Facts per serving: 168 cal., 4 g total fat (1 g sat. fat), 28 mg chol., 410 mg sodium, 27 g carbo., 2 g fiber, 6 g pro. Daily Values: 5% vit. A, 2% vit. C, 11% calcium, 9% iron

**Sweet Onion Wheat
Buns and Ginger-Date
Pumpkin Loaves:**
Whether you crave
savory or sweet, one
of these beguiling
breads will hit
the spot.

CRUNCHY PARMESAN
CORN BREAD

Prep: 30 minutes   Bake: 50 minutes
Makes: 1 loaf (8 servings)   Oven: 375°

1 cup boiling water
¼ cup bulgur
  Yellow cornmeal
1 cup all-purpose flour
1 cup yellow cornmeal
⅓ cup grated Parmesan cheese
2 tablespoons sugar
1 tablespoon baking powder
½ teaspoon fennel seed
½ teaspoon dried basil, crushed

2 beaten eggs
1 cup milk
¼ cup olive oil or cooking oil
⅓ cup sun-dried tomatoes (oil pack),
  drained and chopped, or diced
  pimiento, drained
⅓ cup sliced green onions

1 Pour boiling water over bulgur; let stand for 5 minutes. Drain. Meanwhile, grease bottom and ½ inch up sides of a 6-cup soufflé dish, an 8×4×2-inch loaf pan, or a 9×5×3-inch loaf pan. Sprinkle bottom and sides with cornmeal; set aside.

2 In a large mixing bowl combine flour, the 1 cup cornmeal, the Parmesan cheese, sugar,

Crunchy Parmesan Corn Bread: Flecks of sun-dried tomatoes and green onions give this beautiful bread color and flavor. The "crunch" comes from nutty-flavored bulgur wheat.

baking powder, fennel seed, and basil. Make a well in the center of dry mixture; set aside.

3 **In a medium mixing bowl** combine eggs, milk, and oil. Stir in bulgur and mix well. Add all at once to dry mixture. Stir just until moistened (batter should be lumpy). Fold in tomatoes or pimiento and green onion.

4 **Spoon batter into** prepared dish or pan. Bake in a 375° oven for 50 to 55 minutes or until a wooden toothpick inserted near center comes out clean. (If necessary, cover with foil for the last 10 to 15 minutes of baking to prevent overbrowning.) Remove from dish or pan. Cool on a wire rack for 30 minutes. Serve warm.

Nutrition Facts per serving: 269 cal., 11 g total fat (3 g sat. fat), 59 mg chol., 259 mg sodium, 35 g carbo., 2 g fiber, 8 g pro. Daily Values: 7% vit. A, 9% vit. C, 19% calcium, 13% iron

COMPANY CORN BREAD

Prep: 20 minutes **Bake:** 18 minutes
Makes: 8 to 10 servings **Oven:** 400°

Nobody loves cornbread like a Southerner. This cornbread takes on a Southern accent because it's baked in a skillet. No matter where you hail from, warm wedges of this tender, slightly sweet cornbread will entice you to the table.

  1 **cup all-purpose flour**
  ¾ **cup yellow or white cornmeal**
  2 to 3 **tablespoons sugar**
2½ **teaspoons baking powder**
  ¾ **teaspoon salt**
  1 **tablespoon butter**
  2 **beaten eggs**
  1 **cup milk**
  ¼ **cup melted shortening or cooking oil**

1 **Stir together** the flour, cornmeal, sugar, baking powder, and salt; set aside.

2 **Add butter** to a 10-inch cast-iron skillet.* Place in a 400° oven for about 3 minutes or until butter is melted. Remove from oven and swirl butter in pan to coat bottom and sides of pan.

3 **Meanwhile,** in a bowl combine eggs, milk, and shortening. Add egg mixture all at once to dry mixture. Stir just until moistened. Pour batter into hot skillet. Bake for 18 to 20 minutes or until light brown. Serve warm.

*Note: A 9×1½-inch round baking pan may be substituted for the skillet. Bake as directed.

Nutrition Facts per serving: 219 cal., 10 g total fat (3 g sat. fat), 59 mg chol., 360 mg sodium, 26 g carbo., 1 g fiber, 5 g pro. Daily Values: 6% vit. A, 0% vit. C, 12% calcium, 10% iron

Popovers: Like their close cousin Yorkshire pudding, crisp and eggy popovers taste great when served with roast beef, lamb, or pork.

POPOVERS

Prep: 15 minutes   **Bake:** 40 minutes
Makes: 6 popovers   **Oven:** 400°

Turn plain popovers into breakfast fare: Add ½ teaspoon ground cinnamon to the flour batter. Serve them with honey or preserves.

> **1 tablespoon shortening or**
> **nonstick spray coating**
> **2 beaten eggs**
> **1 cup milk**
> **1 tablespoon cooking oil**
> **1 cup all-purpose flour**
> **¼ teaspoon salt**

1 Using ½ teaspoon shortening for each cup, grease the bottoms and sides of six 6-ounce custard cups or cups of a popover pan. (Or, spray cups with nonstick coating.) Place the custard cups on a 15×10×1-inch baking pan; set aside.

2 In a medium mixing bowl use a wire whisk or rotary beater to beat eggs, milk, and oil until combined. Add flour and salt; beat until smooth.

3 Fill the prepared cups half full with batter. Bake in a 400° oven about 40 minutes or until very firm.

4 Immediately after removing from oven, use the tines of a fork to prick each popover to let steam escape. Turn off the oven. For crisper popovers, return popovers to oven for 5 to 10 minutes or until desired crispness is reached. Remove popovers from cups; serve immediately.

Nutrition Facts per popover: 154 cal., 7 g total fat (2 g sat. fat), 74 mg chol., 130 mg sodium, 17 g carbo., 1 g fiber, 5 g pro. Daily Values: 5% vit. A, 0% vit. C, 5% calcium, 7% iron

---

RISING TO THE OCCASION

Just what is the "pop" in popovers? It's not magic, though it may appear to be: Muffin cups a scant half-full of batter that contains no leavening suddenly explode into airy, cloudlike puffs that are crisp on the outside and delectably soft on the inside. Why? The answer is simple: The heat is on. Popovers pop because of the steam that forms inside of them as they bake.

In the mid-19th century, popovers were one of the few breads cooks could make quickly. They became known as popovers because the batter "popped over" the edge of the pan.

PROVOLONE AND
PEPPER POPOVERS

Prep: 20 minutes **Bake:** 40 minutes
Makes: 6 popovers **Oven:** 400°

Add a bit of bite to these puffs with cracked black pepper. Look for it in the spice section of your supermarket. Better yet, use a mortar and pestle to coarsely crush whole peppercorns.

- 1 tablespoon shortening or nonstick spray coating
- 2 eggs
- 1 cup milk
- 1 tablespoon cooking oil
- 1 cup all-purpose flour
- ¼ teaspoon salt
- ¼ cup finely shredded provolone cheese (1 ounce)
- 1 to 2 teaspoons cracked black pepper

1 Using ½ teaspoon shortening for each cup, grease the bottoms and sides of six 6-ounce custard cups or cups of a popover pan. (Or, spray cups with the nonstick coating.) Place the custard cups on a 15×10×1-inch baking pan; set aside.

2 In a medium mixing bowl use a wire whisk or rotary beater to beat eggs, milk, and oil until combined. Add flour and salt; beat until smooth. Fold in provolone cheese and black pepper.

3 Fill the prepared cups half full with batter. Bake in a 400° oven about 40 minutes or until firm.

4 Immediately after removing from oven, use the tines of a fork to prick each popover to let steam escape. Turn off oven. For crisper popovers, return popovers to oven for 5 to 10 minutes or until desired crispness is reached. Remove popovers from cups; serve immediately.

Nutrition Facts per popover: 171 cal., 8 g total fat (3 g sat. fat), 77 mg chol., 172 mg sodium, 17 g carbo., 1 g fiber, 7 g pro. Daily Values: 6% vit. A, 1% vit. C, 8% calcium, 8% iron

ACHIEVING POPOVER PERFECTION

The popover debate may not rage quite so vociferously as that over, say, chili or barbecue, but there is some disagreement about the best way to ensure the most perfectly formed popovers (some popover fans say putting them in a cold oven is the key, for instance). Forget all of that and just follow the recipe and these few pointers:

- Use large eggs.
- Stir the batter while filling the cups to keep it well mixed.
- Don't add any more cheese or meat than the recipe directs.
- Grease the pans properly to make the popovers easy to remove.
- Don't open the oven door during baking. Cool air can cause the popovers to fall.
- Prevent overbrowning by placing the oven shelf in the lower part of the oven so the custard cups or pan is in the center.
- Bake the popovers for the time indicated or until firm; do not underbake.
- Prick popovers with a fork after removing them from the oven to let steam escape so they don't get soggy. To "crisp" popovers, shut off the oven, return the popovers to the oven for 5 to 10 more minutes, then remove them from the pan while still warm.
- Serve popovers hot from the oven. Place leftovers in a freezer bag and freeze for up to 3 months. Reheat frozen popovers in a shallow baking pan in a 400° oven for 10 to 15 minutes or until warm.

CAKE DOUGHNUTS

Prep: 40 minutes Chill: 2 hours
Fry: 2 minutes per batch
Makes: 13 to 15 doughnuts

3¼ cups all-purpose flour
 2 teaspoons baking powder
 ½ teaspoon ground cinnamon
 ¼ teaspoon salt
 ¼ teaspoon ground nutmeg
 ⅔ cup milk
 ¼ cup butter, melted
 2 beaten eggs
 ⅔ cup granulated sugar
 1 teaspoon vanilla
    Shortening or cooking oil for
       deep-fat frying
 1 recipe Chocolate Glaze
    (see top right), granulated sugar,
    or powdered sugar (optional)

1 **In a large mixing bowl** combine 2¼ cups of the flour, the baking powder, cinnamon, salt, and nutmeg. In medium mixing bowl combine milk and melted butter. In another large mixing bowl combine eggs, the ⅔ cup granulated sugar, and the vanilla; beat with electric mixer until thick. Add the dry mixture and milk mixture alternately to egg mixture, beating just until combined after each addition. Stir in remaining flour. Cover dough; chill in the refrigerator for 2 hours.

2 **Turn dough out** onto lightly floured surface. Roll to ½-inch thickness. Cut with a floured 2½-inch doughnut cutter, dipping cutter into additional flour between cuts. Reroll as necessary.

3 **Fry doughnuts** and doughnut holes, 2 or 3 at a time, in deep hot fat (375°) about 1 minute on each side or until golden, turning once with slotted spoon. Drain on paper towels. If desired, drizzle warm doughnuts with Chocolate Glaze or shake warm doughnuts in bag with granulated or powdered sugar. Cool on wire racks.

Nutrition Facts per doughnut: 288 cal., 15 g total fat (6 g sat. fat), 45 mg chol., 155 mg sodium, 33 g carbo., 1 g fiber, 4 g pro. Daily Values: 6% vit. A, 0% vit. C, 6% calcium, 10% iron

Chocolate Glaze: In saucepan melt 4 ounces semisweet chocolate, cut up, and 3 tablespoons butter over low heat, stirring frequently. Remove from heat. Stir in 1½ cups sifted powdered sugar and 3 tablespoons hot water. If necessary, stir in additional hot water to make drizzling consistency.

BUTTERMILK COFFEE CAKE

BEST-LOVED

Prep: 30 minutes Bake: 35 minutes
Makes: 18 servings Oven: 350°

Also called Cowboy Coffee Cake through the years in Better Homes and Gardens® cookbooks, this classic, with its buttery, nut-crumb topping, is one everyone has tasted—and everyone loves.

2½ cups all-purpose flour
1½ cups packed brown sugar
 ½ teaspoon salt
 ⅔ cup butter or shortening
 2 teaspoons baking powder
 ½ teaspoon baking soda
 ½ teaspoon ground cinnamon
 ½ teaspoon ground nutmeg
 2 beaten eggs
1⅓ cups buttermilk or sour milk
       (see tip, page 329)
 ½ cup chopped nuts

1 **Grease the bottom** and ½ inch up sides of a 13×9×2-inch baking pan; set aside. In a large mixing bowl combine flour, brown sugar, and salt. Cut in butter until mixture resembles coarse crumbs; set aside ½ cup crumb mixture. Stir baking powder, baking soda, cinnamon, and nutmeg into remaining crumb mixture.

2 **In a small mixing bowl** combine eggs and buttermilk. Add egg mixture all at once to dry mixture; mix well. Spoon batter into prepared pan. Stir together reserved crumb mixture and nuts. Sprinkle over batter. Bake in a 350° oven for 35 to 40 minutes or until a wooden toothpick inserted near the center comes out clean. Serve warm.

Nutrition Facts per serving: 214 cal., 10 g total fat (2 g sat. fat), 33 mg chol., 228 mg sodium, 28 g carbo., 1 g fiber, 3 g pro. Daily Values: 7% vit. A, 0% vit. C, 6% calcium, 8% iron

THE PEANUT'S PROGRESS

For more than a century before this country was colonized, African cooks were using peanuts (or groundnuts) in many ways in their creative cooking: as a vegetable fresh from the garden, as the base for a creamy soup, and in a chicken dish served with a peanut sauce.

Southerners (and eventually the whole country) adopted the peanut as a staple in its myriad forms: raw, baked, roasted, or boiled; in peanut soup, peanut gravy, and peanut brittle; and perhaps most beloved of all, whirled into peanut butter.

PEANUT BUTTER
COFFEE CAKE

Prep: 30 minutes **Bake:** 25 minutes
Makes: 9 servings **Oven:** 375°

The makers of the famous candy that combines chocolate and peanut butter know a good thing when they taste it. So go ahead: Get some chocolate in your peanut butter—or peanut butter in your chocolate—and discover how delicious it can be.

  ¼ **cup all-purpose flour**
  ¼ **cup packed brown sugar**
  2 **tablespoons peanut butter**
  1 **tablespoon butter**
  ¼ **cup miniature semisweet**
      chocolate pieces
  ¼ **cup peanut butter**
  2 **tablespoons butter**
  1 **cup all-purpose flour**
  ½ **cup packed brown sugar**
  ½ **cup milk**
  1 **egg**
  1 **teaspoon baking powder**
  ¼ **teaspoon baking soda**
  ¼ **teaspoon salt**
  ¼ **cup miniature semisweet**
      chocolate pieces

1 **Grease an** 8×8×2-inch baking pan; set aside. For streusel topping, in a small mixing bowl combine the ¼ cup flour, the ¼ cup brown sugar, the 2 tablespoons peanut butter, and the 1 tablespoon butter. Stir together until crumbly. Stir in ¼ cup chocolate pieces; set aside.

2 **In a large mixing bowl** beat the ¼ cup peanut butter and the 2 tablespoons butter with an electric mixer on medium to high speed for 30 seconds or until combined.

3 **Add about half** of the 1 cup flour, the ½ cup brown sugar, half of the milk, the egg, baking powder, baking soda, and salt. Beat with an electric mixer on low speed until thoroughly combined, scraping the side of the bowl constantly. Add the remaining flour and remaining milk. Beat on low to medium speed just until combined. Stir in ¼ cup chocolate pieces.

4 **Spread batter evenly** in prepared pan. Sprinkle with the streusel topping. Bake in a 375° oven for 25 to 30 minutes or until a wooden toothpick inserted near the center comes out clean. Cool in pan on a wire rack for 15 minutes. Cut into squares. Serve warm. (Cover any leftovers and store at room temperature or in the refrigerator for up to 3 days.)

Nutrition Facts per serving: 269 cal., 13 g total fat
(4 g sat. fat), 35 mg chol., 243 mg sodium,
36 g carbo., 1 g fiber, 6 g pro. Daily Values: 5% vit. A,
0% vit. C, 6% calcium, 10% iron

RIBBON-OF-FRUIT TEACAKE

Prep: 30 minutes   Bake: 45 minutes
Makes: 8 servings   Oven: 350°

2¼ **cups all-purpose flour**
  ¾ **cup granulated sugar**
  ¾ **cup butter**
  ½ **teaspoon baking powder**
  ½ **teaspoon baking soda**
  ¼ **teaspoon ground nutmeg**
  ⅛ **teaspoon salt**
  1 **beaten egg**
  ⅔ **cup buttermilk or sour milk**
    (see tip, page 329)
  1 **teaspoon vanilla**
1¼ **cups canned fruit pie filling, such**
    as cherry, apricot, raisin,
    strawberry, peach, or blueberry
  1 **recipe Vanilla Icing (see right)**

1 **Grease and flour** an 11-inch fluted tart pan with removable bottom or a 2-quart rectangular baking dish; set aside.

2 **In a large bowl** combine flour and granulated sugar. Cut in butter until mixture resembles coarse crumbs. Set aside ½ cup mixture for topping.

3 **For batter** stir baking powder, soda, nutmeg, and salt into remaining crumb mixture. Make a well in the center. In a small bowl combine egg, buttermilk, and vanilla. Add egg mixture all at once to nutmeg mixture. Stir just until moistened (batter should be lumpy). Set aside 1 cup batter.

4 **Spread remaining batter** onto bottom and 1 inch up sides of prepared pan or dish. Carefully spread the desired pie filling on top. Spoon reserved batter into small mounds on top of filling. Sprinkle with topping.

5 **Bake in** 350° oven about 45 minutes for tart pan or about 40 minutes for baking dish or until golden. (If necessary, cover edges with foil after 30 minutes to prevent overbrowning.)

6 **Cool in pan** on a wire rack for 15 minutes. If using tart pan, remove side and bottom. Drizzle with Vanilla Icing. Serve warm, or cool on wire rack.

Vanilla Icing: Stir together ½ cup sifted powdered sugar, ½ teaspoon vanilla, and enough milk (1 to 2 teaspoons) to make drizzling consistency.

Nutrition Facts per serving: 442 cal., 19 g total fat (4 g sat. fat), 28 mg chol., 310 mg sodium, 64 g carbo., 1 g fiber, 5 g pro. Daily Values: 24% vit. A, 1% vit. C, 3% calcium, 11% iron

---

COFFEE CAKE 101

How to get even the sleepiest heads up and at 'em: Pop a coffee cake into the oven. There's nothing quite like a piece of warm, fresh-baked coffee cake to go with your morning coffee (or tea), as anyone who awakens to the wonderful, homey aroma will heartily agree. Here's how to make a coffee cake just right every time:

■ If you're baking in a metal pan, be sure it's a shiny one. Shiny pans reflect heat, which produces a golden, delicate, and tender crust.

■ Most coffee cakes are at their best served warm. Let your coffee cake cool for 20 to 30 minutes before cutting and serving— it will be at its just-right-for-eating stage.

■ Save leftover coffee cake for an afternoon snack or tomorrow's breakfast in a tightly covered container stored at room temperature. If the coffee cake contains cream cheese, store it in the refrigerator.

■ To reheat coffee cake, wrap it in heavy foil and heat in a 350° oven for about 15 minutes.

Ribbon-of-Fruit Teacake:
A sweet layer of cherry
pie filling swirls through
this streusel-topped quick
bread, but you can choose
another of your favorite
fruit fillings as well.

RASPBERRY-CHEESE
COFFEE CAKE *EASY*

Prep: 20 minutes   **Bake:** 30 minutes
Makes: 12 servings   **Oven:** 350°

Swirls of red preserves make this rich cream cheese coffee cake as eye-catching as it is yummy.

  1 **8-ounce package cream cheese, softened**
  ½ **cup butter**
1¾ **cups all-purpose flour**
  1 **cup granulated sugar**
  2 **eggs**
  ¼ **cup milk**
  1 **teaspoon baking powder**
  ½ **teaspoon baking soda**
  ½ **teaspoon vanilla**
  ½ **cup seedless red raspberry preserves or strawberry preserves**
    Powdered sugar

1 Grease a 13×9×2-inch baking pan; set aside. In a large mixing bowl beat cream cheese and butter with an electric mixer on medium to high speed about 30 seconds or until combined. Add about half of the flour to the cream cheese mixture.

2 Add the granulated sugar, eggs, milk, baking powder, baking soda, and vanilla to cream cheese mixture. Beat on low speed until thoroughly combined, scraping the side of bowl. Beat on medium speed for 2 minutes. Beat in remaining flour on low speed just until combined.

3 Spread batter evenly into prepared pan. Spoon preserves in small mounds on top of the batter. Using a small narrow spatula or knife, gently swirl preserves into the batter to create a marbled effect (see photo, top right).

4 Bake in 350° oven for 30 to 35 minutes or until a wooden toothpick inserted near the center comes out clean.

Using a small narrow metal spatula, swirl or zigzag the preserves into the batter to create a marbled effect. Do not swirl too vigorously or the marbled effect will be lost.

5 Cool in the pan on wire rack for 15 minutes. Sift powdered sugar over coffee cake. Serve warm, or cool on wire rack.

Nutrition Facts per serving: 317 cal., 16 g total fat (7 g sat. fat), 67 mg chol., 224 mg sodium, 40 g carbo., 1 g fiber, 4 g pro. Daily Values: 17% vit. A, 0% vit. C, 5% calcium, 8% iron

PAPAYA STREUSEL
COFFEE CAKE

Prep: 25 minutes   **Bake:** 30 minutes
Makes: 15 servings   **Oven:** 350°

  ⅔ **cup packed brown sugar**
  ⅔ **cup all-purpose flour**
  1 **teaspoon ground cinnamon**
  ¼ **teaspoon ground ginger**
  ⅓ **cup butter**
  3 **cups all-purpose flour**
  1 **cup granulated sugar**
  1 **tablespoon baking powder**
  ¼ **teaspoon salt**
  1 **cup butter**
  2 **beaten eggs**
  ½ **cup milk**
  ½ **cup papaya nectar**
  1 **medium papaya, peeled, halved, cored, and thinly sliced**
  1 **recipe Powdered Sugar Icing (optional) (see page 313)**

1 Grease a 13×9×2-inch baking pan; set aside. For streusel topping, in a medium mixing bowl combine the brown sugar, the ⅔ cup flour, the cinnamon, and ginger. Cut in the ⅓ cup butter until mixture resembles coarse crumbs; set aside.

2 **For batter,** in a medium mixing bowl combine the 3 cups flour, granulated sugar, baking powder, and salt. Cut in the 1 cup butter until mixture resembles fine crumbs. Make a well in the center; set aside. In a small mixing bowl, combine eggs, milk, and papaya nectar. Add egg mixture all at once to dry mixture. Stir just until moistened (the batter should be lumpy).

3 **Spread half of the batter** evenly in the prepared pan. Arrange papaya slices on top of batter. Drop remaining batter by small spoonfuls over papaya. Sprinkle with streusel topping.

4 **Bake in** 350° oven about 30 minutes or until a wooden toothpick inserted near center comes out clean.

5 **Cool in pan** on a wire rack for 15 minutes. If desired, drizzle with Powdered Sugar Icing. Serve warm. (Store any leftovers in refrigerator for up to 3 days.)

Nutrition Facts per serving: 376 cal., 18 g total fat (5 g sat. fat), 50 mg chol., 277 mg sodium, 50 g carbo., 1 g fiber, 4 g pro. Daily Values: 18% vit. A, 34% vit. C, 9% calcium, 12% iron

Powdered Sugar Icing: In a small mixing bowl stir together 1 cup sifted powdered sugar and ¼ teaspoon vanilla. Stir in 1 tablespoon milk. Stir in additional milk, 1 teaspoon, at a time, to make drizzling consistency.

Pear Coffee Cake: Prepare as directed above, except substitute 2 medium ripe pears for the papaya and use pear nectar. Or, use one 8-ounce can of pear halves (juice pack). Drain the pears, reserving juice. Add water to the reserved juice to make ½ cup liquid and use that liquid in place of the pear nectar. Thinly slice the pear halves.

BLUEBERRY BUCKLE

Prep: 25 minutes **Bake:** 50 minutes
Makes: 9 servings   **Oven:** 350°

A comfortable classic, this much-loved recipe has appeared in the Better Homes and Gardens® New Cook Book *since the early 1940s.*

2½ **cups all-purpose flour**
2½ **teaspoons baking powder**
 ¼ **teaspoon salt**
 ½ **cup shortening**
 ¾ **cup sugar**
  1 **egg**
 ½ **cup milk**
  2 **cups fresh or frozen blueberries**
 ½ **cup sugar**
 ½ **teaspoon ground cinnamon**
 ¼ **cup butter**

1 **Grease the bottom and** ½ inch up sides of a 9×9×2-inch or an 8×8×2-inch baking pan; set aside. In a large mixing bowl combine 2 cups of the flour, baking powder, and salt; set aside.

2 **Beat shortening** with an electric mixer on medium speed for 30 seconds. Add the ¾ cup sugar. Beat on medium to high speed until light and fluffy. Add egg; beat well. Add dry mixture and milk alternately to egg mixture, beating until smooth after each addition. Spoon batter into prepared pan. Sprinkle with blueberries.

3 **Combine** remaining flour, ½ cup sugar, and cinnamon. Cut in butter until mixture resembles coarse crumbs. Sprinkle over berries. Bake in a 350° oven 50 to 60 minutes or until golden. Serve warm.

Nutrition Facts per serving: 403 cal., 18 g total fat (6 g sat. fat), 38 mg chol., 228 mg sodium, 58 g carbo., 2 g fiber, 5 g pro. Daily Values: 6% vit. A, 7% vit. C, 10% calcium, 12% iron

---

BUCKLE UP

Perfectly at home on the breakfast table in the morning or on the dessert buffet after dinner, a buckle is a homey, country-style dessert of tender cake, fruit (usually blueberries), and a buttery streusel topping.

Fresh Raspberry Kuchen: Kuchen is a traditional German fruit- or cheese-filled cake served for breakfast or dessert. In this version, a layer of cake is topped with colorful fresh berries and baked in a lemon cream filling.

FRESH RASPBERRY KUCHEN

Prep: 30 minutes Bake: 55 minutes
Chill: 4 hours Makes: 12 servings Oven: 350°

  2 **cups fresh or frozen raspberries***
  1 **cup all-purpose flour**
  ½ **cup sugar**
  1 **teaspoon baking powder**
  ¼ **cup butter, melted**
  2 **egg whites**
  1 **teaspoon vanilla**
1½ **cups plain lowfat or fat-free yogurt**
  2 **tablespoons all-purpose flour**
  ½ **cup sugar**
  2 **slightly beaten egg yolks**
  1 **slightly beaten egg**
1½ **teaspoons finely shredded lemon peel**
  1 **teaspoon vanilla**

1 **If using frozen** raspberries, thaw at room temperature 15 minutes; drain.

2 **In food processor bowl** or medium mixing bowl combine the 1 cup flour, ½ cup sugar, and the baking powder. Add butter, egg whites, and 1 teaspoon vanilla. Cover and process, or stir by hand, until well mixed. Spread onto the bottom of an ungreased 9-inch springform pan; sprinkle with raspberries.

3 **For filling,** place yogurt in a large mixing bowl; sprinkle with the 2 tablespoons flour. Add ½ cup sugar, egg yolks, whole egg, lemon peel, and 1 teaspoon vanilla. Mix until smooth; pour over berries in springform pan.

4 **Bake in a** 350° oven about 55 minutes or until center appears set when shaken gently. Cool in pan on a wire rack for 15 minutes; remove side of pan. Cover; chill in refrigerator for 4 to 24 hours.

5 **To serve,** remove pan bottom. Transfer to a platter. If desired, garnish with lemon leaves.

*Note: Frozen raspberries may make the creamy filling softer because they tend to water out.

Nutrition Facts per serving: 187 cal., 6 g total fat (1 g sat. fat), 55 mg chol., 111 mg sodium, 30 g carbo., 1 g fiber, 4 g pro. Daily Values: 11% vit. A, 9% vit. C, 7% calcium, 5% iron

APRICOT COFFEE CAKE

Prep: 50 minutes   Bake: 25 minutes
Makes: 12 servings   Oven: 350°

  Nonstick spray coating
¾ cup finely snipped dried apricots
½ cup water
 1 5½-ounce can apricot nectar
     (⅔ cup)
⅓ cup cooking oil
 2 cups all-purpose flour
½ cup granulated sugar
 1 package active dry yeast
1½ teaspoons baking powder
½ teaspoon ground cinnamon
¼ teaspoon salt
 2 slightly beaten egg whites
½ cup regular or quick-cooking
     rolled oats
¼ cup packed brown sugar
 2 tablespoons butter, melted

1 **Spray an** 11×7×1½-inch baking pan with nonstick coating. In a small saucepan combine apricots and water; bring to full boil. Remove from heat. Stir in the apricot nectar and oil. Cool mixture for about 25 minutes or until warm but not hot (115° to 120°).

2 **Meanwhile, in a large mixing bowl** combine flour, granulated sugar, yeast, baking powder, cinnamon, and salt. Add apricot mixture and egg whites. Stir just until combined. Spread the batter evenly in prepared pan.

3 **Combine** oats and brown sugar. Stir in butter. Sprinkle over batter. Bake in a 350° oven for 25 to 30 minutes or until brown. Serve warm.

Nutrition Facts per serving: 231 cal., 8 g total fat (2 g sat. fat), 5 mg chol., 122 mg sodium, 36 g carbo., 1 g fiber, 4 g pro. Daily Values: 9% vit. A, 8% vit. C, 4% calcium, 11% iron

DOUBLE-COFFEE COFFEE CAKE

Prep: 25 minutes   Bake: 50 minutes
Makes: 12 servings   Oven: 350°

 6 teaspoons instant coffee crystals
 1 cup chopped walnuts
 2 cups granulated sugar
¼ cup packed brown sugar
 2 teaspoons ground cinnamon
 3 cups all-purpose flour
1½ teaspoons baking powder
1½ teaspoons baking soda
½ teaspoon salt
¾ cup butter
 1 8-ounce carton dairy sour cream
 3 eggs
¼ cup buttermilk or sour milk
     (see tip, page 329)
¼ cup applesauce
 1 teaspoon vanilla

1 **Grease and flour** a 10-inch fluted tube pan; set aside. Dissolve 4 teaspoons of the coffee crystals in 2 teaspoons hot water; set aside. In medium bowl combine nuts, ¼ cup of the granulated sugar, the brown sugar, cinnamon, and remaining coffee crystals; set aside. In another bowl combine flour, baking powder, soda, and salt; set aside.

2 **In a large bowl** beat the butter with an electric mixer on medium speed for 30 seconds. Add the remaining granulated sugar. Beat until light and fluffy. Add reserved coffee-water mixture, sour cream, eggs, buttermilk, applesauce, and vanilla; beat well. Add dry mixture, a little at a time, beating well after each addition.

3 **Pour half** of the batter into the prepared pan. Sprinkle with 1 cup of the nut mixture. Top with remaining batter. Sprinkle with remaining nut mixture. Bake in a 350° oven about 50 minutes or until a wooden toothpick inserted near center comes out clean. Cool in pan on wire rack for 10 minutes. Remove from pan. Serve warm.

Nutrition Facts per serving: 483 cal., 23 g total fat (6 g sat. fat), 62 mg chol., 461 mg sodium, 64 g carbo., 1 g fiber, 7 g pro. Daily Values: 21% vit. A, 0% vit. C, 8% calcium, 14% iron

PANCAKES *EASY*

Prep: 10 minutes   **Cook:** 4 minutes per batch
Makes: 8 to 10 (4-inch) or 36 (2-inch) pancakes

Top these fluffy flapjacks with your favorite syrup, warmed, or fruit and whipped cream.

>   1 **cup all-purpose flour**
>   1 **tablespoon granulated sugar**
>   2 **teaspoons baking powder**
> ¼ **teaspoon salt**
>   1 **beaten egg**
>   1 **cup milk**
>   2 **tablespoons cooking oil**

1 **In a medium mixing bowl** combine the flour, sugar, baking powder, and salt. Make a well in the center of the dry mixture; set aside.

2 **In another medium mixing bowl** combine the egg, milk, and oil. Add egg mixture all at once to the dry mixture. Stir just until moistened (batter should be lumpy).

3 **To make 4-inch pancakes,** pour about ¼ cup batter onto a hot, lightly greased griddle or heavy skillet (see top photo, below). (Or, to make dollar-size pancakes, pour about 1 tablespoon batter onto a hot, lightly greased griddle or heavy skillet.) Cook

over medium heat about 2 minutes on each side or until pancakes are golden, turning to second side when pancakes have bubbly surfaces and edges are slightly dry (see photo, bottom left). Serve warm.

Nutrition Facts per 4-inch pancake: 114 cal., 5 g total fat (1 g sat. fat), 29 mg chol., 181 mg sodium, 14 g carbo., 0 g fiber, 3 g pro. Daily Values: 3% vit. A, 0% vit. C, 10% calcium, 6% iron

Buckwheat Pancakes: Prepare as at left, except substitute ½ cup whole wheat flour and ½ cup buckwheat flour for the all-purpose flour; substitute brown sugar for the granulated sugar.

Buttermilk Pancakes: Prepare as at left, except reduce baking powder to 1 teaspoon and add ¼ teaspoon baking soda to dry mixture; substitute buttermilk or sour milk (see tip, page 329) for milk. If necessary, add more buttermilk or sour milk to thin the batter.

BLUEBERRY PANCAKES

Prep: 10 minutes   **Cook:** 4 minutes per batch
Makes: 8 to 10 (4-inch) pancakes

Cornmeal and cinnamon are an unusual but undeniably yummy combination in these bejeweled-with-blueberries pancakes.

>   1 **cup all-purpose flour**
>   2 **tablespoons cornmeal**
>   1 **tablespoon sugar**
>   1 **teaspoon baking powder**
> ½ **teaspoon baking soda**
> ¼ **teaspoon salt**
> ¼ **teaspoon ground cinnamon**
>   1 **beaten egg**
>   1 **cup buttermilk or sour milk**
>   **(see tip, page 329)**
>   2 **tablespoons cooking oil**
>   1 **cup fresh or frozen blueberries**

1 **In a medium mixing bowl** combine flour, cornmeal, sugar, baking powder, baking soda, salt, and cinnamon. Make a well in center of dry mixture; set aside.

Pour batter onto a hot griddle or skillet. Leave enough space between pancakes for them to expand during cooking.

Pancakes are ready to turn when tops are bubbly all over and a few bubbles are broken. Also, the edges should be slightly dry.

Blueberry Pancakes: Add a little lean smoked bacon or sausage to a plate of these fruit-filled classics and you've got a breakfast hearty enough for a hungry lumberjack but special enough for company.

2 **In another medium mixing bowl** combine the egg, buttermilk, and oil. Add egg mixture all at once to dry mixture. Stir just until moistened (batter should be lumpy). Gently fold in berries.

3 **For each pancake,** pour about ¼ cup of the batter onto a hot, lightly greased griddle or heavy skillet (see top photo, page 316). Cook over medium heat about 2 minutes on each side or until pancakes are golden, turning to second side when pancakes have bubbly surfaces and edges are slightly dry (see bottom photo, page 316). Serve warm.

Nutrition Facts per pancake: 129 cal., 5 g total fat (1 g sat. fat), 28 mg chol., 232 mg sodium, 18 g carbo., 1 g fiber, 4 g pro. Daily Values: 1% vit. A, 4% vit. C, 7% calcium, 6% iron

MAKING THE PERFECT PANCAKE

Pancakes are easy to make and require no tricky techniques, but a few pointers can only make them better:

- Begin by mixing all of the dry ingredients in a mixing bowl and stirring them until they're well combined. Beat eggs and other liquid ingredients in a separate bowl.
- Great pancakes spring from a griddle or skillet that heats evenly and is lightly greased. Put a small amount of shortening on a pastry brush or paper towel and rub it across the griddle surface before heating. Or, give the cold pan a quick spray with nonstick spray coating. If your griddle or skillet has a nonstick surface, it may not be necessary to grease it.

- Test the griddle for readiness by dripping a few drops of water on it. If the water dances over the surface, the griddle is ready.
- Don't crowd your griddle; pancakes will cook better and look better if they don't run together.
- Pancakes are ready to flip when the undersides are golden brown (use the edge of a thin spatula to check) and the top surfaces are covered evenly with tiny, unbroken bubbles (see bottom photo, page 316).
- Pancakes are best piping hot—so keep the first batches warm in a 300° oven while you cook the rest. Loosely cover with aluminum foil.

GERMAN APPLE PANCAKE

Prep: 20 minutes Bake: 20 minutes
Makes: 4 servings Oven: 400°

½ of a 12-ounce package (6 links)
  skinless pork sausage links
3 eggs
½ cup milk
2 tablespoons cooking oil
¼ cup all-purpose flour
¼ cup whole wheat flour
  or all-purpose flour
½ teaspoon apple pie spice
¼ teaspoon salt
1 tablespoon butter
2 tablespoons brown sugar
2 teaspoons cornstarch
½ teaspoon apple pie spice
½ cup apple cider or apple juice
1 tablespoon lemon juice
2 medium cooking apples, cored and
  thinly sliced
¼ cup broken walnuts, toasted
  (optional) (see tip, page 247)

1 **In medium skillet** cook sausage links according to package directions. Drain on paper towels.

2 **For batter,** in a medium mixing bowl combine eggs, milk, and oil. Beat with a wire whisk or rotary beater until combined. Add all-purpose flour, whole wheat flour, ½ teaspoon apple pie spice, and the salt. Beat until smooth.

3 **Place butter** in a 10-inch ovenproof skillet. Place in a 400° oven for 3 to 5 minutes or until butter melts.

4 **Pour the batter** into hot skillet. Bake for 15 minutes. Prick the center area of pancake with tines of fork; bake about 5 minutes more or until puffed and golden.

5 **Meanwhile, for sauce,** in a medium saucepan combine brown sugar, cornstarch, and ½ teaspoon apple pie spice. Add apple cider or juice and lemon juice. Cook and stir until thickened and bubbly. Add apple slices. Cook and stir gently for 3 to 4 minutes or until apples are just tender. Thinly slice sausage links; stir into apple mixture. If desired, stir in nuts. Heat through.

6 **To serve, transfer pancake** to a warm serving plate. Spoon sauce onto top center of pancake. Cut into wedges. Serve immediately.

Nutrition Facts per serving: 358 cal., 21 g total fat (10 g sat. fat), 209 mg chol., 488 mg sodium, 33 g carbo., 3 g fiber, 12 g pro. Daily Values: 12% vit. A, 9% vit. C, 7% calcium, 13% iron

NATIVE-GRAIN
HOTCAKES

Prep: 15 minutes   **Cook:** 2 minutes per batch
Makes: 6 to 8 (5-inch) pancakes

The toasty flavor of buckwheat and the crunch of cornmeal enliven these healthful hotcakes.

    1 cup buckwheat flour
    ¼ cup all-purpose flour
    ¼ cup yellow cornmeal
    1 teaspoon baking powder
    ½ teaspoon salt
    ¼ teaspoon baking soda
    2 beaten eggs
    1½ cups buttermilk or sour milk
    2 tablespoons honey
    1 tablespoon cooking oil
    1¼ cups maple syrup
    ½ cup fresh cranberries

1 **In a mixing bowl** combine buckwheat flour, all-purpose flour, cornmeal, baking powder, salt, and baking soda. Combine eggs, buttermilk, honey, and oil. Add egg mixture all at once to dry mixture. Stir just until moistened (batter should be lumpy).

2 **For each hotcake,** pour about ⅓ cup batter onto hot, lightly greased griddle or heavy skillet (see top photo, page 316). Cook over medium heat for 1 to 2 minutes on each side or until golden, turning to cook second side when hotcakes have bubbly surfaces and edges are slightly dry (see bottom photo, page 316).

3 **Meanwhile, in a saucepan** heat maple syrup with cranberries over medium-high heat about 8 minutes or until berries begin to pop. Serve hotcakes with cranberry mixture.

Nutrition Facts per hotcake with 1 tablespoon berry mixture: 249 cal., 5 g total fat (1 g sat. fat), 73 mg chol., 375 mg sodium, 45 g carbo., 3 g fiber, 8 g pro. Daily Values: 4% vit. A, 0% vit. C, 12% calcium, 12% iron

Native-Grain Hotcakes: Two Native American products—sweet maple syrup and tart fresh cranberries—come together to make a fitting topping for these earthy griddlecakes that feature a native grain, corn.

LEMONY RICOTTA PANCAKES

Prep: 15 minutes
Cook: 4 minutes per batch
Makes: 6 or 7 (5-inch) pancakes

Slather strawberry jam or preserves over these delicate pancakes—it complements the subtle lemon flavor.

  ¾ **cup all-purpose flour**
  1 **teaspoon baking powder**
  ½ **teaspoon salt**
  ½ **teaspoon ground nutmeg**
  2 **beaten eggs**
  1 **cup ricotta cheese**
  ½ **cup milk**
  1 **tablespoon sugar**
  ½ **teaspoon finely shredded lemon
      peel**
  1 **teaspoon lemon juice**

1 **In a large mixing bowl** combine flour, baking powder, salt, and nutmeg; set aside. In a medium mixing bowl combine the eggs and ricotta cheese. Stir in the milk, sugar, lemon peel, and lemon juice. Add egg mixture all at once to dry mixture; stir just until combined.

2 **For each pancake,** pour about ⅓ cup batter onto a hot, lightly greased griddle or heavy skillet (see top photo, page 316). Spread the batter into a 5-inch circle. Cook about 2 minutes on each side or until golden, turning to cook second sides when pancakes have bubbly surfaces and edges are slightly dry (see bottom photo, page 316).

Nutrition Facts per pancake: 154 cal., 6 g total fat
(3 g sat. fat), 85 mg chol., 321 mg sodium,
17 g carbo., 0 g fiber, 9 g pro. Daily Values: 9% vit. A,
1% vit. C, 17% calcium, 7% iron

WAFFLES

Prep: 20 minutes **Bake:** per waffle iron directions
Makes: 12 to 16 (4-inch) waffles

You can bake this batter in a regular waffle iron as well as a Belgian waffle iron.

  1¾ **cups all-purpose flour**
  1 **tablespoon baking powder**
  ¼ **teaspoon salt**
  2 **egg yolks**
  1¾ **cups milk**
  ½ **cup cooking oil**
  2 **egg whites**

1 **In a medium mixing bowl** combine flour, baking powder, and salt. Make a well in center of dry mixture; set aside.

2 **In another medium mixing bowl** beat egg yolks slightly. Stir in milk and oil. Add egg yolk mixture all at once to the dry mixture. Stir just until moistened (batter should be lumpy).

3 **In a small mixing bowl** beat egg whites until stiff peaks form (tips stand straight). Gently fold beaten egg whites into batter, leaving a few fluffs of egg white. Do not overmix.

4 **Pour 1 to 1¼ cups** batter onto grids of a preheated, lightly greased waffle iron. Close lid quickly; do not open until done. Bake according to manufacturer's directions. When done, use a fork to lift waffle off grid. Repeat with remaining batter. Serve warm.

Nutrition Facts per waffle: 172 cal., 11 g total fat
(2 g sat. fat), 38 mg chol., 164 mg sodium,
15 g carbo., 0 g fiber, 4 g pro. Daily Values: 7% vit. A,
0% vit. C, 11% calcium, 6% iron

Easy Waffles: Prepare as above, except do notseparate eggs. In a mixing bowl beat whole eggs slightly. Beat in milk and oil. Add egg mixture all at once to dry mixture. Stir just until moistened (batter should be lumpy).

Buttermilk Waffles: Prepare as above, except reduce baking powder to 1 teaspoon and add ½ teaspoon baking soda. Substitute 2 cups buttermilk or sour milk (see tip, page 329) for milk.

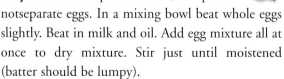

WONDERFUL WAFFLES

There's a little more to the difference between pancakes and waffles than just the way they look. Waffle batter is usually a little higher in fat than pancake batter and often has beaten egg whites folded into it, making for a little lighter texture.

Waffle bakers come in round, square—even heart-shapes. They can be electric or designed for use on top of the range, with regular or nonstick surfaces.

Heating an electric waffle iron is easy—most have a built-in thermostat that heats the unit to a predetermined temperature and signals when it's ready to use (and when your waffles are ready, too).

Because of the grids on waffle irons, the best way to grease them is with a light coating of nonstick spray before you turn the unit on.

While your waffles are underway, keep the ones you've already made warm until serving time by arranging them in a single layer on a wire rack. Set the rack atop a baking sheet and place it in a 300° oven. If you stack freshly baked waffles, they'll get soggy.

GINGERBREAD WAFFLES

Prep: 15 minutes
Bake: per waffle iron directions
Makes: 12 to 16 (4-inch) waffles

Spice-scented waffles and a lively Citrus Sauce team up for a memorable breakfast or holiday brunch treat.

>   1 cup all-purpose flour
>   ¾ cup whole wheat flour
>   1 tablespoon baking powder
>   ½ teaspoon salt
>   ½ teaspoon ground cinnamon
>   ¼ teaspoon ground ginger
>   ⅛ teaspoon ground cloves
>   2 beaten eggs
>   1¾ cups milk
>   ½ cup cooking oil
>   2 tablespoons molasses
>   1 recipe Citrus Sauce (see right)

1 In a mixing bowl combine all-purpose flour, whole wheat flour, baking powder, salt, cinnamon, ginger, and cloves; set aside. In another mixing bowl combine eggs, milk, oil, and molasses. Add egg mixture all at once to dry mixture. Stir just until moistened (batter should be lumpy).

2 Pour 1 to 1¼ cups batter onto grids of a preheated, lightly greased waffle iron. Close lid quickly; do not open until done. Bake according to manufacturer's directions. When done, use a fork to lift waffle off grid. Repeat with remaining batter. Serve with Citrus Sauce.

Citrus Sauce: In a saucepan combine ¾ cup sugar and 2 tablespoons cornstarch. Stir in 1 cup water, ¾ cup orange juice, and ¼ cup lemon juice. Cook and stir over medium heat until thickened and bubbly. Cook and stir 2 minutes more. Remove from heat. Stir in 2 tablespoons butter, 2 teaspoons finely shredded lemon peel, and 2 teaspoons finely shredded orange peel. Serve warm. (Store leftover sauce in refrigerator.)

Nutrition Facts per waffle with about 3 tablespoons sauce: 259 cal., 13 g fat (3 g sat. fat), 43 mg chol., 229 mg sodium, 33 g carbo., 1 g fiber, 4 g pro. Daily Values: 5% vit. A, 18% vit. C, 12% calcium, 8% iron

THREE-GRAIN WAFFLES

Prep: 20 minutes **Chill:** at least 2 hours
Bake: per waffle iron directions
Makes: 12 to 16 (4-inch) waffles

1¼ **cups all-purpose flour**
  1 **cup yellow cornmeal**
  ½ **cup oat bran**
  ¼ **cup sugar**
  1 **package active dry yeast**
  ½ **teaspoon salt**
1¾ **cups milk**
  2 **eggs**
  ⅓ **cup cooking oil**
  1 **teaspoon vanilla**
  1 **recipe Double-Fruit Syrup**
    (optional) (see below)

1 In a large mixing bowl combine the flour, cornmeal, oat bran, sugar, yeast, and salt. Add milk, eggs, oil, and vanilla. Beat with an electric mixer on medium speed about 1 minute or until the batter is thoroughly combined. Cover batter loosely and chill in the refrigerator for 2 to 24 hours or until mixture is bubbly and slightly thickened.

2 Before using, allow batter to stand at room temperature for 1 hour. (Or, to make the waffles without chilling, cover and let mixture stand for 1 hour at room temperature or until bubbly and slightly thickened.)

3 To bake waffles, stir batter. Pour 1 to 1¼ cups batter onto grids of a preheated, lightly greased waffle iron. Close lid quickly; do not open until done. Bake according to manufacturer's directions. When done, use a fork to lift waffle off grid. Repeat with remaining batter. Serve warm. If desired, serve with Double-Fruit Syrup.

Nutrition Facts per waffle: 198 cal., 8 g total fat (2 g sat. fat), 38 mg chol., 118 mg sodium, 27 g carbo., 2 g fiber, 5 g pro. Daily Values: 4% vit. A, 0% vit. C, 4% calcium, 9% iron

Double-Fruit Syrup: In a saucepan stir together 1 cup apricot nectar or orange juice, ⅓ cup coarsely snipped dried apricots, 2 to 3 tablespoons honey, and 2 teaspoons cornstarch. Cook and stir until thickened and bubbly; cook and stir for 2 minutes more. Gently stir in 1 cup sliced fresh strawberries; heat through.

OVERNIGHT BELGIAN WAFFLES

Prep: 15 minutes **Chill:** at least 8 hours
Bake: per waffle iron directions
Makes: 9 (6-inch) waffles

 ½ **cup warm water (105° to 115°)**
  1 **package active dry yeast**
  1 **teaspoon sugar**
  2 **cups milk**
  ⅓ **cup butter, melted and cooled**
  2 **eggs**
  1 **teaspoon sugar**
  ¾ **teaspoon salt**
  2 **cups all-purpose flour**
    Nonstick spray coating

1 In large mixing bowl combine water, yeast, and 1 teaspoon sugar. Let stand for 5 minutes or until foamy. Stir in milk, butter, eggs, 1 teaspoon sugar, and salt. Stir in flour until well mixed. Cover and chill in the refrigerator for 8 hours or overnight (batter will be thin).

2 To bake waffles, spray a Belgian waffle iron with nonstick coating. Add batter and bake according to manufacturer's directions. Serve warm.

Nutrition Facts per waffle: 202 cal., 9 g total fat (5 g sat. fat), 70 mg chol., 288 mg sodium, 23 g carbo., 1 g fiber, 6 g pro. Daily Values: 11% vit. A, 0% vit. C, 6% calcium, 10% iron

---

THIS WAFFLE SPEAKS FLEMISH

A waffle by any other name is still a waffle—it just may be Belgian. The main difference between a Belgian waffle and a standard waffle is its appearance: Belgian waffles are thick and have very large, deep grids or pockets—the better to hold the toppings. A special waffle iron is required to make Belgian waffles, which often are served for dessert.

Fresh berries and whipped cream are the traditional toppings, but the sky's the limit. Consider lemon curd, cooked apples or bananas, jam, or flavored yogurt.

muffins, biscuits,
and scores

English Tea Scones, recipe page 240

MUFFINS, BISCUITS, AND SCONES

MUFFINS

Prep: 15 minutes Bake: 20 minutes
Makes: 10 to 12 muffins Oven: 400°

*With just a twist or two, sweet and savory
muffins are as fitting with your favorite entrée
at dinner as they are with morning coffee.*

1¾ **cups all-purpose flour**
 ⅓ **cup sugar**
 2 **teaspoons baking powder**
 ¼ **teaspoon salt**
 1 **beaten egg**
 ¾ **cup milk**
 ¼ **cup cooking oil**

1 Grease twelve 2½-inch muffin cups or line with
paper bake cups; set aside. In a medium mixing
bowl combine flour, sugar, baking powder, and salt.
Make a well in center of dry mixture; set aside.

2 In another mixing bowl combine egg, milk,
and oil. Add the egg mixture all at once to the
dry mixture (see photo, top right). Stir just
until moistened (batter should be lumpy) (see
photo, above right).

3 Spoon batter into prepared muffin cups,
filling each two-thirds full. Bake in a 400° oven
about 20 minutes or until golden. Cool in muffin
cups on a wire rack for 5 minutes. Remove from
muffin cups; serve warm.

Nutrition Facts per muffin: 164 cal., 6 g total fat (1 g
sat. fat), 23 mg chol., 142 mg sodium, 23 g carbo.,
1 g fiber, 3 g pro. Daily Values: 2% vit. A, 0% vit. C,
7% calcium, 7% iron

Banana Muffins: Prepare as above, except do not
use paper bake cups. Reduce milk to ½ cup. Add
¾ cup mashed banana and ½ cup chopped nuts to
the dry mixture with the egg mixture.

Buttermilk Muffins: Prepare as above, except add
¼ teaspoon baking soda to dry mixture and
substitute buttermilk or sour milk for the milk (see
tip, page 329).

Cheese Muffins: Prepare as above, except stir ½ cup
shredded cheddar or Monterey Jack cheese
(2 ounces) into dry mixture.

Use the back of a wooden spoon to make a well in the center of the dry mixture. Carefully pour liquid mixture into dry mixture all at once.

Using a wooden spoon, stir batter just until ingredients are moistened. Overmixing the batter can cause peaks, tunnels, and a tough texture.

Cranberry Muffins: Prepare as at left, except combine 1 cup coarsely chopped cranberries and 2 tablespoons additional sugar. Fold into batter.

Oatmeal Muffins: Prepare as at left, except reduce flour to 1⅓ cups and add ¾ cup rolled oats to dry mixture.

Poppy Seed Muffins: Prepare as at left, except increase sugar to ½ cup and add 1 tablespoon poppy seed to dry mixture.

A GEM OF A QUICK-BREAD

In the mid-19th century, a special baking pan for muffins was introduced to undoubtedly receptive home cooks. This early pan was an arrangement of iron or tin "gem" cups fastened together by a rack (similar to the set-up of modern-day popover pans). To this day, muffins are called gems in many parts of the country.

SOUR CREAM-CHERRY MUFFINS

Prep: 20 minutes **Bake:** 12 minutes
Makes: 36 muffins **Oven:** 400°

Perfect for teatime, these sweet and diminutive gems are just the right size for nibbling.

  2 **cups all-purpose flour**
  ½ **cup granulated sugar**
  2 **teaspoons baking powder**
  ¼ **teaspoon salt**
  2 **beaten eggs**
  ½ **cup dairy sour cream**
  ½ **cup milk**
  ¼ **cup cooking oil**
  ½ **teaspoon finely shredded lemon peel**
  ¼ **teaspoon almond extract**
  1 **cup dried tart cherries, coarsely chopped**
  ½ **cup chopped almonds**
  1 **recipe Lemon Glaze (see below)**

1 Grease thirty-six 1¾-inch muffin cups or line with miniature paper bake cups; set aside. In a large mixing bowl combine flour, granulated sugar, baking powder, and salt. Make a well in the center of the dry mixture; set aside.

2 In a medium mixing bowl combine eggs, sour cream, milk, oil, lemon peel, and almond extract. Add egg mixture all at once to dry mixture (see top photo, page 325). Stir just until moistened (batter should be lumpy) (see bottom photo, page 325). Fold in dried cherries and almonds.

3 Spoon batter into prepared muffin cups, dividing batter evenly (cups will be full). Bake in a 400° oven for 12 to 15 minutes or until golden. Cool in muffin cups on a wire rack for 5 minutes. Remove from cups. Brush with Lemon Glaze.

Lemon Glaze: Stir together ¾ cup sifted powdered sugar, 2 teaspoons lemon juice, and enough water (2 to 3 teaspoons) to make glazing consistency.

Nutrition Facts per muffin: 82 cal., 4 g total fat (1 g sat. fat), 14 mg chol., 42 mg sodium, 11 g carbo., 0 g fiber, 2 g pro. Daily Values: 3% vit. A, 0% vit. C, 2% calcium, 2% iron

PUMPKIN-PRALINE MUFFINS

BEST-LOVED

Prep: 20 minutes **Bake:** 20 minutes
Makes: 12 to 14 muffins **Oven:** 375°

A favorite of Better Homes and Gardens® editors, these are sure to become a favorite of yours, too.

  ⅓ **cup packed brown sugar**
  2 **tablespoons dairy sour cream**
  ⅔ **cup chopped pecans**
  2 **cups all-purpose flour**
  2 **teaspoons baking powder**
  1 **teaspoon ground cinnamon**
  ½ **teaspoon baking soda**
  ¼ **teaspoon salt**
  ¼ **teaspoon ground nutmeg**
  ⅛ **teaspoon ground cloves**
  1 **beaten egg**
  ¾ **cup buttermilk or sour milk (see tip, page 329)**
  ¾ **cup canned pumpkin**
  ⅔ **cup packed brown sugar**
  ⅓ **cup butter, melted**

1 Grease twelve to fourteen 2½-inch muffin cups or line with paper bake cups; set aside. In a small mixing bowl stir together the ⅓ cup brown sugar and sour cream; stir in pecans. Set aside.

2 In medium mixing bowl combine flour, baking powder, cinnamon, baking soda, salt, nutmeg, and cloves. Make well in center of dry mixture.

3 In another medium mixing bowl combine egg, buttermilk, pumpkin, the ⅔ cup brown sugar, and melted butter. Add pumpkin mixture all at once to the dry mixture (see top photo, page 325). Stir just until moistened (batter should be lumpy) (see bottom photo, page 325).

4 Spoon batter into prepared muffin cups, filling each almost full. Spoon about 2 teaspoons of the pecan mixture on top of each muffin. Bake in a 375° oven for 20 to 25 minutes or until done. Cool in muffin cups on a wire rack for 5 minutes. Remove from muffin cups; serve warm.

Nutrition Facts per muffin: 234 cal., 10 g total fat (4 g sat. fat), 33 mg chol., 237 mg sodium, 33 g carbo., 1 g fiber, 4 g pro. Daily Values: 40% vit. A, 1% vit. C, 8% calcium, 12% iron

Pumpkin-Praline Muffins (top) and Peach-Brown Sugar Muffins: Whatever the weather, there are muffins to suit the season. In the fall, warm up with the pumpkin-spice variety. In summer, take advantage of the peak of peach season by baking a batch of Peach-Brown Sugar Muffins with sweet, juicy, fresh peaches.

PEACH-BROWN SUGAR MUFFINS

Prep: 20 minutes   **Bake:** 20 minutes
Makes: 16 muffins   **Oven:** 400°

Rich with sour cream, this crunchy-topped muffin has been an editor's choice since 1982 when it was in a Better Homes and Gardens® magazine story about farm-fresh recipes.

    2 **cups all-purpose flour**
    2 **teaspoons baking powder**
  ¾ **teaspoon salt**
  ¼ **teaspoon baking soda**
  ¼ **teaspoon ground allspice**
    1 **beaten egg**
    1 **8-ounce carton dairy sour cream**
  ⅓ **cup packed brown sugar**
  ⅓ **cup milk**
  ¼ **cup cooking oil**
    1 **cup chopped peeled fresh, frozen, or canned peaches**
    1 **recipe Streusel Topping (see right)**

1 **Grease sixteen** 2½-inch muffin cups; set aside. In a medium mixing bowl combine flour, baking powder, salt, baking soda, and allspice. Make well in center of dry mixture; set aside. In another bowl combine egg, sour cream, brown sugar, milk, and oil; stir in peaches. Add peach mixture all at once to dry mixture (see top photo, page 325). Stir just until moistened (batter should be lumpy) (see bottom photo, page 325).

2 **Spoon batter into prepared** muffin cups, filling each two-thirds full. Sprinkle batter with Streusel Topping. Bake in a 400° oven for 20 to 25 minutes or until a wooden toothpick inserted in center comes out clean. Cool 5 minutes in muffin cups; serve warm.

Streusel Topping: Mix 3 tablespoons all-purpose flour, 3 tablespoons brown sugar, and ¼ teaspoon cinnamon; cut in 4 teaspoons butter until mixture resembles coarse crumbs.

Nutrition Facts per muffin: 160 cal., 8 g total fat (3 g sat. fat), 23 mg chol., 191 mg sodium, 20 g carbo., 1 g fiber, 3 g pro. Daily Values: 5% vit. A, 1% vit. C, 6% calcium, 6% iron

Giant Blueberry Muffins: There's nothing better than a fresh-baked blueberry muffin with your favorite cup of coffee or tea.

GIANT BLUEBERRY
MUFFINS

Prep: 15 minutes   Bake: 35 minutes
Makes: 6 giant muffins   Oven: 350°

If you prefer your muffins to be a modest size, spoon the batter into twelve 2½-inch muffin cups and bake in a 375° oven about 20 minutes or until golden.

　2　**cups all-purpose flour**
　¾　**cup granulated sugar**
2½　**teaspoons baking powder**
　½　**teaspoon salt**
　2　**beaten eggs**
　¾　**cup milk**
　½　**cup melted butter or cooking oil**
　1　**tablespoon finely shredded orange peel**
　1　**cup fresh or frozen blueberries, thawed**
　　Coarse sugar (optional)

1 **Grease six** 3½-inch muffin cups. Set muffin cups aside.

2 **In a medium mixing bowl** combine flour, granulated sugar, baking powder, and salt. Make a well in the center of dry mixture; set aside.

3 **In another medium mixing bowl** combine eggs, milk, butter or oil, and orange peel. Add egg mixture all at once to the dry mixture (see top photo, page 325). Stir just until moistened (batter should be lumpy) (see bottom photo, page 325). Fold in blueberries.

4 **Spoon batter into prepared** muffin cups, filling each almost full. If desired, sprinkle tops with coarse sugar. Bake in a 350° oven about 35 minutes or until golden. Cool in muffin cups on a wire rack for 5 minutes. Remove from muffin cups; serve warm.

Nutrition Facts per muffin: 425 cal., 18 g total fat (10 g sat. fat), 114 mg chol., 522 mg sodium, 60 g carbo., 2 g fiber, 7 g pro. Daily Values: 19% vit. A, 8% vit. C, 16% calcium, 15% iron

SIZING UP MUFFINS

Muffin cups come in all shapes and sizes, from bite-size minis to standard 2½-inch cups to Texas-size mega-muffins. You'll need to adjust the baking time according to the pan you choose. Mini-muffins will bake about 8 minutes less than standard-size muffins. For jumbo muffins, lower the oven temperature to 350° and bake for about 30 minutes.

Some muffin-lovers like their muffins to be all tops—and there's a special pan for that, too. Muffin-top or muffin-crown pans make flat muffin rounds. Look for these pans in specialty cookware stores or department stores. Bake muffin tops about 10 minutes less than regular-size muffins.

APPLESAUCE-RHUBARB MUFFINS

Prep: 20 minutes   Bake: 18 minutes
Makes: 24 muffins   Oven: 400°

- **2 cups all-purpose flour**
- **1 cup whole wheat flour**
- **2 teaspoons baking powder**
- **2 teaspoons ground cinnamon**
- **½ teaspoon baking soda**
- **½ teaspoon salt**
- **2 beaten eggs**
- **1⅓ cups packed brown sugar**
- **1⅓ cups applesauce**
- **½ cup cooking oil**
- **1½ cups chopped rhubarb**
   Crumbled sugar cubes or cinnamon-sugar

1 **Lightly grease twenty-four** 2½-inch muffin cups or line with paper bake cups.

2 **In a large mixing bowl** combine all-purpose flour, whole wheat flour, baking powder, cinnamon, baking soda, and salt. Make a well in the center; set aside.

3 **In a medium mixing bowl** combine eggs, brown sugar, applesauce, and cooking oil. Add egg mixture all at once to dry mixture (see top photo, page 325). Stir just until moistened (batter should be lumpy) (see bottom photo, page 325). Fold in rhubarb.

4 **Spoon batter into prepared** muffin cups, filling each two-thirds full. Sprinkle with crumbled sugar cubes or cinnamon-sugar. Bake in a 400° oven for 18 to 20 minutes or until a wooden toothpick inserted in center comes out clean. Cool in muffin cups on a wire rack for 5 minutes. Remove from muffin cups; serve warm.

Nutrition Facts per muffin: 361 cal., 13 g total fat (2 g sat. fat), 43 mg chol., 265 mg sodium, 59 g carbo., 3 g fiber, 6 g pro. Daily Values: 2% vit. A, 3% vit. C, 10% calcium, 17% iron

MAKING SOUR MILK

Q Can regular milk be substituted for buttermilk in a recipe in the same amount?

A No—but there's a quick and easy way to make sour milk, which can be a substitute. For each cup of sour milk, place 1 tablespoon lemon juice or vinegar in a glass measuring cup; add enough milk to make 1 cup total liquid. Let the mixture stand 5 minutes before using it in your recipe.

WHEAT BRAN **MUFFINS**

Prep: 20 minutes **Bake:** 20 minutes
Makes: 12 muffins **Oven:** 400°

*There's nutty, delicious whole-wheat flavor in
every healthful bite of these fruit-filled muffins,
made moist with applesauce.*

    Nonstick spray coating
1¼ cups wheat bran or oat bran*
 1 cup all-purpose flour
 2 teaspoons baking powder
 ¼ teaspoon baking soda
 ¼ teaspoon salt
 ¾ cup applesauce
 ½ cup skim milk
 ⅓ cup honey
 ¼ cup refrigerated egg product or
      frozen egg product, thawed
 1 tablespoon cooking oil
 ½ cup raisins, snipped dried apricots,
      or snipped dried apples

1 Spray bottoms of twelve 2½-inch muffin cups
with nonstick coating; set aside. In a mixing
bowl combine wheat or oat bran, flour, baking
powder, baking soda, and salt. Make a well in the
center of the dry mixture; set aside.

2 In another bowl combine applesauce, milk,
honey, egg product, and oil. Add milk mixture
all at once to dry mixture (see top photo, page 325).
Stir just until moistened (batter should be lumpy)
(see bottom photo, page 325). Fold in raisins.

3 Spoon batter into prepared muffin cups,
filling each two-thirds full. Bake in a 400° oven
about 20 minutes or until golden. Cool on wire rack
5 minutes. Remove from muffin cups; serve warm.

*Note: If using oat bran, be sure it's 100% oat bran
with no added ingredients. If oat bran isn't
available, place 1⅓ cups rolled oats in a food
processor bowl or blender container; process until
oats are the consistency of flour. (You should have
about 1 cup.)

Nutrition facts per muffin: 126 cal., 2 g total fat (0 g
sat. fat), 0 mg chol., 148 mg sodium, 28 g carbo., 2 g
fiber, 4 g pro. Daily Values: 1% vit. A, 0% vit. C, 6%
calcium, 10% iron

SMOKED CHEDDAR **MUFFINS**

Prep: 20 minutes **Bake:** 12 minutes
Makes: 12 muffins **Oven:** 425°

*Match the topping of these savory muffins to the
tastes and textures of what you serve them with.*

 1 cup all-purpose flour
 1 cup yellow cornmeal
 ¼ cup sugar
 1 tablespoon baking powder
 ¼ teaspoon salt
 ¼ to ½ teaspoon ground red pepper
 2 beaten eggs
 1 cup milk
 ¼ cup butter, melted
 1 cup shredded smoked cheddar
      cheese (4 ounces)
    Desired toppings, such as sunflower
      seeds, pine nuts, additional
      smoked cheddar cheese, poppy
      seed, sesame seed, or roasted
      red pepper strips

1 Grease twelve 2½-inch muffin cups; set aside.
In a medium mixing bowl combine flour,
cornmeal, sugar, baking powder, salt, and ground
red pepper. Make a well in the center; set aside.

2 In another mixing bowl combine eggs, milk,
and melted butter. Add the egg mixture all at
once to the dry mixture (see top photo, page 325).
Add the 1 cup shredded cheese and stir just until
batter is smooth (do not overbeat).

3 Spoon batter into prepared muffin cups,
filling cups almost full. Sprinkle desired
topping(s) over muffins. Bake in a 425° oven for
12 to 15 minutes or until golden. Cool in muffin
cups on a wire rack for 5 minutes. Remove from
muffin cups; serve warm.

Nutrition Facts per muffin: 193 cal., 9 g total fat (3 g
sat. fat), 47 mg chol., 260 mg sodium, 22 g carbo.,
1 g fiber, 6 g pro. Daily Values: 11% vit. A, 0% vit. C,
15% calcium, 8% iron

Smoked Cheddar Muffins: Try these tender, smoky muffins with your favorite steak, chicken, or fish dish at dinner—or with the perfect omelet or egg casserole at brunch.

Tomato-Rosemary Muffins: Perfect with your favorite pasta or with antipasto and before-dinner drinks, these muffins spiked with tomato sauce, Parmesan cheese, and rosemary have a decidedly Italian accent.

TOMATO-ROSEMARY
MUFFINS

Prep: 20 minutes   Bake: 15 minutes
Makes: 36 mini muffins   Oven: 350°

1¾ cups all-purpose flour
⅓ cup grated Parmesan cheese
2 tablespoons sugar
2 teaspoons baking powder
½ teaspoon dried rosemary, crushed
¼ teaspoon baking soda
⅛ teaspoon garlic powder
⅛ teaspoon pepper
1 beaten egg

½ cup milk
½ cup tomato sauce
⅓ cup olive oil or cooking oil
    Grated Parmesan cheese (optional)

1 Lightly grease thirty-six 1¾-inch muffin cups or grease twelve 2½-inch muffin cups; set aside. In a bowl combine flour, the ⅓ cup Parmesan cheese, sugar, baking powder, rosemary, soda, garlic powder, and pepper. Make a well in center; set aside.

2 In another mixing bowl combine egg, milk, tomato sauce, and oil. Add the egg mixture all at once to the dry mixture (see top photo, page 325). Stir just until moistened (batter should be lumpy) (see bottom photo, page 325).

3 **Spoon batter into prepared** muffin cups, filling each two-thirds full. If desired, sprinkle with additional Parmesan cheese. Bake mini muffins in a 350° oven about 15 minutes or until light brown. (Or, bake regular-size muffins in 350° oven for 20 to 24 minutes or until light brown.) Cool in muffin cups on wire racks for 5 minutes. Remove from muffin cups; serve warm.

Nutrition Facts per mini muffin: 50 cal., 3 g total fat (1 g sat. fat), 7 mg chol., 70 mg sodium, 6 g carbo., 0 g fiber, 1 g pro. Daily Values: 1% vit. A, 0% vit. C, 3% calcium, 2% iron

FRUIT AND HONEY-BRAN MUFFINS

LOW-FAT

Prep: 20 minutes   **Bake:** 15 minutes
Makes: 14 to 16 muffins   **Oven:** 400°

Fresh-baked muffins are at your fingertips anytime with this make-ahead batter.

1½ **cups all-purpose flour**
  1 **cup whole bran cereal**
  ¼ **cup packed brown sugar**
  1 **tablespoon baking powder**
  1 **teaspoon ground cinnamon**
  ¼ **teaspoon salt**

  1 **beaten egg**
1¼ **cups milk**
  ¼ **cup honey**
  ¼ **cup cooking oil**
  ½ **cup raisins or chopped dried fruit
      (apricots, dates, figs, cherries,
      blueberries, or cranberries)**

1 **In a medium mixing bowl** combine flour, cereal, brown sugar, baking powder, cinnamon, and salt. Make well in center of dry mixture; set aside.

2 **In another bowl** combine egg, milk, honey, and oil. Add egg mixture all at once to dry mixture (see top photo, page 325). Stir just until moistened (the batter will be lumpy) (see bottom photo, page 325). Fold in raisins or dried fruit. Store in a covered container in refrigerator for up to 3 days.

3 **To bake,** gently stir batter. Grease desired number of 2½-inch muffin cups or line with paper bake cups. Spoon batter into prepared muffin cups, filling each two-thirds full. Bake in 400° oven for 15 to 20 minutes or until golden. Cool in muffin cups on a wire rack 5 minutes; serve warm.

Nutrition Facts per muffin: 148 cal., 5 g total fat (1 g sat. fat), 17 mg chol., 166 mg sodium, 26 g carbo., 2 g fiber, 3 g pro. Daily Values: 2% vit. A, 8% vit. C, 9% calcium, 10% iron

MUFFINS 101

A basket of warm, fresh-baked muffins on the table is eminently satisfying. Here are a few pointers to make them the best they can be:

- "Ledges on the edges" are those unwanted rims around the edges of your muffins. To get nicely domed muffins without ledges, grease the muffin cups on the bottoms and only halfway up the sides.
- After adding the liquid mixture to the flour mixture, stir just until moistened (see bottom photo, page 325). If you try to stir out all the lumps, your muffins will have peaks, tunnels, and a tough texture.
- Once the batter is mixed, put the muffins in the preheated oven right away. Batters that use baking powder and baking soda need to be baked immediately so the leavening power is not lost.

- Muffins are done when their tops are golden.
- To avoid soggy muffins, cool them in the baking pan only as long as directed in the recipe.
- To store muffins, place them in a plastic bag, seal, and store at room temperature for up to 3 days.
- To freeze muffins, wrap them tightly in heavy foil or place them in freezer bags and freeze for up to 3 months. To reheat frozen muffins, wrap them in heavy foil. Heat them in a 300° oven for 12 to 15 minutes for 1¾-inch muffins; 15 to 18 minutes for 2½-inch muffins; and 25 to 30 minutes for jumbo-size muffins.

Best-Ever Buttermilk Biscuits: This recipe is basic and indispensable. Brighten your family's morning with fresh-from-the-oven biscuits slathered with marmalade, jam, or honey butter.

CHEESE 'N' JALAPEÑO
CORN MUFFINS

Prep: 20 minutes **Bake:** 20 minutes
Makes: 10 to 12 muffins **Oven:** 400°

If you like your muffins fresh and hot in more ways than one, make these muffins with the ground red pepper and the chili peppers.

    1 cup all-purpose flour
    ¾ cup yellow cornmeal
    3 tablespoons sugar
   2½ teaspoons baking powder
    ¼ teaspoon salt
    ⅛ teaspoon ground red pepper
       (optional)
    1 beaten egg
    ¾ cup milk
    ⅓ cup cooking oil
    ½ cup shredded cheddar or Monterey
       Jack cheese (2 ounces)
    2 tablespoons canned chopped
       jalapeño or green chili peppers

1 **Grease twelve** 2½-inch muffin cups; set aside. In a medium mixing bowl combine flour, cornmeal, sugar, baking powder, salt, and, if desired, ground red pepper. Make a well in the center of dry ingredients; set aside.

2 **In another medium mixing bowl** combine egg, milk, and oil. Add egg mixture all at once to the dry mixture (see top photo, page 325). Stir just until moistened (batter should be lumpy) (see bottom photo, page 325). Fold in cheese and chili peppers.

3 **Spoon batter into prepared** muffin cups, filling each two-thirds full. Bake in a 400° oven for 20 to 23 minutes or until golden. Cool in muffin cups on a wire rack for 5 minutes. Remove from muffin cups; serve warm.

Nutrition Facts per muffin: 198 cal., 10 g total fat (3 g sat. fat), 29 mg chol., 195 mg sodium, 22 g carbo., 1 g fiber, 5 g pro. Daily Values: 4% vit. A, 7% vit. C, 12% calcium, 8% iron

BEST-EVER BUTTERMILK BISCUITS

Prep: 15 minutes **Bake:** 10 minutes
Makes: 10 to 12 biscuits **Oven:** 450°

These tender biscuits are as at home split and topped with creamed chicken for dinner as they are spread with butter and jam for breakfast.

> 2 **cups all-purpose flour**
> 1 **tablespoon baking powder**
> 2 **teaspoons sugar**
> ½ **teaspoon cream of tartar**
> ¼ **teaspoon salt**
> ¼ **teaspoon baking soda**
> ½ **cup shortening**
> ⅔ **cup buttermilk**

1 In a medium mixing bowl combine flour, baking powder, sugar, cream of tartar, salt, and baking soda. Using a pastry blender, cut in shortening until mixture resembles coarse crumbs (see top photo, right). Make a well in the center of dry mixture. Add buttermilk all at once to dry mixture. Using a fork, stir just until moistened.

2 Turn dough out onto a lightly floured surface. Quickly knead dough by folding and gently pressing 10 to 12 strokes or until dough is nearly smooth (see bottom photo, right). Pat or lightly roll dough to ½-inch thickness. Cut dough with a floured 2½-inch biscuit cutter, dipping the cutter into flour between cuts.

3 Place biscuits 1 inch apart on an ungreased baking sheet. Bake in a 450° oven for 10 to 12 minutes or until golden. Remove the biscuits from baking sheet; serve warm.

Nutrition Facts per biscuit: 185 cal., 11 g total fat (3 g sat. fat), 1 mg chol., 211 mg sodium, 20 g carbo., 1 g fiber, 3 g pro. Daily Values: 0% vit. A, 0% vit. C, 10% calcium, 8% iron

Use a pastry blender to cut the shortening into the dry mixture. For best results, use a rocking motion to make uniform coarse crumbs.

To knead, fold dough in half toward you. Gently press the two edges together with the heel of your hand. Give dough quarter turn; repeat folding and pressing.

THE BISCUIT OF CHOICE

In this country, even the biscuits have distinguishing accents. Most Northerners prefer a tender, flaky biscuit with large volume. Southerners tend to like a crusty biscuit with a soft, tender, crumbly center that doesn't flake. Southerners also are more likely to add buttermilk or sour milk to their biscuits.

Some of the variance has to do with the kind of flour used. All-purpose flour (made from a combination of soft and hard wheats) contributes to the flakiness of a Northern-style biscuit. Soft-wheat flour is used to produce a Southern-style biscuit.

Across the ocean in the British Isles, a "biscuit" refers not to a small quick bread, but rather to a flat, thin cookie or cracker. The word biscuit comes from the French *bis cuit,* meaning "twice cooked," which is what was done to the original sea biscuits to keep them crisp on long voyages.

LEMON BURST BISCUITS

Prep: 20 minutes **Bake:** 10 minutes
Makes: 10 to 12 biscuits **Oven:** 450°

> **2 cups all-purpose flour**
> **1 tablespoon granulated sugar**
> **2 teaspoons baking powder**
> **2 teaspoons finely shredded lemon peel**
> **¼ teaspoon baking soda**
> **¼ teaspoon salt**
> **½ cup shortening**
> **½ cup buttermilk or sour milk (see tip, page 329)**
> **⅓ cup mayonnaise or salad dressing**
> **1 recipe Lemon Glaze (optional) (see below)**

1 Combine flour, granulated sugar, baking powder, lemon peel, soda, and salt. Using a pastry blender, cut in shortening until mixture resembles coarse crumbs (see top photo, page 335). Make a well in the center of dry mixture.

2 Combine buttermilk and mayonnaise. Add the buttermilk mixture all at once to dry mixture. Using a fork, stir just until moistened.

3 Turn the dough out onto a lightly floured surface. Quickly knead dough by folding and gently pressing for 10 to 12 strokes or until the dough is nearly smooth (see bottom photo, page 335). Pat or lightly roll dough to ½-inch thickness. Cut dough with a floured 2½-inch biscuit cutter, dipping the cutter into flour between cuts.

4 Place biscuits 1 inch apart on an ungreased baking sheet. Bake in a 450° oven for 10 to 12 minutes or until golden. Remove the biscuits from the baking sheet and cool slightly. If desired, drizzle Lemon Glaze over biscuits. Serve warm.

Nutrition Facts per biscuit: 236 cal., 17 g total fat (4 g sat. fat), 3 mg chol., 19 g carbo. 201 mg sodium, 1 g fiber, 3 g pro. Daily Values: 0% vit. A, 0% vit. C, 6% calcium, 7% iron

Lemon Glaze: Stir together 1 cup sifted powdered sugar, 1 tablespoon milk, ½ teaspoon finely shredded lemon peel, and ¼ teaspoon vanilla. Stir in additional milk, 1 teaspoon at a time, until glazing consistency.

SWEET POTATO BISCUITS

LOW-FAT

Prep: 25 minutes **Bake:** 12 minutes
Makes: 12 biscuits **Oven:** 425°

These thyme-scented biscuits are delightful with Southern-style dishes: fried chicken, country ham, and burgoo (stew), to name just a few.

> **2 cups all-purpose flour**
> **2 teaspoons baking powder**
> **2 teaspoons snipped fresh thyme or ½ teaspoon dried thyme, crushed**
> **½ teaspoon baking soda**
> **½ teaspoon salt**
> **¼ cup shortening**
> **1 cup mashed cooked sweet potatoes or mashed canned sweet potatoes**
> **½ cup milk**
> **2 tablespoons brown sugar**

1 In a medium mixing bowl combine flour, baking powder, thyme, soda, and salt. Using a pastry blender, cut in shortening until mixture resembles coarse crumbs (see top photo, page 335). Make a well in the center of dry mixture; set aside.

2 In another medium mixing bowl combine sweet potatoes, milk, and brown sugar. Add sweet potato mixture all at once to dry mixture. Using a fork, stir just until moistened.

3 Turn dough out onto a lightly floured surface. Quickly knead dough by folding and gently pressing dough for 10 to 12 strokes or until dough is nearly smooth (see bottom photo, page 335). Pat or lightly roll dough to ½-inch thickness. Cut dough with a floured 2½-inch round cutter, dipping cutter into flour between cuts.

4 Place biscuits 1 inch apart on an ungreased baking sheet. Bake in a 425° oven for 12 to 15 minutes or until golden. Remove biscuits from baking sheet and serve warm.

Nutrition Facts per biscuit: 149 cal., 5 g total fat (1 g sat. fat), 1 mg chol., 211 mg sodium, 24 g carbo., 1 g fiber, 3 g pro. Daily Values: 47% vit. A, 7% vit. C, 6% calcium, 8% iron

Cottage Cheese-Chive Biscuits: Cottage cheese makes these biscuits moist and a confetti of fresh-snipped chives fills them with flavor. They're the perfect partner for your favorite soup or main-dish salad.

COTTAGE CHEESE-CHIVE
BISCUITS

EASY

Prep: 20 minutes   Bake: 15 minutes
Makes: 12 biscuits   Oven: 425°

Drop-biscuits are a breeze to make, so you can enjoy fresh bread any night of the week.

> 2 **cups all-purpose flour**
> 2½ **teaspoons baking powder**
> ¼ **teaspoon salt**
> 6 **tablespoons butter**
> ¾ **cup small-curd cottage cheese**
> ⅔ **cup milk**
> 2 **tablespoons snipped fresh chives**
>   **or thinly sliced green onion tops**

1 **Line a baking sheet with foil;** grease the foil. Set aside.

2 **In a medium mixing bowl** combine flour, baking powder, and salt. Using a pastry blender, cut in butter until mixture resembles coarse crumbs (see top photo, page 335). Make a well in the center of dry mixture; set aside.

3 **In a small mixing bowl** combine cottage cheese, milk, and chives. Add cottage cheese mixture all at once to dry mixture. Using a fork, stir just until moistened.

4 **Drop dough by generous tablespoonfuls** onto prepared baking sheet. Bake in a 425° oven for 15 to 18 minutes or until golden. Remove from baking sheet; serve warm.

Nutrition Facts per biscuit: 141 cal., 7 g total fat (4 g sat. fat), 18 mg chol., 238 mg sodium, 16 g carbo., 1 g fiber, 4 g pro. Daily Values: 6% vit. A, 0% vit. C, 8% calcium, 6% iron

CRANBERRY-ORANGE
BISCUITS

Prep: 20 minutes   **Bake:** 10 minutes
Makes: 10 biscuits   **Oven:** 450°

Give these festive biscuits holiday flair by cutting them with a star- or tree-shaped cookie cutter.

    2 cups all-purpose flour
    1 tablespoon sugar
    1 tablespoon baking powder
    1 teaspoon finely shredded orange
         peel
    ¼ teaspoon salt
    ¼ teaspoon baking soda
    ½ cup shortening
    ½ cup dried cranberries, finely
         snipped or chopped
    1 8-ounce container orange yogurt
         or vanilla yogurt

1 In a mixing bowl combine flour, sugar, baking powder, orange peel, salt, and soda. Using a pastry blender, cut in shortening until mixture resembles coarse crumbs (see top photo, page 335). Add cranberries; toss until well mixed. Make a well in center of dry mixture. Add yogurt all at once to dry mixture. Using a fork, stir just until moistened.

2 Turn the dough out onto a lightly floured surface. Quickly knead dough by folding and gently pressing dough 10 to 12 strokes or until dough is nearly smooth (see bottom photo, page 335). Pat or lightly roll to ½-inch thickness. Cut with floured 2½-inch biscuit cutter, dipping cutter into flour between cuts.

3 Place biscuits 1 inch apart on an ungreased baking sheet. Bake in a 450° oven for 10 to 12 minutes or until golden. Remove from baking sheet; serve warm.

Nutrition Facts per biscuit: 206 cal., 11 g total fat (3 g sat. fat), 1 mg chol., 207 mg sodium, 24 g carbo., 1 g fiber, 3 g pro. Daily Values: 0% vit. A, 1% vit. C, 11% calcium, 8% iron

BISCUIT AND SCONE BASICS

Light, tender, flaky biscuits and scones are a breeze to make if you follow these basic techniques:

- Stir dry ingredients well to distribute the leavening agent.
- When a recipe calls for butter, make sure it's cold when you begin.
- Mix butter or shortening and flour only until mixture resembles coarse crumbs.
- Stir in the liquid just until moistened.
- Very gently knead the dough by folding and pressing—10 to 12 strokes should be enough to distribute the moisture.
- Cut out as many of the biscuits as possible

from a single rolling of the dough (the second rolling and the additional flour will make them a bit tougher than the first batch).

- Place biscuits and scones close together on the baking sheet for a soft crust; for a crispy crust, place them about 1 inch apart.
- Remove from the oven when top and bottom crusts are an even golden brown.
- Store in a sealed plastic bag at room temperature for 2 or 3 days, or freeze them for up to 3 months.
- Reheat foil-wrapped biscuits or scones in a 300° oven for 10 to 12 minutes; reheat frozen biscuits for 20 to 25 minutes.

Lemon Pepper Biscuit Sticks: Simple enough for every day but special enough for entertaining, these lemony-peppery biscuit sticks are not only delicious with dinner, but before it, too. Pile them high in a linen-lined basket or pretty pot for munching on with pre-dinner drinks.

LEMON PEPPER
BISCUIT STICKS

Prep: 25 minutes Bake: 10 minutes
Makes: 24 biscuit sticks   Oven: 400°

Delicious with fish and perfect with pasta, these biscuit sticks provide a change of pace from traditional garlic bread.

> 2 **cups all-purpose flour**
> 2 **tablespoons sugar**
> 2 **teaspoons baking powder**
> 1 **teaspoon lemon pepper seasoning**
> ¼ **teaspoon baking soda**
> 6 **tablespoons butter**
> 1 **beaten egg**
> ⅓ **cup buttermilk or sour milk**
>   **(see tip, page 329)**
>   **Lemon pepper seasoning (optional)**

1 **In a medium mixing bowl** combine flour, sugar, baking powder, the 1 teaspoon lemon pepper seasoning, and baking soda. Using a pastry blender, cut in butter until mixture resembles coarse crumbs (see top photo, page 335). Make a well in the center of dry mixture; set aside.

2 **In a small mixing bowl** combine egg and buttermilk. Add the egg mixture all at once to dry mixture. Using a fork, stir just until moistened.

3 **Turn dough out** onto a lightly floured surface. Quickly knead dough by folding and gently pressing dough for 10 to 12 strokes or until dough is nearly smooth (see bottom photo, page 335). Pat or lightly roll dough into a 12×6-inch rectangle. Cut dough into twenty-four 6-inch strips.

4 **Place dough strips ½ inch apart** on ungreased baking sheet. If desired, sprinkle with additional lemon pepper seasoning. Bake in a 400° oven for 10 to 12 minutes or until golden. Cool on baking sheet on wire rack for 10 minutes. Remove from baking sheet; serve warm.

Nutrition Facts per stick: 69 cal., 3 g total fat (2 g sat. fat), 17 mg chol., 124 mg sodium, 9 g carbo., 0 g fiber, 1 g pro. Daily Values: 3% vit. A, 0% vit. C, 2% calcium, 3% iron

PARMESAN CHEESE CRESCENTS

Prep: 25 minutes **Bake:** 15 minutes
Makes: 12 crescents **Oven:** 425°

No need to shoot for the moon with these easy-to-assemble, light-as-air crescent rolls flavored with Parmesan cheese and fresh parsley.

2¼ **cups all-purpose flour**
 2 **teaspoons baking powder**
½ **teaspoon salt**
¼ **teaspoon baking soda**
½ **cup shortening**
¾ **cup buttermilk or sour milk**
    (see tip, page 329)
 1 **tablespoon butter, melted**
⅓ **cup grated Parmesan cheese**
 2 **tablespoons finely snipped**
      fresh parsley
   Milk
   Grated Parmesan cheese

1 **In a medium mixing bowl** stir together flour, baking powder, salt, and baking soda. Using a pastry blender, cut in shortening until mixture resembles coarse crumbs (see top photo, page 335). Make a well in center of dry mixture. Add buttermilk all at once to dry mixture. Using a fork, stir just until moistened.

2 **Turn dough out** onto a lightly floured surface. Quickly knead dough by folding and gently pressing dough for 10 to 12 strokes or until nearly smooth (see bottom photo, page 335). Pat or lightly roll dough into a 13-inch circle. Brush with melted butter. Sprinkle with ⅓ cup Parmesan cheese and parsley. Cut into 12 wedges. Roll up each wedge from the wide end to the point.

3 **Place crescents, seam side down,** about 2 inches apart on an ungreased baking sheet, curving to form crescents. Brush with milk and sprinkle with additional Parmesan cheese. Bake in a 425° oven for 15 to 20 minutes or until golden. Remove crescents from baking sheet; serve warm.

Nutrition Facts per crescent: 185 cal., 11 g total fat (3 g sat. fat), 6 mg chol., 264 mg sodium, 18 g carbo., 1 g fiber, 4 g pro. Daily Values: 2% vit. A, 1% vit. C, 10% calcium, 7% iron

ENGLISH TEA SCONES

Prep: 20 minutes **Bake:** 12 minutes
Makes: 16 scones **Oven:** 400°

Traditionally English (right down to the currants) in all but their square shape, these cream scones can be cut in standard wedges, too. Pat or lightly roll the dough to an 8-inch circle; cut into 12 wedges (see photo, page 323).

2½ **cups all-purpose flour**
 2 **tablespoons sugar**
 4 **teaspoons baking powder**
¼ **teaspoon salt**
⅓ **cup butter, cut into pieces**
 2 **beaten eggs**
¾ **cup whipping cream**
½ **cup dried currants or snipped raisins**
   Milk
   Sugar

1 **In a medium mixing bowl** combine flour, the 2 tablespoons sugar, the baking powder, and salt. Using a pastry blender, cut in butter until mixture resembles coarse crumbs (see top photo, page 335). Make a well in the center of dry mixture; set aside.

2 **In a medium mixing bowl** combine eggs, whipping cream, and currants or raisins. Add egg mixture all at once to dry mixture. Using a fork, stir just until moistened.

3 **Turn dough out** onto a lightly floured surface. Quickly knead dough by folding and gently pressing dough for 10 to 12 strokes or until dough is nearly smooth (see bottom photo, page 335). Pat or lightly roll dough into an 8-inch square. Cut into 16 squares.

4 **Place scones 1 inch apart** on an ungreased baking sheet. Brush scones with milk and sprinkle with additional sugar. Bake in a 400° oven for 12 to 14 minutes or until golden. Remove scones from baking sheet; serve warm.

Nutrition Facts per scone: 168 cal., 9 g total fat (5 g sat. fat), 52 mg chol., 176 mg sodium, 20 g carbo., 1 g fiber, 3 g pro. Daily Values: 9% vit. A, 0% vit. C, 8% calcium, 8% iron

GREAT SCOT, IT'S SCONES!

Immigrants from England may have awakened Americans to the scone, but the Scots take most of the credit for creating them. They're thought to have taken their name from the Stone of Destiny (or Scone), the site where Scottish kings were once crowned. Once scones were made with oats and griddle-baked; now they're more likely to be made with flour and baked in the oven.

Travelers to the British Isles invariably return home with a passion for the ritual of scones and tea.

Some scones are savory and biscuitlike, others sweet and cakelike. Traditionally, scones are cut into triangles and served as part of a tea menu in which they're split in half and slathered with butter, jam, or clotted (also called Devonshire) cream, a very thick—almost semisolid—cream.

DRIED CHERRY SCONES

BEST-LOVED

Prep: 30 minutes   Bake: 10 minutes
Makes: 12 scones   Oven: 400°

Be sure to choose dried sweet—not dried tart—cherries for these teatime treats.

- ½ cup snipped dried sweet cherries or raisins
- 2 cups all-purpose flour
- 3 tablespoons brown sugar
- 2 teaspoons baking powder
- ½ teaspoon salt
- ½ teaspoon baking soda
- ¼ cup butter
- 1 teaspoon finely shredded orange peel
- 1 beaten egg yolk
- 1 8-ounce carton dairy sour cream
- 1 recipe Orange Glaze (see right)

1 **In a small mixing bowl** pour enough boiling water over dried cherries to cover. Let stand for 5 minutes; drain well. In large mixing bowl combine flour, brown sugar, baking powder, salt, and baking soda. Using a pastry blender, cut in butter until mixture resembles coarse crumbs (see top photo, page 335). Add drained cherries and orange peel; toss to coat. Make a well in the center; set aside.

2 **In a small mixing bowl** combine egg yolk and sour cream. Add egg mixture all at once to dry mixture. Using a fork, stir until combined (mixture may seem dry).

3 **Turn dough out** onto a lightly floured surface. Quickly knead dough by folding and gently pressing for 10 to 12 strokes or until dough is nearly smooth (see bottom photo, page 335). Pat or lightly roll dough into a 7-inch circle. Cut into 12 wedges.

4 **Arrange wedges 1 inch apart** on an ungreased baking sheet. Bake in a 400° oven for 10 to 12 minutes or until light brown. Cool on a wire rack for 10 minutes. Drizzle warm scones with Orange Glaze. Serve warm.

Orange Glaze: In small mixing bowl stir together 1 cup sifted powdered sugar, 1 tablespoon orange juice, and ¼ teaspoon vanilla. Stir in enough additional orange juice, 1 teaspoon at a time, to make drizzling consistency.

Nutrition Facts per scone: 214 cal., 9 g total fat (4 g sat. fat), 31 mg chol., 249 mg sodium, 32 g carbo., 1 g fiber, 3 g pro. Daily Values: 13% vit. A, 2% vit. C, 7% calcium, 7% iron

BERRY-CORNMEAL SCONES

EASY

Prep: 20 minutes   Bake: 20 minutes
Makes: 10 scones   Oven: 400°

1¼ **cups all-purpose flour**
 ¾ **cup cornmeal**
 ¼ **cup sugar**
 2 **teaspoons baking powder**
 ¼ **teaspoon baking soda**
 ¼ **teaspoon salt**
 ⅓ **cup butter**
 1 **teaspoon finely shredded lemon
    peel**
 1 **cup fresh or frozen blueberries or
    raspberries, thawed**
 ⅔ **cup buttermilk or sour milk
    (see tip, page 329)**
 1 **teaspoon vanilla**

1 **In a medium mixing bowl** stir together flour, cornmeal, sugar, baking powder, baking soda, and salt. Using a pastry blender, cut in butter until mixture resembles coarse crumbs (see top photo, page 335). Add lemon peel. Make a well in center of dry mixture; set aside.

2 **In a medium mixing bowl** combine blueberries or raspberries, buttermilk, and vanilla. Add berry mixture all at once to dry mixture. Using a fork, stir just until moistened.

3 **Turn dough out** onto a lightly floured surface. Quickly knead dough by folding and gently pressing dough for 10 to 12 strokes or until dough is nearly smooth (see bottom photo, page 335). Pat or lightly roll dough into an 8-inch circle on an ungreased baking sheet. Cut dough into 10 wedges, cutting only about halfway through dough to score.

4 **Bake in a 400° oven** for 20 to 25 minutes or until golden. Cut into wedges; remove scones from baking sheet. Serve warm.

Nutrition Facts per scone: 206 cal., 11 g total fat (3 g sat. fat), 1 mg chol., 207 mg sodium, 24 g carbo., 1 g fiber, 3 g pro. Daily Values: 0% vit. A, 1% vit. C, 11% calcium, 8% iron

GOAT CHEESE AND ONION SCONES

LOW-FAT

Prep: 20 minutes   Bake: 15 minutes
Makes: 12 scones   Oven: 400°

Sweet scones may be queen of the tea table, but this savory version will rule at dinner. They're great made with feta and your favorite herb, too.

 2 **cups all-purpose flour**
 1 **green onion, finely chopped**
 2 **teaspoons baking powder**
 ¼ **teaspoon baking soda**
 ¼ **teaspoon salt**
 ¼ **teaspoon freshly ground pepper**
 1 **beaten egg**
 4 **ounces semi-soft goat cheese
    (chèvre), crumbled or cut into
    small cubes**
 ½ **cup buttermilk or sour milk
    (see tip, page 329)**

1 **In a medium mixing bowl** combine flour, green onion, baking powder, soda, salt, and pepper. Make a well in center of dry mixture; set aside.

2 **In a small mixing bowl** stir together the egg, goat cheese, and buttermilk. Add egg mixture all at once to dry mixture. Using a fork, stir just until moistened.

3 **Turn dough out** onto a lightly floured surface. Quickly knead dough by folding and gently pressing dough for 10 to 12 strokes or until dough is nearly smooth (see bottom photo, page 335). Divide dough in half. Pat or lightly roll half of the dough into a 5-inch circle. Cut into 6 wedges. Repeat with remaining dough.

4 **Place scones 1 inch apart** on an ungreased baking sheet. Bake in a 400° oven for 15 to 18 minutes or until golden. Remove scones from baking sheet; serve warm.

Nutrition Facts per scone: 112 cal., 3 g total fat (2 g sat. fat), 27 mg chol., 203 mg sodium, 15 g carbo., 1 g fiber, 5 g pro. Daily Values: 2% vit. A, 0% vit. C, 6% calcium, 7% iron

yeast breads

Tuscan Whole Wheat-Herb Bread,
recipe page 354

YEAST BREADS

WHITE BREAD LOW-FAT

Prep: 40 minutes   Rise: 1¼ hours
Bake: 40 minutes   Makes: 2 loaves (32 servings)
Oven: 375°

5¾ to 6¼ cups all-purpose flour
   1 package active dry yeast
2¼ cups milk or buttermilk or sour
     milk (see tip, page 329)
   2 tablespoons sugar
   1 tablespoon butter or shortening
1½ teaspoons salt

1 In a large mixing bowl combine 2½ cups of the flour and the yeast; set aside. In a medium saucepan heat and stir milk, sugar, butter, and salt just until warm (120° to 130°) and butter almost melts. Add milk mixture to dry mixture. Beat with electric mixer on low to medium speed for 30 seconds, scraping side of bowl constantly. Beat on high speed for 3 minutes. Using a wooden spoon, stir in as much of the remaining flour as you can.

2 Turn dough out onto a lightly floured surface. Knead in enough of the remaining flour to make a moderately stiff dough that is smooth and elastic (6 to 8 minutes total) (see top photo, right). Shape dough into a ball. Place in a lightly greased bowl, turning once to grease surface of the dough. Cover; let rise in a warm place until double in size (45 to 60 minutes) (see second photo, right).

3 Punch dough down. Turn dough out onto a lightly floured surface. Divide dough in half. Cover; let rest 10 minutes. Meanwhile, lightly grease two 8×4×2-inch loaf pans.

4 Shape dough into loaves by patting or rolling (see bottom 2 photos, right). To shape by patting, gently pat and pinch each half of dough into a loaf shape, tucking edges beneath. To shape by rolling, on lightly floured surface, roll each half of dough into a 12×8-inch rectangle. Roll up, jelly-roll style, starting from a short side. Seal with fingertips as you roll.

5 Place the shaped dough in the prepared loaf pans. Cover and let rise in a warm place until nearly double in size (30 to 40 minutes).

6 Bake in a 375° oven about 40 minutes or until bread sounds hollow when you tap the tops with your fingers (if necessary, cover with foil for the last 10 minutes of baking to prevent overbrowning). Immediately remove from pans. Cool on wire racks.

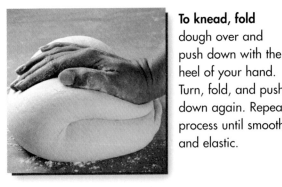

To knead, fold dough over and push down with the heel of your hand. Turn, fold, and push down again. Repeat process until smooth and elastic.

You can tell if dough has doubled by pressing two fingers ½ inch into the dough. Remove your fingers; if the indentations remain, the dough is ready to punch down.

To shape dough, gently pat each half into a loaf, pinching and tucking the edges beneath the loaf. Place each shaped loaf seam side down in a prepared pan.

Or, roll each half of dough into a 12×8-inch rectangle. Tightly roll up, jelly-roll style, starting from a short side. Pinch seam to seal. Place seam side down in pan.

Nutrition Facts per serving: 91 cal., 1 g total fat (0 g sat. fat), 2 mg chol., 112 mg sodium, 17 g carbo., 1 g fiber, 3 g pro. Daily Values: 1% vit. A, 0% vit. C, 2% calcium, 6% iron

Wheat Bread: Prepare as at left, except substitute 2 cups whole wheat flour for 2 cups all-purpose flour. Allow additional rising time (1 to 1½ hours for first rise and 50 to 60 minutes for second rise).

ITALIAN COUNTRY LOAVES

LOW-FAT

Prep: 40 minutes **Stand:** 4 to 24 hours
Rise: 2 hours **Bake:** 40 minutes
Makes: 2 loaves (32 servings) **Oven:** 400°

To replicate the Old World aura of this traditionally wood-fired, oven-baked bread, bake the loaves on a bread stone—and top them off with the aromatic rosemary.

  1 **cup warm water (105° to 115°)**
  1 **package active dry yeast**
9¾ to 10¼ **cups unbleached
      all-purpose flour**
  ⅔ **cup milk**
  1 **teaspoon sugar**
1¾ **cups warm water (105° to 115°)**
  ⅓ **cup olive oil**
  1 **tablespoon snipped fresh rosemary
      or 1 teaspoon dried rosemary,
      crushed**
  2 **cloves garlic, minced**
  2 **teaspoons salt**
      Cornmeal
      Fresh rosemary sprigs (optional)

1 In a large mixing bowl stir together the 1 cup warm water and the yeast. Let stand about 3 minutes or until mixture looks creamy. Stir in 1 cup of the flour, the milk, and sugar. Add another 1 cup of flour, ½ cup at a time. Cover; set in warm place for 4 to 24 hours or refrigerate up to 4 days.

2 Using an electric mixer on low speed or stirring by hand with a wooden spoon, beat the 1¾ cups warm water, the ⅓ cup olive oil, the snipped or dried rosemary, the garlic, and salt into the yeast mixture. Using a wooden spoon, stir in as much of the remaining flour as you can, 1 cup at a time.

3 Turn dough out onto a lightly floured surface. Knead in enough of the remaining flour to make a moderately stiff dough that is smooth and elastic (6 to 8 minutes total) (see top photo, page 345). Rub surface of dough with a little additional flour; shape into a ball. Place in greased bowl; turn once to grease surface. Cover with towel; let rise in warm place until double in size (1 to 1½ hours; allow 2 to 3 hours if yeast mixture was chilled) (see second photo, page 345).

Use a sharp knife to make ¼-inch-deep cuts in a crisscross design in the top of the loaf. If desired, brush rosemary sprigs with olive oil and place on the loaf.

4 Punch dough down. Turn out onto a lightly floured surface. Divide in half. Grease 2 large baking sheets; sprinkle with cornmeal. (Or, cut sheet of parchment paper to fit bread stone.) Shape each half of dough into a ball. Place on the prepared baking sheets or on the parchment paper on a countertop. Flatten each to about 6½ inches in diameter. Cover; let rise until nearly double (about 1 hour).

5 Adjust 2 oven racks so that 1 is in lowest position and other is in middle of oven. If you want bread to have an extra-crisp crust, place a broiler pan on bottom oven rack while oven preheats to 400°. When pan is hot, carefully pour about 1 cup hot tap water into the pan in the oven. Be careful of the hot steam. If using a bread stone, place stone on middle rack and preheat it for 30 minutes. Rub loaves lightly with additional flour. Cut a crisscross design in top of each loaf. If desired, brush rosemary sprigs with additional olive oil and place on loaves.

6 Leave bread on baking sheets or carefully transfer along with parchment paper directly to the preheated bread stone; place in the oven on the middle rack. (If you only have room to bake 1 loaf at a time, cover 1 loaf and place in refrigerator, removing 15 minutes before baking. Repeat heating broiler pan and adding water for second loaf.) Bake in the 400° oven about 40 minutes or until loaves are crusty and deep golden. (The water in broiler pan will evaporate after about 10 minutes of baking time; remove the dry pan to avoid warping.) Transfer loaves to wire racks; cool completely.

Nutrition Facts per serving: 152 cal., 3 g total fat (0 g sat. fat), 0 mg chol., 137 mg sodium, 27 g carbo., 1 g fiber, 4 g pro. Daily Values: 0% vit. A, 0% vit. C, 1% calcium, 11% iron

BAGUETTES LOW-FAT

Prep: 50 minutes   Rise: 3 hours
Bake: 20 minutes
Makes: 4 baguettes (40 servings)   Oven: 450°

The thin, cylindrical baguette was created by Parisian bakers when their customers began demanding more crisp crust from their bread.

2½ cups cool water (70° to 75°)
2 packages active dry yeast
6 to 6¾ cups bread flour or unbleached all-purpose flour
1 egg white
Toasted sesame seed and/or toasted wheat germ (optional)

1 **In a large mixing** bowl stir together the cool water and yeast. Let stand about 3 minutes or until mixture looks creamy. With a freestanding electric mixer or by hand with spoon, beat in 3 to 4 cups of the flour, a little at a time, mixing on low speed at first and then on medium speed. (This will take about 10 minutes.) Sprinkle 2 teaspoons salt over the dough during the last minute of mixing.

2 **Using spoon,** stir in as much of remaining flour as you can. Turn out onto a lightly floured surface. Knead in enough remaining flour to make a stiff dough that is smooth and elastic (8 to 10 minutes total).* Shape dough into ball. Place in large greased bowl; turn once. Cover with plastic wrap; let rise in a warm place until double (1½ to 2 hours). (Or, cover and refrigerate overnight.)

3 **Punch dough** down; knead gently in bowl just a few strokes. Cover; let rise again until nearly double (45 to 60 minutes in warm place, or 1½ to 2 hours in refrigerator). Punch dough down again. Turn out onto a lightly floured surface. Divide into 4 equal portions. Cover and let rest for 10 minutes.

Bring up long edges of dough rectangle; pinch seam to close, gently stretching loaf lengthwise. Keep seam on top of dough; it will become the bottom of the loaf.

Meanwhile, grease 4 baguette pans or 2 large baking sheets; set aside.

4 **To shape loaves,** work with 1 portion dough at a time, leaving others covered. Flatten 1 portion with heel of your hand to about 8×4-inch rectangle, pressing out air bubbles as you go. Bring up long edges; pinch to close seam (see photo, lower left). Pat flat again; repeat pinching and stretching to make a 17-inch-long loaf that is about 2 inches in diameter. (If dough becomes too bouncy and shrinks back as you work with it, let it rest for 5 to 10 minutes and continue with another portion of dough. The dough will be easier to shape after it rests.) Place each loaf, seam side down, in a prepared baguette pan or place loaves 3 to 4 inches apart on prepared baking sheets. Cover with kitchen towel; let rise in a warm place until nearly double (45 to 60 minutes).

5 **Adjust** 2 oven racks so that 1 is in the lowest position and the other is in the middle of the oven. If you want the bread to have an extra-crisp crust, place a broiler pan on the bottom oven rack while the oven preheats to 450°. When the pan is hot, carefully pour about 1 cup hot tap water into the pan in the oven. Be careful of the hot steam.

6 **With a sharp knife** or clean razor blade, cut 4 or 5 diagonal slashes in each loaf, about ¼ inch deep. Combine egg white and 2 tablespoons water; brush on loaves. Dust with additional flour and/or sprinkle with sesame seed or wheat germ.

7 **Place bread** in oven on the middle rack. (If you don't have room to bake all loaves at once, cover others and place in refrigerator; remove 10 minutes before baking. Repeat heating broiler pan and adding water for each batch.) Bake in the 450° oven 20 to 25 minutes or until golden and sounds hollow when you tap tops. (The water in the broiler pan will evaporate after about 10 minutes of baking time; remove dry pan to avoid warping.) Transfer loaves to wire racks; cool completely. Serve within 12 hours.

*Note: If your mixer has a dough hook, continue to add flour, ¼ cup at a time, until the dough clings together and cleans the side of the bowl. Continue mixing on medium speed about 5 minutes to make a stiff dough that is smooth and elastic.

Nutrition Facts per serving: 76 cal., 0 g total fat, 0 mg chol., 109 mg sodium, 15 g carbo., 1 g fiber, 3 g pro. Daily Values: 0% vit. A, 0% vit. C, 0% calcium, 4% iron

RYE BREAD

Prep: 40 minutes   **Rise:** 1½ hours
Bake: 35 minutes
Makes: 2 loaves (24 servings)   **Oven:** 375°

This hearty rye makes a world-class Reuben that rivals that of the finest delicatessen.

3½ **to 4 cups all-purpose flour**
   2 **packages active dry yeast**
   2 **cups warm water (120° to 130°)**
   ¼ **cup packed brown sugar**
   2 **tablespoons cooking oil**
   1 **teaspoon salt**
   2 **cups rye flour**
   1 **tablespoon caraway seed**
      Cornmeal

1 In a large mixing bowl stir together 2¾ cups of the all-purpose flour and the yeast. Add the warm water, brown sugar, oil, and salt. Beat with electric mixer on low to medium speed 30 seconds, scraping side of bowl. Beat on high speed 3 minutes. Using a wooden spoon, stir in rye flour, caraway seed, and as much of the remaining all-purpose flour as you can.

2 Turn dough out onto a floured surface. Knead in enough of the remaining all-purpose flour to make moderately stiff dough that is smooth and elastic (6 to 8 minutes total) (see top photo, page 345). Shape into ball. Place in a greased bowl; turn once. Cover; let rise in warm place until double (about 1 hour) (see second photo, page 345).

3 Punch dough down. Turn dough out onto a floured surface. Divide dough in half. Cover; let rest 10 minutes. Meanwhile, lightly grease baking sheet and sprinkle with cornmeal, or grease two 8×4×2-inch loaf pans.

4 Shape dough by gently pulling each half into a ball, tucking edges beneath. Place on the prepared baking sheet. Flatten each to 6 inches in diameter. (Or, shape each half into a loaf by patting

or rolling. Place in prepared loaf pans.) Cover and let rise in a warm place until nearly double in size (30 to 45 minutes).

5 Bake in a 375° oven 35 to 40 minutes or until done (if necessary, cover loosely with foil for the last 10 minutes of baking to prevent overbrowning). Immediately remove from baking sheet or pans. Cool on wire racks.

Nutrition Facts per serving: 112 cal., 1 g total fat (0 g sat. fat), 0 mg chol., 91 mg sodium, 22 g carbo., 2 g fiber, 3 g pro. Daily Values: 0% vit. A, 0% vit. C, 0% calcium, 7% iron

Peasant Rye Bread: Prepare as above, except reduce rye flour to 1 cup. Stir ½ cup whole bran cereal and ½ cup yellow cornmeal in with the rye flour.

SOURDOUGH BREAD

Prep: 1 hour   **Rise:** 1¼ hours   **Bake:** 30 minutes
Makes: 2 loaves (24 to 36 servings)   **Oven:** 375°

   1 **cup Sourdough Starter**
      (see page 349)
5½ **to 6 cups all-purpose flour**
   1 **package active dry yeast**
1½ **cups water**
   3 **tablespoons sugar**
   3 **tablespoons butter**
   1 **teaspoon salt**
   ½ **teaspoon baking soda**

1 Measure cold Sourdough Starter; let stand at room temperature 30 minutes. Mix 2½ cups of the flour and the yeast; set aside. Heat and stir water, sugar, butter, and salt just until warm (120° to 130°) and butter almost melts; add to dry mixture. Add starter. Beat with electric mixer on low speed 30 seconds, scraping bowl. Beat on high speed 3 minutes.

2 Combine 2½ cups of the remaining flour and the baking soda. Add to yeast mixture. Stir until combined. Stir in as much remaining flour as you can.

3 Turn dough out onto a lightly floured surface. Knead in enough remaining flour to make a moderately stiff dough (6 to 8 minutes total) (see top photo, page 345). Shape dough into a ball. Place dough in a greased bowl; turn once. Cover and let rise in warm place until double in size (45 to 60 minutes) (see second photo, page 345).

4 **Punch dough** down. Turn dough out onto a floured surface. Divide in half. Cover; let rest 10 minutes. Meanwhile, lightly grease baking sheet.
5 **Shape by** gently pulling each half into a ball, tucking edges beneath. Place on prepared baking sheet. Flatten each to about 6 inches in diameter. Using sharp knife, make crisscross slashes across tops of loaves. Cover; let rise in a warm place until nearly double in size (about 30 minutes).
6 **Bake in a** 375° oven for 30 to 35 minutes or until bread sounds hollow when you tap the tops (if necessary, cover loosely with foil for the last 10 minutes of baking to prevent overbrowning). Transfer to wire racks; cool completely.

Nutrition Facts per serving: 131 cal., 2 g total fat (1 g sat. fat), 4 mg chol., 133 mg sodium, 25 g carbo., 1 g fiber, 3 g pro. Daily Values: 1% vit. A, 0% vit. C, 0% calcium, 9% iron

SOURDOUGH STARTER

Prep: 15 minutes   Stand: 5 to 10 days

This starter can be used to make tangy, tuggy-textured Sourdough Bread (page 348) or Lemony Moravian Sugar Bread (page 361).

     1 **package active dry yeast**
2½ **cups warm water (105° to 115°)**
     2 **cups all-purpose flour**
     1 **tablespoon sugar or honey**

The starter will bubble vigorously as it ferments. The fermentation process develops the pleasantly sour and tangy flavor expected in sourdough breads.

1 **Dissolve yeast** in ½ cup of the warm water. Stir in the remaining warm water, the flour, and sugar or honey. Using a wooden spoon, beat until smooth. Cover with 100-percent cotton cheesecloth. Let stand at room temperature (75° to 85°) 5 to 10 days or until mixture has a fermented aroma and vigorous bubbling stops, stirring 2 or 3 times a day (see photo, above). (Fermentation time depends on the room temperature; a warmer room will hasten the fermentation process.)
2 **To store,** transfer Sourdough Starter to a 1-quart plastic container. Cover and refrigerate.
3 **To use,** stir starter. Measure desired amount of cold starter. Bring starter to room temperature. Replenish starter after each use by stirring ¾ cup all-purpose flour, ¾ cup water, and 1 teaspoon sugar or honey into remaining starter. Cover starter with cheesecloth; let stand at room temperature 1 day or until bubbly. Cover with lid; refrigerate for later use. If starter isn't used within 10 days, stir in 1 teaspoon sugar or honey. Continue to add an additional 1 teaspoon sugar or honey every 10 days unless the starter is replenished.

THE SOURDOUGH STORY

There's nothing quite like the tangy taste and tuggy texture of a piece of fresh-baked sourdough bread. The American sourdough story is a rich one. There are tales of naturally occurring yeasts that live in the air around San Francisco—making it difficult to replicate that city's famous bread anywhere else—of starters that have become so much a part of the family they've been given a name, and of 100-year-old sourdough starters more jealously guarded than gemstones.

Back in the days of the Old West, pioneer and cowboy cooks saved a piece of dough from one batch of bread to leaven the next. Because sourdough was the critical ingredient needed for making bread, frontier families considered it their most important possession after the family Bible.

In addition to bread, sourdough was used in flapjacks and biscuits. It also was used to fill cracks in log cabins, to treat wounds, and—some say—even to resole shoes.

Sage-Wheat Bread: Fresh sage, the classic stuffing seasoning, imparts bread with its delightful, smokey flavor. It makes for delicious sandwiches with leftover turkey.

SAGE-WHEAT BREAD

LOW-FAT

Prep: 40 minutes   **Rise:** 1½ hours
Bake: 30 minutes
Makes: 2 loaves (24 servings)   **Oven:** 375°

2¼ to 2¾ **cups all-purpose flour**
  2 **packages active dry yeast**
  1 **tablespoon snipped fresh sage or**
    1 **teaspoon dried sage, crushed**
1¾ **cups milk**
  ¼ **cup packed brown sugar**
  3 **tablespoons butter**
  2 **teaspoons salt**
  2 **cups whole wheat flour**
  ½ **cup yellow cornmeal**
  1 **slightly beaten egg**
    Fresh sage sprigs (optional)

1 In a large mixing bowl combine 2 cups of the all-purpose flour, the yeast, and snipped or dried sage; set aside. In medium saucepan heat and stir milk, brown sugar, butter, and salt just until warm (120° to 130°) and butter almost melts. Add milk mixture to dry mixture. Beat with an electric mixer on low to medium speed for 30 seconds, scraping side of bowl constantly. Beat on high speed for 3 minutes. Using a wooden spoon, stir in the whole wheat flour, cornmeal, and as much of the remaining all-purpose flour as you can.

2 Turn dough out onto a floured surface. Knead in enough of the remaining all-purpose flour to make a moderately stiff dough that is smooth and elastic (6 to 8 minutes total). Shape into a ball. Place in a greased bowl; turn once. Cover; let rise in a warm place until double (1 to 1¼ hours).

3 Punch dough down. Turn out onto a lightly floured surface. Divide in half. Cover and let rest 10 minutes. Lightly grease a large baking sheet and lightly sprinkle with additional cornmeal. Shape each half into a ball. Place on prepared baking sheet. Flatten each to about 5 inches in diameter.

4 Mix egg and 1 tablespoon water; brush on loaves. If desired, place sage sprigs on top of loaves. Cover; let rise until nearly double (30 to 45 minutes).

5 Brush with the egg mixture. Bake in 375° oven for 30 to 35 minutes or until done (if necessary, cover with foil for last 15 minutes of baking to prevent overbrowning). Transfer to wire rack; cool.

Nutrition Facts per serving: 117 cal., 2 g total fat (1 g sat. fat), 14 mg chol., 205 mg sodium, 21 g carbo., 2 g fiber, 4 g pro. Daily Values: 2% vit. A, 0% vit. C, 2% calcium, 7% iron

OLD-WORLD
MULTIGRAIN BREAD

Prep: 40 minutes **Stand:** 3 days **Rise:** 1½ hours
Bake: 30 minutes **Makes:** 2 loaves (32 servings)
Oven: 425°

Though this chewy, delicious bread takes a few days (make the starter three days before you plan to bake the bread) and a little extra effort to make, it's well worth the effort.

  1 **cup milk**
  1 **package active dry yeast**
  1 **cup whole wheat flour**
  2 **cups warm water (105° to 115°)**
  6 to 6½ **cups all-purpose flour**
  1 **cup rye flour**
  1 **tablespoon salt**
    Cornmeal

1 **For the starter,** in a small saucepan heat and stir milk until warm (105° to 115°). Transfer to a large mixing bowl. Stir in yeast and let stand until dissolved. Add the whole wheat flour. Using a wooden spoon, stir until thoroughly combined. Cover loosely with plastic wrap and let stand at room temperature about 24 hours.

2 **On the next day,** uncover the starter and add the warm water. Stir in 2 cups of the all-purpose flour and the rye flour. (The mixture should be thick.) Cover with cheesecloth; let stand about 24 hours.

3 **On day 3,** uncover starter and stir in the salt. Using a wooden spoon, stir in as much of the remaining all-purpose flour as you can, ½ cup at a time. Turn out onto a lightly floured surface. Cover; let rest for 3 to 4 minutes. Knead in enough of the remaining flour to make a stiff dough that is smooth and elastic (8 to 10 minutes total) (see top photo, page 345). Shape into a ball.

4 **Place dough** in a greased large bowl; turn once to grease surface. Cover; let rise in warm place until double (about 1 hour) (see second photo, page 345). Punch dough down. Turn out onto a lightly floured surface. Divide in half. Grease large baking sheet; sprinkle with cornmeal. (Or, cut sheet of parchment paper to fit bread stone.) Shape dough by gently pulling each half into a ball, tucking edges underneath. Place on the prepared baking sheet or on the parchment paper on a countertop. Cover; let rise in a warm place until nearly double in size (about 30 minutes).

5 **Preheat oven** to 425° and adjust 1 oven rack so it is in the middle of the oven. If using a bread stone, place stone on the middle rack and preheat it for 30 minutes. With a sharp knife or clean razor blade, cut 3 parallel slashes in each loaf, making each about 4 inches long and ¼ inch deep.

6 **Leave bread** on baking sheet or carefully transfer along with the parchment paper directly to the preheated bread stone; place in the oven on the middle rack. (If you only have room to bake 1 loaf at a time, cover 1 loaf and place in the refrigerator, removing 20 minutes before baking.) Bake in the 425° oven for 30 to 40 minutes or until loaves are crusty and deep golden. Transfer loaves to wire racks; cool completely.

Nutrition Facts per serving: 107 cal., 0 g total fat, 1 mg chol., 205 mg sodium, 22 g carbo., 2 g fiber, 3 g pro. Daily Values: 0% vit. A, 0% vit. C, 1% calcium, 8% iron

Raisin-Pecan Loaves: Prepare as above, except halfway through kneading, knead in 1 cup toasted chopped pecans and ¾ cup raisins. Let dough rise as above. Divide dough in half; shape into balls. Let rest for 5 minutes.

Using your hands, roll each ball into a 16-inch-long loaf, applying more pressure at the ends. Pinch ends so the center bulges and ends taper. Place on a greased large baking sheet (or, on parchment paper, if using a bread stone). Let rise as above. Make a ¼-inch-deep lengthwise slash down the center of each loaf, stopping 1 inch from ends. Bake as above. Transfer loaves to wire racks; cool completely.

OLD-FASHIONED POTATO BREAD

LOW-FAT

Prep: 50 minutes   **Rise:** 1¼ hours
Bake: 35 minutes   **Makes:** 2 loaves (32 servings)
Oven: 375°

1½ **cups water**
  1 **medium potato, peeled and cubed**
  1 **cup buttermilk or sour milk**
       (see tip, page 329)
  3 **tablespoons sugar**
  2 **tablespoons butter**
  2 **teaspoons salt**
  6 **to 6½ cups all-purpose flour**
  2 **packages active dry yeast**
     All-purpose flour

1 In saucepan bring water and potato to boiling. Cook, covered, about 12 minutes or until potato is very tender; do not drain. Mash potato in the water. Measure potato mixture. If necessary, add additional water to make 1¾ cups total. Return potato mixture to saucepan. Add the buttermilk, sugar, butter, and salt. Heat or cool as necessary until warm (120° to 130°), stirring constantly.

2 In a large mixing bowl combine 2 cups of the flour and the yeast. Add the potato mixture. Beat with an electric mixer on low to medium speed for 30 seconds, scraping the side of the bowl. Beat on high speed 3 minutes. Using a wooden spoon, stir in as much of the remaining flour as you can.

3 Turn dough out onto a lightly floured surface. Knead in enough of the remaining flour to make a moderately soft dough that is smooth and elastic (6 to 8 minutes total) (see top photo, page 345). Shape dough into ball. Place in lightly greased bowl, turning once to grease surface. Cover; let rise in warm place until double (45 to 60 minutes) (see second photo, page 345).

4 Punch dough down. Turn dough out onto a lightly floured surface. Divide dough in half. Cover; let rest for 10 minutes. Meanwhile, lightly grease two 8×4×2-inch loaf pans.

5 Shape each half of the dough into a loaf by gently patting dough into a loaf shape, tucking edges beneath (see third photo, page 345). Lightly dip tops of loaves in additional flour. Place loaves in prepared pans, flour sides up. Cover; let rise in a warm place until nearly double (about 30 minutes).

6 Bake in a 375° oven 35 to 40 minutes or until bread sounds hollow when you tap tops (if necessary, cover loosely with foil for the last 15 minutes of baking to prevent overbrowning). Immediately remove from pans. Cool on wire racks.

Nutrition Facts per serving: 99 cal., 1 g total fat (1 g sat. fat), 2 mg chol., 150 mg sodium, 20 g carbo., 1 g fiber, 3 g pro. Daily Values: 0% vit. A, 0% vit. C, 1% calcium, 7% iron

---

WHY YOU NEED TO KNEAD

Kneading dough may be one of the most satisfying aspects of baking bread. It can be great for working out frustrations, and it's great exercise for your arms. Apart from that, kneading builds a protein structure called gluten, which gives body to the finished bread.

To knead, fold the dough over and push down on it with the heels of your hands, curving your fingers over the dough. Give the dough a quarter turn and repeat the process of folding and pushing down until you have an elastic dough and the stiffness called for in a recipe. Here's how to tell:

- Soft dough is very sticky and used for breads that don't need kneading.
- Moderately soft dough is slightly sticky and is used for rich, sweet breads. This dough is kneaded on a floured surface for about 3 to 5 minutes.
- Moderately stiff dough is not sticky and is slightly firm to the touch. It usually requires 6 to 8 minutes of kneading on a lightly floured surface and is used for nonsweet breads.
- Stiff dough is firm to the touch and will hold its shape after about 8 to 10 minutes of kneading. It's used for breads with a chewy texture, such as French bread.

Challah: This rich, tender loaf of Jewish origin makes an eye-catching showpiece for a holiday buffet or dinner party.

EGG BREAD

LOW-FAT

Prep: 45 minutes **Rise:** 1½ hours
Bake: 25 minutes **Makes:** 2 loaves (32 servings)
Oven: 375°

4¾ to 5¼ cups all-purpose flour
  1 package active dry yeast
1⅓ cups milk
  3 tablespoons sugar
  3 tablespoons butter
½ teaspoon salt
  2 eggs

1 In a large mixing bowl stir together 2 cups of the flour and the yeast; set aside. In a medium saucepan heat and stir milk, sugar, butter, and salt just until warm (120° to 130°) and butter almost melts. Add milk mixture to dry mixture along with eggs. Beat with electric mixer on low to medium speed 30 seconds, scraping side of bowl constantly. Beat on high speed for 3 minutes. Using wooden spoon, stir in as much remaining flour as you can.

2 Turn dough out onto a lightly floured surface. Knead in enough of the remaining flour to make a moderately stiff dough that is smooth and elastic (6 to 8 minutes total) (see top photo, page 345). Shape dough into ball. Place in lightly greased bowl, turning once to grease surface. Cover; let rise in a warm place until double in size (about 1 hour) (see second photo, page 345).

3 Punch dough down. Turn dough out onto a lightly floured surface. Divide dough in half. Cover; let rest for 10 minutes. Meanwhile, lightly grease two 8×4×2-inch loaf pans.

4 Shape dough into loaves by patting or rolling (see bottom 2 photos, page 345). Place dough in prepared pans. Cover; let rise in a warm place until nearly double (about 30 minutes).

5 Bake in a 375° oven for 25 to 30 minutes or until bread sounds hollow when you tap tops (if necessary, cover loosely with foil for the last 10 minutes of baking). Immediately remove from pans. Cool on wire racks.

Nutrition Facts per serving: 87 cal., 2 g total fat (1 g sat. fat), 19 mg chol., 72 mg sodium, 15 g carbo., 1 g fiber, 3 g pro. Daily Values: 2% vit. A, 0% vit. C, 1% calcium, 5% iron

Challah: Prepare as above, except substitute 1¼ cups water for the milk and pareve margarine for the butter. Prepare as directed through step 2. Punch dough down. Divide dough in thirds. Cover; let rest 10 minutes. Roll each third into an 18-inch-long rope. Place ropes on a greased large baking sheet 1 inch apart; braid ropes (see Chocolate Challah on page 290 for braiding directions). Cover; let rise in a warm place until nearly double (about 30 minutes). Brush braid with 1 beaten egg yolk; sprinkle with 2 teaspoons sesame seed and/or poppy seed. Bake as directed above. Makes 1 braid (32 servings).

YEAST BREAD 101

Pulling a perfectly browned, crisp-crusted loaf of homemade bread from the oven is one of life's greatest simple pleasures, and—by heeding these few tips—not hard to achieve:

- When you're dissolving the yeast, check the temperature of the heated mixture with a thermometer to make sure it's just right. If it's too hot, the yeast will die and your bread won't rise. If it's too cold, the yeast won't activate and your bread won't rise, either.
- Start with the minimum amount of flour given in a recipe, and knead in just enough. Never use more than the maximum, or your bread will be heavy and compact.
- Proof (raise) your dough in a draft-free area between 80° and 85° until double for the first rise and just until nearly double for the second.

To use your oven, place the bowl of dough in an unheated oven and set a large pan of hot water underneath on the oven's lower rack.

- Check the dough to see if it has risen enough by pressing two of your fingers ½ inch into the center. If the indentations remain after you remove your fingers, the dough has doubled in size and is ready for the next step (see second photo, page 345).
- For the second rise, don't let the dough rise above the top of the pan because the dough needs room to rise more as it bakes, a phenomenon called "oven spring."
- Check bread for doneness by tapping the top of the loaf with your fingers. If it sounds hollow, the bread is done. (Check rolls and coffee cakes for golden brown tops and sides.)

TUSCAN WHOLE WHEAT-HERB BREAD

LOW-FAT

Prep: 30 minutes **Rise:** 1¼ hours
Bake: 29 minutes
Makes: 1 loaf (12 servings) **Oven:** 425°/375°

Italian bakers call this bread "Pane Integrale." The name refers to the unadulterated nature of whole wheat flour. Enjoy this and other hearty, country-style breads the traditional Italian way—dipped in olive oil sprinkled with cracked pepper, with grated cheese on the side (see photo, page 343).

1⅓ cups warm water (105° to 115°)
  1 package active dry yeast
  1 tablespoon olive oil
  2 teaspoons snipped fresh sage or
     ½ teaspoon dried sage, crushed
1½ teaspoons salt
  1 teaspoon sugar
1½ cups whole wheat flour
  2 to 2½ cups bread flour or
     all-purpose flour

1 **In a large** mixing bowl stir together the warm water, yeast, oil, sage, salt, and sugar. Let mixture stand for 5 minutes.

2 **Using a** wooden spoon, stir in the whole wheat flour, about ½ cup at a time. Stir in 1½ cups of the bread flour or all-purpose flour, a little at a time; stir until most of the flour has been absorbed and the dough begins to form a ball. Turn dough out onto lightly floured surface. Knead in enough of the remaining bread flour or all-purpose flour to make a moderately stiff dough that is smooth and elastic (6 to 8 minutes total) (see top photo, page 345). Shape the dough into a ball. Place in a lightly greased bowl, turning once to grease the surface. Cover; let rise in a warm place until double (45 to 60 minutes) (see second photo, page 345).

3 **Punch dough** down. Turn out onto a lightly floured surface. Cover; let rest for 10 minutes. Meanwhile, lightly grease a baking sheet. Shape dough into an 8×4-inch oval loaf. Place on prepared baking sheet. Sprinkle with additional flour. Cover; let rise until almost double (for 30 to 45 minutes).

With a sharp knife, make cuts in the loaf top about 1½ inches apart and ½ inch deep. As the bread bakes, the cuts will open up and give the loaf an attractive old-world look.

4 Using a sharp knife, slash top of loaf several times, making each cut about ½ inch deep (see photo, above). Place in a 425° oven. For a crisp crust, spray or brush the loaves with cold water every 3 minutes for the first 9 minutes of baking. After 9 minutes, reduce oven temperature to 375°; lightly sprinkle bread with additional flour. Bake about 20 minutes more or until bread sounds hollow when you tap top (if necessary, cover loosely with foil for the last 15 minutes of baking). Transfer bread to wire rack; cool completely.

Nutrition Facts per serving: 134 cal., 2 g total fat (0 g sat. fat), 0 mg chol., 269 mg sodium, 26 g carbo., 3 g fiber, 4 g pro. Daily Values: 0% vit. A, 0% vit. C, 0% calcium, 10% iron

ITALIAN CHEESE
BREAD

LOW-FAT

Prep: 40 minutes   **Rise:** 1¾ hours
Bake: 30 minutes
Makes: 1 loaf (32 servings)   **Oven:** 375°

Bakers in the Italian province of Umbria use pecorino (peh-kuh-REE-noh) cheese in this soft round bread. Pecorino cheese is made from sheep's milk and can vary from soft to hard in texture and from mild to sharp in flavor. For this recipe, choose a firm pecorino cheese that can be shredded easily. You'll find pecorino at Italian grocery stores or meat markets— and at some supermarkets.

4¾ to 5¼ cups all-purpose flour
  1 package active dry yeast
1⅓ cups milk
  3 tablespoons sugar
  2 tablespoons butter

½ teaspoon salt
  2 eggs
1½ cups shredded pecorino or provolone cheese (6 ounces)
  1 egg white
  1 tablespoon water

1 In a large mixing bowl stir together 2 cups of the flour and the yeast; set aside.

2 In a small saucepan heat and stir the milk, sugar, butter, and salt just until warm (120° to 130°) and butter almost melts. Add milk mixture to dry mixture along with the eggs. Beat with an electric mixer on low to medium speed for 30 seconds, scraping the side of bowl constantly. Beat on high speed for 3 minutes. Add the shredded cheese. Using a wooden spoon, stir in as much of the remaining flour as you can.

3 Turn dough out onto a lightly floured surface. Knead in enough of the remaining flour to make a moderately stiff dough that is smooth and elastic (6 to 8 minutes total) (see top photo, page 345).

4 Shape the dough into a ball. Place in a lightly greased bowl, turning once to grease surface. Cover; let rise in a warm place until double in size (about 1 hour) (see second photo, page 345).

5 Punch dough down. Turn out onto a lightly floured surface. Cover; let rest for 10 minutes. Lightly grease a 9- or 10-inch springform pan. Shape the dough into an 8- or 9-inch round loaf. Place in prepared pan. Cover; let rise in warm place until almost double in size (about 45 minutes).

6 In a small bowl stir together the egg white and water; brush onto dough. Bake in a 375° oven for 30 to 35 minutes or until bread sounds hollow when you tap top (if necessary, cover loosely with foil for the last 10 to 15 minutes of baking to prevent overbrowning). Loosen side of pan; remove loaf. Cool on a wire rack.

Nutrition Facts per serving: 103 cal., 3 g total fat (1 g sat. fat), 18 mg chol., 99 mg sodium, 15 g carbo., 1 g fiber, 4 g pro. Daily Values: 3% vit. A, 0% vit. C, 4% calcium, 6% iron

BREAD BOX

Though you may pine for the days when nearly every kitchen had a bread box that held homemade bread, there are better ways to store your bread than in a bread box to keep its fresh-baked taste and texture great.
To store yeast breads for the short term, cool the loaves completely, then place in an airtight container or bag. Store in a cool, dry place for 2 to 3 days. Don't store breads in the refrigerator, as that actually speeds up the going-stale process. If the bread has cheese or meat in it, eat what you can the day it's baked and freeze the rest.
To freeze yeast breads, place completely cooled, unfrosted bread in a freezer container or bag. Freeze for up to 3 months. Thaw the wrapped bread at room temperature for 2 hours. Frost sweet breads after thawing.

SWEDISH LIMPA **BREAD**

Prep: 40 minutes   **Rise:** 1½ hours
Bake: 30 minutes
Makes: 2 loaves (32 servings)   **Oven:** 375°

Caraway seed, fennel seed, and orange peel make this moist loaf fragrant and flavorful.

3¼ **to 3¾ cups all-purpose flour**
  2 **packages active dry yeast**
  2 **teaspoons caraway seed**
  ½ **teaspoon fennel seed, crushed**
     (optional)
  2 **cups milk**
  ½ **cup packed brown sugar**
  2 **tablespoons molasses**
  2 **tablespoons butter**
1½ **teaspoons salt**
  2 **tablespoons finely shredded**
     orange peel
2½ **cups rye flour**
     Milk (optional)
     Caraway seed (optional)

1 In a large mixing bowl combine 2½ cups of the all-purpose flour, the yeast, the 2 teaspoons caraway seed, and, if desired, fennel seed.

2 In a saucepan heat and stir the 2 cups milk, the brown sugar, molasses, butter, and salt just until warm (120° to 130°). Add the milk mixture to dry mixture along with orange peel. Beat with electric mixer on low to medium speed for 30 seconds, scraping bowl constantly. Beat on high speed for 3 minutes. Using a spoon, stir in the rye flour and as much of the remaining all-purpose flour as you can.

3 Turn dough out onto a floured surface. Knead in enough of the remaining all-purpose flour to make a moderately stiff dough that is smooth and elastic (6 to 8 minutes total) (see top photo, page 345). Shape dough into a ball. Place dough in a greased bowl, turning once to grease surface. Cover; let rise in a warm place until double in size (about 1 hour) (see second photo, page 345).

4 Punch dough down. Divide in half. Cover and let rest 10 minutes. Grease a baking sheet. Shape each half of dough into a round loaf. Place on prepared baking sheet. Flatten slightly. Cover and let rise in a warm place until nearly double (about 30 minutes). If desired, brush tops of loaves with a little additional milk and sprinkle lightly with additional caraway seed. Bake in a 375° oven for 30 to 35 minutes or until lightly browned. Transfer loaves to wire rack; cool completely.

Nutrition Facts per serving: 100 cal., 1 g total fat
(1 g sat. fat), 3 mg chol., 118 mg sodium, 20 g carbo.,
1 g fiber, 3 g pro. Daily Values: 1% vit. A, 1% vit. C,
2% calcium, 6% iron

SWEET PEPPER-CHEESE BATTER BREAD EASY

Prep: 25 minutes   **Rise:** 1⅔ hours
Bake: 40 minutes   **Makes:** 1 loaf (16 servings)
Oven: 375°

No cheddar on hand? Substitute Swiss or Monterey Jack, plain or—for a bit of heat—with jalapeño peppers.

  1 **package active dry yeast**
  ¾ **cup warm water (105° to 115°)**
  2 **beaten eggs**
  ½ **cup shredded cheddar cheese**
  ½ **cup finely chopped red sweet or green sweet pepper**
  ¼ **cup finely chopped onion**
  ¼ **cup shortening**
  2 **tablespoons sugar**
  ½ **teaspoon salt**
  ½ **teaspoon dried thyme, crushed**
2⅔ **cups all-purpose flour**

1 In a large mixing bowl dissolve yeast in the warm water. Stir in eggs, cheese, red or green pepper, onion, shortening, sugar, salt, and thyme. Gradually add 2 cups of the flour, beating with an electric mixer on medium speed until smooth. Using a wooden spoon, stir in the remaining flour (batter will be stiff).

2 Cover; let rise in a warm place until double in size (about 1 hour). Stir down dough. Grease a 9×5×3-inch loaf pan. Transfer dough to prepared pan. Smooth top of dough with floured hands. Cover; let rise in a warm place until nearly double in size (about 40 minutes).

3 Bake in a 375° oven for 40 to 45 minutes or until bread sounds hollow when you tap top. Immediately remove loaf from pan. Cool loaf on a wire rack.

Nutrition Facts per serving: 131 cal., 5 g total fat (2 g sat. fat), 30 mg chol., 97 mg sodium, 17 g carbo., 1 g fiber, 4 g pro. Daily Values: 4% vit. A, 8% vit. C, 2% calcium, 7% iron

DILLY BREAD EASY

Prep: 25 minutes   **Rise:** 50 minutes
Bake: 25 minutes   **Makes:** 1 loaf (8 servings)
Oven: 375°

This homey batter bread gets its subtle tang and moistness from cottage cheese and its mild herb essence from dillseed. Serve it with your favorite main-dish soup or salad.

  2 **cups all-purpose flour**
  1 **package active dry yeast**
  2 **teaspoons dillseed**
  ¼ **teaspoon baking soda**
  2 **tablespoons chopped onion**
  1 **tablespoon butter**
  1 **cup cream-style cottage cheese**
  ¼ **cup water**
  2 **tablespoons sugar**
  ½ **teaspoon salt**
  1 **egg**

1 Generously grease a 1½-quart soufflé dish or casserole, or a 9×1½-inch round baking pan. In a large mixing bowl combine ¾ cup of the flour, the yeast, dillseed, and baking soda; set aside.

2 In a medium saucepan cook onion in butter until tender. Add cottage cheese, water, sugar, and salt to onion mixture; heat and stir just until warm (120° to 130°). Add cottage cheese mixture to dry mixture along with egg. Beat with an electric mixer on low to medium speed for 30 seconds, scraping side of bowl constantly. Beat on high speed for 3 minutes. Using a wooden spoon, stir in the remaining flour.

3 Spread batter into the prepared dish, casserole, or pan. Cover; let rise in a warm place until nearly double in size (50 to 60 minutes).

4 Bake in a 375° oven about 25 minutes or until golden (if necessary, cover with foil for the last 10 minutes of baking to prevent overbrowning). Immediately remove from dish, casserole, or pan. Serve warm, or cool on wire rack.

Nutrition Facts per serving: 171 cal., 4 g total fat (2 g sat. fat), 34 mg chol., 302 mg sodium, 27 g carbo., 1 g fiber, 8 g pro. Daily Values: 3% vit. A, 0% vit. C, 2% calcium, 11% iron

DOUBLE-SWIRL APPLE
BREAD

Prep: 50 minutes   Rise: 1½ hours
Bake: 30 minutes   Makes: 2 loaves (32 servings)
Oven: 375°

If you like, omit the coarse sugar and drizzle the baked loaves with Vanilla Glaze (page 379).

5½ to 6 cups all-purpose flour
1 package active dry yeast
1 cup milk
3 tablespoons granulated sugar
3 tablespoons butter
¾ teaspoon salt
2 eggs
1 cup shredded apple
1½ cups finely chopped peeled apple
½ cup finely chopped walnuts or
    pecans, toasted
½ cup packed brown sugar
2 teaspoons ground cinnamon
2 tablespoons butter, softened
1 slightly beaten egg white
1 tablespoon water
    Coarse sugar

1 In a large mixing bowl combine 2 cups of the flour and the yeast; set aside. In a saucepan heat and stir milk, granulated sugar, the 3 tablespoons butter, and the salt until warm (120° to 130°) and butter almost melts. Add milk mixture to dry mixture along with eggs. Beat with an electric mixer on low to medium speed for 30 seconds, scraping side of bowl constantly. Beat on high speed 3 minutes. Stir in shredded apple. Using a wooden spoon, stir in as much remaining flour as you can.

2 Turn dough out onto a lightly floured surface. Knead in enough of the remaining flour to make a moderately stiff dough that is smooth and elastic (6 to 8 minutes total) (see top photo, page 345). Shape into a ball. Place in lightly greased bowl, turning once to grease surface. Cover; let rise in a warm place until double (about 1 hour) (see second photo, page 345). Punch dough down.

3 Turn dough out onto a lightly floured surface. Divide in half. Cover; let rest 10 minutes. Lightly grease two 8×4×2- or 9×5×3-inch loaf pans.

4 Meanwhile, for filling, in a medium mixing bowl combine chopped apple, nuts, brown sugar, and cinnamon; set aside.

5 Roll half of the dough to a 14×9-inch rectangle. Spread with 1 tablespoon of the softened butter; sprinkle with half of the filling. Beginning at both short ends, roll each end up, jelly-roll style, to center. Place loaf, rolled side up, in a prepared loaf pan. For second loaf, repeat with remaining dough, remaining butter, and remaining filling.

6 Cover; let rise until almost double in size (about 30 minutes). Stir together egg white and water. Brush egg white mixture over tops of loaves; sprinkle with coarse sugar. Bake in a 375° oven for 30 to 40 minutes or until bread sounds hollow when you tap tops (if necessary, loosely cover with foil for the last 15 minutes of baking to prevent overbrowning). Immediately remove from pans. Cool on wire racks.

Nutrition Facts per serving: 132 cal., 4 g total fat (1 g sat. fat), 19 mg chol., 79 mg sodium, 22 g carbo., 1 g fiber, 3 g pro. Daily Values: 2% vit. A, 0% vit. C, 1% calcium, 7% iron

FOR A QUICK RISE

Q How can any yeast bread recipe be adapted to using quick-rise yeast?
A Easy. Every recipe in this chapter (with the exception of Sourdough Starter and any yeast doughs requiring a refrigerated rise) can be made with quick-rising active dry yeast. Simply follow the recipe, keeping in mind that the dough should rise in about one-third less time than with regular yeast, especially during the second rising.

Double-Swirl Apple Bread: For a spectacular breakfast treat, toast slices of this fruit- and nut-filled loaf and slather with orange marmalade or apricot preserves.

Pepper-Parmesan Bread: All of the appealing flavor of garlic bread—plus a generous sprinkling of pepper—makes this robust loaf a natural to serve with lasagna or any of your favorite pasta dishes.

PEPPER-PARMESAN
BREAD

Prep: 40 minutes   **Rise:** 1¾ hours
Bake: 40 minutes   **Makes:** 2 loaves (40 servings)
Oven: 375°

For an appetizer, top toasted slices of this spunky bread with some chopped tomato or olives.

5¼ to 5¾ cups all-purpose flour
1½ cups grated Parmesan cheese
  2 packages active dry yeast
1½ teaspoons freshly ground black
     pepper
  1 teaspoon salt
¼ teaspoon garlic powder
  2 cups warm water (120° to 130°)
     Cornmeal
  1 slightly beaten egg white
  1 tablespoon water

1 **In a large** mixing bowl combine 2 cups of the flour, ½ cup of the Parmesan cheese, the yeast, pepper, salt, and garlic powder. Add the 2 cups warm water. Beat with an electric mixer on low to medium speed for 30 seconds, scraping bowl. Beat on high speed for 3 minutes. Using wooden spoon, stir in as much of the remaining flour as you can.

2 **Turn dough** out onto a lightly floured surface. Knead in enough of the remaining flour to make a stiff dough that is smooth and elastic (8 to 10 minutes total) (see top photo, page 345). Shape

into a ball. Place in a lightly greased bowl; turn once. Cover and let rise in a warm place until double (1 to 1½ hours) (see second photo, page 345).

3 **Punch dough** down. Turn out onto a lightly floured surface. Divide in half. Cover and let rest 10 minutes. Meanwhile, grease a baking sheet; sprinkle with cornmeal. Roll out half the dough into a 15×12-inch rectangle. Sprinkle ½ cup of the Parmesan cheese on dough in a narrow row, 3 inches from and parallel to a long side of the rectangle. Starting from the opposite long side, roll up tightly, jelly-roll style. Moisten edges and seal well; taper ends. Repeat with remaining dough and remaining Parmesan cheese. Place loaves, seam sides down, on prepared baking sheet (cheese should be at top of loaves). Cover and let rise until nearly double in size (about 45 minutes).

4 **Stir together** egg white and the 1 tablespoon water. Brush egg white mixture over loaves. Using a sharp knife, make 5 or 6 diagonal cuts, about ¼ inch deep, across top of each loaf.

5 **Bake in a** 375° oven for 40 to 45 minutes or until the loaves sound hollow when you tap tops (if necessary, cover loaves loosely with foil for the last 15 minutes of baking to prevent overbrowning). For a crispier crust, brush loaves again with egg white mixture after 20 minutes of baking. Transfer loaves to a wire rack; cool completely.

Nutrition Facts per serving: 75 cal., 1 g total fat (1 g sat. fat), 3 mg chol., 125 mg sodium, 12 g carbo., 1 g fiber, 3 g pro. Daily Values: 0% vit. A, 0% vit. C, 4% calcium, 5% iron

ANADAMA BREAD

LOW-FAT

Prep: 40 minutes   **Rise:** 1½ hours
Bake: 40 minutes   **Makes:** 2 loaves (32 servings)
Oven: 375°

This bread allegedly was invented by a man whose wife was an incompetent baker. In desperation, he baked his own bread while mumbling, "Anna, damn her!"

4½ **to 5 cups all-purpose flour**
  2 **packages active dry yeast**
  2 **cups cold water**
  1 **cup yellow cornmeal**
½ **cup molasses**
⅓ **cup shortening**
  2 **teaspoons salt**
  2 **eggs**
  2 **tablespoons butter, melted**

1 In a large bowl combine 1 cup of the flour and the yeast. In saucepan combine water and cornmeal. Cook and stir until thickened and bubbly. Remove from heat; stir in molasses, shortening, and salt. Cool just until warm (115° to 120°). Add molasses mixture to dry mixture along with eggs. Beat with electric mixer on low speed 30 seconds, scraping bowl. Beat on high speed 3 minutes. Using spoon, stir in as much remaining flour as you can.

2 Turn dough out onto a lightly floured surface. Knead in enough remaining flour to make moderately stiff dough that is smooth and elastic (6 to 8 minutes total) (see top photo, page 345). Shape into ball. Place in lightly greased bowl; turn once. Cover; let rise in warm place until double (about 1 hour) (see second photo, page 345).

3 Punch dough down. Turn out onto a lightly floured surface. Divide dough in half. Cover; let rest 10 minutes. Grease two 8×4×2-inch loaf pans.

4 Shape dough into loaves (see bottom 2 photos, page 345). Place in prepared pans. Cover; let rise until nearly double (about 30 minutes). Brush with butter. Bake in a 375° oven 20 minutes. Cover with foil. Bake for 20 minutes more. Immediately remove from pans. Cool on wire racks.

Nutrition Facts per serving: 118 cal., 3 g total fat (1 g sat. fat), 15 mg chol., 146 mg sodium, 19 g carbo., 1 g fiber, 3 g pro. Daily Values: 1% vit. A, 0% vit. C, 1% calcium, 8% iron

LEMONY MORAVIAN SUGAR BREAD

BEST-LOVED

Prep: 25 minutes   **Rise:** 1 hour   **Bake:** 20 minutes
Makes: 12 servings   **Oven:** 375°

A Better Homes and Gardens® editors' all-time favorite, this sweet yeast bread comes from the Moravians, a Christian sect that brought their simple, delicious fare to Pennsylvania and North Carolina from Eastern Europe in the 1700s.

  1 **cup Sourdough Starter**
    (see page 349)
3½ **cups all-purpose flour**
  1 **package active dry yeast**
½ **cup granulated sugar**
½ **cup milk**
¼ **cup butter**
  2 **slightly beaten eggs**
  2 **teaspoons shredded lemon peel**
    (set aside)
  2 **tablespoons lemon juice**
¾ **cup packed brown sugar**
⅓ **cup butter**
  1 **teaspoon ground cinnamon**

1 Bring starter to room temperature. In a large bowl mix 1½ cups of the flour and the yeast.

2 In a small saucepan heat and stir granulated sugar, milk, the ¼ cup butter, and ½ teaspoon salt until warm (120° to 130°) and butter almost melts. Add sugar mixture to dry mixture. Add Sourdough Starter, eggs, and lemon juice. Beat with electric mixer on low speed for 30 seconds, scraping bowl. Beat on high speed about 2 minutes. Using spoon, stir in lemon peel and remaining flour.

3 Lightly grease a 13×9×2-inch baking pan. Transfer dough to prepared pan; pat dough evenly into pan with floured hands. Cover; let rise in a warm place until nearly double (about 1 hour).

4 In a saucepan heat and stir brown sugar, the ⅓ cup butter, and cinnamon until smooth. Poke holes in dough with the handle of a wooden spoon. Pour butter mixture over dough. Bake in a 375° oven 20 to 25 minutes or until golden. Serve warm.

Nutrition Facts per serving: 324 cal., 10 g total fat (6 g sat. fat), 60 mg chol., 200 mg sodium, 52 g carbo., 1 g fiber, 6 g pro. Daily Values: 10% vit. A, 2% vit. C, 3% calcium, 16% iron

CHERRY TEA RING

Prep: 50 minutes **Rise:** 2 hours **Bake:** 25 minutes
Makes: 2 rings (24 servings) **Oven:** 350°

1½ **cups milk**
½ **cup butter**
2 **packages active dry yeast**
½ **cup warm water (105° to 115°)**
7 to 7½ **cups all-purpose flour**
½ **cup granulated sugar**
2 **slightly beaten eggs**
1½ **teaspoons salt**
2 **cups water**
2 **cups snipped dried tart cherries**
1 **recipe Cinnamon Filling**
   (see lower right)
1 **recipe Almond Glaze**
   (see lower right)

1 In a small saucepan heat and stir milk and butter until warm and butter almost melts. Cool to lukewarm (105° to 115°).

2 In a large mixing bowl dissolve the yeast in the ½ cup warm water. Stir in the milk mixture, 3½ cups of the flour, the granulated sugar, eggs, and salt. Using a wooden spoon, stir in as much of the remaining flour as you can.

3 Turn dough out onto a lightly floured surface. Knead in enough of the remaining flour to

Use a sharp knife to cut slits from the outside edge of dough ring to center, leaving about 1 inch attached at center. Repeat at 1-inch intervals around dough ring.

Gently grasp a slice and turn it to one side so one of the cut sides is down. Repeat with remaining slices, being careful not to tear the dough or spill the filling.

make a moderately stiff dough that is smooth and elastic (6 to 8 minutes total). Shape into a ball. Place in a greased bowl, turning once to grease surface. Cover; let rise in a warm place until double in size (about 1½ hours).

4 Punch dough down. Turn out onto a lightly floured surface. Divide dough in half. Cover; let rest for 10 minutes.

5 In a medium saucepan bring the 2 cups water to boiling; remove from heat. Add cherries; let stand 5 minutes. Drain, squeezing to remove excess water.

6 Roll half of the dough into a 15×9-inch rectangle. Sprinkle half of the Cinnamon Filling evenly over dough. Sprinkle with half of the cherries. Roll up, jelly-roll style, starting from a long side. Seal seam. Grease a large baking sheet.

7 Place dough roll on prepared baking sheet. Attach ends together to form a circle; pinch seam to seal. Using a sharp knife, cut slits at 1-inch intervals around the ring (see top photo, lower left). Gently turn each slice so 1 of the cut sides is down (see bottom photo, lower left). Cover; let rise until nearly double in size (about 30 minutes). Repeat with remaining dough, remaining Cinnamon Filling, and remaining cherries.

8 Bake in a 350° oven about 25 minutes or until tea rings sound hollow when you tap tops (the centers may be lighter in color) (if necessary, cover rings with foil for the last 5 to 10 minutes of baking to prevent overbrowning). Transfer to wire racks; cool completely. Drizzle with Almond Glaze.

Cinnamon Filling: In a medium mixing bowl stir together ⅔ cup granulated sugar, ⅔ cup packed brown sugar, ⅓ cup all-purpose flour, and 1 tablespoon ground cinnamon. Using a pastry blender or fork, cut in ½ cup butter until crumbly.

Almond Glaze: In small bowl stir together 2½ cups sifted powdered sugar, 2 teaspoons light-colored corn syrup, ½ teaspoon vanilla, and ½ teaspoon almond extract. Stir in enough evaporated milk, half-and-half, or light cream (3 to 4 tablespoons) to make drizzling consistency. If desired, stir a few drops red food coloring into half of the glaze.

Nutrition Facts per serving: 346 cal., 9 g total fat (5 g sat. fat), 40 mg chol., 229 mg sodium, 62 g carbo., 2 g fiber, 5 g pro. Daily Values: 14% vit. A, 0% vit. C, 3% calcium, 13% iron

Cherry Tea Ring: Delightful at brunch or teatime, this beautiful, rich bread will be much-beloved by anyone lucky enough to taste its tart cherry filling and sweet almond glaze.

OVERNIGHT BUBBLE LOAF

Prep: 35 minutes   Chill: 2 to 24 hours
Bake: 35 minutes   Makes: 1 loaf (16 servings)
Oven: 350°

This yeast loaf is a great choice for a brunch menu. It waits in the refrigerator, shaped and ready to bake.

3½ to 4 cups all-purpose flour
  1 package active dry yeast
1⅓ cups milk
  2 tablespoons honey
  1 tablespoon butter
  ¾ teaspoon salt
  1 egg
  ⅔ cup toasted wheat germ
  ¼ cup butter
  ⅔ cup packed brown sugar
  3 tablespoons light-colored corn
     syrup
  ½ teaspoon ground cinnamon
  ⅓ cup chopped walnuts
  ⅓ cup granulated sugar
  1 teaspoon ground cinnamon
  3 tablespoons butter, melted

1 **In a mixing** bowl stir together 1½ cups of the flour and the yeast; set aside. In a saucepan heat and stir milk, honey, the 1 tablespoon butter, and the salt just until warm (120° to 130°). Add milk mixture to dry mixture along with egg. Beat with an electric mixer on low to medium speed for 30 seconds, scraping side of bowl constantly. Beat on high speed for 3 minutes. Stir in wheat germ and as much of the remaining flour as you can.

2 **Turn dough** out onto a floured surface. Knead in enough of the remaining flour to make a moderately soft dough that is smooth and elastic (3 to 5 minutes total) (see top photo, page 345). Place dough in a lightly greased bowl, turning once to grease surface. Cover; let rest 20 minutes.

3 **Meanwhile,** in a saucepan heat and stir the ¼ cup butter, the brown sugar, corn syrup, and the ½ teaspoon cinnamon until smooth; set aside. Grease a 10-inch fluted tube pan; set aside.

4 **Divide dough** into 4 portions. Divide each portion into 4 pieces (16 pieces total). Roll each piece into a ball. Sprinkle walnuts over bottom of prepared pan. In a small bowl combine the ⅓ cup granulated sugar and the 1 teaspoon cinnamon. Dip dough balls in the 3 tablespoons melted butter; coat with sugar mixture. Place half of the coated dough balls in a single layer in prepared pan. Drizzle with about one-third of the brown sugar mixture. Top with remaining coated dough balls and drizzle with remaining brown sugar mixture. Cover lightly with oiled waxed paper, then plastic wrap; refrigerate for 2 to 24 hours.

5 **Uncover.** Let stand at room temperature about 20 minutes. Bake in a 350° oven for 35 to 40 minutes or until bread sounds hollow when you tap top. Cool in pan on a wire rack for 5 minutes. Invert bread onto serving platter. Cool about 45 minutes; serve warm.

Nutrition Facts per serving: 256 cal., 9 g total fat (4 g sat. fat), 30 mg chol., 178 mg sodium, 40 g carbo., 1 g fiber, 6 g pro. Daily Values: 7% vit. A, 1% vit. C, 3% calcium, 14% iron

KUGELHOPF

Prep: 20 minutes   Rise: 3 hours
Bake: 30 minutes   Makes: 1 loaf (16 servings)
Oven: 350°

A Turk's head mold is a tall, fluted ring mold named—presumably—for its turbanlike shape and the ornate swirls it imparts to whatever is baked in it.

  1 package active dry yeast
  ¼ cup warm water (105° to 115°)
  ½ cup milk
  ¼ cup butter
  ½ cup sugar
  2 eggs
2½ cups all-purpose flour
  1 teaspoon salt
  ½ cup golden raisins
  1 teaspoon finely shredded lemon
     peel
  1 tablespoon butter, melted
  3 tablespoons fine dry bread crumbs
    Blanched whole almonds

KUGELHOPF OR GUGELHUPF?

Part bread, part cake, the sweet and rich briochelike *kugelhopf* is an Austrian creation whose popularity swelled in Paris in the 18th century thanks to Marie "Let-Them-Eat-Cake" Antoinette, who had a passion for it.

There are as many versions of kugelhopf as there are ways to spell it—suglhupf, kugelhupf, gugelhupf, and kougloff, to name just a few—but they're all embellished traditionally with whole almonds stuck in each swirling flute and are baked in a pan called a Turk's head mold, presumably named so because of its ornate, turbanlike shape.

1 **Dissolve the yeast** in the warm water. Let stand 5 to 10 minutes to soften. Heat milk almost to boiling. Cool to lukewarm (105° to 115°).

2 **In large** mixing bowl beat butter and sugar with an electric mixer on medium speed until light. Add eggs, 1 at a time, beating after each addition. Add the softened yeast and lukewarm milk. Sift together flour and salt; add to beaten mixture. Beat at medium speed about 2 minutes or until smooth. Stir in raisins and lemon peel. Cover; let rise in warm place until double in size (about 2 hours).

3 **Meanwhile,** brush a 1½-quart Turk's head mold or casserole liberally with the melted butter; sprinkle with bread crumbs, coating well. Arrange almonds in a design in bottom of mold. Stir down the batter; spoon carefully into prepared mold. Let rise in warm place until nearly double in size (about 1 hour). Bake in 350° oven for 30 to 35 minutes or until golden. Cool in mold on wire rack 10 minutes. Remove mold. Cool completely.

Nutrition Facts per serving: 158 cal., 5 g total fat (3 g sat. fat), 37 mg chol., 191 mg sodium, 25 g carbo., 1 g fiber, 4 g pro. Daily Values: 4% vit. A, 0% vit. C, 1% calcium, 7% iron

ARMENIAN FLATBREAD

Prep: 1 hour   Rise: 1½ hours
Bake: 20 minutes per batch
Makes: 14 rounds (14 servings)   Oven: 350°

5¾ to 6¼ cups all-purpose flour
1 package active dry yeast
2 cups water
¼ cup butter
1 tablespoon sugar
¼ cup sesame seed, toasted

1 **In large** bowl combine 2½ cups of the flour and yeast. In saucepan heat and stir water, butter, sugar, and 2 teaspoons salt until warm (120° to 130°) and butter almost melts. Add butter mixture to dry mixture. Beat with electric mixer on low speed for 30 seconds, scraping bowl. Beat on high speed for 3 minutes. Using spoon, stir in half of the sesame seed and as much of the remaining flour as you can.

2 **Turn out** onto lightly floured surface. Knead in enough of the remaining flour to make a moderately stiff dough that is smooth and elastic (6 to 8 minutes total) (see top photo, page 345). Shape dough into ball. Place in lightly greased bowl; turn once. Cover; let rise in a warm place until double (1½ to 2 hours) (see second photo, page 345).

3 **Punch dough** down. Turn out onto a lightly floured surface. Divide dough into 14 portions; shape into balls, tucking edges under. Cover and let rest 10 minutes. Lightly grease baking sheets.

4 **Roll each** ball to 8-inch round; place on prepared sheets. Brush with cold water; sprinkle with remaining seed. Using fork, prick each round well. Do not allow to rise. Bake in 350° oven about 20 minutes or until lightly browned. (Keep remaining rounds in refrigerator until ready to bake.) Transfer to racks; cool (bread will crisp as it cools).

Nutrition Facts per round: 219 cal., 5 g total fat (2 g sat. fat), 9 mg chol., 341 mg sodium, 37 g carbo., 2 g fiber, 6 g pro. Daily Values: 3% vit. A, 0% vit. C, 1% calcium, 16% iron

Garlic-Herb Flatbread: Prepare as above, except use only 2 tablespoons sesame seed; omit brushing bread with water and sprinkling with sesame seed. Brush warm bread with a mixture of ¼ cup butter, melted; 1 tablespoon snipped fresh thyme or oregano; and 1 clove garlic, minced.

DRIED TOMATO
FOCACCIA

Prep: 25 minutes   Rise: 1⅓ hours
Bake: 25 minutes   Makes: 2 rounds (24 servings)
Oven: 375°

3¼ to 3¾ cups bread flour or
    all-purpose flour
1 package active dry yeast
1¼ cups warm water (120° to 130°)
3 tablespoons snipped fresh sage
3 tablespoons olive oil or cooking oil
1 tablespoon dry white wine
1 teaspoon salt
¼ teaspoon cracked black pepper
1 cup dried tomato slices
    (not oil-packed)
¼ cup pitted kalamata olives or ripe
    olives, quartered
½ cup shredded Parmesan cheese
    (2 ounces)

Dust your fingers lightly with flour and press into dough to make ½-inch-deep indentations. Repeat to cover dough round, spacing indentations 1 to 2 inches apart.

1 **In a large mixing** bowl combine 1¼ cups of the flour and the yeast. Add the 1¼ cups water, the sage, 1 tablespoon of the oil, the wine, salt, and pepper to dry mixture. Beat with an electric mixer on low to medium speed 30 seconds, scraping bowl. Beat on high speed 3 minutes. Using spoon, stir in as much of the remaining flour as you can.

2 **Turn dough** out onto a lightly floured surface. Knead in enough remaining flour to make a stiff dough that is smooth and elastic (8 to 10 minutes total) (see top photo, page 345). Shape dough into a ball. Place in a lightly greased bowl; turn once. Cover and let rise in a warm place until double in size (about 1 hour) (see second photo, page 345).

3 **Cover** tomatoes with warm water; soak 10 to 15 minutes or until softened. Drain; set aside. Grease two 12-inch pizza pans or 2 baking sheets. Punch dough down. Turn out onto floured surface. Divide in half. Shape each half into ball. Place on prepared pans or sheets. Cover; let rest 10 minutes.

4 **Using your hands,** flatten each ball to about 12 inches in diameter. Cover; let rise until nearly double (about 20 minutes). Make ½-inch-deep indentations in dough (see photo, left). Brush dough with the remaining oil; top with tomato slices and olives. Sprinkle with Parmesan cheese. Bake in a 375° oven about 25 minutes or until golden. Transfer to wire racks; cool completely.

Nutrition Facts per serving: 100 cal., 3 g total fat (0 g sat. fat), 2 mg chol., 81 mg sodium, 15 g carbo., 1 g fiber, 4 g pro. Daily Values: 0% vit. A, 1% vit. C, 2% calcium, 5% iron

---

ITALY'S FAVORITE FLATBREAD

When the sun rises each morning on the small towns that dot the coast of Liguria—a region in northwest Italy that cradles the Ligurian Sea—the only thing that can be heard is the sound of someone sweeping the stone streets with a broom. There's a singular aroma in the air, too. It is the heavenly scent of focaccia, the olive-oil infused flatbread that is native to this region, baking in the oven of the town bakery.

Focaccia is eaten as an accompaniment to soups and salads, and especially as a mid-morning snack, cut in large wedges or rectangles while it's still warm and wrapped in waxed paper so you can meander the streets, munching as you go.

The toppings for focaccia are myriad: fresh herbs (especially rosemary); coarse salt; olives; tomatoes; roasted peppers; Parmesan, pecorino, Romano, or Gorgonzola cheese; garlic; onion; and toasted nuts are just a few tasty possibilities.

Dried Tomato Focaccia: Heaped high with toppings, this colorful flatbread derives its chewy texture from bread flour and its remarkable flavor from sage and black pepper.

ORANGE-CINNAMON LOAF *EASY*

Prep: 15 minutes
Bake: per bread machine directions

For 1½-Pound Loaf (16 servings):
½ cup buttermilk or sour milk
⅓ cup water
1 egg
3 tablespoons butter, cut up
3 cups bread flour
3 tablespoons granulated sugar
2 teaspoons finely shredded orange peel
¾ teaspoon salt
¾ teaspoon ground cinnamon
1 teaspoon active dry yeast or bread machine yeast
1 recipe Orange Glaze (see below)

For 2-Pound Loaf (22 servings):
⅔ cup buttermilk or sour milk
½ cup water
1 egg
¼ cup butter, cut up
4 cups bread flour
¼ cup granulated sugar
2½ teaspoons finely shredded orange peel
1 teaspoon salt
1 teaspoon ground cinnamon
1½ teaspoons active dry yeast or bread machine yeast
1 recipe Orange Glaze (see below)

1 Select loaf size you want to make. Add all of the ingredients except the Orange Glaze to a bread machine according to manufacturer's directions. Select the basic white bread cycle. Remove hot bread from machine as soon as it is done. Cool completely on wire rack. Drizzle with Orange Glaze.

Orange Glaze: Mix 1 cup sifted powdered sugar and 1 teaspoon vanilla. Stir in enough orange juice (4 to 6 teaspoons) to make a drizzling consistency.

Nutrition Facts per serving: 155 cal., 3 g total fat (2 g sat. fat), 19 mg chol., 134 mg sodium, 28 g carbo., 1 g fiber, 4 g pro. Daily Values: 2% vit. A, 1% vit. C, 1% calcium, 7% iron

WHOLE-GRAIN BREAD *EASY*

Prep: 15 minutes
Bake: per bread machine directions

This is a superb everyday, all-purpose loaf for sandwiches and terrific toast.

For 1½-Pound Loaf (16 servings):
1¼ cups milk
1 egg
4 teaspoons molasses or honey
4 teaspoons butter
¾ teaspoon salt
2 cups bread flour
1¼ cups whole wheat flour
¾ cup four-grain cereal flakes or cornflakes
1 teaspoon active dry yeast or bread machine yeast
⅓ cup shelled unsalted sunflower seeds or chopped pecans

For 2-Pound Loaf (22 servings):
1½ cups milk
2 eggs
2 tablespoons molasses or honey
2 tablespoons butter
1 teaspoon salt
2⅔ cups bread flour
1½ cups whole wheat flour
1 cup four-grain cereal flakes or cornflakes
1½ teaspoons active dry yeast or bread machine yeast
½ cup shelled unsalted sunflower seeds or chopped pecans

1 Add ingredients to a bread machine according to manufacturer's directions. If available, select whole grain cycle, or select basic white bread cycle. Remove hot bread from machine as soon as it is done. Place on wire rack; cool completely.

Nutrition Facts per serving: 144 cal., 4 g total fat (1 g sat. fat), 17 mg chol., 135 mg sodium, 23 g carbo., 2 g fiber, 5 g pro. Daily Values: 3% vit. A, 1% vit. C, 3% calcium, 10% iron

ONION-MILLET
BREAD *EASY*

Prep: 15 minutes
Bake: per bread machine directions

Speckled with millet—a tiny, round yellow cereal grain—this bread has a chewy texture and nutty flavor.

For 1½-Pound Loaf (16 servings):

1 cup milk
2 tablespoons water
1 tablespoon cooking oil
2 cups bread flour
1 cup whole wheat flour
¼ cup millet
2 tablespoons brown sugar
1 tablespoon minced dried onion
¾ teaspoon salt
⅛ teaspoon garlic powder
1 teaspoon active dry yeast or bread machine yeast

For 2-Pound Loaf (22 servings):

1⅓ cups milk
3 tablespoons water
4 teaspoons cooking oil
2⅔ cups bread flour
1⅓ cups whole wheat flour
⅓ cup millet
3 tablespoons brown sugar
4 teaspoons minced dried onion
1 teaspoon salt
⅛ teaspoon garlic powder
1¼ teaspoons active dry yeast or bread machine yeast

1 Select loaf size you want to make. Add the ingredients to a bread machine according to manufacturer's directions. If available, select whole grain cycle, or select basic white bread cycle. Remove hot bread from machine as soon as it is done. Place on wire rack; cool completely.

Nutrition Facts per serving: 121 cal., 2 g total fat (0 g sat. fat), 1 mg chol., 109 mg sodium, 23 g carbo., 2 g fiber, 4 g pro. Daily Values: 0% vit. A, 0% vit. C, 2% calcium, 7% iron

BREAD-MACHINE CONVERSIONS

With less math than you need to balance your checkbook, you easily can convert a conventional yeast bread recipe for use in your bread machine. Here's how:

- Reduce the amount of flour to 2 cups for a 1-pound machine, 3 cups for a 1½-pound machine, or 4 cups for a 2-pound machine.

- Reduce all ingredients by the same proportion, including the yeast (one package equals about 2¼ teaspoons). If a range is given for flour, use the lower amount to figure the reduction proportion. For example, for a 1½-pound bread machine, a recipe calling for 4½ to 5 cups of flour and 1 package of yeast would be decreased by one third—to 3 cups flour and 1½ teaspoons yeast.

- If the bread uses two or more types of flour, add the amounts of flour together and use that total as the basis for reducing the recipe. The total amount of flour used should only be 2, 3, or 4 cups, depending on the size of your machine.

- Use bread flour instead of all-purpose flour, or add 1 to 2 tablespoons gluten flour (available at health food stores) to the all-purpose flour. Rye breads will need 1 tablespoon of gluten flour even when bread flour is used.

- Bring liquids to room temperature before starting a recipe.

- Measure the liquids as you would for any other recipe, but add them in the order specified by the bread-machine manufacturer.

- Add dried fruits or nuts at the raisin-bread cycle, if your machine has one. If not, add according to manufacturer's directions.

- Don't use light-color dried fruits, such as apricots and golden raisins, because the preservatives in them can inhibit yeast performance. Choose another fruit or use the dough cycle and lightly knead the fruit in by hand before shaping the loaves.

- If you are only making the dough in the machine, you might have to knead in a little more flour after removing the dough from the machine and before shaping it. Knead in just enough to make the dough easy to handle. If necessary, let the dough rest 5 minutes before shaping it. The dough is very elastic, and letting it rest makes it easier to shape.

- If a recipe contains whole wheat or rye flour, use the whole-wheat cycle, if your machine has one. For sweet or rich breads, use the light-color setting, if your machine has one.

- The first time you try a new bread in your machine, watch and listen carefully. Check the dough after the first 3 to 5 minutes of kneading. If your machine works excessively hard during the mixing cycle, if the dough looks dry and crumbly (see top photo, below), or if two or more balls of dough form, add additional liquid, 1 teaspoon at a time, until one smooth ball forms.

If the dough has too much moisture and does not form a ball (see middle photo, below), add additional bread flour, 1 tablespoon at a time, until a ball does form. (Keep a record of how much liquid or flour was added.) Bread dough with the correct amount of flour and liquid will form a smooth ball (see photo, left).

EASY YEAST BREAD *EASY*

Prep: 30 minutes   **Chill:** 2 hours to 3 days
Rise: about 30 minutes
Bake: 10 minutes (rolls), 25 minutes (loaves)
Makes: 24 rolls or 2 loaves (24 servings)
Oven: 375°

Homemade bread is minutes away when you have this no-knead bread dough on hand. Mix it up in 20 minutes, then store it in the refrigerator for up to 3 days, or freeze it for up to 3 months. It makes great pizza crust, too.

3¾ cups all-purpose flour
    (or 2¾ cups all-purpose flour
    plus 1 cup whole wheat flour)
  1 package active dry yeast
  ½ teaspoon dried dillweed, or dried
    sage or basil, crushed (optional)
1¼ cups milk
  ¼ cup butter or shortening
  2 to 4 tablespoons sugar
  ½ teaspoon salt
  1 egg or 2 egg whites

1 In a large bowl mix 1½ cups of the all-purpose flour, the yeast, and, if desired, herb; set aside. In saucepan heat and stir milk, butter, sugar, and salt just until warm (120° to 130°) and butter almost melts. Add butter mixture to dry mixture along with egg. Beat with an electric mixer on low to medium speed for 30 seconds, scraping bowl. Beat on high speed for 3 minutes. Stir in the remaining flour.*

2 Cover and refrigerate for at least 2 hours or for up to 3 days. Stir dough down. Divide dough in half. Cover; let rest 10 minutes. Shape into Butterhorns, Cloverleaf Rolls, Rosettes, or Loaves, as desired. Bake in a 375° oven until done. (Allow 10 to 12 minutes or until golden for rolls. Allow 25 to 30 minutes or until bread sounds hollow when you tap tops for loaves. If necessary, cover loaves with foil the last 10 minutes of baking to prevent overbrowning.) Immediately remove from pans. Cool on wire racks.

Butterhorns: Grease baking sheets. Divide each half of dough into 2 portions (4 portions total). On a lightly floured surface, roll each portion to an 8-inch circle. If desired, brush with melted butter. Cut each circle into 6 wedges. Starting at wide end of each wedge, roll toward point. Place, point sides down, on prepared baking sheets. Cover; let rise in warm place until nearly double (30 to 40 minutes). Bake rolls as at left.

Cloverleaf Rolls: Grease twenty-four 2½-inch muffin cups. Divide each half of dough into 2 portions. Divide each portion into 18 pieces (72 pieces total). Shape each piece into a ball, tucking edges under to make smooth tops. Place 3 balls in each prepared muffin cup, smooth sides up. Cover; let rise until nearly double (30 to 40 minutes). Bake as at left.

Rosettes: Grease baking sheets. Divide each half of dough into 12 pieces (24 pieces total). On a floured surface, roll each piece into a 12-inch-long rope. Tie rope in a loose knot, leaving 2 long ends. Tuck top end under knot. Bring bottom end up; tuck into center of knot. Place on prepared baking sheets. Cover; let rise until nearly double (30 to 40 minutes). If desired, brush rolls with a mixture of 1 egg yolk and 1 tablespoon water. Bake rolls as at left.

Loaves: Grease two 8×4×2-inch loaf pans. On a lightly floured surface, roll each half of the dough to a 12×8-inch rectangle. Roll up each, jelly-roll style, starting from a short side. Seal with fingertips as you roll. Place in prepared pans. Cover; let rise in a warm place until nearly double (35 to 45 minutes). Bake as at left.

*Note: You can freeze the dough at this point. Divide the dough in half. Wrap in plastic wrap; place in freezer bags. Seal, label, and freeze for up to 3 months. Before using, thaw for about 2½ hours at room temperature or overnight in the refrigerator. Shape as directed above.

Nutrition Facts per roll or serving: 96 cal., 3 g total fat (1 g sat. fat), 15 mg chol., 73 mg sodium, 16 g carbo., 1 g fiber, 3 g pro. Daily Values: 2% vit. A, 0% vit. C, 1% calcium, 6% iron

BRIOCHE

Prep: 50 minutes   **Rise:** 2¾ hours   **Chill:** 6 hours
Bake: 15 minutes   **Makes:** 24 rolls   **Oven:** 375°

Rich and buttery, brioche traditionally are shaped with elegant topknots.

  1 **package active dry yeast**
¼ **cup warm water (105° to 115°)**
½ **cup butter**
⅓ **cup sugar**
¾ **teaspoon salt**
  4 **cups all-purpose flour**
½ **cup milk**
  4 **eggs**

1 **Dissolve the yeast** in the ¼ cup warm water. Let stand 5 to 10 minutes to soften. In large bowl beat butter, sugar, and salt with electric mixer on low to medium speed until fluffy. Add 1 cup of the flour and the milk. Separate 1 egg. Add the egg yolk and remaining whole eggs to the beaten mixture (refrigerate egg white to use later). Add softened yeast; beat well. Stir in the remaining flour until smooth. Place in a greased bowl. Cover; let rise in warm place until double in size (about 2 hours). Refrigerate dough 6 hours. (Or, omit 2-hour rising time and refrigerate dough for up to 24 hours.)

2 **Grease twenty-four** 2½-inch muffin cups; set aside. Stir dough down. Turn dough out onto a floured surface. Divide dough into 4 portions; set 1 portion aside. Divide each of the remaining 3 portions into 8 pieces (24 pieces total).

3 **To shape,** pull each piece into a ball, tucking edges under to make smooth tops. Place in prepared muffin cups, smooth sides up. Divide reserved dough portion into 24 pieces; shape into balls. Using floured finger, make an indentation in each large ball. Press a small ball into each indentation. Stir together reserved egg white and 1 tablespoon water; brush over rolls. Cover; let rise in a warm place until double in size (45 to 55 minutes).

4 **Bake in** 375° oven 15 minutes or until golden, brushing again with egg white mixture after 7 minutes. Remove from pans. Cool on wire racks.

Nutrition Facts per roll: 130 cal., 5 g total fat
(3 g sat. fat), 46 mg chol., 125 mg sodium,
18 g carbo., 1 g fiber, 3 g pro. Daily Values: 6% vit. A,
0% vit. C, 1% calcium, 7% iron

SIMPLE WHEAT ROLLS

Prep: 25 minutes   **Chill:** 2 to 24 hours
Rise: 40 minutes   **Bake:** 20 minutes
Makes: 24 rolls   **Oven:** 375°

These all-time favorites always are freshly baked. One Better Homes and Gardens® editor likes to take a basketful to Thanksgiving dinner. The dough can be refrigerated for up to 24 hours before baking.

4¼ **cups all-purpose flour**
  ⅓ **cup sugar**
  2 **envelopes active dry yeast**
  2 **teaspoons salt**
  2 **eggs**
  2 **cups warm water (120° to 130°)**
¾ **cup cooking oil**
  2 **cups whole wheat flour**
     Nonstick spray coating or shortening

1 **In a large mixing** bowl mix 3 cups of the all-purpose flour, the sugar, yeast, and salt. Stir together the eggs, water, and oil; add to flour mixture.

2 **Beat with** an electric mixer on low to medium speed for 30 seconds, scraping side of bowl constantly. Beat on high speed for 3 minutes. Using a wooden spoon, stir in remaining all-purpose flour and the whole wheat flour.

3 **Transfer dough** to a very large greased bowl; turn once. Cover; refrigerate for 2 to 24 hours.

4 **Stir dough** down. Let dough rest 10 minutes. Meanwhile, spray a 13×9×2-inch baking pan and an 8×8×2-inch baking pan with nonstick coating, or lightly grease pans with shortening.

5 **Turn dough** out onto a well-floured surface. Roll dough to a 12×8-inch rectangle; cut with a knife or pizza cutter into twenty-four 2×2-inch rolls. Transfer rolls to prepared pans (put 16 rolls in the 13×9-inch pan and 8 rolls in the 8×8-inch pan). Cover; let rise in a warm place until double in size (about 40 minutes).

6 **Bake in a** 375° oven for 20 to 25 minutes or until golden. Serve warm.

Nutrition Facts per roll: 187 cal., 8 g total fat
(1 g sat. fat), 18 mg chol., 185 mg sodium,
26 g carbo., 2 g fiber, 4 g pro. Daily Values: 0% vit. A,
0% vit. C, 0% calcium, 9% iron

PROOF-POSITIVE

There's something soothing about having bread rising as you putter around the house, but if time is of the essence, try using your microwave to speed the proofing process.

- First, do the following test: Place 2 tablespoons butter in a custard cup in the center of your oven. Cook, uncovered, on 10% power (low) 4 minutes. If butter doesn't melt completely, your microwave is proofing-ready. If it does, your microwave puts out too much power even at the low setting and will kill the yeast before the bread has a chance to rise. If so, you'll need to raise your yeast breads conventionally.

- If your oven passed the test, place 3 cups of water in a microwave-safe 4-cup measure. Cook on 100% power (high) 6½ to 8½ minutes or until boiling. Move measure to back of oven. Place kneaded dough in a microwave-safe greased bowl, turning once. Cover with waxed paper and place in the microwave with the hot water. Heat dough and water on 10% power (low) 13 to 15 minutes (15 to 20 minutes for rich breads) or until dough has nearly doubled. Punch it down. Then shape it (for any shape other than loaves, you'll have to do the second proofing conventionally because the pans won't fit in the microwave).

- Place the loaves in microwave-safe dishes. Return to the microwave oven with the hot water. Cover with waxed paper. Heat on low for 6 to 8 minutes (10 to 14 minutes for rich breads) or until nearly doubled.

CRUNCHY PARMESAN-HERB BREADSTICKS

Prep: 40 minutes **Rise:** 1¼ hours
Bake: 30 minutes
Makes: 24 breadsticks **Oven:** 375°/300°

LOW-FAT

Enjoy these plain, or dip them in your favorite mustard, pizza sauce, or sour cream dip.

     2 to 2½ cups all-purpose flour
     ⅓ cup grated Parmesan cheese
     1 package active dry yeast
     1 teaspoon Italian seasoning, crushed
     ¾ cup warm water (120° to 130°)
     1 tablespoon cooking oil
     1 slightly beaten egg white
     1 tablespoon water
        Grated Parmesan cheese

1 In a medium mixing bowl stir together ¾ cup of the flour, the ⅓ cup Parmesan cheese, the yeast, and Italian seasoning. Add the ¾ cup warm water and the oil to dry mixture. Beat with an electric mixer on low to medium speed for 30 seconds, scraping side of bowl constantly. Beat on high speed for 3 minutes. Using a wooden spoon, stir in as much of the remaining flour as you can.

2 Turn dough out onto a lightly floured surface. Knead in enough of the remaining flour to make a stiff dough that is smooth and elastic (8 to 10 minutes total) (see top photo, page 345). Shape into a ball. Place dough in a lightly greased bowl, turning once to grease the surface. Cover; let rise in a warm place until double in size (45 to 60 minutes) (see second photo, page 345).

3 Punch dough down. Turn out onto a lightly floured surface. Divide into 4 portions. Divide each portion into 6 pieces (24 pieces total). Cover; let rest for 10 minutes. Grease baking sheets. To shape breadsticks, roll each piece into an 8-inch-long rope. Place ropes 2 inches apart on prepared baking sheets. Cover; let rise in a warm place until nearly double in size (about 30 minutes).

4 Stir together egg white and the 1 tablespoon water; brush on breadsticks. Sprinkle with additional Parmesan cheese. Bake in a 375° oven for 10 minutes. Reduce oven temperature to 300°. Bake for 20 to 25 minutes more or until golden and crisp. Transfer to wire racks; cool completely.

Nutrition Facts per breadstick: 49 cal., 1 g total fat (0 g sat. fat), 1 mg chol., 33 mg sodium, 8 g carbo., 0 g fiber, 2 g pro. Daily Values: 0% vit. A, 0% vit. C, 2% calcium, 3% iron

AUTUMN GRAPE
CLUSTERS

Prep: 1 hour   Rise: 2¼ hours
Chill: 2 to 24 hours   Bake: 12 minutes
Makes: 10 rolls   Oven: 375°

4½   **cups all-purpose flour**
  1   **package active dry yeast**
  1   **cup milk**
½   **cup butter**
  3   **tablespoons sugar**
  3   **eggs**
  1   **egg yolk**
  1   **teaspoon water**

1 **In large** bowl combine 2 cups of the flour and the yeast. In a medium saucepan heat and stir milk, butter, sugar, and ¾ teaspoon salt until warm (120° to 130°) and butter almost melts. Add milk mixture to dry mixture along with the whole eggs. Beat with an electric mixer on low to medium speed for 30 seconds, scraping bowl. Beat on high speed 3 minutes. Using a spoon, stir in remaining flour.

Arrange balls of dough into loose rows, occasionally making the rows 2 balls high. Decorate each cluster of balls with leaves, a vine, and a stem.

2 **Place dough** in a greased bowl. Cover; let rise in warm place until double (about 2 hours). Punch dough down. Cover with plastic wrap; refrigerate for 2 to 24 hours. Punch down. Turn out onto a lightly floured surface. Divide into 10 portions. Cover; return all but 1 portion to the refrigerator.

3 **To shape a grape cluster,** using kitchen scissors, snip the 1 portion into 20 to 22 pieces, varying the sizes slightly. Set 5 small pieces aside. Grease baking sheets. To make the grapes, roll remaining pieces into balls. Using your finger, rub each ball with a little water as you assemble them together into a grape cluster. On a greased baking sheet, build grape clusters, starting with 4 or 5 balls at the top of the cluster and continuing in loosely organized rows, ending with 1 ball at the bottom of the cluster. Shape the reserved small pieces of dough into 3 leaves, a stem, and a curly vine; arrange on grape cluster (see photo, left). If desired, use a knife to mark veins in the leaves. Continue with the remaining dough portions, keeping dough chilled until needed. When all are assembled, cover grape clusters; let rise in a warm place for 15 minutes.

4 **In a small bowl** combine egg yolk and water; brush on grape clusters. Bake in a 375° oven for 12 to 15 minutes or until golden. Transfer to wire racks; cool completely. Serve the same day. (Or, seal, label, and freeze for up to 1 month.)

Nutrition Facts per roll: 327 cal., 12 g total fat (7 g sat. fat), 112 mg chol., 300 mg sodium, 45 g carbo., 2 g fiber, 9 g pro. Daily Values: 18% vit. A, 0% vit. C, 4% calcium, 18% iron

---

WHEN TWO'S A CROWD

Much of the success of yeast breads hinges on making sure enough air circulates in the oven as the loaves or rolls are baking. When baking several long or round loaves of bread at the same time or a large batch of rolls, you'll need an extra-large baking sheet (about 17×14 inches). If you don't have one this large, you can shape the loaves or rolls on two smaller baking sheets and let them rise as directed. But bake only one at a time, placing the second sheet in the refrigerator. If you bake two smaller sheets at the same time, not enough air will circulate around the bread while in the oven and cause the bread to bake unevenly.

Autumn Grape Clusters: For a captivating centerpiece on a party table, arrange several of these golden loaves on a platter.

SOFT PRETZELS

Prep: 50 minutes   **Rise:** 1¼ hours
Bake: 24 minutes   **Boil:** 2 minutes per batch
Makes: 20 pretzels   **Oven:** 475°/350°

As is done for bagels, briefly boiling the pretzels gives them a tuggy, delightfully chewy texture.

4 to 4½ cups all-purpose flour
1 package active dry yeast
1½ cups milk
¼ cup sugar
2 tablespoons cooking oil
1 teaspoon salt
2 tablespoons salt
3 quarts boiling water
1 slightly beaten egg white
1 tablespoon water
   Sesame seed, poppy seed,
      or coarse salt

1 **In a large mixing** bowl stir together 1½ cups of the flour and the yeast; set aside. In a medium saucepan heat and stir milk, sugar, oil, and the 1 teaspoon salt until warm (120° to 130°). Add milk mixture to dry mixture. Beat with an electric mixer on low to medium speed for 30 seconds, scraping side of bowl constantly. Beat on high speed for 3 minutes. Using a wooden spoon, stir in as much of the remaining flour as you can.

2 **Turn dough** out onto a lightly floured surface. Knead in enough of the remaining flour to make a moderately stiff dough that is smooth and elastic (6 to 8 minutes total) (see top photo, page 345). Shape the dough into a ball. Place dough in a lightly greased bowl, turning once to grease surface. Cover; let rise in a warm place until double in size (about 1¼ hours) (see second photo, page 345).

3 **Punch dough** down. Turn dough out onto a lightly floured surface. Cover dough; let rest for 10 minutes. Meanwhile, lightly grease baking sheets; set aside.

4 **Roll dough into** a 12×10-inch rectangle. Cut into twenty 12×½-inch strips. Gently pull each strip into a 16-inch-long rope. Shape ropes into pretzels (see photo, right).

5 **Carefully** place pretzels on prepared baking sheets. Bake in a 475° oven for 4 minutes. Remove pretzels from oven. Reduce the oven temperature to 350°.

6 **Dissolve the 2 tablespoons salt** in the boiling water. Lower pretzels, 3 or 4 at a time, into the boiling water. Boil for 2 minutes, turning once. Using a slotted spoon, remove pretzels from water; drain on paper towels. Let stand a few seconds. Grease baking sheets well. Place pretzels about ½ inch apart on the prepared baking sheets.

7 **In a small** mixing bowl stir together egg white and the 1 tablespoon water. Brush pretzels with some of the egg white mixture. Sprinkle pretzels lightly with sesame seed, poppy seed, or coarse salt. Bake in the 350° oven for 20 to 25 minutes or until golden. Transfer to wire racks; cool completely.

Nutrition Facts per pretzel: 119 cal., 2 g total fat (0 g sat. fat), 1 mg chol., 226 mg sodium, 21 g carbo., 1 g fiber, 3 g pro. Daily Values: 1% vit. A, 0% vit. C, 2% calcium, 7% iron

Whole Wheat Soft Pretzels: Prepare as above, except substitute 1½ cups whole wheat flour for 1½ cups of the all-purpose flour that is stirred in at the end of step 1.

About 4 inches from each end of a rope, cross one end over the other. Twist once at the crossover point. Fold ends up over the edge of circle. Moisten ends; tuck them under bottom edge of circle. Press to seal.

PRETZEL PARTNERS

Depending on how you choose to top your homemade pretzels before baking them— with coarse salt, sesame seed, poppy seed, or simply egg white—the options for a sweet or savory treat are nearly limitless. Here are some ideas for other fun ways to embellish them.

Just before serving, brush the pretzels with melted butter and sprinkle on grated Parmesan, Romano, or other hard cheese; a Cajun spice mixture; or a cinnamon-sugar mixture.

Though the traditional go-with for soft pretzels is spicy mustard (and there's a whole host of mustards on your supermarket shelf from which to choose), consider other accompaniments, such as a bold cheese sauce or flavored sour cream dips.

HERBED-POTATO
PARKER HOUSE ROLLS

Prep: 40 minutes **Rise:** 1⅓ hours
Bake: 12 minutes **Makes:** 30 rolls **Oven:** 375°

These rolls shaped like little pocketbooks became famous in the late 1800s as a specialty served at the Parker House, a Boston hotel.

  3 to 3½ cups all-purpose flour
  1 package active dry yeast
  3 tablespoons snipped fresh chives
  2 teaspoons snipped fresh dill
  ¾ cup water
  ¼ cup butter
  1 teaspoon sugar
  ½ teaspoon salt
  1 egg
  ¼ cup mashed potatoes
  3 tablespoons butter, melted
    Grated Parmesan cheese

1 **In a large mixing** bowl combine 1½ cups of the flour, the yeast, chives, and dill. In a small saucepan heat and stir the water, the ¼ cup butter, the sugar, and salt until warm (120° to 130°) and butter almost melts. Add butter mixture to dry mixture. Add egg and mashed potatoes. Beat with an electric mixer on low to medium speed for 30 seconds, scraping side of bowl constantly. Beat on high speed for 3 minutes. Using wooden spoon, stir in as much of the remaining flour as you can.

2 **Turn dough** out onto a lightly floured surface. Knead in enough of the remaining flour to make a moderately stiff dough that is smooth and elastic (6 to 8 minutes total) (see top photo, page 345). Shape dough into a ball. Place in a lightly greased bowl, turning once to grease surface. Cover and let rise in a warm place until double in size (about 1 hour) (see second photo, page 345).

3 **Punch dough** down. Turn out onto a lightly floured surface. Divide dough in half. Cover; let rest 10 minutes. Grease baking sheets; set aside. Roll each half of dough to ¼-inch thickness. Using a floured 2½-inch biscuit cutter, cut into rounds. Brush with some of the melted butter.

4 **To shape rolls,** use a wooden spoon handle to make a slightly off-center crease in each round. For each roll, fold large half over small half, overlapping slightly; press folded edge firmly. Place rolls 3 inches apart on prepared baking sheets. Cover; let rise until nearly double in size (about 20 minutes).

5 **Lightly brush tops** of rolls with remaining melted butter. Sprinkle with Parmesan cheese. Bake in a 375° oven for 12 to 15 minutes or until golden. Serve warm.

Nutrition Facts per roll: 71 cal., 3 g total fat (2 g sat. fat), 14 mg chol., 74 mg sodium, 9 g carbo., 0 g fiber, 2 g pro. Daily Values: 2% vit. A, 0% vit. C, 0% calcium, 4% iron

ENGLISH MUFFINS

Prep: 30 minutes **Rise:** 1½ hours
Cook: 25 minutes **Makes:** 12 muffins

5¼ to 5¾ cups all-purpose flour
2 packages active dry yeast
2 cups milk
¼ cup butter or shortening
2 tablespoons sugar
   Cornmeal

1 In a large bowl stir together 2 cups of the flour and yeast; set aside. In saucepan heat and stir milk, butter, sugar, and 1 teaspoon salt just until warm (120° to 130°) and butter almost melts. Add milk mixture to dry mixture. Beat with electric mixer on low speed for 30 seconds, scraping bowl. Beat on high speed for 3 minutes. Using spoon, stir in as much of the remaining flour as you can.

2 Turn dough out onto lightly floured surface. Knead in enough remaining flour to make moderately stiff dough that is smooth and elastic (6 to 8 minutes total). Shape dough into ball. Place dough in lightly greased bowl; turn once. Cover; let rise in warm place until double (about 1 hour).

3 Punch dough down. Turn out onto a lightly floured surface. Cover; let rest for 10 minutes. Roll to slightly less than ½-inch thickness. Using floured 4-inch biscuit cutter, cut dough into rounds, dipping cutter into flour between cuts. Reroll as necessary. Dip both sides of each muffin into cornmeal. (If necessary, to make cornmeal adhere, lightly brush muffins with water.) Cover; let rise in a warm place until very light (about 30 minutes).

4 Cook muffins, 4 at a time, in ungreased electric skillet* at 325° for 25 to 30 minutes or until golden, turning every 5 minutes. (Keep remaining muffins in refrigerator for up to 8 hours.) Cool on wire racks. Split muffins horizontally. To serve, toast or broil muffin halves.

*Note: If you don't have an electric skillet, cook muffins over low heat on an ungreased large griddle or in several skillets for 25 to 30 minutes or until golden, turning frequently.

Nutrition Facts per muffin: 253 cal., 6 g total fat (2 g sat. fat), 8 mg chol., 234 mg sodium, 43 g carbo., 2 g fiber, 7 g pro. Daily Values: 6% vit. A, 0% vit. C, 4% calcium, 17% iron

CINNAMON ROLLS

Prep: 45 minutes **Rise:** 1 hour
Chill: 2 to 24 hours **Stand:** 30 minutes
Bake: 20 minutes **Makes:** 24 rolls **Oven:** 375°

4¾ to 5¼ cups all-purpose flour
1 package active dry yeast
1 cup milk
⅓ cup butter
⅓ cup granulated sugar
½ teaspoon salt
3 eggs
1 recipe Brown Sugar Filling
   (see page 379)
½ cup golden raisins (optional)
½ cup chopped pecans (optional)
1 tablespoon half-and-half or
   light cream
1 recipe Vanilla Glaze (see page 379)

1 In a large mixing bowl combine 2¼ cups of the flour and the yeast. In a saucepan heat and stir milk, butter, granulated sugar, and salt just until warm (120° to 130°) and butter almost melts. Add milk mixture to dry mixture along with eggs. Beat with electric mixer on low speed 30 seconds, scraping bowl. Beat on high speed 3 minutes. Stir in as much of the remaining flour as you can.

2 Turn dough out onto a lightly floured surface. Knead in enough of the remaining flour to make a moderately soft dough that is smooth and elastic (3 to 5 minutes total). Shape into a ball. Place in a greased bowl, turning once. Cover; let rise in a warm place until double (about 1 hour).

3 Punch dough down. Turn out onto a lightly floured surface. Divide in half. Cover; let rest for 10 minutes. Lightly grease two 9×1½-inch round baking pans or 2 baking sheets. Roll each half of dough into a 12×8-inch rectangle. Sprinkle Brown Sugar Filling over dough rectangles. If desired, sprinkle with raisins and pecans. Roll up each rectangle, jelly-roll style, starting from a long side. Seal seams. Slice each roll into 12 pieces. Place, cut sides down, in prepared pans or on prepared baking sheets.

4 Cover dough loosely with clear plastic wrap, leaving room for rolls to rise. Refrigerate for 2 to 24 hours. Uncover; let stand at room temperature

Maple-Nut Rolls: One of the most wonderful features of this recipe is that you can shape the rolls the night before you plan to enjoy them. When you awaken in the morning, just pop the rolls in the oven and serve them warm.

30 minutes. (Or, to bake rolls right away, don't chill dough. Instead, cover loosely; let dough rise in warm place until nearly double, about 30 minutes.)

5 **Break any** surface bubbles with a greased toothpick. Brush dough with half-and-half or light cream. Bake in 375° oven for 20 to 25 minutes or until light brown (if necessary, cover rolls loosely with foil for the last 5 to 10 minutes of baking to prevent overbrowning). Remove from oven. Brush again with half-and-half or light cream. Cool for 1 minute. Carefully invert rolls onto wire rack. Cool slightly. Invert again onto a serving platter. Drizzle with Vanilla Glaze. Serve warm.

Brown Sugar Filling: In a medium mixing bowl stir together ¾ cup packed brown sugar, ¼ cup all-purpose flour, and 1 tablespoon ground cinnamon. Cut in ⅓ cup butter until crumbly.

Vanilla Glaze: In small mixing bowl stir together 1¼ cups sifted powdered sugar, 1 teaspoon light-colored corn syrup, and ½ teaspoon vanilla. Stir in enough half-and-half or light cream (1 to 2 tablespoons) to make drizzling consistency.

Nutrition Facts per roll: 203 cal., 6 g total fat (4 g sat. fat), 42 mg chol., 120 mg sodium, 33 g carbo., 1 g fiber, 4 g pro. Daily Values: 8% vit. A, 0% vit. C, 2% calcium, 10% iron

Apple-Cinnamon Rolls: Prepare as at left, except substitute 1 cup finely chopped, peeled apple for the raisins and nuts.

Chocolate-Cinnamon Rolls: Prepare as at left, except substitute 1 cup semisweet chocolate pieces for the raisins and nuts.

Old-Fashioned Cinnamon Rolls: Prepare as at left, except omit Brown Sugar Filling. Brush dough rectangles with 3 tablespoons melted butter. Combine ⅔ cup granulated sugar and 2 teaspoons ground cinnamon; sprinkle over rectangles. Continue as at left.

Maple-Nut Rolls: Prepare as at left, except omit the Brown Sugar Filling and Vanilla Glaze. Mix ¾ cup packed brown sugar, ¼ cup all-purpose flour, and 1 tablespoon apple pie spice. Using a pastry blender, cut in ¼ cup butter until crumbly. Stir in 1 cup finely snipped dried apricots. Sprinkle over rectangles; top with ½ cup chopped toasted pecans. Continue as at left. Drizzle rolls with 1 recipe Maple Glaze (see below).

Maple Glaze: Heat 3 tablespoons butter over medium-low heat 7 to 10 minutes or until light brown; remove from heat. Stir in 1½ cups sifted powdered sugar and ¼ cup maple or maple-flavored syrup. If needed, stir in milk to make drizzling consistency.

GOOEY CARAMEL-PECAN ROLLS

BEST-LOVED

Prep: 45 minutes **Rise:** 1½ hours
Bake: 20 minutes **Makes:** 12 rolls
Oven: 375°

*Keep plenty of napkins on hand for these
irresistible sticky rolls.*

    4 to 4½ cups all-purpose flour
    1 package active dry yeast
    1 cup milk
    ⅓ cup granulated sugar
    ¼ cup butter
    ½ teaspoon salt
    ¼ teaspoon ground ginger, ground
        nutmeg, ground cinnamon,
        finely shredded orange peel,
        or finely shredded lemon peel
        (optional)
    2 eggs
    ½ cup packed brown sugar
    2 tablespoons granulated sugar
    1 teaspoon ground cinnamon
    ⅓ cup butter
    ⅔ cup packed brown sugar
    3 tablespoons light-colored corn
        syrup
    1 cup chopped pecans
    3 tablespoons butter, melted

1 **In a large mixing** bowl stir together 2 cups of the flour and the yeast; set aside.

2 **In medium** saucepan heat and stir milk, the ⅓ cup granulated sugar, the ¼ cup butter, the salt, and, if desired, a spice or peel just until warm (120° to 130°) and butter almost melts. Add milk mixture to dry mixture along with eggs. Beat with electric mixer on low to medium speed 30 seconds, scraping side of bowl constantly. Beat on high speed for 3 minutes. Using a wooden spoon, stir in as much of the remaining flour as you can.

3 **Turn dough** out onto a lightly floured surface. Knead in enough of the remaining flour to make a moderately soft dough that is smooth and elastic (3 to 5 minutes total) (see top photo, page 345). Shape dough into a ball. Place dough in a lightly greased bowl, turning once to grease surface. Cover; let rise in a warm place until double in size (about 1 hour) (see second photo, page 345).

4 **For filling,** in small bowl stir together the ½ cup brown sugar, the 2 tablespoons granulated sugar, and the 1 teaspoon cinnamon; set aside.

5 **Punch dough** down. Turn out onto a lightly floured surface. Cover; let rest 10 minutes.

6 **While dough** is resting, in a medium saucepan melt the ⅓ cup butter. Stir in the ⅔ cup brown sugar and the corn syrup. Cook and stir until combined. Pour into an ungreased 13×9×2-inch baking pan. Sprinkle pecans evenly over top; set aside.

7 **Roll dough** into an 18×10-inch rectangle. Brush dough with the melted butter. Sprinkle filling over dough rectangle. Roll up, jelly-roll style, starting from a long side. Seal seam. Slice roll into 12 equal pieces. Place, cut sides down, in prepared pan. Cover; let rise in a warm place until nearly double (about 30 minutes). (Or, cover rolls loosely with plastic wrap, leaving room for rolls to rise. Refrigerate for 2 to 24 hours. Uncover and let stand at room temperature for 30 minutes.)

8 **Bake in a** 375° oven for 20 to 25 minutes or until golden. Cool in pan for 5 minutes. Invert rolls onto a wire rack or serving platter. Serve warm.

To Make Ahead: Prepare and bake rolls as above; cool completely. Place the rolls in a freezer container or freezer bag; freeze for up to 3 months. Before serving, wrap the frozen rolls in foil and bake in a 300° oven about 25 minutes or until warm.

Nutrition Facts per serving: 437 cal., 19 g total fat
(8 g sat. fat), 69 mg chol., 238 mg sodium,
61 g carbo., 2 g fiber, 7 g pro. Daily Values:
13% vit. A, 0% vit. C, 5% calcium, 19% iron

BAGELS

Prep: 40 minutes   **Rise:** 20 minutes
Broil: 3 minutes   **Boil:** 7 minutes per batch
Bake: 25 minutes   **Makes:** 12 bagels   **Oven:** 375°

A three-step procedure of broiling, boiling, and baking gives bagels their unique texture.

4¼ to 4¾ cups all-purpose flour
1 package active dry yeast
1½ cups warm water (120° to 130°)
3 tablespoons sugar
1 teaspoon salt
6 cups water
1 tablespoon sugar

1 **In a large mixing** bowl stir together 2 cups of the flour and the yeast. Add the 1½ cups warm water, the 3 tablespoons sugar, and the salt. Beat with an electric mixer on low to medium speed for 30 seconds, scraping side of bowl constantly. Beat on high speed for 3 minutes. Using a wooden spoon, stir in as much of the remaining flour as you can.

2 **Turn dough** out onto a floured surface. Knead in enough of the remaining flour to make a moderately stiff dough that is smooth and elastic (6 to 8 minutes total) (see top photo, page 345). Cover; let rest 10 minutes. Meanwhile, grease a large baking sheet.

3 **Working quickly,** divide dough into 12 portions; shape each into a smooth ball. Punch a hole in center of each ball; pull gently to make a 2-inch hole. Place on prepared baking sheet. Cover; let rise 20 minutes. (Start timing after first bagel is shaped.)

4 **Broil bagels** 5 inches from heat for 3 to 4 minutes, turning once (tops should not brown). Meanwhile, in a deep 12-inch skillet or a large pot bring the 6 cups water and the 1 tablespoon sugar to boiling. Reduce heat. Add bagels, 4 or 5 at a time, and simmer for 7 minutes, turning once. Drain bagels on paper towels. Grease a baking sheet well. Place drained bagels on the prepared baking sheet. Bake in a 375° oven for 25 to 30 minutes or until tops are golden. Transfer to wire rack; cool completely

Nutrition Facts per bagel: 166 cal., 0 g total fat, 0 mg chol., 179 mg sodium, 35 g carbo., 1 g fiber, 4 g pro. Daily Values: 0% vit. A, 0% vit. C, 0% calcium, 13% iron

Onion Bagels: Prepare as above, except stir 2 tablespoons dried minced onion into the flour along with the yeast.

Raisin Bagels: Prepare as above, except add ¾ cup raisins with the all-purpose flour that is stirred in at the end of step 1.

Whole Wheat Bagels: Prepare as above, except substitute 1½ cups whole wheat flour for 1½ cups of the all-purpose flour that is stirred in at the end of step 1.

THE BAGEL'S BEGINNING

Despite the fact that a circle is without end, this chewy, delicious circle with a hole in the center does have a beginning. Though it's not known where the bagel originated, the first written reference to bagels comes out of Krakow, Poland, in 1610. It's a decree outlawing the giving of bagels as gifts except "to midwives and the women present when a pregnant woman gives birth."

It seems odd, yes, but bagels were apparently thought to possess magical powers, and—not wanting to treat the bagel's mystical potency lightly—the city fathers reserved the gift of bagels for the most critical hours of life.

Thank goodness that law didn't last.

KOLACKY

Prep: 45 minutes   **Rise:** 1 hour 35 minutes
Bake: 12 minutes   **Makes:** 24 rolls
Oven: 375°

These Eastern European sweet rolls are as delicious with a poppy seed filling as with this fruit filling. Just purchase poppy seed cake and pastry filling and substitute it for the apricot filling, if you like.

    4 to 4½ cups all-purpose flour
    1 package active dry yeast
    1 cup milk
    ¾ cup butter
    ½ cup granulated sugar
    ½ teaspoon salt
    4 egg yolks
    1 teaspoon finely shredded lemon peel
    1 recipe Apricot Filling (see right)
    2 tablespoons butter, melted, or milk
      Powdered sugar

1 **In a large mixing** bowl combine 2 cups of the flour and the yeast; set aside.

2 **In a medium** saucepan heat and stir the 1 cup milk, the ¾ cup butter, the granulated sugar, and salt just until warm (120° to 130°) and butter almost melts. Add milk mixture to dry mixture along with the egg yolks. Beat with an electric mixer on low to medium speed for 30 seconds, scraping side of bowl constantly. Beat on high speed for 3 minutes. Using a wooden spoon, stir in lemon peel and as much of the remaining flour as you can.

3 **Turn dough** out onto a lightly floured surface. Knead in enough of the remaining flour to make a moderately soft dough that is smooth and elastic (3 to 5 minutes total) (see top photo, page 345). Place dough in a lightly greased bowl, turning once to grease the surface. Cover; let rise in a warm place until double in size (for 1 to 1½ hours) (see second photo, page 345).

4 **Meanwhile,** prepare Apricot Filling. Set filling aside to cool.

5 **Punch dough** down. Turn dough out onto a lightly floured surface. Divide dough in half. Cover; let rest 10 minutes. Grease 2 baking sheets.

6 **Shape each half** of the dough into 12 balls (24 balls total), tucking the edges under to make smooth tops. Place balls 3 inches apart on prepared baking sheets. Flatten each ball to 2½ inches in diameter. Cover; let rise in a warm place until nearly double (about 35 minutes).

7 **Using your thumb,** make an indentation in the center of each dough round. Spoon about 2 teaspoons of the Apricot Filling into each of the indentations. Lightly brush edges of dough with the 2 tablespoons melted butter or milk. Bake in a 375° oven for 12 to 15 minutes or until golden. Transfer to wire racks; cool completely. Lightly sift powdered sugar over the tops. (If desired, store in the refrigerator for up to 2 days.)

Apricot Filling: In a small saucepan combine 1 cup snipped dried apricots and enough water to cover apricots by 1 inch. Bring to boiling; reduce heat. Simmer, covered, 10 to 15 minutes or until apricots are very soft. Drain, reserving 2 tablespoons of the cooking liquid. In a blender container or food processor bowl place the softened apricots, reserved cooking liquid, ¼ cup granulated sugar, 1 teaspoon lemon juice, ¼ teaspoon ground cinnamon, and ⅛ teaspoon ground nutmeg. Cover; blend or process until smooth. Scrape down sides as necessary.

Nutrition Facts per roll: 182 cal., 8 g total fat (5 g sat. fat), 54 mg chol., 120 mg sodium, 25 g carbo., 1 g fiber, 3 g pro. Daily Values: 16% vit. A, 0% vit. C, 2% calcium, 8% iron

---

THE SHAPE OF KOLACKY TO COME

The little fruit-filled sweet breads called kolacky commonly are shaped in circles. To the people of Eastern Europe, where kolacky originated, the circle was a symbol of good luck, prosperity, and eternity. Today, you'll find kolacky that are made not only into circles but squares and diamonds, too. We don't know about their luck-producing ability, but they taste just as delicious.

baking with kids

Cookie-Cutter Cakes, recipe page 394

BAKING WITH KIDS

CANDY BAR COOKIES ON A STICK

Prep: 1 hour   **Bake:** 15 minutes per batch
Makes: about 40 cookies   **Oven:** 325°

What child can resist the fun of shaping dough around candy pieces to create a terrific treat?

  1 cup peanut butter
  ½ cup butter, softened
  ½ cup shortening
1½ cups granulated sugar
  ½ cup packed brown sugar
1½ teaspoons baking soda
  2 eggs
  1 teaspoon vanilla
2¼ cups all-purpose flour
 40 wooden sticks
 40 miniature-size (about 1-inch square) chocolate-coated caramel-topped nougat candy bars (with or without peanuts)
    Small multicolored decorative candies, chopped nuts, and/or colored sugar (optional)

Insert a wooden stick into one end of a candy piece. Take about 2 tablespoons of cookie dough and form it into a ball around the candy and the base of the stick.

1 **To make the cookie dough,** in a large mixing bowl beat peanut butter, butter, and shortening with an electric mixer on medium to high speed about 30 seconds. Add granulated sugar, brown sugar, and baking soda. Beat until combined. Beat in eggs and vanilla until combined. Beat in as much of the flour as you can with mixer. Using wooden spoon, stir in any remaining flour.

2 **To shape the cookies,** insert a wooden stick into each candy bar piece. For each cookie, form about 2 tablespoons dough into a ball and shape it around a piece of candy bar, making sure the candy is completely covered (see photo, above). If desired, roll ball in decorative candies, nuts, or colored sugar, gently pushing candies or nuts into dough.

3 **To bake the cookies,** place cookies 2½ inches apart on ungreased cookie sheets (see photo, above). Bake in a 325° oven for 15 to 20 minutes or until golden and set. Cool on cookie sheets for 5 minutes. Carefully transfer cookies to wire racks; cool completely. Place in an airtight container and store at room temperature for up to 3 days.

Nutrition Facts per cookie: 212 cal., 11 g total fat (4 g sat. fat), 18 mg chol., 131 mg sodium, 27 g carbo., 1 g fiber, 3 g pro. Daily Values: 2% vit. A, 0% vit. C, 2% calcium, 4% iron

---

TOOLBOX: KIDS IN THE KITCHEN

Baking is easy if you have the right tools. Here's a rundown of the equipment you need to bake the recipes in this chapter:
- Cookie sheets
- Cookie cutters, 4- and 5-inch round cutters
- Mixing bowls (large, medium, and small)
- Electric mixer
- Wooden spoons
- Pastry brush
- Spatulas (a rubber one for scraping bowls and pans clean, and a flat-edged metal or plastic one for removing cookies from cookie sheets)

- Wire racks
- Measuring cups and spoons
- Baking pans: an 8×8×2-inch square baking pan, a 13×9×2-inch baking pan, a 15×10×1-inch baking pan, a muffin pan with 2½-inch cups, 2 kid-size (5¾×3×2-inch) loaf pans, a large roasting pan
- Ruler
- Small self-sealing plastic freezer bags
- Wooden sticks
- Scissors
- Rolling pin

Flower Power Cookies: A roll of refrigerated sugar cookie dough grows into a garden of fanciful spring blossoms. Simply color the dough as desired and let kids shape it into their favorite flowers.

FLOWER POWER COOKIES

Prep: 1 hour   Bake: 8 minutes per batch
Makes: about 24 cookies   Oven: 375°

   1 **20-ounce roll refrigerated sugar cookie dough**
½ **cup almond paste**
   Food coloring
   Colored sugars, coarse sugar, or edible glitter

1 **To make the colored dough,** divide sugar cookie dough evenly among 4 small mixing bowls. Add 2 tablespoons almond paste and desired food coloring to each bowl of cookie dough.

2 **Beat each dough** with an electric mixer on medium speed until the color is well mixed, washing the beaters after each color. Break off small pieces of different colors of dough and shape them into desired flowers, spacing cookies 2 inches apart on ungreased cookie sheets. Sprinkle cookies with colored sugars, coarse sugar, or edible glitter.

3 **For daisy- or pansy-style cookies,** shape colored dough into ¼- to ½-inch balls. Use the balls for the flower centers and petals. (Or, flatten the balls to make petals.) If desired, overlap the petals around the center (see photo, lower left).

4 **For tulip-style** cookies, roll colored dough into 2½-inch-long logs. Place 5 logs side by side; pinch the logs together at one end to make the flower stem base. Curl out the tips at the other end to make opening petals (see photo, lower left).

5 **Bake cookies in a 375° oven** for 8 to 10 minutes or until the edges are light brown. Carefully transfer cookies to wire racks; cool completely.

Nutrition Facts per cookie: 133 cal., 6 g total fat (1 g sat. fat), 7 mg chol., 99 mg sodium, 18 g carbo., 0 g fiber, 2 g pro. Daily Values: 0% vit. A, 0% vit. C, 2% calcium, 3% iron

Shape these colorful cookies right on an ungreased cookie sheet. Mix and match pieces of colored dough to create a variety of flower shapes.

PLAYING IT SAFE

Make baking with kids a good time by keeping it safe. Follow these tips:

- Remind everyone to wash hands before starting.
- Keep hot pads handy and near the stove and a damp cloth close by for wiping up spills.
- Provide a step stool to prevent kids from climbing or reaching to get what they need.
- Set up electric appliances away from the sink.

- Explain how to operate the range and all the equipment needed for the recipe before starting.
- Teach kids to keep pan handles turned away from the edge of the range to avoid spills.
- Show kids how to use a cutting board when using a knife and how to cut with the sharp edge pointed away from their bodies.
- Encourage kids to think safety first!

PEANUT BUTTER DINOSAURS

Prep: 1 hour **Bake:** 10 minutes per batch
Makes: about 36 cookies **Oven:** 350°

1 cup shortening
1 cup peanut butter
1 cup granulated sugar
1 cup packed brown sugar
2 teaspoons baking powder
¼ teaspoon salt
2 eggs
1 teaspoon vanilla
2¼ cups all-purpose flour

1 To make the cookie dough, in a large mixing bowl beat shortening and peanut butter with an electric mixer on medium speed for 30 seconds. Add granulated sugar, brown sugar, baking powder, and salt. Beat until well combined. Beat in eggs and vanilla until combined. Beat in as much of the flour as you can with the mixer. Using a wooden spoon, stir in any remaining flour.

2 To shape the cookies, shape dough into balls and ropes. Place shapes on ungreased cookie sheets, pressing and molding with your fingers into dinosaur shapes. Flatten to ¼-inch thickness. Add small pieces of dough for eyes and other details; gently press them into the larger pieces of dough.

3 Bake cookies in a 350° oven for 10 to 12 minutes or until light brown on the edges. Cool on cookie sheets for 1 minute. Carefully transfer cookies to wire racks; cool completely.

Nutrition Facts per cookie: 168 cal., 10 g total fat (2 g sat. fat), 12 mg chol., 75 mg sodium, 19 g carbo. 1 g fiber, 3 g pro. Daily Values: 0% vit. A, 0% vit. C, 2% calcium, 4% iron

Dinosaur Cookies: From left, triceratops, stegosaurus, and brontosaurus rule as dessert or a snack. Start with peanut butter cookie dough, and your kids can create them all and more.

FROSTIES

Prep: 1 hour   **Bake:** 18 minutes per batch
Makes: 24 cookies   **Oven:** 325°

    1 **cup butter, softened**
   ½ **cup sugar**
    1 **teaspoon vanilla**
   ¼ **teaspoon salt**
  2¼ **cups all-purpose flour**
       Miniature semisweet chocolate
          pieces
   24 **gumdrops**
    1 **recipe Decorating Icing**
          (see page 389)
    1 **or 2 pieces rolled fruit leather**

1 **To make the cookie dough,** in a large mixing bowl beat butter with an electric mixer on medium to high speed for 30 seconds. Add sugar, vanilla, and salt. Beat until combined. Beat in as much of the flour as you can with the mixer. Using a wooden spoon, stir in any remaining flour.

2 **For each snowman,** shape dough into 3 balls: one 1-inch ball, one ¾-inch ball, and one ½-inch ball. Place balls on ungreased cookie sheets in decreasing sizes with edges touching. Press together slightly. Insert 2 chocolate pieces, point side down, in the smallest ball for eyes and 1 in the middle ball and 2 in the largest ball for buttons.

3 **Bake cookies in a 325° oven** for 18 to 20 minutes or until bottoms of cookies are light

Frosties: Gumdrop hats, fruit leather scarves, and tiny chocolate chip buttons attire these chubby snowmen. They love a snowy forecast, but they'll melt in your mouth whatever the weather.

brown. Carefully transfer the cookies to wire racks; cool completely.

4 **For hat,** flatten gumdrops into thin oval shapes (about 1½×1 inches each). Roll into cone shapes. Pinch edges together. Roll up bottom edge of each cone to form hat brim. Attach hats to heads with Decorating Icing. Place remaining Decorating Icing in a small self-sealing plastic freezer bag; seal bag and snip small hole in a corner. (Or, place icing in pastry bag fitted with a small round tip.) Pipe on brooms and faces. Cut fruit leather into 3-inch-long thin strips. Tie strips around necks for scarves.

Decorating Icing: Stir together 1 cup sifted powdered sugar and 1 tablespoon milk. Stir in a little additional milk until it reaches piping consistency. Tint with paste food coloring.

Nutrition Facts per cookie: 166 cal., 9 g total fat (2 g sat. fat), 10 mg chol., 77 mg sodium, 21 g carbo., 1 g fiber, 1 g pro. Daily Values: 7% vit. A, 1% vit. C, 0% calcium, 3% iron

JUMBO COMBO COOKIES

BEST-LOVED

Prep: 20 minutes **Cook:** 10 minutes per batch
Makes: 18 cookies **Oven:** 375°

These super-big cookies are extra fun to eat because you load them with your favorite fruit, nuts, or candy.

> 1 cup butter, softened
> 1 cup packed brown sugar
> 1 teaspoon baking powder
> ¼ teaspoon baking soda
> ¼ teaspoon salt
> 2 eggs
> 2 teaspoons vanilla
> 1½ cups all-purpose flour
> 1½ teaspoons finely shredded orange peel (optional)
> 2¼ cups regular or quick-cooking rolled oats
> 1½ cups dried fruit, nuts, and/or candy*

1 **Grease** a cookie sheet; set aside.

2 **To make the cookie dough,** in a large mixing bowl beat butter with an electric mixer on medium to high speed for 30 seconds. Add brown sugar, baking powder, baking soda, and salt. Beat until combined, scraping sides of bowl occasionally. Beat in the eggs and vanilla until combined. Beat in the flour and, if desired, orange peel. Using a wooden spoon, stir in the rolled oats and your choice of dried fruit, nuts, and/or candy.

3 **To make each cookie,** spoon dough into a ¼-cup measure; use a rubber spatula to push the dough out onto the prepared cookie sheet, keeping mounds of dough about 4 inches apart (see photo, below). Using your fingers, gently press each dough mound into a 3-inch circle.

4 **Bake in a 375° oven** 10 minutes or until edges are lightly browned. Cool on pan for 1 minute. Transfer cookies to a wire rack; cool completely.

Nutrition Facts per cookie: 246 cal., 11 g total fat (7 g sat. fat), 51 mg chol., 182 mg sodium, 34 g carbo., 1 g fiber, 4 g pro. Daily Values: 10% vit. A, 0% vit. C, 3% calcium, 9% iron

*Note: Choose from raisins, dried tart cherries, dried blueberries, mixed dried fruit bits, flaked coconut, chopped peanuts, chopped mixed nuts, semisweet chocolate pieces, chocolate-covered raisins, candy-coated milk chocolate pieces, miniature milk chocolate kisses, and/or chocolate-covered toffee pieces.

Either spoon the cookie dough into a ¼-cup measure to mound the cookies or use a large ice-cream scoop.

COCOA CATS   *LOW-FAT*

Prep: 40 minutes   **Chill:** 1 hour
Bake: 7 minutes per batch
Makes: about 48 cookies   **Oven:** 375°

⅓ **cup shortening**
⅓ **cup butter, softened**
¾ **cup sugar**
⅓ **cup unsweetened cocoa powder**
1 **teaspoon baking powder**
1 **egg**
2 **tablespoons milk**
1 **teaspoon vanilla**
1¾ **cups all-purpose flour**
1 **recipe Halloween Icing (see right)**

1 To make the cookie dough, in a large mixing bowl beat shortening and butter with an electric mixer on medium to high speed 30 seconds. Add sugar, cocoa powder, and baking powder. Beat until combined. Beat in egg, milk, and vanilla until combined. Beat in as much flour as you can with the mixer. Using a wooden spoon, stir in any remaining flour. Divide dough in half. Cover; chill in refrigerator 1 to 2 hours or until easy to handle.

2 To shape the cookies, on a lightly floured surface roll 1 dough portion to slightly less than ¼-inch thickness. Using a cat-shaped cutter, cut into shapes. Place shapes 1 inch apart on ungreased cookie sheets. Repeat with remaining dough.

3 Bake cookies in a 375° oven for 7 to 9 minutes or until edges are firm and bottoms are light brown. Carefully transfer cookies to wire racks; cool completely. Decorate with Halloween Icing.

Halloween Icing: In a small mixing bowl stir together 1 cup sifted powdered sugar, ¼ teaspoon vanilla, and enough milk (2 to 3 teaspoons) to make of piping consistency. Stir in enough orange food coloring (or a combination of red and yellow) to color the icing orange. Place icing in a small self-sealing plastic freezer bag; seal and snip a small hole in a corner. (Or, place icing in a pastry bag fitted with a small round tip.)

Nutrition Facts per cookie: 64 cal., 3 g total fat (1 g sat. fat), 8 mg chol., 22 mg sodium, 9 g carbo., 0 g fiber, 1 g pro. Daily Values: 1% vit. A, 0% vit. C, 1% calcium, 2% iron

Sherbet Cookiewiches: Prepare dough and chill as above. Using half of the dough, roll out as directed. (Wrap and freeze remaining dough for up to 3 months.) Using a 2½-inch round cookie cutter, cut dough into approximately 24 circles. Bake as directed but do not decorate with icing.

Line a 13×9×2-inch baking pan with foil, using a piece of foil large enough to overlap opposite 2 edges of the pan. Place 1 quart orange sherbet in a chilled large mixing bowl. Using a wooden spoon, stir sherbet until softened. Stir in ¾ cup miniature semisweet chocolate pieces. Using the wooden spoon, transfer sherbet mixture to the foil-lined pan; spread evenly. Freeze 4 to 6 hours or until firm.

Use the foil to lift the sherbet from the pan. Using the same cookie cutter, cut out 12 sherbet circles. Place leftover sherbet scraps in a freezer bag

Sherbet Cookiewiches: Next Halloween, invite the neighborhood ghosts and goblins in to gobble up a plateful of witches—orange sherbet and chocolate-filled cookiewiches that is.

or container for future use. Place each sherbet circle between 2 cookie circles.

Place cookie sandwiches on a large cookie sheet; loosely cover and freeze until firm. If desired, wrap each sandwich in a 6-inch square piece of freezer wrap and keep frozen for up to 1 month. Makes 12 cookiewiches.

FRUIT CHEWIES *LOW-FAT*

Prep: 25 minutes   **Bake:** 20 minutes
Makes: 20 bars   **Oven:** 350°

Bursting with dried apples and raisins, these spicy bars make a terrific low-fat snack.

  ½ **cup snipped dried apples**
  2 **tablespoons apple juice**
  ⅓ **cup packed brown sugar**
  ⅓ **cup butter**
  1 **egg**
  1 **teaspoon vanilla**
  ⅓ **cup all-purpose flour**
  ¼ **cup toasted wheat germ**
  ¼ **teaspoon baking powder**
  ¼ **teaspoon apple pie spice or ground cinnamon**
  ¼ **cup raisins**
  2 **tablespoons toasted wheat germ Powdered sugar**

1 Grease an 8×8×2-inch baking pan; set aside. In a small mixing bowl stir together dried apples and apple juice; set aside.

2 In a medium saucepan heat and stir the brown sugar and butter over medium heat until butter melts. Remove from heat; let cool 5 minutes.

3 Stir egg and vanilla into butter mixture in saucepan. Using a wooden spoon, beat lightly just until combined. Stir in flour, the ¼ cup wheat germ, the baking powder, and spice.

4 Add undrained apples and raisins to mixture in saucepan. Stir just until combined.

5 Spread the batter in the prepared baking pan. Sprinkle with the 2 tablespoons wheat germ. Bake in a 350° oven about 20 minutes or until top is golden and a wooden toothpick inserted in center comes out clean. Cool in pan on wire rack. Sprinkle top lightly with powdered sugar. Cut into bars.

Nutrition Facts per bar cookie: 71 cal., 4 g total fat (2 g sat. fat), 19 mg chol., 42 mg sodium, 9 g carbo., 0 g fiber, 1 g pro. Daily Values: 3% vit. A, 0% vit. C, 1% calcium, 3% iron

PARENTS, START YOUR BAKERS YOUNG

Baking is a wonderful activity for kids. They learn a bit about art, science, responsibility, and creativity, and fond memories are created when you bake together as a family. Every child, toddler on up, can participate. Let younger kids help add ingredients to a bowl or help with stirring. Four- to 6-year-olds can stir, measure, scrape bowls, fill pans with batter, and use cookie cutters. Bake alongside your children until you feel they are competent baking alone. Even then, make sure you are nearby.

PEANUT BUTTER AND
JELLY BARS

BEST-LOVED

Prep: 20 minutes   Bake: 30 minutes
Makes: 36 bars   Oven: 350°

Let the kids choose the jelly. You can use a different flavor on each half of the pan.

1⅓ **cups all-purpose flour**
1⅓ **cups quick-cooking rolled oats**
 ¾ **cup packed brown sugar**
 ½ **cup granulated sugar**
 1 **teaspoon baking powder**
 ½ **teaspoon baking soda**
 ½ **cup butter**
 ½ **cup peanut butter**
 1 **cup chopped peanuts**
 1 **beaten egg**
 1 **10-ounce jar (1 cup) grape jelly**
   or your favorite jelly

1 To make the crumb mixture, stir together flour, rolled oats, brown sugar, granulated sugar, baking powder, and soda. Using a pastry blender, cut in butter and peanut butter until mixture resembles fine crumbs. Stir in ½ cup of the peanuts. Set aside 1 cup of the crumb mixture for topping.

Sprinkling on nuts and topping is easy for youngsters to handle. Encourage them to sprinkle evenly over the whole surface. Also, warn them not to touch the hot pan.

2 To make crust, stir the egg into the remaining crumb mixture. Press mixture into the bottom of an ungreased 13×9×2-inch baking pan. Bake in a 350° oven for 15 minutes. Carefully spoon the jelly evenly over the partially baked crust. Sprinkle with the remaining peanuts and reserved topping (see photo, lower left).

3 Bake in the 350° oven for 15 to 18 minutes more or until lightly browned around the edges. Cool in the pan on a wire rack. Cut into bars. Store bars in an airtight container in the refrigerator for up to 3 days.

Nutrition Facts per bar cookie: 143 cal., 7 g total fat (2 g sat. fat), 13 mg chol., 75 mg sodium, 19 g carbo., 1 g fiber, 3 g pro. Daily Values: 2% vit. A, 0% vit. C, 1% calcium, 4% iron

CHOCOLATE SYRUP
BROWNIES

 **EASY**

Prep: 15 minutes   Bake: 30 minutes
Makes: 32 brownies   Oven: 350°

Coach from the sideline while your child mixes up these easy cake-style brownies.

 ½ **cup butter, softened**
 ⅔ **cup sugar**
 3 **eggs**
 1 **16-ounce can (1½ cups) chocolate-flavored syrup**
1¼ **cups all-purpose flour**
1½ **cups milk chocolate pieces**

1 Grease a 13×9×2-inch baking pan; set aside. In a large mixing bowl beat butter with electric mixer on medium speed for 30 seconds. Add sugar; beat until combined. Add eggs; beat on low speed just until combined. Pour in chocolate syrup, stirring with a spoon until combined. Stir in flour until combined. Pour into prepared pan; spread evenly.

2 **Bake in a 350° oven** for 30 minutes. Remove from oven; sprinkle with chocolate pieces. Cool slightly; spread melted chocolate over brownies. Cut into bars before chocolate becomes firm. Cool in pan on wire rack. If necessary, cover and refrigerate bars until chocolate is firm enough to serve.

Nutrition Facts per brownie: 136 cal., 6 g total fat (4 g sat. fat), 28 mg chol., 50 mg sodium, 21 g carbo., 0 g fiber, 2 g pro. Daily Values: 4% vit. A, 0% vit. C, 2% calcium, 3% iron

CHERRY POCKETS

Prep: 25 minutes **Bake:** 15 minutes
Makes: 8 pockets **Oven:** 425°

> 1 cup cherry pie filling
> ½ teaspoon almond extract
> 1 15-ounce package (2 crusts) folded
>   refrigerated unbaked piecrust or
>   1 recipe Pastry for Double-Crust
>   Pie (see page 48)
> 2 tablespoons honey

1 **To make the filling,** in a medium bowl combine cherry pie filling and almond extract; set aside.

2 **Let refrigerated** piecrusts stand at room temperature according to package directions. (Or, prepare Pastry for Double-Crust Pie; divide dough in half.) On a lightly floured surface roll each crust or each half of the pastry to an 11-inch circle. Cut four 5-inch circles from each 11-inch circle.

3 **Place about** 2 tablespoons of the filling onto each 5-inch circle. Moisten edge with water using your finger or a pastry brush. Fold dough in half over filling. Press edge with a fork to seal. Place pockets on an ungreased baking sheet. Prick tops several times with a fork.

4 **Bake pockets in a 425° oven** for 15 to 20 minutes or until golden. Carefully transfer pockets to a wire rack; cool 15 minutes. While still warm, brush with honey. Serve warm or cooled.

Nutrition Facts per pocket: 298 cal., 15 g total fat (0 g sat. fat), 15 mg chol., 214 mg sodium, 39 g carbo., 0 g fiber, 2 g pro.

Finish each pie by placing a 5-inch pastry circle over apple filling. Press the edges down with your fingers until the dough circles seal together.

EASY-AS-APPLE PIES

Prep: 20 minutes **Bake:** 18 minutes
Makes: 4 servings **Oven:** 400°

Introduce kids to pie baking with these simple apple-filled miniatures.

> 1 15-ounce package (2 crusts) folded
>   refrigerated unbaked piecrust
> 1 large Granny Smith apple
> 2 tablespoons sugar
> 1 teaspoon cornstarch
> ¼ teaspoon ground cinnamon
> 1 beaten egg or 1 tablespoon milk

1 **Let crusts stand** at room temperature according to package directions.

2 **Peel,** core, and thinly slice apple. In a medium mixing bowl combine sugar, cornstarch, and cinnamon. Stir until mixed. Add apple slices and toss to coat.

3 **Unfold piecrusts;** cut out four 4-inch circles from 1 crust. Place circles on an ungreased baking sheet. Divide apple mixture among circles, spreading mixture up to ½ inch from edges. Cut remaining pastry into four 5-inch circles. Brush egg or milk on bottom crust edges. Place 5-inch circles over apples. Press edges with fingers to seal (see photo, above). Make two 1-inch slits in the top of each. Brush tops with remaining egg or milk.

4 **Bake in a 400° oven** for 18 to 20 minutes or until golden brown. Carefully transfer pies to a wire rack; cool about 20 minutes. Serve warm or cool completely.

Nutrition Facts per serving: 551 cal., 31 g total fat (0 g sat. fat), 83 mg chol., 436 mg sodium, 62 g carbo., 1 g fiber, 6 g pro. Daily Values: 2% vit. A, 2% vit. C, 0% calcium, 1% iron

COOKIE-CUTTER CAKES

Prep: 35 minutes **Bake:** 20 minutes
Cool: 30 minutes **Makes:** 10 servings **Oven:** 350°

For holiday cutouts, use a gingerbread man or Santa cookie cutter (see photo, page 383).

2⅔ **cups all-purpose flour**
1⅓ **cups sugar**
 4 **teaspoons baking powder**
1⅓ **cups milk**
 ½ **cup butter, softened**
 2 **eggs**
 2 **teaspoons vanilla**
 1 **recipe Icing (see below)**
  Assorted tiny candies (optional)

1 Grease a 15×10×1-inch baking pan; set aside. In large bowl combine flour, sugar, and baking powder. Add milk, butter, eggs, and vanilla. Beat with an electric mixer on low speed until combined. Beat on medium speed 1 minute. Pour batter into prepared pan.

2 Bake in a 350° oven for 20 to 25 minutes or until a wooden toothpick inserted in the center comes out clean. Cool in pan on a wire rack.

3 Using deep-sided cookie cutters or a knife, cut cake into desired shapes. Using a small spatula, carefully remove shapes from pan; place on wire rack; drizzle with Icing. Decorate with candies.

Icing: In a medium mixing bowl combine 2 cups sifted powdered sugar, 2 tablespoons milk, and ½ teaspoon vanilla. Stir in additional milk, 1 teaspoon at a time, until of drizzling consistency.

Nutrition Facts per serving: 409 cal., 11 g total fat (6 g sat. fat), 70 mg chol., 269 mg sodium, 73 g carbo., 1 g fiber, 6 g pro. Daily Values: 12% vit. A, 0% vit. C, 15% calcium, 12% iron

WACKY BANANA CAKE

Prep: 20 minutes **Bake:** 30 minutes
Makes: 9 servings **Oven:** 350°

What's wacky about this cake? It's mixed right in the baking pan.

1½ **cups all-purpose flour**
 ¾ **cup sugar**
 1 **teaspoon baking soda**
 ¼ **teaspoon salt**
 ¼ **teaspoon ground cinnamon**
 ⅔ **cup mashed ripe bananas (about 2 medium)**
 6 **tablespoons butter, melted**
 ¼ **cup cold water**
 1 **tablespoon vinegar**
 ½ **cup miniature semisweet chocolate pieces**
 ¼ **cup almond brickle pieces or chopped mixed nuts**

1 In an ungreased 8×8×2-inch baking pan stir together the flour, sugar, baking soda, salt, and cinnamon.

2 Add the bananas, melted butter, cold water, and vinegar to the dry mixture. Stir the mixture just until combined.

3 Sprinkle the chocolate pieces over the top of the cake.

4 Bake in a 350° oven for 30 to 35 minutes or until a wooden toothpick inserted in the center comes out clean. Sprinkle the hot cake with almond brickle pieces or nuts. Cool in pan on a wire rack.

Nutrition Facts per serving: 294 cal., 12 g total fat (5 g sat. fat), 22 mg chol., 304 mg sodium, 46 g carbo., 1 g fiber, 3 g pro. Daily Values: 7% vit. A, 3% vit. C, 0% calcium, 8% iron

---

CURIOUS ABOUT CAKE

Kids are curious by nature. Offer them these science lessons as you bake a cake:
- Eggs help the cake rise and give it a springy texture. Plus, they help bind the ingredients.
- Flour provides structure.

- Baking soda and baking powder help a cake rise high and fluffy.
- Sugar makes a cake sweet and tender.
- Fat, such as butter or vegetable shortening, makes a cake moist and tender.

CANDY-TOPPED
GINGERBREAD LOAVES

Prep: 20 minutes **Bake:** 25 minutes
Makes: 2 loaves (6 servings) **Oven:** 350°

*At Christmas, decorate the loaves with
red and green gumdrops, jelly beans, or other
small candies. At Easter, use pastel-colored ones.*

1½ **cups all-purpose flour**
 1 **teaspoon baking powder**
 1 **teaspoon ground cinnamon**
 ½ **teaspoon ground ginger**
 ¼ **teaspoon baking soda**
 ¼ **teaspoon salt**
 1 **beaten egg**
 ⅓ **cup light-flavored molasses**
 ⅓ **cup cooking oil**
 ¼ **cup packed brown sugar**
 ¼ **cup milk**
 1 **recipe Lemon Icing (see right)**
   **Gumdrops, jelly beans, and/or
     small multicolored decorative
     candies**

1 **Grease bottoms** and halfway up the sides of two
5¾×3×2-inch individual loaf pans;* set aside.

2 **In medium** mixing bowl combine flour, baking
powder, cinnamon, ginger, baking soda, and
salt. Make a well in center of flour mixture; set aside.

3 **In another medium** mixing bowl stir together
egg, molasses, oil, brown sugar, and milk. Add
egg mixture all at once to the flour mixture. Stir just
until moistened (batter will be a little lumpy).
Spoon batter into prepared pans.

4 **Bake in a 350° oven** for 25 to 30 minutes or
until a wooden toothpick inserted near the center comes out clean. Cool in pans on wire racks for
10 minutes. Remove from pans. Cool completely on
wire racks.

5 **Drizzle loaf tops** with Lemon Icing. Decorate
with candies as desired.

Lemon Icing: In a small mixing bowl stir together
1 cup sifted powdered sugar and 1 teaspoon lemon
juice or vanilla. Stir in milk, 1 teaspoon at a time,
until icing is of drizzling or piping consistency.

Nutrition Facts per serving: 369 cal., 13 g total fat
(2 g sat. fat), 36 mg chol., 224 mg sodium,
59 g carbo., 1 g fiber, 4 g pro. Daily Values: 2% vit. A,
1% vit. C, 10% calcium, 17% iron

*Note: To use 5-inch gingerbread-man-shaped pans
instead of individual loaf pans, grease bottoms and
halfway up sides of 6 pans. Spoon batter into pans.
Bake in 350° oven about 15 minutes or until done.

FRUITY YOGURT
MUFFINS *LOW-FAT*

Prep: 12 minutes **Bake:** 20 minutes
Makes: 12 muffins **Oven:** 400°

1¾ **cups all-purpose flour**
 ⅓ **cup granulated sugar**
 2 **teaspoons baking powder**
 ½ **teaspoon ground cinnamon**
 ¼ **teaspoon salt**
 1 **beaten egg**
 ⅔ **cup mashed bananas
     (about 2 medium)**
 ½ **cup strawberry (or your favorite
     fruit flavor) low-fat yogurt**
 ¼ **cup cooking oil**
 ¼ **cup Grape Nuts cereal or
     2 tablespoons brown sugar**

1 **Grease** twelve 2½-inch muffin cups; set aside.
In a medium mixing bowl combine flour, granulated sugar, baking powder, cinnamon, and salt.

2 **In another medium mixing bowl** stir together
egg, mashed bananas, yogurt, and oil. Add egg
mixture all at once to flour mixture. Stir just until
moistened (batter will be a little lumpy). Fill muffin pans three-fourths full. Sprinkle with cereal.

3 **Bake in a 400° oven** for 20 to 25 minutes or
until golden. Cool in muffin pans on a wire rack
5 minutes. Remove from muffin pans; serve warm.

Nutrition Facts per muffin: 165 cal., 5 g total fat
(1 g sat. fat), 18 mg chol., 133 mg sodium,
27 g carbo., 1 g fiber, 3 g pro. Daily Values: 4% vit. A,
3% vit. C, 6% calcium, 7% iron

WHOLE WHEAT ZOO ROLLS

LOW-FAT

Prep: 30 minutes   Rise: 30 minutes
Bake: 15 minutes   Makes: 12 rolls   Oven: 350°

Abracadabra! Frozen bread dough turns into a zoo full of animals—just like that.

1 16-ounce loaf frozen honey wheat
   or whole wheat bread dough,*
   thawed according to package
   directions
1 egg white
1 tablespoon milk
   Sesame seed (optional)

1 **Using kitchen scissors,** divide the thawed bread dough into 12 equal portions (each portion should make 1 animal- or flower-shaped roll). Lightly grease 2 baking sheets; set aside.

2 **Shape dough** into desired shapes on prepared baking sheets. (See ideas on page 397 or create your own shapes.)

3 **Cover the shaped** rolls lightly with a kitchen towel. Let the rolls rise in a warm place (away from cool drafts) until they are nearly double in size (will take 30 to 35 minutes).

4 **Using a fork,** stir together the egg white and milk. Using a pastry brush, gently brush tops of rolls with egg white mixture. If desired, sprinkle rolls with sesame seed.

5 **Bake in a 350° oven** about 15 minutes or until golden on top. (If using two oven racks, switch each pan to the other rack half way through baking to promote even baking. If your oven only has 1 rack, place 1 pan of rolls, covered, in refrigerator until the other pan is done baking.) Carefully transfer rolls to wire racks; let cool slightly. Serve warm.

Nutrition Facts per roll: 100 cal., 2 g total fat (0 g sat. fat), 0 mg chol., 215 mg sodium, 18 g carbo., 2 g fiber, 5 g pro.

*Note: You can substitute frozen white bread dough for the wheat bread dough.

BREAD-BAKING MAGIC

Q What makes bread rise?

A Yeast. Yeast is a tiny organism that eats the sugar and starch in the dough. As it does that, it produces air bubbles, which cause the dough to expand and rise.

Q Why does bread get even bigger after you put it in the oven?

A Heat from the oven makes those same air bubbles produced by the yeast organisms get even bigger—then your bread does, too.

Q Why does bread get a brown, crunchy crust?

A The crust is formed in the oven because the outside of the bread is exposed to the most heat. The crust protects the inside of the bread as it bakes so it stays soft. (Some people think the crust is the best part.)

Snake: Roll a portion of the dough into a 10-inch-long rope. Place the rope on a prepared baking sheet, curving the rope several times so it looks like a moving snake. For the mouth, cut a ¾-inch-long slit in 1 end.

Snail: Roll a portion of dough into a 10-inch-long rope. Wrap into a coil shape and place on a prepared baking sheet. For the head, trim outside end of rope flat; pull it out a little from the coil.

Turtle: Start with a portion of dough and pinch off 6 little pieces of dough for the legs, head, and tail. For the body, roll the remaining large piece of dough into a ball and place on a prepared baking sheet, flattening slightly. Place legs, head, and tail on the baking sheet, touching the body where you think they should go. To make the shell design on the body, use a small knife to cut a crisscross design ¼ inch deep.

Rabbit: Divide 1 portion of the dough into 2 equal pieces. For body, shape 1 piece into a ball; place on a prepared baking sheet. Divide other piece in half, using 1 half for the head and dividing the other half into 2 ears and a tail. Place head on baking sheet, touching body. Place ears and tail on baking sheet touching head and body where you think they should go.

Bear Face: Divide 1 portion of the dough into 2 equal pieces. For the head, shape 1 piece into a ball; place on a prepared baking sheet. Divide other piece into 2 ears and a nose. Place ears on baking sheet, touching bear head. Press nose onto bear head in the middle. For eyes, use a small knife to cut little slits in the dough above the nose.

Flower: Divide 1 portion of the dough into 2 equal pieces. Shape 1 piece into a 5-inch-long rope, then into a coil. Place on a prepared baking sheet. For the petals, divide the remaining piece into 10 balls. Place the balls in a circle around the coil, making sure the balls touch the coil.

Homemade Granola:
Teach kids how to make their own cereal. For breakfast, serve crunchy granola with milk and strawberries. Or, pack it in school lunches as a snack.

HOMEMADE GRANOLA *EASY*

Prep: 20 minutes   **Bake:** 30 minutes
Makes: 7 cups (14 servings)   **Oven:** 300°/350°

2½ **cups regular or quick-cooking rolled oats**
 1 **cup flaked or shredded coconut**
⅓ **cup shelled sunflower seeds**
¼ **cup sesame seed**
¼ **cup butter**
¼ **cup packed brown sugar**
¼ **cup honey**
1½ **teaspoons vanilla**
½ **cup toasted wheat germ**
 1 **cup raisins**

1 **Lightly butter** or grease a large roasting pan. Add oats, coconut, sunflower seeds, and sesame seed; spread evenly. Bake in a 300° oven for 20 minutes, stirring several times.

2 **While the oat mixture** is baking, in a small saucepan combine butter, brown sugar, and honey. Cook and stir over medium heat until butter melts. Remove from heat. Stir in vanilla.

3 **Remove** roasting pan from the oven; place on a wire cooling rack. Increase oven temperature to 350°. Add wheat germ to the oat mixture. Pour warm brown sugar mixture over oat mixture. Using a fork or spatula, stir the oat mixture to coat it with the brown sugar mixture. Bake 5 minutes more.

4 **Stir raisins** into oat mixture. Using a spatula, spread mixture evenly in pan. Bake for 5 to 10 minutes more or until golden. Place pan on a wire cooling rack. Using a spatula, transfer the granola to a large sheet of foil (mixture will be crumbly). Spread evenly. Cool completely. Store in an airtight container for up to 2 weeks.

Nutrition Facts per serving (without milk): 232 cal., 10 g total fat (5 g sat. fat), 9 mg chol., 83 mg sodium, 33 g carbo., 1 g fiber, 5 g pro. Daily Values: 4% vit. A, 1% vit. C, 3% calcium, 12% iron

GETTING THE MOST FROM GRANOLA

Versatile granola can be adjusted to your family's tastes and served in a variety of ways. If someone doesn't like coconut or raisins, substitute slivered almonds for the coconut or dried tart cherries for the raisins. Of course, this crunchy blend of grains, seeds, and fruit makes terrific cereal, but also consider sprinkling it over ice cream for a sundae. Or, improvise a parfait by layering it with fruit-flavored yogurt. For trail mix, add peanuts, milk chocolate pieces, tiny marshmallows, or candy-coated chocolate or peanut-butter-flavored pieces to the cooled granola.

400

MY FAVORITE RECIPES

PAGE NUMBER

METRIC COOKING HINTS

By making a few conversions, cooks in Australia, Canada, and the United Kingdom can use the recipes in *Better Homes and Gardens® New Baking Book* with confidence. The charts on this page provide a guide for converting measurements from the U.S. customary system, which is used throughout this book, to the imperial and metric systems. There also is a conversion table for oven temperatures to accommodate the differences in oven calibrations.

Product Differences: Most of the ingredients called for in the recipes in this book are available in English-speaking countries. However, some are known by different names. Here are some common American ingredients and their possible counterparts:

■ Sugar is granulated or castor sugar.
■ Powdered sugar is icing sugar.
■ All-purpose flour is plain household flour or white flour. When self-rising flour is used in place of all-purpose flour in a recipe that calls for leavening, omit the leavening agent (baking soda or baking powder) and salt.
■ Light-colored corn syrup is golden syrup.
■ Cornstarch is cornflour.
■ Baking soda is bicarbonate of soda.
■ Vanilla is vanilla essence.
■ Green, red, or yellow sweet peppers are capsicums.
■ Golden raisins are sultanas.

Volume and Weight: Americans traditionally use cup measures for liquid and solid ingredients. The chart, below, shows the approximate imperial and metric equivalents. If you are accustomed to weighing solid ingredients, the following approximate equivalents will help.

■ 1 cup butter, castor sugar, or rice = 8 ounces = about 250 grams
■ 1 cup flour = 4 ounces = about 125 grams
■ 1 cup icing sugar = 5 ounces = about 150 grams

Spoon measures are used for smaller amounts of ingredients. Although the size of the tablespoon varies slightly in different countries, for practical purposes and for recipes in this book, a straight substitution is all that's necessary.

Measurements made using cups or spoons always should be level unless stated otherwise.

EQUIVALENTS: U.S. = AUSTRALIA/U.K.

⅛ teaspoon = 0.5 ml
¼ teaspoon = 1 ml
½ teaspoon = 2 ml
1 teaspoon = 5 ml
1 tablespoon = 1 tablespoon
¼ cup = 2 tablespoons = 2 fluid ounces = 60 ml
⅓ cup = ¼ cup = 3 fluid ounces = 90 ml
½ cup = ⅓ cup = 4 fluid ounces = 120 ml
⅔ cup = ½ cup = 5 fluid ounces = 150 ml
¾ cup = ⅔ cup = 6 fluid ounces = 180 ml
1 cup = ¾ cup = 8 fluid ounces = 240 ml
1¼ cups = 1 cup
2 cups = 1 pint
1 quart = 1 liter
½ inch =1.27 cm
1 inch = 2.54 cm

BAKING PAN SIZES

American	Metric
8×1½-inch round baking pan	20×4-cm cake tin
9×1½-inch round baking pan	23×3.5-cm cake tin
11×7×1½-inch baking pan	28×18×4-cm baking tin
13×9×2-inch baking pan	30×20×3-cm baking tin
2-quart rectangular baking dish	30×20×3-cm baking tin
15×10×1-inch baking pan	30×25×2-cm baking tin (Swiss roll tin)
9-inch pie plate	22×4- or 23×4-cm pie plate
7- or 8-inch springform pan	18- or 20-cm springform or loose-bottom cake tin
9×5×3-inch loaf pan	23×13×7-cm or 2-pound narrow loaf tin or pâté tin
1½-quart casserole	1.5-liter casserole
2-quart casserole	2-liter casserole

OVEN TEMPERATURE EQUIVALENTS

Fahrenheit Setting	Celsius Setting*	Gas Setting
300°F	150°C	Gas Mark 2 (slow)
325°F	160°C	Gas Mark 3 (moderately slow)
350°F	180°C	Gas Mark 4 (moderate)
375°F	190°C	Gas Mark 5 (moderately hot)
400°F	200°C	Gas Mark 6 (hot)
425°F	220°C	Gas Mark 7
450°F	230°C	Gas Mark 8 (very hot)
Broil		Grill

*Electric and gas ovens may be calibrated using Celsius. However, for an electric oven, increase the Celsius setting 10 to 20 degrees when cooking above 160°C. For convection or forced-air ovens (gas or electric), lower the temperature setting 10°C when cooking at all heat levels.

MICROWAVE HINTS

■ **Butter, melting:** In a bowl heat butter, uncovered, on 100% power (high) 35 to 45 seconds for 2 tablespoons, 45 to 60 seconds for ¼ cup, or 1 to 1½ minutes (about 45 seconds in high-wattage ovens) for ½ cup.

■ **Butter, softening:** In a bowl heat ½ cup butter, uncovered, on 10% power (low) for 1½ to 2½ minutes (about 45 seconds in high-wattage ovens) or until softened.

■ **Chocolate, melting:** In a bowl heat chocolate, uncovered, on 100% power (high) 1 to 2 minutes for 1 ounce (1½ to 2½ minutes for 1 cup chocolate pieces) or until soft enough to stir smooth, stirring every minute during cooking time.

■ **Coconut, toasting:** In a 2-cup measure cook 1 cup coconut, uncovered, on 100% power (high) for 2½ to 3½ minutes or till toasted, stirring after 1 minute, then stirring every 30 seconds.

■ **Cream cheese, softening:** In a bowl heat cream cheese, uncovered, on 100% power (high) 15 to 30 seconds for 3 ounces (30 to 60 seconds for 8 ounces) or till softened.

■ **Lemons, juicing:** Halve or quarter 1 lemon. Heat on 100% power (high) 20 to 45 seconds. Squeeze lemon to release juice.

■ **Sauces, reheating:** Heat chilled topping, uncovered, on 100% power (high) 30 seconds to 1½ minutes for ½ cup or 60 seconds to 2 minutes for 1 cup.

■ **Muffins and rolls, warming:** Place muffins or rolls on a plate. Heat, uncovered, on 100% power (high) for 10 to 20 seconds for 1 or 2 muffins or 30 to 60 seconds for 4 muffins or until heated through.

■ **Nuts, toasting:** In a 2-cup measure cook nuts, uncovered, on 100% power (high) till toasted, stirring every minute for the first 2 minutes, then stirring every 30 seconds. Allow 2 to 3 minutes for ½ cup almonds or pecans, 2 to 3 minutes for 1 cup almonds, 3 to 4 minutes for 1 cup pecans, 3 to 4 minutes for ½ cup raw peanuts or walnuts, and 3½ to 5 minutes for 1 cup raw peanuts or walnuts. Whole nuts may toast first on the inside, so open a few to check for doneness. At the first sign of toasting, spread whole or chopped nuts on paper towels to cool. They will continue to toast as they stand. Let them stand for at least 15 minutes.

■ **Pie (fruit), warming:** Place 1 slice of fruit pie on a plate. Heat, uncovered, on 100% power (high) 45 to 60 seconds (about 20 seconds in high-wattage ovens) or until heated through.

FREEZER STORAGE

Brownies and Bars (unfrosted)	Up to 3 months
Layer Cakes (unfrosted)	Up to 4 months
Angel Food, Sponge, and Chiffon Cakes (unfrosted)	Up to 3 months
Cheesecakes	Up to 1 month (whole) / Up to 2 weeks (pieces)
Cookie Dough	Up to 6 months
Cookies (unfrosted)	Up to 3 months
Cream Puff Pastry Shells	Up to 2 months
Croissant and Puff Pastry Dough	Up to 3 months
Croissants and Danishes	Up to 2 months
Fruit Pies (baked)	Up to 8 months
Fruit Pies (unbaked)	Up to 3 months
Muffins, Biscuits, and Scones	Up to 3 months
Pie Pastry Dough	Up to 3 months
Quick Breads	Up to 3 months
Yeast Breads	Up to 3 months

TOASTING NUTS, SEEDS, AND COCONUT

Toasting heightens the flavor of nuts, seeds, and coconut. To toast, spread the nuts, seeds, or coconut in a single layer in a shallow baking pan. Bake in a 350° oven for 5 to 10 minutes or until light golden brown, watching carefully and stirring once or twice to brown evenly.

WEIGHTS AND MEASURES

3 teaspoons = 1 tablespoon
4 tablespoons = ¼ cup
5⅓ tablespoons = ⅓ cup
8 tablespoons = ½ cup
10⅔ tablespoons = ⅔ cup
12 tablespoons = ¾ cup
16 tablespoons = 1 cup

1 tablespoon = ½ fluid ounce
1 cup = 8 fluid ounces
1 cup = ½ pint
2 cups = 1 pint
4 cups = 1 quart
2 pints = 1 quart
4 quarts = 1 gallon

1 teaspoon = 5 milliliters
1 tablespoon = 15 milliliters
1 cup = 240 milliliters
1 quart = 1 liter
1 ounce = 28 grams
1 pound = 454 grams

EMERGENCY BAKING SUBSTITUTIONS

Use these substitutions only in a pinch, as they may affect the flavor or texture of your recipe.

If you don't have:	Substitute:
Apple pie spice, 1 teaspoon	½ teaspoon ground cinnamon plus ¼ teaspoon ground nutmeg, ⅛ teaspoon ground allspice, and dash ground cloves or ginger
Baking powder, 1 teaspoon	½ teaspoon cream of tartar plus ¼ teaspoon baking soda
Buttermilk, 1 cup	Sour milk: 1 tablespoon lemon juice or vinegar plus enough milk to make 1 cup (let stand 5 minutes before using); or 1 cup plain yogurt
Chocolate, semisweet, 1 ounce	3 tablespoons semisweet chocolate pieces; or 1 ounce unsweetened chocolate plus 1 tablespoon sugar
Chocolate, sweet baking, 4 ounces	¼ cup unsweetened cocoa powder plus ⅓ cup sugar and 3 tablespoons shortening
Chocolate, unsweetened, 1 ounce	3 tablespoons unsweetened cocoa powder plus 1 tablespoon cooking oil or shortening, melted
Cornstarch, 1 tablespoon (for thickening)	2 tablespoons all-purpose flour
Corn syrup, 1 cup	1 cup granulated sugar plus ¼ cup water
Egg, 1 whole	2 egg whites; 2 egg yolks; or ¼ cup frozen egg product, thawed
Flour, cake, 1 cup	1 cup minus 2 tablespoons all-purpose flour
Flour, self-rising, 1 cup	1 cup all-purpose flour plus 1 teaspoon baking powder, ½ teaspoon salt, and ¼ teaspoon baking soda
Fruit liqueur, 1 tablespoon	1 tablespoon fruit juice
Gingerroot, grated, 1 teaspoon	¼ teaspoon ground ginger
Half-and-half or light cream, 1 cup	1 tablespoon melted butter or margarine plus enough whole milk to make 1 cup
Honey, 1 cup	1¼ cups granulated sugar plus ¼ cup water
Mascarpone cheese, 8 ounces	8 ounces regular cream cheese
Milk, 1 cup	½ cup evaporated milk plus ½ cup water; or 1 cup water plus ⅓ cup nonfat dry milk powder
Molasses, 1 cup	1 cup honey
Pumpkin pie spice, 1 teaspoon	½ teaspoon ground cinnamon plus ¼ teaspoon ground ginger, ¼ teaspoon ground allspice, and ⅛ teaspoon ground nutmeg
Sour cream, dairy, 1 cup	1 cup plain yogurt
Sugar, granulated, 1 cup	1 cup packed brown sugar
Yeast, active dry, 1 package	1 cake compressed yeast